Blackstone's

Police Investigator's Manual

Blackstone's

Police Investigator's Manual

Glenn Hutton

David Johnston

Fraser Sampson

OXFORD

UNIVERSITY PRESS

OXFORD

UNIVERSITY PRESS

Great Clarendon Street, Oxford OX2 6DP

Oxford University Press is a department of the University of Oxford.
It furthers the University's objective of excellence in research, scholarship,
and education by publishing worldwide in

Oxford New York

Auckland Bangkok Buenos Aires Cape Town Chennai
Dar es Salaam Delhi Hong Kong Istanbul Karachi Kolkata
Kuala Lumpur Madrid Melbourne Mexico City Mumbai Nairobi
São Paulo Shanghai Taipei Tokyo Toronto

Oxford is a registered trade mark of Oxford University Press
in the UK and certain other countries

A Blackstone Press Book

© Glenn Hutton, David Johnston, Fraser Sampson, 2004

ISBN 0-19-927102 - X

Typeset by Newgen Imaging Systems (P) Ltd., Chennai, India
Printed in Great Britain
on acid-free paper by
Ashford Colour Press, Gosport, Hampshire

Contents

Table of Cases

Table of Statutes

Table of Statutory Instruments

PART ONE

Property Offences

1.1   **Theft**

1.1.1   **Introduction**

Theft, and the offences associated with it, cover some of the most commonly encountered offences in English—and Welsh—criminal law.

Acquisitive crime makes up a substantial proportion of all recorded crime and therefore takes up a vast proportion of investigators' time.

Given the volume of such crimes, together with the social consequences to victims and the communities in which they live, this area of criminal law has a significant impact on the work of all investigators.

In an attempt to address the high volume crime arising out of vehicle thefts, the government has introduced new legislation in the form of the Vehicles (Crime) Act 2001. The Act received Royal Assent on 10 April 2001, and introduces some of the recommendations of the Vehicle Crime Reduction Team made up of ACPO, the Home Office, the Association of British Insurers, Driver and Vehicle Licensing Agency, and a number of other motor industry groups.

The 2001 Act creates powers to regulate motor salvage businesses in the UK, gives police the right of entry to registered premises without a warrant and makes requirements in relation to suppliers of vehicle number plates.

1.1.2   **Theft**

OFFENCE: **Theft—*Theft Act 1968, s. 1***
> • Triable either way • Seven years' imprisonment on indictment; six months' imprisonment and/or a fine summarily
> *(Arrestable offence)*

The Theft Act 1968, s. 1 states:

> (1) A person is guilty of theft if he dishonestly appropriates property belonging to another with the intention of permanently depriving the other of it; and 'thief' and 'steal' shall be construed accordingly.

KEYNOTE

It is important for all investigators to understand each element of this offence. The Theft Act 1968 provides some detailed guidance as to parts of the above definition, while our common law has clarified some of the others.

In order for an offence of theft to exist, each element of the definition must be proved and those elements are considered in detail below.

This is a 'trigger' offence under s. 63B of the Police and Criminal Evidence Act 1984 which can activate police powers to require a sample from a person in police detention to ascertain the presence of a specified Class A drug in some force areas.

1.1.3   **Dishonestly**

If a person cannot be shown to have acted 'dishonestly', he/she is not guilty of theft. The decision as to whether or not a defendant was in fact dishonest is one for the jury or magistrate(s) but the evidence compiled by investigators will clearly influence that decision significantly. Although there are countless examples of when a person would be acting dishonestly, the 1968 Act sets out a number of specific circumstances where the relevant person will *not* be treated as dishonest.

The Theft Act 1968, s. 2 states:

(1) A person's appropriation of property belonging to another is not to be regarded as dishonest—
   (a) if he appropriates the property in the belief that he has in law the right to deprive the other of it, on behalf of himself or of a third person; or
   (b) if he appropriates the property in the belief that he would have the other's consent if the other knew of the appropriation and the circumstances of it; or
   (c) (except where the property came to him as trustee or personal representative) if he appropriates the property in the belief that the person to whom the property belongs cannot be discovered by taking reasonable steps.

(2) A person's appropriation of property belonging to another may be dishonest notwithstanding that he is willing to pay for the property.

KEYNOTE

In all three instances it is the person's *belief* that is important.

- Under s. 2(1)(a), if a person in dispute with a bookmaker believes he/she has a legal contractual right to take something of a value equal to his/her unpaid winnings from the bookmaker's stand, that person will not be regarded as dishonest—even though gambling debts are not legally enforceable. His/her belief need not even be reasonable, only honestly held, and could be based on a 'mistake' (contrast the general defence of mistake).

- Under s. 2(1)(b), the person appropriating the property must believe both elements, i.e. that the other person would have consented had he/she known of the appropriation *and the circumstances of it*. If a member of a police station tea club is desperate for a cigarette and takes cash from the tea club kitty which colleagues occasionally use for such 'emergencies', the taker might well argue that s. 2(1)(b) applies. If, however, the money is taken to boost the Christmas kitty of another shift, the second condition may defeat them! Although the person need not have given his/her consent to the appropriation, the presence of such consent may be very relevant in establishing the honest existence of the defendant's belief. It is suggested that this element of theft, namely the element of *dishonesty* is where the issue of consent properly belongs and not in the element of 'appropriation' as discussed below.

- Under s. 2(1)(c), the belief has to be in relation to the likelihood of discovering the 'owner' by taking reasonable steps. Both the nature and value of the property, together with the attendant circumstances, will be relevant. The chances of finding the owner of a valuable, monogrammed engagement ring found after a theatre performance would be considerably greater than those of discovering the owner of a can of beer found outside Twickenham stadium following a Six Nations match between Wales and England. Again, it is the defendant's *belief* at the time of the appropriation that is important here, not that the defendant went on to *take* reasonable steps to discover the person to whom the property belongs.

Under s. 2(2), if a person appropriates another's property, leaving money or details of where he/she can be contacted to make restitution will not *of itself* negate dishonesty (see *Boggeln* v *Williams* [1978] 1 WLR 873). The wording of s. 2(2) gives latitude to a court where the defendant was willing to pay for the property. The subsection says that such an appropriation *may* be dishonest, not that it *will always* be dishonest.

1.1.4   **Dishonesty: The Ruling in *Ghosh***

Section 2 will not cater for every circumstance and indeed ss. 2 to 6 only affect the interpretation of the basic elements of theft as set out in s. 1 unless the Act says otherwise (s. 1(3)). Since the case of *R* v *Ghosh* [1982] QB 1053 there has been a requirement for juries to be given some form of direction where the issue of dishonesty is raised. As well as clarifying that the defendant's dishonesty is a matter for a jury to decide, the Court of Appeal in *Ghosh* also identified two aspects which the jury should consider when so deciding. If s. 2 is not applicable or helpful then a jury must decide:

- whether, according to the ordinary standards of reasonable and honest people, what was done was 'dishonest'; and, if it was,
- whether 'the defendant himself must have realised that what was done was dishonest' *by those standards.*

This test against the standards of reasonable and honest people means that a defendant who has a purely *subjective* belief that he/she is doing what is morally right (e.g. an anti-vivisectionist taking animals from a laboratory) can still be 'dishonest'. The ruling applies to other offences under the Theft Act 1968 and the original case arose from charges of deception. The *Ghosh* test is probably the source of the questions so loved by some interviewing officers: 'But what would an *honest* person have done?' or 'What would have been the *honest* thing to do?'

1.1.5   Appropriates

The Theft Act 1968, s. 3 states:

> (1) Any assumption by a person of the rights of an owner amounts to an appropriation, and this includes, where he has come by the property (innocently or not) without stealing it, any later assumption of a right to it by keeping or dealing with it as owner.

KEYNOTE

It is important to note that there can be an 'appropriation' without any criminal liability and appropriation itself does not amount to an offence; it describes one of the circumstances that must exist before a charge of theft can be made out. An appropriation requires no mental state on the part of the appropriator. It is an objective act.

Where an appropriation takes place and is accompanied by the required dishonesty and intention to deprive permanently, there will be a theft.

When and where the particular act amounting to an appropriation took place is therefore of critical importance when bringing a charge of theft; it is also vital when establishing other offences such as robbery (see 1.5), aggravated burglary (see 1.3) and handling stolen goods (see 1.4).

1.1.6   *R v Gomez*

The decision of the House of Lords in *R* v *Gomez* [1993] AC 442 is significant in the development of the meaning of 'appropriation'. Gomez worked in a shop in London. He was approached by a friend who asked him to accept two building society cheques in exchange for some expensive electrical goods from the shop. Knowing the cheques to be stolen, Gomez took them to his store manager asking him to authorise the supply of goods. Gomez assured the manager that the cheques had been confirmed and that they were 'as good as cash'. With this reassurance the manager authorised the supply of the goods. Gomez paid the cheques into the store's account and the large quantity of electrical goods was dispatched to Gomez's friend. Some time later, the cheques were returned with a 'not to pay' order on them as they had been reported stolen.

Gomez was arrested for theft of the electrical goods, together with his friend, and sent for trial. There, counsel for Gomez submitted that there was no case to answer in respect of the theft because the store manager had authorised their supply and therefore there had been no 'appropriation' under s. 3(1) of the Theft Act 1968. The submission was rejected by the trial judge but was upheld on appeal on the grounds that, when Gomez's friend took possession of the electrical goods, he was entitled to do so under the terms of the contract of sale entered into by the store manager. The Court went on to say that, although the contract of sale my have been 'voidable' (that is, the other parties to it could have it set aside because they had been duped into it), nevertheless the goods were transferred to Gomez's friend with the express authority of the 'owner' (the store manager).

On the appeal by the Director of Public Prosecutions to the House of Lords, Lord Keith followed an earlier case (*Lawrence v Metropolitan Police Commissioner* [1972] AC 626). His Lordship disagreed with the argument that an act expressly or impliedly authorised by the owner can never amount to an 'appropriation' and pointed out that the decision in *Lawrence* was a direct contradiction of that proposition. The House of Lords upheld the men's convictions for theft and accepted that there are occasions where property can be 'appropriated' for the purposes of the Theft Act 1968, *even though the owner has given his/her consent or authority*.

A number of issues come from this decision:

- *Taking or depriving*. First, it is not necessary that the property be 'taken' in order for there to be an appropriation, neither need the owner be 'deprived' of the property. Similarly, there is no need for the defendant to 'gain' anything by an appropriation which can also be caused by damaging or destroying property (*R v Graham* [1997] 1 Cr App R 395).

- *Consent*. Secondly, it is irrelevant to the issue of appropriation whether or not the owner consented to that appropriation. This is well illustrated in *Lawrence*, the decision followed by the House of Lords in *Gomez*. In *Lawrence* a tourist gave his wallet full of unfamiliar English currency to a taxi driver for the latter to remove the correct fare. The driver in fact helped himself to ('appropriated') far more than the amount owed. It has held that the fact that the wallet and its contents were handed over freely (with consent) by the owner did not prevent the taxi driver's actions from amounting to an 'appropriation' of it. The Court of Appeal appears—at least on one occasion—to have interpreted *Gomez* as deciding that consent *obtained by fraud* is irrelevant to the issue of appropriation (see *R v Mazo* (1997) 2 Cr App R 518). However, there is no such restriction placed on the decision in *Gomez* and it seems safe to assume that *no* consent given by the owner of property can prevent it being 'appropriated' for the purposes of the Theft Act 1968. This creates a considerable overlap with offences of deception.

- *Interfering with goods*. Our higher courts were greatly concerned for a number of years by the swapping of price labels on goods displayed for sale in shops and whether or not such behaviour amounted to an appropriation. A third point that is now clear from the decision in *Gomez* is that simply swapping the price labels on items displayed for sale in a shop *would* amount to an 'appropriation'. This is because to do so, irrespective of any further intention, involves an assumption of one of the owner's rights in relation to the property. If that appropriation were accompanied by the required circumstances of dishonesty and intention to deprive, then there would be a *prima facie* case of theft.

- *More than one appropriation*. A fourth point apparent from *Gomez* is that there may be an appropriation of the same property on more than one occasion. However, once property has been *stolen* (as opposed to merely appropriated), that same property cannot be stolen again by the same thief (*R v Atakpu* [1994] QB 69). Appropriation can also be a continuing act, that is, it can include the whole episode of entering and ransacking a house and the subsequent removal of property (*R v Hale* (1978) 68 Cr App R 415). Therefore identifying the exact point at which property was appropriated with the requisite intention and accompanying dishonesty can cause practical difficulties, particularly in cases involving cheques and credit transactions. The advice of the Crown Prosecution Service should be sought in such cases.

Summary

The House of Lords was recently asked to rule on whether a person could 'appropriate' property belonging to another where the other person made her an absolute gift of property, retaining no proprietary interest in the property or any right to resume or recover it (*R v Hinks* [2000] 3 WLR 1590). In that case the defendant had befriended a middle aged man of limited intelligence who had given her some £60,000 over a period of time. The defendant was charged with five counts of theft and, after conviction, eventually appealed to the House of Lords. Their Lordships held that:

- in a prosecution for theft it was unnecessary to prove that the taking was without the owner's consent (as in *Lawrence* above);

- it was immaterial whether the act of appropriation was done with the owner's consent or authority (as in *Gomez*); and

- *Gomez* therefore gave effect to s. 3(1) by treating 'appropriation' as a neutral word covering 'any assumption by a person of the rights of an owner'.

Although consistent with earlier cases, this approach creates a few problems. If acceptance of the gift were treated as an 'appropriation', the defendant would seem to have had a belief that she had a right to deprive the donor of the property and therefore she was not 'dishonest'. Further, under s. 5 of the 1968 Act, the prosecution has to prove that, at the time of the alleged appropriation, the relevant property belonged to another. In *Hinks* the defendant had been validly given the property, therefore it is difficult to see how the money still belonged to the donor at the time of appropriation.

These and other concerns were raised by Lord Hobhouse who pointed out that ss. 1 to 6 should be read as a whole and that attempts to 'compartmentalise' each element only lead to contradictions. However, he was in a minority and the case decision stands, compartments and all.

If a person, having come by property—innocently or not—without stealing it, later assumes any rights to it by keeping it or treating it as his/her own, then he/she 'appropriates' that property (s. 3(1)).

An exception to these circumstances is provided by s. 3 which states:

(2) Where property or a right or interest in property is or purports to be transferred for value to a person acting in good faith, no later assumption by him of rights which he believed himself to be acquiring shall, by reason of any defect in the transferor's title, amount to theft of the property.

KEYNOTE

If a person buys a car in good faith and gives value for it (i.e. a reasonable price) but then discovers it has been stolen, his/her refusal to return it to the vendor will not, without more, *attract liability for theft*. Without s. 3(2) the retention of the vehicle would be caught by s. 3(1). This narrow exemption does not mean however that the innocent purchaser gets good title to the car (see *National Employers' Mutual Insurance Association* v *Jones* [1990] AC 24), nor would it provide a defence if the stolen goods are a gift and the 'donor' (recipient) subsequently discovers that they had been stolen.

1.1.7   Property

The Theft Act 1968, s. 4 states:

(1) 'Property' includes money and all other property, real or personal, including things in action and other intangible property.

(2) A person cannot steal land, or things forming part of land and severed from it by him or by his directions, except in the following cases, that is to say—

   (a) when he is a trustee or personal representative, or is authorised by power of attorney, or as liquidator of a company, or otherwise, to sell or dispose of land belonging to another, and he appropriates the land or anything forming part of it by dealing with it in breach of the confidence reposed in him; or

   (b) when he is not in possession of the land and appropriates anything forming part of the land by severing it or causing it to be severed, or after it has been severed; or

   (c) when, being in possession of the land under a tenancy, he appropriates the whole or part of any fixture or structure let to be used with the land.

   For purposes of this subsection 'land' does not include incorporeal hereditaments; 'tenancy' means a tenancy for years or any less period and includes an agreement for such a tenancy, but a person who after the end of a tenancy remains in possession as statutory tenant or otherwise is to be treated as having possession under the tenancy, and 'let' shall be construed accordingly.

(3) A person who picks mushrooms growing wild on any land, or who picks flowers, fruit or foliage from a plant growing wild on any land, does not (although not in possession of the land) steal what he picks unless he does it for reward or for sale or other commercial purpose.

For purposes of this subsection 'mushroom' includes any fungus, and 'plant' includes any shrub or tree.

(4) Wild creatures, tamed or untamed, shall be regarded as property; but a person cannot steal a wild creature not tamed nor ordinarily kept in captivity, or the carcase of any such creature, unless either it has been reduced into possession by or on behalf of another person and possession of it has not since been lost or abandoned, or another person is in course of reducing it into possession.

KEYNOTE

Under s. 4(1), 'things in action' would include patents and trademarks and other things which can only be enforced by legal action as opposed to physical possession. Other intangible property would include software programs and perhaps credits accumulated on 'smart cards'. Confidential information—such as the contents of an examination paper—is not intangible property *per se* (see *Oxford* v *Moss* (1978) 68 Cr App R 183). However, the document itself would be property. It has been accepted by the Court of Appeal that contractual rights obtained by buying a ticket for the London Underground may amount to a 'thing in action' (see *R* v *Marshall* [1998] 2 Cr App R 282), though this view is extremely contentious.

The very high percentage of mobile phones stolen over recent years has led to the enactment of specific legislation to reduce their attractiveness to thieves and robbers. For the Mobile Telephones (Re-programming) Act 2002, **see para. 1.4.7**).

Cheques will be property as they are pieces of paper (albeit of very little intrinsic value). The contents of a bank or building society account, however, are also a 'thing in action' that can be stolen *provided the account is in credit or within the limits of an agreed overdraft facility* (*R* v *Kohn* (1979) 69 Cr App R 395). Therefore, reducing the credit balance in one account, and transferring a like sum into your own account, amounts to an 'appropriation' within the meaning of s. 1. This principle (set out in *Kohn*) was reaffirmed in *R* v *Williams (Roy)* [2001] 1 Cr App R 23 by the Court of Appeal.

Under s. 4(2), you cannot generally steal land even though it is 'property' for the purposes of criminal damage. It also seems that the restrictions relating to land as 'property' under s. 4(2) above do not apply to offences of obtaining property by deception (see *Blackstone's Criminal Practice*, 2003, section B5.27). If you are a trustee or personal representative or someone in a position of trust to dispose of land belonging to another you can be guilty of stealing it if, in such circumstances, you dishonestly dispose of it.

If you are in possession of land under a tenancy then things forming part of that land to be used with it are 'property'. Such fittings and fixtures (including fireplaces, fitted kitchens etc.) would be particularly relevant to agricultural tenants or those occupying council property.

Section 4(3) obliquely includes mushrooms, flowers, fruit and foliage in the ambit of 'property' unless they are growing wild on any land. If they are so growing, then the person picking them must be shown to have done so for reward, sale or other commercial purpose in order to be guilty of theft. It is arguable that, if the person does not have such a *purpose at the time of the picking*, any later intention to sell the fruit etc. may not bring it within the provisions of s. 4(3).

Section 4(4) appears slightly confusing in that the subsection acknowledges that all wild creatures are 'property' but goes on to qualify the occasions when they will be capable of supporting a charge of theft. Once a person has reduced it into possession (say, by trapping, capturing or shooting it), a wild animal can be 'stolen', as it can during the process of so reducing it into possession. If the animal is lost or abandoned after it has been reduced into possession or killed then it cannot be 'stolen'.

These provisos appear to relate more to the concept of 'belonging to another' (see below) than 'property'.

Pets and animals that are tamed or ordinarily kept in captivity are always property for the purposes of theft.

1.1.8   **What is not Property?**

Human bodies are not property (*Doodeward* v *Spence* (1907) 6 CLR 406) although a driver has been convicted of stealing a specimen of his own urine (*R* v *Welsh* [1974] RTR 478). This principle was upheld by the Court of Appeal in *R* v *Kelly* [1999] QB 621, after the conviction of two people involved in the theft of body parts from the Royal College of Surgeons. The court upheld the convictions for theft on the grounds that the process of *alteration* (amputation, dissection and preservation) which the body parts had undergone did make them 'property' for the purposes of the 1968 Act. The common law rule was that there is no property in a corpse and any change to that rule would have to be made by Parliament.

1.1.9   **Belonging to Another**

The Theft Act 1968, s. 5 states:

(1) Property shall be regarded as belonging to any person having possession or control of it, or having in it any proprietary right or interest (not being an equitable interest arising only from an agreement to transfer or grant an interest).

(2) Where property is subject to a trust, the persons to whom it belongs shall be regarded as including any person having a right to enforce the trust, and an intention to defeat the trust shall be regarded accordingly as an intention to deprive of the property any person having that right.

KEYNOTE

Property can be 'stolen' from any person who has possession or control or a right or interest in that property. In one case where the defendant sneaked into a garage to recover his own recently-repaired car, he was convicted of stealing the car which at the time 'belonged to' the garage proprietor who had possession and control of it (*R* v *Turner (No. 2)* [1971] 1 WLR 901). In determining whether or not a person had 'possession' of property for the purposes of s. 5(1), the period of possession can be finite (i.e. for a given number of hours, days etc.) or infinite (*R* v *Kelly* [1998] 3 All ER 741). It is not necessary to show who does own the property—only that it 'belongs to' someone other than the defendant. (For rights of the Crown under the Treasure Act 1996 and other statutes, see *Blackstone's Criminal Practice*, 2003, section B4.18.)

Where money is given by members of the public to charity collectors it becomes the property of the relevant charitable trustees at the moment it goes into the collecting tin (*R* v *Dyke* [2002] Crim LR 153). This will be important when framing the relevant charge or indictment. If in doubt as to the 'ownership' of property that is the subject of a theft, the advice of the Crown Prosecution Service should be sought.

When a cheque is written, that will create a 'thing in action'. That thing in action belongs only to the payee. Therefore a payee of a cheque cannot 'steal' the thing in action which it creates (*R* v *Davies* (1988) 88 Cr App R 347). The piece of paper on which a cheque is printed will also be property—however low in value (see above).

In proving theft, you must show that the property belonged to another *at the time of the appropriation*. This requirement has caused some difficulty where a defendant's decision not to pay for goods has been made *after* property passed to him/her. In such cases (e.g. people refusing to pay for meals after they have eaten or deciding to drive off having filled their car with petrol), the proper charge has been one of deception or making off without payment. But it should be remembered that the appropriation can be an extended and continuing act (*R* v *Atakpu* [1994] QB 69). The House of Lords' ruling in *Gomez* raises some questions over such cases, see above. As the consent of the owner is irrelevant to the issue of 'appropriation', the key element in such cases is whether the property 'belonged to another' at the time of the act of appropriation. If ownership of the property had passed to the defendant *before* he/she appropriated it (e.g. by virtue of the Sale of Goods Act 1979; see *Edwards* v *Ddin* [1976] 1 WLR 942) then this element of theft would not be made out and an alternative charge should be considered.

Obligations Regarding Another's Property

The Theft Act 1968, s. 5 states:

(3) Where a person receives property from or on account of another, and is under an obligation to the other to retain and deal with that property or its proceeds in a particular way, the property or proceeds shall be regarded (as against him) as belonging to the other.

KEYNOTE

'Obligation' means a legal obligation, not simply a moral one (*R v Hall* [1973] QB 126). Whether or not such an obligation exists is a matter of law for a trial judge to decide (*R v Dubar* [1994] 1 WLR 1484).

Instances under s. 5(3) most commonly involve receiving money from others to retain and use in a certain way (e.g. travel agents taking deposits; solicitors holding funds for mortgagees; or pension fund managers collecting contributions (*R v Clowes (No. 2)* [1994] 2 All ER 316)). The Court of Appeal has held that one effect of s. 5(3), is that property can be regarded as belonging to another even where it does not 'belong' to them on a strict inter-pretation of civil law (*R v Klineberg* (1999) 1 Cr App R 427). In that case the defendants collected money from customers in their timeshare business. Although the customers were told that their deposits would be placed with an independent trustee, the defendants paid the sums into their company account, thereby breaching the 'obligation' under s. 5(3) to deal with the money in a particular way. Section 5(3) would also include, say, the owners of shopping malls where coins thrown into a fountain are to be donated to charity; if the owners did not deal with those coins in the way intended, the provisions of s. 5(3) may well apply.

Obligation to Restore Another's Property

The Theft Act 1968, s. 5 states:

(4) Where a person gets property by another's mistake, and is under an obligation to make restora-tion (in whole or in part) of the property or its proceeds or of the value thereof, then to the extent of that obligation the property or proceeds shall be regarded (as against him) as belonging to the person entitled to restoration, and an intention not to make restoration shall be regarded accordingly as an intention to deprive that person of the property or proceeds.

KEYNOTE

Before s. 5(4) was enacted, an employee who was mistakenly credited with extra money in his/her bank account could not be prosecuted for larceny (the predecessor of theft) (*Moynes v Cooper* [1956] 1 QB 439). In such circumstances under s. 5(4) the employee will be liable for stealing the extra money if he/she keeps it (see *Attorney-General's Reference (No. 1 of 1983)* [1985] QB 182 where a police officer's account was credited with money representing overtime which she had not actually worked).

Section 5(4) only applies where someone *other than the defendant* has made a mistake. It is clear that such a mistake can be a mistake as to a material fact; whether or not a mistake as to *law* would be covered is unclear.

Again, the obligation to make restoration is a *legal* one and, as with s. 5(3), an unenforceable or moral obliga-tion will not be covered by s. 5(4). (See *R v Gilks* [1972] 1 WLR 1341 where a betting shop mistakenly paid out winnings against the wrong horse. As gambling debts are not legally enforceable the defendant was not under 'an obligation' to restore the money and therefore s. 5(4) did not apply.)

1.1.10 **Intention of Permanently Depriving**

If you cannot prove an intention permanently to deprive you cannot prove theft (see *R v Warner* (1970) 55 Cr App R 93).

If there is such an intention at the time of the appropriation, giving the property back later will not alter the fact and the charge will be made out (*R v McHugh* (1993) 97 Cr App R 335).

In certain circumstances s. 6 may help in determining the presence or absence of such an intention.

The Theft Act 1968, s. 6 states:

(1) A person appropriating property belonging to another without meaning the other permanently to lose the thing itself is nevertheless to be regarded as having the intention of permanently depriving the other of it if his intention is to treat the thing as his own to dispose of regardless of the other's rights; and a borrowing or lending of it may amount to so treating it if, but only if, the borrowing or lending is for a period and in circumstances making it equivalent to an outright taking or disposal.

KEYNOTE

The key feature of s. 6(1) is the intention to treat 'the thing' as one's own to dispose of regardless of the other's rights. An example of such a case would be where property is 'held to ransom' (*R* v *Coffey* [1987] Crim LR 498). The borrowing or lending of another's property is specifically caught within s. 6(1). If a person takes property from his/her employer (e.g. carpet tiles) and uses it in a way which makes restoration unlikely or impossible (e.g. by laying them in his/her living room), then s. 6(1) will apply (see *R* v *Velumyl* [1989] Crim LR 299).

Similarly, if a person borrowed a season ticket causing the owner to miss a match, s. 6(1) would help prove the required intention because the circumstances of the borrowing make it equivalent to an outright taking.

In a recent case involving robbery (see below), the defendants took the victim's personal stereo headphones from him and broke them in two, rendering them useless before returning them to him. The Administrative Court held that a person who took something and dealt with it for the purpose of rendering it useless in this way demonstrated the intention of treating that article as his/her own to dispose of. The Court did not accept the argument that the property had to be totally exhausted before s. 6 applied (see also *R* v *Fernandes* (1996) 1 Cr App R 175) and held that the magistrates had been wrong to accept the submission of no case to answer on this point (*DPP* v *J* (2002) LTL 20 February).

The Theft Act 1968, s. 6 states:

(2) Without prejudice to the generality of subsection (1) above, where a person, having possession or control (lawfully or not) of property belonging to another, parts with the property under a condition as to its return which he may not be able to perform, this (if done for purposes of his own and without the other's authority) amounts to treating the property as his own to dispose of regardless of the other's rights.

KEYNOTE

Section 6(2) deals with occasions such as pawning another's property. If there is a likelihood that the defendant will be unable to meet the conditions under which he/she parted with another person's property, s. 6(2) would help in proving an intention permanently to deprive.

1.2   **Burglary**

1.2.1   **Section 9(1)(a)**

OFFENCE: **Burglary—*Theft Act 1968, s. 9***
- Triable on indictment if 'ulterior offence' is so triable, or if committed in dwelling and violence used; otherwise triable either way • Fourteen years' imprisonment (if building/part of building is dwelling, otherwise ten years' imprisonment on indictment; six months' imprisonment and/or a fine summarily *(Arrestable offence)*

The Theft Act 1968, s. 9 states:

(1) A person is guilty of burglary if—
  (a) he enters any building or part of a building as a trespasser and with intent to commit any such offence as is mentioned in subsection (2) below; or...

(2) The offences referred to in subsection (1)(a) above are offences of stealing anything in the building or part of a building in question, of inflicting on any person therein any grievous bodily harm or raping any person therein, and of doing unlawful damage to the building or anything therein.

KEYNOTE

There are two types of burglary. The first one is concerned with the defendant's *intentions when entering the building or part of a building*. Entry into a building or part of a building must be 'effective and substantial' (*R* v *Collins* [1973] QB 100). The defendant does not need to get his/her whole body into the building; provided that the entry is deliberate (i.e. not accidental), an entry by part of the body will be sufficient. A defendant may use an object as an extension of themselves to 'enter' and ultimately the question of whether they entered or not will be one of fact for a jury or magistrate(s).

The defendant's entry must be trespassory, that is, without any express or implied permission. Often permission is given conditionally, as with a householder inviting a television engineer to inspect his/her television, or a shopkeeper inviting shoppers to browse through goods on display. In such cases, entry becomes trespassory if someone goes beyond that condition, for instance by taking a TV set (*R* v *Jones* [1976] 1 WLR 672) or going behind the counter in a shop (*R* v *Walkington* [1979] 1 WLR 1169). In order to prove that an entry was trespassory it must be shown that the defendant knew that he/she did not have permission, or was at least reckless as to that fact.

Burglary under s. 9(1)(a) is a crime of *ulterior intent*, that is, in addition to the deliberate entry as a trespasser, the defendant must be shown to have had one of the ulterior intentions listed at s. 9(2). These intentions must coincide with the trespassory entry, that is, they must have been formed in the mind of the defendant by the time he/she enters the building/part of a building. This requirement is a further example of the principle that *mens rea* and *actus reus* must coincide. This requirement for the relevant ulterior intention should be contrasted with burglary under s. 9(1)(b) (**see 1.2.5**) which only requires that the trespasser goes on to do certain things inside the building/part of a building. This distinction is particularly important in relation to defences.

Sections 1 and 2 of the Criminal Evidence (Amendment) Act 1997 extending the power to take non-intimate samples without consent apply to all offences of burglary including aggravated burglary (**see 1.3**).

1.2.2 **Building**

The Theft Act 1968 s. 9 states:

(4) References in subsections (1) and (2) above to a building,...and...to a building which is a dwelling, shall apply also to an inhabited vehicle or vessel, and shall apply to any such vehicle or vessel at times when the person having a habitation in it is not there as well as at times when he is.

KEYNOTE

The effect of s. 9(4) is to include house boats or vehicles used as dwellings. There is a general requirement for 'buildings' to have some degree of permanence (*Norfolk Constabulary* v *Seekings* [1986] Crim LR 167). An unfinished house can be a building for the purposes of burglary (*R* v *Manning* (1871) LR 1 CCR 338), as can an industrial freezer (*B* v *Leathley* [1979] Crim LR 314).

1.2.3   **Intentions at the Time of Entry**

The intentions must be as follows:

- Stealing—this means an intention to commit theft under s. 1. The property which the defendant intends to steal must be in a building or part of a building.

- Inflicting grievous bodily harm—this will present practical difficulties if no grievous bodily harm is ultimately inflicted or if the defendant did not carry a weapon. If grievous bodily harm is inflicted, then the second offence under s. 9(1)(b) below would apply. In proving an intention to commit grievious bodily harm under s. 9(1)(a), it is not necessary to prove that an assault was actually committed (*Metropolitan Police Commissioner* v *Wilson* [1984] AC 242).

- Raping any person—the intended victim may be male or female. Again proof of such an intention will be difficult. Where a person is charged with this offence, the Youth Justice and Criminal Evidence Act 1999 imposes certain restrictions on the introduction of evidence or the asking of questions at trial relating to the victim's sexual behaviour.

- Causing unlawful damage—this includes damage, not only to the building but to anything in it.

1.2.4   **Conditional Intent**

Provided the required intention can be proved, it is immaterial whether or not there is anything 'worth stealing' within the building (*R* v *Walkington* [1979] 1 WLR 1169). Presumably the same will be true if the person whom the defendant intends to rape or to cause serious harm is not in the building or part of the building at the time.

1.2.5   **Section 9(1)(b)**

OFFENCE: **Burglary—*Theft Act 1968, s. 9***
         (see para. 12.4.1)

The Theft Act 1968, s. 9 states:

(1) A person is guilty of burglary if—

...

(b) having entered any building or part of a building as a trespasser he steals or attempts to steal anything in the building or that part of it or inflicts or attempts to inflict on any person therein any grievous bodily harm.

KEYNOTE

The second type of burglary involves a defendant's behaviour *after* entering a building or part of a building.

The defendant must have entered the building or part of a building as a trespasser; it is not enough that he/she subsequently became a trespasser by exceeding a condition of entry (e.g. hiding in the public area of a shop during open hours until the shop closes). However, where a person has entered a particular building (such as a shop or a pub) lawfully and without trespassing, if he/she later moves to *another part* of the building as a trespasser, this element of the offence will be made out.

....

EXAMPLE

D enters a public house near closing time with a friend who buys him a drink from the bar. D's entry onto that part of the premises has been authorised by the implied licence extended to members of the adult public by the publican and therefore D is not a trespasser. D then goes into the lavatories to use them as such. At this point he has entered another part of a building but again his entry is made under the implied licence to customers wishing to use the lavatories. While inside the lavatory area, D decides to hide until closing time in order to avoid buying his friend a drink. He hides inside one of the cubicles. At this point, although D's intention in hiding may be considered a little mean-spirited, he has none of the required intentions for the purposes of s. 9(1)(a) (see above).

Once the publican has shut the pub for the night, D leaves the lavatory and walks into the bar area. Now D has entered *a part of a building as a trespasser* because the licence extended to members of the public by the publican certainly does not cover wandering around in the bar after it has been closed. Having no particular intention at this point, however, D has still not committed an offence of burglary.

On seeing the gaming machines in the public bar, D decides to break into them and steal the money inside. At this point, although he has *two* of the required intentions for s. 9(1)(a) (an intention to steal and an intention to cause unlawful damage), those intentions were formed *after* his entry. Therefore, D has not committed burglary under s. 9(1)(a). Because he has not stolen/attempted to steal or inflicted/attempted to inflict grievous bodily harm on any person therein, D has not committed burglary under s. 9(1)(b) either.

D then breaks open a gaming machine. At this point he commits burglary under s. 9(1)(b). This is because, having entered a part of a building (the public bar area) as a trespasser (because the pub is closed and D knows that to be the case), he *attempts to steal*. If he simply damaged the machine without an intention of stealing the contents, D would not commit this offence because causing unlawful damage is only relevant to the offence under *s. 9(1)(a)*.

....

It has been argued that, if a defendant's intentions at the time of entering a building or part of a building are dishonest, he/she would automatically become a trespasser because any conditional or implied permission from the occupier to enter would not include someone with dishonest intentions. Such an argument would mean that all shoplifters could be charged with burglary (an argument which is unlikely to endear you to your Crime Manager!). Whether or not this argument has any merit, one thing is clear in relation to trespassers in cases of burglary. There is a doctrine at common law that an unlawful act by a person lawfully on premises has a retrospective effect, rendering the person's presence trespassory *ab initio* ('from the outset'). This means that, even if a person has entered the land lawfully, any later wrongdoing would make his/her whole entry and presence on the premises trespassory. Clearly this would have a significant effect on the number of offences that could be classified as burglaries and would support the argument above. Thankfully, the common law doctrine has been held not to apply to burglary (see *R* v *Collins* [1973] QB 100).

Unlike s. 9(1)(a), there are only two further elements to the offence under s. 9(1)(b)—the subsequent theft/ attempted theft of anything in the building or part of it, and the subsequent inflicting/attempted inflicting of grievous bodily harm to any person therein.

1.3   Aggravated Burglary

OFFENCE: **Aggravated Burglary—*Theft Act 1968, s. 10***
 • Triable on indictment • Life imprisonment
 (Arrestable offence)

The Theft Act 1968, s. 10 states:

 (1) A person is guilty of aggravated burglary if he commits any burglary and at the time has with him any firearm or imitation firearm, any weapon of offence or any explosive.

KEYNOTE

The 'time' at which the defendant must have the weapon etc. with him/her is critical and will depend on the type of burglary with which he/she is charged. If the defendant is charged with an offence under s. 9(1)(a), he/ she must be shown to have had the weapon *at the time of entry*. Therefore, if several people are charged with the offence of aggravated burglary, it must be shown that one of the defendants who actually entered the building had the weapon with them (*R* v *Klass* (1998) 1 Cr App R 453). If the charge is brought under s. 9(1)(b), he/she must be shown to have had the weapon *at the time of stealing or inflicting grievous bodily harm (or attempting either)*.

．．

EXAMPLE

A person (X) enters a house as a trespasser intending to steal the contents. While inside, X is disturbed by the occupier. X grabs a kitchen knife from the kitchen and threatens the occupier.

．．

If charged with burglary under s. 9(1)(a), X does not, on these facts alone, commit the offence of aggravated burglary because he did not have the weapon (kitchen knife) *at the time* of the burglary. If, however, X grabs the knife from the kitchen and stabs the occupier, *inflicting grievous bodily harm*, he commits the offence of burglary under s. 9(1)(b) *and at the time* has with him a weapon of offence. (See *R* v *O'Leary* (1986) 82 Cr App R 341.) Therefore X would be guilty of aggravated burglary. Similarly, if X followed the occupier into another part of the house intending to stab him, he would commit aggravated burglary.

'Has with him' will require a degree of immediate control (*R* v *Pawlicki* [1992] 1 WLR 827) and will normally be the same as 'carrying' (*Klass* above).

In cases where a defendant has been found entering a building with a weapon, it will not be necessary to prove any intention to use that weapon during the burglary (*R* v *Stones* [1989] 1 WLR 156).

1.3.1   Firearm/Weapon of Offence/Explosive

The Theft Act 1968, s. 10 states:

> (1) ...and for this purpose—
>   (a) 'firearm' includes an airgun or pistol, and 'imitation firearm' means anything which has the appearance of being a firearm, whether capable of being discharged or not, and
>   (b) 'weapon of offence' means any article made or adapted for use for causing injury to or incapacitating a person, or intended by the person having it with him for such use; and
>   (c) 'explosive' means any article manufactured for the purpose of producing a practical effect by explosion, or intended by the person having it with him for that purpose.

KEYNOTE

The 'person' whom the article is intended to injure or incapacitate under s. 9(1)(b) above need not be a person in the building/part of a building. If a burglar has a weapon that he/she intends to use to injure or incapacitate someone unconnected with the building/part of a building, he/she may be tempted to use that weapon during the course of the burglary; the very consequence behind the creation of this offence (see *Stones* above).

It would appear that the defendant must at least know they have an article with them *and* that the article is in fact a weapon of offence (see *Blackstone's Criminal Practice*, 2003, section B4.80).

Note the additional element of articles made, adapted or intended for 'incapacitating' a person. This is broader than the other legislation defining weapons and would include rope, binding tape, chloroform, handcuffs and CS spray.

1.4   Handling Stolen Goods

OFFENCE: **Handling Stolen Goods—*Theft Act 1968, s. 22***
   • Triable either way • Fourteen years' imprisonment on indictment; six months' imprisonment and/or a fine summarily
   (Arrestable offence)

The Theft Act 1968, s. 22 states:

(1) A person handles stolen goods if (otherwise than in the course of the stealing) knowing or believing them to be stolen goods he dishonestly receives the goods, or dishonestly undertakes or assists in their retention, removal, disposal or realisation by or for the benefit of another person, or if he arranges to do so.

KEYNOTE

Handling can only be committed *otherwise than in the course of stealing*. Given the extent of theft and the fact that it can be a continuing act, it is critical to identify at what point the theft of the relevant property ended. It is also useful, in cases of doubt, to include alternative charges.

You must show that the defendant *knew* or *believed* the goods to be stolen. Mere suspicion, however strong, will not be enough (*R* v *Griffiths* (1974) 60 Cr App R 14). Deliberate 'blindness' to the true identity of the goods would suffice but the distinction is a fine one in practice. It can be very difficult to prove knowledge or belief on the part of, say, a second-hand dealer who 'asks no questions'. Because there are practical difficulties in proving the required *mens rea*, s. 27(3) of the 1968 Act makes special provision to allow evidence of the defendant's previous convictions, or previous recent involvement with stolen goods, to be admitted.

Dishonestly retaining goods may amount to theft, in which case that is the relevant charge.

'Goods' will include money and every other description of property except land, and includes things severed from the land by stealing (s. 34(2)(b) of the Act).

1.4.1 Stolen Goods

The Theft Act 1968, s. 24 states:

(1) The provisions of this Act relating to goods which have been stolen shall apply whether the stealing occurred in England or Wales or elsewhere, and whether it occurred before or after the commencement of this Act, provided that the stealing (if not an offence under this Act) amounted to an offence where and at the time when the goods were stolen; and references to stolen goods shall be construed accordingly.

(2) For purposes of those provisions references to stolen goods shall include, in addition to the goods originally stolen and parts of them (whether in their original state or not),—

   (a) any other goods which directly or indirectly represent or have at any time represented the stolen goods in the hands of the thief as being the proceeds of any disposal or realisation of the whole or part of the goods stolen or of goods representing the stolen goods; and

   (b) any other goods which directly or indirectly represent or have at any time represented the stolen goods in the hands of a handler of the stolen goods or any part of them as being the proceeds of any disposal or realisation of the whole or part of the stolen goods handled by him or of goods so representing them.

(3) But no goods shall be regarded as having continued to be stolen goods after they have been restored to the person from whom they were stolen or to other lawful possession or custody, or after that person and any other person claiming through him have otherwise ceased as regards those goods to have any right to restitution in respect of the theft.

(4) For purposes of the provisions of this Act relating to goods which have been stolen (including subsections (1) to (3) above) goods obtained in England or Wales or elsewhere either by blackmail or in the circumstances described in section 15(1) of this Act shall be regarded as stolen; and 'steal', 'theft' and 'thief' shall be construed accordingly.

The Theft Act 1968, s. 24A states:

(7) Subsection (8) below applies for purposes of provisions of this Act relating to stolen goods (including subsection (4) above).

(8) References to stolen goods include money which is dishonestly withdrawn from an account to which a wrongful credit has been made, but only to the extent that the money derives from the credit.

KEYNOTE

If goods are not stolen there is no handling. Whether they are so stolen is a question of fact for a jury or magistrate(s). There is no need to prove that the thief, blackmailer, deceiver etc. has been convicted of the primary offence before prosecuting the alleged handler, neither is it always necessary to *identify* who that person was.

Goods obtained by deception and blackmail are included in the definition of 'stolen goods' under s. 24(4). Clearly goods gained through robbery or burglary will, by definition, be 'stolen' as theft is an intrinsic element of both offences.

'Wrongful credits' are included within the meaning of stolen goods under certain circumstances (**see 1.11**).

1.4.2 Section 24 Explained

Under s. 24(1) a person can still be convicted of handling if the goods were stolen outside England and Wales but only if the goods were taken under circumstances which amounted to an offence in the other country.

Under s. 24(2), goods will be classed as stolen only if they are the property which was originally stolen or if they have at some time represented the *proceeds* of that property in the hands of the thief or a 'handler'.

Therefore if a video cassette recorder (VCR) is stolen, sold to an unsuspecting party who then part exchanges it for a new one at a high street retailer, the first VCR will be 'stolen' goods, the new one will not. If the person buying the original VCR *knew* or *believed* that it was stolen, the new VCR would be treated as stolen goods.

Tracing the proceeds of theft, deception, blackmail etc. can be complex; proving them to be stolen even more so. There is an overlap between this legislation—which deals with goods that have been stolen—and other legislation such as the Criminal Justice Act 1988 which relates to criminally-obtained property generally or the Drug Trafficking Act 1994. For further guidance see *Blackstone's Criminal Practice*, 2003, section B22.

Under s. 24(3), once goods have been restored to lawful possession they cease to be stolen. This situation formerly caused practical problems when police officers recovered stolen property but waited for it to be collected by a handler (see *Houghton* v *Smith* [1975] AC 476). Since the Criminal Attempts Act 1981 and the common-law rulings on 'impossibility', this has been less problematic. In such cases you may consider:

- Theft—collecting the property will be an 'appropriation'.

- Handling—an *arrangement* to come and collect stolen goods will probably have been made while they were still 'stolen'.

- Criminal attempt—the person collecting the goods has gone beyond merely preparing to handle them.

Section 24(4) widens the occasions on which goods will be deemed to be stolen goods beyond strictly theft-based offences such as burglary and robbery.

1.4.3 Proof that Goods were Stolen

The Theft Act 1968, s. 27 states:

(4) In any proceedings for the theft of anything in the course of transmission (whether by post or otherwise), or for handling stolen goods from such a theft, a statutory declaration made by any person that he dispatched or received or failed to receive any goods or postal packet, or that any goods or postal packet when dispatched or received by him were in a particular state or condition, shall be admissible as evidence of the facts stated in the declaration, subject to the following conditions:—

(a) a statutory declaration shall only be admissible where and to the extent to which oral evidence to the like effect would have been admissible in the proceedings: and

(b) a statutory declaration shall only be admissible if at least seven days before the hearing or trial a copy of it has been given to the person charged, and he has not, at least three days before the hearing or trial or within such further time as the court may in special circumstances allow, given the prosecutor written notice requiring the attendance at the hearing or trial of the person making the declaration.

1.4.4   **Handling**

Despite some views to the contrary, there is only one offence of handling stolen goods (albeit made up of many facets). Therefore to charge a defendant without specifying a particular form of handling is not bad for duplicity (*R* v *Nicklin* [1977] 1 WLR 403). However, the offence can be divided for practical purposes into two parts:

- *receiving/arranging to receive* stolen goods, in which case the defendant acts for his/her own benefit, and

- *assisting/acting for the benefit of another* person, in which case that assistance to another or benefit of another must be proved.

1.4.5   **Receiving**

Often used as shorthand for handling stolen goods generally, this is a specific part of the overall offence. Receiving does not require the physical reception of goods and can extend to exercising control over them. Things in action—such as bank credits from a stolen cheque—can be 'received'.

'Arranging to receive' would cover circumstances which do not go far enough to constitute an attempt—that is, actions which *are* merely preparatory to the receiving of stolen goods may satisfy the elements under s. 22 even though they would not meet the criteria under the Criminal Attempts Act 1981.

If the goods have yet to be stolen, then s. 22 would not apply and the offence of conspiracy should be considered (see *R* v *Park* (1987) 87 Cr App R 164).

1.4.6   **Assisting/Acting for Another's Benefit**

Assisting or acting for the benefit of another can be committed by misleading police officers during a search (see *R* v *Kanwar* [1982] 1 WLR 845).

Disposing of the stolen goods or assisting in their disposal or realisation usually involves physically moving them or converting them into a different form (see *R* v *Forsyth* (1997) 2 Cr App R 299).

If the only person 'benefiting' from the defendant's actions is the defendant himself/herself, this element of the offence will not be made out (*R* v *Bloxham* [1983] 1 AC 109).

Similarly, if the only 'other' person to benefit is a co-accused on the same charge, the offence will not be made out (*R* v *Gingell* (2000) 1 Cr App R 88).

1.4.7   **Re-programming Mobile Phones**

OFFENCE: **Re-programming Mobile Phones—*Mobile Telephones (Re-Programming) Act 2002, s. 1***
  - Triable either way • Five years' imprisonment on indictment; 6 months imprisonment and/or a fine summarily
  (*Arrestable offence*)

The Mobile Telephones (Re-programming) Act 2002, s. 1 states:

(1) A person commits an offence if—
    (a) he changes a unique device identifier, or
    (b) he interferes with the operation of a unique device identifier.
(2) A unique device identifier is an electronic equipment identifier which is unique to a mobile wireless communications device.

(3) But a person does not commit an offence under this section if—

    (a) he is the manufacturer of the device, or

    (b) he does the act mentioned in subsection (1) with the written consent of the manufacturer of the device.

KEYNOTE

The above offence was created in direct response to the burgeoning problem of mobile phone thefts and robberies. By making several offences arising out of re-programming mobile phones (to compliment the system of handset barring that all major network providers have signed up to), the legislation attempts to reduce the attractiveness of such phones as targets for thieves and robbers. The unique device identifier is currently the International Mobile Equipment Identity (IMEI) number which identifies the handset of a mobile phone. It can be found on most mobile phones either behind the battery or by keying in the number *#06#. The wording of the section, however, allows for future development of mobile phones which may use different equipment identifiers. Changing the unique identifier is an offence; so, too, is adding a chip or otherwise interfering with that identifier.

It is the view of the Home Office that the international Global System for Mobiles (GSM) standards make it unnecessary for anyone other than a manufacturer or its agent to alter an IMEI number. For that reason, s. 1(3) creates a statutory defence for manufacturers or people with the *written* consent of the manufacturer.

OFFENCE: **Having or Supplying Anything for Re-programming Mobile Phones—**
Mobile Telephones (Re-programming) Act 2002, s. 2

    • Triable either way • Five years' imprisonment on indictment; 6 months
      imprisonment and/or a fine summarily
    (Arrestable offence)

The Mobile Telephones (Re-programming) Act 2002, s. 2 states:

(1) A person commits an offence if—

    (a) he has in his custody or under his control anything which may be used for the purpose of changing or interfering with the operation of a unique device identifier, and

    (b) he intends to use the thing unlawfully for that purpose or to allow it to be used unlawfully for that purpose.

(2) A person commits an offence if—

    (a) he supplies anything which may be used for the purpose of changing or interfering with the operation of a unique device identifier, and

    (b) he knows or believes that the person to whom the thing is supplied intends to use it unlawfully for that purpose or to allow it to be used unlawfully for that purpose.

(3) A person commits an offence if—

    (a) he offers to supply anything which may be used for the purpose of changing or interfering with the operation of a unique device identifier, and

    (b) he knows or believes that the person to whom the thing is offered intends if it is supplied to him to use it unlawfully for that purpose or to allow it to be used unlawfully for that purpose.

KEYNOTE

Having something in your custody or under your control is slightly narrower than having it in your 'possession'.

The above offences apply to *anything* that may be used for the restricted purposes. It must be shown that, in each case, the defendant had the article, object etc. or supplied/offered to supply it *and* that he/she had the requisite intent or knowledge at the time. For 'knowing or believing', see para 1.4.

The definition of 'unique device identifier' is the same as for the s. 1 offence and a thing is used by a person unlawfully for a purpose if, in using it for that purpose, he/she commits an offence under s. 1.

1.5 **Robbery**

OFFENCE: **Robbery—*Theft Act 1968, s. 8***

> • Triable on indictment • Life imprisonment
> *(Arrestable offence)*

The Theft Act 1968, s. 8 states:

> (1) A person is guilty of robbery if he steals, and immediately before or at the time of doing so, and in order to do so, he uses force on any person or puts or seeks to put any person in fear of being then and there subjected to force.

KEYNOTE

For there to be a robbery, there must be a theft and, consequently, dishonesty (*R* v *Robinson* [1977] Crim LR 173). To be guilty of robbery, the defendant must either:

- Use *force* on any person. If the force used is applied, not to the person directly but to his/her property (such as pulling a shopping basket or handbag from his/her hand), this may still be robbery as the force has still been applied, albeit indirectly (*Corcoran* v *Anderton* (1980) 71 Cr App R 104).

Or

- Put, or seek to put, *any* person in fear of being then and there subjected to force. It is not enough to threaten to use force on some future occasion, or to use force at some place other than at the scene, nor is it enough to show simply that the victim was frightened; you must show that the defendant put or sought to put the victim in fear of being then and there subjected to force (see *R* v *Khan* (2001) LTL 9 April).

As the force must be used *in order to steal*, it would seem to follow that an accidental application of force during a theft would not be enough to prove robbery.

The force used or threatened must be on or towards *any* person, not necessarily the person from whom the theft is committed. Although the wording does not make it clear, it appears that any person means any person *other than the defendant*. Pretending to use force on an accomplice in order to compel a third person to part with his/her property would probably not come within the parameters of the offence as the defendant would not in reality be 'using' force on the accomplice nor seeking to put him/her in fear of being then and there subjected to such force.

Increases in crime prevention technology (such as improved car security devices and locking codes in mobile phones) mean that an unsophisticated thief needs to get his/her hands on the property while it is still in use by its lawful owner. This will often mean using force or threats of force on that owner, thereby turning theft into robbery. This may account for the reported increase in 'carjacking' where drivers are forced out of their cars by would-be thieves. While this will generally amount to robbery if the car is actually 'stolen' as a result, there may be difficulties in proving the offence where there is no attendant element of theft, but a taking without the owner's consent. Whatever charge is settled upon, crime prevention technology may well have turned street robbery into an example of life's (or at least crime's) little ironies.

Whether force has been used or a person so put in fear will be a question of fact for a jury (*R* v *Dawson* (1976) 64 Cr App R 170). If force or the fear of force is proved, it must also be shown that it was used at the time or *immediately* before the theft, and *in order to carry out the theft*. If the defendant used force in order to escape having stolen property from another, then this element would not be satisfied. It is important to remember, however, that appropriation can be regarded as a continuing act. If you can show that when a defendant used force on another, he/she was still in the throes of appropriating property, this element will be satisfied.

For the Mobile Telephones (Re-programming) Act 2002, passed as a result of the very high percentage of mobile phones stolen in robberies, **see para. 1.4.7.**

1.6   **Deception**

Deception offences are closely related to theft and other offences involving dishonesty and may often overlap with those offences. The most important element here is the presence of the operating act of 'deception'.

The Theft Act 1968, s. 15 states:

(4) '...deception' means any deception (whether deliberate or reckless) by words or conduct as to fact or as to law, including a deception as to the present intentions of the person using the deception or any other person.

As deception offences require dishonesty—a largely subjective concept—then the 'recklessness' referred to above should be *subjective*; that is, the defendant must have given some thought to his/her conduct (see *R* v *Goldman* [1997] Crim LR 894). The special provisions of s. 2 of the Theft Act 1968 in relation to dishonesty do not directly apply to deception offences but the *Ghosh* directions as to what might be considered dishonest do apply. Dishonesty and deception are two distinct elements and the presence of a defendant's intention to deceive is not necessarily proof that he/she was dishonest (see *R* v *Clarke* [1996] Crim LR 824).

The general essence of a 'deception' is behaviour that induces someone to believe that something is, or might be, true. For that reason, offences involving falsification of documents are also included in this section (**see 1.10.2**). There are several related offences involving falsification of documents but these have not been included in this manual.

Without more, deception itself is not an offence; there must be other intentions or consequences springing from the deception, together with the element of dishonesty referred to above.

1.7   **Words or Conduct**

The courts have accepted that some omissions can be a deception (e.g. deliberately omitting to fill out forms (*R* v *Shama* [1990] 1 WLR 661)). It is difficult therefore to see how the inclusion of 'words or conduct' adds anything other than a checklist against which to assess a defendant's behaviour when proving the elements of deception. In some circumstances silence and failure to act can amount to 'conduct' for the purposes of supporting a criminal deception (*R* v *Rai* (2000) 1 Cr App R 233). In *Rai* the defendant remained silent when council workers came to his home in order to install a downstairs bathroom for his elderly mother who had lived there. Although his mother had died between the placing of the order and subsequent installation, the defendant failed to tell the workers of this material change in circumstances and allowed them to go ahead with their work. The Court of Appeal held that this behaviour was enough to support a charge of obtaining a service by deception (as to which, see below). In the offences which follow, the particular consequences (such as the parting with property or the provision of a service) must be brought about by the deception.

There are particular difficulties in relation to credit cards and charge cards where the person being 'deceived' is not entirely convinced by the deception or is aware that the deceiver is simply exceeding his/her authorised credit limit. For a discussion of these cases, see *Blackstone's Criminal Practice*, 2003, section B5.9.

If the 'target' of the deception is not actually deceived by the words or conduct then there will only have been an attempted deception. Although there is no clear authority on the issue, it would appear that this requirement means that a machine cannot be deceived and any offences committed by fooling a machine or computer would not amount to deception. Because of this restriction and the increase in the number of commercial transactions carried out solely by interaction with a machine (e.g. purchases of goods and services over the telephone by keying in details of debit cards), there has been some pressure for a change in the law. Despite this pressure, the Law Commission has declined to recommend the creation of a new offence of 'fraud' which would do away with the need for an operating deception. For the time being, therefore, if a person orders goods or services simply by dialing up an automated database and keying in false details of a 'Switch' card over the telephone, he/she does not commit any offence involving deception (though there would clearly be other offences).

If the deceit is practised *after* the desired consequences (e.g. the obtaining of property or services), there will be no operating deception (see *R* v *Collis-Smith* [1971] Crim LR 716), but there may still be other offences (such as making off without payment).

1.8 Fraud

1.8.1 Obtaining Property by Deception

OFFENCE: **Obtaining Property by Deception—*Theft Act 1968, s. 15***
* Triable either way • Ten years' imprisonment on indictment; six months' imprisonment and/or a fine summarily
(Arrestable offence)

The Theft Act 1968, s. 15 states:

(1) A person who by any deception dishonestly obtains property belonging to another, with the intention of permanently depriving the other of it, shall on conviction on indictment be liable...

(2) For purposes of this section a person is to be treated as obtaining property if he obtains ownership, possession or control of it, and 'obtain' includes obtaining for another or enabling another to obtain or to retain.

(3) Section 6 above shall apply for purposes of this section, with the necessary adaptation of the reference to appropriating, as it applies for purposes of section 1.

KEYNOTE

'Property' for these purposes is generally the same as for the offence of theft. However, the restrictions in relation to 'property' contained in s. 4(2)–(4) of the 1968 Act do not appear to apply to this offence. Therefore, it would seem that you can 'obtain' land by deception. Where the property obtained is a bank credit or the offence involves the issuing of a cheque, the situation is complicated by the decision in *R* v *Preddy* [1996] AC 815. Although there may be an offence under s. 15A, which was introduced as a result of *Preddy*, the advice of the Crown Prosecution Service should be sought.

'Obtaining' as defined under s. 15(2) is very broad and also includes enabling another to *retain* property. A defendant practising a deception to enable *himself/herself* to retain property would not fall into this definition.

As mentioned above, you must prove a connection between the deception practised and the obtaining of the property.

....

EXAMPLE

A man (X) goes to the goods collection point in an electrical superstore. Falsely claiming that he has ordered and paid for a computer game for his son's birthday, X says he would like to collect the game but has lost the receipt. The sales assistant believes him and gives him the computer game. The following week X gives the game to his delighted son.

In these circumstances you must prove that:

- X used a *deception*—by both his *words* and *conduct* he *deliberately* misrepresented *facts* about himself and the pre-paid order for goods
- X acted *dishonestly*—implicit in his behaviour
- X *obtained property*—he gained control of (including actual possession) the computer game
- the goods *belonged to another*—the electrical store
- X *intended to deprive* the other of the goods *permanently*—he gave the game to his son (note that s. 6 of the Theft Act 1968 applies to this offence).

....

If the sales assistant had not been fooled by the deception but had felt sorry for X's son and gave him the game anyway, this offence would not be made out. There would, however, have been an attempted deception. Since the House of Lords' decision in *R* v *Gomez* [1993] AC 442, there may also be an offence of theft. In fact, following that ruling, many offences under s. 15 will also be chargeable as offences of theft without the need to prove the operating deception.

If, instead of deceiving the assistant into giving him the game, X had deceived him into giving his son a free session on a coin-operated video game in the store, no *property* would have been obtained. A *service* would have been obtained and the proper charge would be one of obtaining a service by deception under the Theft Act 1978, s. 1.

1.8.2 Obtaining a Pecuniary Advantage

OFFENCE: **Obtaining a Pecuniary Advantage by Deception— *Theft Act 1968, s. 16***

- Triable either way • Five years' imprisonment on indictment; six months' imprisonment and/or a fine summarily

(Arrestable offence)

The Theft Act 1968, s. 16 states:

(1) A person who by any deception dishonestly obtains for himself or another any pecuniary advantage shall on conviction on indictment be liable . . .

(2) The cases in which a pecuniary advantage within the meaning of this section is to be regarded as obtained for a person are cases where—
   (a) [repealed]
   (b) he is allowed to borrow by way of overdraft, or to take out any policy of insurance or annuity contract, or obtains an improvement of the terms on which he is allowed to do so; or
   (c) he is given the opportunity to earn remuneration or greater remuneration in an office or employment, or to win money by betting.

KEYNOTE

The elements of deception and dishonesty are the same as those for s. 15 above. This offence is really about deceiving people in order to bring about certain types of opportunity. Helpfully, the House of Lords have decided that a defendant need not be shown to have actually profited by his/her actions, only that his/her deception brought about the consequences listed at s. 16(2)(b) or (c) (*DPP* v *Turner* [1974] AC 537).

1.8.3 False Accounting

OFFENCE: **False Accounting—*Theft Act 1968, s. 17***

- Triable either way • Seven years' imprisonment on indictment; six months' imprisonment and/or a fine summarily

(Arrestable offence)

The Theft Act 1968, s. 17 states:

(1) Where a person dishonestly, with a view to gain for himself or another or with intent to cause loss to another,—

(a) destroys, defaces, conceals or falsifies any account or any record or document made or required for any accounting purpose; or

(b) in furnishing information for any purpose produces or makes use of any account, or any such record or document as aforesaid, which to his knowledge is or may be misleading, false or deceptive in a material particular;

he shall [commit an offence].

(2) For purposes of this section a person who makes or concurs in making in an account or other document an entry which is or may be misleading, false or deceptive in a material particular, or who omits or concurs in omitting a material particular from an account or other document, is to be treated as falsifying the account or document.

KEYNOTE

This section creates two offences: destroying, defacing etc. accounts and documents; and using false or misleading accounts or documents in furnishing information.

An offence under s. 17 can be committed by omission as well as by an act. Failing to make an entry in an accounts book, altering a till receipt or supplying an auditor with records that are incomplete may, if accompanied by the other ingredients, amount to an offence.

Unlike theft there is no requirement to prove an intention permanently to deprive but there is a need to show dishonesty. As a result, this offence is relatively straightforward to prove once an investigator has identified the *prima facie* evidence.

The misleading, false or deceptive nature of the information furnished under s. 17(1)(b) must be 'material' to the defendant's overall purpose, i.e. the ultimate gaining or causing of loss. Such an interpretation means that the defendant's furnishing of information need not relate directly to an accounting process and could be satisfied by lying about the status of a potential finance customer (see *R* v *Mallet* [1978] 1 WLR 820).

Where the documents falsified are not intrinsically 'accounting' forms, such as insurance claim forms filled out by policyholders, you must show that those forms are treated for accounting purposes by the victim (*R* v *Sundhers* [1998] Crim LR 497).

There is also a further offence (triable and punishable as the above offences), of company officers making false statements with intent to deceive members or creditors (Theft Act 1968, s. 19).

1.9   Theft Act 1978, Sections 1 and 2

1.9.1   Obtaining Services by Deception

OFFENCE: **Obtaining Services by Deception—*Theft Act 1978, s. 1***

• Triable either way • Five years' imprisonment on indictment; six months' imprisonment and/or a fine summarily
(Arrestable offence)

The Theft Act 1978, s. 1 states:

(1) A person who by any deception dishonestly obtains services from another shall be guilty of an offence.

(2) It is an obtaining of services where the other is induced to confer a benefit by doing some act, or causing or permitting some act to be done, on the understanding that the benefit has been or will be paid for.

KEYNOTE

Deception and dishonesty are the same as for those offences under the 1968 Act. The main difference between this and the offence of obtaining property is that here *the person providing the service* must be induced to do so by the deception, that is, he/she must be the 'target' of the deception. Although there is no mention of obtaining a service for *another*, the Court of Appeal has accepted that such behaviour could amount to an offence under s. 1 (*R v Nathan* [1997] Crim LR 835). As with the offence of obtaining property, the deception could be aimed at a third party. Again, there may be some overlap with other deception offences. A service provided by a hotel may include property such as a meal. Conversely, the delivery of goods will include an element of service. To illustrate the possible extent of overlap between deception offences consider the following example.

....

EXAMPLE

A person replies to a job advertisement for a child minder. Falsely claiming to have a recognised qualification in child care, he is offered a job which includes remuneration, accommodation, meals and the use of the family car.

....

By applying for the job and availing himself of the attendant benefits, the person apparently commits many of the offences considered in this section.

Service

There is nothing in the section which requires the service to be a lawful or contractual one.

There were considerable problems involved with prosecuting offences under s. 1 where the service obtained was the granting of a loan. The courts had decided that loan agreements, even those procured by deception, were not covered by s. 1 of the 1978 Act and s. 16 of the 1968 Act only extends to overdraft facilities.

However, Parliament has amended s. 1 of the 1978 Act (Theft (Amendment) Act 1996, s. 4(1)) by inserting s. 1(3) which states:

(3) Without prejudice to the generality of subsection (2) above, it is an obtaining of services where the other is induced to make a loan, or to cause or permit a loan to be made, on the understanding that any payment (whether by way of interest or otherwise) will be or has been made in respect of the loan.

KEYNOTE

This new subsection puts the quite common situation of obtaining a loan by deception squarely within the offence of obtaining services.

1.9.2 **Evading Liability by Deception**

OFFENCE: **Evading Liability by Deception—*Theft Act 1978, s. 2***
- Triable either way • Five years' imprisonment on indictment; six months' imprisonment and/or a fine summarily
(Arrestable offence)

The Theft Act 1978, s. 2 states:

(1) Subject to subsection (2) below, where a person by any deception—
   (a) dishonestly secures the remission of the whole or part of any existing liability to make a payment, whether his own liability or another's; or

     (b) with intent to make permanent default in whole or in part on any existing liability to make a payment, or with intent to let another do so, dishonestly induces the creditor or any person claiming payment on behalf of the creditor to wait for payment (whether or not the due date for payment is deferred) or to forgo payment; or

     (c) dishonestly obtains any exemption from or abatement of liability to make a payment;

     he shall be guilty of an offence.

(2) For purposes of this section 'liability' means legally enforceable liability; and subsection (1) shall not apply in relation to a liability that has not been accepted or established to pay compensation for a wrongful act or omission.

(3) For purposes of subsection (1)(b) a person induced to take in payment a cheque or other security for money by way of conditional satisfaction of a pre-existing liability is to be treated not as being paid but as being induced to wait for payment.

(4) For purposes of subsection (1)(c) 'obtains' includes obtaining for another or enabling another to obtain.

KEYNOTE

Deception and dishonesty have the same meaning as in the other offences above.

This section creates three distinct offences. One feature which all three offences share is the requirement for a *legal liability*. In the case of s. 2(1)(a) and (b) that liability must already be in existence whereas the wording of s. 2(1)(c) makes provision for both existing and newly-created liabilities.

If the liability is not legally enforceable (such as a betting agreement or an agreement to provide an immoral service) none of the three offences will apply.

Section 2(2) excludes any liability to pay compensation in relation to a wrongful act or omission where that liability has not been accepted or established.

Elements of the Offences

To prove the offence under s. 2(1)(a) you must show that a defendant secured a release from all or part of an existing liability to make a payment. If a person orders and accepts delivery of goods and then dishonestly convinces the supplier that they have been paid for, he/she would commit this offence. Note that because the deception in such a case is not committed at the time of the goods being obtained, s. 15 of the 1968 Act (obtaining property by deception) is not applicable. Section 2(1)(a) makes provision for the situation where the liability is *another* person's liability, not just the defendant's.

Under s. 2(1)(b) there is a requirement to prove an intent to make permanent default, that is, not just to put creditors off or to delay payment to them. Perhaps the best examples of such offences are those involving 'dud' cheques which, by virtue of s. 2(3), will amount to an inducement to wait for payment. Section 2(1)(b) makes provision for the situation where the defendant's intentions are to let *another person* make permanent default on *any* existing liability.

An 'abatement' is a reduction in a liability to make a payment. Such an abatement under s. 2(1)(c) might be obtained when someone falsely claims to be a student in order to get into a cinema at a discounted rate. In such circumstances, the person's deception as to his/her status (i.e. as a paid-up member of the Students' Union) may also be an offence under s. 1 (see *R v Adams* [1993] Crim LR 525).

Section 2(1)(c) makes no provision in respect of obtaining an exemption from, or abatement of a liability *for another* to make a payment. It may therefore be argued that, given the specific inclusion of such provisions in s. 2(1)(a) and (b), this was an intentional omission by the legislators. However, the approach of the Court of Appeal in *Nathan* (see above) may also be adopted in such circumstances.

Overlap

As with the other deception offences, there will be occasions when offences under s. 2 of the 1978 Act will overlap. Consider the following example:

....

EXAMPLE

X orders a lawnmower from a mail order catalogue, never intending to pay for it. When it is delivered to X's house some weeks later, the delivery driver asks for both payment in full for the mower and also for the delivery charges. X, who ordered the goods, falsely states that he has already paid a 50 per cent deposit and is only liable for the remainder. He also falsely states that when he placed the order he was told delivery would be free. The delivery driver and the mail order company accept the 50 per cent payment (made with a worthless cheque) and the 'purchaser', X, then sells the lawnmower at a car boot sale.

In these circumstances X may commit:

- Theft—by dishonestly appropriating the mower intending to deprive the supplier of it permanently.
- Obtaining property by deception—by dishonestly deceiving the mail order company from the outset into giving him control of the mower, intending permanently to deprive them of it.
- Obtaining a service by deception—because X never intended to pay for the mower or the delivery service he has induced the mail order company to confer that benefit on the understanding that it had been/will be paid for.
- Evading liability by deception—X has, by his deceptions dishonestly secured a release from his existing liability to pay for the mower and its delivery.
- Dishonestly inducing the company and its agent to wait for payment, intending to make permanent default.
- Dishonestly obtaining an abatement of his liability to pay for the mower and an exemption from paying for its delivery.

Clearly there are some charges which more readily lend themselves to these circumstances, but the example serves to show the potential overlap in even relatively straightforward theft and deception offences. In cases of doubt, the advice of the Crown Prosecution Service should be sought.

....

1.10   Offences Relating to Bank Accounts

There are two recent offences which have been created to deal specifically with circumstances where defendants cause bank or building society accounts to be credited or debited, or where they dishonestly retain funds which have been wrongly credited to their account. The first offence is discussed below. The second one is set out below, followed by an explanation of how the offences relate to each other in practice.

1.10.1   Obtaining Money Transfer

OFFENCE: **Obtaining Money Transfer by Deception—*Theft Act 1968, s. 15A***
- Triable either way • Ten years' imprisonment on indictment; six months' imprisonment and/or a fine summarily
(Arrestable offence)

The Theft Act 1968, s. 15A states:

(1) A person is guilty of an offence if by any deception he dishonestly obtains a money transfer for himself or another.

(2) A money transfer occurs when—
   (a) a debit is made to one account,
   (b) a credit is made to another, and
   (c) the credit results from the debit or the debit results from the credit.

(3) References to a credit and to a debit are to a credit of an amount of money and to a debit of an amount of money.

(4) It is immaterial (in particular)—
    (a) whether the amount credited is the same as the amount debited;
    (b) whether the money transfer is effected on presentment of a cheque or by another method;
    (c) whether any delay occurs in the process by which the money transfer is effected;
    (d) whether any intermediate credits or debits are made in the course of the money transfer;
    (e) whether either of the accounts is overdrawn before or after the money transfer is effected.

KEYNOTE

This offence was introduced by the Theft (Amendment) Act 1996, s. 1, to close a gap in the law relating to deception. In a case involving a complicated mortgage fraud (*R v Preddy* [1996] AC 815), the House of Lords had accepted that there had been no *property belonging to another* to support a charge of obtaining property by deception under s. 15, neither had there been an obtaining of a 'service'. As a result of the Theft (Amendment) Act 1996, s. 4, the provision of a loan *is* now a 'service' for these purposes.

The above offence now caters for such occasions. As this is new law there has been no opportunity for the courts to interpret its application. The Law Commission, however, felt that the wording in s. 15A(2) was wide enough to cover occasions where the amount credited from one account is different from the amount debited or vice-versa. It should also cover circumstances where there is a delay in the debit or credit on either account or where the debit/credit is made in error and later corrected.

'Dishonestly' and 'deception' will have the same meaning as in the other offences in this chapter. Remember that if a person dishonestly presents a cheque from another person's account and that cheque is honoured, there has been an old fashioned appropriation of the contents (which can be 'property'). Therefore, there would be a theft and the principle in *Preddy* would not apply (*R v Williams (Roy)* (2001) 1 Cr App R 23).

An 'account' means an account kept with a bank or a person carrying on a business which falls within s. 15B which states:

A business falls within this subsection if—

(a) in the course of the business money received by way of deposit is lent to others; or

(b) any other activity of the business is financed, wholly or to any material extent, out of the capital of or the interest on money received by way of deposit;

and 'deposit' here has the same meaning as in section 35 of the Banking Act 1987 (fraudulent inducement to make a deposit).

KEYNOTE

An 'account' for the purpose of an offence under s. 15A(1) must be an account kept with a bank or a person carrying on a business that falls within s. 15B. As such, the offence will generally be restricted to transactions involving the crediting and debiting of accounts held with financial institutions.

Relationship Between s. 15A and s. 24A

The offence(s) could be committed in the following ways:

• Where a defendant dishonestly obtains a transfer of funds, by a deception, from the bank account of a friend into his/her own bank account. In such a case there would be two overlapping offences; the offence of obtaining a money transfer by deception (s. 15A, above) and the further offence (s. 24A) of *retaining* the credit once it had been obtained in that way.

• Where a defendant is authorised to operate his/her employer's account and steals funds from it, transferring them to his/her own account. The defendant would commit both theft, and also the offence of dishonestly retaining a wrongful credit (s. 24A).

- Where a defendant uses any form of dishonest deception to get a person to transfer funds from his/her own account into that of a third person. The defendant would commit the offence of dishonestly obtaining a money transfer (s. 15A) and the third party, if they dishonestly failed to take reasonable steps to secure its cancellation, would commit the offence under s. 24A.

- Where a defendant dishonestly obtains a money transfer by deception and then, some-time later, draws the cash out of his/her account. The defendant commits an offence under s. 15A, an offence under s. 24A and theft. The cash will be 'stolen goods' for the purposes of s. 22 and anyone who receives it under the conditions specified in s. 22 will be guilty of 'handling'.

1.10.2 Falsification of Documents and Other Instruments

In addition to the offence of deception, there are a series of closely-related offences which deal with falsification of documents or other 'instruments'. As with some deception offences, there will be circumstances which appear to support charges under several different enactments such as false accounting, using a false instrument or obtaining property by deception.

1.11 Retaining a Wrongful Credit

OFFENCE: **Dishonestly Retaining a Wrongful Credit—*Theft Act 1968, s. 24A***
- Triable either way • Ten years' imprisonment on indictment; six months' imprisonment and/or a fine summarily
(Arrestable offence)

The Theft Act 1968, s. 24A states:

   (1) A person is guilty of an offence if—
     (a) a wrongful credit has been made to an account kept by him or in respect of which he has any right or interest;
     (b) he knows or believes that the credit is wrongful; and
     (c) he dishonestly fails to take such steps as are reasonable in the circumstances to secure that the credit is cancelled.

   (2) References to a credit are to a credit of an amount of money.

   (3) A credit to an account is wrongful if it is the credit side of a money transfer obtained contrary to section 15A of this Act.

   (4) A credit to an account is also wrongful to the extent that it derives from—
     (a) theft;
     (b) an offence under section 15A of this Act;
     (c) blackmail; or
     (d) stolen goods.

   (5) In determining whether a credit to an account is wrongful, it is immaterial (in particular) whether the account is overdrawn before or after the credit is made.

   (6) ...

   (7) Subsection (8) below applies for purposes of provisions of this Act relating to stolen goods (including subsection (4) above).

   (8) References to stolen goods include money which is dishonestly withdrawn from an account to which a wrongful credit has been made, but only to the extent that the money derives from the credit.

   (9) In this section 'account' and 'money' shall be construed in accordance with section 15B of this Act.

KEYNOTE

This offence was prompted by the decision in *R v Preddy* [1996] AC 815. The Law Commission were anxious to ensure that the transferee of funds obtained dishonestly could be charged with 'handling' those funds. As there were considerable problems created by applying the existing legislation under s. 22, these further offences were introduced.

The wrongful credit to an account can occur in two ways: it may come from the circumstances outlined under s. 15A; or it may come from one of the dishonest sources set out in s. 24A(4) above.

Again, the type of 'account' involved is the same as for the offence under s. 15A(1). Therefore, these offences will generally be restricted to transactions involving the crediting of accounts held with financial institutions.

There is a requirement for dishonesty. However, there is no requirement for any *deception*.

The effects of s. 24A(8) are that *money* derived from credit received under ss. 15A and 24A of the Theft Act 1968 may amount to stolen goods. The provisions governing the status of the credit itself (i.e. not as cash but as a 'thing in action') are more complicated. If the proceeds of a theft by A are paid into his/her bank account they are stolen goods because they represent the stolen goods in the hands of the thief (s. 24(4)).

If they are then transferred into B's bank account, they cease to be stolen goods. This is because the 'thing in action' (the credit balance) created by the transfer in B's name is a different 'thing in action' from the one originally created by A (see *R v Preddy* [1996] AC 815). As such, the credit balance in B's name has never represented the proceeds of the theft *in the hands of the thief*. If B withdraws money from the credited account, that money then, by virtue of s. 24A(8), becomes stolen goods once more.

To quote from *Blackstone's Criminal Practice*, 2003, section B4.147:

> It may seem strange that the proceeds of A's original theft can be classed as stolen goods when paid into A's own bank account, cease to be so classified when effectively 'transferred' to B's account, and yet revert to being stolen goods when dishonestly withdrawn as cash by B; but such is now the law.

This offence is also unusual in that the *actus reus* not only *can be* satisfied by an 'omission', but necessarily *involves* an omission or a failure to act.

1.12 **Blackmail**

OFFENCE: **Blackmail—*Theft Act 1968, s. 21***
　　　　　　　• Triable on indictment • Fourteen years' imprisonment
　　　　　　　(Arrestable offence)

The Theft Act 1968, s. 21 states:

(1) A person is guilty of blackmail if, with a view to gain for himself or another or with intent to cause loss to another, he makes any unwarranted demand with menaces; and for this purpose a demand with menaces is unwarranted unless the person making it does so in the belief—
　　(a) that he has reasonable grounds for making the demand; and
　　(b) that the use of the menaces is a proper means of reinforcing the demand.

(2) The nature of the act or omission demanded is immaterial, and it is also immaterial whether the menaces relate to action to be taken by the person making the demand.

KEYNOTE

It might be better—for several reasons—if this offence were to be called 'demands with menaces'. Whatever its name, in proving this offence you must show that a defendant acted either with a view to gain for himself/herself or another or with intent to cause loss to another. The distinction here is important. The phrase 'with a view to' has been held (albeit under a different criminal statute) by the Court of Appeal to be less than 'with intent to' (*R v Zaman* [2002] EWCA Crim 1862). In *Zaman*, the Court accepted that a lesser degree of *mens rea* was required to prove that a defendant acted 'with a view to' something and that this phrase meant simply that the defendant had something in his/her contemplation as *something that realistically might occur*, not that he/she necessarily intended or even wanted it to happen. Clearly this is a very different test from 'intent'. In the above offence then, it appears that the state of mind needed to prove the first element is that the defendant contemplated some gain for himself/herself or for another as being a realistically likely to flow from his/her actions. The alternative is an 'intent' to cause loss—a harder element to prove.

There is no requirement for dishonesty, deception or theft and the offence is aimed at the making of the demands rather than the consequences of them.

Section 34 of the 1968 Act states:

(2) For the purposes of this Act—

(a) 'gain' and 'loss' are to be construed as extending only to gain or loss in money or other property, but as extending to any such gain or loss whether temporary or permanent; and—

(i) 'gain' includes a gain by keeping what one has, as well as a gain by getting what one has not; and

(ii) 'loss' includes a loss by not getting what one might get, as well as a loss by parting with what one has;

KEYNOTE

This is one of those bits of legislation which makes less sense the more you read it. The bottom line is that keeping what you already have can amount to a 'gain'. Similarly, not getting something that you might expect to get can be a 'loss'.

EXAMPLE

Consider an example used later in relation to 'obtaining a pecuniary advantage'. A person makes unwarranted demands with menaces with a view to getting a sports fixture cancelled and thereby to avoid losing money that he has bet on the outcome of that fixture. Here it could be argued that the intention of keeping what the defendant already had (the money at risk on the bet) amounts to 'gain' as defined under s. 34(2). Similarly, the intention of preventing others getting what they might have got (their winnings or the club's earnings) could amount to a 'loss'.

1.12.1 **Criminal Conduct**

The offence of blackmail is complete when the demand with menaces is made. It does not matter whether the demands bring about the desired consequences or not. If a demand is made by letter, the act of making it is complete when the letter is posted. The letter does not have to be received (*Treacy* v *DPP* [1971] AC 537).

The Court of Appeal has held that words or conduct which would not intimidate or influence anyone to respond to the demand would not be 'menaces'. As such, the term requires threats and conduct of such a nature and extent that a person of normal stability and courage might be influenced or made apprehensive so as to give in to the demands (see *R* v *Clear* [1968] 1 QB 670).

Menaces will therefore include threats but these must be significant to the victim. If a threat bears a particular significance for a victim (such as being locked in the boot of a car to someone who is claustrophobic) that will be enough, provided the defendant was aware of that fact. If a victim is particularly timid and the defendant knows it, that timidity may be taken into account when assessing whether or not the defendant's conduct was 'menacing' (*R* v *Garwood* [1987] 1 WLR 319).

1.12.2 **Unwarranted?**

If a defendant raises the issue that his/her demand was reasonable and proper, you will have to prove that he/she did not believe:

– that he/she had reasonable grounds for making the demand; and

– that the use of the particular menaces employed was not a proper means of reinforcing it.

The defendant's *belief* will be a subjective one and therefore could be entirely unreasonable. However, if the threatened action would itself be unlawful (such as a threat to rape the victim) then it is unlikely that the courts would accept any claim by a defendant that he/she believed such a demand to be 'proper' (see *R* v *Harvey* (1980) 72 Cr App R 139).

PART TWO

Assaults, Drugs, Firearms and Defences

2.1 Homicide

2.1.1 Introduction

Homicide covers not only the offences of murder and manslaughter, but also other occasions where a person causes, or is involved in, the death of another. The common law which has grown up around the subject of homicide is important, not only because of the gravity of the offences themselves, but also because the cases have defined a number of key issues in criminal law which are applicable to many other offences.

In all cases of homicide, the general criminal conduct (*actus reus*) is the same—the killing of another person—but there are often complex arguments over causation.

Although offences of homicide are still relatively rare in day-to-day policing, many assaults can turn into homicides simply by the consequent and causally-connected death of the victim. For this reason, it is necessary that police officers have at least a general understanding of the key concepts.

In approaching the offences discussed in this chapter, it is worth noting the statutory duty imposed on chief officers of police and the local probation board for the area, acting jointly as the 'responsible authority' in relation to certain types of offender. Although primarily concerned with sex offenders, that duty (under s. 67 of the Criminal Justice and Court Services Act 2000) also relates to violent offenders and the responsible authority has a duty to establish appropriate 'arrangements' for the purpose of assessing and managing the risks posed in their area by relevant violent offenders.

In considering any offences set out in this chapter, the right to life enshrined in Article 2 of the European Convention on Human Rights may be significant. In particular, the positive obligation imposed on a State to protect the lives of its citizens may be relevant where a person has been killed or an unlawful attempt has been made on his/her life. Article 2 creates both a duty on the State not to take life and also a positive duty to protect the lives of individuals (see *X* v *United Kingdom* (Application 7154/75) (1978) 14 DR 31). The duty of the State to protect people from the criminal actions of others was examined in the case of *Osman* v *United Kingdom* (2000) 29 EHRR 245. There the European Court of Human Rights held that it is possible for an individual to show that the State had violated Article 2 if the police had failed to protect his/her right to life under certain circumstances. Recently, in a case concerning withholding medical treatment, the High Court considered the positive and negative duties under Article 2. The court held that the negative obligation was to refrain from taking a life intentionally. It held that this obligation was not breached by a decision made in the patient's best interests to withdraw life support facilities and that the intentional deprivation of life had to involve a deliberate act as opposed to an omission. In relation to the positive obligation, the court held that this required the relevant public authority to take adequate and appropriate steps to safeguard life. Again, the taking of a responsible clinical decision to withhold treatment that was not in the patient's best interests met the State's positive obligation under Article 2 (*NHS Trust A* v *M* [2001] 2 WLR 942).

2.1.2 Murder

OFFENCE: **Murder—*Common Law***
> • Life imprisonment (mandatory)
> *(Serious arrestable offence)*

Murder is committed when a person unlawfully kills another human being under the Queen's Peace, with malice aforethought (see *Blackstone's Criminal Practice*, 2003, section B1).

KEYNOTE

A conviction for murder carries a mandatory sentence of life imprisonment (in the case of a defendant who is under 18, 'detention at Her Majesty's pleasure': Powers of Criminal Courts (Sentencing) Act 2000, s. 90).

'Unlawful killing' means actively causing the death of another without justification and includes occasions where someone fails to act after creating a situation of danger.

'Another human being' includes a baby who has been born alive and has an existence independent of its mother. If a person injures a baby while it is in its mother's womb and it subsequently dies from those injuries *after being born*, it may be appropriate to bring a charge of murder.

If the defendant intended only to cause serious injury to the mother, that intention cannot support a charge of *murder* in respect of the baby if it goes on to die after being born alive. It may, however, support a charge of *manslaughter*. This departure from the earlier law is clear from the House of Lords' ruling in *Attorney-General's Reference (No. 3 of 1994)* [1998] AC 245, a ruling that overturned the Court of Appeal's previous decision in the same case. The House of Lords ruled that the doctrine of 'transferred malice' does not fully apply in cases of unborn children (*in utero*). Any liability of the defendant for the subsequent death of a child that he/she injured before it was born alive will depend on the defendant's intentions at the time of causing the injury. Clearly an intention to kill the mother could be sufficient in bringing a charge of murder following the subsequent and connected death of the child.

'Under the Queen's Peace' appears to exclude deaths caused during the legitimate prosecution of warfare (see the War Crimes Act 1991). Under the provisions of the Offences Against the Person Act 1861 any British citizen who commits a murder anywhere in the world may be tried in England or Wales.

It should be noted that the only state of mind or mens rea that will support a charge of attempted murder is an intention to kill. Nothing less will suffice (hence the note in the CPS Charging Standards).

Sections 1 and 2 of the Criminal Evidence (Amendment) Act 1997 extending the power to take non-intimate samples without consent apply to this offence and also to conspiracies, attempts or incitements in the circumstances set out in that Act.

Malice Aforethought

This archaic expression both sounds—and was—very complex and daunting until recently. Now, after the cases of *R* v *Moloney* [1985] AC 905 and *R* v *Hancock* [1986] AC 455, the *mens rea* required for murder is an intention:

– to kill, or

– to cause grievous bodily harm.

Murder is therefore a crime of 'specific intent'.

The term 'malice aforethought' is therefore completely misleading and the only place where 'premeditation' is insisted upon is in murder mystery novels.

Year and a Day

Another ancient and awkward rule which no longer applies is the 'year and a day' requirement. Since the Law Reform (Year and a Day Rule) Act 1996 there is no longer a need to show that a victim died within a year and a day of the defendant's actions (s. 1).

If a victim of an alleged murder dies *more than three years after receiving their injury* then the consent of the Attorney-General (or Solicitor-General) is needed before bringing a prosecution (s. 22(b)). That consent is also needed if the defendant has already been convicted of an offence committed under the circumstances connected with the death (s. 22(a)).

2.1.3   Special Defences

As a conviction for murder leaves a judge no discretion in sentencing a defendant, a number of 'special defences' have developed around the offence. These 'defences' are now provided by the Homicide Act 1957 and, rather than securing an acquittal, allow for a conviction of voluntary manslaughter instead of murder. As such these defences fall outside the more common defences that are generally available in respect of criminal offences. While defences in the more general sense are of direct relevance to the police, the special defences discussed below are technical issues that are only really of passing importance to police officers. Many criminal texts approaching their subject from a purely academic perspective devote many pages to this complex area, whereas most police officers will probably never encounter these matters more than once in their careers.

These 'special defences' are:

– diminished responsibility

– provocation

– suicide pact.

Diminished Responsibility

The Homicide Act 1957, s. 2 states:

(1) Where a person kills or is party to the killing of another, he shall not be convicted of murder if he was suffering from such abnormality of mind (whether arising from a condition of arrested or retarded development of mind or any inherent causes or induced by disease or injury) as substantially impaired his mental responsibility for his acts or omissions in doing or being a party to the killing.

(2) On a charge of murder, it shall be for the defence to prove that the person charged is by virtue of this section not liable to be convicted of murder.

(3) A person who but for this section would be liable, whether as principal or as accessory, to be convicted of murder shall be liable instead to be convicted of manslaughter.

(4) The fact that one party to a killing is by virtue of this section not liable to be convicted of murder shall not affect the question whether the killing amounted to murder in the case of any other party to it.

KEYNOTE

'Abnormality of mind' has been held to be 'a state of mind so different from that of ordinary human beings that the reasonable man would term it abornmal' (*R* v *Byrne* [1960] 2 QB 396). This includes the mental inability to exert control over one's behaviour and to form rational judgement.

'Impairment of mental responsibility'—this impairment must be 'substantial'. Whether or not that is the case will be a question of fact for the jury to decide. Minor lapses of lucidity will not be enough. There may be any number of causes of the 'abnormality' of the mind. Examples accepted by the courts to date have included pre-menstrual symptoms (*R* v *Reynolds* [1988] Crim LR 679) and 'battered wives' syndrome' (*R* v *Hobson* (1998) 1 Cr App R 31).

The burden of proving these features lies with the defence and the standard required is one of a balance of probabilities. While this issue of 'reverse onus of proof' has created some inconsistent decisions across different statutory provisions—and in particular its relationship with the European Convention on Human Rights—in *R* v *Lambert* [2001] 2 WLR 211, the Court of Appeal held that this burden of proof did not breach an individual's right to a presumption of innocence or the right to a fair trial under the Convention.

Provocation

The Homicide Act 1957, s. 3 states:

Where on a charge of murder there is evidence on which a jury can find that the person charged was provoked (whether by things done or by things said or by both together) to lose his self-control, the question whether the provocation was enough to make a reasonable man do as he did shall be left to be determined by the jury; and in determining that question the jury shall take into account everything both done and said according to the effect which, in their opinion, it would have on a reasonable man.

KEYNOTE

The question of provocation here is not a general consideration of the ordinary English meaning of the word, but a highly technical pleading that has developed through the common law. The real relevance of this area to police officers will be in the gathering and recording of any evidence that might support or undermine the claim that the defendant was 'provoked'.

The main questions to be considered are:

— Was the defendant actually provoked?

— Might a reasonable person have acted as the defendant did under the same circumstances?

These two tests have attracted different approaches (subjective and objective), with the overall result that the whole area is a shining example of the shortcomings in our current common law system. Whether the defendant was in fact provoked will be a matter for the jury.

It is clear that words (*DPP* v *Camplin* [1978] AC 705) or even sounds (*R* v *Doughty* (1986) 83 Cr App R 319 (baby crying)) have amounted to 'provocation'. It is also clear that the words or acts need not be directed towards the defendant, nor need they originate from the ultimate victim. Therefore a defendant may be sufficiently provoked by things which X says to Y that he/she kills Z and the 'defence' of provocation could be available. In addition to the 'battered wives' syndrome' mentioned above, where the provocation has been endured by the defendant over a prolonged period (such as the abused wife in *R* v *Ahluwalia* [1992] 4 All ER 889), he/she may be able to show an eventual and sudden lack of self-control brought about by that prolonged behaviour or by a particular event which proved to be 'the last straw' (*R* v *Humphreys* [1995] 4 All ER 1008). If a defendant simply panics or acts out of fear, as opposed to losing control, the defence will not be made out. Unlike the general defence of 'duress', there is no defence of 'provocation by circumstances'; the provocation must come from something done by or to a third person (*R* v *Acott* [1997] 1 WLR 306).

If there is no loss of control by the defendant, then the provocation defence will not be available. See, for example, *R* v *Cocker* [1989] Crim LR 740 where the defendant had endured pleas from his chronically-ill wife to kill her. He had not lost control at the time of the killing—quite the reverse—and the judge had no alternative but to pass a life sentence.

As to the 'reasonable person' test, the rules for applying this are now, after much argument, set out in the House of Lords' decision in *R* v *Smith* [2001] 1 AC 146. Those seeking complete clarity on the matter, however, will still be disappointed by some parts of this judgment and a full discussion can be found in *Blackstone's Criminal Practice*, 2003, section B1.20.

Suicide Pact

The Homicide Act 1957, s. 4 states:

(1) It shall be manslaughter, and shall not be murder, for a person acting in pursuance of a suicide pact between him and another to kill the other or be a party to the other being killed by a third person.

KEYNOTE

The defendant must show that:

— a suicide pact had been made, and

— he/she had the intention of dying at the time the killing took place.

'Suicide pact' is defined by the Homicide Act 1957, s. 4(3) as:

> a common agreement between two or more persons having for its object the death of all of them, whether or not each is to take his own life, but nothing done by a person who enters into a suicide pact shall be treated as done by him in pursuance of the pact unless it is done while he has the settled intention of dying in pursuance of the pact.

(See also **para. 2.1.5** for the offence of assisting a suicide.)

2.1.4 Manslaughter

Traditionally, this subject is divided into two classifications—voluntary and involuntary manslaughter. This is not particularly helpful. The real division between the two types of manslaughter centres around the *mens rea*—the state of mind of the defendant.

The three sets of circumstances where 'special defences' may reduce a murder charge to one of manslaughter make up one type or classification of the offence (so-called *voluntary* manslaughter). They have been covered in **para 2.1.3** above. In that sense, voluntary manslaughter is more a finding by a court than an offence with which someone can be charged. The second classification (*involuntary* manslaughter) occurs where the defendant causes the death of another but is not shown to have had the required *mens rea* for murder.

OFFENCE: **Manslaughter—*Common Law***
- Triable on indictment • Life imprisonment
(Serious arrestable offence)

KEYNOTE

Manslaughter, like murder is the unlawful killing of another human being. What it does not require is the intention to kill or to cause grievous bodily harm.

Sections 1 and 2 of the Criminal Evidence (Amendment) Act 1997 extending the power to take non-intimate samples without consent apply to this offence and also to conspiracies, attempts or incitements in the circumstances set out in that Act.

The second classification of manslaughter, that is, those cases which do not involve the 'special defences' under the Homicide Act 1957 (**see para. 2.1.3**) can be separated into occasions where a defendant:

- kills another by an *unlawful act which was likely to cause bodily harm*, or

- kills another by *gross negligence*.

Manslaughter by Unlawful Act

In order to prove manslaughter by an unlawful act (constructive manslaughter), you must prove:

– An unlawful act by the defendant, that is, an act which is unlawful in itself, irrespective of the fact that it ultimately results in someone's death. The act must be inherently unlawful. An act that only becomes unlawful by virtue of the way in which it is carried out will not be enough. A good example is 'driving'. Driving is clearly not an inherently unlawful act but becomes so if done inconsiderately on a road or public place. Therefore if someone drives inconsiderately and thereby causes the death of another, the act of driving—albeit carried out in a way that attracts criminal liability—is not an 'unlawful act' for the purposes of constructive manslaughter (see *Andrews* v *DPP* [1937] AC 576). This is one reason why there are statutory offences addressing most instances of death that are caused by poor standards of driving. The act need not be directed or aimed at anyone and can include acts committed against or towards property (*R* v *Goodfellow* (1986) 83 Cr App R 23).

Generally, if the actions of the victim break the chain of causation between the defendant's unlawful act and the cause of death, the defendant will not be responsible for the death of that victim (see *Blackstone's Crime Manual*, chapter 2).

This is why drug dealers who supply controlled drugs cannot generally be held liable for the ultimate deaths of their 'victims' (See *R v Dalby* [1982] 1 WLR 621 and *R v Armstrong* [1989] Crim LR 149). Although the Court of Appeal accepted that, where a person buys a controlled drug from another and immediately injects it, resulting in his/her death, the supplier might attract liability for bringing about the person's death (*R v Kennedy* [1999] Crim LR 65), by far the greater weight of authorities suggest that the supplier is unlikely to be convicted of manslaughter in such a case unless they have done something more (e.g. helping apply a tourniquet)—see generally *R v Dias* [2001] EWCA Crime 2968.

An *omission* to do something will not suffice. Any unlawful killing caused by an omission would either come under the circumstances outlined in *Blackstone's Police Manual: Crime*, chapter 2, or under those required to prove gross negligence.

- That the act involved a risk of somebody being harmed. That risk will be judged objectively; that is, would the risk be apparent to a reasonable and sober person watching the act? (See *R v Church* [1966] 1 QB 59.) Such acts might include dropping a paving stone off a bridge into the path of a train (*DPP v Newbury* [1977] AC 500), setting fire to your house (*Goodfellow* above) or firing a gun at police officers and then holding someone else in front of you when the officers return fire (*R v Pagett* (1983) 76 Cr App R 279). 'Harm' must be physical; the risk of emotional or psychological harm does not appear to be enough (see *R v Dawson* (1985) 81 Cr App R 150).

- That the defendant had the required mens rea for the relevant 'unlawful act' (e.g. for an assault or criminal damage) which led to the death of a victim. If he/she did not have that *mens rea*, the offence of manslaughter will not be made out. See, for example, *R v Lamb* [1967] 2 QB 981, where the defendant pretended to fire a revolver at his friend. Although the defendant believed that the weapon would not fire, the chamber containing a bullet moved round to the firing pin and the defendant's friend was killed. As Lamb did not have the *mens rea* required for an assault, his conviction for manslaughter was quashed.

There is no logical reason why, if a defendant uses a motor vehicle as a means to commit an 'unlawful act' (e.g. an assault), that he/she cannot be charged with manslaughter as long as the 'act' goes beyond poor driving. There are, however, reasons of policy (see *R v Lawrence* [1982] AC 510) why, in all but the most deliberate of cases, the offence under the Road Traffic Act 1988, as amended, should be used.

Manslaughter by Gross Negligence

Manslaughter is the only criminal offence at common law capable of being committed by negligence. The degree of that negligence has been the source of considerable debate over the years and particular problems have arisen in trying to distinguish the level of negligence required for manslaughter and that required to prove 'recklessness'.

A charge of manslaughter may be brought where a person, by an instance of gross negligence, has brought about the death of another. Thankfully the most difficult task in defining the degree of negligence that will qualify as 'gross' falls to the trial judge when he/she addresses the jury. Whether a defendant's conduct will amount to gross negligence is a question of fact for the jury to decide in the light of all the evidence (*R v Bateman* (1925) 19 Cr App R 8). What is clear from the decided cases is that civil liability, although a starting point for establishing the breach of a duty of care, is not enough to amount to 'gross negligence', neither is 'recklessness' as defined in *Caldwell* (*R v Adomako* [1995] 1 AC 171).

The test in *Adomako* as summarised by Lord Mackay seems to provide the leading authority on the area. Lord Mackay put the test for the jury as being: ... 'whether, having regard to the risk of death involved, the conduct of the defendant was so bad in all the circumstances as to amount in their judgment to a criminal act or omission'.

For the practical difficulties and the inconsistencies in the case law on this area generally, see *Blackstone's Criminal Practice*, 2003, section B1.39.

Corporate Manslaughter

One area that has caused a great deal of speculation—and not a little confusion—is that of corporate manslaughter. The requirement that there be at least some evidence of the state of mind of defendant even in cases involving gross negligence has always presented problems where the defendant is a limited company. As an entirely separate legal 'person', a limited company can clearly be capable of committing criminal offences and it is not unusual for companies to be prosecuted for criminal offences, particularly those involving strict liability. Where the offence in question requires proof of a state of mind by the defendant, however, corporate liability becomes a little more problematic. Companies can still commit such offences, which include manslaughter, a fact made very clear by the prosecution of P&O ferries after the sinking of the *Herald of Free Enterprise* in 1987. However, the problem of identifying a 'directing mind' of an officer of the company has prevented the successful prosecution of corporate liability cases on a number of occasions (including in the P&O case). A recent case that has attracted a great deal of attention in this area followed the Southall rail crash. In *Attorney-General's Reference (No. 2 of 1999)* [2000] 3 WLR 195, the Court of Appeal confirmed that a defendant might be convicted of gross negligence manslaughter without the need to prove his/her particular state of mind at the time provided it is shown:

- that the defendant owed the deceased a duty of care

- that the defendant breached that duty of care, and

- that the breach was so grossly negligent that the defendant could be deemed to have had such a disregard for the life of the deceased as to deserve criminal punishment

(per *R* v *Adomako* [1995] 1 AC 171).

However, the state of mind of the defendant might still be relevant as the jury need to take all the circumstances into account when considering the breach of duty of care above. As a result, a 'corporate defendant' could only be convicted of manslaughter by gross negligence through the mind and will of its directors and senior managers.

Where this area is of direct relevance to police officers is in the early investigation of fatal incidents where the appropriate health and safety standards appear to have been breached. While the investigation of such incidents is primarily the responsibility of the Health and Safety Executive, there will be occasions where it is proper for the police to conduct a manslaughter investigation and to treat the scene as a crime scene (see also *R* v *DPP, ex parte Jones (Timothy)* [2000] Crim LR 858). At the time of writing, the Law Commission is once again considering this area of criminal law very carefully and the government has again raised the creation of a new offence of 'corporate killing'.

2.1.5   **Aiding Suicide**

OFFENCE: **Aiding Another to Commit Suicide—*Suicide Act 1961, s. 2***
> • Triable on indictment • Fourteen years' imprisonment
> *(Arrestable offence)*

The Suicide Act 1961, s. 2 states:

> (1) A person who aids, abets, counsels or procures the suicide of another, or an attempt by another to commit suicide, shall be liable ...

KEYNOTE

This offence is an alternative verdict on a charge of murder/manslaughter (Suicide Act 1961, s. 2(2)). The House of Lords has held that the Suicide Act 1961 is not incompatible with the European Convention on Human Rights; at the same time, it upheld a decision of the Director of Public Prosecutions refusing to undertake not to prosecute in a case where a sufferer of motor neurone disease wanted her husband to help her die. In the case, which attracted a huge amount of publicity, their Lordships held that the DPP had no power to give an undertaking not to prosecute in advance of an offence actually being committed and that, even if he/she *did* have that power, using it in such a way would be an abuse of process because the circumstances of the offence could not possibly be known in advance (*R (on the application of Pretty)* v *DPP* [2001] UKHL 61). The late Mrs Pretty also failed in her attempt to have the ruling overturned at the European Court of Human Rights. Although the news media insisted on referring to these trials as 'right to die' hearings it is important to distinguish issues concerning the 'right' of an individual to die under certain circumstances and the issues arising out of 'assisted suicide' which were decided in Mrs Pretty's case. It was formerly an offence to commit suicide (!) but that was repealed by s. 1 of the 1961 Act. This offence has the unusual feature of creating criminal liability for aiding and abetting *an attempt*.

Given that this offence is linked to the expected death of another, it might be argued that it will always be a 'serious' arrestable offence even though it is not included under s. 116(2) of the Police and Criminal Evidence Act 1984.

2.1.6 Solicitation of Murder

OFFENCE: **Encouraging Another to Murder—*Offences Against the Person Act 1861, s. 4***

  • Triable on indictment • Life imprisonment
  (Arrestable offence)

The Offences Against the Person Act 1861, s. 4 states:

> Whosoever shall solicit, encourage, persuade or endeavour to persuade, or shall propose to any person, to murder any other person, whether he be a subject of Her Majesty or not . . . shall be guilty of a misdemeanour . . .

KEYNOTE

The proposed victim may be outside the United Kingdom.

It does not matter whether or not the person is in fact encouraged to commit murder. This offence may be appropriate in cases where a person is trying to arrange a 'contract killing' (see *R* v *Adamthwaite* (1994) 15 Cr App R (S) 241 where the person 'encouraged' was an undercover police officer). For this reason this offence may be preferred in cases where the defendant has 'conspired' with one other person and that person is an undercover police officer.

The comments in relation to serious arrestable offences above also apply to this offence.

2.2 Offences Against the Person

2.2.1 Introduction

Non-fatal offences against others cover a wide range of behaviour from a raised fist to a calculated wounding. The importance of this subject lies not only in the number of occasions when investigators will need to refer to it, but also because it deals with violence and the fear of violent crime—areas in which victims are particularly traumatised. Violence and threats of violence often accompany other offences (indeed, in some—such as robbery—it is an ingredient of the offence) and it is often with considering an alternative charge of, for instance, assault in such cases. As courts are being urged to focus on the effects of a defendant's conduct upon their victim, the scope for bringing a charge of assault is widening.

2.2.2 Key Issues

2.2.3 Assault and Battery

Assault and battery are, strictly speaking, two separate things. What people generally think of as being an 'assault' (e.g. a punch on the nose) is a 'battery', that is, the infliction of unlawful force on someone else. While it would cover a punch on the nose, an 'assault' in its proper legal sense has a much wider meaning and includes any act whereby the defendant 'intentionally—or possibly recklessly—causes another person to apprehend immediate and unlawful personal violence' (*Fagan* v *Metropolitan Police Commissioner* [1969] 1 QB 439).

2.2.4 Assault or Battery?

Although these terms—assault and battery—have distinct legal meanings they are often referred to as simply 'assaults' or 'common assault'. It is, however, important to separate the two expressions when charging or laying an information against a defendant as to include both may be bad for duplicity (*DPP* v *Taylor* [1992] QB 645).

The term battery, or the application of 'force', creates a misleading impression as a very small degree of physical contact will be enough. That force can be applied directly or indirectly. For example, where a defendant punched a woman causing her to drop and injure a child she was holding, he was convicted of assaulting that child (*Haystead* v *Chief Constable of Derbyshire* [2000] 3 All ER 890). The *actus reus* needed to prove an assault is an act which caused the victim to apprehend the immediate infliction of unlawful force. The force or violence apprehended by the victim does not have to be a 'certainty'. Causing a fear of some possible violence can be enough (see *R* v *Ireland* [1998] AC 147) provided that the violence feared is about to happen in the immediate future (see *R* v *Constanza* (1997) 2 Cr App R 492).

While some offences can be committed by an act or an *omission* (e.g. manslaughter) for a charge of assault to succeed there must be an *act* (*Fagan*).

It also is important to remember that the state of mind of the *victim* in an assault is relevant to the *actus reus*. The victim must apprehend the immediate use of unlawful force. For these reasons, if a defendant threatened someone with an imitation pistol, he/she could still be charged with assault provided the victim *believed* that the pistol was real—the defendant had caused an apprehension of possible immediate force being used (*Logdon* v *Director of Public Prosecutions* [1976] Crim LR 121). These would also be an offence under the Firearms Act 1968, **see para. 2.12**.

Words can amount to an assault provided they are accompanied by the required *mens rea*. This was made clear by the decision in *R* v *Ireland* [1998] AC 147 where it was held that telephone calls to a victim, followed by silences, could amount to an assault. In *Ireland*, the House of Lords accepted that '*a thing said is also a thing done*' and rejected the view that words can never amount to an assault. *Ireland* involved the making of threatening telephone calls which led the victims to fear that unlawful force would be used against them. The House of Lords accepted that, in such cases, even *silence* could fulfil the requirements for the *actus reus* of assault if it brought about the desired consequences (e.g. fear of the immediate use of unlawful force).

Where the words threatening immediate unlawful force come in the form of letters, the Court of Appeal has held that an assault may have been committed *(see Constanza above)*.

As well as constituting an assault, words can also *negate* an assault if they make a conditional threat, e.g. where you attend an incident and one person says to another, '*If these officers weren't here I'd chin you!*'.

Although the force threatened must be immediate, that immediacy is—like most legal interpretation—somewhat elastic. Courts have accepted that, where a person makes a threat from outside a victim's house to the victim who is inside, an assault is still committed even though there will be some time lapse before the defendant can carry out the threat.

In *Ireland* the House of Lords suggested that a threat to cause violence 'in a minute or two' might be enough to qualify as an assault. The victim must be shown to have feared the use of *force*; it will not be enough to show that a person threatened by words—or silence—feared more calls or letters. The fear of force is the key to assault.

2.2.5 Intentionally or Recklessly

The *mens rea* needed to prove common assault is either:

- an intention to cause apprehension of immediate unlawful violence, or

- subjective recklessness as to that consequence.

When considering the *mens rea of* any assault, it is important to separate the assault or battery **(see 2.2.4)** from *any further consequences caused by* that assault or battery. The *mens rea* needed for the assault/battery is set out above. If a defendant's behaviour causes another to fear immediate and unlawful personal violence, he/she commits an 'assault' provided it can be shown that, at the time, the defendant *intended* to cause that fear or was *subjectively reckless* as to whether such a fear would result from his/her actions.

So what happens where the defendant's actions cause more than just fear; they cause more serious injury? Unfortunately that appears to depend on the extent of the injury and the wording of the offence charged. Among the more serious offences under the Offences Against the Person Act 1861 are causing 'atual bodily harm' (s. 47) and 'wounding' or inflicting/causing 'grievous bodily harm' (ss. 18 and 20). The *mens rea* required for an offence under s. 47, causing actual bodily harm, is the same as that required for the basic offence of assault (*R v Savage* [1992] 1 AC 699). This is because s. 47 makes no specific requirement for any greater degree of *mens rea* by the defendant and, in effect, the offence of causing actual bodily harm becomes simply an assault or battery with a more serious outcome. From the defendant's point of view this is really pot luck because there is no requirement for him/her to have intended or even foreseen the actual bodily harm. In the case of woundings and grievous bodily harm, the situation is different because ss. 18 and 20 use the word 'maliciously'. This element introduces the element of intention or subjective recklessness *in relation to the injuries suffered by the victim* (*Savage* above), thereby adding a further requirement to the *mens rea*.

....

EXAMPLE

Take the example of two people in a pub. They are arguing. One person, the defendant, threatens to throw a pint of beer over the other, the victim. At this point the defendant has caused the victim to fear that immediate unlawful personal violence will be used against him—an 'assault'. In order to prove an offence of assault under the Criminal Justice Act 1988, you must show that, at the time of the threat, the defendant either intended to cause the fear of violence or was subjectively reckless in that regard. If such an intention or recklessness cannot be shown, there is no offence of assault.

After the threat, a third person pushes past the defendant, accidentally knocking him into the victim and spilling the beer over him. At this point there has been no 'assault' by the defendant because there has been no *actus reus* by him, irrespective of his intentions.

The defendant continues to argue and then raises his glass and throws the contents over the victim. Clearly there has now been a voluntary application of unlawful force—a 'battery'—which the defendant intended to apply and he commits an offence under the Criminal Justice Act 1988. In the act of throwing the beer, however, the defendant's hand slips and he in fact hits the victim in the face with his beer glass causing a broken tooth. At this point the defendant's actions have gone beyond those intended by him and his victim has suffered injuries which the defendant had neither intended nor considered. Nevertheless, at the time of the assault (and battery) the defendant had the required *mens rea* for the assault/battery and therefore is liable for any actual bodily harm suffered by the victim as a result. Therefore the defendant commits the offence of assault occasioning actual bodily harm under s. 47 of the Offences Against the Person Act 1861, even though he neither intended nor considered the injuries to his victim.

Having a small amount of beer left in the glass, the defendant flicks the 'dregs' from the glass at the victim. The defendant loses his grip on the glass and it flies from his hand, hitting the victim in the eye and breaking on impact. The victim suffers a deep wound to the eye. Although the defendant is still liable for any actual bodily harm, he can only be liable for the more serious offences of wounding and causing/inflicting *grievous* bodily harm if it can be shown that he acted 'maliciously'. Malice for these purposes means that he must have intended to cause the harm or realised that there was a risk of at least some harm being suffered by the victim. If he did realise that the victim was at risk of being harmed by his actions, the defendant may be liable for an offence under s. 20 of the Offences Against the Person Act 1861. If it can be shown that he intended to bring about *serious* harm, the defendant may be liable for the offence under s. 18 of the 1861 Act.

If the victim goes on to die from the injury, the defendant would be guilty of murder, or manslaughter by unlawful or dangerous act, depending on the level of *mens rea* (see **paras 2.1.2 and 2.1.4**).

Given the requirements for *mens rea*, together with the respective penalties, it is not surprising that charges of 'actual bodily harm' might be preferred over charges of malicious wounding or inflicting grievous bodily harm.

....

2.2.6   Consent

A key element in proving an assault is the *unlawfulness* of the force used or threatened. Therefore, you might argue, if a person consents to the use of force, it cannot be unlawful and no assault or battery is committed. If only life were so simple! Although the courts have accepted consent as a feature which negatives any offence, they have been reluctant to accept this feature in a number of notable cases. These cases have developed as a question of public policy and were summarised in the House of Lords in the so-called 'spanner trial' (*R* v *Brown* [1994] 1 AC 212).

That case involved members of a sado-masochist group who inflicted varying degrees of injuries on one another for their own gratification. Charged with many offences against the person, the group claimed that they had consented to the injuries and therefore no assault or battery had taken place. Their Lordships followed an earlier policy that *all assaults which result in more than transient harm will be unlawful unless there is good reason for allowing the plea of 'consent'*. Good reason will be determined in the light of a number of considerations:

- the practical consequences of the behaviour
- the dangerousness of the behaviour
- the vulnerability of the 'consenting' person.

Further difficulties in clarifying what will amount to 'true' or effective consent were added by the decision of the Court of Appeal in *R* v *Wilson* (1996) 2 Cr App R 241. In that case the court accepted that a husband might lawfully brand his initials on his wife's buttocks with a hot knife provided she consented (as she appeared to have done). The reasoning behind the judgment seems to be based on the fact that the branding was similar to a form of tattooing (see below), but also on the policy grounds that consensual activity between husband and wife is not a matter for criminal investigation. This causes several problems, not least of which is the fact that sado-masochistic 'branding' was denounced by the House of Lords in *Brown* above. Therefore, if a situation arose where a husband and wife took part in mutual branding in the privacy of their home, their criminal liability would arguably depend on whether they caused the harm for purposes of sado-masochistic pleasure or out of some affectionate wish to be permanently adorned with the mark of their loved one. It is also unclear how far the policy aspect of the decision in *Wilson* would extend and whether or not it would encompass unmarried or homosexual couples.

Sado-masochistic injury may justifiably be made the subject of criminal law on grounds of the 'protection of health'. It was for this reason that the European Court of Human Rights held that there had been no violation of the defendants' right to private life (under Article 8) in the *Brown* case above. Although the defendants asserted that the interference by the criminal law in their consensual sexual practices amounted to an unnecessary restriction of their individual rights under Article 8, the Court held that this was a justifiable intrusion on the grounds set out above (*Laskey* v *United Kingdom* (1997) 24 EHRR 39).

Clearly there are times when a person may consent to even serious harm such as during properly-conducted sporting events (see *Attorney-General's Reference (No. 6 of 1980)* [1981] QB 715), tattooing and medical operations. Where the activity falls outside those parameters, such as an off-the-ball incident in a football match (*R* v *Lloyd* (1989) 11 Cr App R (S) 36) or an unauthorised prize fight, the plea of consent will not apply.

Other more straightforward policy considerations would include the implied consent by people getting on to crowded tube trains or moving around at a packed concert venue. In these cases it will be a matter of fact to decide whether the behaviour complained of went beyond what was acceptable in those particular circumstances.

Where a dentist who had been suspended by the General Dental Council continued to operate on patients, her failure to inform those patients of her suspension did not affect their true 'consent' and the dentist's actions were not an 'assault' (*R* v *Richardson* (1998) 2 Cr App R 200). The situation would be very different if the dentist had no formal qualifications at all, or if her actions went beyond the proper professional activities of a dentist (e.g. an indecent touching of patients).

2.2.7   Lawful Chastisement

There is an increasingly narrow head under which force might lawfully be applied to children. Those acting in *loco parentis* of a child appear to be able to use reasonable force in controlling the behaviour of that child (see *Blackstone's Criminal Practice*, 2002, section B2.10). What is 'reasonable' is likely to vary widely and would be difficult to define given the breadth and depth of social attitudes and conventions within England and Wales.

In a case involving an allegation of assault by a stepfather on his stepson, the European Court of Human Rights held that the United Kingdom was in breach of its obligation to protect individuals from inhuman or degrading punishment (under Article 3 of the European Convention on Human Rights) because the law in this area was not clear enough (*A* v *United Kingdom* (1999) 27 EHRR 611). The issues of reasonable chastisement and its compatibility with the Convention was examined recently by the Court of Appeal in *R* v *H* [2001] 2 FLR 431. Among other things, the Court held that the defence should be considered in the light of the nature and context of the defendant's behaviour, its duration, its physical and mental effects on the child, the age and personal characteristics of the child, and the reasons for the punishment. Additionally, Protocol 1, Article 2 (the right to education) of the Convention requires a State to have regard to the religious and philosophical convictions of parents in its schools. This requirement was at the centre of a successful challenge against corporal punishment in a State school (*Campbell* v *United Kingdom* (1982) 4 EHRR 293). The School Standards and Framework Act 1998 now outlaws corporal punishment in all British schools, although staff may use reasonable force in restraining violent or disruptive pupils (Education Act 1996, s. 550A). The Divisional Court has held that this legislation removes entirely the defence of reasonable chastisement from any teacher when they are acting as such (*Williamson* v *Secretary of State for Education and Employment* [2002] HRLR 14. In that case it was held that the defendants' belief that corporal punishment should be imposed could not be a 'philosophical or religious conviction' even though it was supported by a religious text. This is the case irrespective of the fact that parents try to delegate authority to use such punishment. In *Williamson*, the Divisional Court held that the defendants' belief that corporal punishment should be imposed could not be a 'philosophical or religious conviction' even though it was supported by a religious text. This finding was confirmed by the Court of Appeal (*Williamson* v *Secretary of State for Education and Employment* [2002] EWCA Civ 1926). The Divisional Court held that the law had always shown a respect for the physical integrity of the individual: any intentional assault was unlawful unless there was a defence of justification. This required a stronger case to justify the right to inflict physical injury than to justify a right not to have it inflicted. The legislation gave effect to a clear Parliamentary intention to abolish corporal punishment in all schools including independent schools and did not infringe the human rights of any of the claimants.

2.2.8   Offences

2.2.9   Common Assault and Battery

OFFENCE: **Common Assault/Battery—*Criminal Justice Act 1988, s. 39***

     • Triable summarily • Six months' imprisonment

OFFENCE: **Racially or Religiously Aggravated—*Crime and Disorder Act 1998, s. 29(1)(c)***

     • Triable either way • Two years' imprisonment and/or a fine on indictment; six months' imprisonment and/or a fine summarily

     (No specific power of arrest)

KEYNOTE

Under certain circumstances the magistrates must issue a certificate of dismissal following the bringing of a charge of common assault (Offences Against the Person Act 1861, ss. 44 and 45). In order for a certificate of dismissal to be issued it must be shown that the party aggrieved (the victim) brought the charge or it was so preferred on the victim's behalf *and* the magistrates find:

- the offence not to have been proved or
- the assault to have been justified or
- the assault to be so trifling that it did not merit any punishment.

The certificate releases the defendant from all further proceedings, civil or criminal, *arising from the same cause*. Therefore, although such a certificate would absolve the defendant from further criminal or civil action in respect of the *actus reus* that amounted to the assault/ battery), it would not protect him/her from further proceedings arising from some distinct but related matter (e.g. acts committed immediately before or after the assault/ battery).

If the prosecution is not brought by or on behalf of the aggrieved party, the certificate will not be applicable.

Common assault was deemed by the legislators to be one of those offences where it was necessary to increase the maximum penalty available to the courts if it was committed under racially or religiously aggravated circumstances (see the Crime and Disorder Act 1998, s. 29(1)(c)). A further effect of the racially or religiously aggravated offence is that it can be tried on indictment without having to be included alongside another indictable offence as is the case with common assaults generally (see the Criminal Justice Act 1988, s. 40).

In a recent decision, the Divisional Court held that the words 'white man's arse licker' and 'brown Englishman' when used to accompany an assault on an Asian victim did not necessarily make the assault 'racially aggravated' and that the prosecution had not done enough to show that the assailants' behaviour fell under the definition set out in s. 28 of the 1998 Act (*DPP* v *Pal* [2000] Crim LR 756).

Under the racially—and now religiously—aggravated public order offences the courts have held that police officers are entitled to the same protection under the legislation as anyone else (see *R* v *Jacobs* (2001) 2 Cr App R (S) 38) and the same principle ought to apply to physical assault.

If an assault upon a police officer is 'racially or religiously aggravated' per the requirements of s. 28 of the Crime and Disorder Act 1998, it may be preferable to consider this offence rather than one of the offences under the Police Act 1996 (as to which, **see 2.2.11**).

It should be noted that there are potential problems with the availability of alternative verdicts in cases of racially or religiously aggravated assault and, in cases of doubt, the advice of the Crown Prosecution Service should be sought.

2.2.10 Assault with Intent to Resist Arrest

OFFENCE: **Assault with Intent to Resist Arrest—*Offences Against the PersonAct 1861, s. 38***

- Triable either way • Two years' imprisonment

(No specific power of arrest)

The Offences Against the Person Act 1861, s. 38 states:

> Whosoever... shall assault any person with intent to resist or prevent the lawful apprehension or detainer of himself or of any other person for any offence, shall be guilty of an offence...

KEYNOTE

This is a crime of *specific intent*. It must be shown that the defendant intended to resist or prevent a lawful arrest. It must also be shown that the defendant knew the arrest was lawful. Provided they were acting within their powers, this offence can apply to arrests made, not only by police officers, but also by store detectives, Benefits Agency staff and custody assistants. There are other specific offences created for the protection of court security officers and prisoner custody officers (not police officers) under the Criminal Justice Act 1991, ss. 78 and 90. If the person assaulted was assisting a police officer in the execution of his/her duty, the offence below may also apply.

Once the lawfulness of the arrest is established, the state of mind necessary for the above offence is an intention to resist/prevent that arrest, accompanied by knowledge that the person assaulted was trying to make or help in the arrest. It is irrelevant whether or not the person being arrested had actually committed an offence. These principles were set out recently by the Court of Appeal in a case where the defendant mistakenly believed that the arresting officers had no lawful power to do so. The Court held that such a mistaken belief does not provide a defendant with the defence of 'mistake'. Similarly, a belief in one's own innocence, however genuine or honestly held, cannot afford a defence to a charge under s. 38 (*R* v *Lee* [2000] Crim LR 991).

2.2.11 Assaults on Police

There is an offence which deals specifically with assaults on police officers.

OFFENCE: **Assault Police—*Police Act 1996, s. 89***

- Triable summarily • Six months' imprisonment and/or a fine

(No specific power of arrest)

The Police Act 1996, s. 89 states:

(1) Any person who assaults a constable in the execution of his duty, or a person assisting a constable in the execution of his duty, shall be guilty of an offence...

KEYNOTE

It is critical to this offence that the officer was acting in the execution of his/her duty when assaulted. Given the almost infinite variety of situations that police officers may find themselves in, it is difficult to define the precise boundaries of the execution of their duty. There have been many instances of officers being assaulted after entering premises as technical 'trespassers' or not following statutory or common law requirements when stopping and questioning people. If it is not proved that the constable was in the execution of his/her duty then part of the *actus reus* will be missing. However, a court may infer from all the circumstances that an officer was in fact acting in the execution of his/her duty (*Plowden* v *DPP* [1991] Crim LR 850).

Where the assault is made in reaction to some form of physical act by the officer, it must be shown that the officer's act was not in itself unlawful. Other than the powers of arrest and detention, police officers have no general power to take hold of people in order to question them or keep them at a particular place while background enquiries are made about them. Therefore, if an officer does hold someone by the arm in order to question them without arresting them, there may well be a 'battery' by that officer (*Collins* v *Wilcock* [1984] 1 WLR 1172). The courts have accepted, however, that there may be occasions where a police officer is justified in taking hold of a person to attract their attention or to calm them down (*Mepstead* v *DPP* (1996) 160 JP 475).

However, where a prisoner is arrested and brought before a custody officer, that officer is entitled to assume that the arrest has been lawful. Therefore, if the prisoner goes on to assault the custody officer, that assault will nevertheless be an offence under s. 89(1) *even if the original arrest turns out to have been unlawful* (*DPP* v *L* [1999] Crim LR 752).

There is no need to show that the defendant knew—or suspected—that the person was in fact a police officer or that he/she was acting in the lawful execution of his/her duty (*Blackburn* v *Bowering* [1994] 1 WLR 1324). However, if the defendant claims to have been acting in self-defence under the mistaken and honestly held belief that he/she was being attacked, there may not be sufficient *mens rea* for a charge of assault.

These offences are simply a form of common assault upon someone carrying out a lawful power of arrest. There is a further offence which deals with behaviour not amounting to an actual assault.

OFFENCE: **Obstruct Police—*Police Act 1996, s. 89***

> • Triable summarily • One month's imprisonment and/or a fine
> *(No specific power of arrest)*

The Police Act 1996, s. 89 states:

(2) Any person who resists or wilfully obstructs a constable in the execution of his duty, or a person assisting a constable in the execution of his duty, shall be guilty of an offence...

KEYNOTE

Resistance suggests some form of physical opposition; obstruction does not and may take many forms. For instance, warning other drivers of a speed check operation (*Betts* v *Stevens* [1910] 1 KB 1, providing misleading information (*Ledger* v *DPP* [1991] Crim LR 439), or deliberately drinking alcohol before providing breath specimen (*Ingleton* v *Dibble* [1972] 1 All ER 275). Obstruction has been interpreted as making it more difficult for a constable to carry out his/her duty (*Hinchcliffe* v *Sheldon* [1955] 1 WLR 1207). Refusing to answer an officer's questions is not obstruction (*Rice* v *Connolly* [1966] 2 QB 414)—unless perhaps the defendant was under some duty to provide information. Any obstruction must be *wilful*, that is the defendant must intend to do it. The obstruction will not be 'wilful' if the defendant was simply trying to help the police, even if that help turned out to be more of a hindrance (*Wilmot* v *Atack* [1977] QB 498).

Obstruction can be caused by omission but only where the defendant was already under some duty towards the police or the officer. There is also a common law offence of refusing to go to the aid of a constable when asked to do so in order to prevent or diminish a breach of the peace (*R v Waugh* (1986) *The Times*, 1 October).

Tipping off people who were about to commit crime has been held to amount to obstruction (*Green v Moore* [1982] QB 1044), and some extreme forms of obstruction may amount to more serious offences such as perverting the course of justice or concealing offences. There are also specific statutory offences of 'tipping off' in relation to money laundering and drug trafficking offences under s. 93D of the Criminal Justice Act 1988 and s. 53 of the Drug Trafficking Act 1994 respectively.

Note that unless the obstruction involves a breach of the peace, there will be no specific power of arrest and more general arrest powers will need to be considered.

2.2.12 Offences Involving Significant or Lasting Injury

If an assailant causes any significant or lasting injury then one of the following offences may apply.

2.2.13 Assault Occasioning Actual Bodily Harm

OFFENCE: **Assault Occasioning Actual Bodily Harm—*Offences Against the Person Act 1861, s. 47***

- Triable either way • Five years' imprisonment on indictment; six months' imprisonment and/or a fine summarily

(Arrestable offence)

OFFENCE: **Racially or Religiously Aggravated—*Crime and Disorder Act 1998, s. 29(1)(b)***

- Triable either way • Seven years' imprisonment and/or a fine on indictment; six months' imprisonment and/or a fine summarily

(Arrestable offence)

The Offences Against the Person Act 1861, s. 47 states:

> Whosoever shall be convicted...of any assault occasioning actual bodily harm shall be liable...to [imprisonment]...

KEYNOTE

It must be shown that 'actual bodily harm' was a consequence, directly or indirectly, of the defendant's actions. Such harm can include shock (*R v Miller* [1954] 2 QB 282) and mental 'injury' (*R v Chan-Fook* [1994] 1 WLR 689).

For a discussion of the relevant *mens rea* for this offence, **see 2.2.5**. The state of mind required is the same as that for an assault or battery.

Examples of what will amount to 'actual bodily harm' can be found in the CPS Charging Standards and include:

- loss or breaking of teeth
- temporary loss of sensory functions
- extensive or multiple bruising
- minor fractures and cuts requiring stitches
- psychiatric injury going beyond fear, distress or panic.

As with common assault, this offence was deemed by the legislators to be one where it was necessary to increase the maximum penalty available to the courts if it was committed under racially aggravated circumstances (see Crime and Disorder Act 1998, s. 29(1)(b)).

Again it should be noted that there are potential problems with the availability of alternative verdicts in cases of racially aggravated assault and, in cases of doubt, the advice of the Crown Prosecution Service should be sought.

Sections 1 and 2 of the Criminal Evidence (Amendment) Act 1997 extending the power to take non-intimate samples without consent apply to this offence and also to conspiracies, attempts or incitements in the circumstances set out in that Act.

2.2.14 Wounding or Inflicting Grievous Bodily Harm

OFFENCE: **Wounding or Inflicting Grievous Bodily Harm—*Offences Against the Person Act 1861 s. 20***

- Triable either way • Five years' imprisonment on indictment; six months' imprisonment and/or a fine summarily

(Arrestable offence)

OFFENCE: **Racially or Religiously Aggravated—*Crime and Disorder Act 1998, s. 29(1)(a)***

- Triable either way • Seven years' imprisonment and/or a fine on indictment; six months' imprisonment and/or a fine summarily

(Arrestable offence)

The Offences Against the Person Act 1861, s. 20 states:

> Whosoever shall unlawfully and maliciously wound or inflict any grievous bodily harm upon any other person, either with or without any weapon or instrument, shall be guilty of [an offence]...

KEYNOTE

Wounding is a breaking of the 'whole' skin or the continuity of the skin. A cut which goes right through all the layers of a person's skin, whether caused externally (e.g. a knife wound) or internally (a punch causing a tooth to puncture the cheek), will amount to a wound.

The word 'inflict' has caused problems in the past. However, the House of Lords in *R v Ireland* [1998] AC 147 has made it clear that no 'assault' is needed for this offence and that harm could be 'inflicted' indirectly (in this case by menacing telephone calls inflicting psychiatric harm). Therefore, there is now little if any difference between inflicting harm and 'causing' harm. It should be enough to show that the defendant's behaviour brought about the resulting harm to the victim.

There have also been many judicial attempts at defining grievous bodily harm. In *R v Saunders* [1985] Crim LR 230 it was held that the expression meant 'serious or really serious harm'. This harm will now include psychiatric harm (*Ireland*). Examples of what will amount to 'grievous bodily harm' can be found in the CPS Charging Standards and include:

- injury resulting in some permanent disability or visible disfigurement

- broken or displaced limbs or bones

- injuries requiring blood transfusion or lengthy treatment.

For a discussion of the relevant *mens rea* for this offence, **see 2.1.5.**

'Maliciously'—although the word maliciously suggests some form of evil premeditation, 'malice' here amounts to subjective recklessness. It means that the defendant must realise that there is a risk of some harm being caused to the victim. The defendant does not need to foresee the degree of harm which is eventually caused, only that his/her behaviour may bring about some harm to the victim.

Section 1 and 2 of the Criminal Evidence (Amendment) Act 1997 extending the power to take non-intimate samples without consent apply to this offence and also to conspiracies attempts or incitements in the circumstances set out in that Act.

As with common assault and assault occasioning actual bodily harm, this offence was deemed by the legislators to be one where it was necessary to increase the maximum penalty available to the courts if it was committed under racially or religiously aggravated circumstances (see Crime and Disorder Act 1998, s. 29(1)(a)).

Again, it should be noted that there are potential problems with the availability of alternative verdicts in cases of aggravated assaults and the advice of the Crown Prosecution Service should be sought.

2.2.15 Wounding or Causing Grievous Bodily Harm with Intent

OFFENCE: **Wounding or Causing Grievous Bodily Harm with Intent—*Offences Against the Person Act 1861, s. 18***
    • Triable on indictment only • Life imprisonment
    (Arrestable offence)

The Offences Against the Person Act 1861, s. 18 states:

> Whosoever shall unlawfully and maliciously by any means whatsoever wound or cause any grievous bodily harm to any person with intent to do some grievous bodily harm to any person, or with intent to resist or prevent the lawful apprehension or detainer of any person, shall be guilty of [an offence] ...

KEYNOTE

This is a crime of *specific intent*. The word 'cause', together with the expression 'by any means whatsoever', seems to give this offence a wider meaning than s. 20. However, the increasingly broad interpretation of the s. 20 offence means that there is little difference in the *actus reus* needed for either offence.

The state of mind for this offence is the same as that for s. 20 with the added intention of bringing about serious harm or to resist/prevent arrest.

Where the intent was to cause grievous bodily harm, the issue of 'malice' will not arise. However, where the intent was to resist or prevent the lawful arrest of someone, the element of maliciousness as set out above will need to be proved.

Sections 1 and 2 of the Criminal Evidence (Amendment) Act 1997 also apply to this offence (and to conspiracies, attempts or incitements in the circumstances set out in that Act).

The provisions of ss. 28 and 29 of the Crime and Disorder Act 1998 in relation to racially or religiously aggravated assaults do not apply to this offence as it was felt by the legislators that there was nothing to be gained by creating a special offence, given that the maximum sentence available is already life imprisonment. However, the courts must still take notice of any element of racial or religious aggravation when determining sentence (s. 153 of the Powers of Criminal Courts (Sentencing) Act 2000).

Perhaps in these cases more than any other, there are potential problems with the availability of alternative verdicts in cases of racially or religiously aggravated assaults and the advice of the Crown Prosecution Service should be sought.

2.3 Threats to Kill

OFFENCE: **Making a Threat to Kill—*Offences Against the Person Act 1861, s. 16***
    • Triable either way • Ten years' imprisonment on indictment; six months'
    imprisonment and/or a fine summarily
    (Arrestable offence)

The Offences Against the Person Act 1861, s. 16 states:

> A person who without lawful excuse makes to another a threat, intending that that other would fear it would be carried out, to kill that other or a third person shall be guilty of an offence ...

KEYNOTE

The proviso that the threat must be made 'without lawful excuse' means that a person acting in self-defence or in the course of his/her duty in protecting life (e.g. an armed police officer) would not commit this offence (provided that his/her behaviour was 'lawful').

You must show that the threat was made (or implied (*R v Solanke* [1970] 1 WLR 1)) with the intention that the person receiving it would fear that it would be carried out. It is the intention of the person who makes the threat which is important in this offence. It does not matter whether the person to whom the threat is made *does* fear that the threat would be carried out, or that the person whose life is threatened so fears (unless that person is the same person to whom the threat is made). The threat may be to kill another person at some time in the future or it may be an immediate threat, but the threatened action must be directly linked with the defendant. Simply passing on a threat on behalf of a third person would probably be insufficient for this offence.

2.4   Child Abduction

There is a Convention between the United Kingdom and many other countries which is designed to help with the civil law practicalities of recovering children from other jurisdictions. The full list of such countries can be found in the Child Abduction and Custody (Parties to Conventions) Order 1986 (SI 1986 No. 1159), as amended.

There are two offences of abducting children, one which applies to people 'connected with the child' and the second by others.

2.4.1   Person Connected with Child

OFFENCE: **Child Abduction—Person Connected with Child—*Child Abduction Act 1984, s. 1***

> • Triable either way • Seven years' imprisonment on indictment; six months' imprisonment and/or a fine summarily
>
> *(Arrestable offence)*

The Child Abduction Act 1984, s. 1 states:

> (1) Subject to subsections (5) and (8) below, a person connected with a child under the age of 16 commits an offence if he takes or sends the child out of the United Kingdom without the appropriate consent.

'Connected with a Child'

The Child Abduction Act 1984, s. 1 states:

> (2) A person is connected with the child for the purposes of this section if—
> (a) he is a parent of a child; or
> (b) in the case of a child whose parents were not married to each other at the time of his birth, there are reasonable grounds for believing that he is the father of the child; or
> (c) he is a guardian of the child; or
> (d) he is a person in whose favour a residence order is in force with respect to the child; or
> (e) he has custody of the child.

'Appropriate Consent'

The Child Abduction Act 1984, s. 1 states:

> (3) In this section 'the appropriate consent' in relation to a child, means—
> (a) the consent of each of the following—
> (i) the child's mother;
> (ii) the child's father, if he has parental responsibility for him;

           (iii) any guardian of the child;

           (iv) any person in whose favour a residence order is in force with respect to the child;

           (v) any person who has custody of the child; or

    (b) the leave of the court granted under or by virtue of any provision of Part II of the Children Act 1989; or

    (c) if any person has custody of the child, the leave of the court which awarded custody to him.

KEYNOTE

This offence can only be committed by those people listed in s. 1(2). To be guilty they must take or send the child out of the United Kingdom. The taking or sending must be shown to have been done without the consent of *each* of those persons listed in s. 1(3)(a) above.

Defence

The Child Abduction Act 1984, s. 1 states:

    (4) A person does not commit an offence under this section by taking or sending a child out of the United Kingdom without obtaining the appropriate consent if—

        (a) he is a person in whose favour there is a residence order in force with respect to the child, and

        (b) he takes or sends him out of the United Kingdom for a period of less than one month.

    (4A) Subsection (4) above does not apply if the person taking or sending the child out of the United Kingdom does so in breach of an order under Part II of the Children Act 1989.

    (5) A person does not commit an offence under this section by doing anything without the consent of another person whose consent is required under the foregoing provisions if—

        (a) he does it in the belief that the other person—

           (i) has consented; or

           (ii) would consent if he was aware of all the relevant circumstances; or

        (b) he has taken all reasonable steps to communicate with the other person but has been unable to communicate with him; or

        (c) the other person has unreasonably refused to consent.

KEYNOTE

Note the specific defence (at s. 1(5))—if the defendant believes that the appropriate person has consented or would have consented had they known of the circumstances.

    A further provision (s. 1(5A)) states that s. 1(5)(c) will not apply if the person who refused to consent is a person:

- in whose favour there is a residence order in force with respect to the child; or

- who has custody of the child; or

- is, by taking or sending the child out of the United Kingdom, acting in breach of a court order in the United Kingdom.

The consent of the Director of Public Prosecutions is needed before a charge of child abduction is brought under this section (s. 4(2)).

2.4.2   **Person Not Connected with Child**

OFFENCE: **Child Abduction—Person Not Connected with Child—*Child Abduction Act 1984, s. 2***

        • Triable either way • Seven years' imprisonment on indictment; six months' imprisonment and/or a fine summarily

        (Arrestable offence)

The Child Abduction Act 1984, s. 2 states:

(1) Subject to subsection (3) below, a person other than one mentioned in subsection (2) below, commits an offence if, without lawful authority or reasonable excuse, he takes or detains a child under the age of 16—
   (a) so as to remove him from the lawful control of any person having lawful control of the child: or
   (b) so as to keep him out of the lawful control of any person entitled to lawful control of the child.

(2) The persons are—
   (a) where the father and mother of the child in question were married to each other at the time of his birth, the child's father and mother;
   (b) where the father and mother of the child in question were not married to each other at the time of his birth, the child's mother; and
   (c) any other person mentioned in section 1(2)(c) to (e) above.

KEYNOTE

This offence requires the taking or detaining of a child under 16 years. This will include keeping a child in the place where he/she is found and inducing the child to remain with the defendant or another person. You must show that the defendant acted without lawful authority or reasonable excuse. Unlike kidnapping, the consent of the victim is irrelevant. Proving the absence of reasonable excuse could be difficult. Clearly a defendant could argue, particularly in the case of a very young child, that he/she was acting in the child's best interests, a claim which might be difficult to refute.

Sections 1 and 2 of the Criminal Evidence (Amendment) Act 1997 extending the power to take non-intimate samples without consent apply to this offence and also to conspiracies, attempts or incitements in the circumstances set out in that Act.

Defence

The Child Abduction Act 1984, s. 2 states:

(3) ... it shall be a defence for [the defendant] to prove—
   (a) where the father and mother of the child in question were not married to each other at the time of his birth—
      (i) that he is the child's father; or
      (ii) that, at the time of the alleged offence, he believed, on reasonable grounds, that he was the child's father; or
   (b) that, at the time of the alleged offence, he believed that the child had attained the age of 16.

KEYNOTE

Section 2(3)(b) provides a defence if the accused can show that he/she believed the child to be 16 or over. Given the appearance, dress and behaviour of children in their early teens, this defence may not be too difficult to establish in many cases. This should be contrasted with some sexual offences involving children.

2.5 False Imprisonment

OFFENCE: **False Imprisonment—*Common Law***
   • Triable on indictment • Unlimited maximum penalty
   (Arrestable offence)

It is an offence at common law falsely to imprison another person.

KEYNOTE

This offence is the first in an ascending order of aggravated offences against the person and is more usually dealt with under civil law or as kidnapping/abduction (see below).

The elements required for this offence are the unlawful and intentional/reckless restraint of a person's freedom of movement (*R* v *Rahman* (1985) 81 Cr App R 349). Locking someone in a vehicle or keeping them in a particular place for however short a time may amount to false imprisonment if done unlawfully. An unlawful arrest may amount to such an offence and it is not uncommon for such an allegation to be levelled at police officers against whom a public complaint has been made.

The state of mind required to prove this offence is 'subjective' recklessness (*R* v *James* (1997) *The Times*, 2 October).

Sections 1 and 2 of the Criminal Evidence (Amendment) Act 1997 apply to this offence and also to conspiracies, attempts or incitements in the circumstances set out in that Act.

2.6 Kidnapping

OFFENCE: **Kidnapping—*Common Law***
   • Triable on indictment • Unlimited maximum penalty
   (Serious arrestable offence)

It is an offence at common law to take or carry away another person without the consent of that person and without lawful excuse.

KEYNOTE

Kidnapping is the second of the aggravated offences described above. The required elements of this offence are the unlawful taking or carrying away of one person by another by force or fraud (*R* v *D* [1984] AC 778). These requirements go beyond those of mere restraint needed for false imprisonment. Parents may be acting without lawful excuse, for instance, if they are acting in breach of a court order in respect of their children.

The taking or carrying away of the victim must be without the consent of the victim. If the victim consents to an initial taking but later withdraws that consent, the offence would be complete. If the victim is a child, the consent will probably be that of the parents but the more appropriate charge in such a case may be one under the Child Abduction Act 1984.

The state of mind required for this offence appears to be the same as that for false imprisonment, indeed the only thing separating the two offences seems to be *actus reus* (*R* v *Hutchins* [1988] Crim LR 379).

Sections 1 and 2 of the Criminal Evidence (Amendment) Act 1997 above also apply to this offence (and to conspiracies, attempts or incitements in the circumstances set out in that Act).

2.7 Public Order Act 1986 Offences

Many of the most common offences regulating public disorder and threats to public order were formerly contained in the Public Order Act 1936. This left several key offences, such as riot and affray to the common law. These provisions were felt to be inadequate and the Public Order Act 1986 was passed in an attempt to codify the law in this area.

2.7.1 Riot

OFFENCE: **Riot—*Public Order Act 1986, s. 1***
   • Triable on indictment • Ten years' imprisonment
   (Arrestable offence)

The Public Order Act 1986, s. 1 states:

(1) Where 12 or more persons who are present together use or threaten unlawful violence for a common purpose and the conduct of them (taken together) is such as would cause a person of reasonable firmness present at the scene to fear for his personal safety, each of the persons using unlawful violence for the common purpose is guilty of riot.

(2) It is immaterial whether or not the 12 or more use or threaten unlawful violence simultaneously.

(3) The common purpose may be inferred from conduct.

(4) No person of reasonable firmness need actually be, or be likely to be, present at the scene.

(5) Riot may be committed in private as well as in public places.

KEYNOTE

This offence requires the consent of the Director of Public Prosecutions before a prosecution can be brought. Although there may be occasions where 12 or more people behave in the way proscribed by s. 1, it still very rare for a charge of riot to be brought. This may have something to do with the provisions of the Riot Damages Act 1886 which enables people who have suffered loss or damage during a riot to claim compensation from the local police budget (s. 2) irrespective of whether there has been any proven negligence on the part of the police. This provision attracted a great deal of criticism following the disturbances in Bradford, Oldham and Burnley in 2001 and, in the same year, the lodging of civil claims following disorder at the Yarl's Wood detention centre.

It is not necessary that all 12 people concerned use or threaten unlawful violence at the same time. However, the courts have held that each defendant must be shown to have *used* unlawful violence and not merely threatened to do so (*R* v *Jefferson* [1994] 1 All ER 270). A defendant must be shown to have *intended* to use/threaten violence or to have *been aware* that his/her conduct may have been violent (s. 6(1)).

The offence may be committed in private as well as in a public place. There is no need to prove that a person of reasonable firmness was actually caused to fear for his/her safety; merely that such a person would be caused so to fear (although clearly one way to prove that element would be by the testimony of those witnessing the behaviour).

Although there must be a common purpose, this need not be part of a pre-determined plan, nor be unlawful in itself. A common purpose to get into a rock concert or even the January sales at a high street store could therefore be enough, provided all other elements are present.

Violence

Section 8 of the Public Order Act 1986 provides guidance on when conduct will amount to 'violence':

'violence' means any violent conduct, so that—

(a) except in the context of affray, it includes violent conduct towards property as well as violent conduct towards persons, and

(b) it is not restricted to conduct causing or intended to cause injury or damage but includes any other violent conduct (for example, throwing at or towards a person a missile of a kind capable of causing injury which does not hit or falls short).

KEYNOTE

It has been held that the use of the term 'unlawful' in the 1986 Act has been included to allow for the general defences—such as self-defence—to be applicable (see *R* v *Rothwell* [1993] Crim LR 626).

Drunkenness

Parliament has specifically catered for self-induced intoxication, not just for the offence of riot, but in relation to other offences under the 1986 Act by s. 6 which states:

(5) For the purposes of this section a person whose awareness is impaired by intoxication shall be taken to be aware of that of which he would be aware if not intoxicated, unless he shows either

that his intoxication was not self-induced or that it was caused solely by the taking or administration of a substance in the course of medical treatment.

(6) In subsection (5) 'intoxication' means any intoxication, whether caused by drink, drugs or other means, or by a combination of means.

2.7.2 Violent Disorder

OFFENCE: **Violent Disorder—*Public Order Act 1986, s. 2***
- Triable either way • Five years' imprisonment and/or a fine on indictment; six months' imprisonment and/or a fine summarily
- *(Arrestable offence)*

The Public Order Act 1986, s. 2 states:

(1) Where 3 or more persons who are present together use or threaten unlawful violence and the conduct of them (taken together) is such as would cause a person of reasonable firmness present at the scene to fear for his personal safety, each of the persons using or threatening unlawful violence is guilty of violent disorder.

(2) It is immaterial whether or not the 3 or more use or threaten unlawful violence simultaneously.

(3) No person of reasonable firmness need actually be, or be likely to be, present at the scene.

(4) Violent disorder may be committed in private as well as in public places.

KEYNOTE

In order to convict any defendant of this offence, you must show that there were three or more people using or threatening violence. If this is not proved then the court should acquit each defendant (*R* v *McGuigan* [1991] Crim LR 719). Ordinarily this will mean that, if there are only three defendants, the acquittal of one will mean the acquittal of all, unless you prove that there were others taking part in the disorder who were not charged (*R* v *Worton* (1989) 154 JP 201).

The requirements as to the hypothetical effects on an equally hypothetical person of reasonable firmness are the same as for the offence of riot. However, there is no requirement to prove a common purpose.

Again, a defendant must be shown to have *intended* to use/threaten violence or to have *been aware* that his/her conduct may have been violent (s. 6(2)) and the offence may be committed in private as well as in a public place. 'Violence' for these purposes can include violent conduct towards property (s. 8).

2.7.3 Affray

OFFENCE: **Affray—*Public Order Act 1986, s. 3***
- Triable either way • Three years' imprisonment and/or a fine on indictment; six months' imprisonment and/or a fine summarily
- *(Statutory power of arrest)*

The Public Order Act 1986, s. 3 states:

(1) A person is guilty of affray if he uses or threatens unlawful violence towards another and his conduct is such as would cause a person of reasonable firmness present at the scene to fear for his personal safety.

(2) Where 2 or more persons use or threaten the unlawful violence, it is the conduct of them taken together that must be considered for the purposes of subsection (1).

(3) For the purposes of this section a threat cannot be made by the use of words alone.

(4) No person of reasonable firmness need actually be, or be likely to be, present at the scene.

(5) Affray may be committed in private as well as in public places.

KEYNOTE

Formerly an offence requiring more than one person, this offence may now be committed by a single defendant although, if he/she acts with another, the conduct of them taken together will be the relevant factor in determining their criminal conduct (s. 3(2)).

The House of Lords has held that, in order to prove the offence of affray, the threat of unlawful violence has to be towards a person(s) present at the scene (*I* v *DPP* [2001] 2 WLR 765). Once this element has been proved, it will be necessary to prove the second element, namely whether the defendant's conduct would have caused a hypothetical person present at the scene to fear for his/her personal safety (*R* v *Sanchez* (1996) 160 JP 321).

The threat cannot be made by words alone (s. 3(3)), therefore there must be some action by the defendant—even if that 'action' consists of utilising something else such as a dog to threaten the violence (*R* v *Dixon* [1993] Crim LR 579).

Although violence is 'not restricted to conduct causing or intended to cause injury or damage but includes any other violent conduct' (s. 8), the expression does not include conduct towards property as it does with the offences under ss. 1 and 2.

Once more, a defendant must be shown to have *intended* to use/threaten violence or to have *been aware* that his/her conduct may have been violent (s. 6).

Power of Arrest

The Public Order Act 1986, s. 3 states:

(6) A constable may arrest without warrant anyone he reasonably suspects is committing affray.

KEYNOTE

The power of arrest here is limited to the present tense, that is, to someone who is reasonably suspected of being in the process of committing an affray. This is the same as the power provided for offences under ss. 4 and 4A (see below). A preventive power can be found under the common law provisions in respect of an apprehended breach of the peace. Other powers may be available in relation to assaults or threats to cause damage.

2.7.4   **Fear or Provocation of Violence**

OFFENCE: **Fear or Provocation of Violence—*Public Order Act 1986, s. 4***
   • Triable summarily • Six months' imprisonment and/or a fine
   (Statutory power of arrest)

OFFENCE: **Racially or Religiously Aggravated—*Crime and Disorder Act 1998, s. 31(1)(a)***
   • Triable either way • Two years' imprisonment and/or a fine on indictment; six
      months' imprisonment and/or a fine summarily
   (Statutory power of arrest)

The Public Order Act 1986, s. 4 states:

(1) A person is guilty of an offence if he—
   (a) uses towards another person threatening, abusive or insulting words or behaviour, or
   (b) distributes or displays to another person any writing, sign or other visible representation which is threatening, abusive or insulting, with intent to cause that person to believe that immediate unlawful violence will be used against him or another by any person, or to provoke the immediate use of unlawful violence by that person or another, or whereby that person is likely to believe that such violence will be used or it is likely that such violence will be provoked.

(2) An offence under this section may be committed in a public or a private place, except that no offence is committed where the words or behaviour are used, or the writing, sign or other visible

representation is distributed or displayed, by a person inside a dwelling and the other person is also inside that or another dwelling.

KEYNOTE

The term 'threatening, abusive or insulting' is not defined but it was interpreted by the courts under the Public Order Act 1936. Whether words or behaviour are threatening, abusive or insulting will be a question of fact for the magistrate(s) to decide in each case (see *Brutus* v *Cozens* [1973] AC 854).

As with many of the other public order offences that follow in this chapter, the effect that an individual's rights (such as the right to freedom of expression under Article 10 of the European Convention on Human Rights) will have here is not yet clear. The problems of balancing such freedom of expression with the expectations and sensibilities of ordinary members of society can be seen in other countries where these individual rights have been specifically protected by a written constitution. To paraphrase one American judge in a case involving the use of obscene language by an anti-Vietnam protester, 'it is often true that one person's vulgarity is another person's lyric' (see *Cohen* v *State of California* 403 US 15 (1971) 25).

It is not enough that conduct is 'offensive' but it has been held that masturbation towards a police officer in a public lavatory is capable of being insulting (*Parkin* v *Norman* [1983] QB 82).

'Immediate' unlawful violence does not have to be instantaneous but it must be shown that the defendant's conduct was likely to lead to more than some form of violence at some later date. Therefore publication and sale of material by the author Salman Rushdie, however insulting it may have been to some people, was not enough on its facts to support a charge against the publishers under s. 4 (*R* v *Horseferry Road Metropolitan Stipendiary Magistrate, ex parte Siadatan* [1991] 1 QB 260). 'Immediate' here requires some close proximity between the acts of the defendant and the apprehended violence, with no intervening occurence.

In this, and the s. 4A offence (below), the victim of the racially or religiously aggravated behaviour can be a police officer and the courts have held that police officers are entitled to the same protection under the legislation as anyone else (see *R* v *Jacobs* (2000) *The Times*, 28 December).

There are a number of ways in which this offence can be committed (see below). In all of these, however, there must be the use of threatening/abusive/insulting words or behaviour (or distribution/display of writing, signs etc.). This must be carried out with the requisite state of mind set out at s. 6(3) which states:

(3) A person is guilty of an offence under section 4 only if he intends his words or behaviour, or the writing, sign or other visible representation, to be threatening, abusive or insulting, or is aware that it may be threatening, abusive or insulting.

In addition, it must be shown that the person further *intended* to bring about the consequences set out below (at (a) and (b)) or that the consequences (at (c) and (d)) were likely.

The offence was broken down into four component parts in *Winn* v *DPP* (1992) 156 JP 881. For each of these parts it must be shown:

(a) that the defendant:
- intended the person against whom the conduct was directed
- to believe
- that immediate unlawful violence would be used
- either against him/her or against anyone else
- by the defendant or anyone else; *or*

(b) that he/she:
- intended to provoke the immediate use of unlawful violence
- by that person or anyone else; *or*

(c) that:
- the person against whom the words or behaviour (or distribution/display of writing etc.) were directed
- was likely to believe
- that immediate unlawful violence would be used; *or*

(d) that:
- it was likely that immediate unlawful violence would be provoked.

In the case at (a) above, it does not have to be shown that the other person *actually believed* that immediate violence would be used; it has to be shown that the defendant *intended to cause* him/her to believe it (*Swanston* v *DPP* (1997) 161 JP 203).

The person in whom the defendant intends to create that belief must be the same person at whom the conduct is directed (*Loade* v *DPP* [1990] 1 QB 1052). Therefore, if the defendant uses threatening behaviour towards person A, intending that this will cause person B to believe that immediate unlawful violence will be used, the offence under s. 4 is not, without more, made out.

The inclusion of this offence within the provisions of the Crime and Disorder Act 1998 attracts a higher maximum sentence (under s. 31(4) of the 1998 Act) where the offence is racially or religiously aggravated.

Unlike some of the other racially or religiously aggravated offences, provisions are specifically made for alternative verdicts in relation to the above public order offence (see s. 31(6) of the 1998 Act).

Under the Public Order Act 1986, s. 8, dwelling is defined as:

> . . . any structure or part of a structure occupied as a person's home or as other living accommodation (whether the occupation is separate or shared with others) but does not include any part not so occupied, and for this purpose 'structure' includes a tent, caravan, vehicle, vessel or other temporary or movable structure.

KEYNOTE

Given that the offence at s. 4 can be committed in private (under the restrictions in relation to dwellings by s. 4(2) above), it appears that the offence could be committed by a person sending out e-mails or other forms of communication from his/her house to other non-dwellings or from his/her place of work to people's houses.

Communal landings which form access routes to separate dwellings have been held not to constitute part of a dwelling even though they could only be entered by way of an entry phone system (*Rukwira* v *DPP* [1993] Crim LR 882).

Power of Arrest

The Public Order Act 1986, s. 4 states:

> (3) A constable may arrest without warrant anyone he reasonably suspects is committing an offence under this section.

KEYNOTE

Section 31(2) of the Crime and Disorder Act 1998 provides a constable with a power of arrest without warrant in respect of anyone whom he/she reasonably suspects to be committing an offence under this section which is racially or religiously aggravated.

2.7.5 **Intentional Harassment, Alarm or Distress**

OFFENCE: **Intentionally Causing Harassment, Alarm or Distress—*Public Order Act 1986, s. 4A***
- Triable summarily • Six months' imprisonment and/or a fine
(Statutory power of arrest)

OFFENCE: **Racially or Religiously Aggravated—*Crime and Disorder Act 1998, s. 31(1)(b)***
- Triable either way • Two years' imprisonment and/or fine on indictment; six months' imprisonment and/or fine summarily
(Statutory power of arrest)

The Public Order Act 1986, s. 4A states:

(1) A person is guilty of an offence if, with intent to cause a person harassment, alarm or distress, he—
   (a) uses threatening, abusive or insulting words or behaviour, or disorderly behaviour, or
   (b) displays any writing, sign or other visible representation which is threatening, abusive or insulting, thereby causing that or another person harassment, alarm or distress.

KEYNOTE

The inclusion of this offence within the provisions of the Crime and Disorder Act 1998 attracts a higher maximum sentence (under s. 31(4) of the 1998 Act) where the offence is racially or religiously aggravated.

For the purpose of the racially or religiously aggravated form of causing fear or provocation of violence, any words used by the defendant have to be construed within the meaning that they are given in England and Wales. In construing those words, the courts should not have any regard to the *defendant's* own racial, national or ethnic origins—or presumably their religious beliefs or lack of such (*R v White (Anthony Delroy)* [2001] 1 WLR 1352). In *White*, the defendant had been challenged by a bus conductor who believed she had seen him reaching into someone's handbag. The defendant called the bus conductor a 'stupid African bitch' and, on his arrest, an 'African cunt'. The defendant had been born in the West Indies and regarded himself as 'African'. He appealed against his conviction on (among other things) the grounds that:

- the expression he had used, however unpleasant, did not involve an imputation of membership of a racial or ethnic group, or of a particular colour;

- Parliament could not have intended to criminalise his conduct because he was of the same racial group as the bus conductor;

- evidence of his conduct when arrested by the police was not covered by the statute and should not have been admitted.

The Court of Appeal held that:

- The defendant's words had to be construed as they were generally used in England and Wales. The court did not have to stick to any precise dictionary definition (*Mandla v Dowell Lee* [1983] 2 AC 548). On that basis, the word 'African' described a racial group defined by reference to race because, although capable of including other groups (such as Egyptians and white South Africans), the word was not generally used to describe such other groups. The word 'Asians' had been similarly recognised (see *DPP v Rishan Kqumar Pal* [2000] Crim LR 756).

- There was no basis in law for the second ground. Although it may make it more difficult to establish hostility of racial, national or ethnic origin where a defendant is of the same racial, national or ethnic group as a victim, it is still possible to do so.

- The defendant's remarks about the bus conductor made upon arrest did not amount to racial aggravation under s. 31 of the 1998 Act because it was not conduct '*at the time of committing the offence or immediately after doing so*'. Nevertheless, admission in evidence of those remarks did not render the trial unfair in these circumstances because the jury was entitled to know the complete sequence of events.

Unlike some of the other racially or religiously aggravated offences, provisions are specifically made for alternative verdicts in relation to the above public order offence (see s. 31(6) of the 1998 Act).

In order to prove this offence you must show that the defendant *intended* to cause harassment, alarm or distress and, it seems, that by so doing, the defendant actually caused some harassment, alarm or distress.

Harassment, alarm or distress are not defined and it would appear that they are to be given their ordinary everyday meaning. A police officer can be caused such harassment, alarm or distress (*DPP v Orum* [1989] 1 WLR 88); and can also be the victim of the racially aggravated form of the offence (see *R v Jacobs* (2000) *The Times*, 28 December); and he/she can feel that harassment, alarm or distress for someone else present (e.g. a child—see *Lodge v DPP* (1998) *The Times*, 26 October).

Whether the use of a particular phrase, in the context and circumstances in which it was used, was intended to cause harassment, alarm or distress for the offences above is a question of fact for the relevant magistrate/jury to decide (see *DPP* v *Weeks, The Independent*, 17 July 2000). Consequently, in that case where the defendant was alleged to have called the victim a 'black bastard' during a heated argument over a business transaction, the magistrates were still entitled to find him not guilty of the aggravated s. 4A offence if they were satisfied that the relevant intention was not present.

Posting a threatening, abusive or insulting letter through someone's letter box is not an offence under this section (*Chappell* v *DPP* (1988) 89 Cr App R 82). It may, however, amount to an offence under the Malicious Communications Act 1988.

Section 4A states:

(2) An offence under this section may be committed in a public place or a private place, except that no offence is committed where the words or behaviour are used, or the writing, sign or other visible representation is displayed, by a person inside a dwelling and the person who is harassed, alarmed or distressed is also inside that or another dwelling.

Defence

The Public Order Act 1986, s. 4A provides a specific defence:

(3) It is a defence for the accused to prove—
   (a) that he was inside a dwelling and had no reason to believe that the words or behaviour used, or the writing, sign or other visible representation displayed, would be heard or seen by a person outside that or any other dwelling, or
   (b) that his conduct was reasonable.

KEYNOTE

If is for the defendant to prove that one of the elements existed at the time of the offence. The standard of proof here will be that of the balance of probabilities, i.e. that it was more likely than not.

Power of Arrest

The Public Order Act 1986, s. 4A states:

(4) A constable may arrest without warrant anyone he reasonably suspects is committing an offence under this section.

KEYNOTE

Section 31(2) of the Crime and Disorder Act 1998 provides a constable with a power of arrest without warrant in respect of anyone whom he/she reasonably suspects to be committing an offence under this section which is racially or religiously aggravated.

2.7.6   **Harassment, Alarm or Distress**

OFFENCE: **Harassment, Alarm or Distress—*Public Order Act 1986, s. 5***
   • Triable summarily • Fine
   (Statutory power of arrest)

OFFENCE: **Racially or Religiously Aggravated—*Crime and Disorder Act 1998, s. 31(1)(c)***
   • Triable summarily • Fine
   (Statutory power of arrest)

The Public Order Act 1986, s. 5 states:

(1) A person is guilty of an offence if he—
    (a) uses threatening, abusive or insulting words or behaviour, or disorderly behaviour, or
    (b) displays any writing, sign or other visible representation which is threatening, abusive or insulting, within the hearing or sight of a person likely to be caused harassment, alarm or distress thereby.

KEYNOTE

Unlike the other racially or religiously aggravated forms of public order offences, the offence under s. 5 remains triable summarily, even if aggravated by the conditions set out in s. 28 of the Crime and Disorder Act 1998 (s. 31(5)).

The racially or religiously aggravated circumstances set out at s. 28(1)(a) of the Crime and Disorder Act 1998 deal with situations where the defendant demonstrates racial or religious hostility at the time of (or immediately before or after) commiting the offence, towards the *victim*. To clarify such situations in relation to the racially or religiously aggravated form of the above offence, s. 31(7) provides that the person 'likely to be caused harassment, alarm or distress' will be treated as the 'victim'. This appears to be a more useful provision than its counterpart in relation to the Criminal Damage Act 1971.

Note that 'disorderly' is not defined and ought to be given its ordinary everyday meaning. It need not be shown that the disorderly behaviour is itself threatening, abusive or insulting, nor that it brought about any feelings of apprehension in the person to whom it was directed (*Chambers* v *DPP* [1995] Crim LR 896). The wording of s. 5 is not limited to rowdy behaviour and will extend to any behaviour that could be construed as threatening, abusive or insulting. 'Insulting' has been held by the Divisional Court to include the actions of a market trader who installed a hidden video camera to film women trying on swimwear (*Vigon* v *DPP* (1998) 162 JP 115).

The discussion above (see 2.6.5) in relation to intentional harassment, alarm or distress also applies to this offence, except here there needs to be a person within whose sight or hearing the conduct takes place.

Quashing a conviction under s. 5, the Administrative Court has held that there is a presumption that a defendant's conduct was protected by Article 10 unless and until it is established that a restriction on their freedom of expression was strictly necessary (*Percy* v *DPP* (2002) *The Times*, 21 January). That case involved the defendant defacing an American flag as part of a political protest at a US air base. The Court held that ss. 5 and 6 of the Act contained the necessary balance between the right of individual freedom of expression and the right of others not to be insulted and/or distressed. However, on the facts of the case itself, the issues of proportionality had not been properly considered ánd therefore the defendant's conviction was quashed.

Section 5 states:

(2) An offence under this section may be committed in a public or a private place, except that no offence is committed where the words or behaviour are used, or the writing, sign or other visible representation is displayed, by a person inside a dwelling and the other person is also inside that or another dwelling.

State of Mind

The Public Order Act 1986, s. 6 states:

(4) A person is guilty of an offence under section 5 only if he intends his words or behaviour, or the writing, sign or other visible representation, to be threatening, abusive or insulting, or is aware that it may be threatening, abusive or insulting or (as the case may be) he intends his behaviour to be or is aware that it may be disorderly.

Defence

The Public Order Act 1986, s. 5 provides a specific defence:

(3) It is a defence for the accused to prove—
    (a) that he had no reason to believe that there was any person within hearing or sight who was likely to be caused harassment, alarm or distress, or

(b) that he was inside a dwelling and had no reason to believe that the words or behaviour used, or the writing sign or other visible representation displayed, would be heard or seen by a person outside that or any other dwelling, or

(c) that his conduct was reasonable.

KEYNOTE

It is for the defendant to prove that one of the elements existed at the time of the offence. The standard of proof here will be that of the balance of probabilities, i.e. that it was more likely than not.

In deciding whether a defendant's conduct was reasonable under s. 5(3)(c) an objective test will be applied (*DPP* v *Clarke* (1991) 94 Cr App R 359).

Power of Arrest

The Public Order Act 1986, s. 5 states:

(4) A constable may arrest a person without warrant if—
   (a) he engages in offensive conduct which a constable warns him to stop, and
   (b) he engages in further offensive conduct immediately or shortly after the warning.

The Crime and Disorder Act 1998, s. 31(3) states:

(3) A constable may arrest a person without warrant if—
   (a) he engages in conduct which a constable reasonably suspects to constitute an offence falling within subsection (1)(c) above;
   (b) he is warned by that constable to stop; and
   (c) he engages in further such conduct immediately or shortly after the warning.
   The conduct mentioned in paragraph (a) above and the further conduct need not be of the same nature.

KEYNOTE

It is no longer necessary that the warning be given by the same officer who later arrests the defendant (s. 1 of the Public Order (Amendment) Act 1996). For a warning to be sufficient, the words must convey to the defendant that to continue with his/her conduct will amount to an offence (*Groom* v *DPP* [1991] Crim LR 713).

The second power of arrest applies to suspected offences which are racially or religiously aggravated.

Police Direction to Prevent Harassment

In response to a number of campaigns against individuals believed to be involved in animal experiments, the Criminal Justice and Police Act 2001 gives the police specific powers to prevent the intimidation or harassment of people in their own or others' homes. Situations envisaged by the legislation typically arise where protestors gather outside a house where a particular individual is believed to be. Under such circumstances s. 42 provides the most senior ranking police officer at the scene with discretionary powers to give directions to people in the vicinity. The power arises where:

• the person is outside (or in the vicinity of) any premises that are used by any individual as his/her dwelling, and

• the constable believes, on reasonable grounds, that the person is there for the purpose of representing or persuading the resident (or anyone else)

• that they should not do something they are entitled or required to do or

• that they should do something that they are under no obligation to do, and

• the constable also believes, on reasonable grounds, that the person's presence amounts to or is likely to result in, the harassment of the resident or is likely to cause alarm or distress to the resident.

Although the premises involved may be in use by any 'individual' (e.g. *not* a company) and the purpose may be to persuade that or any other 'individual', the officer must believe that the ultimate effect will be harassment, alarm or distress of the *resident*. The requirement for 'belief' by the police officer here is greater than mere concern or suspicion. The requirement for reasonable grounds means that their existence or otherwise will be judged objectively and not simply from the personal standpoint of the officer using the power. Nevertheless, the officer is given a great deal of individual discretion in using this power. Given the discretion and the potential impact on the competing rights of all involved, the use and extent of this power must be carefully considered in the light of the principles of the Human Rights Act 1998.

A direction given under s. 42 requires the person(s) to do all such things as the officer specifies as being *necessary* to prevent the harassment, alarm or distress of the resident, including a requirement to leave the vicinity either immediately or after a specified time (s. 42(2) and (4)). The officer may decide that people can remain within a certain distance from the relevant premises and may limit the number or identity of people who can remain in the vicinity (s. 42(5)).

The direction may be given orally and, where appropriate, may be given to a group of people together (s. 42(3)). There is no requirement that the officer giving the direction be in uniform (however, see the power of arrest for contravention of such an order below).

The power under s. 42 cannot be used to direct someone to refrain from conduct made lawful under the Trade Union and Labour Relations (Consolidation) Act 1992, s. 220.

OFFENCE: **Knowingly Contravening a s. 42 Direction—*Criminal Justice and Police Act 2001, s. 42(7)***

- Triable summarily • Three months' imprisonment and/or a fine
(Statutory power of arrest)

The Criminal Justice and Police Act 2001, s. 42 states:

> (7) Any person who knowingly contravenes a direction given to him under this section shall be guilty of an offence.

KEYNOTE

The wording of this offence means that you will have to prove a number of key aspects. First, you will need to show that the person acted 'knowingly' in contravening the direction and secondly that it was 'given to them'. Generally the best proof of this will be to show that the person had received the direction (and the detail of its extent) personally and that they understood it. Therefore, although the section allows for directions to be given to groups, there may be practical benefits in giving personal directions where circumstances allow.

Power of Arrest

The Criminal Justice and Police Act 2001, s. 42(8) states:

> A constable in uniform may arrest without warrant any person he reasonably suspects is committing an offence under this section.

KEYNOTE

This power is restricted to officers in uniform (though it may be appropriate under the circumstances to use another power such as the common law power to prevent an imminent breach of the peace). The power is also limited to those people who are reasonably suspected to be in the act of committing the offence, as opposed to those who may *have committed* the offence.

The Criminal Justice and Police Act 2001 also makes specific provision for protecting the directors (and those who live with them) of certain companies involved in sensitive and emotive operations from harassment in their homes or private lives. Under the 2001 Act (see s. 45), an individual who is (or proposes to be) a director, secretary or permanent representative of a relevant company can apply to the Secretary of State for a 'confidentiality order', exempting the individual's personal details from many of the public records that have to be maintained under the Companies Act 1985. This provision is designed to prevent activists who are opposed to the operations of certain research organisations from gaining access to the personal details of the company's officers through public registers.

2.8 Racially and Religiously Aggravated Offences

Since the offence of inciting racial hatred was created by the Race Relations Act in 1965, various governments have tried to install an effective method by which the criminal law can address offending that is actuated by racism. That, and the many provisions which followed, were found to present a number of practical problems, many relating to the actual or perceived difficulties of proving the various elements of the offences. In addition to the racial hatred offences, there have been other attempts to single out criminal conduct that has an overtly racist element (for example the offences of 'racialist' chanting under the Football (Offences) Act 1991).

For whatever reasons, the various measures introduced since 1965 had not succeeded in preventing a rise in the number of reported 'racial incidents' (as defined by ACPO). Although the Home Affairs Select Committee recommended the creation of a new offence of racially motivated violence, the most immediate response was the amendment of the Public Order Act 1986 (under s. 154 of the Criminal Justice and Public Order Act 1994), inserting a new s. 4A. This created a summary offence of intentionally causing harassment, alarm or distress. Again there has been some dissatisfaction as to the extent to which this additional offence (s. 4A) has addressed the behaviour that it was aimed at curbing. More recently, the Stephen Lawrence inquiry focused a great deal of attention on the many potential sources of racism—particularly those that are not immediately apparent on the surface. The inquiry observed (at para. 45.17) that:

> We believe that the use of the words 'racial' and 'racially motivated' are in themselves inaccurate because we all belong to one human race, regardless of our colour, culture or ethnic origin...

Consequently, the inquiry recommended (para. 45.17) a new definition of a *'racist incident'* namely 'any incident which is perceived to be racist by the victim or any other person'.

That definition does not yet appear in any legislation. However, the Crime and Disorder Act 1998 (passed before the report of the Stephen Lawrence inquiry) re-visited the whole issue of racially aggravated crime. Although adopting the use of the expression 'racially aggravated', the Act sought to address many of the issues of criminal law arising from the Stephen Lawrence inquiry. It sets out certain conditions under which specified offences will be deemed to be 'racially aggravated' and increases the powers available to the courts in the punishment of racist offenders.

The 1998 Act was itself amended to incorporate religiously-aggravated offending in the aftermath of the terrorist attacks on the United States in 2001.

The Powers of Criminal Courts (Sentencing) Act 2000 allows the courts to take account of any element of racial or religious aggravation in an offence coming before them. Although that section formalises an earlier sentencing decision (*R v Ribbans* (1995) 12 Cr App R (S) 698) in requiring a court to take any element of racial or religious aggravation into account when passing sentence, the new statutory requirement means that the court must also state openly that racial or religious aggravation features of the offence have been taken into consideration.

The requirement under s. 153 applies to *any offence other than the new racially or religiously aggravated offences* created by the Act. It was felt by the legislators that, even though some offences carried a high enough maximum penalty under the existing legislation (examples of which might be arson (**see 2.9.4**) or wounding with intent (**see 2.2.15**), s. 153 would make the courts take account of, and draw attention to, any racial or religious aggravation when determining the appropriate sentence in any particular case.

2.8.1   The Offences

Sections 28–33 of the Crime and Disorder Act 1998 did not so much create *new* offences, but rather took *existing* offences and set out circumstances under which those offences will be deemed to be 'aggravated'. Those offences are:

Section 29:

- wounding or grievous bodily harm—Offences Against the Person Act 1861, s. 20
- causing actual bodily harm—Offences Against the Person Act 1861, s. 47
- common assault—Criminal Justice Act 1988, s. 39

Section 30:

- 'simple' criminal damage—Criminal Damage Act 1971, s. 1(1)

Section 31:

- causing fear or provocation of violence—Public Order Act 1986, s. 4
- intentional harassment, alarm or distress—Public Order Act 1986, s. 4A
- causing harassment, alarm or distress—Public Order Act 1986, s. 5

Section 32:

- harassment—Protection from Harassment Act 1997, s. 2
- putting in fear of violence—Protection from Harassment Act 1997, s. 4

This area of the law was changed once again after the terrorist attacks of 11 September 2001 by the Anti-terrorism, Crime and Security Act 2001. Part 5 of that Act amended the Crime and Disorder Act 1998, extending the provisions of what were 'racially aggravated' offences to include 'racially *or religiously* aggravated' offences (as to which, see below).

In order to prove these offences there must be proof of the relevant, substantive offence (e.g. common assault) together with further proof of the aggravating circumstances. Once both conditions have been made out, the offences attract greater maximum penalties and powers.

2.8.2   'Racially or Religiously Aggravated'

The test for racial or religious aggravation is set out at s. 28 of the Crime and Disorder Act 1998:

(1) An offence is racially or religiously aggravated for the purposes of sections 29 to 32 . . . if—
    (a) at the time of committing the offence, or immediately before or after doing so, the offender demonstrates towards the victim of the offence hostility based on the victim's membership (or presumed membership) of a racial or religious group; or
    (b) the offence is motivated (wholly or partly) by hostility towards members of a racial or religious group based on their membership of that group.

(2) In subsection (1)(a) above—

'membership', in relation to a racial or religious group, includes association with members of that group;

'presumed' means presumed by the offender.

(3) It is immaterial for the purposes of paragraph (a) or (b) of subsection (1) above whether or not the offender's hostility is also based, to any extent, on any other factor not mentioned in that paragraph.

(4) In this section 'racial group' means a group of persons defined by reference to race, colour, nationality (including citizenship) or ethnic or national origins.

(5) In this section 'religious group' means a group of persons defined by reference to religious belief or lack of religious belief.

KEYNOTE

The aggravating factors for the purposes of s. 28 can be divided into:

- *demonstration* of hostility by the defendant

- *motivation* by hostility of the defendant.

The second type of situation, where the defendant is *motivated* by racial or religious hostility, is the type at which the government's policies to tackle racism are aimed; it is also by far the harder of the two to prove, even though the relevant offence need only be *partly* motivated by racial or religious hostility.

The revised wording of s. 28 (amended after the events of 11 September, 2001) now includes 'religious groups'. These will include groups of people defined, not only by their religious belief, but also their *lack* of any such belief.

In a case involving abuse and assault of a doorman, the Administrative Court held that a racial insult uttered a few moments before an assault was enough to make the offence racially aggravated for the purposes of s. 29 of the Crime and Disorder Act 1998. The Court also held that the victim's own perception of the words used was irrelevant, as was the fact that he was not personally upset by the situation. Similarly, the fact that the defendant might have been motivated to utter the words merely by frustration rather than racism was also irrelevant (*DPP v Woods* [2002] EWHC Admin 85).

Hostility

Common to both factors under s. 28(1)(a) and (b) is the notion of hostility.

Hostility is not defined. However, in comparison to the problematic expression of 'racial hatred' used in the Public Order Act 1986, hostility may well be much easier to identify and prove. The *Oxford English Dictionary* defines 'hostile' as 'of the nature or disposition of an enemy; unfriendly, antagonistic'. It would seem relatively straightforward to show that someone's behaviour in committing the relevant offences was 'unfriendly or antagonistic'. The difficult bit will come when trying to show that the hostility was *based on* the relevant person's membership of a racial or religious group.

Racial Groups

In each case the hostility must be based on the relevant person's membership of a racial group, i.e. membership of a group of people defined by reference to s. 28(4):

- race

- colour

- nationality (including citizenship)

- ethnic origins

- national origins

This definition is the same as that used in the Public Order Act 1986 (see below). It is also very similar to that used in the Race Relations Act 1976. In determining whether or not a group is defined by *ethnic origins*, the courts will have regard to the judgment in the House of Lords in *Mandla* v *Dowell Lee* [1983] 2 AC 548. In that case their Lordships decided that Sikhs were such a group (for the purposes of the Race Relations Act 1976) after considering whether they as a group had:

- A long shared *history.*

- A *cultural tradition* of their own, including family and social customs and manners, often, but not necessarily, associated with religious observance.

- Either a *common geographical origin* or descent from a small number of *common ancestors.*

- A *common language*, not necessarily peculiar to that group.

- A *common literature* peculiar to that group.

- A *common religion* different from that of neighbouring groups or the general community surrounding the group.

- The characteristic of being a *minority* or an *oppressed* or a *dominant* group within a larger community.

Lord Fraser's *dictum* suggests that the first two characteristics above are essential in defining an 'ethnic group', while the others are at least relevant. His Lordship also approved a decision from New Zealand to the effect that Jews are a group with common ethnic origins (*Kings-Ansell* v *Police* [1979] 2 NZLR 531).

Religion

Lord Fraser's sixth point above refers to religion as a possible defining characteristic of an ethnic group. Although this was a notable omission from the ambit of *racial groups* as defined under the original s. 28(4) of the Crime and Disorder Act 1998, religious groups have now been included as a result of the Anti-terrorsism, Crime and Security Act 2001. This means that the former case law (mostly arising in an employment context) over whether religious groups could also be regarded as racial groups is largely irrelevant. The change means that a purely religious group such as Rastafarians (who have been held not to be members of an ethnic group *per se* (*Dawkins* v *Crown Suppliers* (*Property Services Agency*) (1993) *The Times*, 4 February) are now covered by the aggravated forms of offences. In reality, a number of racial groups will overlap with religious groups in any event—Rastafarians would be a good example. An attack on a Rastafarian might be a racially aggravated offence under s. 28 because it was based on the defendant's hostility towards a *racial group* (e.g. African-Caribbeans) into which many Rastafarians fall. Alternatively, an attack might be made on a white Rastafarian based on the victim's religious beliefs (or lack of religious beliefs), i.e. his 'membership of a religious group'. Muslims have also been held not to be a racial group (*J. H. Walker* v *Hussain* [1996] ICR 291) but Muslims are clearly members of a religious group and, as such, are now covered by the Act.

Although the offences that were made 'racially aggravated' by the Crime and Disorder Act 1998 now include religiously aggravated features as well, the proposal to create a specific offence of incitement to religious hatred by the government was withdrawn. At the time of writing the House of Lords announced a select committee to investigate this area of law more fully. Similarly, there are proposals to extend the civil legislation outlawing discrimination to cover religious groups.

Other Racial Groups

Traditional 'gypsies' (as opposed to travellers) are capable of being a racial group on the basis of ethnic origin (*Commission for Racial Equality* v *Dutton* [1989] QB 783). English and Scottish people have been held to constitute groups defined by reference to national origins and thus as members of 'racial groups' in the broad sense as defined and protected from discrimination under the Race Relations Act 1976 (*Northern Joint Police Board* v *Power* [1997] IRLR 610). This decision ought logically to extend to Irish and Welsh people.

Membership

An important extension of 'racial or religious groups' lies in the inclusion of people who associate with members of that group. 'Membership' *for the purposes of s. 28(1)(a)* will include *association* with members of that group (a slightly circular definition) (s. 28(2)). This means that a white man who has a black female partner would potentially fall within the category of a 'member' of her racial group—and vice versa. Moreover, people who work within certain racial or religious groups within the community could also be regarded as members of those groups for these purposes.

For the purposes of s. 28(1)(a), 'membership' will also include anyone *presumed by the defendant* to be a member of a racial or religious group. Therefore, if a defendant wrongly presumed that a person was a member of a racial or religious group, say a Pakistani Muslim, and assaulted them as a result, the defendant's *presumption* would be enough to make his/her behaviour 'racially or religiously aggravated', even though the victim was in fact an Indian Hindu.

Such a presumption would not extend to the aggravating factors under s. 28(1)(b). The only apparent reason for this would seem to be that the s. 28(1)(a) offence requires hostility to be demonstrated towards a particular person ('the victim') while the offence under s. 28(1)(b) envisages hostility towards members of a racial or religious group generally and does not require a specific victim.

Section 28(3) goes on to provide that it is immaterial whether the defendant's hostility (in either case under s. 28(1)) is also based to any extent on *any other factor*.

This concession in s. 28(3) only prevents the defendant pointing to another *factor* in order to explain his/her behaviour in committing the relevant offence (assault, criminal damage, etc.). Although it removes the opportunity for a defendant to argue that his/her behaviour was as a result of other factors (e.g. arising out of a domestic dispute), the subsection does not remove the burden on the prosecution to show that the defendant either demonstrated racial or religious hostility or was motivated by it.

Demonstration of Hostility

Under s. 28(1)(a) it must be shown that the defendant *demonstrated* the required hostility:

- at the time of the offence
- immediately before, or
- immediately after committing the offence.

No guidance is given as to how *immediately* will be interpreted. It is submitted that whether a defendant's demonstration of hostility came immediately before or after the relevant offence will be a question of fact to be decided in light of all the circumstances.

In deciding the issue of immediacy the courts will have to consider the degree of proximity between the defendant's demonstration of racial or religious hostility and the relevant offence itself. It is submitted that the degree of proximity will have to be very high before the defendant's hostility could be shown to have been *immediately* before or after the *actus reus* of the offence. This might cause problems with offences that are said to be 'continuing' or 'ongoing'.

In the context of the offence under s. 4 of the Public Order Act 1986 the Divisional Court held that, where a court finds that the defendant has committed an offence under s. 4 and used racist, threatening and abusive words, it is immaterial for the purposes of s. 28(1)(a) of the 1998 Act that the defendant might have had additional reasons for using that language (*DPP* v *McFarlane* (2002) LTL 7 March).

It is also necessary, for the purposes of s. 28(1)(a), to show that the defendant demonstrated his/her hostility *towards the victim of the offence*. Again this may be problematic in relation to certain offences, e.g. criminal damage.

Racially or religiously aggravated offences can be committed where the aggravating behaviour is directed at or towards a police officer and police officers are entitled to the protection offered by this offence in the same way as any other person (see *R* v *Jacobs* (2000) *The Times*, 28 December).

2.8.3 Other Offences Involving Racism: Racial Hatred

In addition to the racially or religiously aggravated offences discussed above—and elsewhere in this Manual—there are still several former offences under earlier legislation. Few prosecutions took place under these headings before the passing of the Crime and Disorder Act 1998. However, the Anti-terrorism, Crime and Security Act 2001 has focused greater attention on this area of law: what follows is a summary of the offences.

The Public Order Act 1986 introduced several offences aimed at addressing incidents specifically motivated by racial hatred.

For these purposes 'racial hatred' means hatred against a group of persons defined by reference to colour, race, nationality (including citizenship) or ethnic or national origins (s. 17). This area of criminal law was not specifically extended to cover religious groups.

2.8.4 Use of Words, Behaviour or Display of Written Material

OFFENCE: **Use of Words or Behaviour or Display of Written Material—*Public Order Act 1986, s. 18***
- Triable either way • Seven years' imprisonment and/or a fine on indictment; six months' imprisonment and/or a fine summarily
  (Arrestable offence)

The Public Order Act 1986, s. 18 states:

(1) A person who uses threatening, abusive or insulting words or behaviour, or displays any written material which is threatening, abusive or insulting, is guilty of an offence if—
   (a) he intends thereby to stir up racial hatred, or
   (b) having regard to all the circumstances racial hatred is likely to be stirred up thereby.

(2) An offence under this section may be committed in a public or a private place, except that no offence is committed where the words or behaviour are used, or the written material is displayed, by a person inside a dwelling and are not heard or seen except by other persons in that or another dwelling.

KEYNOTE

This, and the other offences under this part of the Act, may not be prosecuted without the consent of the Attorney-General (or Solicitor-General).

Generally, in order to prove these offences, you must show that a defendant:

- *intended* to stir up racial hatred; or

- that he/she *intended* the relevant words, behaviour or material to be threatening, abusive or insulting; or

- that he/she *was aware* that the relevant words/behaviour/material might be threatening, abusive or insulting.

This offence does not apply to broadcasts in a programme (but see below) and there are exemptions in the case of fair and accurate reports of parliamentary or court proceedings.

Defence

The Public Order Act 1986, s. 18 states:

(4) In proceedings for an offence under this section it is a defence for the accused to prove that he was inside a dwelling and had no reason to believe that the words or behaviour used, or the written material displayed, would be heard or seen by a person outside that or any other dwelling.

Power of Arrest

The Public Order Act 1986, s. 18 states:

(3) A constable may arrest without warrant anyone he reasonably suspects is committing an offence under this section.

2.8.5 Publishing or Distributing Written Material

OFFENCE: **Publishing or Distributing Written Material—*Public Order Act 1986, s. 19***

- Triable either way • Seven years' imprisonment and/or a fine on indictment; six months' imprisonment and/or a fine summarily

(Arrestable offence)

The Public Order Act 1986, s. 19 states:

(1) A person who publishes or distributes written material which is threatening, abusive or insulting is guilty of an offence if—
(a) he intends thereby to stir up racial hatred, or
(b) having regard to all the circumstances racial hatred is likely to be stirred up thereby.
(2) ...
(3) References in this Part to the publication or distribution of written material are to its publication or distribution to the public or a section of the public.

KEYNOTE

This offence has attracted more prominence in the last 12 months and its penalty was increased, along with those for other offences under this part of the Act, by the Anti-terrorism, Crime and Security Act 2001.

Prosecution of this offence needs the consent of the Attorney-General (or Solicitor-General).

Defence

The Public Order Act 1986, s. 19 states:

(2) In proceedings for an offence under this section it is a defence for an accused who is not shown to have intended to stir up racial hatred to prove that he was not aware of the content of the material and did not suspect, and had no reason to suspect, that it was threatening, abusive or insulting.

Other Offences under Part III

Other Public Order Act 1986 offences involving activities intended or likely to stir up racial hatred are:

- presenting or directing a public performance of a play—s. 20
- distributing, showing or playing recordings—s. 21
- providing, producing, directing or appearing in a programme service—s. 22
- possessing written material or recordings with a view to displaying, publishing, distributing and playing in a programme service—s. 23.

Each of these offences is triable either way, carries seven years' imprisonment and has its own specific statutory defence.

2.8.6 Protection from Harassment

The Protection from Harassment Act 1997 was introduced after a number of highly-publicised cases of stalking. Although intended for such situations, the Act's extensive provisions have been applied—and interpreted—widely. In passing the legislation set out below, the government anticipated prosecutions under the 1997 Act to be only several hundred; in fact, many thousands of prosecutions have been brought and the following legislation can be a useful and potent tool for the police.

Some of the 1997 Act's most sweeping provisions have been brought into force by the Crime and Disorder Act 1998.

The Offences

OFFENCE: **Harassment—*Protection from Harassment Act 1997, ss. 1 and 2***
- Triable summarily • Six months' imprisonment and/or a fine
(Arrestable offence)

OFFENCE: **Racially or Religiously Aggravated—*Crime and Disorder Act 1998, s. 32(1)(a)***
- Triable either way • Two years' imprisonment and/or a fine on indictment; six months' imprisonment and/or a fine summarily
(Arrestable offence)

The Protection from Harassment Act 1997, ss. 1 and 2 state:

1.—(1) A person must not pursue a course of conduct—
    (a) which amounts to harassment of another, and
    (b) which he knows or ought to know amounts to harassment of the other.

2.—(1) A person who pursues a course of conduct in breach of section 1 is guilty of an offence.

KEYNOTE

This offence is made an 'arrestable offence' by s. 2(3).

The racially or religiously aggravated offence is made an arrestable offence by s. 32(2) of the Crime and Disorder Act 1998 which adds it to those offences listed under s. 24(2) of the Police and Criminal Evidence Act 1984.

Unlike some of the other racially or religiously aggravated offences, provisions are specifically made for alternative verdicts in relation to harassment (see s. 32(5)).

'Harassment' includes alarming the person or causing them distress (s. 7(1) of the 1997 Act).

The inclusion of alarm or distress is significant as it has been held by the Divisional Court that a person—in this case, a police officer—can be alarmed for the safety of another (*Lodge* v *DPP* (1988) *The Times*, 26 October).

'Course of conduct' must involve conduct on at least two occasions but it can involve speech (s. 7(3) and (4)). The issue of whether two acts of harassment against two different victims would suffice for an offence under s. 2 was raised in *DPP* v *Williams (Michael)*, 27 July 1998, unreported. In that case the defendant had reached in through an open bathroom window while one woman was taking a shower and had then climbed onto a roof to see the woman and a friend through a bedroom window. Unfortunately, the Divisional Court held that there was no need to construe the wording of the Act as one of the women had been involved in both incidents. It is arguable that, under the terms of s. 6 of the Interpretation Act 1978, the requirements of the offence could be met where there are two separate victims. However, this issue was considered again by the Divisional Court in *Lau* v *DPP* [2000] Crim LR 580. In that case the 'course of conduct' involved a battery (slapping across the face) against the complainant on one occasion, followed some time later by a threat being made to the complainant's boyfriend in her presence. In *Lau*, the court held that the evidence of a 'course of conduct' by the defendant was insufficient to convict. The court also said that, in determining whether such a course of conduct had been made out, regard should be had to the number of incidents and the relative times when they took place—the fewer the incidents and the further apart in time that they took place, the less likely it was that a court would find that harassment had taken place. What the court did decide in *Williams*, however, was that the offence was not restricted to acts of 'stalking'.

Although it may be helpful in terms of proving the occurrence of 'a course of conduct', the practice in some police areas of issuing warnings and maintaining a register of the same is not a specific requirement of the Act and may raise some issues of procedural fairness.

In *King* v *DPP* (2000) *The Independent*, 31 July, the Divisional Court considered the situation where a number of incidents had taken place and it was alleged that they amounted to a 'course of conduct'. The court held that, although some individual incidents may not amount to harassment in themselves, they could form a background against which further events were to be viewed. In the particular case, the defendant had approached the victim to strike up conversations and had sent her a gift. The court accepted that, *on their particular facts*, these incidents were not enough to constitute harassment or a course of conduct amounting to harassment. They did, however, provide a background against which the defendant's later behaviour—covertly filming the victim and rummaging through her rubbish—and his state of mind could be considered. The court went on to say that the defendant's filming the victim (even though she had not been aware of it) and rummaging through her rubbish were acts that were capable of amounting to harassment or part of a course of conduct amounting to harassment.

On occasions the courts may accept that two instances of behaviour by the defendant several months apart will suffice. In a recent case, where the defendant wrote two threatening letters to a member of the Benefits Agency staff, the defendant was convicted of harassment even though there had been four and a half months' interval between the two letters. In that case the Divisional Court also refused to endorse the view that people in such public service posts were expected to be more robust and therefore less likely to be distressed or frightened by the content of such personal communications (*Baron* v *Crown Prosecution Service*, 13 June 2000, unreported).

But what of the opposite type of conduct, where the acts complained of are so close together that they are alleged to be one continuing act? What if a defendant makes several calls to the victim's mobile phone in the space of five minutes—is this a 'course of conduct'? According to the High Court in *R* v *Kelly* [2002] EWHC Admin 1428, magistrates were entitled to find that it was. But what if, instead of answering the phone as the calls were made, the victim later listened to the abusive and threatening messages left by the defendant on her voicemail facility, replaying each message one after the other? Again, these were the facts in *Kelly*, above, and the magistrates were entitled to find that this still amounted to a course of conduct. In addition, the court held that it was enough that the victim was alarmed or distressed by the course of conduct as a whole rather than by each act making up the course of conduct. This is a different requirement from the more serious offence under s. 4 (see below) where the victim must be caused to fear violence on at least two occasions.

There is no specific requirement that the activity making up the course of conduct be of the same nature. Therefore two distinctly different types of behaviour by the defendant (e.g. making a telephone call on one occasion and damaging the victim's property on another) may suffice. In a case involving the racially or religiously aggravated offence, the aggravating element will need to be proved in relation to both instances of the defendant's conduct.

Some behaviour will be sufficiently disturbing or alarming for two instances to suffice (e.g. the making of overt threats). If sufficiently alarming or distressing, the behaviour may also amount to an offence in itself under some other legislation. Other behaviour, however, may not be sufficient to establish 'harassment' after only two occasions (e.g. the sending of flowers and gifts) and may require more than the bare statutory minimum of two occasions.

Although it may be helpful in terms of proving the occurrence of two or more acts amounting to 'a course of conduct', the practice in some police areas of issuing warnings and maintaining a register of the same (particularly in relation to their own officers) is not a specific requirement of the Act and may raise some issues of procedural fairness.

A limited company cannot be the 'victim' of harassment, although an individual employee or a clearly defined group of individuals could be—*DPP* v *Dziurzynski* [2002] EWHC 1380.

The definition of harassment in s. 7 of the Protection from Harassment Act 1997 is an inclusive but not exhaustive list. Although the words used in s. 7 are 'alarm **and** distress', the Divisional Court has held that they should be taken disjunctively and not conjunctively, that is, the court need only be satisfied that the behaviour involved one or the other; alarm **or** distress (*DPP* v *Ramsdale* [2001] EWHC Admin 106).

All in all, this has turned out to be a very prosecution-friendly piece of legislation extending to behaviour far beyond that which was probably envisaged by its authors.

The repeated commission of other offences (say, public order offences or against property) involving the same victim may also amount to harassment. In such cases the advice of the Crown Prosecution Service should be sought as to which charge(s) to prefer.

In short, in order to prove this offence you must show that:

- the defendant pursued a 'course of conduct',

- the course of conduct amounted to harassment as defined in s. 7(1), and

- the defendant knew, or ought to have known, that his/her conduct amounted harassment.

In order to avoid the practical difficulties of proving the subjective *intention* of the defendant, the offence focuses on an objective test.

In addition, s. 1(2) states:

(2) For the purposes of this section, the person whose course of conduct is in question ought to know that it amounts to harassment of another if a reasonable person in possession of the same information would think the course of conduct amounted to harassment of the other.

KEYNOTE

Section 1(2) requires the jury/court to consider whether the defendant ought to have known that his/her conduct amounted to harassment by the objective test of what a 'reasonable person' would think. Section 1(3)(c) also imposes an objective test as to whether that conduct was reasonable in the judgment of the jury/court. As a result, the Court of Appeal has held that no characteristics of the defendant can be attached to the word 'reasonable' (*R* v *Colohan* [2001] Crim LR 845).

Although the defendant's mental illness may be relevant to sentence, the protective and preventative nature of the Act together with the objective nature of the tests above means that such illness does not provide a defence.

Aiding and Abetting

As a result of incidents against the directors and staff of life science research companies, the Protection from Harassment Act 1997 was amended (see the Criminal Justice and Police Act 2001, s. 44). Those changes mean that if someone aids, abets, counsels or procures another to commit an offence under the 1997 Act, the conduct of the 'primary' defendant will be taken to be the conduct of the aider, abettor, counsellor or procurer of the offence. This does not prevent the primary defendant's conduct from being relevant; what it does is to make the aider, abettor, etc. of the offence liable for the conduct which he/she has facilitated. The 2001 Act also makes provision for determining the knowledge and intention of aiders, abettors etc. Although the Act refers to this area as 'collective harassment', it overlaps with the whole concept of incomplete offences and the advice of the Crown Prosecution Service should be sought in formulating appropriate charges.

If the person concerned in the course of conduct can show that he/she did so:

- for the purpose of preventing or detecting crime, or
- under any enactment or rule of law to comply with a particular requirement, or
- in circumstances whereby the course of conduct was reasonable

the offence under s. 1(1) will not apply (s. 1(3)).

The burden of proving any of these features or circumstances lies with the defendant.

Examples might be police or DSS surveillance teams, or court officers serving summonses. (See also the defence under s. 12 below.)

Whether a course of conduct is 'reasonable' will be a question of fact for a court to decide in the light of all the circumstances. The wording of s. 1(2) suggests that such a test might be an *objective* one (i.e. as a reasonable bystander) and not one based upon the particular belief or perception of the defendant—otherwise the main effect of the 1997 Act would be considerably diluted.

For the powers of a court to issue a restraining order or injunction in relation to this offence, see below.

Under s. 3(1) conduct or apprehended conduct falling within s. 1 may be the subject of a civil claim by the victim/intended victim. This creates a 'statutory tort' of harassment in addition to the criminal offence.

OFFENCE: **Putting People in Fear of Violence—*Protection from Harassment Act 1997, s. 4***

- Triable either way • Five years' imprisonment and/or a fine on indictment; six months' imprisonment and/or a fine summarily
  (Arrestable offence)

OFFENCE: **Racially or Religiously Aggravated—*Crime and Disorder Act 1998, s. 32(1)(b)***

- Triable either way • Seven years' imprisonment and/or a fine on indictment; six months' imprisonment and/or a fine summarily
  (Arrestable offence)

The Protection from Harassment Act 1997, s. 4 states:

(1) A person whose course of conduct causes another to fear, on at least two occasions, that violence will be used against him is guilty of an offence if he knows or ought to know that his course of conduct will cause the other so to fear on each of those occasions.

KEYNOTE

'Course of conduct' is discussed above.

The defendant's course of conduct must cause the victim to fear that violence *will* (rather than might) be used against him or her. This is quite a strict requirement and showing that the conduct caused the victim to be seriously frightened of what might happen in the future is not enough (*R* v *Henley* [2002] Crim LR 582).

You must show that the defendant knew, or ought to have known that their conduct would cause the other person to fear violence. This may be shown by any previous conversations or communications between the defendant and the victim, together with the victims' response to the defendant's earlier behaviour (e.g. running away, calling the police etc.).

The fear of violence being used against the victim must be present on both occasions. If it is present on one occasion but not the other, the offence under s. 2 above may be appropriate.

The course of conduct for the purpose of s. 4 has to cause a person to fear, on at least two occasions, that violence would be used against *him/her* rather than against a member of their family (*Mohammed Ali Caurti* v *DPP* [2002] Crim LR 131).

Unlike some of the other racially or religiously aggravated offences, provisions are specifically made for alternative verdicts in relation to harassment (see s. 32(6)). Where the racially or religiously aggravated form of the offence is charged, the aggravating element of the defendant's conduct must be shown in relation to both instances.

As with the s. 2 offence, a single instance of behaviour may be enough to support a charge for another offence (e.g. assault or threats to kill).

Again, this offence is not one of *intent* but one which is subject to a test of reasonableness against the standard of an ordinary person in possession of the same information as the defendant.

For the powers of a court to issue a restraining order or injunction in relation to this offence, see below.

Section 4 goes on to state:

(2) For the purposes of this section, the person whose course of conduct is in question ought to know that it will cause another to fear that violence will be used against him on any occasion if a reasonable person in possession of the same information would think the course of conduct would cause the other so to fear on that occasion.

Defence

Section 4(3) states:

(3) It is a defence for a person charged with an offence under this section to show that—
   (a) his course of conduct was pursued for the purpose of preventing or detecting crime,
   (b) his course of conduct was pursued under any enactment or rule of law or to comply with any condition or requirement imposed by any person under any enactment, or
   (c) the pursuit of his course of conduct was reasonable for the protection of himself or another or for the protection of his or another's property.

KEYNOTE

There is a slight difference in the wording of the defence when compared to that under s. 1(3) above. There, the defendant may show that his/her conduct was reasonable in the particular circumstances. In relation to the more serious offence under s. 4, the defendant must show that his/her conduct was reasonable *for the protection of themselves, another person or their own/another's property*. These are the only grounds on which the defendant may argue reasonableness in answer to a charge under s. 4. He/she could not therefore argue, say, that the pursuit of the course of conduct was 'reasonable' in order to enforce a debt or to communicate with the victim.

In addition, s. 12 allows for the Secretary of State to certify that the conduct was carried out by a 'specified person' on a 'specified occasion' related to:

• national security

• the economic well-being of the UK, or

• the prevention or detection of serious crime

on behalf of the Crown. If such a certification is made, the conduct of the specified person will not be an offence under the 1997 Act.

Injunctions

Under s. 3(1) of the Protection from Harassment Act 1997, the High Court or a county court may issue an injunction in respect of civil proceedings brought in respect of an actual or apprehended breach of s. 1. The effect of this is that a defendant may be made the subject of an injunction even though his/her behaviour has not amounted to an offence under the 1997 Act.

Section 3(3) states:

(3) Where—
- (a) in such proceedings the High Court or a county court grants an injunction for the purpose of restraining the defendant from pursuing any conduct which amounts to harassment, and
- (b) the [claimant] considers that the defendant has done anything which he is prohibited from doing by the injunction,

the [claimant] may apply for the issue of a warrant for the arrest of the defendant.

KEYNOTE

Anyone arrested under such a warrant may be dealt with by the court at the time of his/her appearance. Alternatively, the court may adjourn the proceedings and release the defendant, dealing with him/her within 14 days of his/her arrest provided the defendant is given not less than two days' notice of the adjourned hearing (see the Rules of the Supreme Court 1998 (SI 1998 No. 1898) and the County Court (Amended) Rules 1998 (SI 1998 No. 1899)).

This is in contrast to some other injunctions (e.g. under the Family Law Act 1996 and the Housing Act 1996). In a case involving an injunction restraining the actions of an anti-vivisection group, the Divisional Court held that the 1997 Act was not a means of preventing individuals from exercising their right to protest over issues of public interest. Eady J said that such an extension of the law had clearly not been Parliament's intention and that the courts would resist any attempts to interpret the Act widely (*Huntingdon Life Sciences Ltd* v *Curtin* (1997) *The Times*, 11 December).

Of far greater significance is the offence created by s. 3(6) of the Protection from Harassment Act 1997.

OFFENCE: **Breach of Injunction—*Protection from Harassment Act 1997, s. 3(6)***

- Triable either way • Five years' imprisonment and/or a fine on indictment; six months' imprisonment and/or a fine summarily

  (Arrestable offence)

The Protection from Harassment Act 1997, s. 3(6) states:

(6) Where—
- (a) the High Court or a county court grants an injunction for the purpose mentioned in subsection (3)(a), and
- (b) without reasonable excuse the defendant does anything which he is prohibited from doing by the injunction,

he is guilty of an offence.

KEYNOTE

Civil injunctions generally will only involve the police where a power of an arrest has been attached (e.g. under s. 3(3) above). In these cases the role of the police will be to bring the defendant before the court in order that he/she can explain his/her behaviour. There is therefore no investigative or prosecuting function on the part of the officers. Section 3(6), however, creates a specific offence of breaching the terms of an injunction. Like the Anti-Social Behaviour Order (ASBO) (see below) and Sex Offender Order (SOO) this marks a new concept in the criminal law.

If a defendant breaches an injunction and commits the offence under s. 3(6) above, he/she will be dealt with in the way of any other prisoner brought into police detention and will face a prison sentence of five years.

It is important to distinguish the offence under s. 3(6), breaching an injunction, from the provisions of s. 5 which deal with restraining orders.

Restraining Orders

Section 5 of the Protection from Harassment Act 1997 provides that a court dealing with a person convicted of an offence under s. 2 or 4 may make an order (a restraining order).

Such an order can only be made after a defendant's conviction for an offence under s. 2 or 4 of the 1997 Act. It is therefore much more limited than the injunction discussed above. Section 5(2) goes on to state:

> (2) The order may, for the purpose of protecting the victim of the offence, or any other person mentioned in the order, from further conduct which—
> (a) amounts to harassment, or
> (b) will cause a fear of violence,
> prohibit the defendant from doing anything described in the order.

KEYNOTE

The purpose behind these orders is to empower the courts to restrain the conduct of offenders following their conviction—an area that was previously seen as one of particular weakness in the criminal justice system.

Unlike the injunction under s. 3(3), restraining orders can be made in criminal court.

The order may be made for the protection of the victim or anyone else mentioned and it may run for a specified period or until a further order. Any order must identify by name the parties it is intended to protect (*R v Mann* (2000) *The Times*, 11 April).

In a case arising out of protests against fur retailers, the Divisional Court held that restraining orders under the 1997 Act did not generally breach the right to freedom of speech and association as protected by Articles 10 and 11 of the European Convention (*Silverton v Gravett* (2001) LTL 31 October).

The prosecutor, the defendant or anyone else mentioned in the order may apply to the court that made it to have the order varied or discharged (s. 5(4)).

OFFENCE: **Breach of Restraining Order—*Protection from Harassment Act 1997, s. 5(5)***

> • Triable either way • Five years' imprisonment and/or a fine on indictment; six months' imprisonment and/or a fine summarily
> *(Arrestable offence)*

The Protection from Harassment Act 1997, s. 5(5) states:

> (5) If without reasonable excuse the defendant does anything which he is prohibited from doing by an order under this section, he is guilty of an offence.

KEYNOTE

The fact that restraining orders can only be made after a conviction for one of the offences under s. 2 or 4 may affect decisions when selecting appropriate charges arising out of an incident. Substituting or failing to include a charge under s. 2 or 4, removes the court's powers to make a restraining order which may be the main remedy sought by a victim. In any cases of doubt the guidance of the Crown Prosecution Service should be sought.

2.9 Criminal Damage

2.9.1 Introduction

Damage to property has many consequences. As well as the immediate financial impact upon the owner, criminal damage affects:

• The environment.

• Community safety—it is well-documented that graffiti and visible damage to buildings can create a widespread fear of crime and sense of lawlessness. This is particularly true where the nature of the damage and/or the selection of the victim is intended to intimidate and is one of the reasons behind the creation of a 'racially or religiously aggravated' form of criminal damage.

- The economy—in many cases of criminal damage the 'hidden' victims are often insurance companies, businesses and local communities.

All of these areas should be considered when investigating offences of criminal damage, and particularly when submitting compensation schedules with a proposed prosecution file.

The most important recent development in this area is the introduction of racially or religiously aggravated criminal damage under the Crime and Disorder Act 1998.

Of particular concern is the growth in arson, with this offence now being (according to government statistics) the largest single cause of fires in the UK, resulting in many deaths and injuries, as well as an annual cost of £40 million.

A further important development in the area of damage to property can be found in Protocol 1, Article 1 of the European Convention on Human Rights which gives individuals a right to peaceful enjoyment of their property and possessions.

Types of Offence

There are extensive civil remedies available for people whose property is damaged by others. In cases involving a course of conduct or behaviour that causes widespread public nuisance, other offences and remedies may apply. The law regulating *criminal* damage, however, is largely contained within one statute, the Criminal Damage Act 1971. This Act deals with occasions where a person:

- actually damages or destroys the property of another (simple damage)
- damages or destroys his/her own property or that of another where there are 'aggravating' factors or circumstances (aggravated damage)
- threatens to damage or destroy property
- has articles to be used for damaging or destroying property
- commits an offence which is 'racially or religiously aggravated'.

2.9.2 Simple Damage

OFFENCE: **Simple Damage—*Criminal Damage Act 1971, s. 1(1)***
- Triable either way • Ten years' imprisonment on indictment; six months' imprisonment and/or a fine summarily
(Arrestable offence)

OFFENCE: **Racially or Religiously Aggravated—*Crime and Disorder Act 1998, s. 30(1)***
- Triable either way • Fourteen years' imprisonment and/or a fine on indictment; six months' imprisonment and/or a fine summarily
(Arrestable offence)

The Criminal Damage Act 1971, s. 1 states:

(1) A person who without lawful excuse destroys or damages any property belonging to another intending to destroy or damage any such property or being reckless as to whether any such property would be destroyed or damaged shall be guilty of an offence.

KEYNOTE

Although triable either way, if the cost of the property destroyed or the damage done is less than £5,000, the offence is to be tried summarily (Magistrates' Courts Act 1980, s. 22). If the damage in such a case was caused by fire (arson) (see 2.9.4) then this rule will not apply.

The fact that the substantive offence is, by virtue of the value of the damage caused, triable only summarily does not make simple damage a 'summary offence' for all other purposes. If it did, you could only be found guilty of *attempting* to commit criminal damage if the value of the intended damage was more than £5,000 (because the Criminal Attempts Act 1981 does not extend to summary offences. Therefore, where a defendant tried to damage a bus shelter in a way that would have cost far less than £5,000 to repair, his argument that he had only attempted what was in fact a 'summary offence' was dismissed by the Divisional Court (*R v Bristol Magistrates, ex parte* E [1998] 3 All ER 798).

The racially or religiously aggravated form of this offence (see below) is triable either way irrespective of the cost of the damage.

Racially or Religiously Aggravated Damage

The racially or religiously aggravated circumstances set out at s. 28(1)(a) of the Crime and Disorder Act 1998 deal with situations where the defendant demonstrates hostility:

- at the time of

- or immediately before or after

committing the offence, towards the *victim* and that hostility is *based on the victim's membership or presumed membership of a racial or religious group*. To clarify such situations in relation to racially or religiously aggravated damage, s. 30(3) provides that the person to whom the property belongs or is treated as belonging, will be treated as the 'victim'.

This provision is helpful where the aggravated offence is one under s. 28(1)(a)—the 'demonstration' type of aggravation—and the property is privately owned.

Where the property is owned by a corporate body (e.g. a bus shelter or tube station) however, there will clearly be problems in proving that the defendant's hostility was based on the *victim's* membership/presumed membership of a racial or religious group. Even though property for these purposes may be treated as belonging to more than one person (see below) this means that, where the damage is caused by racist graffiti in publicly-owned places or in property owned by large corporations, the most suitable charge will probably be under s. 28(1)(b) of the Act—by far the harder to prove. Harder still would be the situation where any such graffiti is of a *religious* nature and the hostility was based on the victim's membership of a religious group. The revised wording of s. 28 of the Crime and Disorder Act 1998 (amended after the events of 11 September 2001) now includes 'religious groups'—and these will include groups of people defined, not only by their religious belief, but also their *lack* of any such belief.

The provisions of s. 30 of the Crime and Disorder Act 1998 only apply to the offence of 'simple' damage under s. 1(1) of the 1971 Act; they do not apply to any of the other offences in this section.

Lawful excuse

Section 5 of the Criminal Damage Act 1971 provides for two occasions where a defendant may have a 'lawful excuse'. These can be remembered as 'permission' (s. 5(2)(a)) and 'protection' (s. 5(2)(b)). Both involve the belief of the defendant. The wording of s. 5 indicates that these particular defences are not the only ones available to a charge of criminal damage and other general defences may apply.

Permission

A person shall be treated as having lawful excuse under s. 5(2):

(a) if at the time of the act or acts alleged to constitute the offence he believed that the person or persons whom he believed to be entitled to consent to the destruction of or damage to the property in question had so consented, or would have so consented to it if he or they had known of the destruction or damage and its circumstances...

KEYNOTE

An example of 'lawful excuse' under s. 5(2)(a) would be if you, as a police officer, were asked by a motorist to help them get into their partner's car after locking the keys inside. If, during that attempt you damaged the rubber window surround, s. 5(2)(a) would provide you with a statutory defence to any later charge of criminal damage by the owner. The key elements here would be:

- the consent of someone whom you believed to be entitled to consent to that damage, and

- the circumstances under which it was caused.

If the driver was not available and your reason for opening the door was to get a better look at some personal documents for intelligence purposes, it is unlikely that the driver or the owner would have consented, either to the damage or the circumstances in which it was caused. Therefore you could not use this particular defence.

Protection

A person shall be treated as having lawful excuse under s. 5(2):

> (b) if he destroyed or damaged or threatened to destroy or damage the property in question or, in the case of a charge of an offence under section 3 above, intended to use or cause or permit the use of something to destroy or damage it, in order to protect property belonging to himself or another or a right or interest in property which was or which he believed to be vested in himself or another, and at the time of the act or acts alleged to constitute the offence he believed—
>
> (i) that the property, right or interest was in immediate need of protection; and
> (ii) that the means of protection adopted or proposed to be adopted were or would be reasonable having regard to all the circumstances.

KEYNOTE

Situations where such a defence can be used involve causing damage to property in order to protect other property. This defence also applies to the offence of having articles for causing damage. Key features of this defence are the immediacy of the need to protect the property and the reasonableness of the means of protection adopted. In a case involving 'peace campaigners' it was held that the threat presented by a possible nuclear attack in the future did not excuse the carrying of a hacksaw for cutting through the perimeter fence of an airbase (*R* v *Hill* (1988) 89 Cr App R 74).

The 1971 Act goes on to say that it is immaterial whether a 'belief' above was justified as long as it was honestly held (s. 5(3)). This is a largely subjective test as to what was going through a defendant's mind at the time—or perhaps what was *not* going through his/her mind! In *Jaggard* v *Dickinson* [1981] QB 527, the defendant had broken a window to get into a house. Being drunk at the time, she had got the wrong house but the court accepted that her belief (that it was the right house and that the owner would have consented) had been honestly held, and that it did not matter whether that belief was brought about by intoxication, stupidity, forgetfulness or inattention. That is not to say, however, that *any* honestly held belief will suffice. An example of someone claiming—though unsuccessfully—a defence under both s. 5(2)(a) and (b) can be seen in *Blake* v *DPP* [1993] Crim LR 586. There the defendant was a vicar who wished to protest against Great Britain's involvement in the Gulf War. In order to mark his disapproval, the defendant wrote a quotation from the Bible in ink on a pillar in front of the Houses of Parliament. He claimed:

- that he was carrying out God's instructions and therefore had a lawful excuse based on his belief that God was the person entitled to consent to such damage and that He had in fact consented or would have done so (s. 5(2)(a)); and

- that he had damaged the property as a reasonable means of protecting other property located in the Gulf from being damaged by warfare (s. 5(2)(b)).

Perhaps unsurprisingly the Divisional Court did not accept either proposition holding that, in the first case, a belief in The Almighty's consent was not a 'lawful excuse' and, in the second, that the defendant's conduct was too remote from any immediate need to protect property in the Gulf States. The test in relation to the defendant's belief appears then to be largely subjective (i.e. what was/was not going on in his/her head at the time) but with an objective element in that the judge/magistrate(s) must decide whether, on the facts as believed by the defendant, his/her acts were capable of protecting property.

A similar approach has been tried more recently in a case where the defendant was arrested after making 22 cuts in a perimeter fence of a base where nuclear warheads were produced. The defendant claimed that the activity at the base was unlawful in international law and therefore acts to prevent that activity amounted to a lawful excuse under the 1971 Act. The Divisional Court did not accept this argument, nor the argument that the defendant's acts were merely an expression of her opinion under Article 10 of the European Convention on Human Rights (*Hutchinson* v *Newbury Magistrates' Court, The Independent*, 20 November 2000).

The Act also states, at s. 5(4), that a right or interest in property includes any right or privilege in or over land, whether created by grant, licence or otherwise.

Section 5(5) allows for other general defences at criminal law to apply in addition to those listed under s. 5.

It is not an offence to damage your own property unless there are aggravating circumstances (**see 2.9.3**). Even if the intention in doing so is to carry out some further offence—such as a fraudulent insurance claim—this fact still does not make it an offence under s. 1(1) of the Criminal Damage Act 1971 (*R* v *Denton* [1981] 1 WLR 1446). (It may, however, give rise to other offences of dishonesty.)

Mens Rea

An offence of criminal damage under s. 1(1) can be proved by showing that the defendant was 'reckless'. As with most criminal offences requiring recklessness as to consequences, the recklessness here is *objective* which will mean proving that:

- the defendant does an act which *in fact* creates an obvious risk that property will be destroyed or damaged, and
- when doing the act, the defendant either has not given any thought to the possibility of there being such a risk or has recognised that there was some risk involved and has nevertheless gone on to do it

(per Lord Diplock in *Metropolitan Police Commissioner* v *Caldwell* [1982] AC 341).

The risk of damage at the time of the defendant's conduct need only be apparent to a *reasonable* person. It is not necessary to show that the risk would have been obvious to the defendant had he/she stopped to think about what he/she was doing; neither need it be shown that the risk would have been obvious to a person of the same age or state of mind as the defendant (*R* v *Coles* (1995) 1 Cr App R 157).

....

EXAMPLE

A group of youths in a shopping precinct walk up to a grocery display and begin juggling with some apples. They drop several apples, some of which smash on the pavement while others are soiled and bruised.

By juggling with the fruit the youths have created an obvious risk that the apples (property) will be damaged. As the risk to the property would have been obvious to any reasonable bystander watching their antics the youths are 'reckless' for the purposes of the Criminal Damage Act 1971, *whether or not they had given any thought to the risk themselves.*

....

Destroy or Damage

Although a key feature of the 1971 Act, the terms 'destroy' or 'damage' are not defined. The courts have taken a wide view when interpreting these terms. 'Destroying' property would suggest that it has been rendered useless but there is no need to prove that 'damage' to property is in any way permanent or irreparable. In the example above, the apples which were smashed were clearly 'destroyed'; those which were soiled, even though they could be washed, would probably be unfit for sale and therefore 'damaged' for the purposes of s. 1(1).

Whether an article has been damaged will be a question of fact for each court to determine on the evidence before it. Situations where courts have accepted that property has been damaged include the defacing of a pavement by an artist using only water-soluble paint (*Hardman* v *Chief Constable of Avon and Somerset* [1986] Crim LR 330) and the erasure of electronically-stored data on a circuit card (*Cox* v *Riley* (1986) 83 Cr App R 54). It has also been held by the Divisional Court that graffiti smeared in mud can amount to damage, even though it is easily washed off (*Roe* v *Kingerlee* [1986] Crim LR 735).

Property

Property is defined in the 1971 Act by s. 10 which states:

(1) In this Act 'property' means property of a tangible nature, whether real or personal, including money and—
  (a) including wild creatures which have been tamed or are ordinarily kept in captivity and any other wild creatures or their carcasses if, but only if, they have been reduced into possession ... or are in the course of being reduced into possession; but
  (b) not including mushrooms growing wild on any land or flowers, fruit or foliage of a plant growing wild on any land.
  ...

KEYNOTE

This definition has similarities with the definition of 'property' for the purposes of theft but 'real' property (i.e. land and things attached to it) can be damaged even though it cannot be stolen. Trampling flower beds, digging up cricket pitches, chopping down trees in a private garden and even pulling up genetically-modified crops may all amount to criminal damage if accompanied by the required circumstances.

It is important to remember when dealing with disputes involving pets or farm animals that they are property for the purposes of this Act. Cases of horses being mutilated would, in addition to the offence of 'cruelty' itself, amount to criminal damage. There may also be occasions—such as domestic or neighbour disputes—involving harm or cruelty to such animals where it will be more appropriate and effective to consider offences under the 1971 Act, together with the powers which they attract under the Police and Criminal Evidence Act 1984 for arrestable offences.

Belonging to Another

Section 10(2) states:

(2) Property shall be treated for the purposes of this Act as belonging to any person—
  (a) having the custody or control of it;
  (b) having in it any proprietary right or interest (not being an equitable interest arising only from an agreement to transfer or grant an interest); or
  (c) having a charge on it.

KEYNOTE

This extended meaning of 'belonging to another' is similar to that used in the Theft Act 1968. One result is that if a person damages his/her own property, he/she may still commit the offence of simple criminal damage if that property also 'belongs to' someone else.

2.9.3 Aggravated Damage

OFFENCE: **Aggravated Damage—*Criminal Damage Act 1971, s. 1(2)***
> • Triable on indictment • Life imprisonment
> *(Arrestable offence)*

The Criminal Damage Act 1971, s. 1 states:

> (2) A person who without lawful excuse destroys or damages any property, whether belonging to himself or another—
> (a) intending to destroy or damage any property or being reckless as to whether any property would be destroyed or damaged; and
> (b) intending by the destruction or damage to endanger the life of another or being reckless as to whether the life of another would be thereby endangered;
> shall be guilty of an offence.

KEYNOTE

The aggravating factor in this offence, and the reason why it attracts such a heavy maximum sentence, is the ulterior intention of endangering life or recklessness as to whether life is endangered. As such, evidence of self-induced intoxication may provide a defence to a charge under this section. This form of 'aggravation' should not be confused with the 'racially or religiously aggravated' form of criminal damage.

The reference to 'without lawful excuse' does not refer to the statutory excuses under s. 5 which are not applicable here, but to general excuses such as self-defence or the prevention of crime.

In order to prove a defendant's recklessness you will need to apply the objective test used in *Caldwell*, that is, would the risk have been obvious to a reasonable person watching the defendant's behaviour?

You must also show that the defendant either intended or was reckless as to each of the following consequences:

- the damage being caused, and

- the *resultant* danger to life.

It does not matter that the *actual* damage caused by the defendant turned out to be minor. What matters is the *potential* for damage and danger created by the defendant's conduct.

Where a defendant set fire to furniture in a house which was unoccupied at the time, the court nevertheless found him guilty of this offence. The court's reasoning for doing so turned on the fact that, had a reasonable bystander been present, he/she would have seen the possible risk that the fire might cause to the lives of others in the area, even though with hindsight it was shown that there had been no likelihood of the fire spreading to neighbouring properties (*R v Sangha* [1988] 1 WLR 519). In this case there was clearly recklessness as to the damage caused *and* recklessness as to the danger to life *presented by the damage*. In contrast, where a defendant fired a weapon through a window pane he was clearly reckless as to the damage his actions would cause. However, the court felt that, even though two people were standing behind the window and that they were obviously put in some danger, it was the *missile* which endangered their lives and not the result of the damage. Therefore the court held that the defendant was not guilty of this particular offence (*R v Steer* [1988] AC 111). This distinction seems to be a fine one, particularly if you are the person behind the window.

If someone were to smash the windscreen of a moving car or to cause a large display window to collapse into a busy street, this would probably be enough to support a charge under s. 1(2) (see *R v Webster* [1995] 2 All ER 168).

2.9.4 Arson

OFFENCE: **Arson—*Criminal Damage Act 1971, s. 1(3)***
> • Triable either way • Life imprisonment on indictment; where life is not endangered six months' imprisonment and/or a fine summarily
> *(Arrestable offence)*

The Criminal Damage Act 1971, s. 1 states:

(3) An offence committed under this section by destroying or damaging property by fire shall be charged as arson.

KEYNOTE

In any of the above cases of criminal damage, if the destruction or damage is caused by fire, the offence will be charged as 'arson'. Given the potential for extensive damage and danger to life that fire-raising has, the restrictions on the mode of trial for simple damage under s. 1(1) do not apply to cases of arson.

As arson is a 'violent offence' for the purposes of the Powers of Criminal Courts (Sentencing) Act 2000, those convicted of it are covered by the statutory provisions relating to sexual and violent offenders.

Aggravated damage caused by arson is triable only on indictment and carries a maximum penalty of life imprisonment.

Sections 1 and 2 of the Criminal Evidence (Amendment) Act 1997 extending the power to take non-intimate samples without consent apply to this offence and also to conspiracies, attempts or incitements in the circumstances set out in that Act.

2.9.5 **Threats to Destroy or Damage Property**

OFFENCE: **Threats to Destroy or Damage Property—*Criminal Damage Act 1971, s. 2***
- Triable either way • Ten years' imprisonment on indictment; six months' imprisonment and/or a fine summarily
(Arrestable offence)

The Criminal Damage Act 1971, s. 2 states:

A person who without lawful excuse makes to another a threat, intending that that other would fear it would be carried out,—

(a) to destroy or damage any property belonging to that other or a third person; or

(b) to destroy or damage his own property in a way which he knows is likely to endanger the life of that other or a third person;

shall be guilty of an offence.

KEYNOTE

This is an offence of *intention*, that is, the key element is the defendant's intention that the person receiving the threat fears it would be carried out.

The s. 2 offence, which originates from the need to tackle protection racketeers, is very straightforward: there is no need to show that the other person actually feared or even believed that the threat would be carried out. There is no need to show that the defendant intended to carry it out; nor does it matter whether the threat was even capable of being carried out.

....

EXAMPLE

If a person, enraged by a neighbour's inconsiderate parking, shouts over the garden wall, '*When you've gone to bed I'm going to T-cut that heap with paint stripper*!', the offence will be complete, provided you can show that the person making the threat intended the neighbour to fear it would be carried out.

....

Where a group of protestors staged a protest in the pods of the London Eye and threatened to set fire to themselves, their conduct was held by the Court of Appeal to be capable able of amounting to a threat to damage the property of another (contrary to s. 2(a) (*R v Cakmak* (2002) *The Times*, 28 March).

In *Cakmak* the court held that the gist of the offence under s. 2(a) was the making of a threat and that any such threat had to be considered objectively.

Whether:

- there has been such a threat to another
- the threat amounted to 'a threat to damage or destroy property'
- the defendant had the necessary state of mind (*mens rea*) at the time

are all questions of fact for the jury to decide (per *Cakmak*).

2.9.6   **Having Articles with Intent to Destroy or Damage Property**

OFFENCE: **Having Articles with Intent to Destroy or Damage Property—*Criminal Damage Act 1971, s. 3***

> • Triable either way   • Ten years' imprisonment on indictment; six months' imprisonment and/or a fine summarily
> *(Arrestable offence)*

The Criminal Damage Act 1971, s. 3 states:

> A person who has anything in his custody or under his control intending without lawful excuse to use it or cause or permit another to use it—
>
> (a) to destroy or damage any property belonging to some other person; or
>
> (b) to destroy or damage his own or the user's property in a way which he knows is likely to endanger the life of some other person;
>
> shall be guilty of an offence.

KEYNOTE

Often referred to as 'possessing articles' for causing damage, this offence is, in reality, far wider than that. Although it also originates from the need to control organised crime, this offence covers *anything* which a defendant has '*in his custody or under his control*', a deliberately broader term than 'possession'.

As a result, this offence applies to graffiti 'artists' carrying aerosols, advertisers with adhesives for sticking illicit posters and neighbours with paint stripper. The key element, once again, is an *intention*. This time the required intention is that the 'thing' be used to cause criminal damage to another's property or to the defendant's own property in a way which he/she knows is likely to endanger the life of another. Such articles are not 'prohibited' articles for the purposes of the power of stop and search under s. 1 of the Police and Criminal Evidence Act 1984.

If the person's intention is to use the articles for contaminating goods or making it appear that goods have been contaminated, a separate offence exists under the Public Order Act 1986, s. 38(3) (see 2.10).

A conditional intent—that is, an intent to use something to cause criminal damage if the need arises—will be enough (*R v Buckingham* (1976) 63 Cr App R 159).

Just as it is not an offence to damage your own property in a way which endangers no one else, neither is it an offence to have something which you intend to use to cause damage under those circumstances.

....

EXAMPLE

If the owner of a 10-metre high conifer decides to trim the top with a chainsaw and a ladder, putting himself— but no one else—at considerable risk, he commits no offence, either by causing the damage or by having the chainsaw. If he intends to fell the tree in a way which a reasonable bystander would say presents a danger to his neighbours or passers by, then he may commit offences on both counts.

....

Police Powers

In addition to the police powers which this offence attracts (by virtue of its being an arrestable offence, there is a statutory power to apply to a magistrate for a search warrant under s. 6.

2.10 Contamination or Interference with Goods

OFFENCE: **Contamination or Interference with Goods—*Public Order Act 1986, s. 38(1)***
• Triable either way • Ten years' imprisonment and/or a fine on indictment; six months' imprisonment and/or a fine summarily
(Arrestable offence)

The Public Order Act 1986, s. 38 states:

(1) It is an offence for a person, with the intention—
  (a) of causing public alarm or anxiety, or
  (b) of causing injury to members of the public consuming or using the goods, or
  (c) of causing economic loss to any person by reason of the goods being shunned by members of the public, or
  (d) of causing economic loss to any person by reason of steps taken to avoid any such alarm or anxiety, injury or loss,
  to contaminate or interfere with goods, or make it appear that goods have been contaminated or interfered with, or to place goods which have been contaminated or interfered with, or which appear to have been contaminated or interfered with in a place where goods of that description are consumed, used, sold or otherwise supplied.

(2) It is also an offence for a person, with any such intention as is mentioned in paragraph (a), (c) or (d) of subsection (1), to threaten that he or another will do, or to claim that he or another has done, any of the acts mentioned in that subsection.

(3) It is an offence for a person to be in possession of any of the following articles with a view to the commission of an offence under subsection (1)—
  (a) materials to be used for contaminating or interfering with goods or making it appear that goods have been contaminated or interfered with, or
  (b) goods which have been contaminated or interfered with, or which appear to have been contaminated or interfered with.

(4) ...

(5) In this section 'goods' includes substances whether natural or manufactured and whether or not incorporated in or mixed with other goods.

(6) The reference in subsection (2) to a person claiming that certain acts have been committed does not include a person who in good faith reports or warns that such acts have been, or appear to have been, committed.

KEYNOTE

Section 38 creates two offences. The first involves the contamination of, interference with or placing of goods with the intentions set out at s. 38(1)(a)–(d). This is a crime of 'specific' intent and the particular intention of the defendant must be proved.

Section 38(2) involves the making of threats to do, *or* the claiming *to have done* any of the acts in s. 38(1), with any of the intentions set out at s. 38(1)(a), (c) or (d). It is difficult to see how a threat or claim made with the intention of causing injury to the public (s. 38(1)(b)) would not also amount to an intention to cause them alarm or anxiety.

Section 38(6) allows for people to communicate warnings in good faith where such acts appear to have been committed.

Where threats to contaminate goods are made there may also be grounds for charging blackmail. This type of 'product' sabotage is increasing, evidenced by the increasingly elaborate sealing devices used by manufacturers. Perhaps the most notorious example of this offence—and the overlap with blackmail—is the case of *R* v *Witchelo* (1992) 13 Cr App R (S) 371 where the defendant, a police officer, was sentenced to 13 years' imprisonment after obtaining £32,000 from food producers to whom he had sent threatening letters.

Additionally, where the defendant's behaviour is designed to influence the government, to intimidate the public or where it creates a serious risk to health and safety, the offences may fall within the definition of 'terrorism' under the Terrorism Act 2000.

2.11 Misuse of Drugs

2.11.1 Introduction

The misuse of controlled drugs has become such a pervasive feature of western society that it now affects almost every aspect of community life. As such, this subject is one of the most written about, argued about and legislated about in our criminal law. The impact of the misuse of drugs on crime and community safety has become so significant that it is also one of the most frequently encountered areas of criminal law for police officers.

The majority of the law in this area is statutory and is supported by a considerable body of case law.

At the time of writing, the use of drug treatment and testing orders was being extended across forces in England and Wales under new legislation.

2.11.2 Drug Trafficking

The Drug Trafficking Act 1994 addresses (amongst other things) the production, movement and storage of controlled drugs, together with the proceeds of drug trafficking. Although the contents of that and related statutes are beyond the scope of this work, references to it have been included as and where it seems appropriate to do so.

2.11.3 Controlled Drugs

The list of controlled drugs has developed almost as fast as the substances themselves. Schedule 2 to the Misuse of Drugs Act 1971 (see appendix 1 which defines what those drugs are), is a slightly daunting and bewildering table of chemicals. This schedule is updated regularly and the latest statutory instrument should be consulted. The Misuse of Drugs Act 1971 (Modification) Order 2001 (SI 2001 No. 3932) for instance added 36 new substances, all but one of which are 'Class A' drugs (see below). Practically, defendants are unlikely to know that they are selling or buying 1-diphenylpropanecarboxylic acid—neither are police officers. Both, however, are likely to know the 'street' name for the more commonly available controlled drugs, but the important classification for the purposes of investigation and prosecution, is that of Class A, B or C drugs. The street *value* of drugs seized can be important in prosecuting offences involving importation and supply of controlled drugs and evidence as to this value has been held to be admissible on occasions (see e.g. *R v Hogewoning* [2002] EWCA Crim 3093). Several drug testing kits that allow for the initial testing of substances without the need to send them to laboratories have been approved by the Secretary of State. Details of these kits, together with the relevant training providers can be found in Home Office Circular 9/2002.

2.11.4 Classification

Drugs which are subject to the provisions of the Misuse of Drugs Act 1971 are listed in Parts I to II to Schedule 2.

The divisions are made largely on the basis of each substance's potential effects on both the person taking it and society in general.

Classification is important in determining the sentencing powers of the courts.

- Class A—This class includes the most notorious and dangerous drugs such as heroin and morphine, opiates, cocaine, some amphetamines and LSD.
- Class B—This class includes codeine and some amphetamines.
- Class C—This class includes some commonly-abused prescription drugs, for examples of these drugs and, at the time of writing, was about to be altered to include cannabis and cannabis resin.

If the charge alleges possession of one particular drug then that drug must be identified.

It is not necessary, when prosecuting an offence, to distinguish between the various chemical forms in which a drug exists (i.e. as a salt, ester or other form) (*R* v *Greensmith* [1983] 1 WLR 1124).

A defendant's admission may, in some cases, be relied upon to prove his/her knowledge as to what a particular substance is (see *R* v *Chatwood* [1980] 1 WLR 874).

Cannabis

The Misuse of Drugs Act 1971, s. 37 states:

'cannabis' (except in the expression 'cannabis resin') means any plant of the genus Cannabis or any part of any such plant (by whatever name designated) except that it does not include cannabis resin or any of the following products after separation from the rest of the plant, namely—

(a) mature stalk of any such plant,

(b) fibre produced from mature stalk of any such plant, and

(c) seed of any such plant,

'cannabis resin' means the separated resin, whether crude or purified, obtained from any plant of the genus *Cannabis*;

KEYNOTE

There can scarcely have been anyone in England and Wales who failed to notice all the media coverage over the change of class for cannabis. Whatever its classification, as cannabis and cannabis resin are both in the same class for the purposes of the 1971 Act there would be no duplicity if a person is charged with possessing either one or the other in the same charge (*R* v *Best* (1980) 70 Cr App R 21).

Drug Testing

The Criminal Justice and Court Services Act 2000 introduced new powers to enable the police to require urine or non-intimate samples to be taken from adults in police detention under certain circumstances. The purpose of such tests is to ascertain whether the person has any specified Class A drug in their body. The power to require such a sample will be activated in one of two ways:

- the person concerned has been charged with a 'trigger' offence (these offences are identified throughout this and other relevant chapters in this Manual); or
- the person concerned has been charged with any offence and a police officer of the rank of inspector or above has reasonable grounds for suspecting that the misuse by that person of any specified Class A drug caused or contributed to the offence.

The Powers of Criminal Courts (Sentencing) Act 2000 makes further provision for the courts to impose drug treatment and testing orders.

2.11.5 **Possession**

Possession appears to be a straightforward concept. However, as with many other such 'straightforward' concepts, the courts have wrangled over its meaning for so long that it is not so straightforward after all.

A good starting point in understanding 'possession' is to realise that it is a neutral concept, not implying any kind of blame or fault. This is the key feature to understand first before going on to consider specific offences under *any* legislation. In order to be in possession of *anything*, the common law requires physical control of the object plus knowledge of its presence. This requirement is particularly problematic where containers of some sort (whether they be boxes, handbags, cigarette packets or whatever) are involved or where the person claims not to have realised what it was that he/she 'possessed'. In such cases, the common law makes the same requirements; you need to show that the person had physical control of the container together with a knowledge that it contained *something*. Once you have established possession, you then need to show that the substance/object/material possessed was in fact proscribed by the relevant statute.

A defendant recently argued that there was a distinction between a person carrying something *in* a container and a person carrying *something inside something else* in a container! For a moment, things were a little scary and an already complicated situation looked perilously close to becoming completely daft. In that particular case, the defendant was found in possession of a box which contained a safe; inside the safe was a significant quantity of a controlled drug. The defendant argued that this type of possession should be differentiated from the situation where someone simply had possession of a box with drugs in it. Mercifully, the Court of Appeal ruled that there was no difference and the issues of proof were the same (*R v Forsyth* [2001] EWCA Crim 2926).

In relation to controlled drugs, the issue becomes complicated further by the specific defences provided by the 1971 Act. The very reason those defences (**see para. 2.11.7**) have been drafted in this way is to reflect the common law concept of possession and to provide some protection from its effects where drugs are concerned (see *R v Bett* [1999] 1 WLR 2109).

So, if a person has a container with him/her and that container is found to have controlled drugs in it, he/she is in possession of those drugs *provided he/she knew that there was something in the container*. That does not mean that, at this point, the person necessarily commits an offence (and he/she may still have a statutory defence); it means that he/she was in 'possession' of the drugs. This merely satisfies one element of a number of possible offences; just as if you were trying to prove that a person was 'driving' a vehicle. (Driving is also a neutral concept and only satisfies one element within a number of possible offences.)

The Misuse of Drugs Act 1971 creates offences under certain circumstances where a person has been shown to have been in 'possession' of a controlled drug. However, the Act also provides a defence which unfortunately includes a mental element on the part of the defendant. It is true that this situation in relation to possession is impracticable—like many others in our system—and it is not even consistently applied (e.g. in cases of strict liability such as some firearms offences involving 'possession' (see *R v Bradish* [1990] 1 QB 981)). Nevertheless, until the concept of 'possession' at common law is changed to include an element of blame or fault, these rules will continue to apply and presumably statutes will continue to contain defences which, like s. 28 of the 1971 Act, are aimed at correcting any unjust results.

Nevertheless it is clear from the House of Lords' decisions in *Warner v Metropolitan Police Commissioner* [1969] 2 AC 256 and *R v Boyesen* [1982] AC 768, and also the Court of Appeal judgment in *R v McNamara* (1988) 87 Cr App R 246 that the basic elements required are that a person 'knows' that he/she is in possession of something which is, in fact, a prohibited or controlled object or substance.

Some of the further practical difficulties that can arise from this view of 'possession' were highlighted in *Adams* v *DPP* [2002] EWHC 438 (Admin). In that case a small quantity of controlled drugs was found in the defendant's home during the execution of a search warrant. There was no proof that the drugs were owned by the defendant, nor that she was specifically aware of their presence but the defendant *did* know that her home was used by various people who were highly likely to bring controlled drugs into it. She was convicted of possession. In hearing her appeal against conviction by way of case stated, the Administrative Court held that, where knowledge of possession of drugs was limited to the fact that a visitor had brought drugs into the defendant's home intending to take them, that was not sufficient evidence from which it was appropriate to infer that she had control over the drugs.

The court also held that giving consent (explicitly or impliedly) for the use of a controlled drug did not of itself constitute possession. Similarly, an inference that the defendant knew whose drugs had been found in her home did not amount to evidence of control over the drug itself—even though she may well have been able to exercise control over what actually took place in her home.

The court went on to point out that the social concern arising from people permitting the use of drugs on their premises would be addressed by the amended offence under s. 8 of the Misuse of Drugs Act 1971 (**see para. 2.11.8**).

To prove possession of a controlled drug then, you must show that a defendant both:

– *had* a controlled drug in his/her possession; and

– *knew* that he/she had something in his/her possession which was in fact a controlled drug.

The first part of this requirement, the *physical* possession, is fairly obvious. It is the second part, the *mental* element required at common law, which complicates the concept.

....

EXAMPLE

Consider the following circumstances: After a stop and search, a defendant is found with a knife in his pocket. The knife has traces of brown powder on the blade. Later examination shows the powder to be heroin. In order to prove 'possession' of the heroin you must show:

– that the defendant actually had the knife

– that the knife had a substance which was a controlled drug on it and that

– the defendant knew *of the existence of the substance* (i.e. the powder).

....

Quality

You would not have to show that he/she knew what the powder was. That is, you do not need to show that the defendant knew the quality of what he/she possessed.

If the defendant admits to knowing that the powder was there but thought it was sand, he/she is in possession of it (see *R* v *Marriott* [1971] 1 WLR 187).

Therefore if a defendant had a packet of cigarettes with him/her and admitted to knowing that he/she had them, he/she would be in possession of a controlled drug if one cigarette was shown to have contained cannabis. The fact that the defendant thought they contained tobacco would be irrelevant (*Searle* v *Randolph* [1972] Crim LR 779) (although clearly they may be able to raise the defence under s. 28: see below).

Quantity

The *quantity* of a controlled drug, however, may be so small that the defendant could not possibly have known about it; therefore, it could not be 'possessed'.

Each case will have to be decided on its merits but the House of Lords have suggested that if something is 'visible, tangible and measurable', that may be sufficient (*Boyesen*). If the amount recovered is too small to support a charge of possession, it might be used to prove earlier possession of the drug (see *R* v *Graham* [1970] 1 WLR 113n and *Hambleton* v *Callinan* [1968] 2 QB 427 (traces of a controlled drug in a urine sample held to be possible evidence of earlier possession of that drug)).

2.11.6 Misuse of Drugs Regulations 2001

The Misuse of Drugs Regulations 2001 (SI 2001 No. 3998) replaced their 1985 predecessor from 1 February 2002.

The importance of the 2001 Regulations lies in the fact that they exempt certain drugs and certain people—including police officers—from the main offences of possession, supply and importation.

Among the key regulations are:

– Regulation 4—which sets out those controlled drugs which will be exempted from the main offences of importation/exportation when they are contained in medicinal products.

– Regulation 5—allowing people holding a licence issued by the Secretary of State to produce, supply, offer to supply or have in their possession a controlled drug—*provided* that their activities (e.g. of supplying etc.) are carried out in accordance with their licence and any conditions attached to it. If the licence holder goes outside the terms of his/her licence (say by offering to supply a drug that is not covered by it) or fails to comply with any conditions attached to the licence (e.g. by keeping the drugs in a different place from that specified), he/she commits the relevant offence(s) in the ordinary way.

– Regulation 6—this allows anyone who is *lawfully* in possession of a controlled drug to give the drug back to the person from whom he/she obtained it and would cover registered heroin addicts properly returning methadone to a chemist. Regulation 6 also allows others to possess and supply certain controlled drugs under strict conditions.

– Regulation 6 allows police constables to have any controlled drug in their possession, or to supply such a drug to anyone who is lawfully allowed to have it (reg. 6(5)–(7)). These exemptions only apply where the constable is *acting in the course of his/her duty as such*.

Other people who are given the same protection are HM Customs & Excise officers, postal workers and people engaged in conveying the drug to someone who may lawfully possess it. This last category would include civilian support staff, exhibits officers and others who, although not police constables, are nevertheless properly engaged in conveying controlled drugs to others.

The remainder of the regulations are generally concerned with exemptions for doctors, dentists, vets and others who may need to store or supply controlled drugs; the 2001 Regulations also impose requirements on some such people in relation to record keeping and the provision of information when requested.

2.11.7 Defences

Before considering the various offences under the Misuse of Drugs Act 1971 it is useful to address the specific statutory defences provided by ss. 5 and 28 of the Act.

Section 5(4) provides a defence to an offence of unlawful possession:

> (4) In any proceedings for an offence under subsection (2) above in which it is proved that the accused had a controlled drug in his possession, it shall be a defence for him to prove—
>   (a) that, knowing or suspecting it to be a controlled drug, he took possession of it for the purpose of preventing another from committing or continuing to commit an offence in connection

with that drug and that as soon as possible after taking possession of it he took all such steps as were reasonably open to him to destroy the drug or to deliver it into the custody of a person lawfully entitled to take custody of it; or

(b) that, knowing or suspecting it to be a controlled drug, he took possession of it for the purpose of delivering it into the custody of a person lawfully entitled to take custody of it and that as soon as possible after taking possession of it he took all such steps as were reasonably open to him to deliver it into the custody of such a person.

KEYNOTE

This defence envisages two distinct situations. The purpose in taking possession of the controlled drug under s. 5(4)(a) must be to:

— prevent *another*

— from committing (in the future) or

— continuing to commit

an offence in connection with *that* drug.

The first situation might arise where a parent, guardian or carer finds a child in possession of something which appears to be a controlled drug. Provided that that person takes all reasonable steps to destroy the drug or to take it to someone lawfully entitled to possess it (like a general practitioner or police officer), *as soon as possible after taking possession of it*, he/she commits no offence *of unlawful possession*.

The finer technical issues of this defence were recently examined in *R v Murphy* [2002] EWCA Crim 1587. In that case, the defendant found some cannabis in his father's car which was outside a prison at the time. The defendant took the drug and buried it in the hope that it would be destroyed by the forces of nature over time. The Administrative Court held that the trial judge had been right not to leave the s. 5(4)(a) defence to the jury. The defendant had to show that he had taken all steps that were reasonably open to him to destroy the drug directly and relying on the forces of nature did not provide this defence on that occasion.

The second situation (under s. 5(4)(b)) may arise where a person finds what he/she believes to be a controlled drug and he/she takes possession of it *solely for the purpose of delivering it to a person lawfully entitled to take custody of it*. The defendant must prove that this was his/her intention at the time of taking possession (*R v Dempsey and Dempsey* (1986) 82 Cr App R 291).

In either case above, s. 5(4) will not provide a defence to any other offence connected with the controlled drug (e.g. supplying or offering to supply).

General Defence

However, there is a more general defence provided by s. 28 of the Act. Section 28 applies to offences of:

– unlawful production (s. 4(2))

– unlawful supply (s. 4(3))

– unlawful possession (s. 5(2))

– possession with intent to supply (s. 5(3))

– unlawful cultivation of cannabis (s. 6(2))

– offences connected with opium (s. 9).

The defences under s. 28 are not available in cases of conspiracy as they are not offences under the 1971 Act (*R v McGowan* [1990] Crim LR 399). In *R v Lambert* [2001] 3 WLR 206, the House of Lords considered the requirements of the defences under ss. 5(4) and 28 in relation to their effect on the presumption of innocence (imposed at both common law and under Article 6). It was argued that the statutory defence shifted the legal burden of proof from the prosecution onto the defendant and, therefore, was incompatible with the Convention. Their Lordships held that the defences could legitimately be read by the courts in a way that moved the *evidential* burden only onto the defendant. Such an approach, they held, was compatible with the Convention and the Human Rights Act 1998.

Section 28 states:

(2) Subject to subsection (3) below, in any proceedings for an offence to which this section applies it shall be a defence for the accused to prove that he neither knew of nor suspected nor had reason to suspect the existence of some fact alleged by the prosecution which it is necessary for the prosecution to prove if he is to be convicted of the offence charged.

(3) Where in any proceedings for an offence to which this section applies it is necessary, if the accused is to be convicted of the offence charged, for the prosecution to prove that some substance or product involved in the alleged offence was the controlled drug which the prosecution alleges it to have been, and it is proved that the substance or product in question was that controlled drug, the accused—

(a) shall not be acquitted of the offence charged by reason only of proving that he neither knew nor suspected nor had reason to suspect that the substance or product in question was the particular controlled drug alleged; but

(b) shall be acquitted thereof—

(i) if he proves that he neither believed nor suspected nor had reason to suspect that the substance or product in question was a controlled drug; or

(ii) if he proves that he believed the substance or product in question to be a controlled drug, or a controlled drug of a description, such that, if it had in fact been that controlled drug, or a controlled drug of that description, he would not at the material time have been committing any offence to which this section applies.

KEYNOTE

This defence envisages three distinct situations:

– a lack of knowledge by the defendant of some fact which is alleged by the prosecution;

– a general lack of knowledge by the defendant about the drug in question;

– a conditional belief held by the defendant about the drug in question.

These situations are discussed below.

Lack of Knowledge of Some Alleged Fact

Section 28(2) allows a defence where the defendant did not *know, suspect* or *have reason to suspect* the existence of some fact which is essential to proving the case.

....

EXAMPLE

Consider the following example. A youth is stopped in the street by a stranger who asks him to drop off an envelope at a nearby address in exchange for £1. As the youth approaches the address he is arrested for possessing a controlled drug (which had been inside the envelope), with intent to supply.

Section 28(2) would allow the youth to discharge the evidential burden by showing that he neither knew, nor suspected that the envelope contained a controlled drug, and that he neither knew nor suspected that he was supplying it to another. Both of these elements would be facts which the prosecution would have to allege in order to prove the offence.

If the youth knew the person to be a local drug dealer, or the reward for his errand was disproportionately large—say £100—then he may not be able to discharge this, albeit evidential, burden.

It has been held that the test for 'reason to suspect' is an objective one (*R v Young* [1984] 1 WLR 654). Consequently, where a 'reason to suspect' was not apparent to a defendant because he/she was too intoxicated to see it, the defence will not apply.

....

General Lack of Knowledge about Drug in Question

The wording of s. 28(3)(a) prevents defendants from claiming a 'defence' when what they thought was one type of controlled drug was in fact another, different controlled drug.

Section 28(3)(b) however, has two strands, one concerned with the defendant's general lack of knowledge about the drug in question and the other (see below) concerning the defendant's conditional belief.

Section 28(3)(b)(i) will allow a defendant to prove that he/she did not believe or suspect the substance in question to be a controlled drug and that he/she had no reason so to suspect.

This clearly overlaps with s. 28(2) and the youth in the above example would also be able to claim this lack of knowledge. If he believed the envelope to contain amphetamine when it turned out to contain heroin, however, this lack of knowledge would not be permitted as a defence under s. 28(3).

Conditional Belief about Drug in Question

In contrast to s. 28(3)(a), the second strand of s. 28(3)(b) allows a defendant to discharge the evidential burden by showing that he/she did believe the drug in question to be a particular controlled drug. It is then open to them to claim that, had the drug in question actually been the drug which he/she believed it to be, then he/she would not have committed any of the offences in **para. 2.11.7** above.

....

EXAMPLE

A registered heroin addict may have been prescribed methadone. If she collects her prescription from a chemist but is mistakenly given pethidine instead, she may be able to discharge the evidential burden by showing that she *believed* the drug in question to be methadone andthat, if it had been, she would not have committed an offence by possessing it.

....

2.11.8   **Offences Involving the Misuse of Controlled Drugs**

Clearly there are occasions when the production, supply and possession of controlled drugs will be lawful and most of these occasions are addressed in either the Misuse of Drugs Regulations 2001 (SI 2001 No. 3998) or in s. 28 of the Misuse of Drugs Act 1971 (**see para. 2.11.7**).

In the offences which follow, the aspects which generally make the behaviour 'unlawful' are either the lack of authority under the relevant regulations, or the absence of the circumstances outlined in the defences under s. 28.

Production

OFFENCE: **Producing Controlled Drug—*Misuse of Drugs Act 1971, s. 4(2)***
- Triable either way • Class A (life imprisonment and/or fine on indictment; six months' imprisonment and/or prescribed sum summarily); Class B (14 years' imprisonment and/or fine on indictment; six months' imprisonment and/or prescribed sum summarily); Class C (five years' imprisonment and/or fine on indictment; three months' imprisonment and/or fine summarily)
  (Serious arrestable offence)

The Misuse of Drugs Act 1971, s. 4 states:

(2) Subject to section 28 of this Act, it is an offence for a person—
   (a) to produce a controlled drug in contravention of subsection (1) [of section 4] . . . ; or
   (b) to be concerned in the production of such a drug in contravention of that subsection by another.

KEYNOTE

'Produce' means producing by manufacture, cultivation or any other method and 'production' has a corresponding meaning (Misuse of Drugs Act 1971, s. 37).

Converting one form of a Class A drug into another has been held to be 'producing' (*R v Russell* (1992) 94 Cr App R 351) as has harvesting, cutting and stripping a cannabis plant (*R v Harris* (1996) 1 Cr App R 369).

Section 4(2) is a drug trafficking offence for the purposes of the Drug Trafficking Act 1994 (**see para. 2.11.2**). It is also a serious arrestable offence under s. 116(2) of the Police and Criminal Evidence Act 1984.

If committed in relation to specified Class A drugs (heroin, cocaine and 'crack' cocaine), this will be a 'trigger' offence under s. 63B of the Police and Criminal Evidence Act 1984 which can activate police powers to require a sample from a person in police detention in some force areas.

Supply

OFFENCE: **Supplying Controlled Drug—*Misuse of Drugs Act 1971, s. 4(3)***

- Triable either way • Class A (life imprisonment and/or fine on indictment; six months' imprisonment and/or prescribed sum summarily); Class B (14 years' imprisonment and/or fine on indictment; six months' imprisonment and/or prescribed sum summarily); Class C (five years' imprisonment and/or fine on indictment; three months' imprisonment and/or fine summarily)

   (Serious arrestable offence)

The Misuse of Drugs Act 1971, s. 4 states:

   (3) Subject to section 28 of this Act, it is an offence for a person—

      (a) to supply or offer to supply a controlled drug to another in contravention of subsection (1) above; or

      (b) to be concerned in the supplying of such a drug to another in contravention of that subsection; or

      (c) to be concerned in the making to another in contravention of that subsection of an offer to supply such a drug.

KEYNOTE

The word supply 'connotes more than the mere transfer of physical control of [something] from one person to another' (per Lord Keith in *Holmes v Chief Constable of Merseyside Police* [1976] Crim LR 125). The offence of supplying requires a further element, namely that the person receiving the item (the controlled drug) is thereby enabled to apply it to his/her own purposes. Whether or not a person has 'supplied' a controlled drug to another is a question of fact.

'Supplying' includes distributing (s. 37(1)).

   This offence most frequently occurs where one person hands over a controlled drug to another, in which case there is little argument about the meaning of supply.

Where a person leaves a controlled drug with another for safekeeping however, the situation is more problematic. It has been held that, where a person holds on to a controlled drug belonging to another for a short while and then hands it back, there is no 'supply' (although there may be unlawful possession) (*R v Dempsey and Dempsey* (1986) 82 Cr App R 291, see below). If the person looking after the drugs for another is in some way benefiting from that activity, then the return of those drugs to the depositor will amount to 'supplying', and the offences of supplying or possession with intent to supply will be applicable (*R v Maginnis* [1987] AC 303, see below). *Dempsey* involved a registered drug addict who was in lawful possession of a controlled drug and who asked his partner to hold on to some of that drug while he went to administer the remainder of it to himself in a gents' toilet. Both the addict and his partner were arrested, the addict being subsequently charged with 'supplying' his partner with the drug. The Court of Appeal held that, if the partner had simply been given the drug for safekeeping until the addict's return, there would be no 'supplying'. If, however, she had been given the drug for her own use, then there clearly *would* be a 'supplying' of that drug and the offence under s. 4(3)(a) would be complete.

Other situations where the *initial* possession of the controlled drug is itself unlawful have also raised difficult questions. If a drug trafficker leaves drugs with a third person temporarily, what criminal liability is incurred by the third person when he/she returns the drugs to the trafficker? Will returning the drug to its owner under these circumstances, which are different from those in *Dempsey* (above) amount to 'supplying'? This situation was faced by the House of Lords in *R v Maginnis* [1987] AC 303. In that case their Lordships decided that Maginnis would have been 'supplying' the controlled drug had he returned it to the drug trafficker who had left a package of cannabis resin in Maginnis' car. Therefore, he was in possession with intent to supply and so committed an offence under s. 5(3) (see below). Once again, however, the court expressed the view that if the person left with temporary possession of the controlled drug was not benefiting from so possessing it, there would be no 'supplying'. That being the case, it is at least arguable that the third person is *aiding and abetting* the trafficker to possess with intent to supply.

This issue has been further complicated by a decision involving a person who claimed that he had been coerced into holding controlled drugs for unnamed dealers. When found in possession of the drugs, the defendant claimed the defence of duress and said that he had only been an 'involuntary custodian' of them, intending to return them at a later date. The Court of Appeal decided that it was irrelevant whether a person was a voluntary or involuntary custodian of the drugs and that an intention to return them to their depositor amounted to an 'intention to supply' (*R v Panton* (2001) *The Times*, 27 March).

If a police informer provides a controlled drug to another in order that the other be arrested, there will still be a 'supplying' of the drug (*R v X* [1994] Crim LR 827).

Injecting another with his/her own controlled drug has been held not to amount to 'supplying' in a case where the defendant assisted pushing down the plunger of a syringe that the other person was already using. Parker CJ's comments in that case suggest that simply injecting another person with their own drug would not amount to 'supplying' (*R v Harris* [1968] 1 WLR 769). It may, however, amount to an offence of 'poisoning' under s. 23 of the Offences Against the Person Act 1861. The key problem with charging the supplier of drugs for self-injection by someone who then dies as a result lies in the issues of causation. While there are some authorities that say a supplier of a drug for self-injection which leads to the death of the recipient *can potentially* amount to unlawful act manslaughter (see para. 2.1.4) great difficulties have arisen and the general view is that the supplier is unlikely to be held liable for *causing* death in such a case (see *R v Dias* [2003] EWCA Crim 945). Where the defendant carries out the injection as opposed to merely the supply of the drug, liability for causing the death of another in this way can be made out however—even if the drug injected is not a controlled drug (see *R v Andrews* [2002] EWCA Crim 3021—injection of insulin with consent; see also *R v Rogers* [2003] EWCA Crim 2968—applying and holding a tourniquet to the arm of a drug abuser while injecting heroin can amount to the *actus reus* for manslaughter). Section 4(3) is a drug trafficking offence for the purposes of the Drug Trafficking Act 1994 (see para. 2.11.2). It is also a serious arrestable offence under s. 116(2) of the Police and Criminal Evidence Act 1984.

Dividing up controlled drugs which have been jointly purchased will amount to 'supplying' (*R v Buckley* (1979) 69 Cr App R 371).

The Court of Appeal has held that there is no statutory defence of 'religious use' to the above offence and that, even where it was accepted that the supply was for religious purposes, bringing a prosecution for the offence did not amount to an infringement the defendant's rights under Articles 8 and 9 of the European Convention on Human Rights (*R v Taylor* [2001] EWCA Crim 2263).

The offence of offering to supply a controlled drug is complete when the offer is made. It is irrelevant whether or not the defendant actually has the means to meet the offer or even intends to carry it out (see *R v Goodard* [1992] Crim LR 588). If the offer is made by conduct alone (i.e. without any words), it may be difficult to prove this offence. If words are used, the defence under s. 28 (see para. 2.11.7) does not appear to apply (see *R v Mitchell* [1992] Crim LR 723). If the offer is made to an undercover police officer, the offence is still committed and the defendant cannot claim that such an offer was not a 'real' offer (*R v Kray*, 10 November 1998, unreported).

In each case it will be a question of fact for the magistrate(s)/jury to decide whether or not the conduct amounted to a supply or offer to supply.

In order to prove the offence of being concerned in the supply/offer to supply a controlled drug, you must show:

— the actual supply of, or making of an offer to supply, a controlled drug,

— the participation of the defendant in that enterprise, and

— knowledge by the defendant that the enterprise involved the supply of, or making of an offer to supply, a controlled drug

(per the Court of Appeal in *R* v *Hughes* (1985) 81 Cr App R 344).

If the object of a conspiracy is to supply a controlled drug to a co-conspirator, any subsequent charge must make that clear; stating that the defendants conspired to supply the drug to 'another' implies that the supply was to be made to someone *other than any of the conspirators* (*R* v *Jackson* (2000) 1 Cr App R 97n).

If committed in relation to specified Class A drugs (heroin, cocaine and 'crack' cocaine), this will be a 'trigger' offence under s. 63B of the Police and Criminal Evidence Act 1984 which can activate police powers to require a sample from a person in police detention in some force areas.

Possession

OFFENCE: **Possession of Controlled Drug—*Misuse of Drugs Act 1971, s. 5(2)***

    • Triable either way • Class A (seven years' imprisonment and/or fine on indictment; six months' imprisonment and/or prescribed sum summarily); Class B (five years' imprisonment and/or fine on indictment; three months' imprisonment and/or fine summarily)

    (Arrestable offence)

    • Class C (two years' imprisonment and/or fine on indictment; three months' imprisonment and/or fine summarily)

    (No specific power of arrest)

The Misuse of Drugs Act 1971, s. 5 states:

(2) Subject to section 28 of this Act and to subsection (4) below, it is an offence for a person to have a controlled drug in his possession in contravention of subsection (1)...

KEYNOTE

See para. 2.11.5 above for meaning of 'possession'.

The offence of possession of cannabis has been hotly debated in parliament, the courts, the media—and even police training centres—for decades, but never more so than at the time of writing. Amid 'Drug Czars' resigning and various pressure groups and politicians giving forth, cannabis was to be relegated to a Class C drug by July 2002. Such a move (which had yet to be enacted at the time of writing) falls short of 'legalisation' or 'decriminalisation'—any doubt as to that position should be dispelled by the words of the Home Secretary that '*all controlled drugs are harmful, all will remain illegal*'. Nevertheless, this reclassification means that offences involving simple possession of cannabis will no longer be an arrestable offence. That is very different from saying that you cannot be arrested for simple possession because you can (e.g. under the general power of arrest under the Police and Criminal Evidence Act 1984).

If committed in relation to specified Class A drugs (heroin, cocaine and 'crack' cocaine), this will be a 'trigger' offence under s. 63B of the Police and Criminal Evidence Act 1984 which can activate police powers to require a sample from a person in police detention in some force areas.

Possession with Intent to Supply

OFFENCE: **Possession with Intent to Supply—*Misuse of Drugs Act 1971, s. 5(3)***

- Triable either way • Class A (life imprisonment and/or fine on indictment; six months' imprisonment and/or prescribed sum summarily); Class B (14 years' imprisonment and/or fine on indictment; six months' imprisonment and/or prescribed sum summarily); Class C (five years' imprisonment and/or fine on indictment; three months' imprisonment and/or fine summarily) *(Serious arrestable offence)*

The Misuse of Drugs Act 1971, s. 5 states:

(3) Subject to section 28 of this Act, it is an offence for a person to have a controlled drug in his possession, whether lawfully or not, with intent to supply it to another in contravention of section 4(1) of this Act.

KEYNOTE

This is a crime of *specific* intent. By way of a counter-measure to the re-classification of cannabis (see above), the Home Secretary has, at the time of writing, announced that the maximum penalty for possessing a Class C drug with intent to supply is to be increased to 14 years' imprisonment.

It is important to note that the lawfulness or otherwise of the possession is irrelevant; what matters here is the lawfulness of the intended supply. If a vet or a police officer or some other person is in lawful possession of a controlled drug but they intend to supply it unlawfully to another, this offence will be made out.

You must show that the intention was that the *possessor* supply the controlled drug, not some third party in the future (*R v Greenfield* (1984) 78 Cr App R 179n).

If more than one person has possession of the relevant controlled drug, you must show an individual intention to supply it by each person charged; it is not enough to show a joint venture whereby one or more parties simply knew of another's intent (*R v Downes* [1984] Crim LR 552). Given the decision of the Court of Appeal in *Kray* (see above), possession with intent to supply a controlled drug to a person who is in fact an under-cover police officer would appear to amount to an offence under this section.

All that is necessary in proving the offence under s. 5(3) is to show that the defendant had a controlled drug in his/her possession and intended to supply that substance to another. If the substance in the defendant's possession is a Class A drug and he/she intended to supply it to another person, the fact that he/she thought the drug was some other type of drug does not matter (*R v Leeson* (2000) 1 Cr App R 233).

While the possession by a defendant of drugs paraphernalia (e.g. clingfilm, paper, scales, contact details, etc.) will be relevant evidence to show that he/she was an active dealer in drugs generally, it does not prove the intention to supply and the trial judge will give a jury very careful directions as to the probative value of such items found in the defendant's possession (see *R v Haye* [2002] EWCA Crim 2476).

Where a Rastafarian was prosecuted for possessing cannabis with intent to supply others as part of their religious worship, he claimed that his rights under Articles 8 and 9 of the European Convention had been unnecessarily and disproportionately interfered with. The Court of Appeal, while reducing the sentence, held that such a prosecution had been properly brought (*R v Taylor* [2002] Crim LR 314).

In proving an intention to supply you may be able to adduce evidence of the defendant's unexplained wealth (*R v Smith (Ivor)* [1995] Crim LR 940) or the presence of large sums of money with the drugs seized (see *R v Wright* [1994] Crim LR 55).

For the meaning of 'supply', see above.

Section 5(3) is a drug trafficking offence for the purposes of the Drug Trafficking Act 1994 (**see para. 2.11.2**). It is also a serious arrestable offence under s. 116(2) of the Police and Criminal and Evidence Act 1984.

If committed in relation to specified Class A drugs (heroin, cocaine and 'crack' cocaine), this will be a 'trigger' offence under s. 63B of the Police and Criminal Evidence Act 1984 which can activate police powers to require a sample from a person in police detention in some force areas.

Cultivation of Cannabis

OFFENCE: **Cultivation of Cannabis—*Misuse of Drugs Act 1971, s. 6***
- Triable either way • Fourteen years' imprisonment and/or a fine on indictment; six months' imprisonment and/or prescribed sum summarily
(Arrestable offence)

The Misuse of Drugs Act 1971, s. 6 states:

(1) Subject to any regulations under section 7 of this Act for the time being in force, it shall not be lawful for a person to cultivate any plant of the genus Cannabis.

(2) Subject to section 28 of this Act, it is an offence to cultivate any such plant in contravention of subsection (1) above.

KEYNOTE

'Cultivate' is not defined but it appears that you would have to show some element of attention (such as watering or feeding) to the plant by the defendant in order to prove this offence. This offence does not permit police officers to tend plants which have been seized as evidence in order to preserve them as exhibits for court!

In proving the offence, you need only show that the plant is of the genus *Cannabis* and that the defendant cultivated it; you need not show that the defendant knew it to be a cannabis plant (*R v Champ* (1981) 73 Cr App R 367).

A person may be licensed to cultivate cannabis plants by the Secretary of State (under reg. 12 of the Misuse of Drugs Regulations 2001).

Supply of Articles

OFFENCE: **Supplying Articles for Administering or Preparing Controlled Drugs—*Misuse of Drugs Act 1971, s. 9A***
- Triable summarily • Six months' imprisonment and/or fine
(No specific power of arrest)

The Misuse of Drugs Act 1971, s. 9A states:

(1) A person who supplies or offers to supply any article which may be used or adapted to be used (whether by itself or in combination with another article or other articles) in the administration by any person of a controlled drug to himself or another, believing that the article (or the article as adapted) is to be so used in circumstances where the administration is unlawful, is guilty of an offence.

(2) ...

(3) A person who supplies or offers to supply any article which may be used to prepare a controlled drug for administration by any person to himself or another believing that the article is to be so used in circumstances where the administration is unlawful is guilty of an offence.

KEYNOTE

This offence is designed to address the provision of drug 'kits'.

'Supply' for these purposes is likely to be interpreted in the same way as for the earlier sections in the 1971 Act. Hypodermic syringes, or parts of them, are not covered by this offence (s. 9A(2)).

The administration for which the articles are intended must be 'unlawful'. Section 9A states:

(4) For the purposes of this section, any administration of a controlled drug is unlawful except—
  (a) the administration by any person of a controlled drug to another in circumstances where the administration of the drug is not unlawful under section 4(1) of this Act, or
  (b) the administration by any person of a controlled drug to himself in circumstances where having the controlled drug in his possession is not unlawful under section 5(1) of this Act.

(5) In this section, references to administration by any person of a controlled drug to himself include a reference to his administering it to himself with the assistance of another.

Occupiers, etc.

OFFENCE: **Occupier or Manager of Premises Permitting Drug Misuse—***Misuse of Drugs Act 1971, s. 8*

- Triable either way Class A or B (14 years' imprisonment and/or fine on indictment; six months' imprisonment and/or prescribed sum summarily); Class C (five years' imprisonment and/or a fine on indictment; three months' imprisonment and/or fine summarily)

(Arrestable offence)

The Misuse of Drugs Act 1971, s. 8 states:

A person commits an offence if, being the occupier or concerned in the management of any premises, he knowingly permits or suffers any of the following activities to take place on those premises, that is to say—

(a) producing or attempting to produce a controlled drug in contravention of section 4(1) of this Act;

(b) supplying or attempting to supply a controlled drug to another in contravention of section 4(1) of this Act, or offering to supply a controlled drug to another in contravention of section 4(1);

(c) preparing opium for smoking;

(d) smoking cannabis, cannabis resin or prepared opium.

KEYNOTE

The courts have adopted a 'common sense' approach to the interpretation of whether someone is an 'occupier' or not (see *R v Tao* [1977] QB 141). You will not need to prove that a defendant falls within some narrow legal meaning of an occupier. What is important in proving this offence is showing that the defendant had enough control over the premises to prevent the sort of activity listed above (see *R v Coid* [1998] Crim LR 199).

If a person cannot be shown to be an occupier in this sense, it may be that he/she can be shown to be involved in the planning, organising and actual use of the premises by taking part in more than just menial tasks. If so, this level of involvement may amount to 'management' of the premises (see *R v Josephs* (1977) 65 Cr App R 253).

'Premises' is not defined and has not been clarified at common law but the meaning has been given a wide definition elsewhere (such as in the Police and Criminal Evidence Act 1984).

The permitting or suffering of these activities requires a degree of *mens rea*—*Sweet v Parsley* [1970] AC 132—even if that degree is little more than wilful blindness (see *R v Thomas* (1976) 63 Cr App R 65). For the purposes of s. 8(b)—and therefore, presumably, s. 8(a)—it is not necessary to show that the defendant knew exactly which drugs were being produced, supplied etc.; only that they were 'controlled drugs' (*R v Bett* [1999] 1 All ER 600).

The Criminal Justice and Police Act 2001 makes provision to extend this offence. At the time of writing, that Part of the 2001 Act had not been brought into force.

An occupier who permits the growing of cannabis plants also commits this offence (*Taylor v Chief Constable of Kent* [1981] 1 WLR 606).

An occupier will not commit the above offence *in relation to the smoking of cannabis or cannabis resin* if the premises are covered by a research licence from the Secretary of State (see reg. 13 of the Misuse of Drugs Regulations 2001).

This offence is likely also to receive greater attention as a result of the re-classification of cannabis (see above) and the fears that this will lead to the opening of so-called 'cannabis cafes'.

Importation of Controlled Drugs

It is an offence under the Misuse of Drugs Act 1971, s. 3 to import or export a controlled drug unless authorised by the regulations made under the Act. The relevant offences and their respective penalties are contained in the Customs and Excise Management Act 1979.

Schedule 1 to the 1979 Act provides for the following penalties for the improper importation or exportation of controlled drugs:

- Class A—life imprisonment
- Class B—14 years' imprisonment
- Class C—five years' imprisonment.

All are serious arrestable offences.

Assisting or Inducing Offence Outside United Kingdom

OFFENCE: **Assisting or Inducing Misuse of Drugs Offence Outside UK—**
Misuse of Drugs Act 1971, s. 20

> • Triable either way • Fourteen years' imprisonment and/or a fine on indictment;
> six months' imprisonment and/or fine summarily
> _(Arrestable offence)_

The Misuse of Drugs Act 1971, s. 20 states:

> A person commits an offence if in the United Kingdom he assists in or induces the commission in any place outside the United Kingdom of an offence punishable under the provisions of a corresponding law in force in that place.

KEYNOTE

In order to prove this offence, you must show that the offence outside the United Kingdom actually took place. The circumstances where this offence is likely to be committed will clearly overlap with the offences of importation/ exportation (see above).

'Assisting' has been held to include taking containers to another country in the knowledge that they would later be filled with a controlled drug and sent on to a third country (_R_ v _Evans_ (1977) 64 Cr App R 237).

For an offence to amount to one under 'corresponding law' for these purposes, a certificate relating to the domestic law concerned with the misuse of drugs must be obtained from the government of the relevant country (s. 36).

Section 20 is a drug trafficking offence for the purposes of the Drug Trafficking Act 1994 (**see para. 2.11.2**).

Incitement

OFFENCE: **Incitement—_Misuse of Drugs Act 1971, s. 19_**

> • Triable and punishable as for substantive offence incited
> _(Arrestable offence if offence incited is arrestable)_

The Misuse of Drugs Act 1971, s. 19 states:

> It is an offence for a person to incite another to commit such an offense.

KEYNOTE

Although the offence of incitement exists for most other offences generally, the Act makes a specific offence of inciting another to commit an offence under its provisions. On the arguments in _DPP_ v _Armstrong_ [2000] Crim LR 379, it would seem that a person inciting an undercover police officer may commit an offence under s. 19 even though there was no possibility of the officer actually being induced to commit the offence.

Section 19 is a drug trafficking offence for the purposes of the Drug Trafficking Act 1994 (**see para. 2.11.2**).

2.11.9   **Enforcement**

Powers of Entry, Search and Seizure

The Misuse of Drugs Act 1971, s. 23 states:

(1) A constable or other person authorised in that behalf by a general or special order of the Secretary of State (or in Northern Ireland either of the Secretary of State or the Ministry of Home Affairs for Northern Ireland) shall, for the purposes of the execution of this Act, have power to enter the premises of a person carrying on business as a producer or supplier of any controlled drugs and to demand the production of, and to inspect, any books or documents relating to dealings in any such drugs and to inspect any stocks of any such drugs.

(2) If a constable has reasonable grounds to suspect that any person is in possession of a controlled drug in contravention of this Act or of any regulations made there under, the constable may—

(a) search that person, and detain him for the purpose of searching him;

(b) search any vehicle or vessel in which the constable suspects that the drug may be found, and for that purpose require the person in control of the vehicle or vessel to stop it;

(c) seize and detain, for the purposes of proceedings under this Act, anything found in the course of the search which appears to the constable to be evidence of an offence under this Act.

In this subsection 'vessel' includes a hovercraft within the meaning of the Hovercraft Act 1968; and nothing in this subsection shall prejudice any power of search or any power to seize or detain property which exercisable by a constable apart from this subsection.

(3) If a justice of the peace (or in Scotland a justice of the peace, a magistrate or a sheriff) is satisfied by information on oath that there is reasonable ground for suspecting—

(a) that any controlled drugs are, in contravention of this Act or of any regulations made there- under, in the possession of a person on any premises; or

(b) that a document directly or indirectly relating to, or connected with, a transaction or dealing which was, or an intended transaction or dealing which would if carried out be, an offence under this Act, or in the case of a transaction or dealing carried out or intended to be carried out in a place outside the United Kingdom, an offence against the provisions of a corresponding law in force in that place, is in the possession of a person on any premises,

he may grant a warrant authorising any constable acting for the police area in which the premises are situated at any time or times within one month from the date of the warrant, to enter, if need be by force, the premises named in the warrant, and to search the premises and any persons found therein and, if there is reasonable ground for suspecting that an offence under this Act has been committed in relation to any controlled drugs found on the premises or in the possession of any such persons, or that a document so found is such a document as is mentioned in paragraph (b) above, to seize and detain those drugs or that document, as the case may be.

KEYNOTE

This is a very wide statutory provision granting authority for a broad range of enforcement measures in connection with controlled drugs.

Particular care will need to be taken when drafting the application for a warrant under s. 23. Where police officers are on premises under the authority of such a warrant, it will be important to have established—probably at the briefing stage—the precise extent of the warrant. If such a warrant authorises the search of premises only, that in itself will not give the officers authority to search *people* found on those premises unless the officer can point to some other power authorising the search (see e.g. *Chief Constable of Thames Valley Police v Hepburn* [2002] EWCA Civ 1841).

The Police and Criminal Evidence Act 1984, code A, applies to the exercise of any power to search people for controlled drugs specifically included in a warrant issued under s. 23.

Obstruction

OFFENCE: **Obstruction—*Misuse of Drugs Act 1971, s. 23(4)***

• Triable either way • Two years' imprisonment and/or a fine on indictment; six
months' imprisonment and/or fine summarily

(No specific power of arrest)

The Misuse of Drugs Act 1971, s. 23 states:

(4) A person commits an offence if he—
  (a) intentionally obstructs a person in the exercise of his powers under this section; or
  (b) conceals from a person acting in the exercise of his powers under subsection (1) above any
      such books, documents, stocks or drugs as are mentioned in that subsection; or
  (c) without reasonable excuse (proof of which shall lie on him) fails to produce any such books
      or documents as are so mentioned where their production is demanded by a person in the
      exercise of his powers under that subsection.

KEYNOTE

The offence of obstructing a person in the exercise of his/her powers is only committed if the obstruction was
intentional (*R v Forde* (1985) 81 Cr App R 19).

Travel Restriction Orders

The Criminal Justice and Police Act 2001 makes provision for courts to impose travel
restrictions on offenders convicted of drug trafficking offences. Travel restriction orders
prohibit the offender from leaving the United Kingdom at any time during the period
beginning from his/her release from custody (other than on bail or temporary release for
a fixed period) and up to the end of the order. The minimum period for such an order is two
years (s. 33(3)).

Where a court

– has convicted a person of a drug trafficking offence

– and it has determined that a sentence of four years or more is appropriate

it is under a *duty* to consider whether or not a travel restriction order would be appropriate
(s. 33). If the court decides not to impose an order, it must give its reasons for not doing so.

An offender may also be required to surrender his/her UK passport as part of the order.

The offences which are covered by travel restriction orders include the production and
supply of controlled drugs (**see para 2.11.8**), the importation/exportation offences
described at para. 6.8.9 along with attempting, or inciting—either at common law or under
the Misuse of Drugs Act 1971, s. 19 (**see para. 2.11.8**).

The Secretary of State may add to this list (see s. 34(2)).

An offender may apply to the court that made a restriction order to have it revoked or
suspended (s. 35) and the court must consider the strict criteria set out in s. 35 when considering any such suspension or revocation. If an order is suspended, the offender has a legal
obligation to be back in the United Kingdom when the period of suspension ends (s. 35(5)(a)).

The general importance of all this to police officers is the offence below.

OFFENCE: **Contravening a Travel Restriction Order—*Criminal Justice and Police
Act 2001, s. 36***

• Triable either way • Five years' imprisonment and/or a fine on indictment;
six months' imprisonment and/or fine summarily

(Arrestable offence)

The Criminal Justice and Police Act 2001, s. 36 states:

(1) A person who leaves the United Kingdom at a time when he is prohibited from leaving it by a travel restriction order is guilty of an offence . . .

(2) A person who is not in the United Kingdom at the end of a period during which a prohibition imposed on him by a travel restriction order has been suspended shall be guilty of an offence . . .

KEYNOTE

These offences make no specific requirement for a particular state of mind. The first offence simply requires proof of two things—that there was an order in existence in respect of the offender and that he/she left the United Kingdom during the time it was in force. As this is an arrestable offence, a person attempting to leave the United Kingdom in breach of an order could commit an offence. Strangely, there is no requirement that the person leave the United Kingdom *voluntarily* in order to be guilty (although they would have a pretty good argument if they were taken out of the jurisdiction against their will or without their knowledge).

However, travel restriction orders do not prevent the proper exercise of any prescribed power to remove a person from the United Kingdom (see s. 37—the relevant powers are set out in the Travel Restriction Order (Prescribed Removal Powers) Order 2002 (SI 2002 No. 313)). For instance, if the Secretary of State deports someone who is under a travel restriction order, that person would not commit the above offence.

The second offence requires proof that there was a suspended order in existence in respect of the offender and that, at the end of the suspension period, the offender was not in the United Kingdom. Given that this offence simply envisages a set of circumstances (that the defendant is not in the United Kingdom when the suspension order ends) it is interesting—though of no great practical relevance—to consider whether this offence could ever be 'attempted'.

Failing to deliver up a UK passport when required by an order will be a summary offence carrying six months' imprisonment and/or a fine (s. 36(3)).

2.12 Firearms

2.12.1 Introduction

The law regulating the possession, transfer and use of firearms remained largely unchanged between the passing of the main Firearms Act in 1968 and the introduction of the Firearms (Amendment) Act in 1988. During 1997, however, the law underwent significant amendment and what were already fairly stringent controls were reinforced by further restrictions on the ownership and use of firearms generally.

In addition to the primary legislation, s. 53 of the Firearms Act 1968 allows the Secretary of State to make rules in relation to the 1968 Act's implementation (see e.g. the Firearms Rules 1989 (SI 1989 No. 854), as amended. The Home Office has also issued guidance to chief officers on the control and licensing of firearms.

In considering the legislation that follows in this chapter, it is worth bearing in mind the provisions of the Terrorism Act 2000 and, in particular, the offences of providing or receiving instruction in the use of firearms and some other weapons. The leading authority giving guidance in relation to sentencing for offences involving firearms is *R* v *Avis* (1998) 1 Cr App R 420. There it was held that there were four questions a sentencing court had to ask itself when assessing the seriousness of a firearms offence:

– what sort of weapon was involved;

– what use had been made of the weapon;

– with what intention did the defendant possess or use the firearm; and

– what was the defendant's record.

All of these issues should arguably be borne in mind when gathering and presenting evidence in firearms cases. It is also worth noting that, following a report from the National Criminal Intelligence Service (NCIS), a firearms database containing details of all licensed firearm and shotgun holders in Great Britain is being set up. Further amendments to some of the penalties were proposed at the time of writing.

2.12.2   **The 'this' checklist**

When considering any situation involving firearms legislation, whether practically or for the purposes of study, it is useful to apply the 'this' checklist.

The 'this' checklist, which is also useful in other areas of law (**see Road Traffic**), means asking whether:

- **this** certificate/exemption
- covers **this** person
- for **this** activity
- involving **this** firearm/ammunition
- for **this** purpose.

This certificate/exemption

The Firearms Act 1968 provides for people to be authorised by certificate to hold, transfer or buy firearms under specified conditions.

The 1968 Act—and the amending legislation—also contains many exemptions, some generally applicable and others very specific.

In each case, whether considering a certificate or other authority, or a possible exemption, it is critical that you establish what conditions apply.

This person

Certificates will authorise the holder to do certain things (e.g. to buy firearms); other authorities will allow a wider group of people to do things (e.g. borrow the rifle of a certificate holder). In considering offences it is important to establish exactly which person is authorised or is exempt from any liability.

This activity

Certificates and exemptions never grant unlimited authority to undertake any activity with every firearm or ammunition. Certificates will usually specify whether the holder can have a firearm in his/her '*possession*'; which firearms or ammunition he/she can possess; and whether he/she can *sell* or *transfer* firearms *or* ammunition. Exemptions are the same in that they will not apply to everyone in respect of all activities.

This firearm/ammunition

In addition to the restrictions on the activity, certificates and exemptions will only apply to particular firearms and/or ammunition. A person authorised to possess a shotgun is not thereby permitted to have an automatic rifle. Similarly, a person who runs a mini rifle range is not thereby given authority to possess mortar shells!

This purpose

Certificates and exemptions will specify the precise purposes for which they apply. For instance, if a certificate allows a person to possess a firearm for slaughtering animals while at the slaughterhouse, that does not permit the possession of the firearm by the slaughterer while at home or travelling to work.

Similarly, some of the general exemptions apply only to the people concerned while they are involved in *the ordinary course of their business*, whether they are registered firearms dealers or members of the armed forces; possession or use of a firearm outside the particular circumstances will not be covered.

2.12.3 Firearms generally

Section 57 of the Firearms Act 1968 states:

> (1) In this Act, the expression ' description from which any shot, bullet or other missile can be discharged, and includes—
>   (a) any prohibited weapon, whether it is such a lethal weapon as aforesaid or not; and
>   (b) any component part of such a lethal or prohibited weapon; and
>   (c) any accessory to any such weapon designed or adapted to diminish the noise or flash caused by firing the weapon.

KEYNOTE

'Lethal barrelled weapon' is not defined under the 1968 Act.

The way in which the courts have determined whether or not something amounts to such a weapon is by asking:

– Can any shot, bullet or other missile be discharged from the weapon?, or

– Could the weapon be adapted so that any shot, bullet or other missile can be discharged?

– If so, is the weapon a 'lethal barrelled' weapon?

(See *Grace* v *DPP* (1989) 153 JP 491.)

A weapon is a lethal barrelled weapon if it is capable of causing injury, irrespective of the intentions of its maker (*Read* v *Donovan* [1947] KB 326). In determining whether a firearm is in fact a lethal barrelled weapon from which missiles can be discharged a court need not consider any specific evidence of someone who has seen the effects of it being fired. Therefore, where magistrates had heard evidence from a gun shop assistant that an air rifle was in working order, they were entitled to conclude that it fell within the definition even though no evidence was given as to the actual effects of the gun being fired (*Castle* v *DPP* (1998) *The Times*, 3 April).

Air pistols (*R* v *Thorpe* [1987] 1 WLR 383), imitation revolvers (*Cafferata* v *Wilson* [1936] 3 All ER 149) and signalling pistols (*Read* v *Donovan*, above) have all been held to be lethal barrelled weapons. That is not to say, however, that they will always be so and each case must be determined in the light of the evidence available.

Component parts, such as triggers or barrels, are also included in the definition, as are silencers and accessories to hide the muzzle flash of a weapon. If a defendant is found in possession of a silencer which has been manufactured for a weapon that is also in the defendant's possession, that will be enough to bring it under s. 57(1). If, however, the silencer is made for a different weapon, it may still come under the s. 57 definition but the prosecution will have to show that it could be used with the defendant's weapon and that he/she had it for that purpose. This slightly odd result is the result of the Court of Appeal's decision in *R* v *Buckfield* [1998] Crim LR 673. Following that reasoning, a silencer or accessory on its own does not appear to be a firearm for the purposes of s. 57(1). Section 57(1) does not include telescopic sights.

A weapon may cease to be a firearm if it is de-activated in line with the provisions of the Firearms (Amendment) Act 1988, s. 8 which states:

> For the purposes of the principal Act and this Act it shall be presumed, unless the contrary is shown, that a firearm has been rendered incapable of discharging any shot, bullet or other missile, and has consequently ceased to be a firearm within the meaning of those Acts, if—
>
> (a) it bears a mark which has been approved by the Secretary of State for denoting that fact and which has been made either by one of the two companies mentioned in section 58(1) of the principal Act or by such other person as may be approved by the Secretary of State for the purposes of this section; and

(b) that company or person has certified in writing that work has been carried out on the firearm in a manner approved by the Secretary of State for rendering it incapable of discharging any shot, bullet or other missile.

KEYNOTE

For the 'two companies' referred to, **see para. 2.12.4.**

2.12.4 **Definitions**

The law regulating firearms classifies weapons into several categories, each of which is specifically defined. As with offences under road traffic legislation, it is critical that the relevant definition is considered before deciding upon a particular charge or offence.

Prohibited weapon

A prohibited weapon is defined under the Firearms Act 1968, s. 5. The definition formerly covered the more powerful or potentially destructive firearms—and their ammunition—such as automatic weapons and specialist ammunition.

Since the Firearms (Amendment) Acts of 1997, however, s. 5 also covers many small firearms which were formerly covered by other parts of the 1968 Act.

The test as to whether a weapon is a 'prohibited' weapon is a purely objective one and is not affected by the intentions of the defendant. Therefore, where a firearm was capable of successively discharging two or more missiles without repeated pressure on the trigger, that weapon was 'prohibited' irrespective of the intentions of the firearms dealer who was in possession of it (*R v Law* [1999] Crim LR 837).

Whereas a firearms certificate is usually needed in order to possess, buy or acquire firearms and ammunition, the authority of the Secretary of State is needed if the firearm or ammunition is a 'prohibited weapon'.

The full list of prohibited weapons and ammunition under s. 5 of the Firearms Act 1968 is as follows:

(1) ...

   (a) any firearm which is so designed or adapted that two or more missiles can be successively discharged without repeated pressure on the trigger;

   (ab) any self-loading or pump-action rifled gun other than one which is chambered for 0.22 rim-fire cartridges;

   (aba) any firearm which either has a barrel less than 30 centimetres in length or is less than 60 centimetres in length overall, other than an air weapon, a muzzle-loading gun or a firearm designed as signalling apparatus;

   (ac) any self-loading or pump-action smooth-bore gun which is not an air weapon or chambered for 0.22 rim-fire cartridges and either has a barrel less than 24 inches in length or is less than 40 inches in length overall;

   (ad) any smooth-bore revolver gun other than one which is chambered for 9 mm rimfire cartridges or a muzzle-loading gun;

   (ae) any rocket launcher, or any mortar, for projecting a stabilised missile, other than a launcher or mortar designed for line-throwing or pyrotechnic purposes or as signalling apparatus;

   (b) any weapon of whatever description designed or adapted for the discharge of any noxious liquid, gas or other thing;

   (c) any cartridge with a bullet designed to explode on or immediately before impact, any ammunition containing or designed or adapted to contain any such noxious thing as is mentioned in paragraph (b) above and, if capable of being used with a firearm of any description, any grenade, bomb (or other like missile), or rocket or shell designed to explode as aforesaid.

(1A) ...
   (a) any firearm which is disguised as another object;
   (b) any rocket or ammunition not falling within paragraph (c) of subsection (1) of this section which consists in or incorporates a missile designed to explode on or immediately before impact and is for military use;
   (c) any launcher or other projecting apparatus not falling within paragraph (ae) of that subsection which is designed to be used with any rocket or ammunition falling within paragraph (b) above or with ammunition which would fall within that paragraph but for its being ammunition falling within paragraph (c) of that subsection;
   (d) any ammunition for military use which consists in or incorporates a missile designed so that a substance contained in the missile will ignite on or immediately before impact;
   (e) any ammunition for military use which consists in or incorporates a missile designed, on account of its having a jacket and hard-core, to penetrate armour plating, armour screening or body armour;
   (f) any ammunition which incorporates a missile designed or adapted to expand on impact;
   (g) anything which is designed to be projected as a missile from any weapon and is designed to be, or has been, incorporated in—
      (i) any ammunition falling within any of the preceding paragraphs; or
      (ii) any ammunition which would fall within any of those paragraphs but for its being specified in subsection (1) of this section.

KEYNOTE

Therefore, the firearms which will require the authority of the Secretary of State before they can be possessed, acquired, bought, sold or transferred will include:

- automatic weapons

- most self-loading or pump-action weapons

- any firearm which is less than 60 cms long or which has a barrel less than 30 cms long (other than an air weapon or signalling apparatus)

- most smooth-bore revolvers

- any weapon—of whatever description—designed or adapted for the discharge of any noxious liquid, gas or other thing

- military weapons and ammunition including grenades and mortars.

Taking empty washing-up liquid bottles and filling them with a noxious fluid such as hydrochloric acid does not amount to 'adapting' them, neither is such a thing a 'weapon' for the purposes of s. 5(2) (*R v Formosa* [1991] 2 QB 1).

An electric 'stun gun' has been held to be a prohibited weapon as it discharges an electric current (*Flack v Baldry* [1988] 1 WLR 393) and it continues to be such even if it is not working (*R v Brown* (1992) *The Times*, 27 March).

The Secretary of State may amend the list above.

Note that s. 5A of the Firearms Act 1968 creates exemptions under the European Council Directive 91/477/EEC on control of the acquisition and possession of weapons [1991] OJL 256/51 which allows people from Member States to possess some prohibited weapons under certain circumstances (**see para. 2.12.7**).

Shotguns

A shotgun is defined under s. 1(3)(a) of the Firearms Act 1968. Section 1 (amended by Firearms (Amendment) Act 1988 s. 2) states:

(3) ...
   (a) a shotgun within the meaning of this Act, that is to say a smooth-bore gun (not being an airgun) which—
      (i) has a barrel not less than 24 inches in length and does not have any barrel with a bore exceeding 2 inches in diameter;

      (ii) either has no magazine or has a non-detachable magazine incapable of holding more than two cartridges; and

      (iii) is not a revolver gun . . . .

  (3A) A gun which has been adapted to have such a magazine as is mentioned in subsection (3)(a)(ii) above shall not be regarded as falling within that provision unless the magazine bears a mark approved by the Secretary of State for denoting that fact and that mark has been made, and the adaptation has been certified in writing as having been carried out in a manner approved by him, either by one of the two companies mentioned in section 58(1) of this Act or by such other person as may be approved by him for that purpose.

KEYNOTE

A barrel's length is measured from the muzzle to the point at which the charge is exploded on firing the weapon (s. 57(6)(a) of the 1968 Act).

The 'two companies' referred to are the Society of the Mystery of Gunmakers of the City of London and the Birmingham proof house.

Air weapons

Air weapons are defined under s. 1(3)(b) of the Firearms Act 1968 as being 'an air rifle, airgun or air pistol', including a rifle, pistol or gun powered by compressed carbon dioxide (see s. 48 of the Firearms (Amendment) Act 1997).

Some air weapons are deemed to be specially dangerous and therefore subject to stricter control than conventional air weapons. Those which are subject to this stricter control are those declared to be so by the Secretary of State. Listed in r. 2 of the Firearms (Dangerous Air Weapons) Rules 1969 (SI 1969 No. 47 made under Firearms Act 1968 ss. 1 and 53), they include:

(1) [any] air rifle, air gun or air pistol—

    (a) which is capable of discharging a missile so that the missile has, on being discharged from the muzzle of the weapon, kinetic energy in excess, in the case of an air pistol of 6 ft lb or, in the case of an air weapon other than an air pistol, of 12 ft lb. [other than one designed for use when submerged in water, or]

    (b) which is disguised as another object.

Section 1 firearm

There is a group of firearms which, although not a category defined in the 1968 Act, are subject to a number of offences including s. 1 (see below). Firearms which fall into this group are often referred to as 'section 1 firearms' and include all firearms except shotguns (see below) and conventional air weapons (see below). Shotguns which have been 'sawn off' (i.e. had their barrels shortened) are section 1 firearms, as are air weapons declared to be 'specially dangerous'.

Section 1 ammunition includes any ammunition for a firearm except:

– cartridges containing five or more shot, none of which is bigger than 0.36 inch in diameter;

– ammunition for an airgun, air rifle or air pistol; and

– blank cartridges not more than one inch in diameter

(s. 1(4)).

Conversion

Some weapons which began their life as section 1 firearms or prohibited weapons will remain so even after their conversion to a shotgun, air weapon or other type of firearm (see s. 7 of the Firearms (Amendment) Act 1988).

Imitation firearms

Some, though not all, offences which regulate the use of firearms will also apply to *imitation* firearms. Whether they do so can be found either in the specific wording of the offence, or by virtue of the Firearms Act 1982.

Put simply there are two types of imitation firearms:

– general imitations—those which have the appearance of firearms (which are covered by s. 57 of the Firearms Act 1968); and

– imitations of section 1 firearms—those which both have the appearance of a *section 1 firearm* and which can be readily converted into such a firearm (which are covered by ss. 1 and 2 of the Firearms Act 1982).

Where 'imitation firearms' are referred to *in the wording of the offence*, that offence will apply to the first category above, that is, 'anything which has the appearance of being a firearm'. Note that this category does not include anything which resembles a prohibited weapon *under s. 5(1)(b)*. Prohibited weapons under s. 5(1)(b) are those which are designed or adapted to discharge noxious liquid etc. (see above).

In some other offences, *the definition of the 1982 Act is applicable*. These offences are all offences which involve section 1 firearms, except those under ss. 4(3) and (4), 16 to 20 and 47 of the 1968 Act.

If an offence does not come within either of the circumstances above, it will not apply to an imitation firearm.

Whether or not something has the appearance of being a firearm will be a question of fact for the jury/magistrate(s) to decide in each case.

2.12.5   **Possessing etc. firearm or ammunition without certificate**

OFFENCE: **Possessing etc. firearm or ammunition without certificate—*Firearms Act 1968, s. 1***

> • Triable either way • Sentence: see sch. 6, appendix 5
> *(Arrestable offence)*

The Firearms Act 1968, s. 1 states:

(1) Subject to any exemption under this Act, it is an offence for a person—
   (a) to have in his possession, or to purchase or acquire, a firearm to which this section applies without holding a firearm certificate in force at the time, or otherwise than as authorised by such a certificate;
   (b) to have in his possession, or to purchase or acquire, any ammunition to which this section applies without holding a firearm certificate in force at the time, or otherwise than as authorised by such a certificate, or in quantities in excess of those so authorised.

KEYNOTE

This offence relates to those firearms described above as section 1 firearms.

If the firearm involved is a sawn-off shotgun, the offence becomes 'aggravated' (under s. 4(4)) and attracts a maximum penalty of seven years' imprisonment (see sch. 6).

The Firearms Act 1982 applies to this section and therefore the second definition of 'imitation firearms' at **para. 2.12.4** above applies here.

The certificate referred to is issued by the chief officer of police under s. 26. Such certificates may carry significant restrictions on the types of firearms which the holder is allowed, together with the circumstances under which he/she may have them (see s. 44(1) of the Firearms (Amendment) Act 1997).

The purpose of the legislation regulating the licensing of firearms is to provide certainty and consistency in the effective control of such weapons. Therefore, the issue of whether a certificate covers a particular category of weapon is a matter of law for the judge to decide and cannot be affected by the intentions or misunderstanding of the defendant (*R v Paul (Benjamin)* (1998) 95(32) LS Gaz 30).

For the forms to be used in relation to the grant of certificates and permits, see the Firearms Rules 1998 (SI 1998 No. 1941 made under Firearms Act 1968).

A person may hold a European firearms pass or similar document, in which case he/she will be governed by the provision of ss. 32A to 32C of the Firearms Act 1968.

If a person has such a certificate which allows the possession etc. of the firearm in question and under the particular circumstances encountered, no offence is committed.

Possession

As in other areas of criminal law (**see para. 2.11.5**), the meaning of possession is wider here than actual physical custody of the firearm in question. A person can remain in possession of a firearm even if someone else has custody of it (*Sullivan v Earl of Caithness* [1976] QB 966).

Possession for the purposes of this offence does not require any specific knowledge on the part of the defendant. For example, if X knows he is in possession of something (e.g. a box), then X is in possession of its contents, *even though X does not know what those contents are* (*R v Hussain* [1981] 1 WLR 416).

Therefore, there is no need to prove that the defendant knew the nature of the thing which he/she possessed in order to prove this offence (and the offence under s. 19, **see para. 2.12.8**). If a defendant is carrying a rucksack and that rucksack turns out to contain ammunition for a section 1 firearm, the defendant is 'in possession' of that ammunition irrespective of his/her knowledge—or ignorance—of its presence in the rucksack (see *R v Waller* [1991] Crim LR 381). (For a discussion of the situation in respect of drugs, **see para. 2.11.5**)

Acquire

Acquire will include hiring, accepting as a gift and borrowing (s. 57(4) of the Firearms Act 1968).

Exemptions

The offence specifies that it is subject to any exemptions under the 1968 Act. There are three main categories of exemption under the firearms legislation:

– General exemptions—listed below.

– European exemptions—these are made under s. 5A to reflect the European Weapons Directive (**see para. 2.12.7**).

– Special exemptions—which apply to the provisions affecting prohibited weapons under s. 5 (**see para. 2.12.7**).

Many of the exemptions overlap as they follow a fairly common sense approach to the necessary possession and use of firearms/ammunition in the course of work and leisure.

General exemptions

The general exemptions, which apply to the provisions of ss. 1 to 5 of the Firearms Act 1968 are mainly concerned with the various occupations of people whom you might expect to be in contact with firearms in one form or another. They include:

Police permit holders

Under s. 7(1) of the 1968 Act, the chief officer of police may grant a permit authorising the possession of firearms or ammunition under the conditions specified in the permit.

Clubs, athletics and sporting purposes

Section 11 of the 1968 Act provides exemptions for a person:

- borrowing the firearm/ammunition from a certificate holder for sporting purposes only (s. 11(1));
- possessing a firearm at an athletic meeting for the purposes of starting races (s. 11(2));
- in charge of a miniature rifle range buying, acquiring or possessing miniature rifles and ammunition, and using them at such a rifle range (s. 11(4));
- who is a member of an approved rifle club, miniature rifle club or pistol club to possess a firearm or ammunition *when engaged as a club member in target practice* (s. 15(1) of the Firearms (Amendment) Act 1988);
- borrowing a shotgun from the occupier of private premises and using it on those premises in the occupier's presence (s. 11(5) of the 1968 Act);
- using a shotgun at a time and place approved by the chief officer of police for shooting at artificial targets (s. 11(6)).

Borrowed rifle on private premises

Section 16 of the Firearms (Amendment) Act 1988 allows a person to borrow a rifle from the occupier of private premises, provided the person is on those premises and in the presence of the occupier (or his/her servant), as long as the occupier holds a certificate and that the borrowing of the rifle complies with that certificate. The person borrowing the rifle may buy or acquire ammunition for it in accordance with the certificate's conditions.

Visitors' permits

Section 17 of the Firearms (Amendment) Act 1988 provides for issuing of a visitors' permit by a chief officer of police and for the possession of firearms and ammunition by the holder of such a permit.

Visitors' permits will not be issued to anyone without a European firearms pass. It is a summary offence (punishable with six months' imprisonment) to make a false statement in order to get a visitors' permit, and it is a similar offence to fail to comply with any conditions within such a permit (see s. 17(10)).

Antiques as ornaments or curiosities

Section 58(2) of the 1968 Act allows for the sale, buying, transfer, acquisition or possession of antique firearms as *curiosities or ornaments*. Whether a firearm is such an antique will be a question of fact to be determined by the court in each case. Mere belief in the fact that a firearm is an antique will not be enough (*R v Howells* [1977] QB 614).

Authorised firearms dealers

Section 8(1) of the 1968 Act provides for registered firearms dealers (or their employees) to possess, acquire or buy firearms or ammunition in the ordinary course of their business without a certificate. If the possession etc. is not in the ordinary course of their business, the exemption will not apply.

Auctioneers, carriers or warehouse staff

Section 9(1) of the 1968 Act allows auctioneers, carriers, warehousemen or their employees to possess firearms and ammunition in the ordinary course of their business without a certificate.

Section 14(1) of the Firearms (Amendment) Act 1988 makes it a summary offence (punishable by six months' imprisonment) for such people to fail to take reasonable precautions for the safe custody of the firearms and ammunition in their possession, or to fail to report the theft of those firearms and ammunition.

Again, if the possession of the firearm or ammunition is in circumstances which do not fall within the ordinary course of their business, the exemption will not apply.

Licensed slaughterers

Section 10 of the 1968 Act allows licensed slaughterers to have in their possession a slaughtering instrument (or ammunition for it) in any slaughterhouse or knackers' yard in which they are employed.

The exemption will only apply to slaughtering instruments and ammunition while in the places specified. If these conditions are not met, the exemption will not apply.

Theatrical performers

Section 12 of the 1968 Act allows people taking part in theatrical performances or films to possess firearms without a certificate, *during, and for the purpose of*, the performance, rehearsal or production. If performers do anything which falls outside this strict definition, they will not be exempt.

Ships or aircraft equipment

Section 13(1) of the 1968 Act provides for the possession of signalling equipment and firearms/ammunition for that purpose when on board ships or at aerodromes, or when removing the equipment from such places.

Section 13(1)(c) provides for the removal of firearms or signalling apparatus from ships, aircraft and aerodromes where authorised by a police permit to do so. The removal to or from such a place must only be done under the authority of police permit and must only be for the purpose specified therein (e.g. to get the firearm or signalling apparatus repaired).

Crown servants

The effect of s. 54(1) of the 1968 Act is to exclude Crown servants from some of the provisions of the Act relating to possession. This general exemption applies to police officers, members of Her Majesty's armed forces (including cadet corps) and visiting forces from other countries. The exemptions are restricted to certain conditions and again only operate where the relevant person is acting in his/her official capacity.

This exemption extends to people employed by a police authority under the direction and control of a chief officer (e.g. civilian crime scene examiners) and also to members of NCIS and the National Crime Squad (**see chapter 1**).

People on service premises may possess a firearm or ammunition if they are supervised by a member of HM armed forces (s. 16A(1) of the Firearms (Amendment) Act 1988). This provision does not include civilian guards who are engaged in the protection of service premises.

Proof houses

Under s. 58(1) of the 1968 Act, members of the Mystery of Gunmakers of the City of London and the guardians of the Birmingham proof house and the Small Heath range at Birmingham have certain statutory duties involving firearms (**see e.g. para. 2.12.4**). They are therefore exempt from those provisions of the Act which interfere with their statutory functions.

Museums Licence

Section 19 of the Firearms (Amendment) Act 1988 provides for people involved in the management of certain museums to hold a museums firearms licence which allows them to possess, buy or acquire firearms and ammunition under certain circumstances.

There are several summary offences involved in the fraudulent application for such licences and the failure to comply with their conditions (see para. 4 to the schedule to the 1988 Act).

2.12.6 Shotgun offences

OFFENCE: **Possessing shotgun without certificate—*Firearms Act 1968, s. 2(1)***
- Triable either way • Sentence: see sch. 6, appendix 5
(Arrestable offence)

The Firearms Act 1968, s. 2 states:

(1) Subject to any exemption under this Act, it is an offence for a person to have in his possession, or to purchase or acquire, a shotgun without holding a certificate under this Act authorising him to possess shotguns.

KEYNOTE

For the definition of 'shotgun', see para. 2.12.4.

The relevant exemptions above will also apply to shotguns.

A shotgun certificate is granted by a chief officer of police under s. 26 of the 1968 Act and will have certain conditions attached to it. A person failing to comply with those conditions commits the following offence.

OFFENCE: **Failing to comply with conditions of shot gun certificate—*Firearms Act 1968, s. 2(2)***
- Triable summarily • Sentence: see sch. 6, appendix 5
(No specific power of arrest)

The Firearms Act 1968, s. 2 states:

(2) It is an offence for a person to fail to comply with a condition subject to which a shot gun certificate is held by him.

2.12.7 Possessing or distributing prohibited weapons or ammunition

OFFENCE: **Possessing or distributing prohibited weapons or ammunition—*Firearms Act 1968, s. 5***
- Triable either way • Sentence: see sch. 6, appendix 5
(Arrestable offence)

The Firearms Act 1968, s. 5 states:

(1) A person commits an offence if, without the authority of the Secretary of State or the Scottish Ministers, he has in his possession, or purchases, or acquires, or manufactures, sells or transfers [a prohibited weapon or ammunition] . . .

KEYNOTE

See para. 2.12.4 for prohibited weapons. For 'possession', see para. 2.12.5.

'Self-loading' and 'pump-action' mean designed or adapted so that the weapon is either automatically reloaded, or is reloaded by manual operation of the fore-end or forestock (s. 57 of the 1968 Act).

Section 5(7) provides guidance in determining whether certain arms and ammunition will fall within the descriptions in s. 5, including the fact that any folding or detachable butt-stock of a firearm will not count when measuring the weapon's overall length.

Exemptions

The first set of exemptions were discussed in relation to the offence under s. 1 (**see para. 2.12.5**); the second and third set are relevant to the offences under s. 5. Those remaining exemptions are:

– European exemptions—exemptions to conform with the European weapons directive.

– Special exemptions.

European Weapons Directive

The European Weapons Directive (91/477/EEC) was brought into effect in order to adjust our domestic legislation in line with the expansion of the European internal market. Its effect is to create certain additional savings and exemptions in relation to the possession of, or some transactions in, specified firearms and ammunition by people who have the relevant certificates or who are recognised as collectors under the law of another country.

To this end, s. 5A of the Firearms Act 1968 provides for a number of occasions where the authority of the Secretary of State will not be required to possess or deal with certain weapons under certain conditions.

The main areas covered by s. 5A are:

– authorised collectors and firearms dealers possessing or being involved in transactions of weapons and ammunition;

– authorised people being involved in transactions of particular ammunition used for lawful shooting and slaughtering of animals, the management of an estate or the protection of other animals and humans.

Section 57(4A) of the Firearms Act 1968 makes other provisions in relation to the European directive as an authority for certain uses of firearms.

Special exemptions

The list of general exemptions to the offences involving firearms under s. 5(1)(aba) focuses largely on people in jobs where they will need to come into contact with firearms mainly in connection with animals or leisure activities.

The exemptions include:

– **Slaughterers**—A slaughterer, if entitled under s. 10 of the 1968 Act (**see para. 2.12.5**), may possess a slaughtering instrument. In addition, persons authorised by certificate to possess, buy, acquire, sell or transfer slaughtering instruments are exempt from the provisions of s. 5 (s. 2 of the Firearms (Amendment) Act 1997). This is the most common exemption.

– **Humane killing of animals**—A person authorised by certificate to possess, buy or acquire a firearm solely for use in connection with the humane killing of animals may possess, buy, acquire, sell or transfer such a firearm (s. 3 of the Firearms (Amendment) Act 1997).

When determining whether a firearm falls within the meaning of a 'humane killer', the definition of a 'slaughtering instrument' under s 57(4) may be referred to (*R v Paul (Benjamin)* (1998) 95(32) LS Gaz 30).

– **Shot pistols for vermin**—A person authorised by certificate to possess, buy or acquire a 'shot pistol' solely for the shooting of vermin, may possess, buy, acquire, sell or transfer such a pistol (s. 41 of the Firearms (Amendment) Act 1997). A 'shot pistol' is a smooth-bored gun chambered for .410 cartridges or 9 mm rim-fire cartridges (s 4(2)).

- **Treatment of animals**—A person authorised by certificate to possess, buy or acquire a firearm for use in connection with the treatment of animals may possess, buy, acquire, sell or transfer any firearm or ammunition designed or adapted for the purpose of tranquillising or treating any animal (s. 8 of the Firearms (Amendment) Act 1997). This exemption also applies to offences involving firearms under s. 5(1)(b) and (c) (**see para. 2.12.4**).

- **Races at athletic meetings**—A person may possess a firearm at an athletic meeting for the purpose of starting races at that meeting (s. 5(1) of the Firearms (Amendment) Act 1997). Similarly, a person authorised by certificate to possess, buy or acquire a firearm solely for the purposes of starting such races may possess, buy, acquire, sell or transfer a firearm for such a purpose (s. 5(2)).

- **Trophies of war**—A person authorised by certificate to do so may possess a firearm which was acquired as a trophy before 1 January 1946 (s. 6 of the Firearms (Amendment) Act 1997).

- **Firearms of historic interest**—Some firearms are felt to be of particular historical, aesthetic or technical interest. Section 7(4) of the Firearms (Amendment) Act 1997 makes detailed provision for the exemption of such firearms, exemptions which exist in addition to the general exemptions under s. 58 of the Firearms Act 1968 (**see para. 2.12.5**). These provisions are set out in the Firearms (Amendment) Act 1997 (Firearms of Historic Interest) Order 1997 (SI 1997 No. 1537) and the Firearms (Amendment) Act 1997 (Transitional Provisions and Savings) Regulations 1997 (SI 1997 No. 1538).

2.12.8 Further offences

Possession with intent to endanger life

OFFENCE: **Possession with Intent to Endanger Life—*Firearms Act 1968, s. 16***
- Triable on indictment • Sentence: see sch. 6, appendix 5
(Serious arrestable offence)

The Firearms Act 1968, s. 16 states:

It is an offence for a person to have in his possession any firearm or ammunition with intent by means thereof to endanger life or cause serious injury to property, or to enable another person by means thereof to endanger life or cause serious injury to property, whether any injury has been caused or not.

KEYNOTE

There is no reference to imitation firearms in the wording of the offence, neither does the 1982 Act apply, therefore this offence cannot be committed by possessing an imitation firearm (**see para. 2.12.4**).

The offence involves 'possession' (**see para. 2.12.5**); there is no need for the firearm to be produced or shown to another.

This is a crime of 'specific intent'. You will have to show an intention by the defendant to behave in a way that he/she knows will in fact endanger the life of another (*R v Brown* [1995] Crim LR 328).

That intent does not have to be an immediate one and it may be conditional (e.g. an intent to shoot someone if they do not do as they are asked) (*R v Bentham* [1973] QB 357).

The life endangered must be the life of 'another', not the defendant's (*R v Norton* [1977] Crim LR 478) but that other person may be outside the UK (*R v El-Hakkoui* [1975] 1 WLR 396).

The firearm must provide the means by which life is endangered; it is not enough to have a firearm at the time when life is endangered by some other means (e.g. by dangerous driving).

There may be occasions where self-defence can be raised in answer to a charge under s. 16 of the 1968 Act but these circumstances will be very unusual (see *R v Georgiades* [1989] 1 WLR 759).

Possession with intent to cause fear of violence

OFFENCE: **Possession with intent to cause fear of violence—*Firearms Act 1968, s. 16A***

> • Triable on indictment • Sentence: see sch. 6, appendix 5
> *(Arrestable offence)*

The Firearms Act 1968, s. 16A (added by Firearms (Amendment) Act 1994, s. 1) states:

> It is an offence for a person to have in his possession any firearm or imitation firearm with intent—
>
> (a) by means thereof to cause, or
>
> (b) to enable another person by means thereof to cause,
>   any person to believe that unlawful violence will be used against him or another person.

KEYNOTE

This offence includes imitation firearms in the general sense (**see para. 2.12.4**).

This is a crime of 'specific intent'.

As with the offence under s. 16, the offence is committed by possession, accompanied by the required intent; there is no need for the firearm to be produced or shown to anyone. The firearm must provide the 'means' for the threat; possession of a firearm while making a general threat to someone who does not know of its presence is unlikely to fall within this section.

Using firearm to resist arrest

OFFENCE: **Using firearm to resist arrest—*Firearms Act 1968, s. 17(1)***

> • Triable on indictment • Sentence: see sch. 6, appendix 5
> *(Serious arrestable offence)*

The Firearms Act 1968, s. 17 states:

> (1) It is an offence for a person to make or attempt to make any use whatsoever of a firearm or imitation firearm with intent to resist or prevent the lawful arrest or detention of himself or another person.

KEYNOTE

If the defendant has the firearm or imitation firearm with them at the time of resisting or preventing an arrest, they commit the offence under s. 18 (**see below**).

The 'firearm' to which s. 17 refers is that defined at **para. 2.12.3**, except component parts and silencers/flash diminishers (s. 17(4)).

This offence includes imitation firearms in the general sense (**see para. 2.12.4**) but not imitation component parts, etc.

This is a crime of 'specific intent'. It requires proof, not of possession, but of evidence that the defendant made some actual use of the firearm and did so intending to resist/prevent the arrest of themselves or someone else. Any arrest which the defendant intended to prevent/resist must have been 'lawful'.

Possessing firearm while committing a schedule 1 offence

OFFENCE: **Possessing firearm while committing or being arrested for schedule 1 Offence—*Firearms Act 1968, s. 17(2)***

> • Triable on indictment • Sentence: see sch. 6, appendix 5
> *(Arrestable offence)*

The Firearms Act 1968, s. 17 states:

> (2) If a person, at the time of his committing or being arrested for an offence specified in schedule 1 to this Act, has in his possession a firearm or imitation firearm, he shall be guilty of an offence under this subsection unless he shows that he had it in his possession for a lawful object.

KEYNOTE

This offence may be committed in two ways; either by being in possession of the weapon at the time of committing the sch. 1 offence or by being in possession of it at the time of being arrested for such an offence. Clearly in the second case, there may be some time between actually committing the sch. 1 offence and being arrested for it.

Nevertheless, if the defendant is in possession of the firearm at the time of his/her arrest, the offence is committed (unless he/she can show that it was for a lawful purpose).

For this offence, you need to prove that the person was in possession of the firearm but not that they actually *had it with them*. This fine but important distinction was recently reviewed by the Court of Appeal where it was reiterated that the two expressions have different meanings throughout the Act, with possession being a deliberately wider concept than the expression 'has with him' (*R v North* [2001] EWCA Crim 544).

There is no need for the defendant to be subsequently convicted of the sch. 1 offence, nor even to prove the elements of it; all that is needed is to show that the defendant, at the time of his/her arrest for a sch. 1 offence, had a firearm/imitation firearm in his/her possession (*R v Nelson (Damien)* [2001] QB 55 CA).

It is for the defendant to prove that the firearm was in his/her possession for a lawful purpose, presumably on the balance of probabilities.

This offence includes imitation firearms in the general sense (**see para. 2.12.4**).

Schedule 1 Offences

The *main* offences listed in sch. 1 are:

– Damage—s. 1 of the Criminal Damage Act 1971.

– Assaults and woundings—ss. 20 and 47 of the Offences Against the Person Act 1861, assault police (s. 89 of the Police Act 1996) and civilian custody officers (s. 90(1) of the Criminal Justice Act 1991 and s. 13(1) of the Criminal Justice and Public Order Act 1994).

– Rape and 'taking out of possession'—ss. 1, 17, 18 and 20 of the Sexual Offences Act 1956. Part I of the Child Abduction Act 1984.

– Theft, robbery, burglary, blackmail and taking a conveyance—Theft Act 1968.

(D.A.R.T.)

Although covering several types of assault, sch. 1 does not extend to wounding/causing grievous bodily harm with intent. Schedule 1 also covers the aiding, abetting or attempting to commit such offences.

Trespassing with firearms

OFFENCE: **Trespassing with firearm in building—*Firearms Act 1968, s. 20(1)***

> • Triable either way (unless imitation firearm or air weapon) • Sentence: see sch. 6, appendix 5
> *(Arrestable offence unless imitation firearm or air weapon)*

The Firearms Act 1968, s. 20 states:

(1) A person commits an offence if, while he has a firearm or imitation firearm with him, he enters or is in any building or part of a building as a trespasser and without reasonable excuse (the proof whereof lies on him).

KEYNOTE

This offence includes a specific reference to imitation firearms (see para. 2.12.4).

If the relevant firearm is an imitation or an air weapon, the offence is triable summarily.

This offence can be committed either by entering a building/part of a building or simply by being in such a place, in each case as a trespasser while having the firearm. As there is no need for the defendant to have 'entered' the building as a trespasser in every case, the offence might be committed after the occupier has withdrawn any permission for the defendant to be there. (Contrast the offence of trespassing with a weapon of offence.)

For a discussion of the elements of entering a building/part of a building as a trespasser.

For the interpretation of 'has with him', see below.

It will be for the defendant to prove that he/she had reasonable excuse and the standard of that proof will be judged against the balance of probabilities.

The power of entry and search under s. 47 of the 1968 Act applies to this offence (see para. 2.12.10).

OFFENCE: **Trespassing with firearm on land—*Firearms Act 1968, s. 20(2)***

- Triable summarily Sentence: see sch. 6, appendix 5
(No specific power of arrest)

The Firearms Act 1968, s. 20 states:

(2) A person commits an offence if, while he has a firearm or imitation firearm with him, he enters or is on any land as a trespasser and without reasonable excuse (the proof whereof lies on him).

KEYNOTE

The elements of this offence are generally the same as those for the s. 20(1) offence above.

As with the s. 20(1) offence, there is no requirement that the defendant had the firearm/imitation firearm with him/her when entering onto the land (compare with the offence of aggravated burglary under the Theft Act 1968).

'Land' for these purposes will include land covered by water (s. 20(3)).

Although this section does not have a specific power of arrest, there is a power of arrest for a police officer in uniform in relation to a person reasonably suspected of trespassing with a weapon of offence which may be appropriate.

Having firearm with intent to commit indictable offence or resist arrest

OFFENCE: **Having firearm with intent to commit an indictable offence or resist arrest—*Firearms Act 1968, s. 18(1)***

- Triable on indictment • Sentence: see sch. 6, appendix 5
(Serious arrestable offence)

The Firearms Act 1968, s. 18 states:

(1) It is an offence for a person to have with him a firearm or imitation firearm with intent to commit an indictable offence, or to resist arrest or prevent the arrest of another, in either case while he has a firearm or imitation firearm with him.

KEYNOTE

This offence, which overlaps with that under s. 17(1) (**see above**), requires the defendant to have the firearm 'with him'. This is a more restrictive expression than 'possession' (as to which, **see para. 2.12.5**), and requires that the firearm is 'readily accessible' to the defendant (e.g. in a car nearby) (*R v Pawlicki* [1992] 1 WLR 827).

Despite this narrower meaning, the defendant does not have to be shown to have been 'carrying' the firearm (*R v Kelt* [1977] 1 WLR 1365), a decision which now conflicts with the situation relating to identical statutory expressions under the Theft Act 1968 and also under the legislation relating to weapons.

This is a crime of 'specific intent' and, in proving that intent, s. 18(2) states:

> (2) In proceedings for an offence under this section proof that the accused had a firearm or imitation firearm with him and intended to commit an offence, or to resist or prevent arrest, is evidence that he intended to have it with him while doing so.

It is not necessary to show that the defendant intended to use the firearm to commit the indictable offence or to prevent/resist the arrest (*R v Duhaney* (1998) 2 Cr App R 25). (Contrast the offence under s. 17(1); see above.)

An indictable offence includes an offence triable either way (Interpretation Act 1978).

Section 18 does not appear to require that any arrest be 'lawful' and it may be that Parliament intended for this offence to be broader in that respect than the offence under s. 17.

This offence includes imitation firearms in the general sense (**see para. 2.12.4**).

The power of entry and search under s. 47 of the 1968 Act applies to this offence (**see para. 2.12.10**).

Having loaded firearm in public place

OFFENCE: **Having loaded firearm in public place—*Firearms Act 1968, s. 19***
- Triable either way • Sentence: see sch. 6, appendix 5
(Arrestable offence unless air weapon)

The Firearms Act 1968, s. 19 states:

> A person commits an offence if, without lawful authority or reasonable excuse (the proof whereof lies on him), he has with him in a public place a loaded shot gun or loaded air weapon, or any other firearm (whether loaded or not) together with ammunition suitable for use in that firearm.

KEYNOTE

'Public place' includes any highway and any other premises or place to which the public have access at the material time, or to which the public are permitted access at the material time whether on payment or otherwise (see s. 57(4) of the 1968 Act).

'Loaded' here means if there is ammunition in the chamber or barrel (or in any magazine or other device) whereby the ammunition can be fed into the chamber or barrel by the manual or automatic operation of some part of the weapon (see s. 57(6)(b)).

If the weapon is a firearm other than an air weapon or a shotgun, the offence is committed by having suitable ammunition with it; there is no requirement for it to be loaded.

If the weapon is an air weapon the offence is only triable summarily.

The Firearms Act 1982 does not apply here, neither is there any mention of imitation firearms in the wording of the section. Therefore, the offence does not apply to imitation firearms.

For the meaning of 'has with him', **see above**.

This offence is an 'absolute' offence like s. 1 (**see para. 2.12.5**). Therefore, if you can show that the defendant (X) knew he had something with him and that the 'something' was a loaded shotgun/air weapon (or other firearm with ammunition), the offence is complete (*R v Vann* [1996] Crim LR 52).

It is for the defendant to show lawful authority or reasonable excuse; possession of a valid certificate does not of itself provide lawful authority for having the firearm/ ammunition in a public place (*Ross v Collins* [1982] Crim LR 368).

2.12.9 **Possession or acquisition of firearms by certain people**

Sections 21 to 24 of the Firearms Act 1968 place further restrictions on the people who can possess, acquire, receive or otherwise have involvement with firearms. Section 21 deals with people who have been convicted of certain offences while ss. 22 to 24 set out minimum ages in respect of certain firearms and transactions.

Section 21 generally provides that any person who has been sentenced to:

– custody for life, or

– to preventive detention, imprisonment, corrective training, youth custody or detention in a young offender institution for three years or more

must not, *at any time*, have a firearm or ammunition in his/her possession.

Section 21 goes on to provide that any person who has been sentenced to imprisonment, youth custody detention in a young offender institution or a secure training order for three months or more, *but less than three years*, must not have a firearm or ammunition in his/her possession at any time before the end of a five-year period beginning on the date of his/her release.

Date of release means, for a sentence partly served and partly suspended, the date on which the offender completes the part to be served and, in the case of a person subject to a secure training order, the date on which he/she is released from detention (under the various relevant statutes) or the date halfway through the total specified by the court making the order, whichever is the latest (s. 21(2A)).

A person holding a licence under the Children and Young Persons Act 1933 or a person subject to a recognisance to keep the peace or be of good behaviour with a condition relating to the possession of firearms, must not, *at any time during the licence or the recognisance*, have a firearm or ammunition in his/her possession (s. 21(3)).

Where sentences or court orders are mentioned, their Scottish equivalents will also apply and a person prohibited in Northern Ireland from possessing a firearm/ammunition will also be prohibited in Great Britain (s. 21(3A)).

Section 21 does not apply to imitation firearms as there is no express reference to them in the section and because the reference in the Firearms Act 1982 does not apply (**see para. 2.12.4**).

If the person who has been sentenced as set out in s. 21 contravenes the provisions above (e.g. by possessing etc. any firearm), he/she commits an either way offence punishable with a maximum of five years' imprisonment (thereby making it an arrestable offence).

Supplying firearm to person prohibited by section 21

OFFENCE: **Selling or transferring firearm to person prohibited by section 21—*Firearms Act 1968, s. 21(5)***

> • Triable either way • Sentence: sch. 6, appendix 5
> *(Arrestable offence)*

The Firearms Act 1968, s. 21 states:

(5) It is an offence for a person to sell or transfer a firearm or ammunition to, or to repair, test or prove a firearm or ammunition for, a person whom he knows or has reasonable ground for believing to be prohibited by this section from having a firearm or ammunition in his possession.

KEYNOTE

Given that all people are presumed to know the law once it is published, it would seem that the knowledge or belief by the defendant would apply to the convictions of the other person, not the fact that possession by that person was an offence.

What you must show is knowledge by the defendant or at least reasonable ground for believing; this latter requirement is stronger than mere cause to suspect.

Other restrictions on possession or acquisition

In addition to the general provisions relating to possession, acquisition etc., ss. 22 to 24 create a number of summary offences restricting the involvement of people of various ages in their dealings with firearms and ammunition. The table opposite provides a brief summary of some of those provisions. For the full extent of these restrictions and their exemptions, reference should be made to the 1968 Act.

It is a summary offence (punishable by one month's imprisonment and/or a fine) to be in possession of any loaded firearm when drunk (s. 12 of the Licensing Act 1872). There is no requirement that the person be in a public place. This offence carries a power of arrest in relation to any person found committing it. Given the decisions in other cases where similar powers of arrest remain applicable, that power would appear to be available to police officers.

2.12.10 **Police powers**

Section 47 of the Firearms Act 1968 states:

(1) A constable may require any person whom he has reasonable cause to suspect—
    (a) of having a firearm, with or without ammunition, with him in a public place; or
    (b) to be committing or about to commit, elsewhere than in a public place, an offence relevant for the purposes of this section,
to hand over the firearm or any ammunition for examination by the constable.

KEYNOTE

This power has two distinct elements. The first applies where the officer has reasonable cause to suspect that a person has a firearm with him/her in a public place. The second relates to a situation where the officer has reasonable cause to suspect that the person is committing or is about to commit an offence relevant to this section anywhere else.

An 'offence relevant to this section' appears to be an offence under s. 18(1) and s. 20 (see s. 47(6)).

It is a summary offence to fail to hand over a firearm when required under this section (s. 47(2)).

In order to exercise this power, a police officer may search the person and may detain him/her for that purpose (s. 47(3)). The officer may also enter *any place* (s. 47(4)).

If the officer has reasonable cause to suspect that:

— there is a firearm in a vehicle in a public place, or

— that a vehicle is being/about to be used in connection with the commission of an 'offence relevant to this section' (see above),

he/she may search the vehicle and, for that purpose, may require the person driving or in control of the vehicle to stop it (s. 47(4)).

The provisions of the PACE Codes of Practice, Code A, will apply to the exercise of these powers of stop and search.

Age	Restrictions	Applies to imitation?
Under 14 years	Having with them air weapon or ammunition for one (s. 22(4) subject to exception*†).	No
	Possessing any s. 1 firearm or ammunition without lawful authority (except as permitted or sports and shooting clubs etc.).	Yes
	Giving or lending s. 1 firearm or ammunition or parting with possession to such a person except as permitted (for sports and shooting clubs etc.) (s. 24(2)).	Yes
	Giving or parting with possession of air weapon to such a person (unless under permitted circumstances*) (s. 24(4)).	Yes
Under 15 years	Having with them assembled shotgun unless supervised by person aged at least 21 or while shotgun is securely covered (s. 22(3)).	No
	Giving shotgun or ammunition for one to such a person (s. 24(3)).	No
	Under 17 years Buying or hiring any firearm or ammunition (s. 22(1)).	No
	Having with them air weapon in public place except airgun or air rifle, in each case securely covered† (s. 22(5)).	No
	Selling or letting on hire to such a person any firearm or ammunition (s. 24(1)).	No
Under 18 years	Holder of certificate using firearm for purpose not authorised by European Weapons Directive (s. 22(1A)).	No

* Section 23 provides that no offence is committed if the person is under the supervision of another who is at least 21 years old. The person under 14 must not use the air weapon for firing missiles beyond the relevant premises and the supervising person must not allow the air weapon to be so used.

† Section 23 goes on to provide that no offence is committed where a person who is a member of an approved rifle club (or miniature rifle club) has with them an air weapon or ammunition while engaged in target shooting as such, nor where he/she is using the weapon at a shooting gallery where the air weapons or miniature rifles being used do not exceed .23 inch calibre.

Note that s. 24 makes a number of defences where the person giving, lending etc. is mistaken about the true age of the other person concerned.

Section 48 states:

(1) A constable may demand, from any person whom he believes to be in possession of a firearm or ammunition to which section 1 of this Act applies, or of a shot gun, the production of his firearm certificate or, as the case may be, his shot gun certificate.

KEYNOTE

The demand for the relevant documentation may be made where the police officer 'believes' that a person is in possession of a section 1 firearm or ammunition or a shotgun. There is no requirement that the officer's belief be reasonable.

Where the person fails to:

– produce the relevant certificate or

– show that he/she is not entitled to be issued with such a certificate or

– show that he/she is in possession of the firearm exclusively in connection with recognised purposes (collecting/historical/cultural) under the law of another EU member State

the officer may demand the production of the relevant valid documentation issued in another member State under any corresponding provisions (s. 48(1A)).

Failing to produce any of the required documents and to let the officer read it, or failing to show an entitlement to possess the firearm or ammunition triggers (!) the power of seizure under s. 48(2). It also gives the officer the power to demand the person's name and address. This requirement is similar to the provision under s. 170 of the Road Traffic Act 1988 (duty to give details after an accident) where it has been held that the name and address of the person's solicitor would suffice (*DPP v McCarthy* [1999] RTR 323). That decision was based on the purpose behind the Road Traffic Act requirement, namely to allow the respective parties to the accident to get in touch with each other in the future. It is suggested that the purpose of the Firearms Act power is a very different one of regulating the possession of weapons and that the furnishing of details of some convenient administrative location for correspondence would not be enough to satisfy the requirements of this section.

If the person refuses to give his/her name or address or gives a false name and address, he/she commits a summary offence (s. 48(3)).

A person from another Member State who is in possession of a firearm and who fails to comply with a demand under s. 48(1A) also commits a separate summary offence (s. 48(4)).

2.12.11   **Shortening and conversion of firearms**

OFFENCE: **Shortening barrel of shotgun to less than 24 inches—*Firearms Act 1968, s. 4(1)***

- Triable either way • Sentence: see sch. 6, appendix 5

(Arrestable offence)

The Firearms Act 1968, s. 4 states:

(1)   Subject to this section, it is an offence to shorten the barrel of a shot gun to a length less than 24 inches.

OFFENCE: **Shortening barrel of other smooth-bore section 1 firearm to less than 24 inches—*Firearms (Amendment) Act 1988 s. 6(1)***

- Triable either way • Five years' imprisonment and/or a fine on indictment; six months' imprisonment and/or a fine summarily

(Arrestable offence)

The Firearms (Amendment) Act 1988, s. 6 states:

(1)   Subject to subsection (2) below, it is an offence to shorten to a length less than 24 inches the barrel of any smooth-bore gun to which section 1 of the principal Act applies other than one which has a barrel with a bore exceeding 2 inches in diameter; . . .

OFFENCE: **Converting imitation firearm—*Firearms Act 1968, s. 4(3)***

- Triable either way • Sentence: see sch. 6, appendix 5

(Arrestable offence)

The Firearms Act 1968, s. 4 states:

(3)   It is an offence for a person other than a registered firearms dealer to convert into a firearm anything which, though having the appearance of being a firearm, is so constructed as to be incapable of discharging any missile through its barrel.

KEYNOTE

The relevant definitions are considered at **para. 2.12.4**.

The first two offences are concerned with the shortening of barrels while the third involves conversion of anything which has the appearance of a firearm so that it can be fired. Registered firearms dealers (**see para. 2.12.5**) are excluded from the wording of the conversion offence. They are also exempted by ss. 4(2) and 6(2) from the relevant offences involving shortening barrels provided the shortening is done for the sole purpose of replacing a defective part of the barrel *so as to produce a new barrel having an overall length of at least 24 inches.*

The length of the barrel of a weapon will be measured from its muzzle to the point at which the charge is exploded (s. 57(6)(a) of the 1968 Act).

Once the shortening or conversion has taken place, the nature of the firearm will have changed (e.g. from a shotgun into a section 1 firearm or from an imitation into a real firearm), in which case the person will also commit the relevant possession offences unless he/she has the appropriate authorisation.

2.12.12   **Restrictions on transfer of firearms**

The Firearms (Amendment) Act 1997 created a number of offences concerned with the transfer, lending, hiring etc. of firearms and ammunition.

In brief, a person 'transferring' (that is, selling, letting on hire, lending or giving) a section 1 firearm or ammunition to another must:

– produce a certificate or permit entitling him/her to do so (s. 32(2)(a)),

– he/she must comply with all the conditions of that certificate or permit (s. 32(2)(b)), and

– the transferor must personally hand the firearm or ammunition over to the receiver (s. 32(2)(c)).

The 1997 Act also requires any person who is the holder of a certificate or permit who is involved in such a transfer (which includes a lending of the firearm/ammunition for a period exceeding 72 hours) to give notice to the chief officer of police who granted the certificate or permit (s. 33(2)).

Notice is also required of certificate or permit holders where a firearm is lost, de-activated or destroyed or where ammunition is lost, or where firearms are sold outside Great Britain (see ss. 34 and 35).

OFFENCE: **Failing to comply with requirements—*Firearms (Amendment) Act 1997, ss. 32–35***

- Section 1 firearm/ammunition: triable either way • Five years' imprisonment and/or fine on indictment; six months' imprisonment and/or fine summarily

(Arrestable offence)

- Shotguns: triable summarily • Six months' imprisonment and/or a fine

(No specific power of arrest)

OFFENCE: **Trade transactions by person not registered as firearms dealer— *Firearms Act 1968, s. 3(1)***

- Triable either way • Sentence: see sch. 6, appendix 5

(Arrestable offence)

The Firearms Act 1968, s. 3 states:

(1) A person commits an offence if, by way of trade or business, he—

     (a) manufactures, sells, transfers, repairs, tests or proves any firearm or ammunition to which section 1 of this Act applies, or a shot gun; or

     (b) exposes for sale or transfer, or has in his possession for sale, transfer, repair, test or proof any such firearm or ammunition, or a shot gun,

     without being registered under this Act as a firearms dealer.

KEYNOTE

The various definitions are considered above. A registered firearms dealer is a person who, by way of trade or business, manufactures, sells, transfers, repairs, tests or proofs firearms or ammunition to which s. 1 applies, or shotguns (s. 57(4) of the 1968 Act).

If the person undertakes the repair, proofing etc. of a s. 1 firearm or ammunition or a shotgun otherwise than as a trade or business, he/she commits an offence (carrying the same punishment as the s. 3(1) offence above) under s. 3(3) unless he/she can point to some authorisation under the Act allowing him/her to do so.

Section 3 goes on to create further either way offences of selling or transferring a firearm or ammunition to someone other than a registered firearms dealer or someone otherwise authorised under the Act to buy or acquire them and of falsifying certificates with a view to acquiring firearms. These offences also carry the same punishment as the s. 3(1) offence above.

Registration is under s. 33 of the 1968 Act.

'Transferring' is also defined under s. 57(4) and includes letting on hire, giving, lending and parting with possession.

Section 9(2) of the 1968 Act exempts auctioneers from the restrictions on selling and possessing for the purposes of sale of firearms and ammunition where the auctioneer has a permit from the chief officer of police. There are further defences provided by s. 9 (for carriers and warehouse staff) and also under s. 8 (transfer to people authorised to possess firearms without certificate).

2.12.13   Other offences under the Firearms (Amendment) Act 1988

There are two offences under the Firearms (Amendment) Act 1988 introduced to ensure compliance with the European Weapons Directive; ss. 18(6) and 18A(6). Both are summary offences punishable with three months' imprisonment and/or a fine.

Other summary offences under the 1968 Act include:

– A firearms dealer failing to send the required notification within 48 hours to the chief officer of police, after selling a firearm or shotgun (s. 18(5)).

– The transferor of a shotgun to another failing to notify police of the details of that transfer as required by s. 4 (s. 4(5)).

– Selling certain ammunition to a person who is not a registered firearms dealer and is not permitted to have the relevant weapon for the ammunition (s. 5(2)).

– A pawnbroker taking a s. 1 firearm or ammunition as a pawn (s. 3(6)).

– Any person selling or transferring any firearm or ammunition or carrying out repairs or tests on such for another person who is drunk or of unsound mind (s. 25).

2.12.14   Documentation

The enforcement of the firearms legislation depends heavily on the possession and production of the relevant documents and ss. 30A to 30D of the Firearms Act 1968 allow for the revocation or partial revocation of certificates by chief officers of police. There are, therefore, many offences which deal with the application for and obtaining of documents, the falsification of records and documents and the failure to maintain proper records. The offences under the Firearms Act 1968 are under ss. 26(5), 29(3), 30(4), 38(8), 39(1) to (3), 40(5) and 52(2)(c); see sch. 6.

There is also an offence under s. 12(2) of the Firearms (Amendment) Act 1988 of failing to comply with a notice from the chief officer of police for the surrender of a certificate. This is a summary offence punishable with three months' imprisonment and/or a fine.

There are further summary offences which were created to ensure compliance with the European Weapons Directive (see, ss. 32B(5), 32C(6), 42A(3) and 48A(4) of the Firearms Act 1968).

PART THREE

Sexual Offences

3.1   Sexual Offences

3.1.1   Introduction

Sexual offences represent a particularly important area of criminal law for two main reasons: the sensitivity required in their investigation and prosecution and their potential effect on the victim.

Many legal textbooks include sexual offences alongside other 'non-fatal offences against the person'. However, such offences can cause significant emotional harm to the victim, harm which may take far longer to 'heal' than many physical injuries. Most of this area of criminal law is contained in statute and there are many, sometimes overlapping, offences.

A further factor affecting this area of criminal law is the relevance of the European Convention on Human Rights. It is clear that sexual activities are aspects of a person's 'private life' as protected by Article 8 of the Convention (see *Dudgeon* v *United Kingdom* (1981) 4 EHRR 149 and *ADT* v *United Kingdom* [2000] Crim LR 1009). It is also clear that this applies to homosexual relationships as well as heterosexual ones (*X* v *United Kingdom* (1997) 24 EHRR 143).

As such, any attempt by the criminal law to place restrictions on the consensual sexual activities of individuals will have to be considered very carefully in light of the Human Rights Act 1998. Indeed some changes to primary legislation in this area have already been made in response to the 1998 Act.

3.2   Anonymity

Under the Sexual Offences (Amendment) Acts 1976 and 1992, victims of most sexual offences (including rape, incest, buggery and indecency with children) are entitled to anonymity throughout their lifetime. This means that there are restrictions on the way in which trials and cases may be reported and the courts have powers to enforce these provisions. This area has been the subject of many campaigns for legal reform over the last 20 years. Further protection preventing victims from cross-examination by their alleged attackers is provided by the Youth Justice and Criminal Evidence Act 1999.

3.3   Rape

OFFENCE: **Rape—*Sexual Offences Act 1956, s. 1***
> • Triable on indictment • Life imprisonment
> *(Serious arrestable offence)*

The Sexual Offences Act 1956, s. 1 states:

(1) It is an offence for a man to rape a woman or another man.

(2) A man commits rape if—
   (a) he has sexual intercourse with a person (whether vaginal or anal) who at the time of the intercourse does not consent to it; and
   (b) at the time he knows that the person does not consent to the intercourse or is reckless as to whether that person consents to it.

(3) A man also commits rape if he induces a married woman to have sexual intercourse with him by impersonating her husband.

KEYNOTE

Until 1994 the offence of rape could only be committed by a man against a woman. Section 142 of the Criminal Justice and Public Order Act 1994 amended the s. 1 offence to include male victims. A further amendment to the law relating to sexual offences was brought about by the Sexual Offences Act 1993, s. 1 which abolished the presumption that a male under the age of 14 was incapable of sexual intercourse.

In July 2002, the Crown Prosecution Service, Home Office and Court Service issued a plan for the implementation of the many recommendations contained in the joint investigation into rape enquiries and prosecutions conducted by Her Majesty's Inspector of Constabulary and Her Majesty's Crown Prosecution Inspectorate.

3.3.1 Criminal Conduct

To prove rape you must show that the defendant had 'sexual intercourse' with the victim. Sexual intercourse will include any degree of penetration either of the anus or the vagina. It is not necessary to prove the completion of the intercourse 'by emission of seed' (ejaculation) (Sexual Offences Act 1956, s. 44). However, the presence of semen is clearly important in proving the elements of a sexual offence, as is other scientific evidence recovered from the victim, the offender and the scene etc.

Oral sex will not amount to 'sexual intercourse' (*R* v *Gaston* (1981) 73 Cr App R 164) but it can amount to indecent assault (**see 3.5**). Wives are now protected by the offence of rape since the case of *R* v *R* [1992] 1 AC 599, where the House of Lords made it clear that a husband can be convicted of raping his wife even if he is still living with her and has not begun separation or divorce proceedings. In *SW* v *United Kingdom* (1995) 21 EHRR 363, a defendant tried to argue that this change in the common law, which had previously not extended the offence of rape to wives, amounted to a violation of Article 7 of the European Convention on Human Rights. Article 7 prohibits the imposition of punishment without a clear criminal offence being in existence at the time of the defendant's act. In the *SW* case, the Court held that the extension of the law in this area had been sufficiently foreseeable to meet the requirements of Article 7.

A husband can also be guilty of assisting others to rape his wife (*R* v *Cogan* [1976] QB 217), a decision that is only really of historical relevance given the extension of the law by *R* v *R*.

3.3.2 Consent

The issue of consent is a question of fact and is critical to proving the offence of rape. It is also potentially the most difficult aspect of the offence to prove. Whereas the act of intercourse or physical intimacy may be proved or corroborated by forensic evidence, the true wishes of the victim at the time of the offence are much more difficult to prove beyond a reasonable doubt. Any consent given must be 'true' consent, not simply a *submission* induced by fear or fraud. Some people however are not capable of giving the required consent. Someone who has a mental disability may be incapable of providing true consent as might someone who is too drunk to exercise rational judgment (*R* v *Lang* (1975) 62 Cr App R 50) or someone who is asleep (*R* v *Mayers* (1872) 12 Cox CC 311).

There is no requirement that the complainant demonstrate or communicate a lack of consent to the defendant and earlier cases to the contrary need not be followed (*R* v *Malone (Thomas Patrick)* (1998) 2 Cr App R 447). What is required is evidence that the victim did not consent at the time and such evidence might include (as in Malone's case) the fact that the victim was too drunk or insensible to give consent or to understand what was going on.

Even if consent is freely given, it may still be withdrawn at any time. Once the 'passive' party to sexual penetration withdraws consent, any continued penetration can amount to rape (*R v Cooper* [1994] Crim LR 531). 'Consent' obtained by impersonating the victim's partner or by procuration will not be true consent (see Sexual Offences Act 1956, s. 1(3) and ss. 2 and 3 (see below)). Neither will consent to sexual penetration be valid when the act itself is misrepresented (see *R v Williams* [1923] 1 KB 340, where a teacher told the victim that sexual intercourse was a technique to improve her singing voice). If, however, it is not the act that is misrepresented but the *intentions* or *attributes* of the person seeking consent (such as a hollow promise to marry the victim afterwards or a pretence that the victim will be paid (*Papadimitropoulos* v *The Queen* (1957) 98 CLR 249)), the consent so obtained will be valid as it amounts to a sexual consensus. Inducing another into an act of prostitution with no intent of paying will not invalidate 'consent' as to the act of sexual intercourse and therefore will not amount to rape (*R v Linekar* [1995] QB 250).

In *Linekar*, the Court of Appeal also considered the situation of impersonating another person in order to have sexual intercourse. In addition to the statutory provision at s. 1(3) above (impersonating the husband), Morland J held that the common law extended the offence of rape to occasions where the defendant impersonated *any* man to whom the victim was ostensibly giving consent. In the court's view, if the victim's consent extended only to a particular individual and the person with whom she had sexual intercourse was in fact an entirely different person, the element of true consent was missing and the offence of rape would be complete. On this basis, the impersonation of any partner or lover which fools the victim into having sexual intercourse will amount to rape. In these cases it is the *identity of the person to whom consent is granted* that is disguised. This is very different from those cases where the *act of intercourse* is disguised or the later intentions of the defendant (e.g. to pay the victim).

3.3.3 State of Mind

The *mens rea* required for this offence is:

- knowledge that the other person does not consent at the time, or

- recklessness as to whether he/she consents or not.

If a defendant knows that the other person might not be consenting at the time but goes on to have intercourse anyway, that behaviour may amount to 'recklessness' (*R v S (Satnam)* (1983) 78 Cr App R 149). In a rape trial the prosecution does not have to choose whether they are proceeding on the basis of the 'knowing' or 'reckless' elements of the required *mens rea* (*R v Flitter* [2001] Crim LR 328).

The Sexual Offences (Amendment) Act 1976, s. 1 states:

(2) It is hereby declared that if at a trial for a rape offence the jury has to consider whether a man believed that a woman or man was consenting to sexual intercourse, the presence or absence of reasonable grounds for such a belief is a matter to which the jury is to have regard, in conjunction with any other relevant matters, in considering whether he so believed.

Whether a defendant *believed* that the victim was consenting is, therefore, a matter for a jury to decide and the presence or absence of *reasonable grounds* for such a belief will be just one relevant matter to consider in making that decision. An honestly held mistake as to the other person's consent, even if unreasonable, will prevent a conviction for rape.

If it can be shown that the defendant did not in fact believe that the other person was consenting, that absence of belief will amount to recklessness (*R v Gardiner* [1994] Crim LR 455).

Where a defendant is inebriated and, as a result, mistakenly believes that the other person is consenting to sexual intercourse, he cannot rely on that mistake as a defence (*R v Fotheringham* (1988) 88 Cr App R 206).

3.4 Buggery

OFFENCE: **Buggery—*Sexual Offences Act 1956, s. 12***

- Triable on indictment • When committed with person under 16 or an animal (life imprisonment)

  (Serious arrestable offence if person under 16)

- Where the defendant is 21 or over and the other person is under 18 (five years' imprisonment)

  (Arrestable offence)

- Otherwise (two years' imprisonment)

The Sexual Offences Act 1956, s. 12 states:

(1) It is [an offence] for a person to commit buggery with another person otherwise than in circumstances described in subsection (1A) or (1AA) below or with an animal.

(1A) The circumstances first referred to in subsection (1) are that the act of buggery takes place in private and both parties have attained the age of sixteen.

(1AA) The other circumstances so referred to are that the person is under the age of sixteen and the other party has attained that age.

(1B) An act of buggery by one man with another shall not be treated as taking place in private if it takes place—
   (a) when more than two persons take part or are present; or
   (b) in a lavatory to which the public have or are permitted to have access, whether on payment or otherwise.

(1C) In any proceedings against a person for buggery with another person it shall be for the prosecutor to prove that the act of buggery took place otherwise than in private or that one of the parties to it had not attained the age of sixteen.

KEYNOTE

Buggery amounts to anal intercourse with a male, female or animal. It also includes anal *or vaginal* intercourse by a male or female with an animal (e.g. a sheep (see *R v Cozins* (1834) 6 C & P 351)).

To prove buggery you must show evidence of penetration to some degree.

The differences in age limits for lawful consensual sexual activity have been successfully challenged as a violation by the state of an individual's right to private life (Article 8 of the European Convention on Human Rights) and freedom from discrimination (Article 14 of the Convention) on several occasions. The European Commission of Human Rights has held that such age differences *did* amount to a violation of those rights (*Sutherland v United Kingdom* [1998] EHRLR 117). As a result, the government has introduced the Sexual Offences (Amendment) Act 2000. The legislation, some of the most controversial in recent criminal law, created considerable disagreement between the House of Commons and the House of Lords. Nevertheless, the 2000 Act received Royal Assent, reducing the minimum age at which a person, whether male or female, may lawfully consent to buggery from 18 years to 16 years (in England and Wales) as of 8 January 2001, thereby equalising the age of consent for sexual activity whether it be heterosexual or homosexual.

Despite the controversial nature of this legislation, it still fails address some of the issues raised, both by the courts (see *ADT v United Kingdom* [2000] Crim LR 1009) and the Home Office (see *Setting the Boundaries*, July 2000)—principally the issue of privacy. Although the 1956 Act has been amended in relation to the respective *ages* of those involved in buggery and 'gross indecency' (**see** 3.9), there are still restrictions on how many people might be involved at any one time in order for the relevant behaviour between men to be regarded as taking place *in private*—restrictions which do not apply to other types of heterosexual activity. In light of the judgment in *ADT* (above), it will be difficult to defend the fact that acts of buggery/gross indecency involving the participation or even the presence of more than two people are still outlawed. Arguably the imposition of the privacy requirement (see below) still amounts to an unjustifiable interference with an individual's right to respect for private life (under Article 8). Nevertheless, the effect of the new legislation is that consensual buggery between males aged 16 or over, when carried out in private, is not an offence (see the Sexual Offences Act 1967, s. 1). Although s. 12 sets out the—fairly common—occasions when such an act will be deemed not to be in private, other occasions will be a question of fact for the jury/magistrate(s) to decide in the light of all the circumstances. It is worth noting that age is only one of the matters that potentially prevent this type of sexual activity from being an offence; privacy and consent are also key elements.

Where one of the parties to an offence of buggery is under 16 years of age, that person does not commit the offence themselves. This provision reflects the view that, in cases where older men are sexually exploiting minors, it is more appropriate to regard the minors as 'victims' of the adult offender rather than criminalising the behaviour of both. If both parties are under 16, however, that element of exploitation is less likely to be present and both commit the offence.

Anyone suffering from a severe mental handicap is unable to give consent to buggery and buggery without consent amounts to rape (see above).

Other 'homosexual' acts which are carried out in private (i.e. not more than two people present or not in public lavatory) are made lawful provided they are consensual and the parties have reached the age of 16 (Sexual Offences Act 1967, s. 1). 'Homosexual' act is defined at s. 1(7) as being buggery or gross indecency *between men*. For gross indecency, **see** 3.9.

A mistaken belief as to the age of the other person, however reasonable, is no defence.

In any proceedings involving an offence of buggery, the burden of proving the elements of privacy, consent and age falls on the prosecution.

The consent of the Director of Public Prosecutions is required before bringing a prosecution for this offence.

OFFENCE: **Assault with Intent to Commit Buggery—*Sexual Offences Act 1956, s. 16***
  • Triable on indictment • Ten years' imprisonment
  (Arrestable offence)

The Sexual Offences Act 1956, s. 16 states:

It is an offence for a person to assault another person with intent to commit buggery.

KEYNOTE

This is a crime of *specific intent*. As buggery without consent is rape (**see** 3.3), there may be an offence of attempted rape in such circumstances, provided the defendant's actions go beyond mere preparation to commit the substantive offence.

OFFENCE: **Procuring Another to Commit Buggery—*Sexual Offences Act 1967, s. 4***
  • Triable on indictment • Two years' imprisonment
  (No specific power of arrest)

The Sexual Offences Act 1967, s. 4 states:

(1) A man who procures another man to commit with a third man an act of buggery which by reason of section 1 of this Act is not an offence shall be liable [for an offence].

KEYNOTE

Under s. 4(1), the procuration of a man to commit buggery with a third man will amount to an offence even though the intended act of buggery itself is not an offence. This is in contrast with the situation where gross indecency is involved.

3.5 Indecent Assault

OFFENCE: **Indecent Assault—*Sexual Offences Act 1956, ss. 14 and 15***

> • Triable either way • Ten years' imprisonment on indictment; six months' imprisonment and/or fine summarily
> *(Serious arrestable offence where act involves gross indecency; otherwise arrestable offence)*

The Sexual Offences Act 1956, ss. 14 and 15 state:

14.—(1) It is an offence, ... for a person to make an indecent assault on a woman.

(2) A girl under the age of sixteen cannot in law give any consent which would prevent an act being an assault for the purposes of this section.

15.—(1) It is an offence for a person to make an indecent assault on a man.

(2) A boy under the age of sixteen cannot in law give any consent which would prevent an act being an assault for the purposes of this section.

KEYNOTE

Indecent assault is simply an assault committed in circumstances of indecency. For there to be an indecent assault there must be an *assault*. In the well-known case of *Fairclough v Whipp* [1951] 2 All ER 834 the defendant invited a child to touch his penis. The court held that there was no assault (however, see the Indecency with Children Act 1960). However, in keeping with the elements required for an assault, it is not essential that there be an actual *battery*. There need not be any indecent *touching* of the victim—or even a threat of indecent touching (*R v Sargeant* (1997) 161 JP 127).

What must be shown is that the defendant committed an assault under circumstances of indecency.

The assault or the accompanying circumstances must be capable of being regarded as indecent, that is, they must contravene ordinary standards of decency. Words may make an assault 'indecent' but the test remains an objective one and the secret thoughts or perverted intentions of a defendant cannot make an otherwise innocuous act 'indecent' (like a sales assistant gaining gratification from removing a customer's shoe in a shoe shop). However, if the act is inherently indecent (like spanking someone's buttocks), you do not need to show that a victim actually appreciated the 'indecent' nature of the assault (*R v Court* [1989] AC 28). This was reiterated by the Court of Appeal in a recent case where the defendant induced three female victims to take part in a survey of breast cancer. Believing the defendant to be medically qualified, the victims allowed him to examine their breasts. The court held that there had been no true consent to the touching of the women's breasts. As the touching was overtly indecent, the only issue was that of consent and consequently the defendant's appeal was dismissed (*R v Tabassum* [2000] Crim LR 686). These features have caused some practical difficulties in cases involving sado-masochism (see *R v Brown* [1994] 1 AC 212).

Where a child is involved—as in some sensationalised cases of school children 'eloping' with adults—there may be an indecent assault even though the victim 'consents'.

However, the recent decision in *R v K* below will now need to be considered in negating any defences.

In *R v K* [2001] Crim LR 993, the defendant was charged with indecent assault against a girl under s. 14 above. K argued that the sexual activity had been consensual and that the girl had told him that she was 16. Having no reason to disbelieve her, the defendant argued that the prosecution had to prove an absence of genuine belief on his part that the girl was 16 or over. Although the Court of Appeal reversed the judge's decision on the point, the House of Lords later allowed the defendant's appeal, holding that an honest belief in the complainant's age is a defence under s. 14. Such a belief need not be based on 'reasonable grounds' but the more unreasonable the belief, the less likely it is that it will be accepted as 'genuine'. This does not affect the situation where the sexual activity takes place without consent (see comments of Lord Bingham). While this decision has attracted considerable criticism (because it is appears to ignore the intention of Parliament in drafting the offence), the ruling in *K* now puts the defence in line with s. 1 of the Indecency with Children Act 1960 and the decision in *B (A Minor)* v *DPP* (2000) 2 Cr App R 65. Therefore, the belief—and the reasons for it—of a defendant at the time will be a crucial piece of evidence for police officers to establish when dealing with this offence.

Note that the House of Lords said that their decision did not extend to the offences under ss. 5 and 6 because they were provided for differently by the Act.

3.6 Unlawful Sexual Intercourse

3.6.1 Intercourse with Girl under 13

OFFENCE: **Unlawful Sexual Intercourse with Girl under 13—*Sexual Offences Act 1956, s. 5***
  - Triable on indictment - Life imprisonment
  (Serious arrestable offence)

The Sexual Offences Act 1956, s. 5 states:

It is [an offence] for a man to have unlawful sexual intercourse with a girl under the age of 13.

3.6.2 Intercourse with Girl under 16

OFFENCE: **Sexual Intercourse with Girl under 16—*Sexual Offences Act 1956, s. 6***
  - Triable either way - Two years' imprisonment on indictment; six months' imprisonment and/or a fine summarily
  (No specific power of arrest)

The Sexual Offences Act 1956, s. 6 states:

(1) It is an offence, subject to the exceptions mentioned in this section, for a man to have unlawful sexual intercourse with a girl under the age of 16.

(2) Where a marriage is invalid under section two of the Marriage Act 1949 or section one of the Age of Marriage Act 1929 (the wife being a girl under the age of 16), the invalidity does not make the husband guilty of an offence under this section because he has sexual intercourse with her, if he believes her to be his wife and has reasonable cause for the belief.

(3) A man is not guilty of an offence under this section because he has unlawful sexual intercourse with a girl under the age of 16, if he is under the age of 24 and has not previously been charged with a like offence, and he believes her to be of the age of 16 or over and has reasonable cause for the belief. In this subsection, 'a like offence' means an offence under this section or an attempt to commit one...

KEYNOTE

This offence is generally referred to as 'USI' (unlawful sexual intercourse). An offence of having unlawful sexual intercourse with a girl under 16 must be prosecuted within 12 months of the act complained of. Both offences under ss. 5 and 6 are ones of strict liability as to age at the time of intercourse and the common law defence of an honestly held belief in the child's age, as set out in *R v K* [2001] Crim LR 993 is not applicable to the offences under ss. 5 and 6 (**see 3.3**). That element can be proved by documentation or the evidence of a parent. Note the defence under s. 6(3) above only applies to a person under the age of 24 who has unlawful sexual intercourse with a girl who is at least 13 but under 16.

3.7 Administering Drugs for Unlawful Sexual Intercourse

OFFENCE: **Administering Drugs for Unlawful Sexual Intercourse with a Woman—*Sexual Offences Act 1956, s. 4***

> • Triable on indictment • Two years' imprisonment
> *(No specific power of arrest)*

The Sexual Offences Act 1956, s. 4 states:

(1) It is an offence for a person to apply or administer to, or cause to be taken by, a woman any drug, matter or thing with intent to stupefy or overpower her so as thereby to enable any man to have unlawful sexual intercourse with her.

KEYNOTE

This is a crime of *specific intent*, which is particularly relevant if the defendant claims to have been intoxicated in some way at the time. There is nothing to exclude alcohol from the provisions of this offence. If sexual intercourse takes place while the woman is so overpowered or stupefied there will almost certainly be a further *prima facie* offence of rape (**see 3.3**). The use of the so-called 'date-rape' drugs has increased significantly over recent years. For details of the substances currently being sold/used for such purposes, the advice of the National Criminal Intelligence Service should be sought.

3.8 Procuration

OFFENCE: **Procuration—*Sexual Offences Act 1956, ss. 2 and 3***

> • Triable on indictment • Two years' imprisonment
> *(No specific power of arrest)*

The Sexual Offences Act 1956, ss. 2 and 3 state:

2.—(1) It is an offence for a person to procure a woman, by threats or intimidation, to have sexual intercourse in any part of the world.

3.—(1) It is an offence for a person to procure a woman, by false pretences or false representations, to have sexual intercourse in any part of the world.

KEYNOTE

These offences would cover the occasions above where the victim has been conned or induced—by one of the listed conditions—into having sexual intercourse. The victim must actually have sexual intercourse—which may take place any where in the world—*as a result of* the threats, intimidation, false pretences or false representations. An example of this offence can be found in *R v Harold* (1984) 6 Cr App R (S) 30 where the defendant discovered that a woman who had once been a prostitute was working as an employee of a firm. The defendant threatened to tell the woman's employer of her former lifestyle unless she had sexual intercourse with him. He was convicted of an offence under s. 2(1) above.

'Procuring' means persuading the woman by whatever means to have sexual intercourse. The act of procurement is not complete until the desired outcome is achieved (*R v Johnson* [1964] 2 QB 404).

3.9   **Gross Indecency**

OFFENCE: **Gross Indecency—*Sexual Offences Act 1956, s. 13***
- Triable either way • If defendant is 21 or over and other person is under 16 (five years' imprisonment)

(Arrestable offence)

- Otherwise (two years' imprisonment) on indictment; six months' imprisonment and/or fine summarily

(No specific power of arrest)

The Sexual Offences Act 1956, s. 13 states:

It is an offence for a man to commit an act of gross indecency with another man, otherwise than in the circumstances described below, whether in public or private, or to be a party to the commission by a man of an act of gross indecency with another man, or to procure the commission by a man of an act of gross indecency with another man.

The circumstances referred to above are that the man is under the age of sixteen and the other man has attained that age.

KEYNOTE

There is no need to prove actual physical contact in making out this offence.

It is not an offence for men aged 16 or more to engage in acts of gross indecency in private (Sexual Offences Act 1967, s. 1). This age limit was reduced from 18 years by the Sexual Offences (Amendment) Act 2000.

As with the offence of buggery the person who is under 16 years of age does not commit the offence themselves.

In bringing charges under the above section the burden of proving that the act was not in 'private', was not consensual or that a party was under 16 years of age will still rest with the prosecution (Sexual Offences Act 1967, s. 1(6)). 'In private' has the same meaning as the expression under s. 12(1A) and (1B) of the 1956 Act (i.e. no more than two people present and not in a public lavatory).

Whether an act is grossly indecent is a question of fact for the jury/magistrate(s) to determine in each case. If a person carries out an indecent assault (**see 3.3**) which amounts to gross indecency, the offence is classed as a 'serious arrestable offence'.

The consent of the Director of Public Prosecutions is required before bringing a prosecution for this offence.

The Sexual Offences Act 1967, s. 4(3) states:

It shall not be an offence under section 13 of the [Sexual Offences Act 1956] for a man to procure the commission by another man of an act of gross indecency with the first-mentioned man which by reason of section 1 of this Act is not an offence under the said section 13.

KEYNOTE

This means it is not an offence for one man to procure another man to commit an act of gross indecency under the circumstances outlined above (i.e. both are 16 years or more and acting in private). This age was reduced from 18 years to 16 years by the Sexual Offences (Amendment) Act 2000.

3.10   **Indecency with Children**

OFFENCE: **Indecency with Children—*Indecency with Children Act 1960, s. 1***
- Triable either way • Ten years' imprisonment on indictment; six months' imprisonment and/or a fine summarily

(Arrestable offence)

The Indecency with Children Act 1960, s. 1 states:

(1) Any person who commits an act of gross indecency with or towards a child under the age of 16, or who incites a child under that age to such an act with him or another, shall [commit an offence] . . .

(2) . . .

(3) References in the Children and Young Persons Act 1933, to the offences mentioned in the first schedule to that Act shall include offences under this section.

KEYNOTE

This offence was enacted to deal with occasions where no contact is actually made with the child or where the defendant is passive. It can be committed by masturbating in the presence of children (provided the defendant knows that the children are aware of what is going on (*R* v *Francis* (1988) 88 Cr App R 127)) and also by inviting children to touch one's genitals (*R* v *Speck* [1977] 2 All ER 859).

There will be occasions where the distinction between this offence and the more general one of indecent assault is difficult to make (see *R* v *Sargeant* (1997) 161 JP 127).

Following the House of Lords' decision in *B (A Minor)* v *DPP* [2000] 2 WLR 452, an honest belief that the child concerned is 16 will now amount to a defence to a charge under s. 1(1). If the circumstances surrounding the offence (especially the child's appearance) suggest that the defendant's 'belief' was not honestly held, this will be critical evidence for investigating officers to record. This decision reverses earlier decisions of the Divisional Court. This decision is in line with that of the House of Lords in *R* v *K* [2001] Crim LR 993 where the charge was one of indecent assault against a child (s. 14—**see 3.5**).

Leaving notes in a public lavatory trying to encourage young boys to get in touch with the defendant was held not to amount to an attempt at committing the above offence, even though the defendant's ultimate motive in meeting the boys was to commit acts of gross indecency with them (*R* v *Rowley* [1991] 4 All ER 649).

Sections 1 and 2 of the Criminal Evidence (Amendment) Act 1997 also apply to this offence (and to conspiracies, attempts or incitements in the circumstances set out in that Act).

Where a person is charged with this offence, the Youth Justice and Criminal Evidence Act 1999 imposes certain restrictions on the introduction of evidence or the asking of questions relating to the victim's sexual behaviour.

3.11 Indecent Photographs of Children

OFFENCE: **Indecent Photographs—*Protection of Children Act 1978, s. 1***
- Triable either way • Ten years' imprisonment on indictment; six months' imprisonment and/or a fine summarily
  (*Serious arrestable offence*)

The Protection of Children Act 1978, s. 1 states:

(1) It is an offence for a person—
  (a) to take, or permit to be taken or to make, any indecent photograph or pseudo-photograph of a child . . . ; or
  (b) to distribute or show such indecent photographs or pseudo-photographs; or
  (c) to have in his possession such indecent photographs or pseudo-photographs, with a view to their being distributed or shown by himself or others; or
  (d) to publish or cause to be published any advertisement likely to be understood as conveying that the advertiser distributes or shows such indecent photographs or pseudo-photographs, or intends to do so.

(2) For purposes of this Act, a person is to be regarded as distributing an indecent photograph or pseudo-photograph if he parts with possession of it to, or exposes or offers it for acquisition by, another person.

(3) ...

(4) Where a person is charged with an offence under subsection (1)(b) or (c), it shall be a defence for him to prove—

(a) that he had a legitimate reason for distributing or showing the photographs or pseudo-photographs or (as the case may be) having them in his possession; or

(b) that he had not himself seen the photographs or pseudo-photographs and did not know, nor had any cause to suspect, them to be indecent.

(5) References in the Children and Young Persons Act 1933 (except in sections 15 and 99) to the offences mentioned in Schedule 1 to that Act shall include an offence under subsection (1)(a) above.

OFFENCE: **Indecent Photographs—*Criminal Justice Act 1988, s. 160***

- Triable either way • Five years' imprisonment on indictment; six months' imprisonment and/or a fine

(Arrestable offence)

The Criminal Justice Act 1988, s. 160 states:

(1) It is an offence for a person to have any indecent photograph or pseudo-photograph of a child in his possession.

(2) Where a person is charged with an offence under subsection (1) above, it shall be a defence for him to prove—

(a) that he had a legitimate reason for having the photograph or pseudo-photograph in his possession; or

(b) that he had not himself seen the photograph or pseudo-photograph and did not know, nor had any cause to suspect, it to be indecent; or

(c) that the photograph or pseudo-photograph was sent to him without any prior request made by him or on his behalf and that he did not keep it for an unreasonable time.

KEYNOTE

Once the defendant realises, *or should realise*, that material is indecent, any distribution, showing or retention of the material with a view to its being distributed will probably result in an offence under the 1978 Act if the person depicted turns out to be a child (*R v Land* [1999] QB 65). This is because s. 160(4) provides no defence of mistake as to a child's age.

The Criminal Justice Act 1988 makes it an offence simply to possess an indecent photograph of a child.

A person will be a 'child' for the purposes of both Acts above if it appears from the evidence as a whole that he/she was, at the material time, under the age of 16 (Protection of Children Act 1978, s. 2(3) and Criminal Justice Act 1988, s. 160(4)).

However, if the impression conveyed by a pseudo-photograph is that the person shown is a child or where the predominant impression is that the person is a child, that pseudo-photograph will be treated for these purposes as a photograph of a child, notwithstanding that some of the physical characteristics shown are those of an adult (s. 7(8) of the 1978 Act).

'Pseudo-photographs' include computer images and the above offences will cover the situation where part of the photograph is made up of an adult form. These recent amendments to the legislation are designed to tackle the proliferation of child pornography on the Internet and other computer programs. Thankfully, there has been a significant amount of authoritative case law in this area, case law which investigators and police officers ought to be aware of when gathering evidence of these offences. Downloading images from the Internet will amount to 'making' a photograph for the purposes of s. 1(1)(a) of the 1978 Act (*R v Bowden* [2000] 2 WLR 1083). 'Making' pseudo-photographs includes voluntarily browsing through indecent images of children on and from the internet (*R v Smith and Jayson* (2002) *The Times*, 3 April). In *Smith and Jayson*, the Court of Appeal held that a person receiving an unsolicited e-mail attachment containing an indecent image of a child would not commit an offence under s.1(1) by opening it if he/she was unaware that it contained or was likely to contain an indecent image. This was because s. 1(1)(a) does not create an absolute offence (see also

Atkins v *DPP* [2000] 1 WLR 1427). This may create a potential 'loophole' for paedophiles using the Internet, but all the relevant circumstances of their viewing will need to be considered. In proving the 1978 Act offence you have to show that the act of 'making' the image was deliberate and intentional with the knowledge that it was, or was likely to be, an indecent photograph or pseudo-photograph of a child. Any title that accompanied the e-mail, along with the level of IT literacy of the defendant and any subsequent e-mail correspondence that he/she had with the sender after opening the attachment, will be directly relevant to the issue of the defendant's state of mind (*mens rea*) in this offence.

In *Smith and Jayson* the Court of Appeal went on to say that, once an image is downloaded, the length of time it remains on the screen is irrelevant, as it the question of 'retrieval'.

Evidence indicating an interest in paedophile material generally can also be relevant to show that it was more likely than not that a file containing an indecent image of a child had been created deliberately. Such evidence has been held by the Court of Appeal to be relevant for this purpose, along with evidence showing how a computer had been used to access paedophile news groups, chatlines and websites (*R* v *Mould* (2000) *The Times*, 21 October). A further decision on the making of a 'pseudo-photograph' has held that an image consisting of two parts of two different photographs taped together (the naked body of a woman taped to the head of a child) would not suffice (*Goodland* v *DPP* (2000) *The Times*, 8 March). In that case the Divisional Court accepted that such an image, *if photocopied*, could fall within the meaning of a 'pseudo-photograph'—a fine distinction, the practical effect of which seems difficult to defend. The Court of Appeal has confirmed that the offence under s. 1(1)(a) is justified by the requirement to protect children from being exploited and does not contravene Article 8 or Article 10 of the European Convention on Human Rights (*R* v *Smethurst* [2001] Crim LR 657). An area that has not been clarified is the criminal liability of the relevant Internet service providers allowing the proliferation of images of children in the ways described above. It is at least arguable that these organisations and individuals are 'distributing' the images or, if not, that they are aiding and abetting the above offences.

A legitimate purpose for possessing such material might be where someone has the material as an exhibits officer or as a training aid for police officers or social workers. The consent of the Director of Public Prosecutions is needed before prosecuting an offence under the Protection of Children Act 1978.

Distributing will include lending or offering to another.

Note that although the offences include video recordings, possession of exposed but undeveloped film (i.e. film in the form in which it is taken out of a camera) does not appear to be covered. The offence at s. 1(1)(b) and (c) of the 1978 Act can only be proven if the defendant showed/distributed the photograph etc. or intended to show or distribute the photograph etc. *to someone else*. This is clear from the decisions in *R* v *Fellows* (1997) 1 Cr App R 244 and *R* v *T* (1998) *The Times*, 12 February. If no such intention can be proved, or if the defendant only had the photographs etc. for his/her own use, the appropriate charge would be under the 1988 Act.

Sections 1 and 2 of the Criminal Evidence (Amendment) Act 1997 apply to an offence under s. 1 of the Protection of Children Act 1978 (and to conspiracies, attempts or incitements in the circumstances set out in the 1997 Act).

See also s. 49 of the Customs and Excise Management Act 1979 in respect of the importation of indecent material.

3.12 Incest

OFFENCE: **Incest—*Sexual Offences Act 1956, ss. 10 and 11***
- Triable on indictment • Male with girl under 13 (life imprisonment)
(Serious arrestable offence)

- Otherwise (seven years' imprisonment)
(Arrestable offence)

The Sexual Offences Act 1956, ss. 10 and 11 state:

10.—(1) It is an offence for a man to have sexual intercourse with a woman whom he knows to be his grand-daughter, daughter, sister or mother.

(2) In the foregoing subsection 'sister' includes half-sister, and for the purposes of that subsection any expression importing a relationship between two people shall be taken to apply notwithstanding that the relationship is not traced through lawful wedlock.

11.—(1) It is an offence for a woman of the age of sixteen or over to permit a man whom she knows to be her grandfather, father, brother or son to have sexual intercourse with her by her consent.

(2) In the foregoing subsection 'brother' includes half-brother, and for the purposes of that subsection any expression importing a relationship between two people shall be taken to apply notwithstanding that the relationship is not traced through lawful wedlock.

OFFENCE: **Inciting Girl under Sixteen to have Incestuous Sexual Intercourse—** *Criminal Law Act 1977, s. 54*

- Triable either way • Two years' imprisonment on indictment; six months' imprisonment and/or a fine summarily

(No specific power of arrest)

The Criminal Law Act 1977, s. 54 states:

(1) It is an offence for a man to incite to have sexual intercourse with him a girl under the age of sixteen whom he knows to be his grand-daughter, daughter or sister.

(2) In the preceding subsection 'man' includes boy, 'sister' includes half-sister, and for the purposes of that subsection any expression importing a relationship between two people shall be taken to apply notwithstanding that the relationship is not traced through lawful wedlock.

KEYNOTE

For the above offences under the Sexual Offences Act 1956 the consent of the Director of Public Prosecutions is required before prosecution.

As incest is outlawed as much in the interests of genetics as ethics, it can only be committed by sexual intercourse. That is also the reason why the offence is restricted to granddaughters, daughters, sisters and mothers. The offence of incest can only be committed if the intercourse is with a person who the woman knows to be her grandfather, father, brother or son. This again makes the presumption that, while a *grandfather* is generally still capable of fathering more children, a *grandson* is unlikely to reach sexual maturity while his grandmother is still of child-bearing age. Although there have been some well-publicised examples of grandmothers bearing children, it was envisaged as very unlikely by the legislators.

The requirement as to 'knowledge' of the particular familial relationship means that you must prove that element of the *mens rea* in order to convict someone of incest.

Sections 1 and 2 of the Criminal Evidence (Amendment) Act 1997 extending the power to take non-intimate samples without consent apply to this offence and also to conspiracies, attempts or incitements in the circumstances set out in that Act.

3.13 Protection of Children

Although many of the general provisions restricting the behaviour of sex offenders have been targeted at paedophiles, there are several significant areas of legislation which are aimed specifically at the protection of children, in both a sexual context and in other areas where their well-being is jeopardised.

Following the death of Victoria Climbié on 25 February 2000, however, an independent statutory inquiry was conducted by Lord Laming and his report published in January 2003. The

Laming Report made no fewer than 108 recommendations, together with deadlines by which time the appropriate action should have been implemented. Many of the recommendations are matters of policy and inter-agency co-operation, with very clear implications for police officers when facing cases of reported abuse. In particular, the proactive roles of supervisors and managers are highlighted within these recommendations and, although the rest of this chapter summarises some of the legislation in this area, reference to local and national guidance should be consulted whenever and wherever crime against children is in issue.

Criminal Justice and Court Services Act 2000

The Criminal Justice and Court Services Act 2000 introduced a number of measures aimed at preventing unsuitable people from working with children. What follows is a summary of some of the relevant provisions of the Act; for further detail see Home Office Circular 45/2000.

Part II of the 2000 Act introduces the concept of disqualification orders. These orders are aimed at disqualifying people who present a threat to children from working in certain jobs and positions. A key feature of disqualification orders is the fact that a court must impose them when defendants are convicted of certain offences unless, having regard to all the circumstances, the court is satisfied that it is unlikely that the defendant will commit any further offences against any child (ss. 28 and 29). Broadly, the requirement to pass a disqualification order arises when:

– the defendant, being 18 or over, is convicted of an 'offence against a child'. 'Offences against a child' are set out in sch. 4 to the Act and generally include most offences involving sexual activity, the use of violence and some drug-related offences (the list specifically includes the military or service law equivalent of these offences);

– a senior court passes a 'qualifying sentence' on the defendant for that offence. A qualifying sentence is generally a sentence of 12 months' imprisonment or more, a hospital or guardianship order (s. 30). 'Senior court' here means the Crown Court and the Court of Appeal. Again, these concepts are specifically extended to cover sentences imposed under service law by courts-martial and the Courts-Martial Appeal Court.

For most purposes under this part of the Act, 'child' means a person under 18.

A person convicted of an 'offence against a child' will also be automatically prevented from a number of activities involving children including carrying on or being involved in the management of a children's home or from privately adopting children unless special authority is sought first (see the Disqualification from Caring for Children (England) Regulations 2002 (SI 2002 No. 635)).

Once an order is imposed, the person becomes a 'disqualified person' for the purposes of the Act. A person can also become 'disqualified' if he/she appears on a statutory list of unsuitable or unfit people (see below).

OFFENCE: **Applying for Position while Disqualified—*Criminal Justice and Court Services Act 2000, s. 35***

  • Triable either way • Five years' imprisonment on indictment; six months' and/or fine summarily

  (Arrestable offence)

Section 35 states:

(1) An individual who is disqualified from working with children is guilty of an offence if he knowingly applies for, offers to do, accepts or does any work in a regulated position.

(2) An individual is guilty of an offence if he knowingly—

  (a) offers work in a regulated position to, or procures work in a regulated position for, an individual who is disqualified from working with children, or

(b) fails to remove such an individual from such work.

(3) It is a defence for an individual charged with an offence under subsection (1) to prove that he did not know, and could not reasonably be expected to know, that he was disqualified from working with children.

KEYNOTE

There are two offences associated with being a disqualified person. The first offence arises where a disqualified person knowingly applies for, offers to do, accepts or does any work in a regulated position (s. 35(1)). Given the specific defence available (see below), it would seem that the requirement of 'knowingly' here relates to the act of applying, offering or accepting work in a regulated position. The offence would therefore not be made out if the application, offer, etc. were made without the disqualified person's knowledge or agreement. Regulated positions are generally those where the person's normal duties include working with children, whether in the public, private or voluntary sectors and also in certain senior management roles such as social services and children's charities.

The statutory defence to s. 35(1) applies if the defendant can show that he/she neither knew, nor could reasonably have been expected to know that he/she was disqualified (a difficult scenario to envisage let alone prove).

The second offence arises where a person offers or procures work in a regulated position for a person who is disqualified from working with children or fails to remove such an individual from that work (s. 35(2)). This offence is clearly aimed at employers, though it would clearly extend beyond those circumstances and it does not have the statutory defence available. This seems slightly odd given that, of the two, a prospective employer is far less likely to know of a person's disqualification than the person disqualified.

Reviews and Appeals

The Criminal Justice and Court Services Act 2000 makes provision for a person to appeal against the imposition of a disqualification order and also to have such orders reviewed after a minimum period. More significantly for the police, s. 34 makes provision for a chief officer of police (or director of social services) to apply to the High Court to restore a disqualification order if it can be shown that:

- the person who was once subject to the order has acted (either before the order ceased or after) in such a way

- as to give reasonable cause to believe that an order is necessary

- to protect children in general or any children in particular

- from serious harm from that person.

If these conditions are made out, the High Court must reinstate the disqualification order.

In addition to the provisions under the Criminal Justice and Court Services Act 2000, there are several pieces of legislation that exist for the protection of children generally. Three key statutes relating to the protection of children are:

- the Protection of Children Act 1999

- the Education Act 2002

- the Children Act 1989.

Protection of Children Act 1999

The Protection of Children Act 1999 was passed to provide greater safeguards for children and to increase the restrictions on those who would seek to gain access to children in order to exploit them. One of the main pillars of the 1999 Act is the creation of a comprehensive and accessible information network. Such a network will:

– provide a consolidated list of people who are deemed to represent a particular risk to children; and

– make that list more accessible to employers and other agencies whose responsibilities include the protection of children.

The 1999 Act brings together two existing lists currently maintained by the Department of Health (the 'Consultancy List') and the Department for Education and Employment ('List 99') for the purposes of identifying those people who are unsuitable to work with children. It also makes provision for relevant organisations to apply to the Criminal Record Bureau for criminal record certificates and criminal conviction certificates utilising the relevant provisions of the Police Act 1997.

The Consultancy List maintained by the Secretary of State for the Department of Health providing access to employers' records on people considered to be unsuitable for work with children has been held not to infringe the human rights of those included on it (*R* v *Worcester County Council and Secretary of State for the Department of Health, ex parte W* [2000] HRLR 702). The same should therefore apply to any such list maintained by authority of the National Assembly for Wales.

The 1999 Act also creates a number of statutory duties upon child care organisations and those involved in the employment of people in child care positions, as well as establishing a tribunal to hear appeals from individuals whose names appear on the relevant list.

Education Act 2002

The Education Act 2002 provides the Secretary of State with many powers to regulate the provisions of teaching and full-time education of children in England. In particular, s. 142 empowers the Secretary of State to direct that a person may not carry out work that involves 'providing education' (not simply teaching) at a school, further education institution or under a contract of employment with a local education authority. The section also covers taking part in the management of an independent school and other work which brings a person regularly into contact with children. Section 142 provides the same powers to the National Assembly for Wales.

Children Act 1989

The Children Act 1989 represents the most comprehensive piece of legislation affecting children ever enacted in England and Wales. Throughout the Act, which makes provision for the care and treatment of children in virtually every aspect of their development, there is a common theme of the child's rights.

Among those rights are the right to protection from harm and the Act imposes many duties on local authorities. It also provides powers for the protection of children and, in particular, for situations where emergency protection is needed.

Police Protection

Section 46 of the Children Act 1989 states:

(1) Where a constable has reasonable cause to believe that a child would otherwise be likely to suffer significant harm, he may—
   (a) remove the child to suitable accommodation and keep him there; or
   (b) take such steps as are reasonable to ensure the the child's removal from any hospital, or other place, in which he is then being accommodated is prevented.

(2) For the purposes of this Act, a child with respect to whom a constable has exercised his powers under this section is referred to as having been taken into police protection.

KEYNOTE

This highly significant and extensive police power has become the focus of considerable attention in the light of the Laming Report (2003) into the death of Victoria Climbié. As a result of some of the Report's recommendations, there will be a range of policy considerations when using this power and local/national guidelines must be consulted.

As to the legislation itself, for most purposes of the 1989 Act, someone who is under 18 years old is a 'child' (s. 105).

The wording of s. 46(1) means that an officer may use the powers at s. 46(1)(a) and (b) if he/she has reasonable cause to believe that, if he/she does not use them, a child is likely to suffer significant harm. The issues arising from similar wording in relation to powers of arrest have been considered by the courts on a number of occasions (see *General Police Duties*, chapter 2). Generally, tests of reasonableness impose an element of objectivity and the courts will consider whether, in the circumstances, a reasonable and sober person might have formed a similar view to that of the officer.

'Harm' is a very broad term and is defined under s. 31(9). It covers all forms of ill treatment including sexual abuse and forms of ill treatment that are not physical. It also covers the impairment of health (physical or mental) and also physical, intellectual, emotional, social or behavioural development. The definition also extends to impairment suffered from seeing or hearing the ill-treatment of any other person.

When determining whether harm to a child's health or development is ' significant', the child's development will be compared with that which could reasonably be expected of a similar child (s. 31(10)).

The power under s. 46 is split into two parts:

— a power to *remove* a child to suitable accommodation and keep him/her there, and

— a power to take reasonable steps to *prevent* the child's removal from a hospital or other place.

The longest a child can spend in police protection is 72 hours (s. 46(6)).

As soon as is reasonably practicable after taking a child into police protection, the police officer must do a number of things as set out above. These things generally include:

— telling the local authority within whose area the child was found what steps that have been, and are proposed to be, taken and why;

— giving details to the local authority within whose area the child is ordinarily resident of the place at which the child is being kept;

— telling the child (if he/she appears capable of understanding) of what steps have been taken and why, and what further steps may be taken;

— taking such steps as are reasonably practicable to discover the wishes and feelings of the child;

— making sure that the case is inquired into by a 'designated officer' (see below);

— taking such steps as are reasonably practicable to inform:
    — the child's parents,
    — every person who is not his/her parent but who has parental responsibility for the child, and
    — any other person with whom the child was living immediately before being taken into police protection,

of the steps that the officer has taken under this section, the reasons for taking them and the further steps that may be taken with respect to the child.

Where the child was taken into police protection by being removed to accommodation which is not provided by or on behalf of a local authority or as a refuge (under s. 51), the officer must, as soon as is reasonably practicable after taking a child into police protection, make sure that the child is moved to accommodation provided by the local authority. Every local authority must receive and provide accommodation for children in police protection where such a request is made (s. 21).

The requirement under s. 46(3)(c) to give the child information, reflects the 1989 Act's theme that children should have some influence over their own destiny.

Designated Officer

The reference at s. 46(3)(e) of the Act to a 'designated officer' is a reference to the appropriate officer designated for that police station for the purposes of this legislation by the relevant chief officer of police. This is a key role in ensuring the effective use of the statutory framework set up for the protection of children in these circumstances and guidance on the minimum levels of training, experience and rank will be issued following the recommendations of the Laming Report. However, the responsibility for ensuring that the case is inquired into by the designated officer, together with the other responsibilities under s. 46(3) and the responsibility for taking steps to inform people under s. 46(4), clearly rest with the police officer exercising the power under s. 46.

Practically, the designated officer must inquire fully and thoroughly into the case; he/she must also do what is reasonable in all the circumstances for the purpose of safeguarding or promoting the child's welfare (having regard in particular to the length of the period during which the child will be so protected) (s. 46(9)(b)).

Where a child has been taken into police protection, the designated officer must allow:

- the child's parents
- any person who is not a parent of the child but who has parental responsibility for him
- any person with whom the child was living immediately before he/she was taken into police protection
- any person in whose favour a contact order is in force with respect to the child
- any person who is allowed to have contact with the child by virtue of an order under s. 34, and
- any person acting on behalf of any of those persons

to have such contact (if any) with the child as, in the opinion of the designated officer, is both reasonable and in the child's best interests (s. 46(10)).

The designated officer may apply for an 'emergency protection order' under s. 44 (s. 46(7)). Such an order allows the court to order the removal of the child to certain types of accommodation and to prevent the child's removal from any other place (including a hospital) where he/she was being accommodated immediately before the making of the order (s. 44(4)). An emergency protection order gives the applicant 'parental responsibility' for the child while it is in force. It also allows the court to make certain directions in relation to contact with the child and a medical or psychiatric assessment of them. Section 44A allows the court to make an order excluding certain people from a dwellinghouse where the child lives and to attach a power of arrest accordingly.

While the designated officer can apply for an emergency protection order without the local authority's knowledge or agreement (see s. 46(8)), there should be no reason why, given proper multi-agency co-operation and a well-planned child protection strategy, this situation would come about. For further guidance on multi-agency working in the area of child protection, see *Working Together to Safeguard Children* (HMSO 1999).

On completing his/her inquiry into the case, the designated officer must release the child from police protection *unless he/she considers that there is still reasonable cause for believing that the child would be likely to suffer significant harm if released* (s. 46(5)).

While a child is in police protection, neither the officer concerned nor the designated officer will have parental responsibility for him/her (s. 46(9)(a)).

When a local authority is informed that a child is in police protection, they have a duty to make 'such enquiries as they consider necessary to enable them to decide whether they should take any action to safeguard' the child (s. 47(1)(b)). A court may issue a warrant for a constable to assist a relevant person to enter premises in order to enforce an emergency protection order.

OFFENCE: **Acting in Contravention of Protection Order or Power Exercised under s. 46—*Children Act 1989, s. 49***

- Triable summarily Six months' imprisonment
(No specific power of arrest)

The Children Act 1989, s. 49 states:

(1) A person shall be guilty of an offence if, knowingly and without lawful authority or reasonable excuse, he—
  (a) takes a child to whom this section applies away from the responsible person;
  (b) keeps such a child away from the responsible person; or
  (c) induces, assists or incites such a child to run away or stay away from the responsible person.

(2) This section applies in relation to a child who is—
  (a) in care;
  (b) the subject of an emergency protection order; or
  (c) in police protection,
  and in this section 'the responsible person' means any person who for the time being has care of him by virtue of the care order, the emergency protection order, or section 46, as the case may be.

KEYNOTE

Although there is no specific power of arrest, the general arrest condition under s. 25(3)(e) of the Police and Criminal Evidence Act 1984 is likely to apply.

It is arguable that, in the case of a child who is under 16, the person would also commit an offence under the Child Abduction Act 1984.

There is also a power of entry under s. 17(1)(e) of the 1984 PACE Act for 'saving life and limb'.

Where a child is taken in contravention of s. 49 above, the court may issue a 'recovery order' under s. 50. Such an order, which is also available where a child is missing or has run away, requires certain people to produce the child to an authorised person (which includes a constable (s. 50(7)(b)) or to give certain information about the child's whereabouts to a constable or officer of the court (s. 50(3)). It can also authorise a constable to enter any premises and search for the child.

Under s. 102 of the 1989 Act, a court may issue a warrant to enter premises in connection with certain provisions of the Act which regulate children's homes, foster homes, child-minding premises and nursing homes for children. Section 102 allows for constables to assist any person in the exercise of their powers under those provisions. It also makes allowances for a constable to be accompanied by a medical practitioner, nurse or health visitor (s. 102(3)).

3.14   Disclosure of Child's Whereabouts

Where a child is reported missing, problems can arise once he/she is discovered to be safe and well but one of the parents wants the police to disclose the whereabouts of the child. This situation arose in *S* v *S (Chief Constable of West Yorkshire Police Intervening)* [1999] 1 All ER 281, and the Court of Appeal provided some clarification of the issues. In that case, the mother left home with her three-year-old child after a marriage breakdown. The father reported the child's absence to the police, who found the child and her mother in a refuge. At the request of the mother, the police advised the father that both she and the child were safe but refused to disclose their whereabouts. The father applied *ex parte* (i.e. without telling the police) to the County Court, which then made an order under s. 33 of the Family Law Act 1986, requiring the police to disclose the information. The Chief Constable was granted leave to intervene and, following another order from the court to disclose the child's whereabouts, the Chief Constable appealed. Butler-Sloss LJ (one of the key figures behind the drafting of the Children Act 1989) gave the finding of the Court of Appeal. The Court held that it was only in exceptional circumstances that the police should be asked to divulge the whereabouts of a child under a s. 33 order. Their primary role in such cases should continue to be finding missing children and ensuring their safety.

However, Butler-Sloss LJ went on to say that, in such cases:

– The police are *not* in a position to give 'categoric assurances' of confidentiality to those who provide information as to the whereabouts of a child. The most they could say is that, other than by removing the child, it would be most unlikely that they would have to disclose the information concerning the child's whereabouts.

– An order under s. 33 provides for the information to be disclosed to the court, not to the other party or his/her solicitor.

– An order under s. 33 should not normally be made in respect of the police without their being present (*ex parte*).

3.15 People Suffering from Mental Impairment

3.15.1 Sexual Offences against the Mentally Impaired

The Sexual Offences Act 1956 creates certain offences for the protection of people who might be unable to understand the nature of, or to consent to, sexual intimacy. Somewhat politically incorrectly, the Act terms such people as 'defectives', defining them at s. 45 as:

> ...[persons] suffering from a state of arrested or incomplete development of mind which includes severe impairment of intelligence and social functioning.

In addition, there is a specific offence of a man under certain circumstances having sexual intercourse with a psychiatric patient (see below).

OFFENCE: **Sexual Intercourse with Mental Defective—*Sexual Offences Act 1956, s. 7***
> • Triable on indictment • Two years' imprisonment
> *(No specific power of arrest)*

The Sexual Offences Act 1956, s. 7 states:

> (1) It is an offence, subject to the exception mentioned in this section, for a man to have unlawful sexual intercourse with a woman who is a defective.

The defence is stated at s. 7 as:

> (2) A man is not guilty of an offence under this section because he has unlawful sexual intercourse with a woman if he does not know and has no reason to suspect her to be a defective.

OFFENCE: **Procurement—*Sexual Offences Act 1956, s. 9***
> • Triable on indictment • Two years' imprisonment
> *(No specific power of arrest)*

The Sexual Offences Act 1956, s. 9 states:

> (1) It is an offence, subject to the exception mentioned in this section, for a person to procure a woman who is a defective to have unlawful sexual intercourse in any part of the world.

The defence is stated at s. 9 as:

(2) A person is not guilty of an offence under this section because he procures a defective to have unlawful sexual intercourse, if he does not know and has no reason to suspect her to be a defective.

OFFENCE: **Owner/Occupier allowing Woman Mental 'Defective' to Use Premises—*Sexual Offences Act 1956, s. 27***

• Triable on indictment • Two years' imprisonment

(No specific power of arrest)

The Sexual Offences Act 1956, s. 27 states:

(1) It is an offence, subject to the exception mentioned in this section, for a person who is the owner or occupier of any premises, or who has, or acts or assists in, the management or control of any premises, to induce or knowingly suffer a woman who is a defective to resort to or be on those premises for the purpose of having unlawful sexual intercourse with men or with a particular man.

The defence is stated at s. 27 as:

(2) A person is not guilty of an offence under this section because he induces or knowingly suffers a defective to resort to or be on any premises for the purpose mentioned, if he does not know and has no reason to suspect her to be a defective.

KEYNOTE

The legal burden (see Evidence and Procedure, chapter 11) in proving the specific defences shown above falls upon the defence (s. 49 of the 1956 Act).

All the above offences apply to female victims, with the offence under s. 7(1) only being capable of commission by a man. Where the alleged victim is male, the offences of rape or indecent assault may apply.

OFFENCE: **Sexual Intercourse with Patients—*Mental Health Act 1959, s. 128***

• Triable on indictment Two years' imprisonment

(No specific power of arrest)

The Mental Health Act 1959, s. 128 states:

(1) Without prejudice to section seven of the Sexual Offences Act 1956, it shall be an offence, subject to the exception mentioned in this section—

(a) for a man who is an officer on the staff of or is otherwise employed in, or is one of the managers of, a hospital or mental nursing home to have unlawful sexual intercourse with a woman who is for the time being receiving treatment for mental disorder in that hospital or home, or to have such intercourse on the premises of which the hospital or home forms part with a woman who is for the time being receiving such treatment there as an out-patient;

(b) for a man to have unlawful sexual intercourse with a woman who is a mentally disordered patient and who is subject to his guardianship under the Mental Health Act 1983 or is otherwise in his custody or care under the Mental Health Act 1983 or in pursuance of arrangements under Part III of the National Assistance Act 1948 or the National Health Service Act 1977, or as a resident in a residential care home within the meaning of Part I of the Registered Homes Act 1984.

The defence is stated at s. 128 as:

(2) It shall not be an offence under this section for a man to have sexual intercourse with a woman if he does not know and has no reason to suspect her to be a mentally disordered patient.

The Sexual Offences Act 1967, s. 1 states:

(3) A man who is suffering from severe mental handicap cannot in law give any consent which, by virtue of subsection (1) of this section, would prevent a homosexual act from being an offence, but a person shall not be convicted, on account of the incapacity of such a man to consent, of

an offence consisting of such an act if he proves that he did not know and had no reason to suspect that man to be suffering from severe mental handicap.

(3A) In subsection (3) of this section 'severe mental handicap' means a state of arrested or incomplete development of mind which includes severe impairment of intelligence and social functioning.

(4) Section 128 of the Mental Health Act 1959 (prohibition on men on the staff of a hospital, or otherwise having responsibility for mental patients, having sexual intercourse with women patients) shall have effect as if any reference therein to having unlawful sexual intercourse with a woman included a reference to committing buggery or an act of gross indecency with another man.

KEYNOTE

This offence requires the consent of the Director of Public Prosecutions before any prosecution can be brought. It can only be committed by a man who is in some way employed in the hospital or home where the patient is receiving treatment. Given that requirement, it is unlikely that the specific defence in s. 128(2) of the 1959 Act would apply in many cases.

Sections 1 and 2 of the Criminal Evidence (Amendment) Act 1997 also apply to this offence (and to conspiracies, attempts or incitements in the circumstances set out in that Act).

Where a person is charged with this offence, the Youth Justice and Criminal Evidence Act 1999 imposes certain restrictions on the introduction of evidence or the asking of questions relating to the victim's sexual behaviour.

3.15.2   **Abduction**

OFFENCE: **Abduction of Woman Mental Defective from Parent/ Guardian—*Sexual Offences Act 1956, s. 21***

  • Triable on indictment Two years' imprisonment
  (No specific power of arrest)

The Sexual Offences Act 1956, s. 21 states:

(1) It is an offence, subject to the exception mentioned in this section, for a person to take a woman who is a defective out of the possession of her parent or guardian against his will, if she is so taken with the intention that she shall have unlawful sexual intercourse with men or with a particular man.

The defence is stated at s. 21 as:

(2) A person is not guilty of an offence under this section because he takes such a woman out of the possession of her parent or guardian as mentioned above, if he does not know and has no reason to suspect her to be a defective.

KEYNOTE

Although no specific power of arrest is provided, the additional arrestable offence of kidnapping should be considered.

The elements in relation to this offence are the same as those for abduction under s. 19.

3.15.3   **Protection of People Suffering from Mental Disorders**

The Mental Health Act 1983 provides for the care and treatment of people suffering from mental disorders and supplies powers for enforcing some of its provisions.

If those powers are executed in good faith, the 1983 Act also provides some protection against criminal and civil liability for the police officers and care workers who use them (see s. 139).

The 1983 Act is supported by a Code of Practice that sets out guidance for the police and other agencies when dealing with people suffering from mental disorders.

Mentally Disordered People Found in Public Places

Section s. 136 of the Mental Health Act 1983 creates a power for police officers to remove such a person under certain conditions.

Section 136 states:

(1) If a constable finds in a place to which the public have access a person who appears to him to be suffering from mental disorder and to be in immediate need of care or control, the constable may, if he thinks it necessary to do so in the interests of that person or for the protection of other persons, remove that person to a place of safety within the meaning of section 135 above.

(2) A person removed to a place of safety under this section may be detained there for a period not exceeding 72 hours for the purpose of enabling him to be examined by a registered medical practitioner and to be interviewed by an approved social worker and of making any necessary arrangements for his treatment or care.

KEYNOTE

Given the number of people who are suffering from some form of mental disorder and who are receiving 'care in the community', this a significant power which is provided for the protection of the person themselves and of others.

The power places a lot of responsibility and latitude on the officer who must decide whether:

— the person is suffering from mental disorder (see below)

— the person is in immediate need of care or control, and

— it is necessary in the person's interest or for someone else's protection that he/she be removed to a place of safety

before the power is applicable. This power appears to be consistent with Article 5 of the European Convention on Human Rights which sets out the limited circumstances where the detention or arrest of an individual will be permitted.

The definition of 'mental disorder' under s. 1(2) is very wide and means:

— mental illness

— arrested or incomplete development of mind

— psychopathic disorder (a persistent disorder or disability resulting in abnormally aggressive or seriously irresponsible conduct)

— any other disorder or disability of mind.

Under s. 135(6), a 'place of safety' is:

— residential accommodation provided by social services

— a hospital

— a police station

— a mental nursing home, or

— any other suitable place where the occupier is willing to receive the patient temporarily.

Anyone being taken to a place of safety or detained at such a place will be treated as being in legal custody (s. 137(1)). (This expression is only relevant in relation to escaping and assisting in an escape; it is very different from 'in police detention' used under s. 118 of the Police and Criminal Evidence Act 1984. A mentally disordered person removed from a public place is not in police detention even if taken to a police station.)

Although the power to remove a person to a place of safety under s. 136(1) is classed among the powers of arrest preserved by s. 26 and sch. 2 to the Police and Criminal Evidence Act 1984, it is not strictly speaking a power of arrest.

It is an offence to assist someone removed under s. 136 to escape (see s. 128).

Interestingly, in considering the lawfulness of an enforced placement of an old woman in a secure ward under Art. 5(1)(e) of the European Convention, the European Court of Human Rights recently decided that the key issue was whether or not the detention was in the person's 'best interests', rather than whether the precise wording of the article had been complied with (see *HM* v *Switzerland* (2002) LTL 26 February). The court held that, not only was the enforced detention of the woman (who suffered from dementia and was unable to care for herself) against her will lawful, but also that keeping her in a closed ward which she was not allowed to leave did not amount to a deprivation of liberty. Whatever its other implications for mental health law, this approach is at least consistent with the intention and wording of s. 136 which is very much aimed at allowing the State to take immediate, short-term action to protect the best interests of someone who is clearly unable to look after themselves. This element should also be considered alongside the positive obligations of the police and others to protect life (under Art. 2 of the European Convention).

Warrant to Search for Patients

Where there is reasonable cause to suspect that a person believed to be suffering from a mental disorder has been, or is being, ill-treated or neglected or is unable to care for himself/herself and is living alone, a warrant may be issued by a magistrate (s. 135).

The warrant allows a constable to enter any premises specified and to remove the person to a place of safety. In doing so, the officer must be accompanied by a social worker and a doctor (s. 135(4)).

A warrant may also be issued in respect of a patient ordered to be detained by a court.

Power to Retake Escaped Patients

Section 138 provides a power to retake people who have been in legal custody under the 1983 Act.

A person removed to a place of safety under s. 136 or a person removed under a warrant, who subsequently escapes while being taken to or detained in a place of safety, cannot be retaken after 72 hours have elapsed. That time period starts either when the person escapes or when his/her liability to be detained began, whichever expires first (s. 138(3)). This means that, if the person escapes *before* reaching the place of safety, the 72 hours begins then; if the person escapes *from* the place of safety, the 72 hours begins at the time he/she arrived there.

There is also a power for a court to issue a warrant for the arrest of a convicted mental patient who is unlawfully at large (Criminal Justice Act 1967, s. 72(3)).

Ambit of the Mental Health Act 1983

The ambit of the Mental Health Act 1983 was recently reviewed in *St George's Healthcare NHS Trust* v *S* [1998] 3 WLR 936, by the Court of Appeal. There it was held that:

– The 1983 Act should not be invoked to overrule the decision of a patient concerning medical treatment simply because that decision appears to be irrational.

– A person detained under the 1983 Act should not be forced to receive medical treatment which is not connected with his/her mental condition unless his/her capacity to give consent is seriously diminished.

PART FOUR

Evidence

4.1   Presumptions in Law

Facts in issue and relevant facts must generally be proved before a court by admissible evidence before they can be accepted by the court as being true. There are occasions, however, when the courts will allow the proof of a fact or number of facts which lead it to presume the existence of a further fact, without any evidence of that fact being given in evidence. That is, from the facts that have been given in evidence, the court will then presume another fact for which no direct evidence has been given. A presumption is normally a conclusion which can be drawn until, where permissible, the contrary is proved.

There are three types of these 'presumptions':

• irrebuttable presumptions of law;

• rebuttable presumptions of law;

• presumptions of fact.

4.1.1   Irrebuttable Presumptions of Law

This is also known as a conclusive presumption. In these cases, where the courts accept the existence of certain basic fact(s) then they must also assume the existence of another fact and the other party to the proceedings cannot produce evidence questioning its existence.

For instance, s. 50 of the Children and Young Persons Act 1933 states:

It shall be conclusively presumed that no child under the age of ten years can be guilty of any offence.

Where the defence produce a birth certificate for the accused showing he/she is only nine then, from that basic fact, the courts *must* presume that the defendant is not guilty of the offence charged. It is an irrebuttable presumption that a child under ten can never be guilty of an offence and matters not what other evidence the prosecution call. Once the birth certificate is accepted as being that of the defendant, the court will find him/her not guilty.

4.1.2   Rebuttable Presumptions of Law

In these cases, once one party has satisfied the court of the basic fact from which a presumption about other facts must be made, it is for the other party to prove that the presumed fact does not exist. That is, the other party can *rebut* the presumption but, if he/she is unable to do so, the court will draw the appropriate inference from it.

Where the prosecution have to disprove an assumption they must do so beyond reasonable doubt but the defence only have to show on a balance of probabilities that the fact (the presumption) exists.

There are a number of rebuttable presumptions but the most likely to apply to criminal cases are 'presumptions of regularity'.

Presumption of regularity

It is presumed that where evidence shows that a person acted in a public or official capacity, in the absence of contrary evidence, that that person was regularly and properly appointed and the act was regularly and properly performed. A typical example is on a charge of assaulting a police officer in the course of his/her duty. Evidence that the police officer acted in that capacity is sufficient proof of his/her due appointment (*R* v *Gordon* (1789) 1 Leach 515; and see *Cooper* v *Rowlands* [1971] RTR 291).

There is also a presumption that mechanical and other instruments were in working order at the time of their use. For example, automatic traffic signals are presumed to be in proper working order unless the contrary is proved (*Tingle Jacobs & Co.* v *Kennedy* [1964] 1 WLR 638). However, there must be evidence of usually correct operation, for example, in relation to the admissibility of evidence of the results of a breath test in excess alcohol cases, where the reliability of the testing device is in question (*Cracknell* v *Willis* [1988] AC 450 and *Newton* v *Woods* [1987] RTR 41).

4.1.3 Presumptions of Fact

The court may, after evidence is given about certain facts, presume (in the absence of sufficient evidence to the contrary), that another fact exists. This differs from rebuttable presumptions of law in that here the court *may* presume the fact exists from other facts presented to the court. With rebuttable presumptions of fact the court *must* presume the fact exists unless it is proved to the contrary. In reality this is just another way of showing that the courts use circumstantial evidence to infer that a fact is true.

Cases where the courts regularly infer the existence of facts from other circumstantial evidence are labelled 'presumptions of fact'. The following are examples of presumptions of fact:

Presumption of intention

Section 8 of the Criminal Justice Act 1967 states:

> A court or jury in determining whether a person has committed an offence—
>
> (a) shall not be bound in law to infer that he intended or foresaw a result of his actions by reason only of its being a natural and probable consequence of those actions; but
>
> (b) shall decide whether he did intend or foresee that result by reference to all the evidence, drawing such inferences from the evidence as appear proper in the circumstances.

Guilty knowledge in cases of handling and theft

Section 27(3) of the Theft Act 1968 allows for the admissibility of previous misconduct and states:

> (3) Where a person is being proceeded against for handling stolen goods (but not for any offence other than handling stolen goods), then at any stage of the proceedings, if evidence has been given of his having or arranging to have in his possession the goods the subject of the charge, or of his undertaking or assisting in, or arranging to undertake or assist in, their retention, removal, disposal or realisation, the following evidence shall be admissible for the purpose of proving that he knew or believed the goods to be stolen goods—
>
> (a) evidence that he has had in his possession, or has undertaken or assisted in the retention, removal, disposal or realisation of, stolen goods from any theft taking place not earlier than 12 months before the offence charged and
>
> (b) (provided that seven days' notice in writing has been given to him of the intention to prove the conviction) evidence that he has within the five years preceding the date of the offence charged been convicted of theft or of handling stolen goods.

KEYNOTE

This provision applies to all forms of handling (*R* v *Ball* [1983] 1 WLR 801) and can be used where handling is the only offence involved in the proceedings.

The question as to what constitutes recent possession is a matter of fact and degree dependent on the circumstances of each case. This presumption can be rebutted by the person offering a true explanation for the possession (*R* v *Schama* (1914) 84 LJ KB 396; *R* v *Garth* [1949] 1 All ER 773; *R* v *Aves* [1950] 2 All ER 330; and *R* v *Williams* [1962] Crim LR 54).

The term 'recent possession' is not defined and so is a question of fact in each case. In *R* v *Smythe* (1980) 72 Cr App R 8, the Court of Appeal held that property found in the possession of an accused, stolen two or three months earlier during some robberies and burglaries, did not amount to recent possession for the offence of handling stolen goods generally.

Presumption of life

Where evidence that a person was alive on a certain date is given to the court, it may be presumed that he/she was still alive on some subsequent date. Of course, where additional evidence is provided showing that the person was in good health and spirits, the chances of such an inference being made will be greater.

4.2 Criminal Conduct

4.2.1 Introduction

For a person to be found guilty of a criminal offence you must show that they:

- acted in a particular way;
- failed to act in a particular way; or
- brought about a state of affairs.

Known as the *actus reus*, this essential characteristic of any offence is the behavioural element. It is important to remember that the element of *actus reus* can also be proved by showing an *omission* to act in certain circumstances.

4.2.2 *Actus Reus*

Mens rea is what a defendant must have had; *actus reus* is what a defendant must have done—or failed to do.

When proving the required *actus reus* you must show:

- that the defendant's conduct was voluntary; and
- that it occurred while the defendant still had the requisite *mens rea*.

Voluntary Act

Other than in the few specific instances where an 'omission' will suffice (**see 4.2.3**), you must generally show that a defendant acted 'voluntarily', that is, by the operation of his/her own free will.

If a person is shoved into a shop window, he/she cannot be said to have damaged it for the purposes of criminal liability, even though he/she was the immediate physical cause of the damage. Similarly, if a person was standing in front of a window waiting to break it and someone came up and pushed that person into the window, the presence of the requisite *mens rea* would still not be enough to attract criminal liability for the resultant damage. In each case, the person being pushed could not be said to be acting of his/her own volition in breaking the window and therefore could not perform the required *actus reus*.

This aspect of voluntariness becomes important, not just when considering offences committed under physical compulsion, but also where the defendant has lost control of his/her own physical actions. Reflexive actions are generally not classed as being willed or voluntary, hence the (limited) availability of the 'defence' of automatism.

Likewise, the *unexpected* onset of a sudden physical impairment (such as severe cramp when driving; actions when sleepwalking) can also render any linked actions 'involuntary'. If the onset of the impairment could reasonably have been foreseen or anticipated (e.g. where someone is prone to blackouts) the defendant's actions may be said to have been willed in the respect that he/she could have prevented the loss of control or at least avoided the situation (e.g. driving) which allowed the consequences to come about.

Coincidence with *Mens Rea*

Generally, it must be shown that the defendant had the requisite *mens rea* at the time of carrying out the *actus reus*. However, there is no need for that 'state of mind' to remain unchanged throughout the entire commission of the offence. If a person (X) poisons another (Y) intending to kill Y at the time, it will not alter X's criminal liability if X changes his mind immediately after giving the poison or even if X does everything he can to halt its effects (see *R v Jakeman* (1983) 76 Cr App R 223). Similarly, if a person 'appropriates' another's property while having the required *mens rea*, giving it back later will not prevent them from committing theft (*R v McHugh* (1993) 97 Cr App R 335).

Conversely, if the *actus reus* is a continuing act, as 'appropriation' is, it may begin without any particular *mens rea* at the start but the required 'state of mind' may come later while the *actus reus* is still continuing. If this happens, whereby the *mens rea* 'catches up' with the *actus reus*, the offence is complete.

This principle can be seen in the offence of rape. The sexual intercourse may be consensual at the time it starts but, if that consent is later withdrawn, any continued intercourse will amount to an offence (*Kaitamaki v The Queen* [1985] AC 147).

A further illustration can be found in a case where a motorist was being directed to pull his car over to the kerb by a police officer. In doing so, the motorist inadvertently drove onto the officer's foot. Having no *mens rea* at the time of driving onto the officer's foot, the defendant was not at that point guilty of assault. However, once the situation was pointed out to him, the fact that he left the car where it was (the *actus reus*) was then joined by the appropriate *mens rea* and he was convicted of assault (*Fagan v Metropolitan Police Commissioner* [1969] 1 QB 439).

4.2.3 Omissions

Criminal conduct is most often associated with *actions*: damaging or stealing property, injuring or deceiving others. In some cases more than one action is required to give rise to criminal liability (e.g. harassment). But, occasionally, liability is brought about by a failure to act (e.g. constructive manslaughter).

Most of the occasions where failure or omission will attract liability are where a *duty to act* has been created. Such a duty can arise from a number of circumstances the main ones being:

D The creation of a **D**angerous situation by the defendant. See, for example, *R v Miller* [1983] 2 AC 161 where the defendant, having accidentally started a fire in a house, moved to another room taking no action to counteract the danger he had created.

U **U**nder statute, contract or a person's public 'office'. Examples would be where a police officer failed to intervene to prevent an assault (*R v Dytham* [1979] QB 722) or where a crossing keeper omitted to close the gates at a level crossing and a person was subsequently killed by a train (*R v Pittwood* (1902) 19 TLR 37).

T Where the defendant has **T**aken it upon himself/herself to carry out a duty and then fails to do so. Such a duty was taken up by the defendant in *R v Stone* [1977] QB 354 when she accepted a duty to care for her partner's mentally-ill sister who subsequently died.

Y In circumstances where the defendant is in a parental relationship with a child or a **Y**oung person.

Whether or not there is a sufficient proximity between the defendant and the victim brought about by a duty to act will be a question of law (see, generally, *R v Singh* [1999] Crim LR 582 and *R v Khan* [1998] Crim LR 830). A graphic and topical example of where such a duty can be created by the defendant is in the case of a lorry driver smuggling illegal immigrants in the back of his vehicle (*R v Wacker* (2003) 2 WLR 374).

In each situation there may be a *duty* to act. Having established such a duty, you must also show that the defendant has *voluntarily* omitted to act as required or that he/she has not done enough to discharge that duty. If a defendant is unable to act (e.g. because someone else has stopped them) or is incapable of doing more because of their own personal limitations, the *actus reus* will *not* have been made out (see *R v Reid* [1992] 1 WLR 793).

Some statutory offences are specifically worded to remove any doubt as to whether they can be committed by omission as well as by a positive act (e.g. torture under the Criminal Justice Act 1988, s. 134). Other offences have been held by the courts to be capable of commission by both positive acts and by omission (e.g. false accounting under the Theft Act 1968, s. 17). Occasionally, some statutory offences arise where the only *actus reus* involves failing to take action under certain circumstances, such as the offence of retaining a wrongful credit under the Theft Act 1968, s. 24A.

The distinction between acts and omissions was considered by the High Court in a recent case concerning withholding medical treatment from chronically ill patients (*NHS Trust A v M* [2001] 1 All ER 801).

4.2.4 Causal Link

Once the *actus reus* has been proved, you must then show a *causal link* between it and the relevant consequences. That is, you must prove that the consequences would not have happened 'but for' the defendant's act or omission.

In a case of simple criminal damage it may be relatively straightforward to prove this causal link: a defendant throws a brick at a window; the window would not have broken 'but for' the defendant's conduct. Where the link becomes more difficult to prove is when the defendant's behaviour triggers other events or aggravates existing circumstances. For example, in *R v McKechnie* [1992] Crim LR 194 the defendant attacked the victim, who was already suffering from a serious ulcer, causing him brain damage. The brain damage prevented doctors from operating on the ulcer which eventually ruptured, killing the victim. The Court of Appeal, upholding the conviction for manslaughter, held that the defendant's criminal conduct had made a significant contribution to the victim's death even though the untreated ulcer was the actual cause of death.

In a case which had similar facts to our 'simple damage' example above, the defendant entered the house after throwing the brick through the window. Although the defendant did not attack the occupant, an 87-year-old who died of a heart attack some hours later, the Court of Appeal accepted that there could have been a causal link between the defendant's behaviour and the death of the victim. If so, a charge of manslaughter would be appropriate (*R v Watson* [1989] 1 WLR 684).

4.2.5 Intervening Act

The causal link can be broken by a new intervening act provided that the 'new' act is 'free, deliberate and informed' (*R v Latif* [1996] 1 WLR 104).

If a drug dealer supplies drugs to another person who then kills himself/herself by overdose, the dealer cannot, without more, be said to have *caused* the death. Death would have been brought about by the deliberate exercise of free will by the user (see *R v Armstrong* [1989] Crim LR 149). However, the Court of Appeal has accepted that, under certain circumstances, where a person buys a controlled drug from another and immediately injects it, resulting in his/her death, the supplier *can* attract liability for bringing about the person's death (*R v Kennedy*, unreported, 31 July 1998). In that case, the court held that the issue of whether or not the supplier's act did in fact cause the death of the drug user should have been left to the jury.

If the medical treatment which a victim is given results in their ultimate death, the treatment itself will not normally be regarded as a 'new' intervening act (*R v Smith* [1959] 2 QB 35). However, for an exception, see *R v Jordan* (1956) 40 Cr App R 152.

There is also a rule which says defendants must 'take their victims as they find them'. This means that if the victim has a particular characteristic—such as a very thin skull or a very nervous disposition—which makes the consequences of an act against them much more acute, that is the defendant's bad luck. Such characteristics (e.g. where an assault victim died after refusing a blood transfusion on religious grounds (*R v Blaue* [1975] 1 WLR 1411)) will not break the causal link.

Actions by the victim will sometimes be significant in the chain of causation such as where a victim of a sexual assault was injured when jumping from her assailant's car (*R v Roberts* (1976) 56 Cr App R 95). Where such actions take place, the victim's behaviour will not necessarily be regarded as introducing a new intervening acts. If the victim's actions are those which might reasonably be anticipated from any victim in such a situation, there will be no new and intervening act and the defendant will be responsible for the consequences flowing from them. If, however, the victim's actions are done entirely of his/her own volition (as in *Armstrong* above) or where those actions are, in the words of Stuart-Smith LJ 'daft' (see *R v Williams* [1992] 1 WLR 380), they *will* amount to a new intervening act and the defendant cannot be held responsible for them.

4.2.6   Principals and Accessories

Once you have established the criminal conduct and the required state of mind, you must identify what degree of involvement the defendant had.

There are two ways of attracting criminal liability for an offence: either as a *principal* or an *accessory*.

A principal offender is one whose conduct has met all the requirements of the particular offence. An accessory is someone who helped in or procured the commission of the offence. If an accessory 'aids, abets, counsels or procures' the commission of an offence, he/she will be treated by a court in the same way as a principal offender for an indictable offence (Accessories and Abettors Act 1861, s. 8) or for a summary offence (Magistrates' Courts Act 1980, s. 44). The expression 'aid, abet, counsel and procure' is generally used in its entirety when charging a defendant, without separating out the particular element that applies. However, if you are trying to show that a defendant *procured* an offence you must show a causal link between his/her conduct and the offence (*Attorney-General's Reference (No. 1 of 1975)* [1975] QB 773). 'Counselling' an offence requires no causal link (*R v Calhaem* [1985] QB 808). As long as the principal offender is aware of the 'counsellor's' advice or encouragement, the latter will be guilty as an accessory, even if the principal would have committed the offence anyway (*Attorney-General v Able* [1984] QB 795).

State of Mind for Accessories

Although the concept of 'state of mind' was addressed in the previous chapter, it is necessary to consider the particular requirements in relation to accessories here.

Generally, the state of mind (*mens rea*) which is needed to convict an accessory is: 'proof of intention to aid as well as of knowledge of the circumstances' (*National Coal Board v Gamble*

[1959] 1 QB 11 at p. 20). The *minimum* state of mind required of an accessory to an offence is set out in *Johnson* v *Youden* [1950] 1 KB 544. In that case the court held that, before anyone can be convicted of aiding and abetting an offence, he/she must at least know the essential matters that constitute that offence. Therefore, the accessory to an offence of drink/driving must at least have been aware that the 'principal' (the driver) had been drinking (see *Smith* v *Mellors* (1987) 84 Cr App R 279).

There must also be a further mental element; namely, an intention to aid the principal. Whether there was such an intention to aid the principal is a question of fact to be decided in the particular circumstances of each case. An example of such a case can be seen in *Gillick* v *West Norfolk & Wisbech Area Health Authority* [1986] AC 112. The case concerned the question as to whether a doctor who prescribed a contraceptive pill for a girl under the age of 16 could be charged with being an accessory to an offence by the girl's partner of having unlawful sexual intercourse.

You can see from this requirement that the wider notions of recklessness and negligence are not enough to convict an accessory.

Occasionally, statutes will make specific provision for the state of mind and/or the conduct of accessories and principals. An example can be found in s. 7 of the Protection from Harassment Act 1997.

Joint Enterprise

If an accessory is present at the scene of a crime when it is committed, his/her presence may amount to *encouragement* which would support a charge of aiding, abetting, counselling or procuring. For instance, someone who has paid to watch a dog fight or other illegal event may be convicted as an accessory to the principal offence (see *R* v *Jefferson* [1994] 1 All ER 270).

Particular problems have been encountered where one person involved in a joint venture goes beyond that which was agreed or contemplated by the other(s).

....

EXAMPLE

A person (the 'accessory'), accompanies a friend (the 'principal'), to a public house where the principal intends to attack a third party. When the two arrive at the public house, the principal produces a knife and stabs the third person. Is the accessory liable for the wounding of the victim? The answer will depend on the nature and extent of the offence that was agreed and contemplated by the accessory and the principal when they set out on their joint enterprise. If the accessory knew that the principal intended to attack the victim, but knew nothing about a knife or any intention to stab the victim, the accessory will generally be liable for the resultant injuries caused by the principal. This is because the joint venture envisaged a physical attack on the third person and the stabbing was simply an 'unusual consequence' arising from the execution of that enterprise (see *R* v *Anderson* [1966] 2 QB 110). If, however, in the example above, the joint enterprise had involved, not an attack on the victim but the theft of his car, then the accessory would not be liable if the principal unexpectedly stabbed a witness or the owner of the car who happened to get in the way. This is because the principal would be going 'beyond what has been tacitly agreed as part of the common enterprise' (*Anderson* above) and therefore the accessory could not be held liable for the consequences of such an 'unauthorised' act.

What would be the liability of the accessory if, in the above example, the victim had subsequently died from his injuries? This situation has caused further problems for the courts and there are many authorities setting out the liability of accessories in such cases. The overall conclusion appears to be that, if at the time they set out on their joint enterprise, the accessory realised:

- that the principal *might* kill someone and
- that, when killing, the principal might have the *intention* to kill or
- an intention to cause *grievous bodily harm*

then the accessory will be liable for murder (*R* v *Powell* [1997] 3 WLR 959).

This is a particularly complex area of criminal liability; its relevance to police officers lies mainly in the gathering of evidence—especially evidence in interview of all the parties concerned. In proving joint enterprise in assaults, the intentions of the defendants will be highly relevant, but so too will any foresight of probable or likely consequences. It will not only be necessary to gather any evidence of what harm a defendant or his/her colleagues *intended* to do; it will also be critical to obtain any evidence showing that a defendant envisaged a degree of harm being caused by the others, even though he/she did not wish to bring such harm about themselves. The Court of Appeal has held that the issue in joint enterprise generally is not a 'state of mind' or intention, but an objective act which it was contemplated by a defendant would or might be done (*R v Day* [2002] Crim LR 984). There are areas of concern in this approach (see the comments in the *Criminal Law Review* accompanying the case report) but, so far as investigators are concerned, the need to establish any available evidence of foresight or contemplation of the consequences is probably the most important point.

If the principal cannot be traced or identified, the accessory may still be liable (see *Hui Chi-ming* v *The Queen* [1992] 1 AC 34). Similarly, an accessory may be convicted of procuring an offence even though the principal is acquitted or has a valid defence for his/her actions. The reasoning for this would seem to be that the principal often supplies the *actus reus* for the accessory's offence. If the accessory also has the required *mens rea*, the offence will be complete and should not be affected by the fact that there is some circumstance or characteristic preventing the principal from being prosecuted.

Additionally, if the accessory had some responsibility and the actual ability to control the actions of the principal, his/her failure to do so may attract liability (e.g. a driving instructor who fails to prevent a learner driver from driving without due care and attention (*Rubie* v *Faulkner* [1940] 1 KB 571)).

Particular care needs to be taken when charging defendants with joint enterprise in outbreaks of public disorder (see *R v Flounders and Alton* [2002] EWCA Crim 1325).

A person whom the law is intended to protect from certain types of offence cannot be an accessory to such offences committed against them. For example, a girl under 16 years of age is protected (by the Sexual Offences Act 1956) from people having sexual intercourse with her. If a 15-year-old girl allows someone to have sexual intercourse with her she cannot be charged as an accessory to the offence (*R v Tyrrell* [1894] 1 QB 710).

4.2.7 Corporate Liability

Companies which are 'legally incorporated' have a legal personality of their own, that is they can own property, employ people and bring law suits: they can therefore commit offences. There are many difficulties associated with proving and punishing criminal conduct by companies. However, companies have been prosecuted for offences of strict liability (see *Alphacell Ltd* v *Woodward* [1972] AC 824); offences requiring *mens rea* (*Tesco Supermarkets Ltd* v *Nattrass* [1972] AC 153); and offences of being an 'accessory' (see *R v Robert Millar (Contractors) Ltd* [1970] 2 QB 54, which concerns aiding and abetting the cause of death by reckless (now dangerous) driving). There are occasions where the courts will accept that the knowledge of certain employees will be extended to the company (see e.g. *Tesco Stores Ltd* v *Brent London Borough Council* [1993] 1 WLR 1037).

Clearly there are some offences that would be conceptually impossible for a legal corporation to commit (e.g. some sexual offences) but, given that companies can be guilty as accessories (see *Robert Millar* above), they may well be capable of aiding and abetting such offences even though they could not commit the offence as a principal.

A company (OLL Ltd) has also been convicted, along with its Managing Director, of manslaughter (following the school canoeing tragedy at Lyme Bay in 1994) (*R v Kite and OLL Ltd, The Independent*, 9 December 1994).

4.2.8 Vicarious Liability

The general principle in criminal law is that liability is *personal*. There are, however, rare occasions where liability can be transmitted *vicariously* to another.

The most frequent occasions are cases where a statutory duty is breached by an employee in the course of his/her employment (see e.g. *National Rivers Authority* v *Alfred McAlpine Homes (East) Ltd* [1994] 4 All ER 286), or where a duty is placed upon a particular individual such as a licensee who delegates some of his/her functions to another. The purpose behind this concept is generally to prevent individuals or organisations from evading liability by getting others to carry out unlawful activities on their behalf. A common law exception to the rule that liability at criminal law is personal can be found in the offence of public nuisance.

4.3 Bail

4.3.1 Introduction

The Bail Act 1976 is the primary source of legislation in relation to bail both by courts and the police. Important amendments to the 1976 Act have been made by the Police and Criminal Evidence Act 1984, the Criminal Justice and Public Order Act 1994, the Crime and Disorder Act 1998 and the Criminal Justice and Police Act 2001. The Human Rights Act 1988 gives further effect to the rights and freedoms guaranteed under the European Convention on Human Rights and the implications of these have been incorporated into this section.

It is important to remember that where a person is seeking bail in criminal proceedings, in most cases he or she has not been found guilty of the offence(s) that he or she faces. Therefore the law generally—and the human rights legislation in particular—controls any restrictions on a suspect's freedom very carefully.

Investigators should also bear in mind the potential influence that the prospect of getting/ not getting bail may have on a suspect and the need to avoid, wherever possible, the appearance of undue influence being exerted on a suspect in this way.

The meaning of 'bail in criminal proceedings' is contained in s. 1 of the Bail Act 1976 which states:

(1) In this Act 'bail in criminal proceedings' means—
   (a) bail grantable in or in connection with proceedings for an offence to a person who is accused or convicted of the offence, or
   (b) bail grantable in connection with an offence to a person who is under arrest for the offence or for whose arrest for the offence a warrant (endorsed for bail) is being issued.

(2) In this Act 'bail' means bail grantable under the law (including common law) for the time being in force.

(3) Except as provided by section 13(3) of this Act, this section does not apply to bail in or in connection with proceedings outside England and Wales.

   ...

(5) This section applies—
   (a) whether the offence was committed in England or Wales or elsewhere, and
   (b) whether it is an offence under the law of England and Wales, or of any other country or territory.

(6) Bail in criminal proceedings shall be granted (and in particular shall be granted unconditionally or conditionally), in accordance with this Act.

KEYNOTE

Section 1(5) provides that bail can be granted immaterial of whether the offence was committed in 'England or Wales or elsewhere', and immaterial as to which country's law the offence relates.

4.3.2 Bail without Charge

Where one of the following conditions apply then the custody officer must release a detained person either unconditionally or on bail:

- there is insufficient evidence to charge and the officer is not willing to authorise detention for questioning, etc. (s. 37(1) and (2) of the Police and Criminal Evidence Act 1984);

- the officer conducting the review concludes that the detention without charge can no longer be justified (s. 40(8) of the 1984 Act);

- at the end of 24 hours' detention without charge, unless the detained person is suspected of a serious arrestable offence and continued detention up to 36 hours is authorised by a superintendent (s. 41(7) of the 1984 Act).

In relation to s. 41(7) above, where continued detention is authorised for up to 36 hours, the detained person must be released with or without bail at or before the expiry of this time. Alternatively, an application can be made to a magistrates' court for a warrant of further detention (s. 42(10) of the 1984 Act).

4.3.3 Bail after Charge

Where a person is charged at the police station (otherwise than on a warrant backed for bail), the custody officer must make a decision:

- to keep the person in custody until he/she can be brought before a magistrates' court, or to release the person; and

- to release the person either unconditionally or on bail

(s. 38(1) of the 1984 Act).

This is a review of the person's detention and therefore the person or his/her legal representative should be given an opportunity to make representations to the custody officer. The review should be conducted with regard to PACE Code of Practice, Code C, paras 15.1 to 15.6 (**see appendix 3**). Where the detained person is a juvenile, an opportunity to make representations should also be given to the 'appropriate adult'.

Where the decision is made to release a person who has been charged, it would be usual for the person to be released on bail being required to attend at the magistrates' court on a specified day.

With the exception of the circumstances set out below in s. 25 of the Criminal Justice and Public Order Act 1994, a person charged with an offence will be given bail unless certain conditions (contained in s. 38 of the 1984 Act) exist allowing the custody officer to refuse bail.

4.3.4 Bail Restrictions

The decision to deny any unconvicted person bail is a significant one, both personally and constitutionally. Every person has a general right not to be subject to unnecessarily onerous bail conditions, a right which has existed since the Magna Carta in the thirteenth century.

Section 25 of the Criminal Justice and Public Order Act 1994 states:

(1) A person who in any proceedings has been charged with or convicted of an offence to which this section applies in circumstances to which it applies shall be granted bail in those proceedings only if the court or, as the case may be, the constable considering the grant of bail is satisfied that there are exceptional circumstances which justify it.

(2) This section applies, subject to subsection (3) below, to the following offences, that is to say—
   (a) murder;
   (b) attempted murder;

(c) manslaughter;

(d) rape; or

(e) attempted rape.

(3) This section applies to a person charged with or convicted of any such offence only if he has been previously convicted by or before a court in any part of the United Kingdom of any such offence or of culpable homicide and, in the case of a previous conviction of manslaughter or of culpable homicide, if he was then sentenced to imprisonment or, if he was then a child or young person, to long-term detention under any of the relevant enactments.

(4) This section applies whether or not an appeal is pending against conviction or sentence.

(5) In this section—

'conviction' includes—

(a) a finding that a person is not guilty by reason of insanity;

(b) a finding under section 4A(3) of the Criminal Procedure (Insanity) Act 1964 (cases of unfitness to plead) that a person did the act or made the omission charged against him; and

(c) a conviction of an offence for which an order is made placing the offender on probation or discharging him absolutely or conditionally;

and 'convicted' shall be construed accordingly; and

'the relevant enactments' means—

(a) as respects England and Wales, section 91 of the Powers of Criminal Courts (Sentencing) Act 2000;

(b) as respects Scotland, sections 205(1) to (3) and 208 of the Criminal Procedure (Scotland) Act 1995;

(c) as respects Northern Ireland, section 73(2) of the Children and Young Persons Act (Northern Ireland) 1968.

KEYNOTE

Section 25 provides that bail may not be granted where a person is charged with murder, attempted murder, manslaughter, rape or attempted rape if they have been convicted of any of these offences *unless* there are exceptional circumstances.

Section 25 appears to conflict with the European Convention's presumption of an individual's right to liberty. However, the European Commission has suggested that all the factors for and against the granting of bail should be considered, giving special weight to those contained within s. 25 (*CC* v *United Kingdom* [1999] Crim LR 228, *Caballero* v *United Kingdom* [2000] Crim LR 587).

In all other cases the custody officer must consider the issue of bail and s. 38(1) of the 1984 Act sets out the occasions where bail can be refused (**see 4.3.5**). Where bail is refused, the custody officer must inform the detained person of the reasons why and make an entry as to these reasons in the custody record (s. 38(3) and (4)).

In accordance with PACE Code C, para. 1.8, if one of the following conditions apply to the detained person he/she must be informed of the decision to refuse bail as soon as practicable. The conditions are that the detained person:

• is incapable of understanding what is said;

• is too violent, or likely to become violent; or

• is in need of medical attention.

In reaching a decision as to whether a person should be refused bail the custody officer should consider whether the same objective can be achieved by imposing conditions to the bail, that is, for the person to appear at an appointed place at an appointed time. If conditions attached to a person's bail are likely to achieve the same objective as keeping the person in detention, bail must be given.

In *Gizzonio* v *Chief Constable of Derbyshire* (1998) *The Times*, 29 April, Gizzonio had been remanded in custody in respect of certain charges which had not ultimately been pursued. Damages (for the wrongful exercise of lawful authority) were sought on the basis that the police had wrongly opposed the grant of bail. It was held that the decision regarding bail is part of the process of investigation of crime with a view to prosecution and so the police enjoyed immunity in that respect.

4.3.5 Grounds for Refusing Bail

Section 38(1) of the Police and Criminal Evidence Act 1984 provides that a custody officer need not grant bail to an unconvicted accused who is charged with an offence if one or more of the following grounds apply.

Name and Address cannot be Ascertained

If there are reasonable grounds for doubting whether the accused's name and address is correct, these doubts would have to be recorded, along with the decision to refuse bail, on the custody record. If the person refuses to give his/her name, this does not automatically satisfy the requirements of s. 38. The actual wording of the section is that the name *or* address *cannot be ascertained* or that which is given is doubted.

Risk of Absconding

If there are reasonable grounds for believing that the accused will fail to appear at court if bailed, there are certain factors which the custody officer should consider when taking a decision to refuse bail under this section. These factors include:

- the nature and seriousness of the offence;
- the character, antecedents, associations and community ties of the accused;
- the accused's 'record' for having answered bail in the past;
- the strength of the evidence against the accused.

Interference with Administration of Justice

There may be reasonable grounds for believing that detention is necessary to prevent the detained person from interfering with the administration of justice or with the investigation of offences or a particular offence.

This ground would not apply for the purpose of the police making further enquiries or where other suspects are still to be arrested. It is generally intended to protect witnesses, keeping them free from fear of intimidation or bribery and enabling other evidence to be properly obtained.

Commission of Further Offences (Imprisonable Offences Only)

If there are reasonable grounds for believing that bail should be refused to prevent the accused committing other offence(s) the custody officer should give due weight to whether the accused had committed offences when previously on bail and also the 'factors' outlined above.

Risk of Injury to Another etc. (Non-imprisonable Offences Only)

There may be reasonable grounds for believing that detention is necessary to prevent the accused causing physical injury to another or causing loss or damage to property.

Own Protection

There may also be reasonable grounds for believing that detention is necessary for the accused's own protection. 'Own protection' can relate to protection from themselves, such as people who are suicidal, alcoholic, drug addicted or mentally unstable, or protection from others, such as in child abuse cases where there is a lot of public anger directed at the suspect.

Juvenile: Welfare

Reasonable grounds for believing that detention is necessary for the juvenile's own welfare provide another reason whereby bail may be denied.

The expression 'welfare' has a wider meaning than just 'protection' and could apply to juveniles who, if released, might be homeless or become involved in prostitution or vagrancy.

In respect of the above conditions, the custody officer must have regard to the same considerations that a court has to consider in taking the corresponding decisions under sch. 1, part I, para. 2 to the Bail Act 1976 (s. 38(2A) of the Police and Criminal Evidence Act 1984). This relates to imprisonable offences where a court need not grant bail if it is satisfied there are *substantial* grounds for believing the accused would:

- fail to surrender to custody;
- commit an offence; or
- interfere with witnesses or otherwise obstruct the course of justice, whether in relation to himself/herself or any other person.

4.3.6 Bail Conditions

The Criminal Justice and Public Order Act 1994 allows the police to impose conditions on bail given to people charged with an offence. These conditions are the same as those which the courts can impose under the Bail Act 1976 with certain modifications outlined below.

General Provisions

The general provisions as to bail are contained in s. 3 of the Bail Act 1976, which states:

(1) A person granted bail in criminal proceedings shall be under a duty to surrender to custody, and that duty is enforceable in accordance with section 6 of this Act.

(2) No recognisance for his surrender to custody shall be taken from him.

(3) Except as provided by this section—
(a) no security for his surrender to custody shall be taken from him,
(b) he shall not be required to provide a surety or sureties for his surrender to custody, and
(c) no other requirement shall be imposed on him as a condition of bail.

(4) He may be required, before release on bail, to provide a surety or sureties to secure his surrender to custody.

(5) He may be required, before release on bail, to give security for his surrender to custody. The security may be given by him or on his behalf.

(6) He may be required to comply, before release on bail or later, with such requirements as appear to the court to be necessary to secure that—
(a) he surrenders to custody,
(b) he does not commit an offence while on bail,
(c) he does not interfere with witnesses or otherwise obstruct the course of justice whether in relation to himself or any other person,
(d) he makes himself available for the purpose of enabling inquiries or a report to be made to assist the court in dealing with him for the offence,
(e) before the time appointed for him to surrender to custody, he attends an interview with an authorised advocate or authorised litigator, as defined by section 119(1) of the Courts and Legal Services Act 1990;
and, in any Act, 'the normal powers to impose conditions of bail' means the powers to impose conditions under paragraph (a), (b) or (c) above.

(6ZAA) Subject to section 3AA below, if he is a child or young person he may be required to comply with requirements imposed for the purpose of securing the electronic monitoring of his compliance with any other requirement imposed on him as a condition of bail.

(6ZA) Where he is required under subsection (6) above to reside in a bail hostel or probation hostel, he may also be required to comply with the rules of the hostel.

(6A) In the case of a person accused of murder the court granting bail shall, unless it considers that satisfactory reports on his mental condition have already been obtained, impose as conditions of bail—

(a) a requirement that the accused shall undergo examination by two medical practitioners for the purpose of enabling such reports to be prepared; and

(b) a requirement that he shall for that purpose attend such an institution or place as the court directs and comply with any other directions which may be given to him for that purpose by either of those practitioners.

(6B) Of the medical practitioners referred to in subsection (6A) above at least one shall be a practitioner approved for the purposes of section 12 of the Mental Health Act 1983.

(7) If a parent or guardian of a child or young person consents to be surety for the child or young person for the purposes of this subsection, the parent or guardian may be required to secure that the child or young person complies with any requirement imposed on him by virtue of subsection (6), (6ZAA) or (6A) above but—

(a) no requirement shall be imposed on the parent or the guardian of a young person by virtue of this subsection where it appears that the young person will attain the age of 17 before the time to be appointed for him to surrender to custody; and

(b) the parent or guardian shall not be required to secure compliance with any requirement to which his consent does not extend and shall not, in respect of those requirements to which his consent does extend, be bound in a sum greater than £50.

(8) Where a court has granted bail in criminal proceedings that court or, where that court has committed a person on bail to the Crown Court for trial or to be sentenced or otherwise dealt with, that court or the Crown Court may on application—

(a) by or on behalf of the person to whom bail was granted, or

(b) by the prosecutor or a constable,

vary the conditions of bail or impose conditions in respect of bail which has been granted unconditionally.

(8A) Where a notice of transfer is given under a relevant transfer provision, subsection (8) above shall have effect in relation to a person in relation to whose case the notice is given as if he had been committed on bail to the Crown Court for trial.

(8B) Subsection (8) above applies where a court has sent a person on bail to the Crown Court for trial under section 51 of the Crime and Disorder Act 1998 as it applies where a court has committed a person on bail to the Crown Court for trial.

(9) This section is subject to subsection (3) of section 11 of the Powers of Criminal Courts (Sentencing) Act 2000 (conditions of bail on remand for medical examination).

(10) This section is subject, in its application to bail granted by a constable, to section 3A of this Act.

(10A) In subsection (8A) above 'relevant transfer provision' means—

(a) section 4 of the Criminal Justice Act 1987, or

(b) section 53 of the Criminal Justice Act 1991.

KEYNOTE

Section 3(6)(e) was added by s. 54(2) of the Crime and Disorder Act 1998 which provides a court granting bail with a further condition not available to the police. This condition, for the accused to attend an interview with an authorised advocate, was introduced to limit the occasions where an accused attended a first hearing and an adjournment was required for such legal advice to be obtained. This condition does not affect the right of an accused to represent himself/herself in court.

Subsection 6ZAA (electronic monitoring) was added by s. 131 of the Criminal Justice and Police Act 2001. A new s. 3AA has also been added by this Act. This section provides the conditions that must be satisfied before a court can order electronic monitoring in relation to a child or young person, i.e. that:

- the alleged offender has attained the age of 12 years; and
- the child or young person has been charged or convicted of a violent or sexual offence, or an offence punishable in the case of an adult with 14 years' imprisonment or more, or has a recent history of repeatedly committing imprisonable offences while remanded on bail or to local authority accommodation; and
- electronic monitoring arrangements are available in that area; and
- the youth offending team has sanctioned its use for the individual.

Police Bail

Section 3A of the Bail Act 1976 applies to bail granted specifically by a custody officer thereby amending s. 3 of the Act:

(1) Section 3 of this Act applies, in relation to bail granted by a custody officer under part IV of the Police and Criminal Evidence Act 1984 in cases where the normal powers to impose conditions of bail are available to him, subject to the following modifications.

(2) Subsection (6) does not authorise the imposition of a requirement to reside in a bail hostel or any requirement under paragraph (d) or (e).

(3) Subsections (6ZAA), (6ZA), (6A) and (6B) shall be omitted.

(4) For subsection (8), substitute the following—
    '(8) Where a custody officer has granted bail in criminal proceedings he or another custody officer serving at the same police station may, at the request of the person to whom it was granted, vary the conditions of bail and in doing so he may impose conditions or more onerous conditions'.

(5) Where a constable grants bail to a person no conditions shall be imposed under subsections (4), (5), (6) or (7) of section 3 of this Act unless it appears to the constable that it is necessary to do so for the purpose of preventing that person from—
    (a) failing to surrender to custody, or
    (b) committing an offence while on bail, or
    (c) interfering with witnesses or otherwise obstructing the course of justice, whether in relation to himself or any other person.

(6) Subsection (5) above also applies on any request to a custody officer under subsection (8) of section 3 of this Act to vary the conditions of bail.

KEYNOTE

The modifications to s. 3, in relation to bail granted by custody officers, are:

- no authority to order electronic monitoring of a child or young person (s. 3(6ZAA));
- no authority to bail to a bail hostel or probation hostel (s. 3(6ZA));
- no authority to bail for court reports (s. 3(6)(d));
- no authority to bail for medical reports (s. 3(6A)).

Bail Conditions

Section 3A(5) of the Bail Act 1976 provides for the occasions when a custody officer can consider imposing bail conditions. These are where it appears to be necessary to prevent the person from:

- failing to surrender to custody; or
- committing an offence while on bail; or
- interfering with witnesses or otherwise obstructing the course of justice, whether in relation to himself/herself or any other person.

Where the custody officer decides to grant bail and considers one or more of the requirements in s. 3A(5)(a) to (c) apply, one or more of the following conditions can be imposed:

- the accused is to live and sleep at a specified address;
- the accused is to give notification any changes of address;
- the accused is to report periodically (daily, weekly or at other intervals) to his/her local police station;
- the accused is restricted from entering a certain area or building or to go within a specified distance of a specified address;
- the accused is not to contact (whether directly or indirectly) the victim of the alleged offence and/or any other probable prosecution witness;
- the accused is to surrender his/her passport;
- the accused's movements are restricted by an imposed curfew between set times (i.e. when it is thought the accused might commit offences or come into contact with witnesses);
- the accused is required to provide a surety or security.

Where conditions are imposed, an accused may make application to the same custody officer or another custody officer serving at the same police station to have the conditions varied or removed. When such an application is received the matter should be considered on its merits at that time. The custody officer can vary the conditions, including making them more onerous, if this can be justified, or leave them the same (s. 5A(2)).

The custody officer either imposing or varying the conditions of bail imposed 'shall include a note of those reasons in the custody record and shall give a copy of that note to the person in relation to whom the decision was taken' (s. 5A(4)).

The application for varying conditions can also be made to a magistrates' court (s. 5A(2)).

A custody officer must record the reasons for imposing and varying bail conditions and indicate details of the relevant risk. Guidance to courts when approaching the decision to grant bail was given in *R v Mansfield Justices, ex parte Sharkey* [1985] QB 613, where it was held that any relevant risk (e.g. of absconding etc.) must be a 'real' risk, not just a fanciful one. *Ex parte Sharkey* concerned the probability of a striking miner during the NUM dispute picketing unlawfully and, it is submitted, any future decision would have to take into account the lawfulness of the person's conduct under the European Convention on Human Rights.

Surety and Sureties

Section 3(4) of the Bail Act 1976 provides that before a person is granted bail he/she may be required to provide one or more sureties to secure his/her surrender to custody. A custody officer is entitled (as a court) to require such sureties.

The question of whether or not sureties are necessary is at the discretion of the custody officer (or court) but this condition can be applied only where it is believed the accused may abscond, commit further offences, interfere with witnesses, etc., (sch. 1, part I). It should be noted that sureties have no responsibilities (liability) in relation to an accused committing further offences or interfering with witnesses etc. whilst on bail.

The suitability of sureties is provided by s. 8 of the 1976 Act and provides for the following considerations as to a surety's suitability:

- financial resources
- character and previous convictions
- relationship to the accused.

The decision as to the suitability of individual sureties is a matter for the custody officer.

The normal consequence for a surety if the accused does not answer bail is that the surety is required to forfeit the entire sum in which he/she stood surety. The power to forfeit recognisances is a matter for the court and is contained in s. 120(1) to (3) of the Magistrates' Courts Act 1980 and rr. 21 and 21A of the Crown Court Rules 1982.

It is not necessary to prove that the surety had any involvement in the accused's non-appearance (*R* v *Warwick Crown Court, ex parte Smalley* [1987] 1 WLR 237). However, where a surety has taken all reasonable steps to ensure the appearance of an accused it was held that the recognisance ought not to be forfeited (*R* v *York Crown Court, ex parte Coleman* (1987) 86 Cr App R 151). In *R* v *Stipendiary Magistrate for Leicester, ex parte Kaur* (2000) 164 JP 127, it was held that the means of the surety *at the time of enforcement* must be taken into account when the court decides whether or not to remit the whole or part of the forfeited recognisance. Section 7(3)(c) of the Bail Act 1976 provides for a surety to notify a constable *in writing* that the accused is unlikely to surrender to custody and that for that reason the surety wishes to be relieved of his/her obligations as a surety. Such an action may well be determined to be 'reasonable steps'.

Security

Section 3(5) of the Bail Act 1976 provides that, before a person is granted bail, he/she may be required to give security for his/her surrender to custody. As with sureties, a custody officer is entitled (as a court) to require such security, as far as s. 3(6)(a) to (c) (surrender to custody, not commit an offence on bail, interfere with witnesses, etc.) applies. The security required may be a sum of money or other valuable item and may be given either by the accused or someone on his/her behalf.

As with sureties, where an accused absconds this would result in forfeiture of the security. This would not be the case if there appears reasonable cause for the (accused's) failure to surrender to custody (s. 5(7) to (9) of the 1976 Act).

The Human Rights Act 1998

Generally, the approach of European Court and Commission is that an accused person should be released unconditionally unless factors that would otherwise lead to a refusal of bail can be met by imposing bail conditions.

Against this background the Court has accepted:

- use of sureties (*Schertenlieb* v *Switzerland* (1980) 23 DR 137);

- surrender of a passport (*Stögmüller* v *Austria* (1969) 1 EHRR 155);

- restrictions on movement (*Schmid* v *Austria* (1985) 44 DR 195).

In the case of *Neumeister* v *Austria* (1968) 1 EHRR 91, the Court considered that it would be a violation of the Convention where the amount of a surety was set by reference to the losses allegedly caused by the person charged.

4.3.7 **Appointment of Court Date**

There is a statutory requirement on a custody officer in relation to when a person must appear before a magistrates' court when he/she is being released on bail.

Section 47 of the Police and Criminal Evidence Act 1984 states:

> (3A) Where a custody officer grants bail to a person subject to a duty to appear before a magistrates' court, he shall appoint for the appearance—
> > (a) a date which is not later than the first sitting of the court after the person is charged with the offence; or

(b) where he is informed by the clerk to the justices for the relevant petty sessions area that the appearance cannot be accommodated until a later date, that later date.

4.3.8 Juveniles Refused Bail

Under s. 38(6) of the Police and Criminal Evidence Act 1984, where a juvenile has been refused bail, the custody officer must try and make arrangements for the detained juvenile to be taken into the care of a local authority in order that he/she can be detained pending appearance in court.

Two exceptions are provided:

• where the custody officer certifies that it is impracticable to do so, or

• in the case of a juvenile of at least 12 years of age, where no secure accommodation is available and there is a risk to the public of serious harm from that juvenile which cannot be adequately protected by placing the juvenile in other local authority accommodation.

The certificate signed by the custody officer must be produced when the juvenile first appears at court (s. 38(7)).

PACE Code C, Note 16B, makes it clear that the availability of secure accommodation is only a factor in relation to a juvenile aged 12 or over, when the local authority accommodation would not be adequate to protect the public from serious harm from the juvenile.

The obligation to transfer a juvenile to local authority accommodation applies equally to a juvenile charged during the daytime as it does to a juvenile to be held overnight, subject to a requirement to bring the juvenile before a court in accordance with s. 46 of the 1984 Act (see below).

4.3.9 Treatment of People Refused Bail

The custody officer must continue to comply with the PACE Codes of Practice in relation to the treatment of the person while detained pending his/her appearance at court or any latter decision to give bail. Even though a decision to refuse bail may have been taken properly at the time, the circumstances may change and bail may become appropriate. It may be that bail has been refused because of the fear that the person may interfere with a witness. If that witness then informs the police that he/she is going to stay with friends abroad, it may be sufficient to protect the witness by granting bail on the condition that the accused surrenders his/her passport.

Section 40 of the 1984 Act requires that a person who has been refused bail must have his/her detention reviewed by the custody officer *within nine hours of the last decision to refuse bail*. This can only be delayed if the custody officer is not available to carry out the review and then it must be carried out as soon as practicable. Any reason for the delay must be recorded in the custody record along with the decision. If detention can no longer be justified, the person should be bailed with or without conditions as appropriate.

A person charged with an offence and refused bail must be brought before a magistrates' court in accordance with s. 46 of the 1984 Act. Section 46 states:

(1) Where a person—
    (a) is charged with an offence; and
    (b) after being charged—
        (i) is kept in police detention; or
        (ii) is detained by a local authority in pursuance of arrangements made under section 38(6) above,

    he shall be brought before a magistrates' court in accordance with the provisions of this section.

(2) If he is to be brought before a magistrates' court for the petty sessions area in which the police station at which he was charged is situated, he shall be brought before such a court as soon as is practicable and in any event not later than the first sitting after he is charged with the offence.

(3) If no magistrates' court for that area is due to sit either on the day on which he is charged or on the next day, the custody officer for the police station at which he was charged shall inform the clerk to the justices for the area that there is a person in the area to whom subsection (2) above applies.

(4) If the person charged is to be brought before a magistrates' court for a petty sessions area other than that in which the police station at which he was charged is situated, he shall be removed to that area as soon as is practicable and brought before such a court as soon as is practicable after his arrival in the area and in any event not later than the first sitting of a magistrates' court for that area after his arrival in the area.

(5) If no magistrates' court for that area is due to sit either on the day on which he arrives in the area or on the next day—
   (a) he shall be taken to a police station in the area; and
   (b) the custody officer at that station shall inform the clerk to the justices for the area that there is a person in the area to whom subsection (4) applies.

(6) Subject to subsection (8) below, where a clerk to the justices for a petty sessions area has been informed—
   (a) under subsection (3) above that there is a person in the area to whom subsection (2) above applies; or
   (b) under subsection (5) above that there is a person in the area to whom subsection (4) above applies,
   the clerk shall arrange for a magistrates' court to sit not later than the day next following the relevant day.

(7) In this section 'the relevant day'—
   (a) in relation to a person who is to be brought before a magistrates' court for the petty sessions area in which the police station at which he was charged is situated, means the day on which he was charged; and
   (b) in relation to a person who is to be brought before a magistrates' court for any other petty sessions area, means the day on which he arrives in the area.

(8) Where the day next following the relevant day is Christmas Day, Good Friday or a Sunday, the duty of the clerk under subsection (6) above is a duty to arrange for a magistrates' court to sit not later than the first day after the relevant day which is not one of those days.

(9) Nothing in this section requires a person who is in hospital to be brought before a court if he is not well enough.

KEYNOTE

The person must be brought before the next available court (it is for the clerk of the court to decide when the next available court is sitting (*R v Avon Magistrates, ex parte Broome* [1988] Crim LR 618)). If no court is sitting on the next day after charging, (other than Sundays, Christmas Day or Good Friday), the custody officer must inform the clerk of the court. If the court in which the person is to appear is in another area, the person must be taken to the area as soon as practicable and then be taken to that court at the next available sitting. Section 46(9) provides an exception to this requirement if the person is in hospital and is not fit to appear.

The detained person need not be granted bail if the custody officer is satisfied that there are 'substantial grounds' for believing that the defendant, if released on bail (whether subject to conditions or not) would:

- fail to surrender to custody; or

- commit an offence while on bail; or

- interfere with witnesses or otherwise obstruct the course of justice, whether in relation to himself/herself or any other person.

The detained person may also be refused bail for his/her own protection. Where the accused is a juvenile, bail may also be refused if he/she should be kept in custody for his/her own welfare.

4.3.10 **Offence of Absconding**

Section 6 of the Bail Act 1976 Act creates an offence of absconding and states:

(1) If a person who has been released on bail in criminal proceedings fails without reasonable cause to surrender to custody he shall be guilty of an offence.

(2) If a person who—
   (a) has been released on bail in criminal proceedings, and
   (b) having reasonable cause therefor, has failed to surrender to custody,
   fails to surrender to custody at the appointed place as soon after the appointed time as is reasonably practicable he shall be guilty of an offence.

KEYNOTE

The burden of proof in relation to showing 'reasonable cause' (s. 6(1)) is a matter for the accused (s. 6(3)).

A person who has 'reasonable cause' still commits the offence if he/she fails to surrender 'as soon after the appointed time as is reasonably practicable'. In *Laidlaw* v *Atkinson* (1986) *The Times*, 2 August, it was held that being mistaken about the day on which one should have appeared was not a reasonable excuse.

Section 6(4) also states:

A failure to give to a person granted bail in criminal proceedings a copy of the record of the decision shall not constitute reasonable cause for that person's failure to surrender to custody.

Failure to Comply with Bail

There are occasions where a person who has been bailed to return to a police station at a later date or to appear at court may be arrested without warrant. These occasions are dealt with by s. 46A of the Police and Criminal Evidence Act 1984 and s. 7 of the Bail Act 1976.

Section 46A of the Police and Criminal Evidence Act 1984 states:

(1) A constable may arrest without a warrant any person who, having been released on bail under this Part of this Act subject to a duty to attend at a police station, fails to attend at that police station at the time appointed for him to do so.

(2) A person who is arrested under this section shall be taken to the police station appointed as the place at which he is to surrender to custody as soon as practicable after the arrest.

(3) For the purposes of—
   (a) section 30 above (subject to the obligation in subsection (2) above), and
   (b) section 31 above,
   an arrest under this section shall be treated as an arrest for an offence.

KEYNOTE

The offence for which the person is arrested under subsection (1) above is the offence for which he/she was originally arrested (s. 34(7) of the 1984 Act). This power of arrest applies only where the person *has* failed to attend the police station at the appointed time; it does not extend to situations where there is a 'reasonable suspicion' that the person has failed to attend.

Failure to Appear at Court (or Expected Not to Appear)

Section 7 of the Bail Act 1976 states:

(1) If a person who has been released on bail in criminal proceedings and is under a duty to surrender into the custody of a court fails to surrender to custody at the time appointed for him to do so the court may issue a warrant for his arrest.

(2) If a person who has been released on bail in criminal proceedings absents himself from the court at any time after he has surrendered into the custody of the court and before the court is ready to begin or to resume the hearing of the proceedings, the court may issue a warrant for his arrest but no warrant shall be issued under this subsection where that person is absent in accordance with leave given to him by or on behalf of the court.

(3) A person who has been released on bail in criminal proceedings and is under a duty to surrender into the custody of a court may be arrested without warrant by a constable—
   (a) if the constable has reasonable grounds for believing that that person is not likely to surrender to custody;
   (b) if the constable has reasonable grounds for believing that that person is likely to break any of the conditions of his bail or has reasonable grounds for suspecting that that person has broken any of those conditions; or
   (c) in a case where that person was released on bail with one or more surety or sureties, if a surety notifies a constable in writing that that person is unlikely to surrender to custody and that for that reason the surety wishes to be relieved of his obligations as a surety.

KEYNOTE

Section 7 therefore provides a power of arrest without warrant if the constable:

- has reasonable grounds for believing that the person is not likely to surrender to custody;

- has reasonable grounds for believing that the person is likely to break, or reasonable grounds for suspecting that the person has broken, any conditions of bail; or

- is notified by a surety in writing that the person is unlikely to surrender to custody and for that reason the surety wishes to be relieved of his/her obligations as a surety.

Where a person is arrested under s. 7, he/she shall be brought before a magistrate in the petty sessions area where he/she was arrested as soon as practicable and in any event within 24 hours (s. 7(4)(a)).

This section requires that a detainee be brought not merely to the court precincts or cells but actually before a justice of the peace within 24 hours of being arrested. This requirement is absolute and, since the justice's jurisdiction under s. 7(5) to remand a detainee in custody only arises once s. 7(4) has been complied with, a detainee who is brought before the justices out of time cannot be remanded in custody (*R* v *Governor of Glen Parva Young Offender Institution, ex parte G (a minor)* [1998] QB 887).

Where a person is arrested within 24 hours of the time appointed for him/her to surrender to custody he/she must be brought before the court at which he/she was to have so surrendered (s. 7(4)(b)). In reckoning the 24-hour period no account is to be taken of Christmas Day, Good Friday or any Sunday (s. 7(4)).

In dealing with a person brought before the court under subsection (4), if the magistrate is of the opinion that the person is not likely to surrender to custody or has broken or is likely to break any bail conditions he/she may:

- remand or commit the person to custody;

- grant bail subject to the same or different conditions.

Where the justice is not of such an opinion, he/she shall grant bail with the same conditions (if any) as were originally imposed (s. 7(5)).

Where the person being dealt with is a child or young person and the justice does not grant bail, he/she should remand such person to the care of the local authority (s. 7(6)).

4.3.11 **Courts and Bail**

Where a person is accused of an offence and appears before a magistrates' court or Crown Court and applies to the court for bail there is a presumption (under s. 4(1) of the Bail Act 1976) in favour of granting bail:

A person to whom this section applies shall be granted bail except as provided in schedule 1 to this Act.

(**See 4.3.12** for sch. 1.)

In addition to a person appearing before the court in connection with proceedings for an offence, s. 4(1) also applies to adjournments for reports before sentencing and persons being dealt with for an alleged breach of a requirement in a community rehabilitation, community punishment, community punishment and rehabilitation or curfew order.

With the exception of s. 4(2) (adjournment for report of a convicted person), s. 4(1) does not apply where a person has been convicted and is seeking bail pending an appeal or has been committed to the Crown Court for sentence. In such cases the granting or refusal of bail is at the discretion of the court. If bail were to be granted by the court it would be subject to s. 1(1) of the Bail Act 1976, 'bail in criminal proceedings'.

The Criminal Justice and Police Act 2001 has amended s. 5 of the Bail Act 1976 and now requires that, wherever a magistrates' court or the Crown Court grants bail to a person to whom s. 4 of the Act applies, the court must give reasons for its decision in any case where the prosecutor makes representations against the granting of bail on any conditions (s. 5(2A)). It also requires the court to give the prosecutor, on request, a copy of the note of the reasons for its decision (s. 5(2B)).

Bail by Magistrates' Courts

A magistrates' court may remand an accused person in custody or on bail (ss. 5(1), 10(1) and 18(4) of the Magistrates' Courts Act 1980). In exercising their powers of remand or bail the magistrates must do so in accordance with the Bail Act 1976 (s. 128(1) of the 1980 Act). These provisions relate to the magistrates' jurisdiction to adjourn and remand a case. Such jurisdiction applies when the court is:

- inquiring into an offence as examining justices;
- trying an information summarily; or
- determining mode of trial for an offence triable either way.

The Bail (Amendment) Act 1993 provides that where a magistrates' court has granted bail, the prosecution may appeal to a judge of the Crown Court against the granting of bail. For this to apply the accused must be charged or have been convicted of an offence punishable by imprisonment of five years or more or offences of taking a conveyance without authority or aggravated vehicle-taking (ss. 12 and 12A of the Theft Act 1968 respectively) and the prosecution must have opposed bail before it was granted.

The prosecution are required to give oral notice of appeal at the end of the proceedings following which the court is required to remand the accused in custody pending the appeal outcome. The prosecution are then required to serve a written notice of appeal on the court and accused within two hours of the conclusion of the proceedings. The appeal must be heard within 48 hours from the date of the oral notice (excluding weekends and public holidays). In *R* v *Middlesex Guildhall Crown Court, ex parte Okoli* (2001) 1 Cr App R 1, it was held that the 48 hours' period was from the date and not the time the oral notice was given.

Bail by the Crown Court

Section 81(1)(a) to (g) of the Supreme Court Act 1981, lists the persons to whom the Crown Court may grant bail. Section 81(1) states:

(1) The Crown Court may grant bail to any person—
    (a) who has been committed in custody for appearance before the Crown Court or in relation to whose case a notice of transfer has been given under section 4 of the Criminal Justice Act 1987 or who has been sent in custody to the Crown Court for trial under section 51 of the Crime and Disorder Act 1998; or
    (b) who is in custody pursuant to a sentence imposed by a magistrates' court, and who has appealed to the Crown Court against his conviction or sentence; or

(c) who is in the custody of the Crown Court pending the disposal of his case by that court; or

(d) who, after the decision of his case by the Crown Court, has applied to that court for the statement of a case for the High Court on that decision; or

(e) who has applied to the High Court for an order of certiorari to remove proceedings in the Crown Court in his case into the High Court, or has applied to the High Court for leave to make such an application; or

(f) to whom the Crown Court has granted a certificate under section 1(2) or 11(1A) of the Criminal Appeal Act 1968 or under subsection (1B) below; or

(g) who has been remanded in custody by a magistrates' court on adjourning a case under section 11 of the Powers of Criminal Courts (Sentencing) Act 2000 (remand for medical examination) or—

(i) section 5 (adjournment of inquiry into offence);

(ii) section 10 (adjournment of trial); or

(iii) section 18 (initial procedure on information against adult for offence triable either way) of the Magistrates' Courts Act 1980;

and the time during which a person is released on bail under any provision of this subsection shall not count as part of any term of imprisonment or detention or detention under his sentence.

KEYNOTE

Subsection (1)(g) relates to an accused who is remanded in custody by the magistrates' court and makes an application for bail to the Crown Court. The reference to ss. 5, 10 and 18 of the Magistrates' Courts Act 1980 relates to adjournments before inquiring into an offence as examining justices and adjournments for medical reports respectively. The magistrates' court is required to provide a certificate to the Crown Court that, before refusing bail, it heard full argument.

Section 25 of the Criminal Justice and Public Order Act 1994 (occasions where bail cannot be granted) relates to all the powers of the Crown Court to grant bail (see **4.3.4**).

Bail by the High Court

The High Court has jurisdiction to grant bail to the following people in the following circumstances:

- people refused bail by the magistrates' court (s. 22(1) of the Criminal Justice Act 1967);

- people who have applied to the Crown Court to state a case for opinion or seeking an order to quash that court's decision (s. 37(1)(b) of the Criminal Justice Act 1948);

- people convicted or sentenced by the magistrates' court and seeking an order to quash that decision (s. 37(1)(d) of the 1948 Act).

There is, therefore, some overlap with applications for bail before a Crown Court judge. In practice, such applications to the High Court are rarer than those to the Crown Court because public funding is not available.

As with the Crown Court, s. 25 of the Criminal Justice and Public Order Act 1994 (occasions where bail cannot be granted) applies to bail by the High Court (see **4.3.4**).

Bail by Court of Appeal

The Court of Appeal may grant bail to a person who has served notice of appeal or notice of application for leave to appeal against conviction and sentence in the Crown Court (s. 19 of the Criminal Appeal Act 1968). People appealing from the Court of Appeal to the House of Lords can also be granted bail (s. 36 of the 1968 Act).

The provisions of s. 25 of the Criminal Justice and Public Order Act 1994 apply equally to the Court of Appeal (see **4.3.4**).

4.3.12 Courts Refusing Bail

The considerations of the court in relation to granting bail are similar to those of the custody officer (**see 4.3.5**) and can be divided into the same two groups, namely:

- those offences that are imprisonable; and

- those offences that do not carry a sentence of imprisonment.

Imprisonable Offences

The Bail Act 1976 (sch. 1, part I, paras 2 to 5) lists the five grounds where a court need not grant bail to an unconvicted accused charged with an imprisonable offence:

2. The defendant need not be granted bail if the court is satisfied that there are substantial grounds for believing that the defendant, if released on bail (whether subject to conditions or not) would
    (a) fail to surrender to custody, or
    (b) commit an offence while on bail, or
    (c) interfere with witnesses or otherwise obstruct the course of justice, whether in relation to himself or any other person.

2A. The defendant need not be granted bail if—
    (a) the offence is an indictable offence or an offence triable either way; and
    (b) it appears to the court that he was on bail in criminal proceedings on the date of the offence.

3. The defendant need not be granted bail if the court is satisfied that the defendant should be kept in custody for his own protection or, if he is a child or young person, for his own welfare.

4. The defendant need not be granted bail if he is in custody in pursuance of the sentence of a court or of any authority acting under any of the Services Acts.

5. The defendant need not be granted bail where the court is satisfied that it has not been practicable to obtain sufficient information for the purpose of taking the decisions required by this part of this schedule for want of time since the institution of the proceedings against him.

KEYNOTE

In para. 3, where the defendant is being kept in custody for his/her own protection, or where the defendant is a child or young person (under the age of 17 (s. 2(2))), the detention is 'for his/her own welfare'.

There are two further grounds where the court need not grant bail:

- where the defendant has been arrested for absconding or breaking conditions of bail (sch. 1, part I, para. 6);

- where the court wishes further inquiries or a report to be made and is satisfied that the only practical way of achieving this is to remand the defendant in custody (sch. 1, part I, para. 7).

Non-imprisonable Offences

The Bail Act 1976 (sch. 1, part II, paras 2 to 4) lists the four grounds where a court need not grant bail to an unconvicted accused charged with an imprisonable offence:

2. The defendant need not be granted bail if
    (a) it appears to the court that, having been previously granted bail in criminal proceedings, he has failed to surrender to custody in accordance with his obligations under the grant of bail and
    (b) the court believes, in view of that failure, that the defendant, if released on bail (whether subject to conditions or not) would fail to surrender to custody.

3. The defendant need not be granted bail if the court is satisfied that the defendant should be kept in custody for his own protection or, if he is a child or young person, for his own welfare.

4. The defendant need not be granted bail if he is in custody in pursuance of the sentence of a court or of any authority acting under any of the Services Acts.

KEYNOTE

There is one further ground (the same as for imprisonable offences) where the court need not grant bail. That is:

- where the defendant has been arrested for absconding or breaking conditions of bail (sch. 1, part II, para. 5).

In addition, s. 58 of the Criminal Justice and Court Services Act 2000, inserted a new subsection (9) into s. 4 of the Bail Act 1976. This new subsection provides that in taking any decisions required by Part I or II of sch. 1 the court should also have regard to any misuse of controlled drugs by the defendant.

When considering bail, the courts also need to take account of the provisions of Article 5 of the European Convention on Human Rights (right to liberty and security) as already outlined in relation to bail by the police (see above).

In *Letellier* v *France* (1991) 14 EHRR 83, it was held that the task of any court in considering bail is to:

> ... examine all the facts arguing for or against the existence of a genuine requirement of public interest justifying, with due regard to the principle of the presumption of innocence, a departure from the rule of respect for individual liberty and set them out in their decisions on applications for release.

The European Court has also held that where a person is subject to pre-trial detention, this should be reviewed at reasonable intervals. An interval of one month was considered reasonable (*Bezicheri* v *Italy* (1989) 12 EHRR 210).

4.3.13 Detention of Adults and Juveniles

Where an accused is aged 21 or over and a court refuses bail, that person is detained in prison until the next hearing.

In relation to an accused under 17 years old, where a court remands them or commits them for trial or sentence without bail, that person must be remanded to local authority accommodation unless the criteria laid down in s. 23(5) of the Children and Young Persons Act 1969 are satisfied (s. 23(1)).

Section 23(5) states:

(5) This subsection applies to a young person who has attained the age of fifteen, but only if—
   (a) he is charged with or has been convicted of a violent or sexual offence, or an offence punishable in the case of an adult with imprisonment for a term of fourteen years or more; or
   (b) he is charged with or has been convicted of one or more imprisonable offences which, together with any other imprisonable offences of which he has been convicted in any proceedings—
      (i) amount, or
      (ii) would, if he were convicted of the offences with which he is charged, amount,
   to a recent history of repeatedly committing imprisonable offences while remanded on bail or to local authority accommodation,

   and (in either case) the condition set out in subsection (5AA) below is satisfied.

(5AA) The condition mentioned in subsection (5) above is that the court is of the opinion, after considering all the options for the remand of the person, that only remanding him to local authority accommodation with a security requirement would be adequate—
   (a) to protect the public from serious harm from him, or
   (b) to prevent the commission by him of imprisonable offences.

KEYNOTE

Section 23(5) applies to boys and girls aged 12 to 16 (Secure Remands and Committals Prescribed Description of Children and Young Persons) Order 1999 (SI 1999 No. 1265).

In *R* v *Croydon Crown Court, ex parte G* (1995) *The Times*, 3 May, 'serious harm' was held to be assessed by reference to the nature of the offences charged and the surrounding circumstances.

Section 23A of the Children and Young Persons Act 1969 provides the police with a power of arrest where a constable has reasonable grounds for suspecting that a person is breaking his/her conditions (i.e. remanded or committed to local authority accommodation). Where the arrested person cannot be brought before the court, before which he/she was to have appeared, within 24 hours then he/she must 'be brought as soon as practicable and in any event within 24 hours after his arrest before a justice of the peace for the petty sessions area in which he was arrested' (s. 23A(2)).

4.3.14 Remands in Police Custody

As outlined above, where a person is remanded in custody it normally means detention in prison. However, s. 128 of the Magistrates' Courts Act 1980 provides that a magistrates' court may remand a person to police custody:

- for a period not exceeding three days (24 hours for persons under 17) (s. 128(7));

- for the purpose of inquiries into offences (other than the offence for which he/she appears before the court) (s. 128(8)(a));

- as soon as the need ceases he/she must be brought back before the magistrates (s. 128(8)(b));

- the conditions of detention and periodic review apply as if the person was arrested without warrant on suspicion of having committed an offence (s. 128(8)(c) and (d)).

This option is colloquially referred to as a 'three day lie down'.

4.3.15 The Human Rights Act 1998

Custody officers need to be aware and give consideration to the rights and freedoms guaranteed under the European Convention on Human Rights when reaching a decision as to bail.

Article 5 of the Convention relates to the right to liberty and security. Article 5(3) provides that a person arrested under Article (5)(1)(c) is entitled to 'trial within a reasonable time or to release pending trial'. Article 5(1)(c) states:

> the lawful arrest or detention of a person effected for the purpose of bringing him before the competent legal authority on reasonable suspicion of having committed an offence or when it is reasonably considered necessary to prevent him committing an offence or fleeing after having done so.

It should be noted that 'trial within a reasonable time' and 'release pending trial' have been held not to be alternatives (*Wemhoff* v *Germany* (1968) 1 EHRR 55).

The Convention requires that every arrested person be brought 'promptly' before a judge or other judicial officer. The meaning of 'promptly' is not specified but in *Brincat* v *Italy* (1992) 16 EHRR 591, the European Court held that a person who had been detained for four days on blackmail charges before being brought before a court was not treated in accordance with the Article. However it is likely that the periods of detention provided by the Police and Criminal Evidence Act 1984 would be acceptable for most purposes of the Convention.

Article 5(3) provides the right to be released pending trial where a person's continuing detention ceases to be reasonable (*Neumeister* v *Austria* (1968) 1 EHRR 91). Bail should only be refused where there are 'relevant' and 'sufficient' reasons and in all cases these reasons should be provided (*Wemhoff* v *Germany*, above; *Tomasi* v *France* (1992) 15 EHRR 1). In *Yagci and Sargin* v *Turkey* (1995) 20 EHRR 505, the European Court were sceptical about what it referred to as 'stereotyped' reasons for refusing bail and it is likely that our domestic courts will take a similar view to anything other than a genuine consideration of each person's individual circumstances.

In *R (DPP)* v *Havering Magistrates' Court* [2001] 1 WLR 805, no oral evidence was available to prove the breach of bail conditions. It was held that such a hearing does not equate to facing a criminal charge and therefore Article 6 (right to a fair trial) does not apply. Also, Article 5 would not necessarily be breached as evidence could be considered which was not admissible in the strict sense and the case did not need to be proved beyond reasonable doubt.

The European Court and Commission have identified four grounds where the refusal of bail may be justified under the Convention:

- fear of absconding
- interference with the course of justice
- the prevention of crime
- the preservation of public order.

These will be considered in turn.

Fear of Absconding

The seriousness of the offence alone has been deemed not to be a sufficient reason to suppose a person will necessarily abscond (*Yagci and Sargin* v *Turkey* (1995) 20 EHRR 505). Regard must be taken of other factors including the character of the detained person, their background, status, etc. (*W* v *Switzerland* (1993) 17 EHRR 60).

Interference with the Course of Justice

As with s. 38(1) of the Police and Criminal Evidence Act 1984 (**see 4.3.5**), this would apply where there are reasonable grounds for believing that detention is necessary to prevent the interference with the administration of justice or with the investigation of offences or a particular offence.

The approach in some European cases has been that where further evidence is obtained and statements taken, the risk of interference diminishes and further detention under this ground is difficult to justify (*W* v *Switzerland*, above). Also, if the detained person has previously been bailed and there was no evidence of interference with the course of justice, using this ground would be very difficult to justify (*Ringeisen* v *Austria* (1971) 1 EHRR 455).

The Prevention of Crime

Again, this is similar to the condition contained in s. 38(1) of the Police and Criminal Evidence Act 1984, where the custody officer has reasonable grounds for believing that the detained person will commit other offence(s) if bailed. It was held in *Matznetter* v *Austria* (1979–80) 1 EHRR 198 and *Toth* v *Austria* (1991) 14 EHRR 551 that a reasonable risk of the person committing further offences whilst on bail was a valid reason for refusal.

In considering a person's previous convictions, the European Court has held that, where these were not comparable either in nature or seriousness with the offence(s) charged, their use as grounds for refusing bail would not be acceptable for the purposes of Article 5 (*Clooth* v *Belgium* (1991) 14 EHRR 717).

The Preservation of Public Order

This provides for the temporary detention of a person where the particular gravity of the offence(s) and the likely public reaction is that the release may give rise to public disorder

(*Letellier* v *France* (1991) 14 EHRR 83). This may be difficult to reconcile with the recent approach of the Court in *Redmond-Bate* v *DPP* (1999) 163 JP 789, where the predicted unlawful acts of others were held not to be a reason for arresting and detaining the individual whose lawful behaviour was antagonising them.

4.4 Pace Codes of Practice

PACE Codes of Practice A–F are included in Appendices 1–6 on pages 319–432.

4.4.1 Introduction

The powers to detain people who have been arrested and the manner in which they must be dealt with are primarily contained in the Police and Criminal Evidence Act 1984 and the PACE Codes of Practice whose creation and status come from s. 66 of the Act. The 1984 Act provides directions to police officers in how detained persons should be treated. The main responsibility for detained persons lies with the custody officer, however it is important that *all* officers, including everyone involved in investigations and dealing with detained persons, are aware of the provisions of the Act and the Codes. Failure to follow the requirements could lead to prosecutions failing because evidence is excluded, civil claims against forces, bad publicity and the possibility of disciplinary action or even criminal proceedings against the investigators themselves.

The Human Rights Act 1998 which came into force in October 2000 makes it even more important to comply with the 1984 Act and its associated Codes of Practice. This can be seen from the case of *R* v *Chief Constable of Kent Constabulary, ex parte Kent Police Federation Joint Branch Board* (2000) 2 Cr App R 196, where it was held that while Article 5 of the European Convention on Human Rights was not then part of the domestic law of England and Wales, the Article embodied important and basic rights which English law recognised and protected, and any deprivation of liberty must be in accordance with the law. The court went on to say that the 1984 Act and the Codes of Practice represented the balance between the important duty of the police to investigate crime and apprehend criminals and the rights of the private citizen. A breach of Code C is fundamental in affecting the fairness of any evidence obtained and presented (see *R* v *Aspinall* (1999) 2 Cr App R 115).

The Human Rights Act 1998 incorporates the European Convention into UK legislation and as such domestic legislation still applies, but will be interpreted so as to incorporate the Articles of the Convention and the relevant case law. Where there is a conflict between domestic law and the Convention, it will be for Parliament to change domestic legislation to come into line with the Convention. The main Articles which need to be considered in relation to the detention of a person include Articles 3, 5, 6 and 8.

The custody officer carries the main responsibility towards prisoners who are brought to the police station. Initially the custody officer must decide whether the person should be detained as a prisoner at the police station. If there are grounds to detain him/her then the detention period must be *for those reasons only*. Once a decision to detain a person has been made, the manner in which he/she must be treated while in detention is set out in the PACE Codes. These Codes are intended to protect the basic rights of detained people. If these Codes are followed it is more likely that evidence obtained while people are in custody will be admissible. The provisions of the 1984 Act give guidance in numerous areas including:

- length of time in detention;
- information about the detained person's arrest;
- searching;

- taking of samples;

- interviewing of suspects;

- identification methods;

- charging; and

- bail.

The PACE Codes set out the minimum standard of treatment that a detained person can expect. These requirements may be extended with the incorporation of the European Convention on Human Rights and its associated case law. The maximum length of detention is also prescribed by the 1984 Act, as are the requirements for charging, bailing and appearances at court.

The following chapter outlines some of the requirements of the legislation and the powers police have in relation to detained people. The chapter is aimed at providing guidance when using the legislation and it is intended to point the reader to the correct sections of the 1984 Act and the PACE Codes of Practice when dealing with detained people and investigations.

Whilst it is common practice for custody officers to have gaolers to assist in managing detained people, it is still the custody officer's responsibility to ensure that PACE is complied with. However, the Police Reform Act 2002 allows the role of support staff to be expanded in this regard.

4.4.2   Designated Police Stations

Section 30 of the Police and Criminal Evidence Act 1984 requires that a person who has been arrested must be taken to a police station *as soon as practicable* after arrest. However, not all police stations have charge rooms or facilities for dealing with prisoners, so the 1984 Act requires that prisoners who will be detained (or who are likely to be detained) for more than six hours must go to a 'designated' police station. A designated police station is one that has enough facilities for the purpose of detaining arrested people. Section 35 requires the Chief Officer of Police to designate sufficient police stations to deal with prisoners. It is for the Chief Officer to decide which stations are to be designated stations and these details are then published. Police stations can be designated permanently or for any specified periods provided that they are not designated for part of a day.

4.4.3   Custody Officers

Custody officers are responsible for the reception and treatment of prisoners brought to the police station.

The role of the custody officer is to act independently of those conducting the investigation, thereby ensuring the welfare and rights of the detained person. This requirement is contained in s. 36(5) of the 1984 Act. PACE Code C, para. 3.4 also supports this point in that it makes it clear that the custody officer must not ask a detained person any questions regarding his/her involvement in any offence. The custody officer should not make any comment which may be seen as placing a value judgment on what the person is alleged to have done, nor should he/she make any other comment which in any way casts doubt on his/her impartiality.

Section 36 requires that one or more custody officers must be appointed for each designated police station. However, in *Vince* v *Chief Constable of Dorset* [1993] 1 WLR 415, it was held that there does not have to be a custody officer available all the time at such a police station. The provision of the facility of a custody officer must be reasonable. Section 36(3) states that a custody officer must be an officer of at least the rank of sergeant. However, s. 36(4) allows constables to perform the functions of a custody officer if a sergeant is not readily available to perform them. The effect of s. 36(3) and (4) is that the practice of allowing constables to perform the role of custody officer where a sergeant (*who has no other role to perform*) is in the police station must therefore be unlawful. Should a decision be made to use acting sergeants or untrained custody officers, this may lead to a claim in negligence by the officer or the detained person where there is a breach of the Codes or someone is injured as a result of the failure to manage the custody suite effectively.

For cases where arrested people are taken to a non-designated police station, s. 36(7) states that an officer of any rank not involved in the investigation should perform the role of custody officer. If no such person is at the station, the arresting officer (or any other officer involved in the investigation) should perform the role. In these cases, an officer of at least the rank of inspector at a designated police station must be informed. It is suggested that once informed, that officer should consider the circumstances of the detained person.

The role of the custody officer is crucial to the effective and fair operation of the criminal justice system. In addition to protecting the rights of detained people the role, if performed properly, should also prevent evidence being declared inadmissible because of a violation of the rules. In order to provide as full a record as possible about the detention of a person, the custody officer is required to open a custody record for each detained person (Code C, para. 2.1) and entries should be recorded *as soon as practicable*. Guidance on the completion of custody records is given in Code C, paras 2.1 to 2.7. Custody officers must become very familiar with this guidance, as they are responsible for the accuracy and completeness of the custody record (para. 2.3). It is important that all entries in the custody record are timed and signed by the maker (Code C, para. 2.6). If a person is requested to sign an entry in accordance with the Codes and refuses, this too should be recorded (Code C, para. 2.7).

It is also recognised that the role of custody officer is very demanding and, on occasions, the time restraints created by the legislation can become unrealistic. For this reason Code C, para. 1.1A states that a custody officer will not be in breach of the Codes if a delay in taking some action was justifiable and steps had been taken to prevent the delay.

However, if that delay was not 'reasonable', it could lead to actions for unlawful detention and false imprisonment and any evidence obtained as a result may be held to be inadmissible (*Roberts* v *Chief Constable of Cheshire Constabulary* [1999] 1 WLR 662).

Where a custody officer feels that he/she is unable to comply with the minimum standards of detention as required by PACE, it is suggested that he/she should draw this to the attention of the line manager and/or the superintendent responsible for the custody suite. Custody officers should be mindful of Article 5 of the Convention in considering whether they are able to manage the number of detained persons in their custody to ensure that their detention is not any longer than needed.

4.4.4 Police Detention and the Treatment of Detained Persons

Depriving a person of his/her liberty is a serious step. The legislation and the PACE Codes of Practice are intended to ensure that where a person's liberty is taken it is for no longer than is necessary. There is a growing trend towards civil claims against the police for unlawful detention and false imprisonment, some of which is as a result of a failure to follow the guidelines. There are strict limits on a person's detention period and the best defence to such cases is to ensure that the 1984 Act and its Codes of Practice are followed.

Meaning of Police Detention

Police detention is defined by s. 118 of the Police and Criminal Evidence Act 1984 which states:

(2) A person is in police detention for the purposes of this Act if—
    (a) he has been taken to a police station after being arrested for an offence or after being arrested under section 41 of the Terrorism Act 2000, or
    (b) he is arrested at a police station after attending voluntarily at the station or accompanying a constable to it,

and is detained there or is detained elsewhere in the charge of a constable, except that a person who is at a court after being charged is not in police detention for those purposes.

KEYNOTE

Paragraph 22 of sch. 4 to the Police Reform Act 2002 refers to power to transfer persons into custody of investigating officers; para. 34(1) relates to designated escort officers taking an arrested person to a police station; and para. 35(3) deals with a designated escort officer transferring a detainee from one police station to another.

PACE Code of Practice C also states:

1.10 ... Section 15 applies solely to people in police detention, e.g. those brought to a police station under arrest or arrested at a police station for an offence after going there voluntarily.

1.11 People in police custody include anyone detained under the Terrorism Act 2000, schedule 8 and section 41, having been taken to a police station after being arrested under the Terrorism Act 2000, section 41. In these cases, reference to an offence in this Code includes the commission, preparation and instigation of acts of terrorism.

1.12 This Code's provisions do not apply to people in custody:
   (i) arrested on warrants issued in Scotland by officers under the Criminal Justice and Public Order Act 1994, section 136(2), or arrested or detained without warrant by officers from a police force in Scotland under section 137(2). In these cases, police powers and duties and the person's rights and entitlements whilst at a police station in England or Wales are the same as those in Scotland;
   (ii) arrested under the Immigration and Asylum Act 1999, section 142(3) in order to have their fingerprints taken;
   (iii) whose detention is authorised by an immigration officer under the Immigration Act 1971;
   (iv) who are convicted or remanded prisoners held in police cells on behalf of the Prison Service under the Imprisonment (Temporary Provisions) Act 1980;
   (v) detained for examination under the Terrorism Act 2000, schedule 7 and to whom the Code of Practice issued under that Act, schedule 14, paragraph 6 applies;
   (vi) detained for searches under stop and search powers except as required by Code A.
      The provisions on conditions of detention and treatment in sections 8 and 9 must be considered as the minimum standards of treatment for such detainees.

KEYNOTE

The last two lines of Code C, para. 1.12 above, make it clear that the way such prisoners are treated should be of no lower standard than that for other detained people. If in doubt as to whether a person falls within the definition of a detained person, it is suggested that he/she should be afforded all the rights and privileges outlined in the Codes of Practice. A similar approach should be adopted when it comes to reviewing a detainee's detention.

With the exception of those groups listed in Code C, para. 1.12, Code C applies to people in custody at police stations in England and Wales, whether or not they have been arrested, and to those removed to a police station as a place of safety under the Mental Health Act 1983, ss. 135 and 136.

Right to Have Someone Informed

Section 56 of the Police and Criminal Evidence Act 1984 provides that a person arrested and held in custody at a police station or other premises may, on request, have one person known to him/her or who is likely to take an interest in his/her welfare, informed at public expense of his/her whereabouts as soon as practicable (Code C, para. 5.1). (If the detainee's first choice cannot be contacted, see Code C, para. 5.1 and Notes 5C and 5D.) This fundamental human right is known as the right not to be held *incommunicado* and guidance on this right is contained in Code C, paras 5.1 to 5.8. If a person transfers to another police station, the same right applies at the next police station (Code C, para. 5.3), even if they have already had someone informed at the previous places of detention.

This right can only be delayed if the offence is a 'serious arrestable offence' and an officer of the rank of superintendent or above (whether or not connected to the investigation) authorises the delay (see Code C, Annex B) (see below). Where a person has to be given information under the Code but is not in a fit state to understand it, it is to be given to him/her as soon as practicable but only when he/she is in a fit state to understand it (Code C, para. 1.8). The delay can only be for a maximum of 36 hours (48 hours in cases involving terrorism), and the 36-hour period is calculated from the 'relevant time' (see below). In the case of a juvenile, the power to authorise the delay does not apply to the appropriate adult, but only to any other person the juvenile wishes to have informed (Code C, para. 3.13).

There may be occasions where officers wish to conduct a search under s. 18 of the 1984 Act and the detained person has requested to have someone informed. Clearly if such a person is informed before the search is conducted, vital evidence or property may be lost. Often the custody officer has two methods by which he/she can inform the person requested about the detained person's detention; either in person or on the phone. Contacting the person by telephone is likely to be the quickest, however, there is no requirement to use the quickest method in order to pass on this information. While there is no case law on this point, Code C, Note 5D, supports the view that, where the s. 18 search is to be conducted relatively quickly after the request is made by the detained person, it would be permissible to inform that person at the time the s. 18 search is conducted. Where the search is not to be conducted straightaway, it is suggested that consideration would have to be given to obtaining the authority of a superintendent to delay the notification as outlined below. A lengthy delay may be seen as a breach of this right, which may lead to a stay of proceedings or a claim for damages as a breach of the detained person's human rights.

Detained people may also be allowed to speak to a person on the telephone for a reasonable time or send letters. If a person has an interpreter, he/she can do this on the detained person's behalf. This right can be denied or delayed in the case of arrestable and serious arrestable offences by an officer of the rank of inspector or above (Code C, para. 5.6). The grounds are the same as those regulating the holding of people *incommunicado* (see below). Where a person is allowed to make a telephone call or send a letter, the procedure in Code C, para. 5.7 should be followed. Should there be any delay in complying with a request by a detained person to have someone informed of his/her detention or to communicate with someone, the detained person should be informed of this and a record kept (s. 56(6) of the 1984 Act). The custody officer also has a discretion to allow visits to the detained person at the police station (Code C, para. 5.4 and Note 5B). It is suggested that with the Codes of Practice outlining the limited rights for the detained person to make telephone calls and the right to restrict these calls, that if the person has a mobile telephone it can be seized for the period of their detention. There is no case law on this point and any force policy should be followed.

There are also special requirements for juveniles and detained people from other countries.

Juveniles

In the case of juveniles, where practicable, a person who is responsible for a juvenile's welfare must be informed of his/her arrest. This person may be the appropriate adult (see Code C, para. 1.7(a)) but if not, an appropriate adult must also be arranged to attend the police station to look after the interests of the juvenile. This action must be undertaken regardless of whether the juvenile wishes to have someone informed or has requested that some other person other than the appropriate adult be informed.

Code C, para. 3.13 states:

3.13 If the detainee is a juvenile, the custody officer must, if it is practicable, ascertain the identity of a person responsible for their welfare. That person:
  – may be:
  – the parent or guardian;
  – if the juvenile is in local authority or voluntary organisation care, or is otherwise being looked after under the Children Act 1989, a person appointed by that authority or organisation to have responsibility for the juvenile's welfare;
  any other person who has, for the time being, assumed responsibility for the juvenile's welfare.
  – must be informed as soon as practicable that the juvenile has been arrested, why they have been arrested and where they are detained. This right is in addition to the juvenile's right in section 5 not to be held incommunicado. See Note 3C

KEYNOTE

If a juvenile known to be subject to a court order under which a person or organisation is given any degree of statutory responsibility to supervise or otherwise monitor them, reasonable steps must also be taken to notify that person or organisation (the 'responsible officer'). The responsible officer will normally be a member of a Youth Offending Team, except for a curfew order which involves electronic monitoring when the contractor providing the monitoring will normally be the responsible officer (Code C, para. 3.14).

Detained persons—special groups

If the detainee appears to be deaf or there is doubt about his/her hearing or speaking ability or ability to understand English, and the custody officer cannot establish effective communication, the custody officer must, as soon as practicable, call an interpreter for assistance to go through the detainee's rights under Code C, paras 3.1–3.5 (Code C, para. 3.12).

If the detainee is a mentally disordered person or is otherwise mentally vulnerable, the custody officer must, as soon as practicable, inform the appropriate adult of the grounds for their detention and their whereabouts. The appropriate adult should also be asked to come to the police station to see the detainee (Code C, para. 3.15). In managing mentally disordered or otherwise mentally vulnerable persons detained under the Mental Health Act 1983, s. 136, the custody officer must be mindful that it is imperative that the detainee is assessed as soon as possible (Code C, para. 3.16).

Detained People from Other Countries

Citizens of independent commonwealth countries or foreign nationals may communicate with their High Commission, Embassy or Consulate as soon as practicable (Code C, para. 7.1). If the country is included on the list at Annex F of Code C, the High Commission, Embassy or Consulate must be informed unless the detained person is a political refugee or is seeking political asylum (para. 7.1).

Where a person who is a friend, relative or a person with an interest in the detained person's welfare, makes enquires about that person, the detained person should be asked whether he/she agrees to the person being informed prior to any information being given (Code C, para. 5.5). The information must not be given if a delay has been authorised.

Right to Legal Advice

Section 58 of the Police and Criminal Evidence Act 1984 provides an almost inalienable right for a person arrested and held in custody at a police station or other premises to consult privately with a solicitor free of charge if he/she requests it (or the appropriate adult makes the request (Code C, para. 3.19)). This provision is very similar to that of s. 56 of the

1984 Act; the right to have a person informed of the arrest. This right to consult a solicitor is considered to be so important that a detained person must be informed of the right when he/she first arrives at the police station and asked for reasons if he/she declines to exercise this right. Detainees are also reminded of this right at other times, e.g. prior to interview and when detention is being reviewed. In *R v Alladice* (1988) 87 Cr App R 380 the Court of Appeal made it clear that:

> no matter how strongly and however justifiably the police may feel that their investigation and detection of crime is being hindered by the presence of a solicitor ... they are nevertheless confined to the narrow limits imposed by section 58.

In *R v Aspinall* [1999] 2 Cr App R 115 the court stated that the right to access to legal advice was a fundamental right under Article 6 of the European Convention on Human Rights and even greater importance had to be attached to advice for a vulnerable person.

Code C, Annex B provides only two exceptions to this right to legal advice:

- Cases where an officer of the rank of superintendent or above (whether or not connected to the investigation) authorises the exercise of the right to be delayed. This only applies if the offence is a serious arrestable offence and Code C, Annex B applies.

- Where the person is held under the prevention of terrorism legislation (Terrorism Act 2000) and the conditions in Code C, Annex B apply. Here a uniformed officer of at least the rank of inspector not connected with the case may be present if authorised by an Assistant Chief Constable or Commander.

The delay can only be for a maximum of 36 hours (48 hours from the time of arrest in terrorism cases) or until the time the person will first appear at court, which ever is the sooner (see below). The 36-hour period is calculated from the 'relevant time' (see below). The authorisation can initially be made orally either in person or by telephone but must be recorded in writing as soon as practicable. Where a delay is authorised then this restricts the drawing of adverse inferences from silence (see Code C, para. 6.6).

The consultation with a solicitor can be either on the telephone, in person or in writing and it must be in private (Code C, para. 6.1). This right to have a private consultation is a good example of where a person's rights under the European Convention need to be considered. In many custody suites this is difficult to comply with (see Code C, Note 6J) but could lead to adverse comment, particularly if officers act on what they heard the detained person say whilst consulting with their legal representative. Code C, Note 6J, gives clear indication that the normal expectation should be that facilities will be available for the detainee to speak in private to a solicitor. This right to have a private consultation also apples to juveniles who, should they wish to have a private consultation without the appropriate adult being present, must be permitted to do so (Code C, Note 1E). This point was considered in *R (on the application of M (A Child)) v Commissioner of the Police of the Metropolis* [2002] Crim LR 215, where the court said that ideally there ought be a consultation room at every police station and facilities for private telephone calls to be made for legal consultations. However, there was no breach of Article 6(3) of the European Convention where it could not be shown that a detainee had been denied adequate facilities for the preparation of his defence.

Once a person has indicated a wish to have a solicitor, and has not yet been advised by a solicitor, he/she can only be interviewed in limited circumstances as set out in Code C, para. 6.6, but it is not necessary to delay taking breath, blood or urine samples from a motorist until a solicitor arrives nor delay searching the detainee or the taking of non-intimate samples without consent for evidential purposes (Code C, Note 3E). Of particular note is Code C, para. 6.6(b). This allows an officer of the rank of superintendent or above to allow an interview to take place or continue without a solicitor being present, if he/she has reasonable grounds for believing that:

(i) the consequent delay might:
- lead to interference with, or harm to, evidence connected with an offence;
- lead to interference with, or physical harm to, other people;
- lead to serious loss of, or damage to, property;
- lead to alerting other people suspected of having committed an offence but not yet arrested for it;
- hinder the recovery of property obtained in consequence of the commission of an offence.

(ii) when a solicitor, including a duty solicitor, has been contacted and has agreed to attend, awaiting their arrival would cause unreasonable delay to the process of investigation.

Another exception is in relation to the drink drive procedure for s. 7 of the Road Traffic Act 1988. In *DPP* v *Noe* [2000] RTR 351 a request to see a solicitor or alternatively to consult a law book to verify the legality of the police request for a specimen of breath was not a reasonable excuse under s. 7. This decision has not been affected by the enactment of the Human Rights Act 1998. This is confirmed by *Campbell* v *DPP* [2003] Crim LR 118, which held that it was entirely proportionate to allow a police officer to require a member of the community to provide a specimen albeit that legal advice had not been obtained.

Code C, para. 6.6 provides two further occasions where the interview may go ahead without a solicitor being present provided the consent of an officer of inspector rank or above has been obtained. Paragraph 6.6(c) deals with the situation where the solicitor the detainee has nominated or selected from a list cannot be contacted, has previously indicated they do not wish to be contacted, or having been contacted, has declined to attend; and the detainee has been advised of the Duty Solicitor Scheme but has declined to ask for the duty solicitor. Paragraph 6.6(d) deals with the situation where the detainee changes his/her mind, about wanting legal advice. In these circumstances the interview may be started or continued provided that the detainee agrees to do so, in writing or on tape. In this case the officer of inspector rank or above must inquire about the detainee's reasons for their change of mind. Paragraph 6.6(d) outlines what information must be recorded in the taped or written interview record.

Where an interview has started without the solicitor being present and access has not been refused under Code C, Annex B, the solicitor must be allowed to be present when he/she arrives at the station unless Code C, para. 6.6(b) applies or he/she has been excluded because of his/her conduct (Code C, para. 6.10).

In considering whether to conduct an interview in these circumstances, guidance is given Code C, Note 6A.

A solicitor for these purposes means a solicitor who holds a current practising certificate, a trainee solicitor, a duty solicitor representative or an accredited representative included on the register of representatives maintained by the Community Legal Service (Code C, para. 6.12). A non-accredited or probationary representative may also attend and give advice unless an officer of the rank of inspector or above considers that such a visit will hinder the investigation of crime and directs otherwise and once admitted he/she should be treated as any other legal adviser (Code C, para. 6.12A).

In deciding whether to admit a non-accredited or probationary representative, the officer should take into account in particular whether the identity and status of the non-accredited or probationary representative have been satisfactorily established; whether he/she is of suitable character to provide legal advice (a person with a criminal record is unlikely to be suitable unless the conviction was for a minor offence and is not of recent date); and any other matters in any written letter of authorisation provided by the solicitor on whose behalf the person is attending the police station (Code C, para. 6.13). The Law Society has advised solicitors that if a non-accredited or probationary representative is refused admission, a written reason for the decision should be requested. If access is refused or a decision is taken that such a person should not be permitted to remain at an interview, he/she must forthwith notify a solicitor on whose behalf the non-accredited or probationary representative was to have acted or was acting, and give him/her an opportunity to make alternative arrangements. The detained person must also be informed and the custody record noted (Code C, para. 6.14 and Note 6F).

Authority to Delay Rights under ss. 56 or 58 (Code C, Annex B)

An officer of the rank of superintendent or above (for s. 56 of the 1984 Act it is likely that this will be lowered to an officer of the rank of inspector, but at the time of writing this has not yet been introduced) can only authorise a delay if he/she has reasonable grounds for believing that by exercising the right it will:

- interfere with or cause harm to evidence connected with a serious arrestable offence or interfere with or cause physical injury to other people; or
- alert other people suspected of having committed such an offence but not yet arrested for it; or
- hinder the recovery of property obtained as a result of such an offence.

The delay may also be re-authorised under s. 56 and/or s. 58, where the person is detained for a serious arrestable offence and has benefited from his criminal conduct in circumstances where the recovery of the value of the property constituting the benefit will be hindered by telling the named person of the arrest or his/her right of access to legal advice (s. 56(5A) for delay in notification and s. 58(8A) for access to legal advice).

For these purposes whether a person has benefited from his/her criminal conduct is to be decided in accordance with Part 2 of the Proceeds of Crime Act 2002. Briefly, criminal conduct is conduct which constitutes an offence in England and Wales, or would constitute such an offence if it occurred in England and Wales. A person benefits from conduct if he/she obtains property as a result of or in connection with the conduct.

In cases where the person is detained under the Terrorism Act 2000, an officer of the rank of superintendent or above may delay the exercise of either right or both if he/she has reasonable grounds for believing that the exercise of the right will lead to any of the consequences of:

- interference with or harm to evidence of a serious arrestable offence;
- interference with or physical injury to any person;
- the alerting of persons who are suspected of having committed a serious arrestable offence but who have not been arrested for it;
- the hindering of the recovery of property obtained as a result of a serious arrestable offence or in respect of which a forfeiture order could be made;
- interference with the gathering of information about the commission, preparation or instigation of acts of terrorism;
- the alerting of a person and thereby making it more difficult to prevent an act of terrorism;
- the alerting of a person and thereby making it more difficult to secure a person's apprehension, prosecution or conviction in connection with the commission, preparation or instigation of an act of terrorism;
  - the detained person has benefited from his/her criminal conduct, and the recovery of the value of the property constituting the benefit will be hindered by informing the named person of the detained person's detention or access to legal advice. For these purposes whether a person has benefited from his/her criminal conduct is to be decided

in accordance with Part 2 of the Proceeds of Crime Act 2002. Briefly, criminal conduct is conduct which constitutes an offence in England and Wales, or would constitute such an offence if it occurred in England and Wales. A person benefits from conduct if he/she obtains property as a result of or in connection with the conduct

(Code C, Annex B, paras 8 and 9).

These powers were amended on 24 March 2003 where the Proceeds of Crime Act 2002 amended ss. 56 and 58 of the 1984 Act. These changes are not reflected in the latest Codes of Practice which must be read in conjunction with the above sections.

If the delay is authorised the detained person must be given the reason for the delay which must correspond to one of the above grounds and an entry must be made in the custody record.

Once the reason for authorising the delay has ceased, the detained person must be allowed to exercise his/her rights. Once this point has been reached, the detained person must as soon as practicable be asked if he/she wishes to exercise the right (or rights), the custody record must be noted accordingly, and the relevant action taken (Code C, Annex B, para. 4).

The fact that the grounds for delaying notification of arrest may be satisfied does not automatically mean that the grounds for delaying access to legal advice will also be satisfied (Code C, Annex B, para. 5), considered separately, and, if authority to delay the right to notify a person is given, it does not automatically mean that the right to legal advice can be delayed.

When considering whether to deny access to a solicitor, the fact that he/she might advise the person not to answer any questions or that the solicitor was initially asked to attend the police station by someone else, provided that the person himself/herself then wishes to see the solicitor, is not a reason for delaying access to a solicitor (Code C, Annex B, para. 3). When considering the delay of access to a solicitor, the authorising officer must bear in mind that access to a solicitor is 'a fundamental right of a citizen' (*R* v *Samuel* [1988] 2 WLR 920). The authorising officer must actually believe that by allowing access to the solicitor, he/she will intentionally or inadvertently alert other suspects. There must also be objective reasons upon which the officer authorising the delay can base his/her beliefs. If the reason for authorising the delay of access to a solicitor is because there are concerns with the particular solicitor who has been requested or is offering his/her services to the detained person the officer should offer the detained person access to a solicitor (who is not the specific solicitor referred to above) on the Duty Solicitor Scheme (Code C, Annex B, Note B4). In deciding whether such an interview will be admissible the court will consider how reliable it is and will consider how the refusal to allow that particular detained person access to a solicitor affected their decision to make a confession. One such case where the confession was excluded is *R* v *Sanusi* [1992] Crim LR 43, where a person from another country was denied access to a solicitor and the court held that his right to advice was particularly significant due to his lack of familiarity with police procedures.

In terrorism cases a direction may be given by an officer of at least the rank of Commander or Assistant Chief Constable which may provide that a detained person who wishes to exercise the right to consult a solicitor may do so only in the sight and hearing of a qualified officer, this person being a constable from the authorising officer's force.

Relevant Time

As discussed above, there are limits on how long a person can be detained. The Police and Criminal Evidence Act 1984 and the Codes of Practice talk of the 'relevant time'. This is the time from which the limits of detention are calculated. The relevant time of a person's detention starts in accordance with s. 41(2) to (5) of the 1984 Act. Section 41 states:

(2) The time from which the period of detention of a person is to be calculated (in this Act referred to as 'the relevant time')—

(a) in the case of a person to whom this paragraph applies, shall be—

(i) the time at which that person arrives at the relevant police station; or

(ii) the time 24 hours after the time of that person's arrest,

whichever is the earlier;

(b) in the case of a person arrested outside England and Wales, shall be—

(i) the time at which that person arrives at the first police station to which he is taken in the police area in England or Wales in which the offence for which he was arrested is being investigated; or

(ii) the time 24 hours after the time of that person's entry into England and Wales, whichever is the earlier,

(c) in the case of a person who—

(i) attends voluntarily at a police station; or

(ii) accompanies a constable to a police station without having been arrested, and is arrested at the police station, the time of his arrest;

(d) in any other case, except where subsection (5) below applies, shall be the time at which the person arrested arrives at the first police station to which he is taken after his arrest.

(3) Subsection (2)(a) above applies to a person if—

(a) his arrest is sought in one police area in England and Wales;

(b) he is arrested in another police area; and

(c) he is not questioned in the area in which he is arrested in order to obtain evidence in relation to an offence for which he is arrested;

and in sub-paragraph (i) of that paragraph 'the relevant police station' means the first police station to which he is taken in the police area in which his arrest was sought.

(4) Subsection (2) above shall have effect in relation to a person arrested under section 31 above as if every reference in it to his arrest or his being arrested were a reference to his arrest or his being arrested for the offence for which he was originally arrested.

(5) If—

(a) a person is in police detention in a police area in England and Wales ('the first area'); and

(b) his arrest for an offence is sought in some other police area in England and Wales ('the second area'); and

(c) he is taken to the second area for the purposes of investigating that offence, without being questioned in the first area in order to obtain evidence in relation to it, the relevant time shall be—

(i) the time 24 hours after he leaves the place where he is detained in the first area; or

(ii) the time at which he arrives at the first police station to which he is taken in the second area,

whichever is the earlier.

KEYNOTE

Note that under s. 41(5), the detainee has, in effect, two detention clocks running. It is important to note that the second clock will start earlier if the detained person is questioned about the offence under investigation in the other police area.

For those detained under the Terrorism Act 2000, the detention clock starts from the time the person is arrested; not the time they arrive at the police station.

Some situations occur where a person is arrested at one police station and has been circulated as wanted by another police station in the same force area. In these cases, where the person is not wanted on warrant, the detention clock for the second offence starts at the same time as for the original offence for which they were arrested. Consideration will need to be given as to how to protect the detention period for the second offence while officers are dealing with the first matter. Options that might be considered would include bailing the person for one of the offences or conducting both investigations at the same station. Here there may be a risk of 'confusing' the suspect, which may allow him/her to retract or qualify any confession he/she might make.

In *Henderson* v *Chief Constable of Cleveland* [2001] 1 WLR 1103 the court considered the policy of not executing a court warrant until after other matters for which the person had been detained were completed. The court held that, once a warrant was executed, there was a requirement to follow the directions of the warrant. The police however had a discretion as to *when* to execute the warrant. This may be relevant where a person has been arrested for one offence and it is discovered that he/she is also wanted for another offence or where there are warrants in existence for that person at more than one court. In such cases, if the warrant is executed immediately, the direction on the warrant tells officers to take the person before the next available court, an action which could interfere with the investigation. If *Henderson* is followed there is no requirement to execute the warrant straightaway and the other matters can be dealt with before the requirement to produce the person at court under the warrant applies.

Detention of People under Arrest

People who have been arrested, or voluntarily given themselves up at a police station, will be brought before a custody officer who must decide whether the person should be detained at the police station or released. People who attend police stations voluntarily to assist the police with their investigations are not subject to this procedure; their treatment is dealt with by PACE Code C, paras 3.21 and 22.

The arresting officer informs the custody officer of the reasons for arrest. This will include *what* offence the person was arrested for and brief details of the *grounds* for the arrest, e.g. the arrest is for robbery and the accused was seen to punch the victim in the face and steal his holdall. In the case of a non-arrestable offence, an example might be that the detained person was seen to drive his car through a red light and has refused to give his name and address, thereby making it impossible to serve a summons. As this information must be given to the person on arrest—in most cases—the details given to the custody officer should be fresh in the mind of the arresting officer; they should also accord with the reasons and grounds given to the person on arrest! If the reasons were not given at the time of arrest (under justifiable grounds) the custody officer should consider whether the arrested person is now in a position to be given the reasons for the arrest. If the reasons for arrest were not given when they should have been the arrest is unlawful regardless of what information is given later (*Wilson* v *Chief Constable of Lancashire* (2000) LTL 23 November).

Having heard the details of and for the arrest, the custody officer must then decide whether or not there are reasons which justify authorising that person's detention (s. 37 of the Police and Criminal Evidence Act 1984 deals with the procedures to be followed before a person is charged). Some commentators have suggested that it is also the role of the custody officer to establish that the arrest itself was lawful. While this would seem to be sensible and good practice, the custody officer's duty is confined to acting in accordance with the requirements set out in s. 37 of the 1984 Act. These duties do not appear to include considering whether the arrest was lawful unless this is relevant to the main question of whether there is sufficient evidence to charge the suspect. The view is supported by the decision of the Divisional Court in *DPP* v *L* [1999] Crim LR 752, where the court held that there was no express or implied requirement imposing a duty on a custody officer to inquire into the legality of an arrest and in that case the custody officer was therefore entitled to assume that it was lawful. A subsequent finding that the arrest was unlawful did not invalidate the decision of the custody officer to hold the person in custody. However, where the custody officer is aware that the arrest is unlawful, he/she will need to consider whether continued detention is justifiable, particularly in light of the Human Rights Act 1998.

Section 37 of the 1984 Act states:

(1) Where—
   (a) a person is arrested for an offence—
      (i) without a warrant; or
      (ii) under a warrant not endorsed for bail, or
   the custody officer at each police station where he is detained after his arrest shall determine whether he has before him sufficient evidence to charge that person with the offence for which he was arrested and may detain him at the police station for such period as is necessary to enable him to do so.

(2) If the custody officer determines that he does not have such evidence before him, the person arrested shall be released either on bail or without bail, unless the custody officer has reasonable grounds for believing that his detention without being charged is necessary to secure or preserve evidence relating to an offence for which he is under arrest or to obtain such evidence by questioning him.

(3) If the custody officer has reasonable grounds for so believing, he may authorise the person arrested to be kept in police detention.

(4) Where a custody officer authorises a person who has not been charged to be kept in police detention, he shall, as soon as is practicable, make a written record of the grounds for the detention.

(5) Subject to subsection (6) below, the written record shall be made in the presence of the person arrested who shall at that time be informed by the custody officer of the grounds for his detention.

(6) Subsection (5) above shall not apply where the person arrested is, at the time when the written record is made—
   (a) incapable of understanding what is said to him;
   (b) violent or likely to become violent; or
   (c) in urgent need of medical attention.

KEYNOTE

If the person is arrested on a warrant, any directions given by the court in the warrant must be followed. Consideration can always be given to contacting the court to get a variation on the conditions of the warrant. (If the warrant was issued for the arrest of a person who has not yet been charged or summonsed for an offence, he/she should be dealt with as any other person arrested for an offence without warrant unless there are any additional directions on the warrant that must be followed.)

Authorising a Person's Detention

A custody officer can authorise the detention of a person when there is sufficient evidence to charge and, in some circumstances, when there is *not* sufficient evidence to charge the suspect. If there is insufficient evidence to charge, the custody officer must decide if the detention is necessary to secure or preserve evidence relating to an offence for which the person is under arrest or to obtain such evidence by questioning him/her.

If a person representing the detained person does not feel the detention is lawful, he/she can apply to the court for the detainee's release (*habeas corpus*). A detainee may also be able to make an application for release or damages following the incorporation of the European Convention on Human Rights. Article 5(4) states:

> Everyone who is deprived of his liberty by arrest or detention shall be entitled to take proceedings by which the lawfulness of his detention shall be decided speedily by a court and his release ordered if the detention is not lawful.

Sufficient Evidence to Charge

Here the custody officer is looking at the evidence in order to satisfy himself/herself that no further investigation is needed before the person can be charged. If this is the case, detention may be authorised. In considering whether this position has been reached it is worth considering Code C, para. 16.1 which states:

> When an officer considers that there is sufficient evidence to prosecute a detained person, and that there is sufficient evidence for a prosecution to succeed, and that the person has said all that he wishes to say about the offence, he shall without delay ... bring him before the custody officer who shall then be responsible for considering whether or not he should be charged ...

KEYNOTE

Code C, para. 16.1 suggests that a charge should not be brought until there is sufficient evidence for a prosecution to succeed. This might require the person being bailed while advice is sought from the Crown Prosecution Service.

Where there is sufficient evidence for a prosecution to succeed, under s. 37(7) of the Police and Criminal Evidence Act 1984, the custody officer must charge the person or release him/her without charge, either on bail or without bail. Often the reason for not charging the person will be to allow a decision to be made by the Crown Prosecution Service as to whether to charge the person, caution them or not to proceed with the case. In these circumstances s. 37(8) requires the custody officer to inform the person that a decision to charge has not yet been made.

Where there is sufficient evidence to charge, a delay in bringing charges may be seen to be unreasonable under Article 6 of the European Convention on Human Rights (*D* v *HM Advocate* (2000) *The Times*, 14 April).

In deciding whether there is sufficient evidence to charge for the purposes of authorising detention or when a person's detention is reviewed; where there is a conflict between the detained person's account and victims' or witnesses' accounts it is reasonable to be in possession of at least one witness statement in the English language before preferring charges (*R* v *Chief Constable of Hertfordshire, ex parte Wiles* [2002] EWHC Admin 387). There is no breach of the Police and Criminal Evidence Act in keeping the detained person in police detention while a statement is translated. It is suggested that the translation needs to be completed expeditiously.

Under s. 37(9) release can be delayed if the person is not in a fit state to be released (e.g. he/she is drunk), until he/she is fit. Where a person is detained for charge, the custody officer should record the grounds for detention in the custody record in the presence of the detained person if practicable (Code C, para. 3.23).

Insufficient Evidence to Charge

This creates two separate criteria for detention, that is to say, where detention is necessary to:

- secure and preserve evidence relating to an offence for which the person is arrested; and/or

- obtain such evidence by questioning the detained person.

If the custody officer has determined that there is not sufficient evidence to charge the person, the person must be released unless the custody officer has *reasonable grounds* for believing that the person's detention is necessary to preserve or to obtain such evidence by questioning the person. 'Reasonable grounds for believing' requires a greater amount of evidence than 'reasonable cause to suspect' and the custody officer must be able to justify any decision not to release a person from detention.

When deciding if detention should be authorised in order to preserve evidence by questioning, the case of *R* v *McGuinness* [1999] Crim LR 318 should be considered. There the court held that the words 'sufficient evidence to prosecute' and 'sufficient evidence for a prosecution to succeed', in Code C, para. 16.1, had to involve some consideration of any explanation, or lack of one, from the suspect. While an interview may not be needed in all cases, questioning of detained people before they are charged may be necessary, particularly where intention or dishonesty is involved or where there may be a defence. It may also be important to put questions to the person about the offence or his/her explanation, as this may be important to negate any defence the person raised at court (see s. 34 of the Criminal Justice and Public Order Act 1994).

Where initial suspicion rests on several people, it may be appropriate to hold all suspects until they all are interviewed before deciding whether there is enough evidence to warrant a charge against any of them. Detention for questioning where there are reasonable grounds for suspecting that an offence has been committed is lawful so long as the suspicion has not been dispelled in the interim and the questioning is not unnecessarily delayed (*Clarke* v *Chief Constable of North Wales, The Independent,* 22 May 2000).

Article 5 of the European Convention on Human Rights makes the decision to authorise detention even more crucial, as it states:

1. Everyone has the right to liberty and security of person. No one shall be deprived of his liberty save in the following cases and in accordance with a procedure prescribed by law:
    (a) the lawful detention of a person after conviction by a competent court;
    (b) the lawful arrest or detention of a person for non-compliance with the lawful order of a court or in order to secure the fulfilment of any obligation prescribed by law;
    (c) the lawful arrest or detention of a person effected for the purpose of bringing him before the competent legal authority on reasonable suspicion of having committed an offence or when it is reasonably considered necessary to prevent his committing an offence or fleeing after having done so ...

The custody officer can detain the person for such period as is necessary in order to make this decision (s. 37(1) of the 1984 Act). Clearly any such period must be 'reasonable' in all the circumstances. For instance, where there are several prisoners waiting to be dealt with it may be reasonable that the last prisoner is not dealt with for 30 minutes because the custody officer is busy with the other prisoners (Code C, para. 1.1A and Note 1H). For the custody officer to be able to make this decision, the arresting officer needs to give sufficient detail about the offence. The account given by the arresting officer should be made in the presence of the arrested person (Code C, para. 3.4) and any comment made by that person in response should be recorded in the custody record (unless the person is violent or it is impractical to do so for some other reason, in which case this fact should also be recorded).

The mere fact that a person needs to be interviewed about the offence is not of itself justification for authorising detention. The question that has to be asked is whether the person can be bailed prior to the interview. Factors which might be relevant in making this decision include whether the person may interfere with witnesses; whether he/she is likely to return if bailed; where there is more than one suspect, that they would have an opportunity to confer before their interviews; whether there is outstanding property; whether the person's name and address is verified. The fact that the officers and any legal representative will be ready to start the interview shortly may also be relevant when making this decision.

Section 37(4) and (5) of the 1984 Act require the custody officer to make a written record of the grounds of detention and to make that record in the presence of the detained person, informing him/her at the same time of the grounds of his/her detention (unless s. 37(6) applies). It is suggested that the custody officer record all the reasons for authorising the person's detention. For example: 'To obtain statements from the victim and witnesses as this information will be needed before interview to fully put the allegation to the suspect and then to allow the suspect to be interviewed about the allegation. If bailed prior to interview he/she may interfere with the witnesses, who are known to the suspect.' It is suggested that detail of at least this minimal level should be included, as it may be necessary in any criminal or civil proceedings. Indeed, it will be difficult for the custody officer to explain his/her decision without such information.

Section 37(6) states:

(6) Subsection (5) above shall not apply where the person arrested is, at the time when the written record is made—

    (a) incapable of understanding what is said to him;

    (b) violent or likely to become violent; or

    (c) in urgent need of medical attention.

Additional Action to be Taken by the Custody Officer

The action to be taken by the custody officer when receiving detained people is set out in Code C, paras 3.1 to 3.5A.

Paragraph 3.1 sets out the information the detained person is entitled to. These are *continuing* entitlements and can be requested at any time during the person's detention.

Paragraph 3.2 deals with written notices which must be given to the detained person in relation to his/her rights. (Code C, para. 1.2 requires that a copy of the Codes of Practice must also be readily available to detained persons should they request it.) There should be versions of these rights in languages other than English available in the custody suite.

Paragraph 3.5 requires the custody officer to establish whether the detained person wishes to have a solicitor at this stage. If he/she declines, the custody officer should ask the person the reason why and, if any reasons are given, these should be recorded in the custody record (Code C, para. 6.5). The detained person must still be asked if they require a solicitor even if they are to be held *incommunicado*.

4.4.5   Limits on Detention and Review

Once detention has been authorised, this does not mean that a person can be detained indefinitely. Section 34 of the Police and Criminal Evidence Act 1984 requires the custody officer to release a person if he/she becomes aware that the grounds for detention no longer apply and that no other grounds exist for the continuing detention (unless the person appears to be unlawfully at large). If there are additional grounds, these should be recorded in the custody record and the person informed of these additional grounds in the same way as when a person is first detained. For example, this could be for new offences or it could be that it becomes necessary to preserve evidence by questioning the detained person.

It is only the custody officer who can authorise the release of a detained person (s. 34(3)). It is a breach of the PACE Codes of Practice for anyone else to release a detained person without first obtaining the authority of the custody officer. In addition to the requirement to release a person should the grounds for detention no longer exist, there are also maximum time limits for which a person can be detained without charge (see below). Once this limit has been reached, it will be necessary to proceed by summons or by warrant. There are also limits on the time a person can be kept in custody after being charged, refused bail and appearing at court (see below).

Time Limits: Without Charge

While a person is in police detention there is a requirement that his/her continuing detention is reviewed. This is dealt with below. There are minimum time requirements for when these reviews must be conducted, with the timing of the first review being calculated from the time detention is authorised. This time can be considered as the 'review time'. The question of whether a person should be kept in custody is a continuous one and the review process is intended as an added protection to the detained person.

The maximum period that a person can be detained without charge (with the exception of suspected acts of terrorism, in which case it is seven days) is 96 hours. The necessity for the continued detention of the person must be reviewed throughout this time. The period of detention is calculated from the 'relevant time' which can be calculated from the chart below. (*Do not confuse the relevant time with the time from which reviews are due.*) The relevant time 'clock' will always start before, or at the same time as the review 'clock'. This is because the review clock does not start until detention has been authorised which clearly cannot happen until the person is brought before the custody officer which, as can be seen from the chart below, is at the very latest, the time the prisoner walks into the custody suite (*with the exception of where the person has been under arrest for 24 hours but has not yet been taken to a police station*).

This relevant time period (that is, the maximum period a person can be detained for) relates to the actual time spent in custody and not a 24-hour period in time. This means that every time the person is bailed the clock stops and usually continues from the time that the person returns to custody for the offence(s) for which he/she was bailed.

Where a person has been released and re-arrested for an offence, it is possible that the relevant time will start again. This is covered by s. 47(7) of the 1984 Act:

> (7) Where a person who was released on bail subject to a duty to attend at a police station is re-arrested, the provisions of this Part of this Act shall apply to him as they apply to a person arrested for the first time but this subsection does not apply to a person who is arrested under section 46A above or has attended a police station in accordance with the grant of bail (and who accordingly is deemed by section 34(7) above to have been arrested for an offence).

KEYNOTE

In cases where this subsection applies, the relevant time starts again and a fresh clock starts. This will apply where the person has been re-arrested for the same offence because of some new evidence (except at such time as when he/she is returning on bail at the appointed time) under s. 41(9) or 47(2).

Section 41 states:

> (9) A person released under subsection (7) above shall not be re-arrested without a warrant for the offence for which he was previously arrested unless new evidence justifying a further arrest has come to light since his release; but this subsection does not prevent an arrest under section 46A below.

Section 47 states:

> (2) Nothing in the Bail Act 1976 shall prevent the re-arrest without warrant of a person released on bail subject to a duty to attend at a police station if new evidence justifying a further arrest has come to light since his release.

KEYNOTE

The issue will be whether new evidence has come to light since the grant of bail and it will be a question of fact as to what the new evidence is. It is suggested that this must be evidence which was not available at the time the person was last in detention or which would not have been available even if all reasonable enquiries had been conducted.

It will always be important to check how much time is left on the person's 'relevant time' and when his/her next review is due.

The Three Stages of Pre-charge Detention

After the custody officer has authorised detention but before a person has been charged there are three distinct stages of detention. These are distinguished by the level at which authorisation for continuing detention is required.

The three stages of detention under the 1984 Act are:

- The basic period of detention, which is the period of detention up to 24 hours, as first authorised by the custody officer.
- Those authorised by an officer of the rank of superintendent or above (s. 42) up to 36 hours.
- Those authorised by a magistrates' court (ss. 43 and 44) up to a maximum of 96 hours.

Each of these is examined in detail below.

The Basic Period of Detention

The majority of people detained by the police are detained for less than six hours; most other cases are dealt with within 24 hours. If a person's continued detention is not authorised beyond 24 hours and the person is not charged with an offence, he/she *must* be released (with or without bail) and cannot be re-arrested for the offence unless new evidence comes to light (s. 41(7) and (9) of the 1984 Act). New evidence is not defined by the 1984 Act but it is suggested that it covers evidence which was not available at the time the person was detained, or which would not have been available if the investigating officers had conducted reasonable enquiries.

During this period of detention the custody officer has a responsibility to monitor whether the grounds for detention still exist. An officer of at least the rank of inspector not involved in the investigation (s. 40(1)(b)) must review the person's detention *at least once in the first six hours* and then, after the first review, *within nine hours of that review*. Further reviews must then be conducted *no later than nine hours after the last review* was conducted, until the person is either charged or released. The detention of persons in police custody not subject to the statutory review requirement in Code C, para. 15.1 should still be reviewed periodically as a matter of good practice (Code C, Note 15B).

If a detained person is taken to hospital for medical treatment, the time at hospital and the period spent travelling to and from the hospital does not count towards the relevant time unless the person is asked questions for the purpose of obtaining evidence about an offence. Where questioning takes place, this period would count towards the relevant time and therefore the custody officer must be informed of it (s. 41(6)).

Detention Authorised by an Officer of the Rank of Superintendent

Under s. 42(1) of the Police and Criminal Evidence Act 1984, detention can only be authorised beyond 24 hours and up to a maximum of 36 hours from the relevant time if:

- an offence being investigated is a 'serious arrestable offence' (see s. 116 of the 1984 Act); *and*
- an officer of the rank of superintendent or above who is responsible for the station at which the person is detained (referred to here as the authorising officer); *and*
- that that senior officer is satisfied that:
  - there is not sufficient evidence to charge; *and*
  - the investigation is being conducted diligently and expeditiously; *and*
  - that the person's detention is necessary to secure or preserve evidence relating to the offence or to obtain such evidence by questioning that person.

At this stage if the authorising officer considers that there is sufficient evidence to charge, he/she cannot authorise further detention beyond 24 hours unless the detained person is in custody for another serious arrestable offence for which further detention can be, authorised (*R v Samuel* [1988] QB 615 and Code C, para. 16.1).

The grounds for this continuing detention are the same as those when the custody officer made the initial decision to detain, with the additional requirements that the case has been

Maximum Periods of Detention for non Terrorism Act Offences

Arrest	Relevant time starts	Review clock starts	24 hours from relevant time
Arrested locally	24 hours from arrest or arrival at police station whichever earliest.		All offences other than serious arrestable offences.
Arrested outside England and Wales	Time first arrives at police station in police area where matter being investigated or 24 hours after first entered England or Wales whichever earliest.	Time custody officer authorises detention.	Release unless s. 41(1) applies.
Arrested for an offence in one police area in England or Wales then transferred to another police area for separate offence in that second police area which is also in England or Wales	24 hours from time he/she leaves the police station in the first police area or the time he/she arrives at the first police station in second police area where the crime is being investigated or the first time questioned about the offence, whichever is the earliest.	This timing applies where the person was in detention for an offence in the first police area (s. 41(5)).	
Voluntarily attends police station or accompanies constable to station but not under arrest	Time of arrest.		
Arrested in one police area in England or Wales for an offence in another police area in England or Wales, there being no 'local' offence(s) for which he/she has been arrested	From time the suspect arrives at the first police station in the area he/she is being sought or from 24 hours after the time he/she is arrested or first time questioned about the offence whichever is the earliest.		

24 to 36 hours' detention	36 to 42 hours' detention	42 to 78 hours' detention	up to 96 hours' detention
Only serious arrestable offences.	Only serious arrestable offences.	Only serious arrestable offences.	Only serious arrestable offences.
Detention authorised by superintendent or above (s. 42).	Where delay in applying for warrant of further detention is reasonable (s. 43(5)).	First warrant for further detention issued by magistrates' court (s. 42).	Further warrants of detention issued by magistrates' court (s. 43).
	See pp. 206–7 for the dangers of not applying within the 36-hour period.	Remember the warrant can be applied for at any stage of detention.	

conducted diligently and expeditiously. It is suggested that Article 5 of the European Convention requires this to be a consideration at all times of detention as a person's right to freedom is one of his/her human rights and any unnecessary periods of detention might be considered actionable. To be able to satisfy the senior officer of this, it will be necessary for the custody record to be available for inspection and details of what inquiries have been made and evidence that the investigation has been moving at a pace that will satisfy the senior officer that the inquires should not already have been completed.

The authorising officer (which here must be an officer of the rank of superintendent or above who is responsible for the station at which the person is detained) can authorise detention up to a maximum of 36 hours from the 'relevant time' of detention. The period can be shorter than this and can then be further authorised by that officer or any other officer of the rank of superintendent or above who is responsible for the station at which the person is detained to allow the period to be further extended up to the maximum 36-hour period (s. 42(2)). Code C, Note 15E gives guidance as to which officers this would include.

The extension of a person's detention by a superintendent or above must be made within 24 hours of the relevant time and cannot be made before at least two reviews have been carried out by a review officer under s. 40 of the 1984 Act (i.e. those normally carried out by an inspector) (s. 42(4)) (Code C, para. 15.2). If an extension to the period of detention is authorised, a record must be made and shall state the number of hours and minutes by which the detention period is extended or further extended (Code C, para. 15.16).

Section 42(5) to (8) mirrors the responsibility on the authorising officer at this stage with those of the review officer during the 'general period' of detention with regard to allowing representations, informing the detained person of the decision to authorise further detention and the need to record the decision. The main difference here is that the authorising officer must look into how the case is being investigated and whether this is being done diligently and expeditiously. Consequently, the authorising officer must also consider any representations on these points and these points should also be covered in any record as to whether detention should continue. When considering whether to authorise further detention the authorising officer must check whether the detained person has exercised his/her right to have someone informed and to consult with a legal representative. If these options have not been taken, s. 42(9) requires the authorising officer to inform the detained person of these rights and also whether he/she will be allowed to exercise these rights if it is a serious arrestable offence and the right has so far been delayed as per Code C, Annex B. The authorising officer should record the detainee's decision in the custody record and the grounds for denying the person those rights where appropriate.

If it is proposed to transfer a detained person from one police area to another for the purpose of investigating the offences for which he/she is detained, the authorising officer may take into consideration the period it will take to get to the other police area when deciding whether detention can go beyond 24 hours (s. 42(3)).

Detention Authorised by a Magistrates' Court

Once the 36-hour limit has been reached, a person's detention can only continue with the authority of the courts through the issuing of a warrant of further detention. If a person's continued detention is not authorised beyond 36 hours by a court and the person is not charged with an offence, he/she must be released with or without bail and cannot be re-arrested for the offence unless new evidence comes to light.

Warrants of Further Detention

Applications for warrants of further detention are made at the magistrates' court. Initially, the magistrates can issue a warrant for further detention for a period of up to 36 hours. This can be extended by the courts on further applications by police up to a maximum total period of detention of 96 hours. The warrant will specify what period of further detention the court has authorised. If detention of the person is required for any longer period, further applications can be made to the court up to a maximum of 96 hours' detention. The grounds on which the court must decide whether to grant a warrant authorising further detention are the same as those that must be considered by a 'superintendent's review' (see above).

Should it be necessary to apply for a warrant it is important that the time restraints are kept in mind at all times and the application procedure followed closely.

Procedure

The application is made in the magistrates' court and both the detained person and the police must be in attendance (s. 43(1) and (2) of the Police and Criminal Evidence Act 1984). The application is made by laying an information before the court. The officer making the application does so on oath and is subject to cross-examination. Under s. 43(14) the information must set out:

- the nature of the offence;
- the general evidence on which the person was arrested;
- what inquiries have been made;
- what further inquiries are proposed; and
- why it is believed that continuing detention is necessary for the proposed inquiries.

It will be important to be able to demonstrate why the person needs to remain in detention while additional inquiries are made, for instance, that further facts need to be verified before further questioning of the suspect can continue and that this cannot be done effectively if the person is released. The detained person must be provided with a copy of the information before the matter can be heard (s. 43(2)). He/she is also entitled to be legally represented. If the person is not legally represented but then requests legal representation at court, the case must be adjourned to allow representation (s. 43(3)). In cases where the person is not represented it may be prudent to remind the person of his/her right to legal representation prior to the court hearing and to make a record of this in the custody record. Should the detained person choose to be legally represented at court, and thereby try and delay the police investigation, s. 43(3)(b) allows the person to be taken back into police detention during the adjournment.

Timing of the application

If it appears likely that the investigation of the serious arrestable offence requires the person's detention to go beyond 36 hours, then thought must be given as to when to make the application to the magistrates' court. Section 43(5) allows the application to be made before the expiry of the 36-hour period (calculated from the relevant time) or, where it has not been practicable for the court to sit within the 36-hour period, the application can be made within the next six hours. There are dangers in applying outside the 36-hour period in that if the court feels that it would have been reasonable to make the application within the

36-hour period then it must refuse the application for the warrant regardless of the merits of the case (s. 43(7)).

The court may either refuse the application or adjourn the hearing until such time as it specifies up to the end of the 36-hour period of detention (s. 43(8)). If the application is refused, the person must be charged or released with or without bail at the expiry of the current permissible period of detention (s. 43(15)).

The application for the warrant can be made at any time, *even before a superintendent's review has been carried out*. If the application is made within the 36-hour period and it is refused, it does not mean the person must be released straight away. Section 43(16) allows the person to be detained until the end of the current detention period (24 hours or 36 hours). The benefit of an early application has to be set against the risk that, once the court has refused an application, it is not allowed to hear any further applications for a warrant of further detention unless new evidence has come to light since the application was refused (s. 43(17)). Code C, Note 15B gives guidance on when an application should be made to the court. Note 15B states:

> An application for a warrant of further detention or its extension should be made between 10 am and 9 pm, and if possible during normal court hours. It will not be practicable to arrange for a court to sit specially outside the hours of 10 am to 9 pm. If it appears possible that a special sitting may be needed (either at a weekend, Bank/Public Holiday or on a weekday outside normal court hours but between 10 am and 9 pm) then the clerk to the justices should be given notice and informed of this possibility, while the court is sitting if possible.

In *R* v *Slough Justices, ex parte Stirling* [1987] Crim LR 576, the 36-hour period expired at 12.53 pm. The case was not heard by the justices until 2.45 pm. The Divisional Court held that the police should have made their application between 10.30 am and 11.30 am, even though this was before the 36-hour time limit had been reached.

In monitoring a person's detention, officers should be mindful of whether a warrant for further detention may be required and, if it is, consider whether a court will be available to hear the application. If a court will not be available then consideration should be given to making an earlier application. The process the magistrates go through in deciding the merits of the application also provides some safeguards in that the person's continued detention has been considered by the courts and therefore may reduce the likelihood of the defence suggesting that detention was not justified.

Further Warrants of Detention

Under s. 44 of the 1984 Act, the process for further warrants follows the same procedure as for the initial warrant, with the exception that the application *must be* made before the expiry of the extension given in the previous warrant. Once the period of detention that has been authorised has expired, and no other applications have been made, the detained person must be charged or released with or without bail.

Terrorism Cases

In terrorism cases the application to the magistrates' court is very similar except that the application must be made by a superintendent. The officer who makes the application may also apply to the court for an order that specified information upon which he/she intends to rely should be withheld from the person to whom the application relates and anyone representing him/her. Section 75 of the Criminal Justice and Police Act 2001 allows for the use of video links for proceedings about Terrorism Act 2000 detention. This will only apply where there are reasonable grounds for believing that if the information were disclosed:

- evidence of an offence under any of the provisions mentioned in s. 40(1)(a) of the Terrorism Act 2000 would be interfered with or harmed;
- the recovery of property obtained as a result of an offence under any of those provisions would be hindered;
- the recovery of property in respect of which a forfeiture order could be made under s. 23 of the Terrorism Act 2000 would be hindered;
- the apprehension, prosecution or conviction of a person who is suspected of committing offences under the Terrorism Act 2000 would be made more difficult as a result of his/her being alerted;
- the prevention of an act of terrorism would be made more difficult as a result of the person being alerted;
- the gathering of information about the commission, preparation or instigation of an act of terrorism would be interfered with; or
- a person would be interfered with or physically injured;
  - the detained person has committed an offence to which Part VI of the Criminal Justice Act 1988 applies (any indictable offence and others listed in sch. 4 to the Criminal Justice Act 1988), has benefited from the offence, and the recovery of the value of that benefit would be hindered if the information were disclosed (sch. 8, pt III to the Terrorism Act 2000).

The Review

While a person is in police detention before charge, his/her detention must be reviewed by an officer of the rank of inspector or above (inspector reviews). This review acts as another safeguard to protect the detained person's right to be detained for only such periods as are necessary to allow for the investigation of an offence. Reviews of police detention are covered by s. 40 of the Police and Criminal Evidence Act 1984.

Section 40(3) sets out the times when reviews must be conducted:

(3) Subject to subsection (4)...—
  (a) the first review shall be not later than six hours after the detention was first authorised;
  (b) the second review shall be not later than nine hours after the first;
  (c) subsequent reviews shall be at intervals of not more than nine hours.

KEYNOTE

Review officer for the purposes of ss. 40 and 40A of the 1984 Act means, in the case of a person arrested but not charged, an officer of at least inspector rank not directly involved in the investigation and, if a person has been arrested and charged, the custody officer. In cases under the Terrorism Act 2000, the review officer means an officer not directly involved in the investigation connected with the detention and of at least inspector rank, for reviews within 24 hours of the detainee's arrest or a superintendent for all other reviews.

It is suggested that even where a detainee is not in police detention as defined by s. 118 of the 1984 Act, consideration should be given to reviewing his/her detention. A case that supports this view is *Chief Constable of Cleveland Police* v *McGrogan* [2002] 1 FLR 707. This was a case involving a person detained at a police station overnight after having been arrested for breach of the peace, the Court of Appeal held the need to regularly review the person's detention was required even though breach of the peace was not an 'offence' for the purpose of s. 118.

The periods set out in s. 40(3) are the *maximum* periods that a review can be left; should the review officer wish to review before this time for operational reasons etc., the review could be brought forward. The first review must be made within six hours of the custody officer authorising detention (this, it must be remembered, is not the time from which the 24-hour clock starts, i.e. the time the detainee came into the station, but the time at which the custody officer authorised detention). Thereafter, each review must be made within nine hours of the last review.

Section 40(4) does allow reviews to be delayed if it is not practicable to carry out the review. Conducting late reviews should be avoided where at all possible (see *Roberts* v *Chief Constable of Cheshire Constabulary* [1999] 1 WLR 662). If delayed, the grounds for and extent of any delay must be recorded (Code C, para. 15.13). Section 40(4) provides two other occasions where it may be justified to delay the review:

– if at that time the person in detention is being questioned by a police officer and the review officer is satisfied that an interruption of the questioning for the purpose of carrying out the review would prejudice the investigation in connection with which he/she is being questioned;

– if at that time no review officer is readily available.

It is suggested that it will be necessary to justify why no review officer was available and it is suggested that where it is known that a review may fall during an interview that it is conducted prior to the interview where appropriate.

In *Roberts*, the defendant had his first review conducted 8 hours, 20 minutes after his detention had been authorised. The Court of Appeal held that under s. 40(1)(b) of the 1984 Act a review of his detention should have taken place by an officer of the rank of inspector or above six hours after detention was first authorised. Section 34(1) was mandatory and provided that a person must not be kept in police detention except in accordance with the relevant provisions of the Act. Therefore, the respondent's detention had been unlawful unless some event occurred to have made it lawful.

The court made it clear that the 1984 Act existed in order to ensure members of the public were not detained except in certain defined circumstances. In the absence of a review, the time spent in detention between 5.25 am, and 7.45 am meant that for that period the defendant's detention was unlawful and amounted to a false imprisonment.

Where a review is due under s. 40 and the detainee has not been charged, the review officer, in limited circumstances, may conduct the review by telephone. The conditions where this is permissible are: that the use of video conferencing facilities does not apply or it is not reasonably practicable to use such facilities (s. 45A of the 1984 Act but not yet in force) and it is not reasonably practicable for the review officer to attend the station holding the detainee, e.g. when severe weather conditions or an unforeseen operational emergency prevent the review officer form attending (Code C, para. 15.9 and Note 15F). Where this review is done by telephone, an officer at the station holding the detainee must fulfil the reviewing officer's obligations under PACE (see Code C, para. 15.10). Code C, para. 15.11 identifies the methods that can be used to ensure that the right of the detainee, appropriate adult and solicitor to make representations to the reviewing officer under Code C, para. 15.3 are satisfied: for example by fax, email message or orally by telephone. The use of telephone to conduct reviews does not include reviews to extend the period of detention beyond the 24-hour clock. Where the review is conducted by telephone, a record must be made of the following: the reason the review officer did not attend the station holding the detainee; the place the review officer was; and the method representations were made to the review officer (Code C, para. 15.14).

Telephone reviews do not apply to reviews of detention after charge by the custody officer or to reviews under the Terrorism Act 2000, sch. 8, pt II in terrorism cases (Code C, Note 15F).

If the review is delayed then it must still be conducted as soon as practicable and the reason for the delay must be recorded in the custody record by the review officer. In these circumstances the nine-hour period until the next review is calculated from the latest time the review should have been carried out and not from the time it was actually carried out. For instance, if the review was due at 3.15 pm and was delayed until 4 pm, the next review would have to be conducted no later than 12.15 am and not 1 am. When the review is conducted the review officer does not have to authorise detention for the full nine-hour period; he/she could decide that the case should be reviewed again within a shorter period and the review decision would reflect this.

When reviewing the detention of a person the review officer goes through the same process as the custody officer did when detention was first authorised (s. 40(8)), namely by asking:

- Is there sufficient evidence to charge? If 'yes', charge or release the person with or without bail. If 'no', then:
- Is detention necessary in order to secure or preserve evidence or is it necessary to detain the person in order to obtain such evidence by questioning him/her? If 'yes', authorise continued detention. If 'no', release the person with or without bail.

The situation may arise where the review officer considers that there is sufficient evidence to charge and authorises detention to charge even though the custody officer disagrees. In this case it is suggested that the custody officer must either charge or release the person with or without bail. The custody officer may wish to refer the matter to an officer of the rank of superintendent or above responsible for the station for advice.

It is suggested that the reviewing officer (or any other officer other than a superintendent or above) cannot tell the custody officer what they must do. The reviewing officer may wish to give advice but it will be for the custody officer to decide whether to take that advice. Clearly failure to do so could lead to internal criticism but legally there is no requirement to follow that advice.

If there is not sufficient evidence to charge, the review officer may want to consider the question: 'If this person is bailed what evidence will be lost'? If the answer is none, continued detention would seem unlawful.

As stated above, it is suggested that Article 5 of the European Convention requires that an investigation must be conducted diligently and expeditiously in order to minimise the time a person is deprived of his/her liberty (particularly where the case does not lead to a prosecution). In order to monitor the effectiveness of the investigation and the time spent in custody, the reviewing officer should consider the period of detention since the last review to ensure that any defect in the person's treatment is corrected, and where necessary, take steps to speed up the investigation.

In cases where it has been decided that a person should be charged but he/she has been detained because he/she is not in a fit state to be charged (s. 37(9)), the review officer must determine whether the person is yet in a fit state. If the detainee is in a fit state, the custody officer should be informed that the person should be charged or released. If the detainee is not in a fit state, detention can be authorised for a further period (s. 40(9)). In such cases, if the person is still unfit, it may be prudent to consider the welfare of the detained person.

During the process of reviewing a person's detention, the review officer must give the detained person (unless he/she is asleep) or any solicitor representing the detained person who is available at the time of the review, an opportunity to make representations about his/her continued detention (s. 40(12)). If the detained person is likely to be asleep at the time the review is to be carried out, the review should be brought forward to allow the detained person to be present at the time of the review (Code C, Note 15C). If the detainee is asleep when the reviewing officer authorises his/her continued detention, the detainee must be informed of the decision when he/she wakes (Code C, para. 15.7) and the details of the officer that informed the detainee of the decision should also be recorded (Code C, para. 15.16). If the detainee makes a comment it may be necessary to inform the reviewing officer (or his/her replacement) of the comment (Code C, para. 15.5). The review officer must also ensure that the detained person is reminded of his/her right to free legal advice and that this reminder is recorded in the custody record (Code C, para. 15.4). In the case of juveniles, the appropriate adult should also be allowed to make representations and the review officer has the discretion to allow other people having an interest in the welfare of the detained person to make representations (Code C, para. 15.3). These representations may be in writing or oral (s. 40(13)). If made in writing, the document should be retained (Code C, para. 15.15). The review officer can refuse to hear oral representations from the detained person if the review officer considers that the person is unfit to make such representations, either because of his/her condition or behaviour (e.g. drunk or violent) (Code C, para. 15.3B). A detainee who is not asleep during the review must be present when the grounds for his/her continued detention are recorded and must at the same time be informed of those grounds unless the review officer considers the person is incapable of understanding what is said, is violent or likely to become violent or in urgent need of medical attention (Code C, Note 15C); any comment made by the detainee should be recorded (Code C, para. 15.5). However, the review officer must not put any questions to the person about his/her comments (Code C, para. 15.6). Also, as the role of review officer is intended to be independent of the investigation, he/she should not put any questions to the person about his/her involvement in any offence; this mirrors the instruction to custody officers (Code C, para. 15.6).

If at any stage an officer of a rank higher than the review officer gives directions which are at variance with a decision made or action taken by the review officer, or which would have been made by the review officer but for the directions by the more senior officer, then s. 40(11) requires the matter to be referred *at once* to an officer of the rank of superintendent or above who is *responsible for the police station*.

It is important to understand the difference between the action of authorising an extension to the 'detention clock' and the role of the review officer. These are two distinct roles and both need to be carried out. When an officer of the rank of superintendent or above extends the 'relevant time' period this is not automatically a review (although there is nothing to stop that officer from conducting the review). This means that the 'reviewing' officer may still have to conduct a review even though the relevant time has only recently been extended, unless the officer of the rank of superintendent or above extending the relevant time has shown the review as having been conducted in the custody record.

Terrorism Act Reviews

In cases where the person has been detained under the Terrorism Act 2000, the first review should be conducted as soon as reasonably practicable after his/her arrest and then at least every 12 hours; after 24 hours it must be conducted by an officer of the rank of superintendent or above. Once a warrant of further detention has been obtained there is no requirement to conduct further reviews. If an officer of higher rank than the review officer gives directions relating to the detained person, and those directions are at variance with the performance by the review officer of a duty imposed on him/her, then he/she must refer the matter at once to an officer of at least the rank of superintendent.

A review officer may only authorise a person's continued detention if he/she is satisfied that it is necessary:

- in order to obtain relevant evidence whether by questioning the person or otherwise;
- to preserve relevant evidence;
- pending a decision whether to apply to the Secretary of State for a deportation notice to be served on the detained person;
- pending the making of an application to the Secretary of State for a deportation notice to be served on the detained person;
- pending consideration by the Secretary of State whether to serve a deportation notice on the detained person; or
- pending a decision whether the detained person should be charged with an offence.

In all cases the review officer must be satisfied that the matter is being dealt with diligently and expeditiously. Where the detained person's rights to a solicitor have been withheld or he/she is being held *incommunicado* at the time of the review, the review officer must consider whether the reason or reasons for which the delay was authorised continue to exist. If in his/her opinion the reason or reasons no longer exist, he/she must inform the officer who authorised the delay of his/her opinion. When recording the grounds for the review the officer must also include his/her conclusion on whether there is a continuing need to withhold the detained person's rights.

In cases where the person is detained under the Terrorism Act 2000 and the review officer does not authorise continued detention, the person does not have to be released if an application for a warrant for further detention is going to be applied for or if an application has been made and the result is pending (s. 41 and sch. 8).

4.4.6   Cautioning

There are occasions where a person for whom there is sufficient evidence to charge may be cautioned as an alternative method of disposing with the case. *R* v *Chief Constable of Lancashire Constabulary, ex parte Atkinson* (1998) 162 JP 275 is a case which considered the level of evidence required before a caution can be considered. There the court said that, provided it was clear that there had been an admission of guilt, it was not necessary, for the purposes of administering a caution, to show that the admission had been obtained in circumstances which satisfied the Codes of Practice. That was not to say that police authorities would not be well advised to take precautions which would satisfy the Code, but it did not follow that in every case there had to be a formal interview. However, police officers would be well advised to take precautions that would satisfy Code C. It would be both fairer and more reliable for a formal interview to take place.

Before making a case disposal decision it is essential that the matter has been fully investigated in order to reach an informed decision. In *Omar* v *Chief Constable of Bedfordshire Constabulary* (2002) unreported, the Divisional Court quashed a caution that had been administered in order to allow a prosecution to be pursued. The court held that a number of reasonable lines of enquiry had not been made, for instance, the police had failed to take a statement from the victim's friend or obtained CCTV that was available or fully investigated the victim's injuries. Further, that the length of time in custody (17 hours) should not have been a relevant consideration and that the suspect's admission was ambiguous. Therefore, it was in the public interest that a decision to caution rather that to change should not prevent the subsequent pursuit of the prosecution of the offender.

While there is no general obligation on the police to disclose material prior to charge, there may be a need to make some disclosure to a suspect's legal representative in order that he/she can advise on whether a caution should be accepted (*DPP* v *Ara* [2001] 4 All ER 559). In *Ara*, the suspect had been interviewed without a legal representative being present but the officers refused to disclose the terms of the interview.

Guidance as to the use of cautioning is provided by Home Office Circular 18/94. The guidelines should be considered carefully in all cases as any decision can be challenged by judicial review.

Sections 65 and 66 of the Crime and Disorder Act 1998 have made new provisions for reprimands and warnings for children and young persons.

In order to show consistency and, if necessary, to justify the decision to give or refuse to give a caution, the grounds for the decision should be recorded.

There is only one exception to the rule that reprimands and warnings replace cautions, and that is in respect of prostitutes' cautions. This approach to dealing with child prostitutes recognises that they are victims of abuse, and do not consent freely to prostitution. Joint guidance issued by the Home Office and the Department of Health sets out the appropriate way to deal with children in prostitution. That treatment aims to divert children away from prostitution, rather than to prosecute them.

4.4.7   Charging

The custody officer must decide whether there is sufficient evidence to charge a person when he/she is first brought to the police station (s. 37(1) of the 1984 Act) and when an officer informs them that he/she considers there is sufficient evidence to provide a realistic prospect of the detainee's conviction (Code C, para. 16.1). If the custody officer decides that there is sufficient evidence to charge, then he/she must charge that person or release him/her without charge, unless officers are still investigating other offences for which the person is in police detention. Similarly, if the custody officer considers that detention is not required, or is no longer required in order to obtain or secure evidence, the person should be released with or without bail attached to the release (s. 37(2)).

It is the custody officer's responsibility to ensure that there is sufficient evidence to charge the person. Where a person is charged in the absence of sufficient evidence (particularly if they are kept in custody), this could lead to a breach of Article 5 of the European Convention, as well as a breach of the PACE Codes of Practice.

Where a detained person is not in a fit state to be charged or released in accordance with s. 34(7) (for instance because he/she is drunk), he/she may be kept in custody until fit (but medical care may have to be considered).

Even where there is sufficient evidence to prosecute successfully, the detained person may be released without charge because it is felt that a charge is not in the public interest or the person has been cautioned or a decision has not yet been made about prosecuting the person.

In this case, the person must be informed when he/she is released that the decision to prosecute has not yet been made (s. 37(8)).

In cases where a person is bailed without being charged, the custody officer cannot impose conditions on that bail (s. 47(1A)).

If a decision is taken to charge the detained person, Code C, para. 16 sets out the procedures to be followed by the custody officer. When a detained person is charged with, or informed that he/she may be prosecuted for an offence, para. 16.2 requires him/her to be cautioned. The caution varies slightly from that when arrested or interviewed (see General Police Duties, chapter 2) and is as follows:

> You do not have to say anything. But it may harm your defence if you do not mention now something which you later rely on in court. Anything you do say may be given in evidence.

The above caution should not be used in circumstances where the detained person has been denied access to a solicitor (see para. 17.3) in which case the following cautions should be used:

> You do not have to say anything, but anything you do say may be given in evidence.

At the time a person is charged, he/she shall be given a written notice as set out in Code C, para. 16.3 and a record shall be made of anything the person says when charged (para. 16.8). Where the person being charged is a juvenile or is mentally disordered or mentally impaired, the appropriate adult should be present and the notice given to him/her (paras 16.3 and 16.6).

Once the person has been charged with or informed that he/she may be prosecuted for an offence, fingerprints can be taken if it is a recordable offence and he/she has not had his/her fingerprints taken during the course of the investigation (s. 61(3)(b)) (see chapter 16). Photographs may also be taken and in some cases DNA samples may be taken (see para. 16.7).

If fingerprints are taken, the person must be informed of the reason why and that those prints may be used for a speculative search concerning other crimes (see para. 16.5). The reasons should also be recorded in the custody record, along with confirmation that the detained person has been given the required information. If the person's photograph is taken, this should also be recorded in the custody record.

Once a person has been charged or informed that he/she may be prosecuted for an offence (which does not include the service of the Notice of Intended Prosecution under ss. 1 and 2 of the Road Traffic Offenders Act 1988; see Road Traffic, chapter 3), generally the person cannot be questioned or spoken to about the matter. Code C, paras 16.4 and 16.5 set out occasions where further investigation involving the person may be allowed and para. 16.9 sets out the procedure to be adopted. It should only be in these circumstances that the custody officer allows any further inquiries involving the detained person to be made. Paragraphs 16.4 and 16.5 deal with:

- written statements made by other people which the investigating officers may wish to show to another person charged;

- questions necessary for the purpose of preventing or minimising harm or loss to some other person or to the public or for clearing up an ambiguity in a previous answer or statement;

- where it is in the interests of justice that the person should have put to him/her—and have an opportunity to comment on—information concerning the offence which has come to light since he/she was charged or informed that he/she might be prosecuted.

4.4.8   Bail

If the person is charged then the custody officer has to decide whether the person is going to be bailed to appear at court or whether bail will be refused and the person kept in custody until the next available court. This is a review of the person's detention and therefore the person or his/her solicitor should be given an opportunity to make representations to the custody officer. The review should be conducted with regard to Code C, paras 15.1 to 15.6.

Where bail has been refused this decision must be reviewed by the custody officer at least every nine hours until the person is taken to court in the same manner required by a review officer.

In addition to the grounds for refusing bail covered in chapter 5, the custody officer may also detain the person after charge if he/she has reasonable grounds for believing that the detention of the person is necessary to enable a sample to be taken from him/her under s. 63B of the Police and Criminal Evidence Act 1984. The custody officer may not authorise a person to be kept in police detention for a period exceeding six hours beginning when the person was charged with the offence.

For occasions where the custody officer refuses bail of a juvenile after charge, see Code C, para. 16.7.

For a full discussion of bail, **see 4.3**.

In *Williamson* v *Chief Constable of West Midlands, The Times*, 11 March 2003, the Court of Appeal clarified the point that breach of the peace is not a criminal offence. Consequently, as there is no power in the Bail Act 1976 to grant bail except in criminal proceedings, no power exists to grant bail for breach of the peace. This means that if the person is bailed, there is no power to arrest the person or obtain a warrant for his/her failure to appear at court under the Bail Act 1976.

4.4.9   Special Groups and Appropriate Adults

In cases where the detained person is a juvenile or a person who is mentally handicapped or appears to be suffering from mental disorder, the custody officer must inform an appropriate adult as soon as possible (this must be done in the case of a juvenile regardless of whether he/she is held *incommunicado* (Code C, para. 3.7). In the case of a juvenile who is the subject of a supervision order, the person supervising the juvenile should also be informed. If the custody officer has any doubt as to the mental state or capacity of a person detained, an appropriate adult should be called (Code C, Note 1G).

A juvenile for the purpose of the 1984 Act is any person who is under the age of 17 or who appears to be under the age of 17 until it is established that he/she is 17 or over (Code C, para. 1.5).

Note 1G defines 'mental disorder' as having the same meaning as in s. 1(2) of the Mental Health Act 1983, as 'mental illness, arrested or incomplete development of mind, psychopathic disorder and any other disorder or disability of mind'. For the purposes of the Codes 'mental disorder' and 'mental handicap' are dealt with similarly throughout. Paragraph 1.4 also states:

> If an officer has any suspicion, or is told in good faith, that a person of any age may be mentally disordered or mentally handicapped, or mentally incapable of understanding the significance of questions put to him or his replies, then that person shall be treated as a mentally disordered or mentally handicapped person for the purposes of this code.

An appropriate adult is defined by para. 1.7 as:

(a) in the case of a juvenile:

    (i) his parent or guardian (or, if he is in care, the care authority or voluntary organisation … ;

    (ii) a social worker; or

    (iii) failing either of the above, another responsible adult aged 18 or over who is not a police officer or employed by the police.

(b) in the case of a person who is mentally disordered or mentally handicapped:

    (i) a relative, guardian or other person responsible for his care or custody;

    (ii) someone who has experience of dealing with mentally disordered or mentally impaired persons but who is not a police officer or employed by the police (such as an approved social worker as defined by the Mental Health Act 1983 or a specialist social worker); or

    (iii) failing either of the above, some other responsible adult aged 18 or over who is not a police officer or employed by the police.

KEYNOTE

The role of the appropriate adult is to assist and advise the detained person. Care should be taken when considering the suitability of an appropriate adult. Code C, Note 1E gives guidance for choosing the appropriate adult. Evidence obtained whilst a person is in custody where the person called as an appropriate adult does not have that person's best interests in mind or is not capable of assisting them could be excluded.

An appropriate adult is not required for a 17 year old (*R* v *Stratford Youth Court, ex parte Harding* [2001] EWHC Admin 615).

In *R* v *Aspinall* [1999] 2 Cr App R 115, the Court of Appeal emphasised the importance of appropriate adults. There it was held that an appropriate adult played a significant role in respect of a vulnerable person whose condition rendered him/her liable to provide information which was unreliable, misleading or self-incriminating.

It is also important to consider the welfare of the appropriate adult. This is demonstrated by the case of *Leach* v *Chief Constable of Gloucestershire Constabulary* [1999] 1 All ER 215. Here L was asked by a police officer to attend police interviews of a murder suspect who was also thought to be mentally disordered, as an 'appropriate adult' per the requirement of the PACE Codes. She was told only that the suspect was a 52-year-old male, and was not informed of the nature of the case. The suspect was in fact Frederick West, who was being questioned in connection with murders committed in particularly harrowing and traumatic circumstances. For many weeks L acted as an appropriate adult, accompanying the officer and suspect to murder scenes and on many occasions being left alone in a locked cell with the suspect. She claimed to be suffering from post-traumatic distress and psychological injury as well as a stroke as a result of her experiences. The Court of Appeal said that the Frederick West case was notorious amongst modern crimes and it was forseeable that psychiatric harm might arise. Whilst there was no requirement to pre-select or warn appropriate adults as to the nature of the case, in some cases, however, counselling or trained help should be offered.

4.5 Identification

4.5.1 Introduction

A critical issue in the investigation and prosecution of offences is the identification of the offender and this, like all other facts in issue, must be proved beyond a reasonable doubt. Many different methods of identification exist but the main feature which must be considered in relation to each is its *reliability*.

4.5.2 Code D

Identification evidence is governed by Code D of the PACE Codes of Practice (**see appendix 4**). These Codes were amended on 1 April 2003.

Generally, the methods of identification covered by Code D can be divided into two:

- occasions where the identity of the suspect is known; and

- occasions where the identity of the suspect is not known.

Although a breach of Code D (or any of the other Codes of Practice) will not automatically result in the evidence being excluded (*R* v *Khan* [1997] Crim LR 584), the judge or magistrate(s) will consider the effects of any breach on the fairness of any subsequent proceedings. The Codes are intended to provide protection to suspects and, if it is felt that the breach of Code D has resulted in unfairness or other prejudicial effect on the defendant, the court may exclude the related evidence under s. 78 of the Police and Criminal Evidence Act 1984.

Check 'This'

Conversely, even if Code D is followed, that is no guarantee that evidence obtained will be admissible. In each case the ultimate purpose of any identification procedure should be borne in mind and the 'this' test should be applied to any proposed procedure by asking:

> How reliable is *this* piece of evidence in proving, or disproving, *this* person's involvement in *this* offence?

This approach should be adopted even if the provisions of Code D are followed. A good example of a situation where such an approach may have helped is *R* v *Hickin* [1996] Crim LR 584. This case was decided under the old Codes of Practice before it was necessary to obtain a first description from a witness. In the case, a group of some 14 suspects were arrested following an attack on two men at night. Clearly it would have been impracticable to arrange identification parades or group identifications for each suspect at that time, thereby allowing for a direct confrontation (see below). However, witnesses could have been asked to provide initial descriptions of suspects before being used in the confrontation. The witnesses' comments at the time of the confrontation could also have been noted and some witnesses might have been asked to remain behind to take part in some later identification parades. As these things were not done, the Court of Appeal held that the identification evidence obtained by the confrontation procedure was unfairly prejudicial, *even though the provisions of Code D had been followed.*

4.5.3 Methods of Identification

Visual

The visual identification of suspects by witnesses is one of the most common forms of identification; it is also one of the most unreliable. Even under research conditions, the recall of eye witnesses is inconsistent; where the witness sees or experiences the spontaneous commission of a crime, that reliability is reduced even further.

It was for these reasons that the *Turnbull* guidelines were set out, together with the provisions of Code D.

Problems of reliability in identification can arise even where the person accused is known to the witness. See, for example, *R* v *Conway* (1990) 91 Cr App R 143 (see below).

A lot will depend on the individual circumstances of each case but it is essential that these issues are covered in any interview or other evidence gathering process.

'Dock identifications', where the witness's first identification of the accused involves pointing out the person in the dock, are often dramatised by film makers but, in practice, are generally disallowed as being unreliable and unfair.

The rules for identification differ between cases where the suspect *is known* and those where suspect is *not known*. Code D, para. 3.4 defines the terms as:

> ... a suspect being 'known' means there is sufficient information known to the police to justify the arrest of a particular person for suspected involvement in the offence. A suspect being 'available' means they are immediately available or will be within a reasonably short time and willing to take an effective part in at least one of the following which it is practicable to arrange;
>
> – video identification;
>   identification parade; or
> – group identification.

Code D requires that a first description provided of a person suspected of a crime (regardless of the time it was given) must be recorded (para. 3.1). This must also be disclosed to the defence in the pre-trial procedure in all cases and, in particular, before any identification procedures take place. This record must be made and kept in a form which enables details of that description to be accurately produced from it, in a visible and legible form (Code D, para. 3.1), which can be given to the suspect or the suspect's solicitor. Such a record could be made electronically or paper-based. The Code also makes provision for the disclosure of materials previously released to the media in relation to an enquiry and for witnesses to be asked if they saw such material before any identification procedure.

Identification where there is a Known Suspect

Where the suspect is known, there are four possible methods of identification provided for in Code D (paras 3.4 to 3.23). These are:

– video identification;

– identification parades;

– group identification; and

– confrontation (this is only of limited use and value).

The modifications to the PACE Codes of Practice alter the hierarchy of identification procedures in cases of disputed identification. Under the previous provisions, the preferred method of identification was the identification parade. Only in cases where an identification parade had been refused by the suspect, or was considered impracticable, could a group identification be considered. It was only if that form of identification was refused or impracticable, that a video identification could be considered, and, as a last resort, a confrontation could be held.

It is crucial that once the person becomes a known suspect, any witnesses, *including police officers*, who might be used at an identification parade, are kept apart from the suspect, as any contact could jeopardise a conviction. In *R* v *Lennon*, 28 June 1999, unreported, a suspect was arrested for public order offences after his description was circulated by the police officers that witnessed the offence. The suspect was placed in a van and the officers accidentally went in the van and identified the suspect. The court held that the person was a known suspect and the identification evidence should have been excluded. Paragraph 3.4 gives guidance as to when a suspect will become 'known' or 'available'. Code D, Note 3D gives guidance where a person deliberately makes themselves unavailable.

The Code also makes provision for the disclosure of materials previously released to the media in relation to an enquiry and for witnesses to be asked if they saw such material before any identification procedure. When a witness has previously been shown photographs or computerised or artist's composite or similar likeness, the suspect and their solicitor must be informed of this fact before the identification procedure takes place. It is the responsibility of the officer in charge of the investigation to make the identification officer aware that this is the case (Code D, Annex E, para. 9).

The Codes recognise that the showing of films or photographs to the public through the national or local media, or to police officers for the purposes of recognition and tracing suspects, may be necessary. However, Code D, para. 3.28, provides that when such material is shown to potential witnesses, including police officers, to obtain identification evidence, it shall be shown on an individual basis to avoid any possibility of collusion, and, as far as possible, the showing shall follow the principles for video identification if the suspect is known, or identification by photographs if the suspect is not known (see Code D, paras 3.4 and 3.3).

When a broadcast or publication is made, a copy of the relevant material released to the media for the purposes of recognising or tracing the suspect must be kept. The suspect or their solicitor, provided it is practicable and would not unreasonably delay the investigation, must be allowed to view such material before any identification procedure is carried out. Each witness involved in the procedure shall be asked, after they have taken part, whether they have seen any broadcast or published films or photographs relating to the offence or any description of the suspect and their replies shall be recorded. This paragraph does not affect any separate requirement under the Criminal Procedure and Investigations Act 1996 to retain material in connection with criminal investigations (Code D, para. 3.29).

Where it has been decided that an identification procedure is to be held (see Code D, para. 3.12), the identification officer and the officer in charge of the investigation must consult each other to determine which procedure is to be offered (Code D, para. 3.14). The suspect shall initially be offered a video identification unless:

– an identification parade is both practicable and more suitable than a video identification; or

– a video identification is not practicable; or

– the officer in charge of the investigation considers a group identification is more satisfactory than a video identification or an identification parade and the identification officer considers it practicable to arrange (Code D, para. 3.16).

An identification parade may not be practicable because of factors relating to the witnesses, such as their number, state of health, availability and travelling requirements. A video identification would normally be more suitable if it could be arranged and completed sooner than an identification parade.

If a suspect refuses the identification procedure first offered, the suspect shall be asked to state their reason for refusing and may get advice from their solicitor and/or if present, their appropriate adult. The suspect, solicitor and/or appropriate adult may make representations about why another procedure should be used. A record should be made of the reasons for refusal and any representations made. If appropriate, the identification officer will arrange for the suspect to be offered an alternative which the officer considers suitable and practicable. If the officer decides it is not suitable and practicable to offer an alternative identification procedure, the reasons for that decision must be recorded (Code D, para. 3.15).

Where a suspect is identified by witnesses, other evidence should still be sought to strengthen the case (or to prove the person's innocence) as identification evidence is often challenged at court. Such supporting evidence may include admissions by the suspect that links him/her to the identification evidence; for example, that he/she owns the vehicle that was driven at the time of the offence *(R v Ward* [2001] Crim LR 316).

When must an Identification Procedure be Held?

Identification procedures should be held for the benefit of the defence as well as the prosecution (*R v Waile* [1998] Crim LR 68). The Codes give guidance on when an identification parade must or may be held. Code D, paras 3.12 and 3.13 state:

3.12 Whenever:

(i) a witness has identified a suspect or purported to have identified them prior to any identification procedure set out in paragraphs 3.5 to 3.10 having been held; or

(ii) there is a witness available, who expresses an ability to identify the suspect, or where there is a reasonable chance of the witness being able to do so, and they have not been given an opportunity to identify the suspect in any of the procedures set out in paragraphs 3.5 to 3.10,

and the suspect disputes being the person the witness claims to have seen, an identification procedure shall be held unless it is not practicable or it would serve no useful purpose in proving or disproving whether the suspect was involved in committing the offence. For example, when it is not disputed that the suspect is already well known to the witness who claims to have seen them commit the crime.

3.13 Such a procedure may also be held if the officer in charge of the investigation considers it would be useful.

Code D, para. 3.12(ii) provides that there is no need to go through any of the identification procedures where, in all the circumstances, it would serve no useful purpose in proving or disproving whether the suspect was involved in committing the offence. This view is supported by the Court of Appeal decision *R v Chen* (2001) *The Times*, 17 April. The defence in that case was one of duress but the appeal was based on the failure of the police to hold identification parades. The Court of Appeal stated that this was not a case about identification as none of the defendants denied their presence at the scene. What they denied was their criminal participation in the activities that took place. It followed, therefore, that Code D did not apply. Other examples would be where it is not in dispute that the suspect is already well-known to the witness who saw the suspect commit the crime or where there is no reasonable possibility that a witness would be able to make an identification.

There have been a number of Court of Appeal cases recently concerning the requirement to hold identification parades. It is suggested that these should be applied to the revised Code regardless of which form of identification procedure is used. The leading case is *R v Forbes* [2001] 2 WLR 1, which was based on the previous Code of Practice. The House of Lords held that if the police are in possession of sufficient evidence to justify the arrest of a suspect, and that suspect's identification depends on eye-witness identification evidence, even in part, then if the identification is disputed, the Code requires that an identification parade should be held with the suspect's consent, unless one of the exceptions applies. The exceptions are set out in Code D, para. 2.15. This is particularly so where the suspect disputes identification.

The House of Lords went on to say that this mandatory obligation to hold an identification parade applies even if there has been a 'fully satisfactory', 'actual and complete' or 'unequivocal' identification of the suspect.

Despite the wording of Code D, it has been held that a suspect's right to have an identification parade is not confined to cases where a dispute over identity has already arisen; that right also applies where such a dispute might reasonably be anticipated (*R v Rutherford* (1993) 98 Cr App R 191). Similarly, a suspect's failure to request an identification parade does not mean that the police may proceed without one (*R v Graham* [1994] Crim LR 212).

It is important to consider the distinction between identification of a suspect and the suspect's clothing or other features. In *D v DPP* (1998) *The Times*, 7 August, a witness had observed two youths for a continuous period of five to six minutes and then informed the police of what he had seen, describing the age of the youths and the clothes that they were wearing. The court held that there had not been an identification within the terms of the Codes of Practice because the witness had at no stage identified the defendant or the co-accused. He had described only their clothing and their approximate ages and the police, acting on that information, had made the arrests. An identification parade could have served no useful purpose since the clothing would have been changed and those persons used for the parade would have been the same approximate age.

The *key factor* to consider when deciding whether to hold an identification parade is whether *a failure to hold a parade could be a matter of genuine potential prejudice to the suspect*. If it is decided to hold an identification procedure, it should be held as soon as it is practical (Code D, para. 3.11).

The question for the court will be whether it is fair to admit the identification evidence. When looking at this issue the court will consider how reliable that identification evidence is.

Any decision to proceed without an identification parade must be capable of justification later to the relevant court. The courts have taken different approaches to justification based on practical difficulties. In an early case, the submissions of the identification officer that it was impracticable to find enough people who sufficiently resembled the defendant were treated fairly dismissively by the trial judge (*R v Gaynor* [1988] Crim LR 242). In later cases, however, the courts have been more lenient, accepting that the time scales involved in arranging identification parades may render them 'impracticable' (see *R v Jamel* [1993] Crim LR 52 where the court refused an objection by the defence to a group identification). A group identification was used in *Jamel* because a parade using mixed-race volunteers would have taken too long to arrange. All reasonable steps must be taken to investigate the possibility of one identification option before moving on to an alternative, and an offer from a suspect's solicitor to find volunteers to stand on a parade is such a 'reasonable' step (*R v Britton and Richards* [1989] Crim LR 144).

Recognition Cases

Recognition cases, that is to say, those cases where the witness states that they know the person who committed the offence as opposed to only being able to give a description, need to be carefully considered. In *R v Ridley* (1999) *The Times*, 13 October, the Court of Appeal stated that there has never been a rule that an identification parade had to be held in all recognition cases and that it will be a question of fact in each case whether or not there is a need to do so. The view that an identification procedure is not required in these cases is supported by para. 3.12(ii).

The facts in *Ridley*, which it is suggested is not uncommon amongst patrolling officers, were that two police officers in a marked police vehicle noticed a car, which had been stolen earlier that day, drive past them. Both officers said that they recognised the defendant driving the car. The officers gave chase and gave evidence that the car was speeding and being driven dangerously. They decided that it was unsafe to continue pursuit, but arrested the suspect six days later. One of the officers claimed to have recognised the suspect because she had interviewed him for some 20 minutes five months previously and had seen him about town. She gave evidence that she had a view of the suspect in the car for about nine seconds. The other officer said that he recognised the suspect from a photograph but could not say when he had seen that photograph. He said that he had seen the suspect in the car for about two seconds. The Court found that the female police officer's identification had been complete and there was no requirement for her to have further identified the suspect.

Ridley can be contrasted with *R v Conway* (1990) 91 Cr App R 143, where the witnesses' evidence was not as strong. There the witnesses stated that they recognised the accused simply because they knew him. The defence argument was that the witnesses did not actually know the accused and so could not have recognised him at the time of the offence. His conviction was quashed because of the prejudice caused by the absence of a parade.

A case can still amount to one of recognition even where the witness does not know the name of the suspect but later obtained those details from a third party, for example where the witness and the suspect went to the same school and the witness became aware of the suspect's full names from other pupils at the school *(R v C; R v B* (2003) unreported).

In *H v DPP* (2003) unreported, the court accepted that it was reasonable for the police not to undertake an identification procedure. In the circumstances of the case the police had every reason to believe that the claimant and the victim were well known to each other. The claimant had accepted that the victim knew her. There was no question of doubt as to the victim's ability to recognise the claimant and as such this was a case of pure recognition where it was futile to hold an identification parade.

Care must be taken in cases where it is believed that the case is one of recognition not requiring an identification procedure. In *R v Harris* [2002] EWCA Crim 174, the witness stated that he recognised the suspect as being someone with whom he went to school. The suspect gave a prepared statement in which he disputed the suggestion that he was well known to the witness. Here the court held that an identification procedure should have been undertaken, as the circumstances of the case did not fall within the general exception of the Code, that it would serve no useful purpose in proving or disproving whether the suspect had been involved in committing the offence.

When a suspect is filmed committing an offence, it is admissible to give evidence of identification by way of recognition from a witness not present at the scene but who knew the defendant and who, having seen the film, identified the suspect as being the defendant *(Attorney-General's Reference (No. 2 of 2002)* [2003] Crim LR 192).

Another common identification problem is that of disqualified drivers and being able to satisfy the court that the person charged with disqualified driving is the same person who was disqualified by the court. This is because s. 73 of the Police and Criminal Evidence Act 1984 requires proof that the person named in a certificate of conviction as having been convicted is the person whose conviction is to be proved. There has been some guidance from the courts as to how this can be achieved. In *R v Derwentside Justices, ex parte Heaviside* [1996] RTR 384, the court stated that this could be done by:

- fingerprints under s. 39 of the Criminal Justice Act 1948;

- the evidence of a person who was present in court when the disqualification order was made;

- admission of the defendant (preferably in interview) *(Moran v CPS* (2000) 164 JP 562).

The methods outlined in *Ex parte Heaviside* are not exhaustive, but just suggested methods (*DPP* v *Mansfield* [1997] RTR 96). A good example of where the police were able to satisfy s. 73 of the 1984 Act came in the case of *Olakunori* v *DPP* [1998] COD 443. In this case, Olakunori was charged with driving whilst disqualified. He had been stopped by police officers and gave a false name and a false date of birth. At the police station, after he was arrested, he gave a different false name and false date of birth to the custody officer. When he was interviewed, he confirmed his surname was Olaktunori. A man named Olatokubo Olakunori, born 20 July 1974, had previously been disqualified from holding and obtaining a driving licence for an offence of driving without a valid certificate of insurance. Olakunori denied all knowledge of the previous disqualification. The prosecution argued that Olakunori had given false names in order to avoid detection for the offence and there was sufficient evidence to establish that Olakunori was the person who had been previously disqualified. This included the court register of the previous convictions, Olakunori's birth certificate which was in the name of Olatunji Olatokunbo Adeola Olakunori, showing his date of birth as 20 July 1974, and his passport which was in the name of Olatokunbo Olakunori. The Court held that the justices had been entitled to find that the false names which the appellant had given were a deliberate attempt to avoid the charge, were relevant to the material issues and that there was no innocent explanation why they had been given. The lies supported the conclusion that the appellant was guilty and accordingly the justices had been entitled to take them into account. Such evidence would be useful to obtain from suspects being investigated for offences of disqualified driving.

Control of the Identification Process

The arrangements for and conduct of identification procedures is the responsibility of an officer not below the rank of inspector who is not involved with the investigation ('the identification officer'). However, except where the Codes expressly state otherwise, the identification officer may allow an 'approved person' to make arrangements for, and to conduct any of the identification procedures in paras 3.11 and 2.21. When the identification officer delegates these procedures, he/she must be able to supervise effectively and either intervene or be able to be contacted for advice.

It is important to note that no officer or any other person involved with the investigation of the case against the suspect, may take any part in these procedures or act as the identification officer. However, the identification officer may consult the officer in charge of the investigation in order to determine which procedure to use.

If the identification officer considers that it is not practicable to hold a video identification or identification parade, the reasons shall be recorded and explained to the suspect (para. 3.15). Should the suspect fail or refuse to co-operate in a video identification, identification parade or group identification, a record should be made including any reasons (paras 3.15 and 3.27).

Before a video identification, an identification parade or group identification is arranged, para. 3.17 outlines a number of matters that must be explained to the suspect and must be recorded in a written notice and handed to the suspect. Paragraph 3.17 must be completed by the identification officer or if it is proposed to hold an identification procedure at a later date and an inspector is not available to act as the identification officer, it can be performed by the custody sergeant before the suspect leaves the station.

Which Identification Procedure should be Used?

Initially the choice should be between a video identification or an identification parade (para. 3.14). However, a group identification could be used where the officer in charge of the investigation considers that in the particular circumstances it is more satisfactory (para. 3.16).

The identification officer and the officer in charge of the investigation shall consult each other to determine which of these two options is the most suitable and practicable in the particular case. Paragraphs 3.14 to 3.16 gives guidance as to factors to consider.

Whilst the choice of procedure is for the police, the suspect, solicitor and/or appropriate adult shall be allowed to make representations as to why another procedure should be used (para. 3.15). If a suspect refuses the identification procedure which is first offered, he/she must be asked to state his/her reasons for refusing and may obtain advice from his/her solicitor and appropriate adult if present (para. 3.15).

Even where a person refuses to take part in an identification procedure, it is still possible to use covert video identification, covert group identification or confrontation (paras 3.21 and 3.24). If the identification officer and the officer in charge of the investigation have reasonable grounds to suspect that the person will take steps to avoid being seen by a witness in any identification procedure, the identification officer has a discretion to arrange for images of him/her to be obtained for use in a video identification procedure. If images of the suspect are obtained in these circumstances, the suspect may, for the purposes of a video identification procedure, co-operate in providing suitable images which shall be used in place of those previously taken (para. 3.20).

Section 64A of the Police and Criminal Evidence Act 1984 provides powers to take photographs and images of suspects detained at police stations and allows the photographs and images so taken to be used to assist with arranging the identification process, the investigation of offences or the conduct of prosecutions by, or on behalf of, police or other law enforcement and prosecuting authorities inside and outside the United Kingdom. After being so used or disclosed, they may be retained but can be used or disclosed only for the same purposes (Code D, para. 3.30).

Code D, paras 3.31 to 3.33 provide further guidance on the destruction and retention of photographs and images taken for the purpose of or in connection with identification procedures. It should be noted that the powers to retain photographs of suspects who have not be detained and moving images of anyone whether detained or not are limited to the situations set out in Code D, para. 3.31.

Where a known suspect is not available (or has ceased to be available for any reason), the identification officer has a discretion to make arrangements for a video identification to be conducted. This must be done in accordance with the provisions applicable to covert video identification (para. 3.21 and Note 3D).

If necessary, the identification officer may follow the video identification procedures but using still images. Any suitable moving or still images may be used and these may be obtained covertly if necessary. Any covert activity should be strictly limited to that necessary to test the ability of the witness to identify the suspect. Alternatively, the identification officer may make arrangements for a group identification. These provisions may be applied to juveniles where the consent of their parent or guardian is either refused or reasonable efforts to obtain that consent have failed (Code D, paras 3.21 and 3.22).

It is only if none of the other options are practicable that the identification officer may arrange for the suspect to be confronted by the witness. A confrontation does not require the suspect's consent. In *R* v *McCulloc*, 6 May 1999, unreported, the Court of Appeal made it clear that confrontations between suspects and witnesses should only be carried out if no other procedure is practicable (see below).

Conduct of Identification Parades

Identification evidence can be crucial to the success of a prosecution. There are clear guidelines that must be followed. Where such guidelines are not followed it is likely that the defence will strongly attempt to have the identification evidence excluded. In *R* v *Jones* (1999)

The Times, 21 April, identification evidence was excluded as the officers told the suspect that if he did not comply with the procedure, force would be used against him.

The conduct of identification parades was criticised in the Stephen Lawrence Inquiry. The McPherson report stated that the timing of any identification parade during an investigation must also be considered carefully:

> Where there are a number of suspects and witnesses and where identification evidence may be crucial this can only emphasise the extreme need for careful planning and foresight. ... The ID parades were delayed until about the middle or end of May partly because of the delay in making the arrests of the suspects. If the arrests had been made earlier it can be said that there would have been more prospect of successful identification, since the passage of time inevitably blunts the memory of the features or look of somebody who has been seen committing a crime.

The need for the identification procedure to be conducted as soon as possible is now recognised by the Codes (para. 3.11).

Annexes A to E of Code D set out in detail the procedures and requirements which must be followed in conducting identification procedures. There is also guidance concerning documentation and retention of material.

Although the courts are aware of the many practical difficulties involved in organising and running identification procedures (see e.g. *R* v *Jamel* above), any flaws in the procedure will be considered in the light of their potential impact on the defendant's trial. Serious or deliberate breaches (such as the showing of photographs to witnesses before the parade), will invariably lead to any evidence so gained being excluded (*R* v *Finley* [1993] Crim LR 50). The key question for the court will be whether the breach of the Codes is likely to have made the identification less reliable. Officers must therefore fully understand and follow the Codes of Practice and relevant Annex for the procedure being used.

Breaches which appear to impact on the safeguards imposed by Annexes A to D to separate the functions of investigation and identification (e.g. where the investigating officer becomes involved with the running of the parade in a way which allows him/her to talk to the witnesses (*R* v *Gall* (1989) 90 Cr App R 64)) will also be treated seriously by the court.

The case of *R* v *Marrin* (2002) *The Times*, 5 March provides some guidance as to methods that could be used to get a suitable pool of participants for an ID parade. The court held that there was nothing inherently unfair or objectionable in some colouring or dye being used on the facial stubble of some volunteers to make them look more like the suspect. However, care needed to be taken with such measures because the procedure would be undermined if it was obvious to the witness that make-up had been used. Another point raised was that it may sometimes be appropriate for those on parade to wear hats, but if possible the wearing of hats should be avoided if hats had not been worn during the offence because this would make it more difficult for a witness to make an identification. However, there could be circumstances where the wearing of hats could help to achieve a resemblance and might be desirable to minimise differences. Finally an identification of a suspect was not invalidated by the witness's request for the removal of a hat. There was nothing unfair in that taking place and there was no breach of any code, either. Under para. 18 of Annex B, a witness could ask for any parade member to adopt any specified posture or that he/she should move.

It is important to follow the guidance in the Codes regardless of what agreement is obtained from the suspect or his/her solicitor. In *R* v *Hutton* [1999] Crim LR 74, at the suggestion of the suspect's solicitor, all the participants in the identification parade wore back to front baseball caps and had the lower part of their faces obscured by material. That identification was the only evidence against the defendant on that count. The court excluded the evidence and did not accept the fact that the decision had been agreed.

It will be essential that any photographs, photofits or other such material is stored securely in a manner that restricts access so as to be able to demonstrate to the court that the material cannot have been viewed by any of the witnesses and that copies have not been made that have not been accounted for.

Identification where Suspect is Not Known

If the suspect is not known, Code D provides for witnesses (including police officers) to be shown photographs (Annex E) or taken to a place where the suspect might be (paras 3.2 and 3.3).

If photographs are to be shown, the procedure set out at Annex E must be followed. Once a witness has made a positive identification from the photographs, computerised or artist's composite, no further witnesses should be shown photographs (para. 3.3) (unless the person identified is eliminated from the enquiry (Annex E, para. 6)).

Using photographs from police criminal records can affect the judgment of a jury and nothing should be done to draw their attention to the fact that the defendant's photograph was already held by the police (*R v Lamb* (1979) 71 Cr App R 198). This rule does not apply if the jury are already aware of the defendant's previous convictions (*R v Allen* [1996] Crim LR 426).

The showing of a CCTV film used for security purposes is addressed at para. 3.28 of Code D.

If a film which has been shown to a witness is later lost or unavailable, the witness may give evidence of what he/she saw on that film but the court will have to consider all the relevant circumstances in deciding whether to admit that evidence *and* what weight to attach to it. (For a discussion of those circumstances, see *Taylor* v *Chief Constable of Cheshire* [1986] 1 WLR 1479.) This is particularly so as the Codes require that the film is retained (Annex A, para. 15 and para. 3.29).

Videos or photographs can be shown to the public at large through the national or local media, or to police officers for the purposes of recognition and tracing suspects. However, when such material is shown to potential witnesses (including police officers) it should be shown on an individual basis so as to avoid any possibility of collusion, and the showing shall, as far as possible, follow the principles for video identification if the suspect is known (paras 3.28, 3.29 and Annex A) or identification by photographs if the suspect is not known (see paras 3.4, 3.3 and Annex E).

Identification at the Scene

There are occasions where the identification is made immediately after the alleged offence. This usually happens when the witness is taken round a particular area to try and find the suspect (in which case Code D, para. 3.2 must be complied with). The need for 'scene identifications' was recognised by Lord Lane CJ in *R v Oscar* [1991] Crim LR 778 and by the Court of Appeal in *R v Rogers* [1993] Crim LR 386.

In *Oscar*, the court held that there had been no requirement for an identity parade in that case and Lord Lane pointed out that, in any case, a later parade where the suspect was dressed differently would be of no value at all. In *Rogers*, the suspect was found near a crime scene and was confronted by a witness who positively identified him. The court held that the identification in that case was necessary for an arrest to be made, although the court felt a later parade could have been carried out.

In such cases, where the meeting of the suspect and the witness takes place soon after the event, wherever possible the officers should comply with para. 3.2. Matters to consider before doing a 'scene identification' include:

- where practicable, a record shall be made of any description of the suspect given by the witness as in para. 3.1(a);
- care should be taken not to direct the witness's attention to any individual unless, having regard to all the circumstances, this cannot be avoided;

- if there is more than one witness, try to keep them separate;

- once there is sufficient information to justify the arrest of a suspect, a formal identification procedure must be adopted;

- the officer or approved person accompanying the witness must make a record in his/her pocket book of the action taken as soon as practicable and in as much detail as possible.

The admissibility of identification evidence obtained when carrying out a 'scene identification' may be compromised if before a person is identified, the witness's attention is specifically drawn to that person.

Careful consideration must be given before a decision to identify a suspect in this manner is used. If there is sufficient evidence to arrest the suspect without using a witnesses identification, then it is likely the courts will find that an identification method outlined above should have been used and the evidence may be excluded. Confrontations between witnesses and suspects on the street can be useful at times, but where this takes place it defeats the formal identification process and needs to be carefully considered. The reason for this is that, even if the suspect is picked out on the identification parade by that witness, the defence will be able to argue that the identification was from the confrontation after the incident and not at the time of the commission of the offence. If there is more than one witness available and a decision is taken to use a witness to try and identify a suspect at the scene, other witnesses should be moved away, so as to reduce the possibility of a chance encounter with the suspect. Where possible, these witnesses should be kept apart until the identification parade and ideally should not discuss the matter between themselves.

An example where a street identification was appropriate is *R v El-Hannachi* (1998) 2 Cr App R 226. Here an affray took place in the car park of a public house. A witness had seen the man earlier in the pub and she had had an unobstructed view in good light before the attack. The witness described the attacker's clothing to the police and then identified a group of men who had been stopped by other officers a short distance away. The court accepted that this was the correct approach. The defendants were not known suspects when they were stopped by the police prior to the witness's identification. The court also accepted that it had not been practicable for a record to have been made of the witness's description, as required by Code D, para. 3.1, prior to the identification. Where a record has been made prior to the identification this may support the identification itself. It should be remembered, however, that the description does not now have to be recorded in writing and could be recorded by some quicker method (e.g. tape recording) (para. 3.1).

A not uncommon situation is where police officers chase a suspect who is arrested by other officers on the description circulated by the chasing officer, who then attends the scene to confirm the person's identity. The case of *R v Nunes*, 31 October 2001, unreported covers this point and points out the dangers of this practice. The facts of the case were that a police officer saw a man inside a house and circulated a description on his radio. A person fitting the description was seen and arrested. The first officer arrived on the scene and identified the arrested person as the man he had earlier seen in the house. The Court of Appeal held that on the particular facts of this case the identification amounted to a breach of the Code. By the time of the identification, the man had been arrested for suspected involvement in the offence and, on his arrest, the identity of the suspect was known to the police. Therefore, by the time the witnessing officer arrived on the scene, the case involved 'disputed identification evidence' because the suspect had said that he had not done anything while the police had told him he matched the description of a suspected burglar. That said, the court did go on to hold that the judge had the discretion to allow the identification evidence to be adduced notwithstanding the breach of the Codes.

Photographs, Image and Sound Reproduction Generally

The use of photographic and computer-generated images (such as E-Fit) to identify suspects has increased considerably over the last few years. Although the courts will exercise considerable caution when admitting such evidence (see *R v Blenkinsop* [1995] 1 Cr App R 7), these methods of identification are particularly useful. Expert evidence may be admitted to interpret images on film (see e.g. *R v Stockwell* (1993) 97 Cr App R 260) and police officers who are very familiar with a particular film clip (e.g. of crowd violence at a football match) may be allowed to assist the court in interpreting and explaining events shown within it (see *R v Clare* (1995) 159 JP 142).

Logically, E-Fit and other witness-generated images would be treated as 'visual statements', in that they represent the witness's recollection of what he/she saw. However, the Court of Appeal has decided that they are not to be so treated (*R v Cook* [1987] QB 417) and therefore the restrictions imposed by the rule against hearsay will not apply (see also *R v Constantinou* (1989) 91 Cr App R 74, where this ruling was followed in relation to a photofit image).

Voice identification from what a suspect on an identification parade says, is dealt with under para. 18 of Annex B to Code D. In *R v Gummerson* [1999] Crim LR 680, it was held that PACE Code D related only to *visual* identification.

Generally, a witness may give evidence identifying the defendant's voice (*R v Robb* (1991) 93 Cr App R 161), while expert testimony may be admitted in relation to tape recordings of a voice which is alleged to belong to the defendant. In the latter case, the jury should be allowed to hear the recording(s) so that they can draw their own conclusions (*R v Bentum* (1989) 153 JP 538).

4.5.4 Fingerprints

Fingerprint is defined by Code D, para. 4.1 and s. 65(1) of the Police and Criminal Evidence Act 1984 as any record, produced by any method, of the skin pattern and other physical characteristics or features of a person's fingers or palms. Fingerprints can be taken electronically provided that they are taken using such devices as the Secretary of State has approved for the purposes of electronic fingerprinting (s. 61(8A) of the 1984 Act). Where a person's fingerprints are to be taken without their consent, under the powers set out in Code D, paras 4.3 and 4.4, reasonable force may be used if necessary.

Before Conviction

The taking of finger and palm prints is governed by ss. 61 and 63A of the Police and Criminal Evidence Act 1984.

Section 61 states:

(1) Except as provided by this section no person's fingerprints may be taken without the appropriate consent.

(2) Consent to the taking of a person's fingerprints must be in writing if it is given at a time when he is at a police station.

KEYNOTE

Fingerprints of a person detained at a police station may be taken without that person's consent in the following circumstances:

- where an officer of at least the rank of superintendent authorises them to be taken; or

- where the person has been charged or reported for a recordable offence

where the person has been charged or reported for a recordable offence (see Code D, Note 4A);

- the person's fingerprints have not already been taken in the course of the investigation of the offence by the police or the fingerprints taken do not constitute a complete set of fingerprints or some, or all, of the fingerprints are not of sufficient quality to allow satisfactory analysis, comparison or matching; and

- from a person who has been bailed to appear at a court or a police station if the person has answered to bail for a person whose fingerprints were taken previously and there are reasonable grounds for believing they are not the same person; or who has answered to bail claims to be a different person from a person whose fingerprints were previously taken (the court or an officer of inspector rank or above, authorises the fingerprints to be taken at the court or police station), s. 61(4A)

(s. 61(3) and Code D, para. 4.3).

An inspector may only give authority for fingerprints to be taken if he/she has reasonable grounds:

- for suspecting the person is involved in a criminal offence;

- for believing that the person's fingerprints will tend to confirm or disprove his/her involvement;

- will facilitate ascertaining his/her identity (for what this means see s. 54A of the Police and Criminal Evidence Act 1984)

(s. 61(4) and Code D, para. 4.3(a)).

However, an authorisation shall not be given for the purpose only of facilitating the person's identity except where he/she has refused to identify themselves or the officer has reasonable grounds for suspecting that he/she is not who he/she claims to be.

The inspector's authority may be given orally or in writing, but if given orally he/she shall confirm it in writing as soon as is practicable (s. 61(5) and Code D, para. 4.8).

Before any fingerprints are taken the person must be informed of the reason their fingerprints are to be taken, if para. 4.3(a) or (c) apply the grounds on which the relevant authority has been given, that their fingerprints may be retained and may be subject of a speculative search (unless destruction of the fingerprints is required in accordance with Annex F, Part (a)), and that if their fingerprints are required to be destroyed, they may witness their destruction as provided for in Annex F, Part (a) Code D, para. 4.7).

A record must be made when a person has been informed of the possibility that their fingerprints may be subject of a speculative search (Code D, para. 4.9). A record must also be made, as soon as possible, of the reason for taking a person's fingerprints without consent and if force is used, the circumstances and those present (Code D, para. 4.8).

Where the suspect does consent to their fingerprints being subject of such a speculative search, the consent must be in writing. Note 6E provides an example of a basic form of words. Once the suspect has given consent for the sample to be retained and used, he/she cannot withdraw this consent. See Code D, Annex F regarding the retention and use of fingerprints and samples taken with consent for elimination purposes.

Note 4B explains what a speculative search means. Code D, paras 4.10 to 4.15 deal with the taking of fingerprints in connection with immigration enquires and Annex F, para. 5 deals with their retention and destruction.

After Conviction

Fingerprints may be taken with the appropriate consent, where a person refuses to give that consent, fingerprints can only be taken if s. 61(6) of the 1984 Act applies, i.e. from a person who has been:

- convicted of a recordable offence;

- given a caution in respect of a recordable offence which, at the time of the caution, the person admitted; or

- warned or reprimanded under s. 65 of the Crime and Disorder Act 1998 for a recordable offence.

For the purposes of taking fingerprints, the meaning of appropriate consent is in relation to:

- a person 17 or over, his/her consent;
- a person 14 to 17, the consent of that person or his/her parent or guardian;
- a person under 14, the consent of his/her parent or guardian.

Section 27 of the 1984 Act provides that a person may be required to attend a police station to have his/her fingerprints taken if he/she:

- has been convicted of a recordable offence; given a caution in respect of a recordable offence which, at the time of the caution, the person admitted; or warned or reprimanded under s. 65 of the Crime and Disorder Act 1998, for a recordable offence; and
- the fingerprints taken on the previous occasion do not constitute a complete set of his/her fingerprints; or some or all of the fingerprints taken on the previous occasion are not of sufficient quality to allow satisfactory analysis, comparison or matching.

The requirement must be made within one month of the date the person is convicted, cautioned, warned or reprimanded and the person must be given a period of at least seven days within which to attend. This seven-day period need not fall during the month allowed for making the requirement. If a person fails to comply with the requirement, he/she can be arrested without warrant (Code D, para. 4.4).

Before any fingerprints are taken with or without consent as above, the person must be informed of the reason his/her fingerprints are to be taken. Before any fingerprints are taken at the police station, the person must also be informed that his/her fingerprints may be retained and may be subject of a speculative search against other fingerprints. Code D, Note 4B explains what a speculative search means (Code D, para. 4.7). A record must be made when a person has been informed of the possibility that his/her fingerprints may be subject of a speculative search (Code D, para. 4.9). A record must also be made, as soon as possible, of the reason for taking a person's fingerprints without consent and if force is used, a record must be made of the circumstances and those present (Code D, para. 4.8).

KEYNOTE

In terms of the disposal of the case, cautioning a person for an offence is the equivalent of a conviction at court. Therefore, if the person has been in police detention and has not had his/her fingerprints taken prior to the caution, there is no power to take that person's fingerprints under the 1984 Act. This is also the case where a person is released and subsequently summonsed.

It should be noted that s. 64 of the 1984 Act, as amended by the Criminal Justice and Police Act 2001, has removed the requirement to destroy fingerprints of suspects who are not convicted and custody officers should no longer inform detained persons of the right to destruction (see Code D, Annex F). The Act removes this obligation in relation to fingerprints and samples where the person is cleared of the offence for which they were taken or a decision is made not to prosecute. The obligation to destroy is replaced by a rule to the effect that any fingerprints or samples retained can only be used for the purposes related to the prevention and detection of crime, the investigation of any offence or the conduct of any prosecution. This means that if a match is established between an individual who has been cleared of an offence at a subsequent crime scene the police are able to use this information in the investigation of the crime. The system of retaining DNA samples and fingerprint evidence after a suspect had been cleared of the offence that gave rise to the collection of those items of evidence is compatible with both Article 8 and Article 14 of the European Convention on Human Rights (*R v Chief Constable of South Yorkshire, ex parte Marper* (2002) *The Times*, 4 April).

Fingerprints and samples taken from a person suspected of committing a recordable offence but not arrested, charged or informed they will be reported for it, may be subject to a speculative search only if the person consents in writing. Code D, Note 4B gives an example of the wording to be used for the consent. Once taken, the sample or fingerprints will be retained and used for purposes related to the prevention and detection of a crime, the investigation of an offence or the conduct of a prosecution either nationally or internationally. Once the person gives consent for the sample to be retained, it cannot be withdrawn.

Where a person, who is not a suspect, provides a sample or fingerprints voluntarily, e.g. for the purposes of elimination, there is no obligation for him/her to allow the samples or fingerprints to be retained or used other than for the purpose for which they were taken. Where consent is not given the fingerprints or samples must be destroyed and the information derived from them cannot be used in evidence against the person concerned or for the purposes of investigation of any offence. When seeking consent from a person for elimination samples and fingerprints the consents should be obtained separately and whether the person is consenting to their use and retention needs to be fully explained. Code D, Annex F, Note F1 should be followed when consent is being requested.

Expert evidence on fingerprints is admissible from suitably qualified individuals who have at least five years' experience in that field.

Whether fingerprint evidence is admissible as evidence tending to prove guilt, depends on:

— the experience and expertise of the witness,

— the number of similar ridge characteristics (if there are fewer than eight ridge characteristics matching the fingerprints of the accused with those found by the police, it is unlikely that a judge would exercise his/her discretion to admit such evidence),

— whether there are dissimilar characteristics,

— the size of print relied on, and

— the quality and clarity of print relied on.

The jury should be warned that expert evidence is not conclusive in itself and that guilt has to be proved in the light of all evidence (*R v Buckley* (1999) 163 JP 561).

Criminal Record and Conviction Certificates

Under the Police Act 1996, in certain circumstances the Secretary of State issues certificates concerning an individual's previous convictions. In some cases the Secretary of State will not do this until he/she has been able to verify the person's identity, which can be done through the taking of their fingerprints. Where this is the case, the Secretary of State may require the police officer in charge of the specified police station, or any other police station he/she reasonably determines, to take the applicant's fingerprints at the specified station at such reasonable time as the officer may direct and notify to the applicant.

If fingerprints are taken in these circumstances they must be destroyed as soon as is practicable after the identity of the applicant is established to the satisfaction of the Secretary of State. The destruction can be witnessed by the person giving the fingerprints if he/she requests and/or the person can ask for a certificate stating the fingerprints have been destroyed. The certificate must be issued within three months of the request.

In the case of an individual under the age of 18 years the consent of the applicant's parent or guardian to the taking of the applicant's fingerprints is also required.

4.5.5 **Body Samples and Impressions**

The taking of samples and impressions is governed by ss. 62 to 63A of the Police and Criminal Evidence Act 1984, together with Code D (paras 6.1 to 6.12).

Inferences from a defendant's refusal to consent to the taking of certain samples may be drawn by a court.

DNA Profiles

The purpose behind the taking of many samples is to enable the process of DNA profiling. Very basically, this involves an analysis of the sample taken from the suspect (the first sample), an analysis of samples taken from the crime scene or victim (the second sample) and then a comparison of the two. Both the process and the conclusions which might be drawn from the results are set out by Lord Taylor CJ in *R v Deen* (1994) *The Times*, 10 January.

The matching process involves creating 'bands' from each sample and then comparing the number of those bands which the two samples share. The more 'matches' that exist between the first and second samples, the less probability there is of that happening by pure chance. A 'good match' between the two samples does not of itself prove that the second sample came from the defendant. In using such samples to prove identification the prosecution will give evidence of:

- the *probability* of such a match happening by chance; and

- the *likelihood* that the person responsible was in fact the defendant.

When applying the 'this' test a jury must consider the second issue, that is, the likelihood of the defendant's being responsible.

The jury's task was set out by Phillips LJ in *R v Doheny* (1997) 1 Cr App R 369. In that case, involving a semen sample, his Lordship said:

> If you accept the scientific evidence called by the Crown, that indicates there are probably only four or five white males in the United Kingdom from whom that semen stain could have come. The defendant is one of them. The decision you have to reach, on all the evidence, is whether you are sure that it was the defendant who left that stain or whether it is possible that it is one of that other small group of men who share the same DNA characteristics.

(See also *Blackstone's Criminal Practice*, 2003, section F18.)

In most cases there will be other evidence against the defendant, evidence which clearly increases the likelihood of his/her having committed the offence.

It will be for the prosecution to produce other facts to the court which reduces the 'chance' of the DNA sample belonging to someone other than the defendant. This may require further enquiries linking the suspect to the area or circumstances of the crime or may come from questions put to the suspect during interview. In *R v Lashley*, 25 February 2000, unreported, the sole evidence against the defendant for a robbery was DNA evidence from a half-smoked cigarette found behind the counter of the post office. The DNA matched a sample obtained from the suspect and would have matched the profile of seven to ten other males in the United Kingdom. The court held that the significance of DNA evidence depended critically upon what else was known about the suspect. Had there been evidence that the suspect was in the area, or normally lived there, or had connections there, at the material time, then the jury could have found that the case was compelling. This, the court said, would be because it may have been almost incredible that two out of seven men in the United Kingdom were in the vicinity at the relevant time.

It is also important to ensure that there is no cross-contamination of DNA evidence between crime scenes, victims and suspects as was seen in the infamous American case of OJ Simpson's murder trial. It will be important to ensure that any allegations that officers may have contaminated evidence through handling/being present at several crime scenes can be successfully challenged It is suggested that the best evidence here will be through records of crime scene logs and, where suspects have are being held in custody, records of who visited the custody suite. It will also be important that suspects and victims are kept apart.

4.5.6 Intimate and Non-intimate Samples

As discussed earlier, there are three key ways to prove a person's involvement in a criminal offence:

- witnesses

- confessions

- scientific evidence.

Given the inherent problems and weaknesses of the first two, together with the advances being made in scientific procedures, the last of these is becoming more and more important in criminal evidence.

The analysis of intimate and non-intimate samples may provide essential evidence in showing or refuting a person's involvement in an offence. However, the courts have made it clear that DNA evidence alone will not be sufficient for a conviction and that there needs to be other supporting evidence to link the suspect to the crime. Such evidence may include confessions, that the suspect was near the crime scene at the time of the offence, that the suspect lived in the locality or had connections in the area.

The police powers to obtain intimate and non-intimate samples are provided by the Police and Criminal Evidence Act 1984 and were extended by amendments made by the Criminal Justice and Public Order Act 1994. Further guidance as to the exercise of these powers is contained within Code D of the PACE Codes of Practice.

Intimate and Non-intimate Samples Defined

Code D, para. 6 1 provides the definition of intimate and non-intimate samples:

(a) an 'intimate sample' means, a dental impression or sample of blood, semen or any other tissue fluid, urine, or pubic hair, or a swab taken from a person's body orifice other than the mouth;

(b) a 'non-intimate sample' means:
 (i) a sample of hair, other than pubic hair, which includes hair plucked with the root, see Note 6A;
 (ii) a sample taken from a nail or from under a nail;
 (iii) a swab taken from any part of a person's body including the mouth but not any other body orifice;
 (iv) saliva;
 (v) a skin impression which means any record, other than a fingerprint, which is a record, in any form and produced by any method, of the skin pattern and other physical characteristics or features of the whole, or any part of, a person's foot or of any other part of their body.

Code D, Note 6A sets out advice for taking non-intimate hair samples and states:

> Where hair samples are taken for the purpose of DNA analysis (rather than for other purposes such as making a visual match) the suspect should be permitted a reasonable choice as to what part of the body he wishes the hairs to be taken from. When hairs are plucked they should be plucked individually unless the suspect prefers otherwise and no more should be plucked than the person taking them reasonably considers necessary for a sufficient sample.

Intimate Samples

Section 62 of the Police and Criminal Evidence Act 1984 sets out police powers to take intimate samples. Code D of the PACE Codes of Practice provides additional guidance as to the exercise of the powers. The provisions of s. 62 together with Code D describe the circumstances and manner in which intimate samples can be taken. These can be understood by considering a number of key issues.

Consent

Before an intimate sample can be taken from a person in police detention, the consent of an officer of the rank of superintendent is necessary, *together with the consent of the person*. Without the consent of *both*, such a sample cannot be taken.

Taking a sample without the relevant authority may amount to inhuman or degrading treatment under Article 3 of the European Convention on Human Rights. It may also amount to a criminal offence of assault and give rise to liability at civil law.

Where a person is not in police detention, an intimate sample may be taken where that person has already provided two (or more) samples in the course of the investigation of the offence, which have proved insufficient for *the same means of analysis*. Should this pre-condition apply then the consent of both a superintendent and the person concerned is necessary, as in the case of a person in police detention (Code D, para 6.2).

Note 6C of Code D recognises that a sample may be taken from a person not in police detention, for the purposes of elimination, providing his/her consent is given.

In all cases where an intimate sample is to be taken from a young person aged 14 but under 17, the consent of his/her parents or guardian is also necessary. If the person is a child under 14, the consent of his/her parents or guardian is necessary only.

Grounds for Authorisation

Regardless of whether the person is in police detention or not, a superintendent may only give his/her authorisation if he/she has reasonable grounds:

- for suspecting the involvement of the person from whom the sample is to be taken in a recordable offence; *and*

- for believing that the sample will tend to confirm or disprove the person's involvement in the offence.

Information to be Given to the Suspect

Where an authorisation has been given and it is proposed to take a sample, an officer shall inform the suspect that the authorisation has been given *and* of the grounds for it being given (including the nature of the offence which the person is suspected of committing). If the person is at a police station then, in addition to the above, an officer must also inform the suspect, before the sample is taken, that the sample may be subject to a 'speculative search' (Code D, para 6.8).

(A speculative search is a check made against other samples and information derived from other samples contained in records or held by or on behalf of the police or held in connection with or as a result of an investigation of an offence.)

Paragraph 6.3 of Code D also requires that, before the sample is given, the suspect must be warned that if he/she refuses without good cause, that refusal may harm his/her case if it comes to trial. Where the suspect is in police detention, or is at the police station voluntarily, the officer shall also explain the entitlement to legal advice.

Recording the Authorisation

A superintendent's authorisation may be given orally but, if so given, it must be confirmed in writing as soon as practicable. The authorisation from the suspect must be given in writing (Code D, para 6.10).

Other Information to be Recorded

Where an intimate sample is taken, certain information should be recorded. This information includes:

- the reasons for taking a sample or impression and if applicable, of its destruction must be made as soon as practicable;

- if force is used, the circumstances of the use of force and those present;

- whether the person gave written consent;

- if they are a suspect that they have been warned that if they refuse without good cause, their refusal may harm their case if it comes to trial;

- if they are in police detention that they have been reminded of their right to legal advice;

- that the person has been informed that samples may be subject of a speculative search.

This information shall be recorded as soon as possible after the sample has been taken. Where a suspect is in police detention the information shall be recorded in the custody record.

Refusal of a Suspect to Give Consent

Where a suspect refuses, without good cause, to provide an intimate sample then, in proceedings against that person for an offence, the court may draw such inferences as appear proper. The court may use such an inference for the purposes of determining:

- guilt;
- whether there is a case to answer;
- whether to commit for trial;
- whether an application to dismiss charges should be granted (where a notice of transfer from a magistrates' court to a Crown Court has been given earlier).

Taking an Intimate Sample

Dental impressions may only be taken by a registered dentist. Intimate samples, other than urine, may only be taken by a registered medical practitioner or a registered health care professional (Code D, para 6.4).

Paragraph 6.9 of Code D sets out the provisions to be followed where clothing needs to removed in circumstances likely to cause embarrassment. These are:

- no person of the opposite sex may be present (other than a medical practitioner or registered health care professional);
- only people whose presence is necessary for the taking of the sample should in fact be present;
- in the case of a juvenile or mentally disordered or mentally vulnerable person, an appropriate adult of the opposite sex may be present *if specifically requested by the person and the person is readily available*;
- in the case of a juvenile, clothing may only be removed in the absence of an appropriate adult if the person signifies (in the presence of the appropriate adult) that he/she prefers his/her absence and the appropriate adult agrees.

Non-intimate Samples

The taking by police of non-intimate samples is governed by s. 63 of the Police and Criminal Evidence Act 1984. Additional guidance in the exercise of the powers is provided by Code D of the PACE Codes of Practice. The key requirements of these provisions are:

Consent

A person may consent to the taking of a non-intimate sample. If he/she does so, the consent must be given in writing.

A non-intimate sample may be taken without consent under the following conditions:

- where a person is in police detention or being held in custody by the police under the authority of a court and an officer of the rank of superintendent authorises it to be taken;
- where a person has been charged with a recordable offence (or told he/she is to be reported for such an offence) and has not provided a non-intimate sample in the course of the investigation of the offence *or* where the person *has* had an non-intimate sample taken but that sample has either proved not suitable for the same means of analysis, or it has proved insufficient;
- where a person has been convicted of a recordable offence.

'Recordable offences' are generally those offences punishable by imprisonment, together with several others designated by statutory instrument (see Code D, Note 4A).

In order to close a gap in the legislation, the Criminal Evidence (Amendment) Act 1997 was passed, allowing the taking of non-intimate samples without consent in the case of people serving sentences for certain sexual, violent or other specified offences.

The effect of ss. 1 and 2 of the 1997 Act is to allow the taking of such samples from people serving a sentence of imprisonment or being detained under a hospital order (under the Mental Health Act 1983) if they were convicted of a recordable offence listed at sch. 1 before 10 April 1995. The provisions also extend to people who were not convicted by reason of their insanity or their unfitness to plead but who were detained at the relevant time under the Mental Health Act 1983.

Grounds for Authorisation

An officer of at least the rank of inspector may only give authority for the taking of a non-intimate sample if he/she has reasonable grounds:

- for suspecting the involvement of the person from whom the sample is to be taken in a recordable offence; *and*
- for believing that the sample will tend to confirm *or disprove* the person's involvement in the offence; *and*
  - where the sample consists of a skin impression that a skin impression of the same part of the body has not already been taken from that person in the course of the investigation of the offence and if one has already been taken that it had not proved to be sufficient.

Information to be Given to the Suspect

Where an authorisation has been given by a superintendent and it is proposed to take a sample, an officer shall inform the suspect that the authorisation has been given *and* of the grounds for it being given (including the nature of the offence the person is suspected of committing).

Where a non-intimate sample is taken as a result of the suspect being charged, informed he/she is to be reported or following conviction for a recordable offence, he/she must be told of the reason why the sample is to be taken.

In cases where a person is in police detention, he/she must be informed—before the sample is taken—that the sample may be subject to a 'speculative search' (Code D, para. 6.8).

Recording the Authorisation

An officer of at least the rank of inspector's authorisation may be given orally, but if so given, must be confirmed in writing as soon as practicable. The consent from the suspect must be given in writing (Code D, para. 6.10).

Other Information to be Recorded

Where a non-intimate sample is taken as a result of a superintendent's authority, the following information should be recorded:

- the *authorisation* by virtue of which the sample was taken;
- the *grounds* for the authorisation;
- the fact that the person has been informed that the sample may be subject to a *speculative search*.

This information must be recorded *as soon as possible* after the sample has been taken.

In other cases where a sample is taken without the person's consent, the reason shall be recorded as soon as practicable after the sample is taken.

Where a suspect is in police detention, the information shall be recorded in the custody record (Code D, paras 6.10 to 6.12).

Use of Force

Paragraph 6.7 of Code D provides that force may be used if necessary to obtain non-intimate samples in the circumstances described. Where force is used, a record should be made of the circumstances and those present at the time.

Taking a Non-intimate Sample

Where clothing needs to be removed in order to take a non-intimate sample, para. 6.9 of the Code D should be applied to prevent embarrassment.

Power to Require Persons to Attend a Police Station to Provide Samples

In addition to the powers outlined, s. 63A of the Police and Criminal Evidence Act 1984 also provides for a constable to require a person to attend a police station for samples to be taken. The circumstances under which this requirement can be made are summarised as follows.

When Can the Requirement be Made?

A constable may make the requirement:

- where a person has been charged with a recordable offence or informed that he/she will be reported, or
- where the person has been convicted of a recordable offence

and, in either case, the person has not had a sample taken in the course of the investigation into the offence, or he/she has had a sample taken but it proved either unsuitable for the same means of analysis or the sample was insufficient.

The Period during which a Constable may Make the Requirement

The requirement to attend a police station must be made:

- within one month of the date of charge or of conviction; or
- within one month of the appropriate officer being informed that the sample is not suitable or has proved insufficient for analysis.

In making the requirement the officer:

- shall give the person at least seven days within which the person must attend; and
- may direct the person to attend at a specified time of day or between specified times of day.

Failure to Comply with the Requirement

Should a person fail to comply with the requirement, a constable may arrest the person without a warrant.

An appropriate officer is:

- the officer investigating the offence in the case of a person charged or told he/she will be reported;
- the officer in charge of the police station from which the investigation was conducted in the case of a person convicted.

For the corresponding power to take finger and palm prints, **see 4.5.4**.

Destruction of Samples

Code D, Annex F deals with the destruction and the speculative searches of fingerprints and samples. It is important that the Annex is followed particularly in relation to obtaining consent and explaining to volunteers what they are consenting to. Annex F, Note F1 provides suggested wordings that can be used when obtaining a person's consent to provide fingerprints or DNA samples for elimination purposes. It is important to use the correct wording depending on what the person has volunteered to, for example whether it is just to allow the fingerprint or sample to be used only for the purposes of a specific investigation; or for that investigation *and* retained by the police for future use. Such future use is limited to purposes related to the prevention or detection of crime, the investigation of an offence or the conduct of a prosecution in, as well as outside, the UK and may also be subject to a speculative search. This includes checking finger prints and samples against other fingerprints and DNA records held by, or on behalf of, the police and other law enforcement authorities in, as well as outside, the UK.

When fingerprints or DNA samples are taken from a person in connection with an investigation and the person is not suspected of having committed the offence, the fingerprints and/or sample must be destroyed as soon as they have fulfilled the purpose for which they were taken unless:

– they were taken for the purposes of an investigation of an offence for which a person has been convicted; and

– fingerprints or samples were also taken from the convicted person for the purposes of that investigation.

The reason why fingerprints and samples are retained is to allow for all fingerprints and samples in a case to be available for any subsequent miscarriage of justice investigation. They may not be used in the investigation of any offence or in evidence against the person who is, or would be, entitled to the destruction of the fingerprints and samples unless the person gives their written consent for their fingerprints or sample to be retained and used after they have fulfilled the purpose for which they were taken.

Annex F, para. 3 details what must be done when a person's fingerprints or sample are to be destroyed, this includes all copies of the fingerprints.

Annex F, para. 5 deals with the retention and destruction of fingerprints taken in connection with Immigration Service enquiries.

Terrorism Offences

There are additional powers and procedures for those suspects arrested in connection with terrorism which are contained in the Terrorism Act 2000.

With the exception of fingerprints, non-intimate samples or intimate samples, a constable may take any steps which are reasonably necessary for:

• photographing the detained person,

• measuring him/her, or identifying him/her

(sch. 8, para. 10(4) to the 2000 Act).

Fingerprints and Non-intimate Samples

Fingerprints and non-intimate samples may be taken from a detained person only if they are taken by a constable either:

• with the consent of the detained person given in writing; or

• where he/she is detained at a police station and a police officer of at least the rank of superintendent authorises the fingerprints or sample to be taken; or

- where the person has been convicted of a recordable offence and, where a non-intimate sample is to be taken, he/she was convicted of the offence on or after 10 April 1995

(sch. 8, para. 10(1)–(4) to the 2000 Act).

Intimate Samples

An intimate sample may be taken from a detained person only if:

- he/she is detained at a police station;
- the appropriate consent is given in writing;
- a police officer of at least the rank of superintendent authorises the sample to be taken

(sch. 8, para. 10(5) to the 2000 Act).

An intimate sample other than a sample of urine or a dental impression may be taken only by a registered practitioner/registered health professional acting on the authority of a constable. An intimate sample which is a dental impression may be taken only by a registered dentist acting on the authority of a constable.

The grounds for which an authorisation may be given under the Terrorism Act 2000 are:

- the officer reasonably suspects that the person has been involved in an offence under any of the provisions mentioned in s. 40(1)(a) of the Terrorism Act 2000 and the officer reasonably believes that the fingerprints or sample will tend to confirm or disprove his/her involvement; or
- the officer is satisfied that the taking of the fingerprints or sample from the person is necessary in order to assist in determining whether he/she is or has been concerned in the commission, preparation or instigation of acts of terrorism (s. 40(1)(b) of the Terrorism Act 2000); or
  - the officer is satisfied that the taking of fingerprints of the detained person will facilitate the ascertainment of that person's identity (or showing that he/she is not a particular person): and that person has refused to identify himself/herself or the officer has reasonable grounds for suspecting that that person is not who he/she claims to be.

Section 40(1)(a) of the Terrorism Act 2000 refers to offences of:

- membership to a proscribed organisation;
- arranging, managing or assisting in arranging or managing a meeting to support a proscribed organisation or to further the activities of a proscribed organisation;
- addressing a meeting for the purpose of encouraging support for a proscribed organisation or to further its activities;
- fund-raising for the purposes of terrorism;
- using and possessing money or other property for the purposes of terrorism or making arrangements for its use;
- money laundering;
- providing instruction or training in the making or use of weapons;
- directing terrorist organisation;
- possession of articles for terrorist purposes;
- collection or possession of information of a kind likely to be useful to a person committing or preparing an act of terrorism;
- inciting terrorism overseas.

Before fingerprints or a sample are taken from a person he/she must be informed that the authorisation has been given, the grounds upon which it has been given and, where relevant, of the nature of the offence in which it is suspected that he/she has been involved.

Where appropriate written consent to the taking of an intimate sample from a person is refused without good cause, in any proceedings against that person for an offence, the court, in determining whether to commit him for trial or whether there is a case to answer, may draw such inferences from the refusal as appear proper, and the court or jury, in determining whether that person is guilty of the offence charged, may draw such inferences from the refusal as appear proper.

It should be noted that s. 63A, as amended by the Criminal Justice and Police Act 2001, widens the extent that fingerprints and DNA profiles can be cross searched against those held by another UK or Island force. This has been extended to other police forces (for example, foreign police forces, the Ministry of Defence and the Armed Forces police forces) on the same basis that already exists between UK and Island forces. This also applies to fingerprints and samples obtained under the Terrorism Act 2000.

Where a sample proves to be insufficient there are provisions for obtaining further samples; this must be authorised by an officer of the rank of superintendent or above.

4.6 Interviews

4.6.1 Introduction

Much of an investigator's time is often spent interviewing witnesses and suspects. In relation to the latter, confessions are often seen by the police to be an important part of the prosecution case but they are frequently a target for attack by the defence. The power imbalance between a detained person and his/her custodians has been an issue which has often brought into question the reliability of any confession, particularly as it had, until recently, been almost the absolute right of an individual detainee to remain silent without any adverse inferences being drawn. However, the 'power imbalance' in a suspect interview is still generally seen as being tilted in the favour of the investigator. The PACE Codes of Practice C and E are intended to provide some protection to people being interviewed and lay down guidelines as to how interviews should be conducted. One result of this protection is that confessions may be held to be inadmissible because of:

- the conduct of the interviewing officers (s. 76(2)(a) of the Police and Criminal Evidence Act 1984);
- the unreliability of the confession itself (s. 76(2)(b)); or
- perceived unfairness in the proceedings (s. 78).

It may seem to the investigator that the balance is in favour of the detained person. However while a person may still remain silent and the rules remain to preserve this right, inferences may now be drawn from a person's silence in some circumstances.

In order to provide safeguards against the risk of evidence from questioning being rendered unreliable or obtained in a manner that breaches an individual's remaining right to silence, there are restrictions and guidelines on police questioning. These rules can be found throughout Codes C and E of the PACE Codes of Practice, giving guidance on the questioning of people by police officers. Failure to follow these rules may lead to evidence being excluded and/or disciplinary charges and ultimately could lead to civil claims for compensation. If any evidence obtained in an interview is later excluded by the relevant court, everyone's time has been wasted, irrespective of any other sanctions that may follow.

4.6.2   **What is an Interview?**

Not all discussions between the police and members of the public will be protected or governed by the PACE Codes of Practice. Code C, para. 11.1A defines an interview as:

> ...the questioning of a person regarding his involvement or suspected involvement in a criminal offence or offences which...is required to be carried out under caution.

KEYNOTE

Whether an interaction between a police officer and a member of the public is defined as an interview by the court can be crucial as to whether it will be admissible in evidence. It is therefore essential to understand the definition of an interview for the purposes of PACE and when a caution must be given (for cautions, see **4.6.3**).

 If a person is asked questions for reasons *other than obtaining evidence about his/her involvement or suspected involvement in an offence*, this is not an interview (and a caution need not be given). (For the use of cautions, see **4.6.3**.) This point is confirmed in the case of *R* v *McGuinness* [1999] Crim LR 318, where the court confirmed that it was only when a person was suspected of an offence that the caution must be administered before questioning. Consequently, in *R* v *Miller* [1998] Crim LR 209 the court held that asking a person the single question, 'Are these ecstasy tablets?' criminally implicated the person and therefore the conversation was an interview (i.e. it would not be necessary to ask such a question if there were no suspicion that the tablets were a controlled substance).

 In *Whelehan* v *DPP* [1995] RTR 177, a police officer, without giving a caution, asked questions of a person, who was sitting in the driving seat of his stationary vehicle with the key in the ignition switch, to establish that the person had been drinking and had driven to the spot. The officer went on to require a breath test. The court held that the magistrates were entitled to rule that the constable's suspicion as to the commission of the offence arose only after taking the breath test and the caution had been correctly administered.

 Whelehan should be compared with *R* v *Wyna*, 6 April 2000, unreported, where police had carried out a long-term surveillance operation. As a result of these observations the suspect was followed by police. He drove to central London where a man was seen to place an item in the boot of his car. The appellant then drove to the motorway heading north and was stopped by the police. A package containing over 4 kg of heroin was found in the boot. When the suspect was stopped, the reason given was that of speeding and when questioned about the drugs at the roadside he provided an innocent explanation. In this case even the Crown conceded that the police had reasonable grounds to suspect that the man had committed an arrestable offence when they stopped him at the roadside, and on that basis, under Code C, para. 10.1, they should have cautioned him immediately before asking him any questions.

Guidance on when questions do not amount to an interview is given by Code C, para. 10.1:

> ...A person need not be cautioned if questions are for other necessary purposes, e.g.:
>
> (a) solely to establish their identity or ownership of any vehicle;
>
> (b) to obtain information in accordance with any relevant statutory requirement, see paragraph 10.9;
>
> (c) in furtherance of the proper and effective conduct of a search, e.g. to determine the need to search in the exercise of powers of stop and search or to seek co-operation while carrying out a search;
>
> (d) to seek verification of a written record as in paragraph 11.13;
>
> (e) when examining a person in accordance with the Terrorism Act 2000, Schedule 7 and the Code of Practice for Examining Officers issued under that Act, Schedule 14, paragraph 6.

KEYNOTE

Before a person can be interviewed about their involvement in an offence, that person must be cautioned. So it might be said that an interview is any questioning of a person after such time as a caution has been or should have been administered. Where a person is arrested for an offence, he/she must also be cautioned, as any questioning will amount to an interview.

4.6.3 **The Caution**

In *Murray* v *United Kingdom* (1996) 22 EHRR 29, it was held that adverse inferences may not be drawn from the silence of a person who wants legal advice if they have not been allowed an opportunity to receive it. As a result of this decision Code C, Annex C sets out the restriction on drawing adverse inferences from silence and the terms of the caution when the restriction applies. Adverse inferences from silence are restricted in some cases where the detainee has not had legal advice. In these cases the caution that must be given to the person has been amended in order to remove the infringement on the person's right to remain silent.

In all cases other than those where the restriction on drawing adverse inferences apply, the caution to be given is set out in Code C, para. 10.5:

> You do not have to say anything. But it may harm your defence if you do not mention when questioned something which you later rely on in Court. Anything you do say may be given in evidence.

The occasions where the alternative caution is required are set out in Code C, Annex C, para. 1, that is occasions where the restriction on drawing an adverse inference apply.

This restriction applies:

– to any detainee at a police station who has asked for legal advice and not been allowed an opportunity to consult a solicitor and has not changed their mind;

– to any detainee at a police station who has had their right to consult a solicitor suspended by an officer of the rank of superintendent or above (Code C, Annex B);

– where an officer of superintendent rank or above has authorised an interview without waiting for the detainee to consult with a solicitor as set out in Code C, para. 6.6(b)(ii);

– where the interview goes ahead without a solicitor, including a duty solicitor, because awaiting their arrival would cause unreasonable delay to the process of the investigation and the person has not changed their mind about wanting a solicitor (Code C, para. (6.6(b)(ii));

– where a person has been charged with, or informed they may be prosecuted for an offence; and
  – has had brought to their notice a written statement made by another person or the content of an interview with another person which relates to that offence,
  – is interviewed about that offence, or
  – makes a written statement about that offence.

Annex C, para. 2 sets out the alternative terms of the caution to be used when the restriction on drawing adverse inferences from silence applies:

> You do not have to say anything, but anything you do say may be given in evidence.

The situation is likely to occur during a detainee's detention where it will be necessary to administer both of these cautions at various times during his/her detention. As there is a significant difference between them in relation to the right to silence, it will be important to make it clear which caution applies to the detainee during any interview or charge procedure. Guidance as to what the detainee should be told, is provided by Code C, Annex C, Note C2, this paragraph gives sample explanations that need to be explained to the detainee before the change is caution is given.

Full caution already given (in most cases given when arrested)	Detainee's access to legal advice restricted as per Code C, Annex C, para. 1. Need to give alternative caution	Explain change in caution as set out at Code C, Annex C Note C2(a)(i)	Give caution as set out at Annex C, para. 2
Full caution already given	Detainee has been charged but is further interviewed (Code C, Annex C, para. 1). Need to give alternative caution	Explain change in caution as set out at Code C, Annex C, Note C2(a) (ii)	Give caution as set out at Annex C, para. 2
Caution as set out at Annex C, para. 2, given	Detainee has now had access to a solicitor or changed their mind. Need to give alternative caution	Explain change in caution as set out at Code C, Annex C, Note C2(b)	Give caution Code C, para. 10.5

Where Code C, Annex C, para. 1 applies (i.e. the detainee has not been given access to a solicitor) and the detainee is charged with an offence or informed they may be prosecuted, the caution at Annex C, para. 2 should be used, on all other occasions the caution at Code C, para. l6.2 should be used:

> You do not have to say anything. But it may harm your defence if you do not mention now something which you later rely on in court. Anything you do say may be given in evidence.

If a person is questioned without being cautioned when a caution should have been given, any admissions made by that person are likely to be inadmissible in evidence. One of the main reasons for this is that a person has a right to remain silent and if the caution has not been given, the suspect has not been warned of this right nor of the risks of self-incrimination. Conversely, if a caution is not required and one is given, the person may not make admissions which he/she might otherwise have made. Consequently, it is important to be aware of when to administer a caution and, in cases of doubt, to err on the side of caution. Should an interview be excluded, this may have implications on other evidence obtained as a consequence of the confession.

An appropriate caution should be administered to all people who are:

– arrested for an offence, and/or

– where Code C, para. 10.1 applies.

Code C, para. 10.1 states:

> A person whom there are grounds to suspect of an offence, see Note 10A, must be cautioned before any questions about an offence, or further questions if the answers provide the grounds for suspicion, are put to them if either the suspect's answers or silence, (i.e. failure or refusal to answer or answer satisfactorily) may be given in evidence to a court in a prosecution...

KEYNOTE

If a person does not appear to understand the caution, the officer who has given it should go on to explain it in his/her own words (Code C, Note 10C).

The caution must be given where there are 'grounds to suspect the person of an offence'. Normally the 1984 Act and the Codes of Practice refer to 'reasonable grounds', whereas here the reference is simply to 'grounds'.

This would suggest that the level of evidence/suspicion needed before a caution is given to a suspect may be *lower* than that needed to arrest the person. This would mean that a person may need to be cautioned when spoken to about offences for which there is no power of arrest or on occasions where there is a power of arrest but the officer's level of suspicion is not sufficient to justify an arrest.

The courts have given some guidance as to when a caution should be administered. There must be real *grounds* for suspicion; a mere hunch is not sufficient. The grounds have to be such as to lead to suspicion that an offence has been committed by that person. This view is confirmed in *Batley v DPP* (1998) *The Times*, 5 March, where the court accepted that, in general terms, where police officers had nothing more than a hunch that an offence was being committed, there would not be enough to activate the Code. However, it was necessary to caution a person before asking questions which went to the very heart of the issue as to whether he/she might be committing an offence, especially since the suspect was being invited to incriminate himself/herself.

In *Fox v United Kingdom* (1990) 13 EHRR 157, the court stated that reasonable suspicion arises from facts or information which would satisfy an objective observer that the person concerned may have committed the offence. Clearly there will be a need to record this information in detail to inform the court of the facts, as known at the time of the decision to caution or not to caution.

Further guidance was provided in *R v Smith* [2001] 1 WLR 1031, where the court held that establishing a reasonable suspicion was an objective test and an honest belief by a police officer was not required. Suspicion could take into account evidence that could not be adduced, such as hearsay. Except where evidence had been obtained in blatant breach of a statute, improperly obtained information could still be relied on.

Where the questions go beyond issues raised by Code C, para. 10.1 and go to the question of guilt, this is likely to be an interview for the purposes of the Police and Criminal Evidence Act 1984. In *Crown Prosecution Service v O'Shea*, 11 May 1998, unreported, police were called to a road traffic accident. O'Shea, the owner of the vehicle, was near the car, exhibiting signs of drunkenness and there was no one else in the vicinity who might have been driving the vehicle. The officer said to O'Shea the words, '*An accident has just happened that is alleged was your fault*'. The court held that it was clear than when the officer had asked O'Shea whether he was driving his vehicle at the time of the accident, the officer had known that he was the owner of the vehicle and therefore the question was not solely to establish whether he was the owner. Accordingly, the thrust of the question was whether he had committed an offence. The defendant's subsequent answer was held to be inadmissible as the PACE Codes of Practice had not been complied with.

O'Shea can be contrasted with *R v Maguire* [1989] Crim LR 815 where the court held that Code C does not prevent a police officer from asking questions at or near the scene of the crime to elicit an explanation which if true or accepted, would clear the suspect.

Once a person has been cautioned, consideration of further cautions must be given. The need for additional cautions is provided for by the PACE Codes of Practice. In addition, in *R v Miller* [1998] Crim LR 209, the court said that one caution was not necessarily enough, and before other questions are asked of a suspect at a later stage, a further caution may be necessary.

In addition to the duty to caution a suspect, there will be occasions where a person arrested for an offence will have to be given a 'special warning' in interview. Special warnings are concerned with a person's right to silence (see ss. 34 to 37 of the Criminal Justice and Public Order Act 1994). As mentioned above, this will only apply where the detainee has had the opportunity to seek legal advice.

Unsolicited Comments

There will be occasions where suspects make unsolicited comments implicating them in an offence before they are suspected of any involvement and therefore before they are cautioned (or further cautioned if already suspected). Such statements are likely to be admissible provided the PACE Codes of Practice are complied with. Code C, paras 11.13 and 11.14 state:

> 11.13 A written record shall be made of any comments made by a suspect, including unsolicited comments, which are outside the context of an interview but which might be relevant to the offence. Any such record must be timed and signed by the maker. When practicable the

suspect shall be given the opportunity to read that record and to sign it as correct or to indicate how they consider it inaccurate. See Note 11E

11.14 Any refusal by a person to sign an interview record when asked in accordance with this Code must itself be recorded.

Note 11E states:

When a suspect agrees to read records of interviews and of other comments and to sign them as correct, they should be asked to endorse the record with *e.g.* 'I agree that this is a correct record of what was said' and add their signature. If the suspect does not agree with the record, the interviewer should record the details of any disagreement and ask the suspect to read these details and sign them to the effect that they accurately reflect their disagreement. Any refusal to sign should be recorded.

KEYNOTE

It is particularly important to record the comment and give the person an opportunity to see what has been recorded and to comment/endorse it. Where the person has had this opportunity and signs the record then it will strengthen the evidence and if he/she declines to sign it, this may assist in establishing what the defence case may be.

In *R* v *Miller* (above) the court held that Code C, para. 11.13 requires a written record, timed and signed by the suspect as correct or an opportunity for the suspect to indicate which parts were inaccurate.

Whilst it is suggested that this should be done at early opportunity, in *Batley* v *DPP* (1998) *The Times*, 5 March, it was held that as the Code did not require an *immediate* endorsement and no time factor was laid down, there was nothing to constrain the police from returning the next day to get their endorsement.

4.6.4 Interview of Person Not Under Arrest

If a person has not been arrested then he/she can be interviewed almost anywhere (but an officer intending to interview a person on private property must consider whether he/she is trespassing). If the interview with a person not under arrest takes place in a police station, Code C, para. 3.21 and Note 1A must be followed.

If the interview is to be with a juvenile, Code C, para. 11.16, gives guidance as to when interviews should take place at a juvenile's place of education. This should only be in exceptional circumstances and with the agreement of the principal or the principal's nominee. The juvenile's parent(s) or person(s) responsible for his/her welfare and the appropriate adult (if a different person) should be notified of the interview and be afforded reasonable time in which to attend. The principal or nominee can act as the appropriate adult where waiting for an appropriate adult would cause unreasonable delay. This is not the case where the juvenile is suspected of an offence against his/her educational establishment (Code C, para. 11.15). Code C, paras 11.18 to 11.20 and Note 11C outline the limited circumstances when a juvenile may be interviewed without an appropriate adult being present.

In cases where the person is not under arrest, certain information must be given to him/her. This is covered by Code C, para. 10.2 which states:

Whenever a person not under arrest is initially cautioned, or reminded they are under caution, that person must at the same time be told they are not under arrest and are free to leave if they want to. See Note 10C.

KEYNOTE

For the situation where a person is a police station voluntarily and not under arrest, see Code C, para. 3.21.

When carrying out an interview, officers should be mindful of how they treat the person, this it is suggested, also applies to witnesses as well as suspects. For instance in *L* v *Reading Borough Council*, 12 March 2001, unreported, the court stated that it was arguable that when interviewing a young child victim there was an assumption of responsibility and a special relationship was created. Part of the responsibility was to protect the child from future harm that could ensue from the manner of the investigation. Following this line, failure to protect the victims/witnesses could lead to a claim for damages if they suffer harm.

4.6.5   Interview of Person Under Arrest

Any interview of a person who is under arrest must take place at a police station (Code C, para. 11.1) or other authorised place of detention unless waiting until the interview can be conducted at such a place is likely to:

- lead to interference with or harm to evidence connected with an offence or interference with or physical harm to other people or serious loss of, or damage to, property; or
- lead to the alerting of other people suspected of having committed an offence but not yet arrested for it; or
- hinder the recovery of property obtained in consequence of the commission of an offence.

Code C requires that interviewing in any of these circumstances shall cease once the relevant risk has been averted or the necessary questions have been put in order to attempt to avert that risk (para. 11.1). There is a danger in these cases of continuing the interview past the point where the risk has been averted, this could lead to the whole interview being excluded.

The courts have recognised that there may be times when a person who is under arrest will be asked questions other than when at the police station. One such example is where the arrested person is present while officers search his/her address. In *R v Hanchard*, 6 December 1999, unreported, the court recognised that searches of premises could not be conducted in complete silence. The court stated that it would be unfair and unreasonable not to put any questions to owners of premises undergoing a search, however, what questions can be asked will be a matter of fact and degree in each individual case. Where questions go beyond that needed for the immediate investigation it would be a breach of the Codes. In *Hanchard*, the questions which were admissible included whether cannabis at the address belonged to the suspect and where a large quantity of money had come from.

If a person has been arrested by one police force on behalf of another and the lawful period of detention in respect of that offence has not yet begun (in accordance with s. 41 of the Police and Criminal Evidence Act 1984), no questions may be put to him/her about the offence while he/she is in transit between the forces except in order to clarify any voluntary statement made by him/her (Code C, para. 14.1).

If a person is in police detention at a hospital, he/she may not be questioned without the agreement of a responsible doctor (Code C, para. 14.2). If an interview does take place, the interviewing officer must inform the custody officer (Note 14A).

If questioning does take place in any of these circumstances it will affect the suspect's 'detention clock'. The custody officer must be informed of such an interview as it may affect the lawfulness of the suspect's detention.

It is essential to comply with the rules on interviewing after arrest, as a failure could jeopardise any future admissions made in interview. In *R v Webster*, 12 December 2000, unreported, the police evidence was that during the search of his house the defendant, having been arrested but not cautioned, had made admissions as to where the drugs were located in his house and as to the amount of drugs that he possessed. No contemporaneous note was taken of the search. The defendant was then interviewed on the same basis as his answers to the questions which had been asked during the search. The court held that the later interview at the police station did not cure the breaches of the Codes of Practice which had occurred during the search.

4.6.6 **Person Charged with an Offence**

Once a person has been charged with an offence generally he/she cannot be interviewed about the offence unless it is necessary:

- to prevent or minimise harm or loss to some other person or to the public; or
- to clear up an ambiguity in a previous answer or statement; or
- in the interest of justice that the person should have questions put to him/her and have an opportunity to comment on information concerning the offence which has come to light since he/she was charged or informed that he/she might be prosecuted.

It should be noted that the service of the Notice of Intended Prosecution under ss. 1 and 2 of the Road Traffic Offenders Act 1988, does not amount to informing a person that he/she may be prosecuted for an offence and so does not preclude further questioning in relation to that offence (Code C, Note 16B).

If a person is interviewed for any other reason, the interview is likely to be inadmissible in evidence.

Where a person is interviewed after charge, Code C, para. 16.5 states:

...Before any such interview, the interviewer shall:

(a) caution the detainee, 'You do not have to say anything, but anything you do say may be given in evidence.';

(b) remind the detainee about their right to legal advice.

See Note 16B

This caution does not restrict the right to silence. It is not unusual for a person who has been charged with offences (and therefore his/her detention is for other reasons, e.g. because bail has been refused) to be paid a 'social visit' or to be spoken to for debrief intelligence purposes. Clearly there is a risk that the person may provide additional evidence about the offences for which he/she has been detained on other matters. *R* v *Williams* (1992) *The Times*, 6 February, recognised that this practice did occur but gave some guidance. The court held that investigating officers should avoid paying 'social visits' to people in custody whose conduct was under investigation. If, after being charged with an offence, a suspect of his/her own volition said that he/she wished to make a statement admitting or giving details of the offence, after properly cautioning the person and complying with the rest of the Codes of Practice, investigating officers were not debarred from recording what he/she had to say. Prior to a person being visited in his/her cell, the custody officer must give his/her authority and the visit must be recorded in the detained person's custody record.

4.6.7 **When Must an Interview be Held?**

Code C, para. 16.1 states:

When the officer in charge of the investigation reasonably believes there is sufficient evidence to provide a realistic prospect of the detainee's conviction, see paragraph 11.6, they shall without delay, and subject to the following qualification, inform the custody officer who will be responsible for considering whether the detainee should be charged...

KEYNOTE

It is suggested that, in a case where a suspect has not been interviewed about an offence, Code C, para. 16.1, requires that person to be asked if he/she has anything further to say about the matter, in which case this will be an interview.

This view is supported by the case of *R* v *Pointer* [1997] Crim LR 676 which held that giving a suspect the opportunity to say something more when the officer already has enough evidence to charge is an interview within the definition of Code C, para. 11.1A, and, therefore, an event which attracts the protection of a caution, legal representation and tape recording.

Interviews in these circumstances are conducted to allow the suspect to make any additional comments and for the interviewing officers to follow up on those responses. If the interview is held for any other reason it is likely to be inadmissible. This was the case in *Pointer* where the court held that there was sufficient evidence to charge prior to the interview and consequently Code C, para. 16.1 had not been complied with. Such an interview may assist the investigating officer to make reasonable lines of enquiry which support the defence.

4.6.8 Conducting and Recording Interviews

The conduct of officers and the proper treatment of the suspect during an interview are essential if an interview is to be admissible in evidence. If an interview is not conducted properly, confessions made during the interview may be excluded. The PACE Codes of Practice are there to afford suspects proper protection from false confessions and treatment which may lead a court to the conclusion that the confession may not be reliable. It is essential, therefore, that officers are fully aware of the relevant Codes and comply with them. For evidential purposes interviews need to be recorded. An accurate record must be made of each interview with a person suspected of an offence, whether or not the interview takes place at a police station (Code C, para. 11.7).

Interviews fall into two main groups:

- those that are tape recorded; and
- those where the only record will be made in writing.

If a suspect makes unsolicited comments which are outside the context of an interview but which might be relevant to the offence, those comments should be recorded and Code C, para. 11.13 should be followed. Code C, Note 11E gives guidance as to what must be included in the record and when the record should be made. As the relevance of the comment may not be obvious at the time it is made, it is suggested that all comments are recorded.

When Interviews Must Be Taped

The interviewing of suspects is governed by PACE Code of Practice E. Code E, paras 3.1 and 3.4 set out which interviews at a police station must be tape recorded. The most noticeable absence from this list is for interviews about matters which can only be tried summarily. These requirements do not *preclude* other interviews being tape recorded. Investigators may well be advised to tape record interviews concerning summarily only offences as it may be more difficult for the defence to suggest any confession was fabricated. If these interviews are tape recorded, they must follow the requirements of tape recorded interviews (see Code E, Note 3A).

The whole of each interview shall be recorded, including the taking and reading back of any statement (Code E, para. 3.5).

All interviews listed in Code E, para. 3.1 conducted at a police station must be tape recorded *unless* the custody officer authorises the interviewing officer not to tape record the interview. If the custody officer authorises the interview to go ahead without being tape recorded, the interview must be recorded in writing. A custody officer authorising this may have to justify the decision at court and the reasons for his/her decision should be recorded.

Code E, para. 3.3 allows the custody officer to make this decision where:

- It is not reasonably practicable to tape record the interview because of:
  - failure of the equipment; or
  - the non-availability of a suitable interview room or recorder; and
  - the custody officer considers on reasonable grounds that the interview should not be delayed until the failure has been rectified or a suitable room or recorder becomes available;

- or it is clear from the outset that no prosecution will ensue;

- where the custody officer has authorised that the detainee can be interviewed in his/her cell (Code E, para. 3.4).

Further, Code E, para. 3.1 does not apply to:

- certain interviews involving terrorism (Code E, para. 3.2).

For cases where a person objects to the interview being tape recorded, see Code E, para. 4.8.

As of September 2002, where persons are held in police detention at Basingstoke, Portsmouth, Southampton, Chatham, Gravesend, Tonbridge, Bromley, Colindale, Edmonton, Redditch, Telford, Worcester, Colchester, Harlow and Southend police stations any interviews held by police officers must be visually recorded. Codes of Practice for the visual recording of interviews have been produced for use at these police stations.

Preparation before Interview at Police Station

Preparation is essential before any interview (indeed it is the first step in the PEACE interviewing model). This preparation should include the following points:

- Decide where the interview will be conducted. Consider the availability of a room and the timing of the interview.

- The location must have a seat for the person being interviewed (Code C, para. 12.6) and should be adequately lit, heated and ventilated (Code C, para. 12.4). The detained person must also have clothing of a reasonable standard of comfort and cleanliness (Code C, para. 8.5). (It will be a question of fact as to what amounts to adequate clothing and it is suggested that if the clothing is such as to degrade the detained person or make him/her uncomfortable, it may lead to the confession being held to be unreliable.)

- If the interview is being taped, ensure that there are sufficient tapes for the anticipated length of the interview (or at least until the first break period). If the interview is being recorded in writing, ensure there are enough forms.

- If the interview is being taped, ensure the notice as set out in Code E, para. 4.19 is available to be given at the end of the interview.

- In deciding the timing of the interview, consideration must be given to the detainee's rest period, which should not be interrupted or delayed unless Code C, para. 12.2 applies. Where the interview goes ahead during the rest period under Code C, para. 12.2(a), a fresh rest period must be allowed. Before a detainee is interviewed, the custody officer, in consultation with the officer in charge of the investigation and appropriate health care professionals as necessary, shall assess whether the detainee is fit enough to be interviewed (Code C, para. 12.3 and Annex G).

- If legal advice has been requested you must arrange for the legal representative to be present at the interview unless Code C, para. 6.6 applies.

- If a person has asked for legal advice and an interview is initiated in the absence of a legal adviser (e.g. where the person has agreed to be interviewed without his/her legal adviser being present or because of the urgent need to interview under Code C, para. 11.1), a record must be made in the interview record (Code C, para. 6.17).

- If an appropriate adult should be present, arrange for his/her attendance. (For the definition of appropriate adult, see Code C, para. 1.7.)

- If an interpreter is needed for the interview, arrange for his/her attendance.

It is also important to draw up an interview plan and to include any relevant areas that may provide a general or specific defence.

– Look at the evidence available and identify any significant statement or silence by the suspect in order that it can be put to him/her in interview (Code C, para. 11.4).

Starting Interviews

In order to interview a detained person, the interviewing officer must obtain permission from the custody officer. An entry must be made in the custody record to record that the interviewing officer accepts responsibility for the detained person. If the request to hand over the detained person is declined, the custody officer must record this fact and the reasons why on the custody record (Code C, para. 12.9). The responsibility for the detained person at this stage rests with the officer to whom the transfer is made and remains with this person until the detained person is returned to the custody officer (s. 39(2) of the Police and Criminal Evidence Act 1984). Section 39 of the 1984 Act states:

(2) If this custody officer, in accordance with any code of practise issued under this Act, transfers or permits the transfer of a person in police detention—
   (a) to the custody of a police officer investigating an offence for which that person is in police detention; or
   (b) to the custody of an officer who has charge of that person outside the police station, the custody officer shall cease in relation to that person to be subject to the duty imposed on him by subsection (1)(a) above; and it shall be the duty of the officer to whom the transfer is made to ensure that he is treated in accordance with the provisions of this Act and of any such codes of practice as are mentioned in subsection (1) above.

Before allowing a detainee to be interviewed the custody officer shall undertake a risk assessment in order to ensure that conducting the interview will not significantly harm the detainee's physical or mental state or that their physical or mental state might result in the them saying something in the interview about their involvement or suspected involvement in the offence being considered unreliable in subsequent court proceedings (Code C, Annex G, paras 1 and 2). The risk assessment should be done, where necessary, in consultation with the officer in charge of the investigation and appropriate health care professionals. Annex G, para. 3 sets out a number of factors that must be considered when conducting this risk assessment. Where risks are identified, the custody officer must determine what safeguards are needed to minimise those risks in order to allow the interview to take place. It should be remembered that vulnerable suspects listed at Code C, para. 11.18 must always be treated as if being at some risk during an interview and therefore may not be interviewed except in accordance with Code C, paras 11.18 to 11.20 (Code C, para. 12.3). Code C, Annex G provides guidance to help police officers and health care professionals assess whether a detainee might be at risk in an interview.

The risk assessment can be very important in terms of ensuring that any confession in an interview is admissible. In *R v Utip* (2003) unreported, the court held that the law required that where there were grounds to suspect mental illness, a defendant should be examined by a doctor to establish whether he/she was fit for interview. Where a defendant had been assessed as fit to be interviewed by a psychiatrist and had his/her interests protected by an appropriate adult and solicitor, there was no unfairness in allowing evidence of the interview to go before the jury.

Preliminary Issues for Interviews Not Being Tape Recorded

Before an interview begins the following points must be dealt with:

- Immediately before the commencement of the interview remind the suspect of his/her right to legal advice (Code C, para. 11.2) and make a note of this reminder and any response in the interview record.

- For the interview record, identify all officers present in the interview as required by Code C, para. 12.7.

- If an appropriate adult is present, inform that person of his/her role (Code C, para. 11.17).

- Administer the caution (Code C, para. 10.1) (and re-administer where appropriate).

Preliminary Issues for Interviews Being Tape Recorded

Before an interview commences the following points must be dealt with:

- Break open tape seals in the presence of the suspect (Code E, para. 4.3).

- Load tapes in the presence of the suspect and set to record (Code E, para. 4.3).

- Inform the suspect about the tape recording in accordance with Code E, para. 4.4.

- Verbally identify all persons present at the interview for the tape (Code E. para. 4.4).

- Administer the relevant caution (Code E, para. 4.5) (and re-administer where appropriate).

- Remind the suspect of his/her right to free legal advice (Code E, para. 4.5 and Code C, paras 6.1 and 6.5) and ensure that the response is recorded on the tape (for instance a nod of the head would not be picked up by a tape recorder).

What Should be Disclosed to the Solicitor

It is important not to confuse the duty of disclosure to a person once charged with the need to disclose evidence to a suspect before interviewing them. After a person has been charged, and before trial, the rules of disclosure are clear and almost all material must be disclosed to the defence.

However, this is not necessarily the case at the interview stage of the investigation. There is no specific provision within the Police and Criminal Evidence Act 1984 for the disclosure of any information by the police at the police station, with the exception of the custody record and, in identification cases, the initial description given by the witnesses. Further, there is nothing within the Criminal Justice and Public Order Act 1994 that states that information must be disclosed before an inference from silence can be made. Indeed, in *R* v *Imran* [1997] Crim LR 754, the court held that it is totally wrong to submit that a defendant should be prevented from lying by being presented with the whole of the evidence against him/her prior to the interview.

In *R* v *Argent* [1997] Crim LR 346, the court dismissed the argument that an inference could not be drawn under s. 34 of the Criminal Justice and Public Order Act 1994 because there had not been full disclosure at the interview. However, the court did recognise that it may be a factor to take into account, but it would be for the jury to decide whether the failure to answer questions was reasonable.

In *R* v *Roble* [1997] Crim LR 449, the court suggested that an inference would not be drawn where a solicitor gave advice to remain silent where, for example, the interviewing officer had disclosed too little of the case for the solicitor usefully to advise his/her client, or where the nature of the offence, or the material in the hands of the police, was so complex or related to matters so long ago that no sensible immediate response was feasible.

It was not uncommon in the past for solicitors to advise on no comment interviews and this has been relied on by defendants to avoid adverse inferences being drawn from their silence. The courts and legal advisers are now very aware of the consequences of advising a suspect to offer no comment. In *R v Morgan* [2002] ECWA Crim 445, the Court of Appeal stated that a court was entitled to assume that a solicitor would advise his/her client about the adverse inferences rule. In *R v Ali* [2002] ECWA Crim 683, the court stated that the question was not whether the advice to remain silent was good advice but whether it provided an adequate reason for failing to answer questions.

There is a balance to be struck between providing the solicitor with enough information to understand the nature of the case against his/her client and keeping back material which, if disclosed, may allow the suspect the opportunity to avoid implicating himself/herself. For instance in *R v Thirlwell* [2002] EWCA Crim 286, the Court of Appeal agreed that the solicitor had not been entitled to provisional medical evidence as to possible causes of death in a murder case. The disclosure of material may well be a factor which the defendant relies on in showing that the failure to mention possible defences was reasonable. If the officers are not hoping to draw inferences from silence then tactically they may decide not to disclose as much information—it will be a question of fact in each case.

Conduct During Interview

All Interviews

- Code C, para. 11.5 reiterates the fact that officers must not act oppressively.
  - If a complaint is made by the suspect concerning the provisions of the codes the interviewing officer must inform the custody officer and follow Code C, para. 12.9. If the complaint is not concerning the codes, Code E, Note 4F applies.
- Officers should only indicate the possible effect of refusing to answer questions or of answering questions if he/she is asked about those possible effects by the suspect *unless this is done as part of a special warning* (see Code C, paras 10.10, 10.11 and 11.15).
  - Code E, para. 4.8 provides guidance where the person objects to the interview being taped.
- Code C, Note 11C reminds officers of the risks associated with the reliability of interviewing juveniles or people who are mentally disordered or suffering from mental impairment.

At the start of the interview the investigating officer should put to the suspect any significant statement or silence which occurred before his/her arrival at the police station and ask the suspect whether he/she confirms the earlier statement or silence and whether he/she wishes to add anything. Code C, para. 11.4A defines a 'significant' statement or silence. This aspect of the interview is very important in terms of establishing whether the facts are disputed. If they are not disputed at this stage, it is unlikely that they will be challenged at any later court hearing and, if challenged, the defence will have to explain why this was not done at the time of the interview. The courts may also view this failure to put the statement to the suspect in a more sinister light. In *R v Allen*, 10 July 2001, unreported, the court were concerned that the police failed to put the admission to the suspect in interview, despite thorough questioning, which they felt clearly placed a question mark over its reliability. If the suspect remains silent in relation to a 'significant silence', that silence may give rise to an adverse inference being drawn under s. 34 of the Criminal Justice and Public Order Act 1994 if the person raises it in his/her defence at court. (As this is very important issue, it may be necessary to delay the interview until the arrest notes are completed or the officers witnessing the offence/arrest have been consulted to ensure that all matters are put to the suspect at this stage.) Consideration should be given to putting questions to a suspect who makes no comment, or even where the legal representative has stated that the suspect will make no comment, as this may allow the court to draw inferences against a defence that the suspect raises at court. The interviewer may wish to go through any significant statement or silence again if during earlier interviews adverse inferences could not be drawn.

Issues Specific to Tape Recorded Interviews

- If the equipment fails, rectify the fault quickly if possible. If this is not possible, look for an alternative recording machine or room. If none available, seek the authority of the custody officer to continue without the interview being tape recorded (see Code E, para. 4.15).

- If a tape breaks, follow Code E, Note 4H.

- When the tapes are removed from the recorder they must be retained (see Code E, para. 4.16) and the procedure at para. 4.18 followed.

- If you need to change tapes during interview, follow Code E, para. 4.11.

- If a suspect objects to the interview being tape recorded at any stage of the interview, the procedure in Code E, para. 4.8 must be followed and Note 4D should be taken into account in deciding whether to continue to record the interview on tape.

- If a suspect indicates that he/she wishes to tell the police about matters not connected with the offence(s) being investigated but does not wish this information to be recorded on tape, Code E, para. 4.10 requires this to be dealt with at the conclusion of the formal interview. Any comment by the suspect would still need to be recorded in writing.

Breaks

Breaks from interviewing must be made at recognised meal times or at other times that take account of when the person last had a meal (Code C, para. 12.7). Short breaks for refreshment must also be provided at intervals of approximately two hours. Code C, Note 12B gives guidance on how long breaks should be. Code C, para. 12.8 sets out the exceptions to the requirement to provide breaks. These exceptions exist where to break the interview would:

- involve a risk of harm to people or serious loss of, or damage to property;

- delay unnecessarily the person's release from custody; or

- otherwise prejudice the outcome of the investigation.

Any decision to delay a break during an interview must be recorded, with grounds, in the interview record (either on the written record or on the tape) (Code C, para. 12.12).

Solicitors and Legal Advice

A 'solicitor' for the purposes of the Codes of Practice means:

- a solicitor holding a current practising certificate;

- a trainee solicitor;

- a duty solicitor representative or an accredited representative included on the register of representatives maintained by the Community Legal Aid Service (Code C, para. 6.12).

Where a solicitor is available at the time the interview begins or while it is in progress, the solicitor must be allowed to be present while the person in interviewed (Code C, para. 6.8). (This applies unless the suspect states that he/she does not want the solicitor to be present or where access is denied under s. 58 of the 1984 Act; see Code C, Annex B.)

If a solicitor arrives at the station to see a suspect, the suspect must be asked whether he/she would like to see the solicitor *regardless of what legal advice has already been received*. The solicitor's attendance and the suspect's decision must be recorded in the custody record (Code C, para. 6.15).

If the investigating officer considers that a solicitor is acting in such a way that he/she is unable properly to put questions to the suspect, he/she will stop the interview and consult an officer not below the rank of superintendent, if one is readily available. Otherwise, an officer not below the rank of inspector who is not connected with the investigation is to decide whether that solicitor should be excluded from the interview. The interview may also have to be stopped in order to allow another solicitor to be instructed (Code C, para. 6.10). For the proper role of the legal representatives, see Code C, Note 6D. Code C, para. 6.6 sets out those occasions where a person can be interviewed without a solicitor being present even though he/she has requested a solicitor. Any authority to exclude a solicitor will need to be justified to the court if necessary (Code C, Note 6E).

With regard to the exclusion of a trainee/probationer solicitor this has to be considered in relation to the specific investigation and whether that person is likely to interfere with the investigation. The decision can take into account the character of the person. Internal advice could also provide guidance as to what the decision should be but the decision has to be made in relation to each individual case. It is not permissible to have blanket bans on such persons (*R* v *Chief Constable of the Northumbria Constabulary, ex parte Thompson* [2001] 1 WLR 1342).

If a request for legal advice is made during an interview, the interviewing officer must stop the interview and arrange for legal advice to be provided. If the suspect changes his/her mind again, the interview can continue provided Code C, para. 6.6 is complied with.

It is important to remember that Code C, para. 6.4 reminds officers that they should *not* try and dissuade the detained person from obtaining legal advice.

When Must the Interview be Concluded?

Guidance is provided by Code C, para. 11.6 as to when an interview should be concluded. Paragraph 11.6 states that the interview shall cease if the investigating officer considers that:

- all the questions relevant to obtaining accurate and reliable information about the offence have been put to the suspect, this includes allowing the suspect an opportunity to give an innocent explanation and asking questions to test if the explanation is accurate and reliable;
- he/she has taken account of any other available evidence; and
- there is sufficient evidence to provide a realistic prospect of conviction for that offence if the person was prosecuted for it.

The investigating officer shall then bring the detained person before the custody officer for charge.

The interview may continue until the above conditions are satisfied with regard to other offences being investigated (Code C, para. 16.1).

It is important to remember that the interview should not be concluded at the point when there is sufficient evidence to prosecute but when there is sufficient evidence for a prosecution to succeed. (In *Prouse* v *DPP* [1999] All ER (D) 748, the question was said to be not how much evidence there is but the quality of it.) Once there is enough evidence to prosecute, it may still be necessary to cover those other points in the interview that may be relevant to the defence case. If these points are not covered in the interview, the defence may surprise the prosecution case with matters that the prosecution have not covered or with issues that may result in the loss of an inference being drawn from the suspect's silence. This was considered in *R* v *McGuinness* [1999] Crim LR 318, where the court held that the words 'sufficient evidence to prosecute' and 'sufficient evidence for a prosecution to succeed' in Code C, para. 11.4, must involve some consideration of any explanation, or lack of one, from the suspect. It would depend on the facts of a case whether the stage where a suspect ought to be charged has been reached. As a word of caution, the court also said that under Code C, paras 16.1 and 11.4, it was not open for a suspect to be questioned beyond the point when he/she ought to have been charged. If the suspect was questioned beyond that point, then the interview was liable to be ruled inadmissible and the content would not be available to support the prosecution case.

Paragraph 3.4 of the Code of Practice to the Criminal Procedure and Investigations Act 1996 says that in conducting an investigation, the investigator should pursue all reasonable lines of enquiry, whether these point towards or away from the suspect. What is reasonable will depend on the particular circumstances. Interviewers should keep this in mind when deciding what questions to ask in an interview.

Special Groups

As a confession can be very damning evidence against a defendant, it is important to provide safeguards that give all suspects the same level of protection. The PACE Codes of Practice recognise certain groups as being in need of additional protection. These groups include juveniles, people who do not speak English, those suffering from a mental impairment and those who are deaf. Such suspects must not be interviewed without the relevant person being present.

For juveniles and those suffering from a mental impairment (or who appear to be such), an appropriate adult must be present (Code C, para. 11.15).

Under Code C, para. 13.2, a person capable of acting as interpreter is required where:

- the suspect has difficulty in understanding English;
- the interviewing officer cannot speak the person's own language; and
- the suspect wishes an interpreter to be present.

If the suspect appears to be deaf or there is any doubt about his/her hearing or speaking ability, an interpreter should be found (unless he/she agrees *in writing* to proceed without an interpreter) (Code C, para. 13.5). This requirement also applies in the case of the appropriate adult who appears to be deaf or there is doubt about his/her hearing or speaking ability (Code C, para. 13.6).

There are limited circumstances where an interview may be conducted without an interpreter or appropriate adult being present. These are set out in Code C, paras 11.1 and 11.15. Once those conditions no longer apply, the interview must be suspended until the appropriate person is present.

Where interpreters are required, Code C, paras 13.3 to 13.11 are to be followed.

If an interpreter who can translate straight from the detained person's language to English cannot be found then more than one interpreter should be used to bridge the language gap. It is the *interviewer* who is responsible for ensuring that the detained person can understand and be understood (*R* v *West London Youth Court, ex parte J* [2000] 1 All ER 823).

Taped Interviews and Special Groups

If the suspect is deaf or there is doubt about his/her hearing ability, a contemporaneous written record should be made as well as the tape recording. This record should be the same as where there is no taped record of the interview (Code E, para. 4.7).

Special Warnings

Now that inferences can be drawn from a suspect's silence (albeit in limited circumstances), it is necessary to warn the person of the dangers of remaining silent. For this reason the 'special warning' was introduced where there is potentially incriminating evidence relating to objects, marks or substances; or relating to the accused's presence at a particular place. If the special warning is not given, inferences from silence will not be allowed to boost the prosecution case but the evidence may still be admissible. Code C, paras 10.5A to 10.5C must be followed if any questions are to be put to the arrested suspect about:

- any object, marks or substances found on the him/her, or
- in or on his/her clothing or footwear, or
- otherwise in his/her possession, or
- in the place where he/she was arrested.

These provisions also apply to any questions about why the suspect was:

- at the scene of the offence,
- at or near the time of the offence for which the constable who saw the suspect there arrested him/her, and
- unable to account for his/her presence at or near the scene of the offence.

It must be made clear to the suspect what matters he/she is being asked to answer and the consequences of remaining silent on each occasion.

See Code C, Annex C for occasions when special warnings and adverse inferences do not apply.

Conclusion of Interview

All Interviews

- The person interviewed (and the appropriate adult or the suspect's solicitor if present during the interview (Code C, para. 11.12)) must be given an opportunity to read the interview record and to sign it as correct or to indicate the respects in which he/she considers it inaccurate (Code C, para. 11.11). If the person concerned cannot read or refuses to read the record or to sign it, the senior police officer present shall read it to him/her (Code C, para. 11.11). If there is any delay in recording the interview, if practicable, the suspect should still be given an opportunity to read the statement.
- Any refusal to sign the record must be recorded (Code C, para. 11.14).
- If an interpreter has been present at the interview, he/she should be given an opportunity to read the record and certify its accuracy (Code C, para. 13.7).
- If the person is in police detention, return him/her to the custody officer, informing that officer whether the Codes have been complied with, if any incidents occurred and whether there were any breaches of the Codes (s. 39(3) of the Police and Criminal Evidence Act 1984).

Tape Recorded Interviews

- The person interviewed must be offered the opportunity to clarify anything he/she has said during the interview and to add anything he/she may wish (Code E, para. 4.17). This may be important when the case comes to court and the defence try to explain why certain things were said during the interview.
- Turn off the tape and seal it with a master tape label (Code E, para. 4.18). If the seal on the tape needs to be broken for any reason, follow Code E, para. 6.2 or, if decision has been made not to institute criminal proceedings, follow Code E, para. 6.3.
- Sign the label and ask the suspect and any third party present to sign it also. If the suspect or third party refuses to sign it, an inspector, or if not available a custody officer, shall be called into the interview room and asked to sign it (Code E, para. 4.18).
- Hand the suspect the notice which explains the use which will be made of the tape recording and the arrangement for access to it (Code E, para. 4.19).
- Make a personal notebook entry about the interview as required by Code E, para. 5.1 (see Code E, para. 1.10).

- Follow force standing orders or local procedures in relation to tape security whether or not the person is charged (Code E, paras 6.1 and 5.2).

4.6.9 Statements from Suspects

Statements under caution, particularly of a detained person, are less common than interviews. If a person has been interviewed on tape or an interview has been recorded contemporaneously in writing, a statement under caution should only normally be conducted at the person's express wish (Code C, Note 12A). A statement must not be elicited by the use of oppression (Code C, para. 11.5) and, if written at the police station, the statement must be on the correct forms (Code C, para. 12.13). Code C, Annex D sets out how the statement should be taken and matters that must be included in the statement whether it is written by the suspect or a police officer. See Code C, Annex C for restrictions on drawing inferences and the variable declarations the person must include in his/her statements.

When completing the statement, the person must always be invited to write down what he/she wants to say and should be allowed to do so without any prompting, except that a police officer may indicate which matters are material or question any ambiguity in the statement. In the case of a person making a statement in a language other than English, Code C, para. 13.4 states:

(a) the interpreter shall take down the statement in the language in which it is made;

(b) the person making the statement shall be invited to sign it;

(c) an official English translation shall be made in due course.

(In these cases, para. 13.4 means that the person will not be invited to write the statement themselves which is an exception to the guidance in Annex D.)

A juvenile or a person who is mentally disordered or mentally handicapped, *whether suspected or not*, must not be asked to provide or sign a written statement in the absence of the appropriate adult unless Code C, paras 11.18 or 11.20 or Annex C applies (Code C, para. 11.15). Statements made by an accused under caution to the police are confidential. It is clearly implicit in the relationship between the police and the accused that the information, before being used in open court, is used only for the purposes for which it is provided and not for extraneous purposes, such as the media. However, the obligation of confidentiality (which is now included in the Police Code of Conduct) in respect of such a statement will be brought to an end where the contents of the statement are already in the public domain (*Bann v British Broadcasting Corporation and Another* (1998) 148 NLJ 979).

Interviews on Behalf of Scottish Forces and Vice Versa

The Crown Prosecution Service, in consultation with the Scottish Crown Office, has produced guidelines in relation to the potential admissibility of interview evidence when officers from England and Wales conduct interviews on behalf of Scottish forces and vice versa. These interviews relate to people subject to cross-border arrest as provided by ss. 136–140 of the Criminal Justice and Public Order Act 1994.

Suspects in Scotland: Interview Evidence Required for Prosecutions in England and Wales

Under the legislation governing prosecutions in Scotland, the suspect is not entitled to legal representation during an interview. Suspects are not warned that a failure to answer questions may harm their defence. Failure to answer questions cannot harm their defence. Interviews under caution are, however, subject to guidelines which incorporate judicial precedent fairness to the accused.

In investigations of any great seriousness, English/Welsh constables should attend in Scotland, arrest the suspect and bring him/her back to their jurisdiction for interview. If such an arrest is made, the arrested person must be taken either to the nearest designated police station in England or a designated police station in a police area in England and Wales in which the offence is being investigated (s. 137(1) and (7)(a) of the 1994 Act).

Scottish officers do not have any statutory or common law powers to detain or arrest a suspect without warrant who is believed to have committed an offence in England and Wales. If there is insufficient evidence for the issue of a warrant, and the case is not sufficiently serious to justify officers travelling to Scotland, Scottish officers can be requested to invite the suspect to attend a police station on a voluntary basis for interview under caution.

When it has not been practicable for an English/Welsh constable to make an arrest, but a constable has gone to Scotland to interview a suspect following arrest or detention by a Scottish constable for Scottish offences, or a person has voluntarily agreed to be interviewed, the English/Welsh constable should comply, insofar as it is practical, with the PACE Codes of Practice, in particular:

- A suspect not under arrest or detention should be told that he/she is not under arrest or detention and that he/she is free to leave.

- A suspect should be told that he/she may seek legal advice and that arrangements are made for legal representation when required. An appropriate adult should also be present when interviewing a youth or a mentally disordered or mentally handicapped person.

- Administer an English/Welsh law caution. When appropriate officers should warn arrested suspects of the consequences of failure or refusal to account for objects, substances or marks (s. 36 of the 1994 Act) and the failure or refusal to account for their presence in a particular place (s. 37).

- Tape record the interview if possible.

- If it is not possible to tape record the interview, a contemporaneous written record of the interview should be made. The suspect must be given the opportunity to read the record and to sign it.

- Also, fingerprints etc. and non-intimate samples may be taken from an arrested or detained person with the authority of an officer of a rank no lower than inspector (s. 18 of the Criminal Procedure (Scotland) Act 1995).

Scottish constables interviewing suspects in Scotland when they are aware that the interview is required for a prosecution in England and Wales, should comply with Scottish law. In addition, insofar as it is practical:

- A suspect should be told that he/she may seek legal advice and that arrangements are made for legal representation when required. A solicitor may be present during any subsequent interview if the suspect requires. An appropriate adult should also be present when interviewing a youth or a mentally disordered or mentally handicapped person.

- When it is certain that the interview evidence will only be used in English/Welsh courts, the English/Welsh caution should be used.

- Tape record the interview if possible.

- If it is not possible to tape record the interview, a written contemporaneous record of the interview should be made. The suspect must be given the opportunity to read the record and to sign it.

English/Welsh officers should assist interviewing Scottish officers by providing a schedule of points to be covered in an interview. This could include a list of appropriate questions.

Suspects in England and Wales: Interview Evidence Required for Prosecutions in Scotland

- English officers do not have any statutory or common law powers to detain or arrest a suspect without warrant who is believed to have committed an offence in Scotland. If there is insufficient evidence for the issue of a warrant, and the case is not sufficiently serious to justify Scottish officers travelling to England or Wales to exercise their cross-border powers under the Act, English or Welsh officers can be requested to invite the suspect to attend an interview on a voluntary basis for interview under caution. See Code C, para. 1.12(i) and Code D, para. 2.17(iv).

- Where a Scottish officer has attended to interview the suspect, the Scottish form of caution should be given.

- English and Welsh constables interviewing suspects in England/Wales when they are aware that the interview is required for a prosecution in Scotland, should comply with the PACE Codes of Practice, save that a Scottish caution should be used in the following terms: 'You are not obliged to say anything but anything you do say will be noted and may be used in evidence.'

The use of the English/Welsh caution may render the interview inadmissible in Scotland.

Scottish officers should assist the interviewing officers by providing a schedule of points to be covered in an interview and a possible list of appropriate questions.

In all circumstances officers should ensure that suspects fully understand the significance of a caution or warning.

4.7 Incomplete Offences

4.7.1 Introduction

There are circumstances where defendants are interrupted or frustrated in their efforts to commit an offence. Such circumstances might come about as a result of police intervention (e.g. where intelligence suggests that a serious offence is to take place on a given date) or as a result of things not going as the defendants had hoped (e.g. the property which they intended to steal not being where they thought it was). In these and other cases several general offences, often called inchoate or incomplete offences, may be used to ensure that the defendant's conduct does not go unpunished.

Note that some incomplete offences (i.e. incitements, conspiracies and attempts) will be drug trafficking offences for the purposes of the Drug Trafficking Act 1994.

4.7.2 Incitement

OFFENCE: **Incitement—*Common Law***

> • Triable as per offence incited • Unlimited maximum penalty on indictment; penalty per offence incited on summary conviction (Criminal Law Act 1977, ss. 28(1) and 30(4)).
> *(Arrestable offence if indictable)*

It is an offence unlawfully to incite another to commit an offence.

KEYNOTE

Incitement involves encouraging or pressurising someone to commit an offence. The other person need not actually commit the substantive offence or even form the intention to do so—though if they do go on to commit the offence, the inciter will become a secondary party.

There are also some specific statutory incitements such as inciting someone to commit an offence under the Misuse of Drugs Act 1971.

Encouraging motorists to break the speed limit by advertising a radar detector has been held to be 'incitement' (*Invicta Plastics Ltd* v *Clare* [1976] RTR 251).

Incitement to murder is punishable under the Offences Against the Person Act 1861, s. 4.

As with accessories a defendant cannot incite another to commit an offence which exists for the defendant's own protection (e.g. a girl under 16 inciting a man to have unlawful sexual intercourse with her (*R* v *Tyrrell* [1894] 1 QB 710)).

A defendant cannot incite another to commit conspiracy (Criminal Law Act 1977, s. 5(7)).

A defendant cannot incite another to aid, abet, counsel or procure an offence which is not ultimately committed (*R* v *Bodin* [1979] Crim LR 176).

4.7.3 Conspiracy

Conspiracies can be divided into statutory and common law conspiracies.

Statutory Conspiracy

OFFENCE: **Statutory Conspiracy — *Criminal Law Act 1977, s. 1***
- Triable on indictment • Where conspiracy is to commit murder, an offence punishable by life imprisonment or any indictable offence punishable with imprisonment where no maximum term is specified—life imprisonment. In other cases, sentence is the same as for completed offence.

(Arrestable offence where substantive offence is arrestable)

The Criminal Law Act 1977, s. 1 states:

(1) Subject to the following provisions of this Part of this Act, if a person agrees with any other person or persons that a course of conduct will be pursued which, if the agreement is carried out in accordance with their intentions, either—
   (a) will necessarily amount to or involve the commission of any offence or offences by one or more of the parties to the agreement; or
   (b) would do so but for the existence of facts which render the commission of the offence or any of the offences impossible,
   he is guilty of conspiracy to commit the offence or offences in question.

KEYNOTE

A charge of conspiracy can be brought in respect of an agreement to commit indictable or summary offences. Conspiracy is triable only on indictment even if it relates to a summary offence (in which case the consent of the Director of Public Prosecutions will be required). Offences of conspiracy are committed at the time of the agreement; therefore it is immaterial whether or not the substantive offence is ever carried out.

Agreeing with Another

For there to be a conspiracy there must be an agreement. Therefore there must be at least two people involved. Each conspirator must be aware of the overall common purpose to which they all attach themselves. If one conspirator enters into *separate* agreements with different people, each agreement is a separate conspiracy (*R* v *Griffiths* [1966] 1 QB 589).

A person can be convicted of conspiracy even if the other conspirators are unknown (as to the affect of the acquittal of one party to a conspiracy on the other parties, see the Criminal Law Act 1977, s. 5(8)).

A defendant cannot be convicted of a statutory conspiracy if the only other party to the agreement is:

- his/her spouse
- a child/children under 10 years of age
- the intended victim

(Criminal Law Act 1977, s. 2(2)).

A husband and wife can both be convicted of a statutory conspiracy if they conspire with a third party (not falling into the above categories) (*R* v *Chrastny* [1991] 1 WLR 1381). The 'end product' of the agreement must be the commission of an offence by *one or more of the parties to the agreement*. Once agreed upon, any failure to bring about the end result or an abandoning of the agreement altogether will not prevent the statutory conspiracy being committed. For the situation where the only other conspirator is an undercover officer.

Note that if an agreement to commit a *summary offence which is not punishable by imprisonment* is done in contemplation or furtherance of a trade dispute, it must be disregarded (Trade Union and Labour Relations (Consolidation) Act 1992, s. 242).

Conspiracy, Incitement and Attempts to Commit Offences Abroad

The law regulating the territorial jurisdiction over offences abroad is complex and has been changed by a number of recent pieces of legislation. The following is only a brief outline of some of that legislation and the advice of the Crown Prosecution Service should be sought in any such cases.

The Criminal Law Act 1977

A conspiracy under the provisions of the Criminal Law Act 1977 must involve an agreement by the respective parties to commit an offence triable under the law of England and Wales. Although this condition (under s. 1(4)) generally restricts statutory conspiracy to an agreement to commit an offence that is to be committed in England and Wales (or to offences planned to be committed on British vessels or aircraft), there are several offences that can be tried by our courts even though they are committed abroad. An example would be manslaughter committed by a British citizen. Therefore a conspiracy in England or Wales to commit such an offence abroad would be triable here.

The Criminal Justice (Terrorism and Conspiracy) Act 1998

In addition, the Criminal Justice (Terrorism and Conspiracy) Act 1998, makes provision to deal with conspiracies in England and Wales to carry out acts outside the United Kingdom. Despite its name, the 1998 Act is not limited to terrorist offences. If the object of the conspiracy would amount to an offence under the jurisdiction of the relevant country *and* of England and Wales, the conspiracy may be tried under the Criminal Law Act 1977, s. 1A. There are, however, procedural restrictions on the prosecution of these conspiracies and the consent of the Attorney-General (or Solicitor- General) must be given before a prosecution can take place.

The Criminal Justice Act 1993

The Criminal Justice Act 1993 (which was only brought into force—in part—in June 1999) implements some of the recommendations of the Law Commission Report 'Jurisdiction over Offences of Fraud and Dishonesty with a Foreign Element' (Law Com. No. 180; 27 April 1989). Section 1(2) sets out a group of substantive offences ('Group A' offences) that can be tried in England and Wales if any relevant act or omission on the part of the defendant took place in England and Wales. Among the offences in Group A are:

- theft
- obtaining property and services by deception
- blackmail
- handling stolen goods
- obtaining a money transfer by deception and retaining a wrongful credit.

This list also contains other offences involving deception, fraud and forgery/counterfeiting.

Section 1(3) sets out another group of offences ('Group B') and this group covers conspiracies, attempts and incitement to commit a Group A offence, together with conspiracies to defraud.

Both lists, Group A and B, may be amended by the Secretary of State (s. 1(4)).

Section 3 sets out the rules to determine the relevance or otherwise of a defendant's nationality or whereabouts at the time of the commission of a Group A or B offence. This then allows the court to establish whether or not it has jurisdiction over the relevant offence.

Section 5 inserts another section (s. 1A) into the Criminal Attempts Act 1981 (see below) and makes further provision in relation to acts that are 'more than merely preparatory' towards the commission of an offence outside England and Wales.

Conspiracy Abroad to Commit Offences in England and Wales

If people conspire abroad to commit offences in England and Wales they may, under certain circumstances, be indicted under English and Welsh law even, it seems, if none of the conspirators enters the jurisdiction to do so (see *R* v *Manning* [2001] QB 330).

Common Law Conspiracies

OFFENCE: **Conspiracy to Defraud—*Common Law***
>   • Triable on indictment • Ten years' imprisonment and/or a fine
>   (*Arrestable offence*)

Conspiracy to defraud involves:

. . . an agreement by two or more [persons] by dishonesty to deprive a person of something which is his or to which he is or would or might be entitled [or] an agreement by two or more by dishonesty to injure some proprietary right [of the victim] . . .

(*Scott* v *Metropolitan Police Commissioner* [1975] AC 819.)

(See also *Blackstone's Criminal Practice*, 2003, section A6.25.)

KEYNOTE

The common law offence of conspiracy to defraud can be divided into two main types. The first is contained in the *dictum* of Viscount Dilhorne in *Scott* above, the second involves a dishonest agreement to *deceive* another into acting in a way that is contrary to his/her duty (see *Wai Yu-Tsang* v *The Queen* [1992] 1 AC 269).

Although the requirement for an agreement between at least two people is the same, this offence is broader than statutory conspiracy. There is no requirement to prove that the end result would amount to the commission of *an offence*, simply that it would result in depriving a person of something under the specified conditions or in injuring his/her proprietary right.

You must show *intent* to defraud a victim (*R* v *Hollinshead* [1985] AC 975).

You must also show that a defendant was *dishonest* as set out in *R* v *Ghosh* [1982] QB 1053.

Clearly there will be circumstances where the defendant's behaviour will amount to both a statutory conspiracy and a conspiracy to defraud. The Criminal Justice Act 1987, s. 12 makes provision for such circumstances and allows the prosecution to choose which charge to prefer.

Examples of common law conspiracies to defraud include:

- Buffet car staff selling their own home-made sandwiches on British Rail trains, thereby depriving the company of the opportunity to sell their own products (*R* v *Cooke* [1986] AC 909).

- Directors agreeing to conceal details of a bank's trading losses from its shareholders (*Wai Yu-Tsang* above).

- Making unauthorised copies of commercial films for sale (*Scott* above).

4.7.4   Attempts

The Criminal Attempts Act 1981, s. 1 states:

  (1) If, with intent to commit an offence to which this section applies, a person does an act which is more than merely preparatory to the commission of the offence, he is guilty of attempting to commit the offence.

    ...

  (2) A person may be guilty of attempting to commit an offence to which this section applies even though the facts are such that the commission of the offence is impossible.

  (3) In any case where—
    (a) apart from this subsection a person's intention would not be regarded as having amounted to an intent to commit an offence; but
    (b) if the facts of the case had been as he believed them to be, his intention would be so regarded, then, for the purposes of subsection (1) above, he shall be regarded as having had an intent to commit that offence.

  (4) This section applies to any offence which, if it were completed, would be triable in England and Wales as an indictable offence, other than—
    (a) conspiracy (at common law or under section 1 of the Criminal Law Act 1977);
    (b) aiding, abetting, counselling, procuring or suborning the commission of an offence;
    (c) offences under section 4(1) (assisting offenders) or 5(1) (accepting or agreeing to accept consideration for not disclosing information about an arrestable offence) of the Criminal Law Act 1967.

KEYNOTE

Most attempts at committing criminal offences will be governed by s. 1. Although some statutory exceptions apply, the sentence generally for such attempts will be:

- for murder—life imprisonment

- for indictable offences—the same maximum penalty as the substantive offence

- for either way offences—the same maximum penalty as the substantive offence *when tried summarily*.

If the attempted offence is triable summarily only, it cannot be an offence under s. 1. However, if the only reason the substantive offence is triable summarily is because of a statutory limit imposed in some cases (e.g. criminal damage to property of a low value) the offence can be attempted. Some summary offences include an element of attempt (e.g. drink drive offences).

  If the offence attempted is triable only on indictment, the attempt will be triable only on indictment. Similarly, if the offence attempted is an 'either way' offence, so to will the attempt be triable either way (s. 4(1)).

  Many other statutory offences contain references to 'attempts', including:

- Theft Act 1968, s. 9 (burglary)

- Firearms Act 1968, s. 17 (using firearm to resist arrest)

- Official Secrets Act 1920, s. 7 (encouraging others to commit offences).

  Section 3 of the Criminal Attempts Act 1981 deals with such statutory provisions and they will generally be governed by the same principals as those set out here.

Offences having Similar Effects

Other situations where a person tries to bring about a particular result or consequence are addressed by statutory offences which, although not falling within the category of 'criminal attempts' nevertheless have a similar effect.

For example, offences under s. 1 of the Computer Misuse Act 1990 can be committed by causing a computer to perform a function under certain circumstances. Under the 1990 Act a defendant could, for example, commit the substantive offence by trying to log-on under someone else's user code or password. Such *actus reus* (criminal conduct) is more often associated with 'incomplete' offences like criminal attempts than substantive offences. Other examples can be found in offences requiring a particular intention such as offences under the Offences Against the Person Act 1861, s. 58 which is almost an 'attempt' to procure an abortion, and an offence of 'attempting' to cause an explosion under the Explosive Substances Act 1883, s. 3.

In some cases, acts which *are* merely preparatory towards a given end can still amount to an offence under the relevant statute, the best example of which is probably arranging to 'receive' stolen goods under the Theft Act 1968, s. 22.

Section 1(4) precludes the 'attempting' of some other incomplete offences. It does not *preclude* statutory offences involving 'procurement' (e.g. under the Sexual Offences Act 1956) or attempting to aid and abet the suicide of another. Note that a defendant can be convicted of attempting to incite.

More than merely preparatory

A defendant's actions must be shown to have gone beyond mere preparation towards the commission of the substantive offence. Whether the defendant did or not go beyond that point will be a question of fact for the jury/magistrate(s). There is no specific formula used by the courts in interpreting this requirement. Courts have accepted an approach of questioning whether the defendant had 'embarked on the crime proper' (*R* v *Gullefer* [1990] 1 WLR 1063) but there is no requirement for him/her to have passed a point of no return leading to the commission of the substantive offence. However, to prove an 'attempt' you must show an *intention* on the part of the defendant to commit the substantive offence.

This requirement means that a higher level or degree of *mens rea* may be required to prove an attempt than for the substantive offence. For instance, nothing less than an *intent* to kill can support a charge of attempted murder (*R* v *Whybrow* (1951) 35 Cr App R 141), while in proving the substantive offence, an intention to cause grievous bodily harm will suffice. However, although this general rule applies to the *consequences* of a defendant's conduct, it does not always apply to the *circumstances* in which the offence is committed. Therefore, in an offence of attempted rape, you must show that the defendant *intended* to carry out the act of intercourse—consequence—but it will be enough to show that he was *reckless* as to whether or not the victim was consenting—circumstances (*R* v *Khan* [1990] 1 WLR 813). As with much in this subject area, this is more a matter for the Crown Prosecution Service. A defendant's intention may be *conditional*; that is, he/she may only intend to steal from a house if something worth stealing is later found inside. The conditional nature of this intention will not generally prevent the charge of attempt being brought and the defendant's intentions will, in accordance with s. 1(3) above, be judged *on the facts as he/she believed them to be*. However, careful drafting of the charge may be required in cases where there is doubt as to the precise extent of the defendant's knowledge at the time he/she was caught (see *R* v *Husseyn* (1977) 67 Cr App R 131n).

Although 'intent to commit' the offence is required under s. 1(1), there are occasions where a state of mind that falls short of such a precise intention may suffice. For instance, in cases of attempted rape the courts have accepted that recklessness as to whether the victim is consenting is sufficient *mens rea* for attempted rape because it is sufficient for the substantive offence (*R v Khan* [1990] 1 WLR 813).

In proving an 'attempt' it is enough to show that a defendant was in one of the states of mind required for the substantive offence and that he/she did his/her best, so far as he/she was able, to do what was necessary for the commission of the full offence (*Attorney-General's Reference (No. 3 of 1992)* [1994] 1 WLR 409).

For acts that are more than merely preparatory towards the commission of an offence outside England and Wales, **see 4.7.3.**

Interfering with Vehicles

OFFENCE: **Interfering with Motor Vehicles—*Criminal Attempts Act 1981, s. 9***
- Triable summarily - Three months' imprisonment and/or a fine
(No specific power of arrest)

The Criminal Attempts Act 1981, s. 9 states:

(1) A person is guilty of the offence of vehicle interference if he interferes with a motor vehicle or trailer or with anything carried in or on a motor vehicle or trailer with the intention that an offence specified in subsection (2) below shall be committed by himself or some other person.

(2) The offences mentioned in subsection (1) above are—
    (a) theft of the motor vehicle or trailer or part of it;
    (b) theft of anything carried in or on the motor vehicle or trailer; and
    (c) an offence under section 12(1) of the Theft Act 1968 (taking and driving away without consent);

    and, if it is shown that a person accused of an offence under this section intended that one of those offences should be committed, it is immaterial that it cannot be shown which it was.

(3)–(4) ...

(5) In this section 'motor vehicle' and 'trailer' have the meanings assigned to them by [section 185(1) of the Road Traffic Act 1988].

KEYNOTE

'Interference' is not defined and there are no conclusive cases on the subject at the time of writing. This offence is one of specific intent and you must prove that the defendant interfered with the vehicle etc. with one of the intentions listed—(note, however, that it is not necessary to show which *particular* intention).

4.7.5 **Impossibility**

Practical difficulties have arisen where, despite the best (or worst) efforts of the defendant, his/her ultimate intention has been impossible (such as trying to extract cocaine from a powder which is, unknown to the defendant, only talc). Impossibility is now far clearer following the Criminal Attempts Act 1981 and its interpretation through the courts. It differs however in some incomplete offences.

....

EXAMPLE

Taking an example of someone who tries to handle goods which are not in fact stolen, the following rules would apply:

- A defendant could *not* be guilty of inciting another, nor of common law conspiracy to defraud in these circumstances. The *physical* impossibility of what they sought to do would preclude such a charge.

- A defendant *could* be guilty of a statutory conspiracy with another to handle 'stolen' goods and also of attempting to handle 'stolen' goods under these circumstances. The physical impossibility would not prelude such charges as a result of the Criminal Attempts Act 1981 and the House of Lords' decision in *R* v *Shivpuri* [1987] AC 1. The only form of impossibility which would preclude liability under the Criminal Attempts Act 1981 or for a statutory conspiracy would be the *legal* impossibility—for instance if the defendants attempted to commit an offence of 'handling vegetables on a Sunday', an offence which is a clear *legal* impossibility (at least to the author's knowledge).

4.8 Offences Against the Administration of Justice and Public Interest

4.8.1 Introduction

A very real consideration when investigating any crime with a view to prosecution is the potential interference with the component parts of that process. This section deals with the various offences which can be seen as an interference with the machinery of justice. Some offences, such as perjury and tendering false statements in evidence, affect the administration of justice directly while others like corruption have an indirect effect on the public interest.

4.8.2 Perjury

OFFENCE: **Perjury in Judicial Proceeding—*Perjury Act 1911, s. 1***
> • Triable on indictment • Seven years' imprisonment
> *(Arrestable offence)*

The Perjury Act 1911, s. 1 states:

(1) If any person lawfully sworn as a witness or as an interpreter in a judicial proceeding wilfully makes a statement material in that proceeding, which he knows to be false or does not believe to be true, he shall be guilty of perjury . . .

(2) The expression 'judicial proceeding' includes a proceeding before any court, tribunal, or person having by law power to hear, receive, and examine evidence on oath.

(3) Where a statement made for the purposes of a judicial proceeding is not made before the tribunal itself, but is made on oath before a person authorised by law to administer an oath to the person who makes the statement, and to record or authenticate the statement, it shall, for the purposes of this section, be treated as having been made in a judicial proceeding.

KEYNOTE

To commit this offence a defendant must have been *lawfully sworn* (see the Evidence Act 1851, s. 16). The statement made in 'judicial proceeding' can be one given orally before the court or tribunal, or it can be given in the form of an affidavit (sworn statement). If a witness tenders a false statement (MG 11) used under the Criminal Justice Act 1967, s. 89 he/she commits a separate, lesser offence (see 4.8.3).

'Wilful' in this case means deliberate as opposed to accidental.

A 'statement material in that proceeding' means that the content of the evidence tendered in that case must have some importance to it and not just be of passing relevance. Whether something is material to a case is a question of law for a judge to decide. Whether a motorist had taken a drink between the time of his/her having a road traffic accident and being breathalysed would be such a material issue, and to get a witness to provide false evidence about that matter would be a 'statement material in that proceeding' (*R* v *Lewins* (1979) 1 Cr App R (S) 246).

To prove perjury you must also show that the defendant *knew* the statement to be false or *did not believe it to be true*. Technically, many defendants who are convicted after entering a 'not guilty' plea commit perjury but it would hardly be practical to investigate and prosecute each occasion where that happens!

Evidence of an opinion provided by a witness who does not genuinely hold such an opinion may also be perjury.

Perjury may be proved by using a court transcript or the evidence of others who were present at the proceeding in question (see Perjury Act 1911, s. 14).

Corroboration is required in cases of perjury (see Perjury Act 1911, s. 13). The requirement for corroboration is solely in relation to the *falsity* of the defendant's statement. There is no requirement under s. 13 for corroboration of the fact that the defendant *actually made* the alleged statement, nor that he/she knew or believed it to be untrue. However, as that corroboration can be documentary and may even come from the defendant's earlier conduct (*R v Threlfall* (1914) 10 Cr App R 112) this requirement does not appear to present much of a hurdle to the prosecution.

Evidence given by live TV link under the provisions of the Criminal Justice Act 1988, s. 32 is also subject to the offence of perjury.

Aiding and Abetting

OFFENCE: **Aiding and Abetting Perjury—*Perjury Act 1911, s. 7***
- If principal offence is contrary to s. 1 triable on indictment • Seven years' imprisonment

(Arrestable offence)

- Otherwise either way • Two years' imprisonment on indictment; six months' imprisonment and/or a fine summarily

(No specific power of arrest)

The Perjury Act 1911, s. 7 states:

(1) Every person who aids, abets, counsels, procures, or suborns another person to commit an offence against this Act shall be liable to be proceeded against, indicted, tried and punished as if he were a principal offender.

(2) Every person who incites ... another person to commit an offence against this Act shall be guilty of [an offence].

KEYNOTE

'Subornation' is the same as procuring. This specific section does not appear to add anything to the general offences of aiding and abetting principal offenders.

4.8.3   **Offences Similar to Perjury**

OFFENCE: **False Testimony of Unsworn Child Witness—*Children and Young Persons Act 1933, s. 38(2)***
- Triable summarily • Punishment as per text of subsection

(No specific power of arrest)

The Children and Young Persons Act 1933, s. 38 states:

(2) If any child whose evidence is received unsworn ... wilfully gives false evidence in such circumstances that he would, if the evidence had been given on oath, have been guilty of perjury, he shall be liable on summary conviction to be dealt with as if he had been summarily convicted of an indictable offence punishable in the case of an adult with imprisonment.

OFFENCE: **False Statements in Criminal Proceedings—*Criminal Justice Act 1967, s. 89***
- Triable either way • Two years' imprisonment and/or a fine on indictment; six months' imprisonment and/or a fine summarily

(No specific power of arrest)

The Criminal Justice Act 1967, s. 89 states:

(1) If any person in a written statement tendered in evidence in criminal proceedings by virtue of section...9 of this Act, or in proceedings before a court-martial...wilfully makes a statement material in those proceedings which he knows to be false or does not believe to be true, he shall be liable...

(2) The Perjury Act 1911 shall have effect as if this section were contained in that Act.

OFFENCE: **False Statements in Criminal Proceedings—*Magistrates' Courts Act 1980, s. 106***
- Triable either way • Two years' imprisonment and/or a fine on indictment; six months' imprisonment and/or a fine summarily
(No specific power of arrest)

The Magistrates' Courts Act 1980, s. 106 states:

(1) If any person in a written statement tendered in evidence in criminal proceedings by virtue of section 102 above wilfully makes a statement material in those proceedings which he knows to be false or does not believe to be true, he shall be liable...

(2) The Perjury Act 1911 shall have effect as if this section were contained in that Act.

OFFENCE: **False Statements on Oath—*Perjury Act 1911, s. 2***
- Triable either way • Seven years' imprisonment and/or a fine on indictment; six months' imprisonment and/or a fine summarily
(Arrestable offence)

The Perjury Act 1911, s. 2 states:

If any person—

(1) being required or authorised by law to make any statement on oath for any purpose, and being lawfully sworn (otherwise than in a judicial proceeding) wilfully makes a statement which is material for that purpose and which he knows to be false or does not believe to be true;...he shall be [guilty of an offence].

KEYNOTE

The first two offences cover witnesses who tender false statements, either in criminal proceedings themselves (Criminal Justice Act 1967) or in place of depositions at a committal hearing (Magistrates' Courts Act 1980). The third offence covers the making of false statements under an oath which is not sworn in connection with a judicial proceeding.

The offence under s. 38 of the Children and Young Persons Act 1933 will be replaced by s. 57 of the Youth Justice and Criminal Evidence Act 1999, when it comes into force.

The Perjury Act 1911 makes further provision for the making of false statements in relation to mariage licences (s. 3) and the making of false statements in relation to the registration of births and deaths (s. 4). Both sections carry seven years' imprisonment on indictment and are therefore *arrestable offences*.

The 1911 Act also creates offences of making false declarations and of suppressing documents. For a full discussion of these offences, see *Blackstone's Criminal Practice*, 2003, section B14.

4.8.4 Perverting the Course of Justice

OFFENCE: **Perverting the Course of Justice—*Common Law***
- Triable on indictment • Life imprisonment and/or a fine
(Arrestable offence)

It is an offence at common law to do an act tending and intended to pervert the course of public justice.

KEYNOTE

'The course of public justice' includes the process of criminal investigation (see *R* v *Rowell* (1977) 65 Cr App R 174).

Although traditionally referred to—and charged—as 'attempting' to pervert the course of justice, it is recognised that behaviour which is *aimed* at perverting the course of public justice does just that and the substantive offence should be charged (see *R* v *Williams* (1991) 92 Cr App R 158).

One way in which this offence is commonly committed is where a prisoner uses a false identity when he/she is arrested. Although the offence of perverting the course of justice may be made out in these—or similar—circumstances in connection with a number of other substantive offences, the Court of Appeal has held that, in many cases, the addition of such a charge is unnecessary and only serves to complicate the sentencing process (*R* v *Sookoo* [2002] EWCA Crim 800). Where, as in *Sookoo*, a defendant makes an unsophisticated attempted to hide their identity and fails, the Court felt that a specific separate count of perverting the course of justice should not be laid. If it was shown that there were serious aggravating features, for instance where a lot of police time and resources had been involved or innocent members of the public had been arrested as a result, a specific charge may be appropriate and could be justified (for the specific offence of wasting police time, see 4.8.8).

Perverting the course of justice requires positive acts by the defendant, not merely standing by and allowing an injustice to take place. The offence will include cases where evidence is deliberately destroyed, concealed or falsified as well as cases where witnesses and jurors are intimidated (see 4.8.5).

Admitting to a crime to enable the true offender to avoid prosecution would fall under this offence (*R* v *Devito* [1975] Crim LR 175), as would abusing your authority as a police officer to excuse someone of a criminal charge (*R* v *Coxhead* [1986] RTR 411). Other examples include:

- making a false allegation of an offence (*R* v *Goodwin* (1989) 11 Cr App R (S) 194 (rape))

- giving another person's personal details when being reported for an offence (*R* v *Hurst* (1990) 12 Cr App R (S) 373)

- destroying and concealing evidence of a crime (*R* v *Kiffin* [1994] Crim LR 449).

It is important that the requisite intention is proved in every case as that intention cannot be implied, even from admitted facts (*R* v *Lalani* (1999) 1 Cr App R 481).

Where a person makes a false allegation to the police justifying a criminal investigation with the possible consequences of detention, arrest, charge or prosecution and that person intends that the allegation be taken seriously, the offence of perverting the course of justice is *prima facie* made out—whether or not the allegation is capable of identifying specific individuals. This is clear from *R* v *Cotter and Others* [2002] EWCA Crim 1033, a case involving the boyfriend of a well-known black Olympic athlete who claimed to have been attacked as part of a racist campaign.

4.8.5 **Intimidating Witnesses and Jurors**

Great care is needed by police officers in handling witnesses. Any behaviour that is seen as interfering with witnesses (or potential witnesses) by promises of favours and rewards or by threats will be a contempt of court (see *R* v *Kellett* [1975] 3 All ER 468). However, there is no 'property' in a witness. Protecting witnesses is one thing but trying to restrict the way in which defendants and/or their legal advisers obtain evidence for their defence—e.g. by properly approaching witnesses—can also amount to a contempt of court (see *Connelly* v *Dale* [1996] 1 All ER 224).

There are several statutory measures designed to protect witnesses, jurors and others involved in the judicial process. These can be separated into measures aimed at protecting those involved in *criminal* trials and/or investigations and offences aimed at protecting those involved in other proceedings.

The first measure can be found in the Criminal Justice and Public Order Act 1994.

OFFENCE: **Intimidating Witnesses and Jurors—*Criminal Justice and Public Order Act 1994, s. 51***

- Triable either way • Five years' imprisonment and/or a fine on indictment; six months' imprisonment and/or a fine summarily

(Arrestable offence)

The Criminal Justice and Public Order Act 1994, s. 51 states:

(1) A person commits an offence if—
   (a) he does an act which intimidates, and is intended to intimidate, another person ('the victim'),
   (b) he does the act knowing or believing that the victim is assisting in the investigation of an offence or is a witness or potential witness or a juror or potential juror in proceedings for an offence, and
   (c) he does it intending thereby to cause the investigation or the course of justice to be obstructed, perverted or interfered with.

(2) A person commits an offence if—
   (a) he does an act which harms, and is intended to harm, another person or, intending to cause another person to fear harm, he threatens to do an act which would harm that other person,
   (b) he does or threatens to do the act knowing or believing that the person harmed or threatened to be harmed ('the victim'), or some other person, has assisted in an investigation into an offence or has given evidence or particular evidence in proceedings for an offence, or has acted as a juror or concurred in a particular verdict in proceedings for an offence, and
   (c) he does or threatens to do it because of that knowledge or belief.

(3) For the purposes of subsections (1) and (2) it is immaterial that the act is or would be done, or that the threat is made—
   (a) otherwise than in the presence of the victim, or
   (b) to a person other than the victim.

(4) The harm that may be done or threatened may be financial as well as physical (whether to the person or a person's property) and similarly as respects an intimidatory act which consists of threats.

(5) The intention required by subsection (1)(c) and the motive required by subsection (2)(c) above need not be the only or the predominating intention or motive with which the act is done or, in the case of subsection (2), threatened.

KEYNOTE

As discussed above, this section is aimed at protecting people involved in the investigation or trial of criminal offences.

These offences are designed to exist alongside the common-law offence of perverting the course of justice (see **4.8.4**) and there will be circumstances which may fall under both the statutory and the common-law offences. Such behaviour may also be punishable as a contempt of court, see *Blackstone's Criminal Practice*, 2003, section B14.59 and **4.8.9** below.

The wording of s. 51(1) to (3) was altered by sch. 4 to the Youth Justice and Criminal Evidence Act 1999, to reflect the courts' interpretations of the elements of the offence. This part of sch. 4 came into force on 14 April 2000.

This is an offence of 'specific intent' or perhaps even multiple intent as it must be shown that the act was done with the intentions set out in s. 51(1)(a) and (c). It must also be shown that the defendant knew or believed the other person to be assisting in the investigation of an offence or that he/she was going to testify/appear on the injury in proceedings for an offence.

For 'knowing or believing' in this context the prosecution must present evidence that an investigation was in fact being carried out at the time of the alleged offence (*R* v *Singh* (2000) 1 Cr App R 31).

Section 51(2) provides a similar offence for acts done or threatened in the knowledge or belief that the person, *or another person*, has so assisted or taken part in proceedings. Doing acts to third parties in order to intimidate or harm the relevant person is also covered by this offence (s. 51(3)). Making threats by telephone will amount to 'doing an act to another' (*DPP* v *Mills* [1997] QB 300).

Section 51(8) creates a statutory presumption under certain circumstances that the defendant had the required motive at the time of his/her actions or threats.

Making a *threat* via a third person knowing it will be passed on and that the ultimate recipient would be intimidated by it amounts to an offence under s. 51(1) (*Attorney-General's Reference (No. 1 of 1999)* (1999) 149 NLJ 975).

The intention to obstruct, pervert or interfere with the course of justice need not be the only or even the main intention (s. 51(5)).

Intimidation of Witnesses in Other Proceedings

In addition to the measures aimed at protecting those involved in the investigation and trial of criminal offences, there are further statutory measures designed to protect witnesses and others who are (or may become) involved in other proceedings. Guidance on the practical application of these measures can be found in Home Office Circular 12/2001.

OFFENCE: **Intimidation of Witnesses—*Criminal Justice and Police Act 2001, s. 39***

- Triable either way • Five years' imprisonment on indictment; six months'
  imprisonment and/or fine summarily
(Arrestable offence)

The Criminal Justice and Police Act 2001, s. 39 states:

(1) A person commits an offence if—
 (a) he does an act which intimidates, and is intended to intimidate, another person ('the victim');
 (b) he does the act—
  (i) knowing or believing that the victim is or may be a witness in any relevant proceedings; and
  (ii) intending, by his act, to cause the course of justice to be obstructed, perverted or interfered with;
and
 (c) the act is done after the commencement of those proceedings.

KEYNOTE

This offence has some similarities to the Criminal Justice and Public Order Act 1994 offence in the earlier paragraph. References to doing an act include threats—against a person and/or their property—and the making of any other statement (s. 39(6)). The key difference is that this offence is concerned with protecting people who are in some way connected with 'relevant proceedings' which are '*any proceedings in or before the Court of Appeal, the High Court, the Crown Court or any county or magistrates' court which are not proceedings for an offence*' (s. 41(1)). This means that the offence will be relevant if the proceedings involved are civil proceedings in the higher courts or the county court or if they are non-offence proceedings in the Crown Court or magistrates' court. Examples of the latter would be a hearing to deal with a breach of a community order or an application for an anti-social behaviour order. You must show that the relevant proceedings had already commenced by the time of the offence.

As with the Criminal Justice and Public Order Act offence, this requires proof of 'multiple' intent in that, as well as showing the intimidatory act, it must also be shown that the elements set out at s. 39(1)(a)–(c) are present. However, if you can prove that the defendant:

- did any act that intimidated, and was intended to intimidate, another person, and

- that he/she did that act knowing or believing that that other person was or might be a 'witness' in any relevant proceedings that had already commenced,

there will be a presumption that the defendant did the act with the intention of causing the course of justice to be obstructed, perverted or interfered with (s. 39(3)). This presumption is, however, rebuttable. 'Witness' here is a very wide expression and extends to anyone who provides, or is able to provide, any information, document or other thing which might be used in evidence in those proceedings (see s. 39(5)).

In proving the offence it is immaterial whether the act:

- is done in the presence of the victim
- is done to the victim him/herself or to another person

or whether or not the intention to obstruct, pervert or interfere with the course of justice is the main intention of the person doing it (s. 39(2)).

This offence is intended to exist alongside the common law offence of perverting the course of justice (as to which, **see 4.8.4**) and came into force on 1 August 2001.

OFFENCE: **Harming Witnesses—*Criminal Justice and Police Act 2001, s. 40***
- Triable either way • Five years' imprisonment on indictment; six months' imprisonment and/or fine summarily
- *(Arrestable offence)*

The Criminal Justice and Police Act 2001, s. 40 states:

(1) A person commits an offence if in circumstances falling within subsection (2)—
  (a) he does an act which harms, and is intended to harm, another person; or
  (b) intending to cause another person to fear harm, he threatens to do an act which would harm that other person.

(2) The circumstances fall within this subsection if—
  (a) the person doing or threatening to do the act does so knowing or believing that some person (whether or not the person harmed or threatened or the person against whom harm is threatened) has been a witness in relevant proceedings; and
  (b) he does or threatens to do that act because of that knowledge or belief.

KEYNOTE

A distinction between this and the s. 39 offence is that the offence above refers to someone who *has been* (or is believed to have been) a witness in relevant proceedings. Again, 'witness' is very wide and extends to anyone who has provided any information, document etc. which was (or might have been) used in evidence in those proceedings (see s. 40(7)). For 'relevant proceedings' see the s. 39 offence. This offence is aimed is the general protection of people who have been involved in relevant proceedings. Therefore there is no requirement here for any intention to pervert or interfere with the course of justice. The harm caused or threatened does not have to directed towards the witness themselves; the key element is the motivation of the defendant. In relation to that motivation, the Act creates a presumption as follows. If you can prove that, between the start of the proceedings and one year after they are concluded, the defendant:

- did an act which harmed, and was intended to harm, another person, or
- threatened to do an act which would harm another person intending to cause that person to fear harm

with the knowledge or belief required by s. 40(2)(a) above, he/she will be presumed to have acted because of that knowledge or belief (s. 40(3)). Again, this is rebuttable. It is immaterial whether the act or threat is made (or would be carried out) in the presence of the person who is or would be harmed, or of the person threatened or whether the motive mentioned in s. 40(2)(b) is the main motive. The harm done or threatened can be physical or financial and can be made to a person or property (s. 40(4)). This offence came into force on 1 August 2001.

4.8.6 **Assisting Offenders**

OFFENCE: **Assisting Offenders—*Criminal Law Act 1967, s. 4***
- Triable on indictment; either way if original offence is either way • Where sentence for original offence is fixed by law (ten years' imprisonment and/or a fine on

indictment; six months' imprisonment and/or a fine summarily) • Where sentence
for original offence is fourteen years (seven years' imprisonment and/or a fine on
indictment; six months' imprisonment and/or a fine summarily) • Where sentence
for original offence is ten years (five years' imprisonment and/or a fine on
indictment; six months' imprisonment and/or a fine summarily)
(Arrestable offence)

- Otherwise (three years' imprisonment and/or a fine on indictment; six months'
imprisonment and/or a fine summarily)
(No specific power of arrest)

The Criminal Law Act 1967, s. 4 states:

(1) Where a person has committed an arrestable offence, any other person who, knowing or
believing him to be guilty of the offence or of some other arrestable offence, does without lawful
authority or reasonable excuse any act with intent to impede his apprehension or prosecution
shall be guilty of an offence.

(1A) In this section and section 5 . . . 'arrestable offence' has the meaning assigned to it by section 24
of the Police and Criminal Evidence Act 1984.

KEYNOTE

This offence must involve some positive act by the defendant; simply doing or saying nothing will not suffice.

Although there is no duty on people to assist the police in their investigations generally, this offence and the
one below create a negative duty not to interfere with investigations after an offence has taken place.

For there to be an offence under s. 4 or 5 (see **4.8.7**), there must first have been an arrestable offence
committed by someone. That arrestable offence must, in the case of the above offence, have been committed by
the 'assisted' person.

The defendant can commit the offence before the person he/she has assisted is convicted of committing the
relevant arrestable offence.

It must be shown that the defendant knew or believed the person to be guilty of that, *or some other* arrestable
offence. Therefore, if the defendant believed that the 'assisted' person had committed a robbery when in fact
he/she had committed a theft, that mistaken part of the defendant's belief will not prevent a conviction for this
offence.

By analogy with the requirements for handling stolen goods mere *suspicion*, however strong, that the
'assisted' person had committed an arrestable offence will not be enough.

This offence requires the consent of the Director of Public Prosecutions before a prosecution is brought (s. 4(4)).

A procedural problem arises where the 'arrestable offence' assisted is taking a conveyance under s. 12 of the
Theft Act 1968. As that offence is triable only summarily, it would seem that *assisting* the offence would have to
be tried on indictment.

This offence cannot be 'attempted' (Criminal Attempts Act 1981, s. 1(4)).

Sections 1 and 2 of the Criminal Evidence (Amendment) Act 1997 extending the powers to take non-intimate
samples without consent apply to this offence if the arrestable offence assisted is murder and also to conspiracies and incitements in the circumstance set out in that Act.

4.8.7 Concealing Arrestable Offences

OFFENCE: **Concealing Arrestable Offences—*Criminal Law Act 1967, s. 5***

- Triable on indictment; either way if original offence is triable either way • Two years'
imprisonment on indictment; six months' imprisonment and/or a fine summarily
(No specific power of arrest)

The Criminal Law Act 1967, s. 5 states:

(1) Where a person has committed an arrestable offence, any other person who, knowing or believing that the offence or some other arrestable offence has been committed, and that he has information which might be of material assistance in securing the prosecution or conviction of an offender for it, accepts or agrees to accept for not disclosing that information any consideration other than the making good of loss or injury caused by the offence, or the making of reasonable compensation for that loss or injury, shall be liable . . .

KEYNOTE

This offence also requires the consent of the Director of Public Prosecutions before a prosecution can be brought (s. 5(3)).

It is also excluded from the provisions of the Criminal Attempts Act 1981 (s. 1(4)).

Again, someone must have committed an arrestable offence before this particular offence can be committed. The main focus of this offence is:

- the acceptance of, or agreement to accept 'consideration' (i.e. anything of value)

- beyond reasonable compensation for loss/injury *caused by the arrestable offence*

- in exchange for not disclosing material information.

'Disclosure' does not appear to be confined to information passed to the police. It would probably extend to other agencies with a duty to investigate offences but is perhaps even wider than that.

This offence requires proof, not only of the defendant's knowledge or belief that an arrestable offence had been committed, but also that he/she has information that might be of material assistance in securing the *prosecution or conviction* of *an offender* for it. Given this very broad wording, the possession of information that might provide useful intelligence in an investigation into arrestable offences may meet the requirements of s. 5, although *proving* that the defendant had the required knowledge or belief presents considerable practical problems.

4.8.8   **Miscellaneous Offences Relating to Offenders**

OFFENCE: **Escaping—*Common Law***
- Triable on indictment • Unlimited punishment
(Arrestable offence)

It is an offence at common law to escape from legal custody.

KEYNOTE

The 'custody' from which a person escapes must be shown to have been lawful. The offence applies to both police custody (or police detention—see the Police and Criminal Evidence Act 1984, s. 118) or custody following conviction.

Whether a person was 'in custody' is a question of fact and the word 'custody' is to be given its ordinary and natural meaning—*E* v *DPP* (2002) LTL 26 February. (See also *Richards* v *Director of Public Prosecutions* (1988) QB 701.) In proving that a person was in custody at a particular time it should be shown that their liberty was restricted in a way that meant that he or she was confined by another and that their freedom of movement was controlled; it is not necessary, however, to show that the person's actual ability to move around was physically impeded e.g. in secure accommodation (*E* v *DPP* above).

People may be in lawful custody even if not directly in the custody of a sworn police officer (for example, those people who are being dealt with by investigating officer or escort officers under sch. 4 to the Police Reform Act 2002).

People detained under the Mental Health Act 1983, s. 36, are also in lawful custody.

If a defendant uses force to *break out* of a prison or a police station, he/she may commit an offence of prison breach, again at common law and attracting the same punishment and mode of trial as escaping.

Under the Prisoners (Return to Custody) Act 1995, s. 1, a person who has been temporarily released under the Prison Act 1952 commits a summary offence if he/she remains unlawfully at large or fails to respond to an order of recall to prison.

Escort officers designated under sch. 4 to the Police Reform Act 2002 have a duty to prevent the escape of people in their charge who they are escorting in accordance with their statutory powers (see the Police Reform Act 2002, sch. 4, part 4, para. 35).

OFFENCE: **Assisting Escape—*Prison Act 1952, s. 39***
- Triable on indictment • Ten years' imprisonment
(Arrestable offence)

The Prison Act 1952, s. 39 states:

Any person who aids any prisoner in escaping or attempting to escape from a prison or who, with intent to facilitate the escape of any prisoner, conveys any thing into a prison or to a prisoner or places any thing anywhere outside a prison with a view to its coming into the possession of a prisoner, shall be guilty of [an offence].

OFFENCE: **Harbouring Offenders—*Criminal Justice Act 1961, s. 22(2)***
- Triable either way • Ten years' imprisonment and/or a fine on indictment; six
  months' imprisonment and/or a fine summarily
(Arrestable offence)

The Criminal Justice Act 1961, s. 22 states:

(2) If any person knowingly harbours a person who has escaped from a prison or other institution to which the said section thirty-nine applies, or who, having been sentenced in any part of the United Kingdom or in any of the Channel Islands or the Isle of Man to imprisonment or detention, is otherwise unlawfully at large, or gives to any such person any assistance with intent to prevent, hinder or interfere with his being taken into custody, he shall be liable . . .

KEYNOTE

The offences under s. 39 of the 1952 Act and s. 22 of the 1961 Act do not apply to a prisoner who escapes while in transit to or from prison (*R* v *Moss* (1985) 82 Cr App R 116).

There is a particular offence, punishable by two years' imprisonment, of inducing or assisting a patient detained in a mental hospital to escape or to absent themselves without leave (Mental Health Act 1983, s. 128).

It also appears that there is a common law offence of forcibly rescuing another from lawful custody (see *Blackstone's Criminal Practice*, 2003, section B14.57).

OFFENCE: **Wasting Police Time—*Criminal Law Act 1967, s. 5(2)***
- Triable summarily • Six months' imprisonment and/or a fine
(No specific power of arrest)

The Criminal Law Act 1967, s. 5 states:

(2) Where a person causes any wasteful employment of the police by knowingly making to any person a false report tending to show that an offence has been committed, or to give rise to apprehension for the safety of any persons or property, or tending to show that he has information material to any police inquiry, he shall be liable . . .

KEYNOTE

It is widely thought that there is a minimum number of hours which must be wasted before a prosecution can be brought for this offence. There is no reliable authority on this point. Consideration should also be given to the offence of perverting the course of justice (**see 4.8.4**). This offence is a 'penalty offence' for the purposes of s. 1 of the Criminal Justice and Police Act 2001.

This is slightly odd given that, at the time of writing, the consent of the DPP was required before a prosecution could be brought.

It is unclear whether this offence will extend to any wasted activities of non-sworn police personnel such as those designated under the Police Reform Act 2002.

4.8.9   **Contempt of Court**

Acts which amount to contempt of court can be divided into criminal and civil contempt. Criminal contempt is defined at common law as 'behaviour involving interference with the due administration of justice' (*Attorney-General* v *Newspaper Publishing plc* [1988] Ch 333 and see *Blackstone's Criminal Practice*, 2003, section B14.59).

Contempt can be committed in many different ways including misbehaviour in court, publication of matters prejudicial to a trial and taking photographs inside a court building. For a full explanation of the subject together with the extensive powers of courts to deal with contempt, see *Blackstone's Criminal Practice*, 2003, section B14.59 *et seq.*

4.9   **Disclosure of Evidence**

4.9.1   **Introduction**

The need for the prosecution to provide the defence with material relating to the charge(s) in a case has been recognised by the courts and the government to be crucial in ensuring that defendants gets a fair trial. This point is further enforced with the introduction of the Human Rights Act 1998 which incorporates the ECHR and in this area brings in Article 6.

Article 6(3):

3. Everyone charged with a criminal offence has the following minimum rights:
    (a) to be informed promptly, in a language which he understands and in detail, of the nature and cause of the accusation against him;
    (b) to have adequate time and facilities for the preparation of his defence;
    (c) to defend himself in person or through legal assistance of his own choosing or, if he has no sufficient means to pay for legal assistance, to be given it free when the interests of justice so require;
    (d) to examine or have examined witnesses against him and to obtain the attendance and examination of witnesses on his behalf under the same conditions as witnesses against him

In *Rowe and Davis* v *UK* (2000) 30 EHRR 1, the European Court of Human Rights emphasised that the right to a fair trial means that the prosecution authorities should disclose to the defence all material evidence in their possession for and against the accused. Only such measures restricting the rights of the defence to disclosure as are strictly necessary are permissible under the ECHR, Article 6(1). *Rowe and Davis* is an important decision in relation to the disclosure of material in criminal cases and the principles that apply. This can be summarised as follows:

- It is a fundamental aspect of the right to a fair trial that criminal proceedings, including the elements of such proceedings which relate to procedure, should be adversarial and that there should be equality of arms between the prosecution and defence.

- The right to an adversarial trial means, in a criminal case, that both the prosecution and defence must be given the opportunity to have knowledge of and comment on the observations filed and the evidence adduced by the other party.

- Article 6(1), in common with English law, requires that the prosecution authority should disclose to the defence all material evidence in their possession for or against the accused.

- The entitlement of disclosure of relevant evidence is not an absolute right.

- Only such measures restricting the right of the defence which are strictly necessary are permissible under Article 6(1).

- Moreover, to ensure that the accused receives a fair trial, any difficulties caused to the defence by limitation on its rights must be sufficiently counter balanced by the procedures followed by the judicial authorities.

- Decision-making procedure must, so far as is possible, comply with the requirements to provide adversarial proceedings and equality of arms, and incorporate adequate safeguards to protect the interests of the accused.

The requirement to provide the defence with material can be divided between that required prior to the person pleading, which is known as advanced information and that which is required once the defendant has pleaded not guilty in the magistrates' court or committed/transferred to the Crown Court. The second stage assumes that the defence has been provided with the prosecution case and therefore any evidence that is left is material and that it will remain unused by the prosecution. This is usually referred to as 'disclosure'. These two stages are considered below.

4.9.2 Advanced Information

Advance information refers to the material that the defence are entitled to have in order to consider whether to plead guilty or not guilty. In some cases it is not a question of whether the defendant committed the crime but whether the prosecution are in a position to prove the offence and, in order to consider this, the defence are unlikely to agree to plead or decide on the mode of trial without knowing the strength of the prosecution case. It is clearly in the public interest that guilty pleas are entered or indicated as soon as possible (*R v Calderdale Magistrates' Court, ex parte Donahue* [2001] Crim LR 141) and often this cannot be achieved unless advanced information has been provided. The need to know as early as possible whether a defendant is going to plead not guilty can be particularly important as there are time limits by which the courts have to set trials and committals. Often these can be delayed because the prosecution have not complied with their disclosure duties.

The prosecution is required, on request, to supply the defence with a summary of the prosecution case and/or copies of the statements of the proposed prosecution witnesses. (In indictable and either way offences this is covered by the Magistrates' Courts (Advance Information) Rules 1985 and in summary only cases by the Attorney-General's Guidelines: Disclosure of Information in Criminal Proceedings (**see appendix 7**). Whilst the rules state that advanced information is only required when requested by the defence, in practice, this should, where possible be made available to the CPS at the first hearing.

It is suggested that Article 6 of the European Convention of Human Rights supports the need to provide advanced information to the defence and that this should be done as soon as possible:

Article 6(3)(a) states that a person is:

to be informed promptly ... and in detail, of the nature and cause of the accusation against him;

Article 6(3)(b), states that an accused is entitled to:

have adequate time ... for the preparation of his defence.

The point concerning advanced information in summary cases was considered in *R v Stratford Justices, ex parte Imbert* (1999) 2 Cr App R 276, where the court gave their opinion that Article 6 does not give an absolute right to pre-trial disclosure, it will be a question of whether the defendant can have a fair trial. Clearly it will be easier to satisfy this test where advanced information as been provided to the defence.

Advanced information might also include the following and so consideration should be had to providing this material to the prosecutor so that he/she can forward it to the defence where appropriate (ensuring the addresses and other details of witnesses and victims are protected):

- copy of the custody record;
- copies of any interview tape(s);
- copy of any first descriptions where relevant;
- significant information that might affect a bail decision or that might enable the defence to contest the committal proceedings (A–G's Guidelines para. 34);
- any material which is relevant to sentence (e.g. information which might mitigate the seriousness of the offence or assist the accused to lay blame in whole or in part upon a co-accused or another person) (A–G's Guidelines para. 44);
- statements and/or a summary of the prosecution cases;
- copy of any video evidence.

Where a person has made several statements but all the relevant evidence for the prosecution case is contained in one statement, it is only that one statement which needs to be disclosed. In order to comply with advanced information the defence needs to be either given a copy of the document or allowed to inspect the document (or a copy of it).

Where the OIC considers that providing advanced information might lead to a witness being intimidated or some other interference with the course of justice he/she should consult with the CPS as the rules allow the prosecutor to limit disclosure of some or all the prosecution case.

4.9.3 Disclosure and the Criminal Procedure and Investigations Act 1996

As stated above this stage assumes that the defence has already been informed of the details of the prosecution case. In most investigations there will be material that has come to the attention of the police which will not be used as evidence to prove the prosecution case but which might be useful to the defence. It is through the disclosure rules that this information will be provided to the defendant. The rules of disclosure are governed by the Criminal Procedure and Investigations Act 1996. The 1996 Act puts the prosecution duty to disclose information to the defence on a statutory footing, and also introduced a new concept in criminal law where the defence have a duty to advise the prosecution of certain matters relating to their case. This is also supported by the 1996 Act Code of Practice, the Attorney-General's Guidelines on Disclosure and the Joint Police and CPS Disclosure Project (JOPI) publication (extracts from which appear in **appendix 8**).

The 1996 Act is further recognition of the need to disclose material to each side to allow the case to be dealt with fairly. This point as well as the need for timely disclosure of material, is further reinforced by Article 6(3) of the European Convention on Human Rights.

In *Jasper v United Kingdom* (2000) 30 EHRR 441 the Court expressed the importance of equality of arms being a fundamental aspect of a fair trial; both the defence and the prosecution must be given the opportunity to have knowledge of and comment on filed observations and evidence adduced by the other party. The Court did recognise that the entitlement to disclosure of relevant evidence was not an absolute right but could be restricted as was strictly necessary (**see 4.9.24**).

4.9.4 The Criminal Procedure and Investigations Act 1996

The Criminal Procedure and Investigations Act 1996 is made up of seven parts. It is the first two parts which are of interest to the police:

- part I sets out the procedures for disclosure and the effects of failing to comply with the Act; and
- part II sets out the duties of police officers in relation to the disclosure provisions.

4.9.5 Aims of the 1996 Act

The aim of the disclosure rules within the Criminal Procedure and Investigations Act 1996 is to make sure that a defendant gets a fair trial and speeds up the whole trial process. This was confirmed by *R* v *Stratford Justices, ex parte Imbert* (1999) 2 Cr App R 276, where the court said that the legislation was to try to ensure that nothing which might assist the defence was kept from the accused.

Paragraph 2 of A–G's Guidelines states that:

> The scheme set out in the Criminal Procedure and Investigations Act 1996 (the Act) is designed to ensure that there is fair disclosure of material which may be relevant to an investigation and which does not form part of the prosecution case. Disclosure under the Act should assist the accused in the timely preparation and presentation of their case and assist the court to focus on all the relevant issues in the trial. Disclosure which does not meet these objectives risks preventing a fair trial taking place.

The Act places a responsibility on the prosecution to make *primary* disclosure of material to the defence; a responsibility for the defence—under certain conditions—to disclose their case to the prosecution with a further responsibility on the prosecution to make a *secondary* disclosure to the defence. As a 'catch all' the prosecution also have a continuing duty to review the material they have disclosed.

There is a duty placed on the prosecutor to disclose to the defence material which may prove helpful to defendant's case. This has to be balanced against the risk of disclosing so much material under their duty to disclose that the defence collapses under the sheer volume of paperwork. Alternatively, allowing the defence relentless requests for material which may be of no real value ('fishing expeditions') could lead to situations where a guilty person is acquitted.

While the duty of disclosure is placed on the prosecutor, the police have a responsibility to assist in this process. It is therefore vital that police officers understand, not only the statutory requirements made of them, but also the extent of their role within the whole disclosure process. This view is supported by the A–G's Guidelines. Paragraph 5 states:

> Investigators and disclosure officers must be fair and objective and must work together with prosecutors to ensure that disclosure obligations are met.

4.9.6 Jurisdiction of the 1996 Act

The Criminal Procedure and Investigations Act 1996 is primarily concerned with the disclosure of material which does not form part of the prosecution case resulting from a criminal investigation (i.e. 'unused material'). A criminal investigation is defined by s. 1(4) of the 1996 Act and para. 2.1 of the Code of Practice. In order to satisfy the disclosure requirements police officers should consider recording and retaining material in the early stages of an investigation, including investigations:

- to detect a crime *after* it has been committed and in order to bring a prosecution;
- to discover *whether* a crime has been committed, for instance where a motorist is stopped and then enquiries are made as to whether the car has been stolen;
- that are the result of a belief/information that an offence *might be* committed.

In these cases the investigation may well have started some time before the defendant became a suspect. In such cases all the material from the investigation/operation would have to be considered to see if it was relevant to the defence case. In cases where there is a surveillance operation or observation point, it may be that the details of the observation point and the surveillance techniques would not be revealed but it would be necessary to retain material generating from it (**see 4.9.24**).

4.9.7   Failure to Comply

Compliance with the rules of disclosure, by both the defence and prosecution, is essential if the 1996 Act is to have any real value. First, in cases where the defence are obliged to make disclosure to the prosecution, failure to do so may lead to the court or jury drawing such inferences as appear proper in deciding the guilt or innocence of the accused (s. 11(3)). Should the prosecution fail to comply with their obligations then an accused does not have to make defence disclosure and no such inference can be made. Secondly, failure by the prosecution to comply with the rules could lead to the court staying the proceedings on the grounds that there has been an abuse of process (s. 5(1)(b) and s. 10). It could also lead to an action for damages or such other relief as the court sees fit under the Human Rights Act 1998, particularly in relation to Article 6 of the European Convention and the right to a fair trial.

Additionally, where the prosecution have not made disclosure on time or fully, a stay on the proceedings or a further adjournment is possible. It is suggested that the more adjournments in a case, the more likely that witnesses will get fed up with the delays and will fail to attend on the next occasion and the case could therefore be lost!

Even if there has been a failure to comply with disclosure the case will not automatically be stayed and therefore any failings should be brought to the attention of the CPS so that the matter can be considered. In *R v Feltham Magistrates' Court, ex parte Ebrahim; Mouat v DPP; R v Feltham Magistrates' Court, ex parte DPP* [2001] 1 WLR 1293, the court stated that:

> It must be remembered that it is a commonplace in criminal trial for the defendant to rely on holes in the prosecution case. If in such a case, there is sufficient credible evidence, apart from the missing evidence, which, if believed, would justify safe conviction then the trial should proceed, leaving the defendant to seek to persuade the jury or magistrates not to convict because evidence might otherwise have been available was not before the court through no fault of the defendant.

Failure to disclose may result in convictions being overturned, for instance in *R v Poole* (2003) *The Times*, 26 June, the Court of Appeal allowed appeals against convictions for murder because the non-disclosure of prosecution evidence influenced the jury's assessment of the reliability of the evidence of a key eyewitness. In this case the witness gave an account that was false in a material particular. However, the police did not follow up those inconsistencies and they failed to inform the CPS that his evidence was unreliable.

4.9.8   Part I of the 1996 Act: Rules of Disclosure

4.9.9   Application of the Disclosure Provisions

Section 1 of the Criminal Procedure and Investigations Act 1996 defines in which type of cases the disclosure provisions apply. In reality this applies to all cases other than those where the defendant pleads guilty at the magistrates' court. These rules only apply where no criminal investigation into the alleged offence took place before 1 April 1997. If an investigation began before 1 April 1997, then it will be necessary to refer to the common law rules, however ACPO have stated that the 1996 Act should be followed in all cases when considering disclosure.

Some guidance is given by the case of R v *Uxbridge Magistrates' Court, ex parte Patel* (2000) 164 JP 209, as to the time an investigation begins. There it was said that the phrase 'criminal investigation' in s. 1(3) of the 1996 Act means that a criminal investigation could begin into an offence before it was committed. This could be so in a surveillance case or where a series of cases was committed, some before and some after the appointed day. Whether in any given case that was the correct view would be a question of fact for the court to determine.

Section 1 also defines a criminal investigation and states:

(4) For the purposes of this section a criminal investigation is an investigation which police officers or other persons have a duty to conduct with a view to it being ascertained—

    (a) whether a person should be charged with an offence, or

    (b) whether a person charged with an offence is guilty of it.

Consequently, this part of the Act also applies to other people, besides the police, who carry out investigations where they have a duty to ascertain whether criminal offences have been committed (e.g. HM Customs and Excise; Benefits Agency investigators). It does not apply to those whose primary responsibility does not relate to criminal offences (e.g. local authorities and schools). It also includes the situation where an investigation is started before any offence has been committed, for instance where a surveillance operation is being conducted with a view to gathering prosecution evidence. In this case it is only the information obtained and not the surveillance operation that is disclosable.

4.9.10 Primary Disclosure by Prosecutor

This is covered by s. 3 of the Criminal Procedure and Investigations Act 1996. This section talks about material which '*might undermine the prosecution case against the accused*'. The courts are likely to consider this to include material which has an adverse affect on the strength of the prosecution case.

Prior to the Criminal Procedure and Investigations Act 1996, in cases where disclosure was required the prosecution had to disclose all material that was relevant to the case. Under the 1996 Act, while a schedule of all relevant material must be provided, only material that undermines the prosecution case must be disclosed at the primary disclosure stage. There is only limited case law in this area but it is likely that such material will consist mainly of material which raises question marks over the strength of the prosecution case, the value of evidence given by witnesses and issues relating to identification. If officers feel that the material is not relevant to the prosecution case but may be useful to the defence in cross-examination, it may well come within the category of material which undermines the prosecution case. Disclosure of previous convictions and other matters that might affect the credibility of a witness may 'undermine the prosecution case' as it may limit the value of the witness's testimony. This factor may not be apparent at the time but may come to light after primary disclosure, such as where it becomes known that the witness has a grudge against the defendant. This is one reason why the 1996 Act requires the decision as to whether material undermines the prosecution case to be continuously monitored throughout the case.

The Code of Practice at para. 3.4 states that:

In conducting an investigation, the investigator should pursue all reasonable lines of inquiry, whether these point towards or away from the suspect. What is reasonable in each case will depend on the particular circumstances.

In *R v Feltham Magistrates' Court, ex parte Ebrahim; Mouat v DPP; R v Feltham Magistrates' Court, ex parte DPP* [2001] 1 WLR 1293, the court stated that the extent of the investigation should be proportionate to the seriousness of the matter being investigated. What is reasonable in a case may well depend on such factors as the staff and resources available, the seriousness of the case, the strength of evidence against the suspect and the nature of the line of inquiry to be pursued. If in doubt it is suggested the CPS are contacted for guidance.

Paragraph 2.22 of the JOPI Guidelines makes important observations concerning negative results when making enquiries 'negative results can sometimes be as significant to an investigation as positive ones'. It is impossible to define precisely when a negative result may be significant, as every case is different. However it will include the result of any enquiry that differs from what might be expected, given the prevailing circumstances. Not only must material or information which points towards a fact or an individual be retained, but also that which casts doubt on the suspect's guilt, or implicates another person. Examples of negative information include:

- where a number of people present at a particular location at the particular time that an offence is alleged to have taken place state they saw nothing unusual;
- where a fingermark from a crime scene cannot be identified as belonging to a known suspect, or is of insufficient value to determine identity;
- any other failure to match a crime scene sample with one taken from a known suspect.

The prosecution only have to disclose material relevant to the prosecution in question. For instance, surveillance logs concerning another matter would not need to be disclosed (*R v Dennis*, 13 April 2000, unreported). It is up to the prosecutor to decide on the format in which material is disclosed to the accused. If material is to be copied, s. 3(3) leaves the question of whether this should be done by the prosecutor or the police open. The prosecutor must also provide the defence with a schedule of all non-sensitive material (s. 4(2)). This includes all other information in police possession, or material that has been examined by the police other than 'sensitive material' (this is disclosed to the prosecutor separately). 'Sensitive material' (**see 4.9.24**) is material which is not in the public interest to disclose and material obtained as a result of a warrant under s. 2 of the Interception of Communications Act 1985. Such material must not be disclosed to the accused or his/her representatives (s. 3(6) and (7)). At this stage the defence is not entitled to inspect items on the schedule that have not been disclosed.

Material must not be disclosed to the extent that the court concludes it is not in the public interest to disclose it and orders accordingly or it is material whose disclosure is prohibited by s. 17 of the Regulation of Investigatory Powers Act 2000.

Time Period for Primary Disclosure

While there are provisions to set specific time periods by which primary disclosure must be met none currently exist. Until such times primary disclosure must be made as soon as practicable after the duty arises. Where disclosure is not made within a reasonable period it could lead to the case being lost. In *R v Bourimech* [2002] EWCA Crim 2089, the defendant sought disclosure following the service of his defence statement of a previous crime report made by the victim. One day before the trial was scheduled to begin, the crime report relating to that incident was served amongst other papers on the defence. This report escaped the notice of the defence until the final day of the trial. The court held that the defect in disclosure amounted to unfairness in the proceedings and the court could not be confident that if the victim had been cross-examined in relation to the previous allegation the jury might have been influenced by the credit and credibility of the witness.

The 1996 Act in effect only applies once the defendant has been committed/transferred to the crown court or is proceeding to trial in the magistrates'/youth court. In most cases prosecution disclosure can wait until after this time without jeopardising the defendant's right to a fair trial. However, the prosecutor must always be alive to the need to make advance disclosure of material that should be disclosed at an earlier stage (*R v DPP, ex parte Lee* [1999] 2 All ER 737). Examples include:

- previous convictions of a complainant or a deceased if that information could reasonably be expected to assist the defence when applying for bail;
- material that might enable a defendant to make a pre-committal application to stay the proceedings as an abuse of process;
- material that might enable a defendant to submit that he/she should only be committed for trial on a lesser charge, or perhaps that he/she should not be committed for trial at all;
- depending on what the defendant chooses to reveal about his/her case at this early stage, material that would enable the defendant and his/her legal advisers to make preparations for trial that would be significantly less effective if disclosure were delayed; for example, names of eye witnesses whom the prosecution did not intend to use.

It should be noted that any disclosure by the prosecution prior to committal would not normally exceed the primary disclosure which, after committal, would be required by s. 3 of the 1996 Act (material which in the prosecutor's opinion might undermine the case for the prosecution (*R v DPP, ex parte Lee*)).

4.9.11 **Disclosure by the Defence**

The duty on the defence to make disclosure only arises *after* the prosecution has made the primary disclosure (s. 5(1)). This duty falls into two categories:

- compulsory;
- voluntary.

The disclosure required by the defence is limited to material that they intend to use at trial.

Compulsory Disclosure by Defence (s. 5)

The duty for the defence to make disclosure does not apply to cases being tried summarily. The duty on the defence, whether the accused is represented or not, is to provide a defence statement to the court and the prosecutor within 14 days of the prosecution making primary disclosure (this period can be extended by the courts).

The defence statement should outline the defence case in general terms. In addition, those issues, relevant to the case, which the accused disputes with the prosecution must be set out with reasons. This requirement to give reasons is intended to stop the defence going on a 'fishing expedition' to speculatively look at material in order to find some kind of defence.

Where the defence case involves an alibi, the statement must give details of the alibi, including the name and address of any alibi witness. In cases where there are co-accused, there is no duty to disclose this information to the other defendants, although this could be done voluntarily.

Voluntary Disclosure by Defence (s. 6)

The purpose of s. 6 of the 1996 Act is to allow the defence, in cases where the case is being tried summarily, to obtain further disclosure from the prosecution after the primary disclosure.

This is only likely to happen where:

- the defence is not satisfied with the material disclosed at the primary disclosure stage or where they wish to examine items listed in the schedule of non-sensitive material;
- the defence wish to show the strength of their case in order to persuade the prosecution not to proceed.

If the defence decide to make a defence statement they must comply with the same conditions imposed on compulsory defence disclosure.

Effect of Failure in Defence Disclosure

If the defence fails to give a defence statement under s. 5 or where a defence statement is provided it is:

- outside the time limits;
- sets out inconsistent defences in a defence statement or at trial puts forward a different defence; or
- at trial adduces evidence in support of an alibi without having given particulars of the alibi in a defence statement, or calls a witness in support of an alibi without providing details of the witness or information that might help trace the witness;

then following sanctions may apply:

- the court or, with the leave of the court, any other party may make such comment as appears appropriate;
- the court or jury may draw such inferences as appear proper in deciding whether the accused is guilty of the offence concerned (but there must also be other evidence to convict the defendant).

4.9.12 Secondary Disclosure by Prosecutor (s. 7)

Once a defence statement has been provided (whether compulsorily or voluntarily), the prosecution must disclose any prosecution material that:

- might be reasonably expected to assist the accused's defence; and
- has not already been disclosed.

It will be a question of fact whether material in police possession might be reasonably expected to assist the defence case. If the court feels that material that was not disclosed would to any reasonable person have been expected to help the defence case, the case may fail. The test for secondary disclosure is wider than primary disclosure in that this test is objective in that it requires disclosure where any reasonable person would expect the material to assist the defence whereas primary disclosure talks of 'the prosecutor's opinion'.

If there is no additional material to be disclosed then the prosecutor must give a written statement to this effect. It is not the responsibility of the prosecutor or the police to examine material held by third parties which the defence have stated they wish to examine (the defence can request this from the third party or apply for a witness summons). However, there may be occasions where matters disclosed in the defence statement lead investigators to look at material held by third parties as it might impact on the prosecution case. This stage of the disclosure process may require further inquiries prompted by the defence statement. The result of those enquiries may then have to be disclosed because it either undermines the prosecution case or it assists the accused's defence.

If the defence is not satisfied that the prosecution have disclosed all they should have, s. 8 of the 1996 Act allows for the defence to apply to the court for further disclosure.

Material must not be disclosed to the extent that the court concludes it is not in the public interest to disclose it and orders accordingly or it is material whose disclosure is prohibited by s. 17 of the Regulation of Investigatory Powers Act 2000.

4.9.13 Continuing Duty of Prosecutor to Disclose (s. 9)

There is duty on the prosecution to continue to review the disclosure of prosecution material right up until the case is completed (acquittal, conviction or discontinuance of the case).

The duty to review is in two stages:

- after primary disclosure the prosecutor must review material not disclosed in terms of whether it might undermine the prosecution case (s. 9); and
- after secondary prosecution disclosure (s. 7).

The review of the material must also be in terms of whether material might be reasonably expected to assist the accused's defence as disclosed by the defence statement. This responsibility is mirrored in the Code of Practice. This is a continuous duty even after secondary disclosure has been made, failure to review could lead to an acquittal, abuse of process or even acquittal at a later appeal.

4.9.14 Roles and Responsibilities under the 1996 Act

The Code of Practice (**see appendix 7**))identifies certain roles within the disclosure process:

- prosecutor;
- officer in charge of the case (OIC);
- disclosure officer;
- investigator;
- supervisor of OIC and disclosure officer.

In addition, it is the responsibility of the chief officer of police of each force to put arrangements in place to ensure that the identity of the OIC and disclosure officer is recorded for each criminal investigation (Code of Practice, para. 3.2). Force policy should be followed in recording this information.

The roles described within the 1996 Act are independent of each other but all must be completed for the disclosure provisions to work (para. 3.1). All police officers involved in an investigation are likely to have to comply with the role of investigator.

Some investigations may involve a large quantity of material, both used and unused. Examples of cases where this may occur include substantial frauds; large-scale conspiracies; drug related offences involving manufacture, importation or supply; homicide or other major enquiries. These are often large or complex cases and additional guidance for these cases is provided in the JOPI Guidelines from para. 2.113 to 2.117.

Although the police roles are independent they may be combined, and the OIC may also be an investigator and, depending on the complexity of the case, may also be the disclosure officer. Whether there is one officer involved in the case or several, each role can be considered separately and must be completed fully in order that the right information can be given to the prosecutor who, ultimately, is responsible for the disclosure of material to the defence. It is important that all officers consult fully in order that the disclosure officer can complete his/her task properly. Each role is considered below as if undertaken by a different person.

4.9.15 **Prosecutor**

This role is defined by s. 2(3) of the 1996 Act as being 'any person acting as prosecutor whether an individual or a body'. In other words, the person who will be taking the case to court. On most occasions this will be the Crown Prosecution Service. It would also apply to the Serious Fraud Office or the Data Protection Registrar. In the case of private prosecutions, the prosecutor is obliged to comply with the disclosure provisions of the 1996 Act but does not have to comply with the Code of Practice. The prosecutor is responsible for ensuring that primary disclosure is made to the defence and, where appropriate, secondary disclosure. The prosecutor should also be available to advise the OIC, disclosure officer and investigators on matters relating to the relevance of material recorded and retained by police, sensitive material and on any other disclosure issues that might arise.

Should there need to be an application to the court to withhold material because of public interest (**see 4.9.24**), this will be done through the prosecutor.

A more detailed explanation of the roles and responsibilities of the prosecutor are set out in the CPS/Police Joint Operational Instructions (JOPI) Guidelines (2003).

4.9.16 **Officer in Charge of the Case (OIC)**

This role may be performed by a person directly involved in the investigation or by person who has been given the role of overseeing the investigation (Disclosure Code, paras 3.1 and 3.3). Whoever has this role is both responsible and accountable for the investigation (para. 3.3). (See also JOPI Guidelines, para. 2.4).

The Attorney-General's Guidelines state that an individual must not be appointed as disclosure officer, or continue in that role, if that is likely to result in a conflict of interest, for instance, if the disclosure officer is the victim of the alleged crime which is the subject of criminal proceedings. It is suggested that the same approach should also be taken when identifying the OIC. This is an important consideration as it should be remembered that the officer is a victim and may be in need of support.

The OIC is responsible for ensuring that proper procedures are in place for the recording of information and that records and materials are retained for the required period (**see 4.9.23**). Paragraph 4.1 of the Code requires that the material is recorded in a durable and retrievable form and that, where possible, the record is made contemporaneously. If not, the record must be made as soon as practicable. Guidance is given in para. 5.4 of the Code para. 6 and of the A–G's Guidelines. These requirements to record information should be paramount in the mind of all investigators, as well as the OIC.

The need for contemporaneous records is also required under the Police and Criminal Evidence Act 1984 and if not complied with could affect the admissibility of important evidence (see s. 78 of the 1984 Act). Note that, under para. 4.3, relevant material to be recorded includes *negative* material. Such material might include the fact that several people at the scene of a crime were spoken to and claimed to have seen nothing, or that they saw several other people at the scene as well. This last point reiterates the position at common law; that police officers have a duty to get to the truth and allow a suspect a fair trial, a duty which includes recording and retaining material which helps the defence.

Having made sure that material is recorded and retained by the investigators in the case, the OIC must make the material available to the disclosure officer (Code, para. 3). Where the function of disclosure officer is carried out by the OIC, there is little problem as the OIC should have a full understanding of the case and the implication of all the material collected, in terms of it being adverse to the case or being of a sensitive nature. In cases where the roles are performed by different people, it is important that the OIC and the disclosure officer consult fully about the material in order that the disclosure officer has as full an understanding of the case as he/she can in order to carry out his/her functions properly (para. 3.1). This must be done in order that the disclosure officer can complete the certification stage (paras 3.1 and 9). These responsibilities can be delegated to other police officers or non-police staff but it remains the responsibility of the OIC to ensure that the tasks are completed (para. 3.3). It may be necessary to demonstrate to the court that these powers have been carried out.

As with all people involved in the disclosure process, s. 9 of the 1996 Act places a duty on the OIC to review material in the case. This duty is emphasised by para. 5.3 of the Code so that, where the OIC becomes aware that previously examined material which has not been disclosed has since become relevant to the case, he/she must take steps to ensure that the material is retained and inform the prosecutor so that disclosure can be made to the defence. At this stage it will be for the OIC to decide in which format that material should be retained (para. 4.1), considering the need to be able to produce it for inspection by the court.

4.9.17 Disclosure Officer

The disclosure officer creates the link between the investigation team and the prosecutor (Crown Prosecution Service) and is therefore very important to the disclosure process. For investigations carried out by the police, generally speaking there is no restriction on who performs this role. It could be the OIC or, equally, it could be performed by unsworn support staff (Code, paras 2.1 and 3.3). The disclosure officer is responsible for providing information and material to the prosecutor at the primary disclosure stage (para. 7.1) and, where necessary, carrying out any additional work requested by the prosecutor before the primary disclosure is made (para. 7.4). It is important that the disclosure officer does not have a conflict of interest, this is set out in the A–G's Guidelines at para. 7:

> An individual must not be appointed as disclosure officer, or continue in that role, if that is likely to result in a conflict of interest, for instance, if the disclosure officer is the victim of the alleged crime which is the subject of criminal proceedings. The advice of a more senior officer must always be sought if there is doubt as to whether a conflict of interest precludes an individual acting as the disclosure officer. If thereafter the doubt remains, the advice of a prosecutor should be sought.

In some cases it will be desirable to appoint a disclosure officer at the outset of the investigation. In making this decision, the OIC should have regard to the nature and seriousness of the case, the volume of material which may be obtained or created, and the likelihood of a committal or a not guilty plea. If not appointed at the start of an investigation, a disclosure officer must be appointed in sufficient time to be able to prepare the unused material schedules for inclusion in the full file submitted to CPS (JOPI Guidelines, para. 2.10).

The disclosure officer is responsible for examining all material retained by the police during the investigation (Code, para. 2.1). The first step is to establish that all material which has been retained in relation to the case has been recorded and made available for examination. The disclosure officer should verify with the OIC that all material has been made available to him/her.

Disclosure officers, or their deputies, must inspect, view or listen to all material that has been retained by the investigator, and the disclosure officer must provide a personal declaration to the effect that this task has been done. The obligation does not apply in circumstances as set out in para. 9 of the A–G's Guidelines. In such cases a section 9 statement must be made explaining why the material has not been examined (A–G's Guidelines, para. 8).

There will occasionally be cases where the police investigation has been intelligence led, there may be an additional disclosure officer appointed just to deal with intelligence material which, by its very nature, is likely to be sensitive. In cases where more than one disclosure officer has been appointed to deal with different aspects of the case, a principal disclosure officer should be identified as the single point of contact for the prosecutor. Where an officer other than the principal disclosure officer submits a disclosure schedule to the prosecutor, that officer should inform the principal disclosure officer. (JOPI Guidelines, paras 2.139 and 2.140).

Should the disclosure officer fail to provide information to the prosecutor within a reasonable time or to comply with any requests made by the prosecutor for additional material, this could lead to the defence not having to provide a defence statement or adverse remarks being made in court. At worse it could lead to a stay of proceedings for an abuse of process (s. 10 of the 1996 Act; see s. 5(4)).

Duties of the Disclosure Officer: Primary Disclosure

Under s. 3 of the 1996 Act all previously undisclosed material that might undermine the prosecution case must be disclosed to the defence. If there is no such material, then the accused must be given a written statement to that effect. This applies to all material in possession of the police or that has been inspected under the provisions of the Disclosure Code of Practice. This therefore requires the disclosure officer to know what material exists and what material has already been made available to the defence.

Where disclosure is required, the first task is to create a schedule of all *non-sensitive material*, which has been retained by the police and which does not form part of the prosecution case, which may be relevant to the investigation (Code, para. 6.3). If in doubt, the prosecutor should be consulted so that they can advise on the relevance of material (para. 6.1). This schedule must be endorsed by the disclosure officer to the effect that, to his/her best ability, it does not contain any sensitive material.

Initially, these schedules only have to be produced where the person is charged with an indictable offence, where the offence is triable either way or where the defendant will be tried summarily and is likely to plead not guilty. If the offence is witnessed by a police officer, or the person has admitted an either way or summary offence, then a schedule is not required unless the person then pleads not guilty. This provision has been added to avoid preparing material which will never be needed. If the person then pleads not guilty the schedule must be prepared as soon as practicable (Code, para. 6.8). However, some forces may require the schedule to be prepared in all cases.

The next step is to create a separate schedule of all sensitive material, which must include the reasons why the disclosure officer believes the material is of a sensitive nature (para. 6.4). Paragraph 6.12 gives examples of the type of material that would be classed as sensitive. If all material has been disclosed and there is no sensitive material, then a statement to that effect should be included on the main schedule. The schedule(s) should include all material, excluding that which forms part of the prosecution case (para. 6.2).

There may be cases where material is so sensitive that the disclosure officer or other investigators consider that it should not even appear on the schedule (**see 4.9.24**). In these cases the prosecutor should be informed of these separately (para. 6.4). It is the responsibility of the investigator who knows the details of the sensitive material to inform the prosecutor.

Once the schedules have been completed, the disclosure officer must decide what material, if any (whether listed on the schedules or not), might undermine the prosecution case. There will be a great reliance placed on the opinion of the disclosure officer as to what material might undermine the prosecution case. It is only material that falls into this category that the defence can inspect at this stage. Should the defence wish to inspect any other material on the schedule, this can only happen after the defence statement (outlining the defence case and giving reasons why they wish to inspect other items on the schedule) has been received. The disclosure officer must draw this information to the attention of the prosecutor and the reasons why he/she believes that the material undermines the prosecution case (para. 7.2). This creates a catch all provision and presumably requires the disclosure officer to make enquires of the other officers in the case to ensure all material is included.

The A–G's Guidelines give guidance as to what material might potentially undermine the prosecution case. Paragraph 36 states that:

> This will include anything that tends to show a fact inconsistent with the elements of the case that must be proved by the prosecution. Material can have an adverse effect on the strength of the prosecution case:
>
> (a) by the use made of it in cross-examination; and
> (b) by its capacity to suggest any potential submissions that could lead to:
>   (i) the exclusion of evidence;
>   (ii) a stay of proceedings;
>   (iii) a court or tribunal finding that any public authority had acted incompatibly with the defendant's rights under the ECHR.

This would include any material individually or when viewed with other factors. Examples are material which:

- casts doubt upon the accuracy of any prosecution evidence;
- may point to another person, whether charged or not (including a co-accused) having involvement in the commission of the offence;
- casts doubt upon the reliability of a confession;
- might go to the credibility of a prosecution witness;
- might support a defence that is either raised by the defence or apparent from the prosecution papers;
- may have a bearing on the admissibility of any prosecution evidence;
- relates to the defendant's mental or physical health, his/her intellectual capacity;
- relates to any ill-treatment which the defendant may have suffered when in the investigator's custody;

(A-G's Guidelines, paras 37 and 38).

Completing the Schedules

It is important that the schedules themselves are completed fully. Guidance is given by paras 6.9 to 6.11 of the Code and in detail in the JOPI Guidelines, paras 2.53 to 2.62. The schedule should have each item numbered consecutively with a description of the item in sufficient detail to allow the prosecutor, when examining the schedule to make an informed decision about the importance of the item, and whether it needs to be disclosed to the defence, in addition to the items suggested by the disclosure officer, as undermining the prosecution case (A–G's Guidelines, para. 10). Whilst items should be listed separately, there may be occasions where items are similar or the same, in which case these may be listed together (A–G's Guidelines, para. 9). This also applies to sensitive schedules, in so far as is possible without compromising the confidentiality of the information (see also JOPI Guidelines, paras 2.74 to 2.85). Paragraph 9 of the A–G's Guidelines also allow in some circumstances, because of the large volumes of material, not to examine all the material. If such material is not examined by the investigator or disclosure officer, and it is not intended to examine it, its existence should be made known to the accused in general terms. A Section 9 statement must be completed by the investigating officer or disclosure officer describing the material by general category and justifying it not having been examined.

The schedules and copies of any material which is considered to undermine the prosecution case should be given to the prosecutor (Code, paras 7.1 to 7.3). The disclosure officer should include an explanation as to why they consider that the material should be disclosed (para. 7.2). As it is unlikely that the prosecutor will have a chance to examine all the material, it is important that the disclosure officer gives clear reasons in his/her report. For the type of material which might undermine the prosecution case, **see 4.9.22**.

In addition to the schedules and copies of material which undermine the prosecution case, para. 7.3 requires the disclosure officer to provide a copy of any material, *whether or not they consider it to undermine the prosecution case*, which is:

- a record of the first description of a suspect given to the police by a potential witness, *whether or not the description differs from that of the alleged offender*;
- information provided by an accused person which indicates an explanation for the offence with which he/she has been charged;
- any material casting doubt on the reliability of a confession;
- any material casting doubt on the reliability of a witness.

The following items should also be considered when deciding on primary disclosure in cases where the disclosure is in the public interest (that is where they are not '*sensitive material*'). The material is (A–G's Guidelines, para. 40):

(i) Those recorded scientific or scenes of crime findings retained by the investigator which: relate to the defendant; and are linked to the point at issue; and have not previously been disclosed;

(ii) Where identification is or may be in issue, all previous descriptions of suspects, however recorded, together with all records of identification procedures in respect of the offence(s) and photographs of the accused taken by the investigator around the time of his arrest;

(iii) Information that any prosecution witness has received, has been promised or has requested any payment or reward in connection with the case;

(iv) Plans of crime scenes or video recordings made by investigators of crime scenes;

(v) Names, within the knowledge of investigators, of individuals who may have relevant information and whom investigators do not intend to interview;

(vi) Records which the investigator has made of information which may be relevant, provided by any individual (such information would include, but not be limited to, records of conversation and interviews with any such person).

The disclosure officer must certify that, to the best of his/her knowledge, all material which has been retained by police and made available to them has been revealed to the prosecutor in accordance with the para. 9.1 of the Code. While the disclosure officer may not always be able to know if all material has been made available to him/her, he/she should consult with the OIC to verify as far as possible that it has been (para. 3.1). Guidance as to primary disclosure revelation is also given in the JOPI Guidelines from para. 2.90 onwards. The disclosure officer should be mindful of the need to demonstrate that he/she has taken all reasonable steps should it transpire that full disclosure had not been made.

Often the police may not possess all the material that could become relevant in a case. It may be that this material has been inspected and a decision made that the material is not relevant to the case at this stage, or that it was not necessary to inspect the material. To cover the risk of material being lost, the disclosure officer should inform third parties of the investigation and invite them to retain material. The disclosure officer should inform the prosecutor that third parties may have such material (para. 3.1). (**See 4.9.25** for third party material.)

Under para. 8 of the Code, information provided by the disclosure officer may be accepted by the prosecutor or might be returned with requests for additional information or for amendments to be made to the schedule or items to be disclosed to the defence. The disclosure officer should comply with any instructions given by the prosecutor and any request for the inspection or copying of material should be met (para. 7.4). If the disclosure officer and OIC consider that material is so sensitive it should not be copied, the disclosure officer should inform the prosecutor and make arrangements for the prosecutor to inspect the material instead (para. 7.4). If copies of materials which are not in writing are requested, the disclosure officer and prosecutor must agree on the format of how it will be provided to the prosecutor (para. 7.5).

It should be remembered that the prosecutor is required to advise the disclosure officer of any omissions or amendments or where there are insufficient or unclear descriptions, or where there has been a failure to provide schedules at all. The disclosure officer must then take all necessary remedial action and provide properly completed schedules to the prosecutor. Failure to do so may result in the matter being raised with a senior officer. (JOPI Guidelines, para. 2.91). There may also be occasions where schedules need to be edited, this is covered in the JOPI Guidelines at para. 2.97.

Once this stage is complete, the prosecutor is able to make primary disclosure to the defence. It will be the responsibility of the disclosure officer to disclose material to the defence if requested to do so by the prosecutor (Code, para. 10.1).

The defence do not have to provide a defence statement until such times as primary disclosure has been made, they then (subject to an extension from the court) have 14 days in which to serve their defence statement. Clearly the sooner primary disclosure is made the more time, in theory, the disclosure officer will have to complete his/her responsibilities under secondary disclosure.

Duties of the Disclosure Officer: Secondary Disclosure

Once primary disclosure has been made the defence may provide a defence statement setting out their case, together with reasons why they wish to inspect additional items on the schedule which have not been disclosed. Under para. 8.2 of the Code, once the defence statement has been provided, the disclosure officer must:

- review the material which is contained on the schedules; and
- inform the prosecutor of any material which might reasonably be expected to assist the defence as disclosed by the defence statement.

This role will often be performed in conjunction with the prosecutor and, at times, may even be undertaken by the prosecutor. However, the Code of Practice does require the disclosure officer to carry out this function and as such there is a duty to review this material even if it is also done by the prosecutor. This responsibility remains with the disclosure officer and must be complied with. It should be remembered that the review of disclosure is based on the defence statement, not a full investigation.

After the material has been reviewed, secondary disclosure can be made to the defence. As with the primary disclosure stage, the disclosure officer must certify that, to the best of his/her knowledge, all material which has been retained by the police and made available to them has been revealed to the prosecutor in accordance with para. 9.1 of the Code. Again, while the disclosure officer may not always know if all material has been made available to him/her, he/she should consult with the OIC to verify as far as possible that it has been (Code, para. 3.1). Guidance as to secondary disclosure revelation is also given in the JOPI Guidelines from para. 2.130 onwards.

Where the defence statement points the prosecution to other lines of inquiry e.g. the investigation of an alibi, or where forensic expert evidence is involved, the disclosure officer should inform the officer in charge of the investigation and copy the defence statement to him or her, together with any CPS advice provided if appropriate (JOPI Guidelines para. 2.113).

Continuing Duty of Disclosure Officer

Once primary disclosure has been made, the disclosure officer has a continuing duty to review material for items that should be disclosed to the defence as undermining the prosecution case. This continuing duty also applies after secondary disclosure in relation to material which might assist the defence case as disclosed in the defence statement (Code, para. 8.3).

Disclosing Material to the Defence

The disclosure officer may also be involved in the actual disclosure of material to the defence which is covered in para. 10 of the Code of Practice. This is material which the prosecutor has agreed that the disclosure officer will disclose to the defence because it falls within the material disclosed:

- at the primary disclosure stage (adverse to prosecution case);
- at the secondary disclosure stage (it assists the defence case); or
- where the court has ordered disclosure after an application by the defence; or
- where, through the continuing duty to review material, it has been disclosed because it has been decided it might undermine the prosecution case or assist the defence case.

The court can also order disclosure of material which the prosecution contend is sensitive. In such cases it may be appropriate to seek guidance on whether to disclose the material or offer no evidence thereby protecting the sensitive material or the source of that material (e.g. where informants or surveillance techniques are involved).

The disclosure officer can make disclosure to the defence by either:

- providing copies of the material; or
- allowing the defence to inspect the material.

Where a request is made for copies, the material must be provided unless it is not practicable or desirable to do so. Examples of such occasions are given in para. 10.3 of the Code. In cases where the material is not recorded in a written format (for instance an audio or video tape) then the disclosure officer has a discretion whether to provide a copy of the item or transcript of what is contained on the tape. This must be certified as a true copy of the tape (para. 10.4). For further guidance see the JOPI Guidelines from para. 2.152 onwards. Forces may have instructions as to providing further copies when requested by the defence in relation to procedures and costs. It is suggested that where copies are provided, some proof of delivery should be obtained.

4.9.18 Duties of Investigators

The roles of investigator may involve just one officer or several officers. An 'investigation' may be completed in a very short time, e.g. from stopping a car, discovering it was stolen, arresting the suspect, obtaining a victim statement and charging the suspect. Alternatively, the case may involve a long, protracted enquiry with several officers, various witnesses and numerous suspects, arrests and interviews.

An officer who is classed as an investigator must make all reasonable lines of enquiry (Code, para. 3.4) and having done so retain all material which is relevant to the case (see **4.9.23**), whether or not it is helpful to the prosecution (A-G's Guidelines, para. 5.1). The investigator also has a responsibility to identify material that could be sensitive and bring this to the attention of the CPS (see **4.9.24**). Where material is identified steps must be taken to record and retain the material. For information recorded on computers see the JOPI Guidelines from para. 2.33 onwards.

The issue of sensitive material is discussed below (see **4.9.24**). Often it is only the investigator who obtained the evidence who will be fully aware of the sensitive nature of the material. In order to balance the need to protect sensitive material yet give the prosecutor full details of why the material is sensitive, para. 6.14 of the Code places the responsibility of informing the prosecutor of details of sensitive material on the investigator. The investigator must take steps to ensure the prosecutor can inspect the material. This does not mean that the disclosure officer or any other officer cannot carry out this function; simply that the investigator must ensure that it is carried out.

When completing the disclosure schedules the investigating officer must be mindful that there may be cases where material is so sensitive that he/she or other investigators consider that it should not even appear on the schedule (such as where disclosure would be likely to lead directly to the loss of life or directly threaten national security (para. 6.13)). It is the responsibility of the investigator who knows the details of the sensitive material to inform the prosecutor.

Continuing Duty of Investigators

The continuing duty of disclosure imposed by ss. 7 and 9 of the 1996 Act mean that investigators have a corresponding duty to keep under review the revelation of material which meets the test for disclosure. It is therefore important that investigators are aware of which material might undermine the prosecution case and which might assist the defence case. It is also important therefore that investigators are aware of the content of defence statements provided after primary disclosure. This will therefore require consultation between OICs, disclosure officers and investigators. If investigators do not carry out their function property, this has an impact on all the others involved in the disclosure process and may lead to disclosure on the defence being defective, which in turn could lead to a miscarriage of justice or stay of proceedings.

4.9.19 Supervisor of OIC and Disclosure Officer

In all cases there must be an OIC and a disclosure officer. If for any reason, either the OIC or the disclosure officer can no longer perform their respective tasks, para. 3.6 of the Code places a responsibility on that person's supervisor to assign another person to take over that role. It is suggested, that this requires a supervisor to know what cases their staff are involved in and who the OIC and disclosure officer is in each of those cases.

4.9.20 Definitions

Paragraph 2.1 of the Code provides definitions to be used when considering the Code and some additional guidance is provided below.

4.9.21 Relevant Material

The 1996 Act is concerned with the disclosure of material which is obtained during the course of a criminal investigation and which may be relevant to the investigation. Material can be in any form and should be widely interpreted. This applies to any material coming to the knowledge of officers involved in the case at any stage of the investigation or even after a suspect has been charged. This is material which the investigator, OIC or disclosure officer consider has some bearing on any offence being investigated or any people being investigated for those offences or any of the surrounding circumstances.

The material will be *relevant* whether it is beneficial to the prosecution case, weakens the prosecution case or assists the defence case. It is not only material that will become 'evidence' in the case that should be considered, any information, record or thing which may have a bearing on the case can be material for the purposes of disclosure. The way in which evidence has been obtained in itself may be relevant.

What is relevant to the offence is once again a question of fact and will not include everything. In *DPP* v *Metten*, 22 January 1999, unreported, it was claimed that the constables who had arrested the defendant had known the identities of potential witnesses to the arrest and these had not been disclosed. The court said that this was not relevant to the case as it did not fall within the definition of an investigation in s. 2(1) of the Criminal Proceedings and Investigations Act 1996 in that it concerned the time of arrest not what happened at the time the *offence* was committed. Paragraph 5.4 of the Code gives guidance on items that might be considered to be relevant material in a case, they include:

- crime reports (including crime report forms, relevant parts of incident report books or police officers' notebooks);
- custody records;
- records which are derived from tapes of telephone messages (for example, 999 calls) containing descriptions of an alleged offence or offender;
- final versions of witness statements (and draft versions where their content differs from the final version), including any exhibits mentioned (unless these have been returned to their owner on the understanding that they will be produced in court if required);
- interview records (written records, or audio or video tapes, of interviews with actual or potential witnesses or suspects);
- communications between the police and experts such as forensic scientists, reports of work carried out by experts, and schedules of scientific material prepared by the expert for the investigator, for the purposes of criminal proceedings;
- any material casting doubt on the reliability of a confession;
- any material casting doubt on the reliability of a witness.

Relevant material may relate to the credibility of witnesses such as previous convictions, the fact that they have a grudge against the defendant or even the weather conditions for the day if relevant to the issue of identification. It may include information that house to house inquiries were made and that no one witnessed anything.

It should be noted that where material is available to police from a particular source, e.g. local authority records, a decision that some of the material is relevant does not mean that it all has to be disclosed. This point is reinforced by the case of *R* v *Abbott* where the Court of Appeal held that the defendant was not entitled to blanket disclosure of all the files. He was certainly not entitled to documents which were not relevant to the case.

4.9.22 **Material that Undermines the Prosecution Case**

There is only limited case law in this area but it is likely that such material will consist mainly of material which raises question marks over the strength of the prosecution case, the value of evidence given by witnesses and issues relating to identification. If officers feel that the material is not relevant to the prosecution case but may be useful to the defence in cross-examination, it may well come within the category of material which undermines the prosecution case.

Disclosure of previous convictions and other matters that might affect the credibility of a witness may 'undermine the prosecution case' as it may limit the value of the witness's testimony. This factor may not be apparent at the time but may come to light after primary disclosure, such as where it becomes known that the witness has a grudge against the defendant. This is one reason why the 1996 Act requires the decision as to whether material undermines the prosecution case to be continuously monitored throughout the case. If in doubt advice should be sought from the CPS.

4.9.23   Retention of Material

Clearly in order to disclose material to the defence there is a need first to find it and secondly retain it. Retention of material applies to documents and other evidence including videos. Failure to retain material could lead to the prosecution losing the case, particularly where the court feel its absence will lead to the defendant not being able to receive a fair trial. In *Mouat* v *DPP* [2001] 1 WLR 1293 the defendant had been charged with speeding. Police officers had recorded a video of the defendant driving at speed and had showed the video to the defendant prior to charge but had later recorded over it. The defendant contended that he had been intimidated by the unmarked police car being driven only inches from his rear bumper. The policy of the force was to keep videos for 28 days, unless they recorded an offence, in which case they were kept for 12 months. The court held that the police were under a duty to retain the video tapes at least until the end of the suspended enforcement period, during which time the defendant was entitled to consider whether he wished to contest his liability in court.

In considering what material should be retained in an investigation consideration should be given to any force orders, what powers there are to seize and retain the said material, as well as the Disclosure Code and the A-G's Guidelines. Where an investigator discovers material that is relevant to the case, he/she must record that information or retain the material (Code, para. 4.1). Once again, this duty to record and retain material relevant to the case includes material that would be regarded as negative to the prosecution case (Code, para. 4.3). This does not just mean witness statements and evidence from inquiries but would include arrest notes, custody records, forensic reports, records of interview and all other material the investigator is aware of that might be relevant to the investigation. To this end, para. 5.1 of the Code places a duty on the investigator to retain all relevant material. Paragraph 5.1 of the Code states that:

> The investigator must retain material obtained in a criminal investigation which may be relevant to the investigation. This includes not only material coming into the possession of the investigator (such as documents seized in the course of searching premises) but also material generated by him (such as interview records). Material may be photographed, or retained in the form of a copy rather than the original, if the original is perishable, or was supplied to the investigator rather than generated by him and is to be returned to its owner.

Often, particularly at the early stages of an investigation (sometimes not until the defence statement is provided outlining the defence case), it will not be possible to know whether material is relevant. If in doubt it should be recorded and placed on the schedule of undisclosed material. Throughout the case, investigators and all others involved should continually review the material in the light of the investigation. Any material which becomes relevant and which has not been disclosed should be disclosed and, where it has not been retained, the OIC should be informed in order that he/she can decide what action to take (Code, para. 5.3).

When deciding if the material should be retained the A-G's Guidelines provide that: 'investigators should always err on the side of recording and retaining material where they have any doubt as to whether it may be relevant' (para. 6).

It is important to note that the material itself does not have to be admissible in court for it to undermine the prosecution case. This point was made in *R v Preston* (1994) 98 Cr App R 405, where it was said that:

> In the first place, the fact that an item of information cannot be put in evidence by a party does not mean that it is worthless. Often, the train of inquiry which leads to the discovery of evidence which is admissible at a trial may include an item which is not admissible, and this may apply, although less frequently, to the defence as well as the prosecution.

In cases where officers are in doubt as to whether material should be recorded and retained, the prosecutor should be consulted. If this cannot be done, the material should be retained and recorded. If the material is not in a format that it can be retained (for instance because it was said orally), material should be recorded in a durable and retrievable form (Code, paras 4.1 and 4.2).

If during the lifetime of a case, the OIC becomes aware that material which has been examined during the course of an investigation, but not retained, becomes relevant as a result of new developments, para. 5.3 of the Code will apply. That officer should take steps to recover the material wherever practicable, or ensure that it is preserved by the person in possession of it (JOPI Guidelines, para. 2.37).

CCTV

CCTV is becoming more prevalent in towns and cities, both from 'in store' cameras and those run through local authorities. The likelihood of an incident being caught on CCTV can be quite strong, which raises the question as to the responsibility of the police to investigate the possibility of there being a tape and retaining the tape. This point was considered in *R v Feltham Magistrates' Court, ex parte Ebrahim; Mouat v DPP* [2001] 1 WLR 1293. These cases related to the obliteration of video evidence. In coming to their judgment, the court considered a number of previous decisions where the police were not required to retain CCTV evidence. The general question for the court was whether the prosecution had been under a duty to obtain or retain video evidence. If there was no such duty, the prosecution could not have abused the process of the court simply because the material was no longer available (as to whether they were under a duty to obtain the evidence, **see 4.9.18**). The joined cases show that CCTV does not necessarily have to be retained in all cases. *R v Dobson* [2001] EWCA Crim 1606, unreported, followed *Ebrahim*. Dobson had been convicted of arson with intent to endanger life, his defence being that he was elsewhere at the time. There had been a strong possibility that the route that Dobson claimed to have taken would have been covered by CCTV but it would have depended on which side of the road he had been using and which way the cameras were pointing at the time. Dobson's solicitors had not asked for the tapes to be preserved at interview and the police confirmed that the possibility of investigating the tapes had been overlooked. The tapes had been overwritten after 31 days. In following the principles set down in *Ebrahim*, the police, by their own admissions, had failed in their duty to obtain and retain the relevant footage. Whilst there was plainly a degree of prejudice in Dobson being deprived of the opportunity of checking the footage in the hope that it supported his case, that prejudice was held not to have seriously prejudiced his case given the uncertainty of the likelihood that it would assist and the fact that Dobson had equally been in a position to appreciate the possible existence and significance of the tapes. The fact that there was no suggestion of malice or intentional omission by the police was also an important consideration for the court.

Complaints Against Police Officers Involved in a Case

Not only might the credibility of witnesses undermine the prosecution case, but so too might complaints against officers involved the case, together with any occasions where officers have not been believed in court in the past. In these cases, it will be necessary to decide whether this information should be disclosed to the defence and if disclosed, in how much detail. This question is probably best answered by the following extract from advice given to prosecutors by the Director of Public Prosecutions:

> It is, of course, necessary in the first instance for the police to bring such matters to the notice of the prosecutor, but it is submitted that the prosecutor should have a greater element of discretion than with the disclosure of previous convictions. With convictions against prosecution witnesses, disclosure normally follows, whereas in relation to disciplinary findings regard should be had to the nature of the finding and its likely relevance to the matters in issue. Findings which involve some element of dishonesty should invariably be disclosed, while matters such as disobedience to orders, neglect of duty and discreditable conduct will often have no relevance to the officer's veracity or the guilt or otherwise of a defendant. Certainly, there should be no duty on the prosecution to disclose details of unsubstantiated complaints even though this is a popular type of inquiry from some defence representatives. The imposition of such a duty would only encourage the making of false complaints in the hope that they might be used to discredit an officer in the future.

The prosecutor should be informed if officers involved in a case have discipline matters on their record. This may well appear on the schedule in order that the prosecutor can consider the matter and amend the schedule if necessary. It is suggested that advice should be sought from the prosecutor as to what information is included on the schedule and if disclosure is to be made, advice on what information to be included should also be sought.

Some guidance is given by the courts. In *R v Edwards* [1991] 2 All ER 266, the court held that a disciplinary finding and reprimand of a DCI for countersigning interview notes which had been wrongly re-written in another case should have been disclosed to the defence. *R v Guney* (1998) Cr App R 242 followed *Edwards*, in *Guney* six police officers went to the defendant's home with a warrant to search for drugs. Three of the officers had formerly been members of No. 3 Area Drugs Squad based at Stoke Newington, which had been subject to 'considerable internal police interest'. The court held that the defence was not entitled to be informed of every occasion when any officer had given evidence 'unsuccessfully' or whenever allegations were made against him/her. In this case the information should have been disclosed. The court went on to say that the records available to the CPS should include transcripts of any decisions of the Court of Appeal Criminal Division where convictions were quashed because of the misconduct or lack of veracity of identified police officers as well as cases stopped by the trial judge or discontinued on the same basis. The systematic collection of such material was preferable to the existing haphazard arrangement.

Once again, if in doubt advice should be sought from the Crown Prosecution Service.

Disclosure of Statements in Cases of Complaints against the Police

Statements made by witnesses during an investigation of a complaint against a police officer are disclosable, however the timing of the disclosure may be controlled. In *R v Police Complaints Authority, ex parte Green* (2002) *The Times*, 6 May, the Court of Appeal stated that there is no requirement to disclose witness statements to eyewitness complainants during the course of an investigation. The evidence of such complainants could be contaminated and, therefore, disclosure would risk hindering or frustrating the very purpose of the investigation. A complainant's legitimate interests were appropriately and adequately safeguarded by his/her right to a thorough and independent investigation, to contribute to the evidence, to be kept informed of the progress of the investigation and to be given reasoned conclusions on completion of the investigation. However, a complainant had no right to participate in the investigation as though he/she was supervising it. The general rule was that complainants, whether victims or next of kin, were not entitled to the disclosure of witness statements used in the course of a police investigation until its conclusion at the earliest.

Police complaints and disciplinary files may also fall within sensitive material that does not have to be disclosed (*Halford* v *Sharples* [1992] 1 WLR 736). However this would not apply to written complaints against the police prompting investigations or the actual statements obtained during the investigations, although immunity may be claimed in the case of a particular document by reason of its contents (*Chief Constable of the West Midlands Police, ex parte Wiley* [1995] 1 AC 274). However, the working papers and reports prepared by the investigating officers do form a class which is entitled to immunity, and therefore production of such material should be ordered only where the public interest in disclosure of their contents outweighs the public interest in preserving confidentiality (*Taylor* v *Anderton* [1995] 1 WLR 447).

See also JOPI, Annex A.

4.9.24 Sensitive Material

This is material which the investigator believes is not in the public interest to disclose. While the general principle that governs the 1996 Act and Article 6 of ECHR is that material should not be withheld from the defence, sensitive material is an exception to this. In *Van Mechden* v *Netherlands* (1997) 25 EHRR 647, the court stated that in some cases it may be necessary to withhold certain evidence from the defence so as to preserve the fundamental rights of another individual or to safeguard an important public interest. However, only such measures restricting the rights of the defence which are strictly necessary are permissible under Article 6. However it should be noted that the court did recognise that the entitlement of disclosure of relevant evidence was not an absolute right but could only be restricted as was strictly necessary. In *R v Keane* [1994] WLR 746 Lord Taylor CJ stated that 'the judge should carry out a balancing exercise, having regard both to the weight of the public interest in non-disclosure and to the importance of the documents to the issues of interest, present and potential, to the defence, and if the disputed material might prove a defendant's innocence or avoid a miscarriage of justice, the balance came down resoundingly in favour of disclosure'.

Decisions as to what should be withheld from the defence is a matter for the court and where necessary an application to withhold the material must be made to the court (*R v Ward* [1993] 1 WLR 619). Such applications will usually be made at the primary or secondary disclosure stages Once material is considered to be sensitive then it should only be disclosed if the pubic interest application fails (unless abandoning the case is considered more appropriate) or with the express written approval of the Treasury Solicitor. Such material is not as wide as it seems, for instance it does not mean evidence which might harm the prosecution case. This category is quite limited and the Code of Practice, at para. 6.12, gives a number of examples of such material. It will be for the disclosure officer to decide what material, if any, falls into this category.

Paragraph 6.12 states that depending on the circumstances, examples of such material may include the following among others:

- material relating to national security;
- material received from the intelligence and security agencies;
- material relating to intelligence from foreign sources which reveals sensitive intelligence gathering methods;
- material given in confidence;
- material which relates to the use of a telephone system and which is supplied to an investigator for intelligence purposes only;
- material relating to the identity or activities of informants, or under-cover police officers, or other persons supplying information to the police who may be in danger if their identities are revealed;
- material revealing the location of any premises or other place used for police surveillance, or the identity of any person allowing a police officer to use them for surveillance;

- material revealing, either directly or indirectly, techniques and methods relied upon by a police officer in the course of a criminal investigation, for example covert surveillance techniques, or other methods of detecting crime;

- material whose disclosure might facilitate the commission of other offences or hinder the prevention and detection of crime;

- internal police communications such as management minutes;

- material upon the strength of which search warrants were obtained;

- material containing details of persons taking part in identification parades;

- material supplied to an investigator during a criminal investigation which has been generated by an official of a body concerned with the regulation or supervision of bodies corporate or of persons engaged in financial activities, or which has been generated by a person retained by such a body;

- material supplied to an investigator during a criminal investigation which relates to a child or young person and which has been generated by a local authority social services department, an Area Child Protection Committee or other party contacted by an investigator during the investigation.

Many of these items are included within the common law principles of public interest immunity. The case law in this area will still apply to decisions regarding the disclosure of such material. These groups are not exclusive and the areas most likely to apply will be those concerning the protection of intelligence and intelligence methods. In any consideration as to what should be withheld the provisions of Part II of the Regulation of Investigatory Powers Act 2000 should be referred to. Part II of the Act will make provision, not only for the gathering and recording of intelligence, but also disclosure of any material gained and methods used. Claims to withhold material may be made by parties other than the prosecutor (who would do so on behalf of the police). In some cases, the relevant minister or the Attorney-General may intervene to claim immunity. Alternatively, the claim to immunity may be made by the party seeking to withhold the evidence, either on its own initiative or at the request of the relevant government department.

Guidance is also provided in paras 41 and 42 of the A-G's Guidelines, even where an application is made to the court to withhold material a prosecutor should aim to disclose as much of the material as he/she properly can (by giving the defence redacted or edited copies of summaries). *R v Davis* (1993), unreported, sets out further guidance when applying for immunity from disclosure. The court said that the procedure to be adopted in such cases depended upon the sensitivity of the material for which public interest immunity was claimed. In most cases where the prosecution sought to avoid disclosure the matter could be resolved by an *inter partes* hearing but in ultra sensitive cases the prosecution should notify the defence of an *ex parte* application which it would make. Where, however, disclosure of the category of material for which immunity was to be claimed would 'let the cat out of the bag' the prosecution might apply to the court without putting the defence on notice. Where the court ruled for non-disclosure before the hearing, the decision was not necessarily final as the situation might change and issues might emerge so that the public interest in non-disclosure was eclipsed by the need to secure fairness for the defendant. The court would therefore have to continually monitor the issue and it was desirable that the same judge who made the ruling, heard the whole case or, if that was impossible, the court must continually keep in mind the ruling which had been made. If there was such a change the prosecution must be told so that it could decide whether to disclose or offer no further evidence.

Where police consider that material should not be disclosed due to the sensitive nature the JOPI Guidelines should be followed. These are covered at paras 2.77 to 2.82.

Some of the key points from these paragraphs include:

- Consultation should take place at a senior level, and a senior officer (who may be independent of the investigation) should be involved.

- The consultation should cover:
  - the reasons why the material is said to be sensitive;
  - the degree of sensitivity said to attach to the material i.e. why it is considered that real harm would be caused to the public interest by disclosure;
  - the consequences of revealing to the defence:
    (a) the material itself,
    (b) the category of the material,
    (c) the fact that an application is being made;
  - the significance of the material to the issues in the trial;
  - the involvement of any third parties in bringing the material to the attention of the police;
  - where the material is likely to be the subject of an order for disclosure, what police views are regarding continuance of the prosecution.

- Any submission that is to be made to the c4ourt will be signed by the prosecutor, and by the senior officer, who will state that to the best of his/her knowledge and belief the assertions of fact on which the submission is based are correct.

Informants

The courts recognise the need to protect the identity of informants to ensure that the supply of information about criminal activities does not dry up and for their own safety. However there may be occasions where if the case is to continue the identity of the informant will have to be disclosed.

> ...if the judge should be of opinion that the disclosure of the name of the informant is necessary or right in order to show the prisoner's innocence, then one public policy is in conflict with another public policy, and that which says that an innocent man is not to be condemned when his innocence can be proved is the policy that must prevail. (*Marks* v *Beyfus*(1890) 25 QBD 494, per Lord Esher MR at p. 498).

This is particularly so where there is a suggestion that an informant has participated in the events constituting, surrounding or following the crime, the judge must consider whether this role so impinges on an issue of interest to the defence, present or potential, as to make disclosure necessary (*R* v *Turner* [1995] 1 WLR 264).

In *R* v *Agar* [1990] 2 All ER 442 the court held that if a defence was manifestly frivolous and doomed to failure, a trial judge might conclude that it must be sacrificed to the general public interest in the protection of informers. But if there was a tenable defence the rule of public policy protecting informants was outweighed by the stronger public interest in allowing a defendant to put forward a case. In this case the defendant alleged that the police had arranged with an informer to ask the accused to go to the informer's house, where drugs allegedly found on him had been planted by the police and the court ruled that the disclosure of the informant should have been made.

The need to disclose details of informants has been considered by the Court of Appeal in two recent cases. The first case, *R* v *Denton* [2002] EWCA Crim 72, concerned a defendant who was a police informer. The defendant was charged with murder and alleged that he had been told by his police handlers not to tell his lawyers about his status. The Court held that there was no duty for the Crown to disclose to the defence, nor to seek a ruling from the judge, as to any information regarding an accused being a police informer. On any common sense view the material had already been disclosed to the defendant and the Crown had no duty to supply the defendant with information with which he was already familiar. This last point may also be relevant to other situations. The second case, *R* v *Dervish* [2001] EWCA Crim 2789, unreported, concerned an undercover operation that was commenced after an informant gave information. The court held in this case that the public interest in protecting the identification of an informant had to be balanced against the right of the defendant to a fair trial, if there was material that might assist the defence, the necessity for the defendant to have a fair trial would outweigh the other interests in the case and the material would have to be disclosed or the prosecution discontinued. There had been no such material in this case.

Observation Points and the *Johnson* Ruling

R v Rankine [1986] 2 WLR 1075 considering previous cases stated that it was the rule that police officers should not be required to disclose sources of their information, whether those sources were paid informers or public spirited citizens, subject to a discretion to admit to avoid a miscarriage of justice and that observation posts were in this rule.

In *R v Johnson* [1988] 1 WLR 1377, the appellant was convicted of supplying drugs. The only evidence against him was given by police officers, who testified that, while stationed in private premises in a known drug-dealing locality, they had observed him selling drugs. The defence applied to cross-examine the officers on the exact location of the observation posts, in order to test what they could see, having regard to the layout of the street and the objects in it. In the jury's absence the prosecution called evidence as to the difficulty of obtaining assistance from the public, and the desire of the occupiers, who were also occupiers at the time of the offence, that their names and addresses should not be disclosed because they feared for their safety.

The judge ruled that the exact location of the premises need not be revealed. The appeal was dismissed; although the conduct of the defence was to some extent affected by the restraints placed on it, this led to no injustice. The jury were well aware of the restraints, and were most carefully directed about the very special care they had to give to any disadvantage they may have brought to the defence. *Johnson* was applied and approved in *R v Hewitt* (1992) 95 Cr App R 81 (see also *R v Grimes* [1994] Crim LR 213).

In *Johnson* Watkins LJ at pp. 1385–6 gave the following guidance as to the minimum evidential requirements needed if disclosure is to be protected:

(a) The police officer in charge of the observations to be conducted, no one of lower rank than a sergeant should usually be acceptable for this purpose, must be able to testify that beforehand he visited all observation places to be used and ascertained the attitude of occupiers of premises, not only to the use to be made of them, but to the possible disclosure thereafter of the use made and facts which could lead to the identification of the premises thereafter and of the occupiers. He may of course in addition inform the court of difficulties, if any, usually encountered in the particular locality of obtaining assistance from the public.

(b) A police officer of no lower rank than a chief inspector must be able to testify that immediately prior to the trial he visited the places used for observations, the results of which it is proposed to give in evidence, and ascertained whether the occupiers are the same as when the observations took place and whether they are or are not, what the attitude of those occupiers is to the possible disclosure of the use previously made of the premises and of facts which could lead at the trial to identification of premises and occupiers.

Such evidence will of course be given in the absence of the jury when the application to exclude the material evidence is made. The judge should explain to the jury, as this judge did, when summing up or at some appropriate time before that, the effect of his ruling to exclude, if he so rules.

The guidelines in *Johnson* do not require a threat of violence before protection can be afforded to the occupier of an observation post; it suffices if the occupier is in fear of harassment (*Blake v DPP* (1993) 97 Cr App R 169).

This extended the rules established in *R v Rankine* [1986] QB 861 and is based on the protection of the owner or occupier of the premises, and not on the identity of the observation post. Thus, where officers have witnessed the commission of an offence as part of a surveillance operation conducted from an unmarked police vehicle, information relating to the surveillance and the colour, make and model of the vehicle should not be withheld (*R* v *Brown* (1987) 87 Cr App R 52). Hodgson J said in *Brown*:

> We do not rule out the possibility that with the advent of sophisticated methods of criminal investigation, there may be cases where the public interest immunity may be successfully invoked in criminal proceedings to justify the exclusion of evidence as to police techniques and methods. But if and when such an argument is to be raised, it must, in the judgment of this court, be done properly.... It would seem clear that if such a contention is put forward the judge must be given as much information as possible and the application will have to be supported, not by the instructions of the junior officer in charge of the case, but by the independent evidence of senior officers.

4.9.25 Third Party Material

Third party material can be considered in two categories:

(a) that which is or has been in the possession of the police or which has been inspected by the police;

(b) all other material not falling under (a).

Material that which falls into the first category is covered by the same rules of disclosure as any other material the police have. Where police do not have material that they believe may be relevant to the case, para. 3.5 of the Code provides that:

> If the officer in charge of an investigation believes that other persons may be in possession of material that may be relevant to the investigation, and if this has not been obtained under paragraph 3.4 above, he should ask the disclosure officer to inform them of the existence of the investigation and to invite them to retain the material in case they receive a request for its disclosure. The disclosure officer should inform the prosecutor that they may have such material. However, the officer in charge of an investigation is not required to make speculative enquiries of other persons: there must be some reason to believe that they may have relevant material. That reason may come from information provided to the police by the accused or from other inquiries made or from some other source.

In the vast majority of cases the third party will make the material available to the investigating officer. However, there may be occasions where the third party refuses to hand over the material and/or allow it to be examined.

If the OIC, the investigator or the disclosure officer believes that a third party holds material that may be relevant to the investigation, that person or body should be told of the investigation. They should be alerted to the need to preserve relevant material. Consideration should be given as to whether it is appropriate to seek access to the material, and if so, steps should be taken to obtain such material. It will be important to do so if the material or information is likely to undermine the prosecution case, or to assist a known defence. A letter should be sent to the third party together with the explanatory leaflet, specimens of which are provided in the JOPI Guidelines at Annex J.

Where access to the material is declined or refused by the third party and it is believed that it is reasonable to seek production of the material before a suspect is charged, the investigator should consider making an application under sch. 1 of the Police and Criminal Evidence Act 1984 (special procedure material). The investigator may seek advice of the prosecutor before such an application is made (JOPI Guidelines, para. 2.45).

Where the suspect has been charged and the third party refuses to produce the material then in these cases application will have to be made to the court for a witness summons. In the magistrates' court this is covered by s. 97(1) of the Magistrates' Courts Act 1980 and in the crown court it is covered by s. 2(2) of the Criminal Procedure (Attendance of Witnesses) Act 1965. The third party may still wish to resist the requirement to produce the material and the point was considered in *R* v *Brushett* [2001] Crim LR 471 (this was a case that concerned Social Services Department files relating to a children's home). The court considered a number of earlier cases and established some central principles as follows:

- To be material evidence documents must be not only relevant to the issues arising in the criminal proceedings, but also documents admissible as such in evidence.

- Documents which are desired merely for the purpose of possible cross-examination are not admissible in evidence and, thus, are not material for the purposes of s. 97.

- Whoever seeks production of documents must satisfy the justices with some material that the documents are 'likely to be material' in the sense indicated, likelihood for this purpose involving a real possibility, although not necessarily a probability.

- It is not sufficient that the applicant merely wants to find out whether or not the third party has such material documents. This procedure must not be used as a disguised attempt to obtain discovery.

- Where social services documents are supplied to the prosecution, the prosecution should retain control of such material as part of the disclosure regime. That is envisaged by the rules. It cannot be acceptable to return material to social services to avoid the obligations arising under the rules. In any event, the obligation would arise in relation to the notes taken and retained.

- The obligation laid on the prosecution by statute and rules cannot be avoided by a third party making an agreement with the prosecution that the prosecution will abrogate any duties laid upon it by either common law or statute.

- If circumstances arise where it would be unjust not to allow disclosure of certain other material, so a defendant would not receive a fair trial, in the sense that he/she could not establish his innocence where he/she might otherwise do so, then that material must be disclosed.

- The fact that the prosecution have knowledge of the third party material may be a relevant factor to allow the defence access.

- Material concerning false allegations in the past may be relevant material.

- If the disputed material might prove the defendant's innocence or avoid a miscarriage of justice, the weight came down resoundingly in favour of disclosing it. (*R* v *Reading Justices, ex parte Berkshire County Council* (1996) 1 Cr App R 239).

The A-G's Guidelines also deal with materials held by third parties (including government agencies) in paras 29 to 33. Paragraph 29 deals with material held by Government departments or other Crown bodies and suggests that reasonable steps should be taken to identify and consider material that may be relevant to an issue in the case. Paragraph 30 examines the circumstances in which the prosecution should take steps to obtain access to material or information in the possession of other third parties. In such cases consideration should be given to take steps to obtain such material or information. It will be important to do so if the material or information is likely to undermine the prosecution case, or assist a known defence. Paragraph 31 deals with the situation where the police or prosecutor meet with a refusal by the third party to supply such material or information. If, despite the reasons put forward for refusal by the third party, it still appears reasonable to seek its production, a witness summons requiring the third party to produce the material should be applied for (such an application can also be made by the defence). The third party can then argue at court that it is not material, or that it should not be disclosed on grounds of public interest immunity.

4.9.26 Confidentiality

The defence may only use material disclosed to them under the 1996 Act for purposes related to the defence case; any other use will be a contempt of court. Once evidence has been given in open court, however, the material is available for other purposes.

4.9.27 Retention Periods

Material must be retained in all cases until a decision is taken whether to institute proceedings against a person for an offence. Where a decision is taken to institute proceedings material must then be retained until the case has been dealt with. The Code gives specific guidance in cases where a person is convicted as to how long material must be retained for. Paragraphs 5.6 to 5.10 set out the retention periods where a person has been convicted. All material which may be relevant must be retained at least until:

- the person is released from custody or discharged from hospital in cases where the court imposes a custodial sentence or hospital order;
- in all other cases, for six months from the date of conviction.

If the person is released from the custodial sentence or discharged from hospital earlier than six months from the date of conviction, the material must be retained for at least six months from the date of conviction. If an appeal is in progress at the end of one of these periods, or an application is being considered by the Criminal Cases Review Commission, the period is extended until:

- the appeal is concluded; or
- the Commission decide not to refer the application to the Court of Appeal; or
- the Court of Appeal determines the appeal resulting from the reference.

In these cases, if material was seized from its owner it may be returned (Code, para. 5.10).

Where material has been seized under the powers provided by the Police and Criminal Evidence Act 1984, para. 5.2 confirms that retention of the material should reflect the provisions of s. 22 of the 1984 Act.

4.10 Documentary Records and Business Documents

4.10.1 Documentary Records

Section 23 of the Criminal Justice Act 1988 states:

(1) Subject—
    (a) to subsection (4) below; and
    (b) to paragraph 1A of Schedule 2 to the Criminal Appeal Act 1968 (evidence given orally at original trial to be given orally at retrial),
    a statement made by a person in a document shall be admissible in criminal proceedings as evidence of any fact of which direct oral evidence by him would be admissible if—
    (i) the requirements of one of the paragraphs of subsection (2) below are satisfied; or
    (ii) the requirements of subsection (3) below are satisfied.

(2) The requirement mentioned in subsection (1)(i) above are—
    (a) that the person who made the statement is dead or by reason of his bodily or mental condition unfit to attend as a witness;
    (b) that—
        (i) the person who made the statement is outside the United Kingdom; and
        (ii) it is not reasonably practicable to secure his attendance; or

    (c) that all reasonable steps have been taken to find the person who made the statement, but that he cannot be found.

(3) The requirements mentioned in subsection (1)(ii) above are—

    (a) that the statement was made to a police officer or some other person charged with the duty of investigating offences or charging offenders; and

    (b) that the person who made it does not give oral evidence through fear or because he is kept out of the way.

(4) Subsection (1) above does not render admissible a confession made by an accused person that would not be admissible under section 76 of the Police and Criminal Evidence Act 1984.

KEYNOTE

In *Trivedi* v *United Kingdom* (1997) 89A DR 136, it was held not to be a violation of Article 6 of the European Convention on Human Rights (right to a fair trial) where an elderly witness's statement was read out due to his deteriorating intellect.

Subject to s. 23(1)(a) to (c), a statement made by a person in a document shall be admissible if any one of the requirements detailed in s. 23(2) is satisfied, or both of the requirements detailed in s. 23(3) are satisfied.

In relation to s. 23(3)(b), it was held in *R* v *H* [2001] Crim LR 815, that a statement made by a witness to a police officer or other individual with a duty to investigate crime is admissible when the witness does not give evidence personally through fear.

In relation to s. 23(2)(c), where a witness cannot be found and their statement is read out in court, the judge is required to make the jury aware of the drawbacks for the defence and to explain the significance of having the evidence tested and the importance of cross-examination (*R* v *McCoy* [1999] All ER (D) 1410; [2002] 6 *Arch News* 2).

14.10.2   Business Documents

Section 24 of the Criminal Justice Act 1988 states:

(1) Subject—

    (a) to subsections (3) and (4) below; and

    (b) to paragraph 1A of Schedule 2 to the Criminal Appeal Act 1968, and

    (c) to section 69 of the Police and Criminal Evidence Act 1984,

    a statement in a document shall be admissible in criminal proceedings as evidence of any fact of which direct oral evidence would be admissible, if the following conditions are satisfied—

        (i) the document was created or received by a person in the course of a trade, business, profession or other occupation, or as the holder of a paid or unpaid office; and

        (ii) the information contained in the document was supplied by a person (whether or not the maker of the statement) who had, or may reasonably be supposed to have had, personal knowledge of the matters dealt with.

(2) Subsection (1) above applies whether the information contained in the document was supplied directly or indirectly but, if it was supplied indirectly, only if each person through whom it was supplied received it—

    (a) in the course of a trade, business, profession or other occupation; or

    (b) as the holder of a paid or unpaid office.

(3) Subsection (1) above does not render admissible a confession made by an accused person that would not be admissible under section 76 of the Police and Criminal Evidence Act 1984.

(4) A statement prepared otherwise than in accordance with section 3 of the Criminal Justice (International Co-operation) Act 1990 below or an order under paragraph 6 of Schedule 13 to this Act or under section 30 or 31 . . . for the purposes—

    (a) of pending or contemplated criminal proceedings; or

    (b) of a criminal investigation,

shall not be admissible by virtue of subsection (1) above unless—

   (i)   the requirements of one of the paragraphs of subsection (2) of section 23 above are satisfied; or

   (ii) the requirements of subsection (3) of that section are satisfied; or

   (iii) the person who made the statement cannot reasonably be expected (having regard to the time which has elapsed since he made the statement and all the circumstances) to have any recollection of the matters dealt with in the statement.

KEYNOTE

Subject to the provisions of s. 24(1)(a) to (c), a statement in a document will be admissible if both conditions (i) and (ii) of subsection (1) are satisfied. A statement:

- other than a statement obtained on request outside the United Kingdom (s. 3 of the Criminal Justice (International Co-operation) Act 1990),

- for use in a Service court (sch. 13 of the 1988 Act),

- an expert's report (s. 30), or

- provision of material to help members of a jury to understand complicated issues or technical terms (s. 31),

will only be admissible if one of the requirements of (i) to (iii) of s. 24(4) are satisfied.

4.11   Criminal Justice Act 1967, Sections 9 and 10

4.11.1   Admissibility of Written Statements in Summary Proceedings

Section 9 of the Criminal Justice Act 1967 states:

(1) In any criminal proceedings, other than [committal proceedings], a written statement by any person shall, if such of the conditions mentioned in the next following subsection as are applicable are satisfied, be admissible as evidence to the like extent as oral evidence to the like effect by that person.

(2) The said conditions are—

   (a) the statement purports to be signed by the person who made it;

   (b) the statement contains a declaration by the person to the effect that it is true to the best of his knowledge and belief and that he made the statement knowing that, if it were tendered in evidence, he would be liable to prosecution if he wilfully stated in it anything which he knew to be false or did not believe to be true;

   (c) before the hearing at which the statement is tendered in evidence, a copy of the statement is served, by or on behalf of the party proposing to tender it, on each of the other parties to the proceedings; and

   (d) none of the other parties or their solicitors, within seven days from the service of the copy of the statement, serves a notice on the party so proposing objecting to the statement being tendered in evidence under this section:

Provided that the conditions mentioned in paragraphs (c) and (d) of this subsection shall not apply if the parties agree before or during the hearing that the statement shall be so tendered.

KEYNOTE

The declaration at s. 9(2)(b) need not be separately signed.

Note that s. 9(2)(c) and (d) need not apply if the parties so agree before or during the hearing. In other words, a statement can still be tendered in evidence even though the other parties have not had copies or the seven-day requirement has not been observed.

Section 9 goes on to state:

(3) The following provisions shall also have effect in relation to any written statement tendered in evidence under this section, that is to say—

   (a) if the statement is made by a person under the age of [eighteen], it shall give his age;

   (b) if it is made by a person who cannot read it, it shall be read to him before he signs it and shall be accompanied by a declaration by the person who so read the statement to the effect that it was so read; and

   (c) if it refers to any other document as an exhibit, the copy served on any other party to the proceedings under paragraph (c) of the last foregoing subsection shall be accompanied by a copy of that document or by such information as may be necessary in order to enable the party on whom it is served to inspect that document or a copy thereof.

(4) Notwithstanding that a written statement made by any person may be admissible as evidence by virtue of this section—

   (a) the party by whom or on whose behalf a copy of the statement was served may call that person to give evidence; and

   (b) the court may, of its own motion or on the application of any party to the proceedings, require that person to attend before the court and give evidence.

(5) ...

(6) So much of any statement as is admitted in evidence by virtue of this section shall, unless the court otherwise directs, be read aloud at the hearing and where the court so directs an account shall be given orally of so much of any statement as is not read aloud.

(7) Any document or object referred to as an exhibit and identified in a written statement tendered in evidence under this section shall be treated as if it had been produced as an exhibit and identified in court by the maker of the statement.

(8) A document required by this section to be served on any person may be served by—

   (a) delivering it to him or to his solicitor; or

   (b) by addressing it to him or leaving it at his usual or last known place of abode or place of business or by addressing it to his solicitor and leaving it at his office; or

   (c) by sending it in a registered letter or by recorded delivery service or by first class post addressed to him at his usual or last known place of abode or place of business or addressed to his solicitor at his office; or

   (d) in the case of a body corporate, by delivering it to the secretary or clerk of the body at its registered or principal office or sending it in a registered letter or by the recorded delivery service or by first class post addressed to the secretary or clerk of that body at that office.

KEYNOTE

The provisions of s. 9 of the Criminal Justice Act 1967, had a major impact on both witness's time (particularly the police) and the cost of court cases. The section allows for evidence to be admitted without the necessity of physically calling the witness who gave the statement.

Victim Personal Statements

On 1 October 2001; the victim personal statements scheme was introduced by the Lord Chief Justice (*Practice Direction (CA Crim Div): Victim Personal Statements*) [2001] 1 WLR 2038). This scheme gives victims of crime the opportunity to provide a statement saying how the crime has affected them and enables the court to take the statement into account when determining sentence.

When taking a statement from a victim a police officer is required to inform the victim of the scheme. The decision as to whether to make such a statement is entirely a matter for the victim. A victim personal statement may be made or updated at any time prior to the disposal of the case.

4.11.2 **Formal Admissions**

Where a fact is accepted by the defence, there is a process by which this can be formally admitted under s. 10 of the Criminal Justice Act 1967. In such formal admissions the fact ceases to be an issue.

Section 10 states:

(1) Subject to the provisions of this section, any fact of which oral evidence may be given in any criminal proceedings may be admitted for the purpose of those proceedings by or on behalf of the prosecutor or defendant, and the admission by any party of any such fact under this section shall as against that party be conclusive evidence in those proceedings of the fact admitted.

(2) An admission under this section—
   (a) may be made before or at the proceedings;
   (b) if made otherwise than in court, shall be in writing;
   (c) if made in writing by an individual, shall purport to be signed by the person making it and, if so made by a body corporate, shall purport to be signed by a director or manager, or the secretary or clerk, or some other similar officer of the body corporate;
   (d) if made on behalf of a defendant who is an individual, shall be made by his counsel or solicitor;
   (e) if made at any stage before the trial by a defendant who is an individual, must be approved by his counsel or solicitor (whether at the time it was made or subsequently) before or at the proceedings in question.

(3) An admission under this section for the purpose of proceedings relating to any matter shall be treated as an admission for the purpose of any subsequent criminal proceedings relating to that matter (including any appeal or retrial).

(4) An admission under this section may with the leave of the court be withdrawn in the proceedings for the purpose of which it is made or any subsequent criminal proceedings relating to the same matter.

KEYNOTE

Where the accused enters a not guilty plea at a plea directions hearing, both the prosecution and defence are expected to inform the court of facts which are to be admitted and which are then accepted in written form in accordance with s. 10(2)(b) of the 1967 Act (see *Practice Direction (Crown Court: Plea and Directions Hearings)* [1995] 1 WLR 1318, para. 10(f)).

Formal admission may be made by counsel or a solicitor during court proceedings. In such cases the admission is written down and signed by or on behalf of the party making the admission. This procedure applies for the purpose of summary trial or proceedings before magistrates acting as examining justices (r. 71 of the Magistrates' Courts Rules 1981).

4.12 Criminal Justice and Public Order Act 1994, Sections 34–37

Having considered the various elements of a wide range of offences it is now necessary to turn to the means by which those offences may be proved—or disproved. Although the earlier sections dealing with substantive offences considered some evidential aspects, it is important to address the basics of evidence here. Evidence can be described as information that may be presented to a court so that it may decide on the probability of some facts asserted before it, that is information by which facts in issue can be proved or disproved. There are several types of evidence by which facts are open to proof—or disproof—and these are discussed below.

4.12.1 **Weight and Admissibility of Evidence**

The three questions that need to be applied to any evidence are:

- is it admissible?
- if so, for what purpose(s)?
- what weight will it carry?

The question of admissibility, to be decided by the judge in all cases, is whether the evidence is relevant to a fact in issue. All evidence of facts in issue and all evidence which is sufficiently relevant to prove (or disprove) facts in issue are potentially admissible.

The admissibility of evidence is very important to the outcome of any trial as it is from this that a person's guilt is decided. When collecting evidence in a case it should always be a consideration whether the evidence being collected is the best available, whether it will be admissible and, if so, for what purpose.

However, once it is established that evidence is admissible, it is put before the court to determine what weight to attach to the evidence; that is, how much effect does it have on proving or disproving the case? And although there is a tendency when studying this subject to concentrate on admissibility, the weight of any evidence is just as important.

Evidence Gathering

The word evidence must not be confused with information. In relation to preparing an offence file, the investigation of the offence will result in the collection of information. What is and what is not evidence can be decided at a later stage with the help of the Crown Prosecution Service. The importance of this distinction is that rules of evidence should not restrict the initial collection of information, otherwise a fact vital to the outcome of the case may be disregarded as irrelevant and/or inadmissible and criminal intelligence may be lost.

Reasons for Excluding Admissible Evidence

Even though evidence may be admissible in criminal cases, at common law, the trial judge has a general discretion to exclude legally admissible evidence tendered by the prosecution. This can be seen in *R* v *Sang* [1980] AC 402, where it was held that:

- A trial judge, as part of his/her duty to ensure that an accused receives a fair trial, always has a discretion to exclude evidence tendered by the prosecution if in his/her opinion its prejudicial effect outweighs its probative value. In deciding if the evidence should be admitted, the question the judge asks him/herself is whether it is fair to allow the evidence not whether it is obtained fairly or by unfair means.

- With the exception of admissions and confessions and generally with regard to evidence obtained from the accused after the commission of the offence (here s. 76 of PACE applies), the judge has no discretion whether to exclude relevant admissible evidence on the ground that this was obtained by improper or unfair means.

Evidence may also be excluded for the following reasons:

- the incompetence of the witness;
- it relates to previous convictions, the character or disposition of the accused;
- it falls under hearsay;
- it is non-expert opinion evidence;

- it is privileged information;
- it is withheld as a matter of public policy.

There is also a power to exclude evidence under ss. 76 and 78 of the Police and Criminal Evidence Act 1984.

4.12.2 Facts in Issue

In a criminal case, facts in issue are those facts which must be proved by the prosecution in order to establish the defendant's guilt, or those facts which are the essential elements of a defence.

Such facts will include:

- the identity of the defendant;
- the *actus reus*;
- any necessary knowledge or intent.

The relevant criminal conduct (*actus reus*) and state of mind (*mens rea*) will always be facts in issue, and it is therefore essential that these features are understood, both as general concepts and also in relation to the particular offence being investigated.

4.12.3 Burden of Proof

The facts in issue fall into two distinct categories:

- The facts that the *prosecution* bear the burden of proving or disproving in order to establish the defendant's guilt;
- the facts which, in exceptional circumstances, the *defence* need to prove to show that the defendant is not guilty.

Duty of the Prosecution

'Throughout the web of the English criminal law one golden thread is always to be seen; that is the duty of the prosecution to prove the prisoner's guilt.' This famous passage is taken from the House of Lords' decision in *Woolmington* v *DPP* [1935] AC 462. The underlying principle was perhaps best explained by Geoffrey Lawrence QC in an address to the jury in a murder trial:

> The possibility of guilt is not enough, suspicion is not enough, probability is not enough, likelihood is not. A criminal matter is not a question of balancing probabilities and deciding in favour of probability.

> If the accusation is not proved beyond reasonable doubt against the man accused in the dock, then by the law he is entitled to be acquitted, because that is the way our rules work. It is no concession to give him the benefit of the doubt. He is entitled by law to a verdict of not guilty.

(See Brian Harris, *The Literature of the Law*, Blackstone Press, 1998.)

Therefore the duty to prove guilt is always on the prosecution. The standard of proof *is beyond all reasonable doubt*.

In *Evans* v *DPP* (2001) *The Times*, 9 July, it was held that the justices had applied *the balance of probabilities* in finding the defendant guilty rather than the criminal standard of proof.

Where the defendant enters a plea of not guilty to the charge, the onus is on the prosecution to prove the whole of their case. This includes 'the identity of the accused, the nature of the act and the existence of any necessary knowledge or intent' (*R* v *Sims* [1946] KB 531).

Generally the onus is on the prosecution in the first instance to establish particular facts to prove the accused's guilt beyond all reasonable doubt. However, once a prima facie case is made out, the defence has to establish particular facts in order to rebut the prosecution evidence. Here there is a shift of the onus to establish particular facts.

Article 6(2) of the European Convention on Human Rights guarantees the right to everyone charged with a criminal offence to be 'presumed innocent until proved guilty according to law'. It follows from this that the burden of proof in criminal proceedings is on the prosecution (*Austria* v *Italy* (1963) 6 YB 740). In a more recent European Court of Human Rights case it was held that a court could not convict an individual solely on the grounds that he/she has failed to prove his/her innocence; it was the duty of the prosecution to prove the accused's guilt (*Bundesgericht* (2001) SJZ 200).

Duty on the Defence

The standard of proof for the defence is less rigorous than for the prosecution when establishing guilt (beyond all reasonable doubt). The defence will succeed if the court or jury are satisfied that the defence evidence is more probably true than false. This standard of proof is referred to as *the balance of probabilities*.

Generally the prosecution bear the duty of proving or disproving certain facts and, if they fail to do so, the defence need say nothing; the prosecution fails and the defendant is acquitted.

In a number of cases, however, the particular statute may impose a burden on the defence to prove certain facts. In these cases, it is said that an *evidential* burden is placed upon the defendant. This does not mean that the defendant has to show that he/she did not commit the offence. That would be contrary to the presumption of innocence that is imposed by both the common law (see *Woolmington* above) and also Article 6 of the European Convention on Human Rights. What it means, in the words of Lord Steyn in *R* v *Lambert* [2001] 3 WLR 206, is that: '...the accused must...put evidence before the court which, if believed, could be taken by a reasonable jury to support his defence'.

This evidential burden can be seen in many cases, e.g. the law relating to the carrying of weapons. Once the prosecution have proved (beyond a reasonable doubt) that a defendant was carrying an offensive weapon, the burden then shifts to the defence to prove (on the balance of probabilities) that he/she had lawful authority or reasonable excuse.

In the area of human rights, Strasbourg's position appears to complement the UK's domestic law in relation to duties on the prosecution and defence. In the first instance the duty to prove guilt is clearly on the prosecution (*Austria* v *Italy* (1963) 6 YB 740). However, where the accused is seeking to establish a specific defence, the burden of proof may transfer from the prosecution to the defence (*Lingens* v *Austria* (1981) 4 EHRR 373).

4.12.4 Inferences from Silence

At common law, when being questioned about involvement in a criminal offence, a person is under no obligation to answer any of the questions. This is another key feature of the criminal justice system in England and Wales and is the reason behind the cautioning of suspects required by the Police and Criminal Evidence Act 1984. However, ss. 34 to 38 of the Criminal Justice and Public Order Act 1994, now contain the substance of the law in relation to the accused's silence.

Sections 34 to 37 permit the court to draw 'such inferences as appear proper' against the accused in the circumstances contained within the sections.

4.12.5   **Inferences from Silence when Questioned or Charged**

Section 34 of the Criminal Justice and Public Order Act 1994 provides that inferences can be drawn if, when questioned by the police under caution, charged or officially informed that he/she may be prosecuted, the accused fails to mention a fact on which he/she later relies in his defence, and which he/she could reasonably have been expected to mention at the time. Section 34 states:

(1)   Where, in any proceedings against a person for an offence, evidence is given that the accused—
   (a) at any time before he was charged with the offence, on being questioned under caution by a constable trying to discover whether or by whom the offence had been committed, failed to mention any fact relied on in his defence in those proceedings, or
   (b) on being charged with the offence or officially informed that he might be prosecuted for it, failed to mention any such fact,
   being a fact which in the circumstances existing at the time the accused could reasonably have been expected to mention when so questioned, charged or informed, as the case may be, subsection (2) below applies.

(2)   Where this subsection applies—
   (a) a magistrates' court inquiring into the offence as examining justices;
   (b) a judge, in deciding whether to grant an application made by the accused under—
      (i)   section 6 of the Criminal Justice Act 1987 (application for dismissal of charge of serious fraud in respect of which notice of transfer has been given under section 4 of the Act); or
      (ii) paragraph 5 of Schedule 6 to the Criminal Justice Act 1991 (application for dismissal of charge of violent or sexual offence involving child in respect of which notice of transfer has been given under section 53 of that Act);
   (c) the court, in determining whether there is a case to answer; and
   (d) the court or jury, in determining whether the accused is guilty of the offence charged, may draw such inferences from the failure as appear proper.

(2A) Where the accused was at an authorised place of detention at the time of the failure, subsections (1) and (2) above do not apply if he had not been allowed an opportunity to consult a solicitor prior to being questioned, charged or informed as mentioned in subsection (1) above.

(3)   Subject to any directions by the court, evidence tending to establish the failure may be given before or after evidence tending to establish the fact which the accused is alleged to have failed to mention.

(4)   This section applies in relation to questioning by persons (other than constables) charged with the duty of investigating offences or charging offenders as it applies in relation to questioning by constables; and in subsection (1) above 'officially informed' means informed by a constable or any such person.

(5)   This section does not—
   (a) prejudice the admissibility in evidence of the silence or other reaction of the accused in the face of anything said in his presence relating to the conduct in respect of which he is charged, in so far as evidence thereof would be admissible apart from this section; or
   (b) preclude the drawing of any inference from any such silence or other reaction of the accused which could properly be drawn apart from this section.

(6)   This section does not apply in relation to a failure to mention a fact if the failure occurred before the commencement of this section.

KEYNOTE

A judgment of the European Court of Human Rights in the case of *Murray v United Kingdom* (1996) 22 EHRR 29 directly lead to the introduction of s. 34(2A) by the Youth Justice and Criminal Evidence Act 1999. The court held that inferences being drawn from the silence of an accused when denied access to legal advice constituted a breach of Article 6(1) in conjunction with Article 6(3) of the European Convention on Human Rights (right to a fair trial).

Where a defendant says that advice was received from his/her solicitor not to answer questions, the accused is entitled to give evidence of the conversation with the solicitor prior to interview to rebut any allegation of post-interview fabrication. The defendant is also entitled to call the solicitor to give evidence of the advice given before interview (*R* v *Daniel* (1998) 162 JP 578).

In *R* v *Argent* (1997) 2 Cr App R 27, the court stated that personal factors which might be relevant to an assessment of what an individual could reasonably have been expected to mention were age, experience, mental capacity, state of health, sobriety, tiredness and personality.

In *R* v *Flynn* (2001) *The Times*, 8 June, the court held that the police are entitled to conduct a second interview with a suspect, having obtained evidence from their witnesses which was not available in the first interview, and adverse inference could be drawn from the suspect's silence.

Section 34 differs from the other 'inference' sections in that the questioning need not occur at a police station and therefore the presence of a legal representative is not required. However, it appears clear that, should the prosecution seek to draw any inferences of an accused's silence where such questioning has occurred, the questions would need to be asked of the suspect again once he/she had access to legal advice.

A requirement to caution the person is contained in s. 34(1)(a) to make it clear of the risks connected with a failure to mention facts which later form part of the defence.

In relation to s. 34, the accused cannot be convicted solely on an inference drawn from a failure or refusal (s. 38(3) of the 1994 Act) (see **4.12.9**).

Guidance has been provided by the government (Home Office Circular 53/1998). This requires that where access to legal advice has been delayed in accordance with Annex B of PACE Code C (**see appendix 3**), the procedures for conducting the interview at the police station should be as follows:

- the interviewing officer should conduct any interview with the suspect at the police station in accordance with PACE Code C, para. 11.2A;

- the interviewing officer should make a written note of those questions which the suspect has failed or refused to answer;

- once the suspect has had the opportunity of access to legal advice, the interviewing officer should put these questions to the suspect again; and ask the suspect whether he/she wishes to say/add anything further.

4.12.6 Inferences from Silence at Trial

Section 35 of the Criminal Justice and Public Order Act 1994 provides that inferences can be drawn from an accused's failure to give evidence or refusal to answer any question, without good cause, where the person has been sworn. Section 35 states:

(1) At the trial of any person who has attained the age of fourteen years for an offence, subsections (2) and (3) below apply unless—
   (a) the accused's guilt is not in issue; or
   (b) it appears to the court that the physical or mental condition of the accused makes it undesirable for him to give evidence;
   but subsection (2) below does not apply if, at the conclusion of the evidence for the prosecution, his legal representative informs the court that the accused will give evidence or, where he is unrepresented, the court ascertains from him that he will give evidence.

(2) Where this subsection applies, the court shall, at the conclusion of the evidence for the prosecution, satisfy itself (in the case of proceedings on indictment, in the presence of the jury) that the accused is aware that the stage has been reached at which evidence can be given for the defence and that he can, if he wishes, give evidence and that, if he chooses not to give evidence, or having been sworn, without good cause refuses to answer any question, it will be permissible for the court or jury to draw such inferences as appear proper from his failure to give evidence or his refusal, without good cause, to answer any question.

(3) Where this subsection applies, the court or jury, in determining whether the accused is guilty of the offence charged, may draw such inferences as appear proper from the failure of the accused to give evidence or his refusal, without good cause, to answer any question.

(4) This section does not render the accused compellable to give evidence on his own behalf, and he shall accordingly not be guilty of contempt of court by reason of a failure to do so.

(5) For the purposes of this section a person who, having been sworn, refuses to answer any question shall be taken to do so without good cause unless—
   (a) he is entitled to refuse to answer the question by virtue of any enactment, whenever passed or made, or on the ground of privilege; or
   (b) the court in the exercise of its general discretion excuses him from answering it.

(6) Where the age of any person is material for the purposes of subsection (1) above, his age shall for those purposes be taken to be that which appears to the court to be his age.

(7) This section applies—
   (a) in relation to proceedings on indictment for an offence, only if the person charged with the offence is arraigned on or after the commencement of this section;
   (b) in relation to proceedings in a magistrates' court, only if the time when the court begins to receive evidence in the proceedings falls after the commencement of this section.

KEYNOTE

Section 35 only applies to a person who has attained the age of 14 years; this is not contained in the other 'inference' sections. This also applies to those whose 'physical or mental condition make it undesirable' for them to give evidence. However, there are rare cases where this may not apply.

In *R* v *Friend* [1997] 1 WLR 1433, the accused was aged 15 with a mental age of nine and an IQ of 63. It was held that the accused's mental condition did not make it 'undesirable' for him to give evidence and it was right that inferences be drawn under s. 35(3).

As with s. 34, in relation to s. 35 the accused cannot be convicted solely on an inference drawn from a failure or refusal (s. 38(3)) (see **4.12.9**).

4.12.7   **Inferences from Silence: Failure to Account for Objects, Substances and Marks**

Section 36 of the Criminal Justice and Public Order Act 1994 provides that inferences can be drawn from an accused's failure to give evidence or refusal to answer any question about any object, substance or mark which may be attributable to the accused in the commission of an offence.

Section 36 states:

(1) Where—
   (a) a person is arrested by a constable, and there is—
      (i)   on his person; or
      (ii) in or on his clothing or footwear; or
      (iii) otherwise in his possession; or
      (iv) in any place in which he is at the time of his arrest,
   any object, substance or mark, or there is any mark on any such object; and

   (b) that or another constable investigating the case reasonably believes that the presence of the object, substance or mark may be attributable to the participation of the person arrested in the commission of an offence specified by the constable; and
   (c) the constable informs the person arrested that he so believes, and requests him to account for the presence of the object, substance or mark; and
   (d) the person fails or refuses to do so,
   then if, in any proceedings against the person for the offence so specified, evidence of those matters is given, subsection (2) below applies.

(2) Where this subsection applies—
    (a) a magistrates' court inquiring into the offence as examining justices;
    (b) a judge, in deciding whether to grant an application made by the accused under—
        (i) section 6 of the Criminal Justice Act 1987 (application for dismissal of charge of serious fraud in respect of which notice of transfer has been given under section 4 of that Act); or
        (ii) paragraph 5 of Schedule 6 to the Criminal Justice Act 1991 (application for dismissal of charge of violent or sexual offence involving child in respect of which notice of transfer has been given under section 53 of that Act);
    (c) the court, in determining whether there is a case to answer; and
    (d) the court or jury, in determining whether the accused is guilty of the offence charged,
    may draw such inferences from the failure or refusal as appear proper.

(3) Subsections (1) and (2) above apply to the condition of clothing or footwear as they apply to a substance or mark thereon.

(4) Subsections 1 and 2 above do not apply unless the accused was told in ordinary language by the constable when making the request mentioned in subsection (1)(c) above what the effect of this section would be if he failed or refused to comply with the request.

(5) This section applies in relation to officers of customs and excise as it applies in relation to constables.

(6) This section does not preclude the drawing of any inference from a failure or refusal of the accused to account for the presence of an object, substance or mark or from the condition of clothing or footwear which could properly be drawn apart from this section.

(7) This section does not apply in relation to a failure or refusal which occurred before the commencement of this section.

KEYNOTE

As with s. 37 below, an inference may only be drawn where four conditions are satisfied:

- the accused has been arrested;
- a constable reasonably believes that the object, substance or mark (or the presence of the accused (s. 37)) may be attributable to the accused's participation in a crime (s. 36 (an offence 'specified by the constable') or s. 37 (the offence for which he/she was arrested));
- the constable informs the accused of his/her belief and requests an explanation;
- the constable tells the suspect (in ordinary language) the effect of a failure or refusal to comply with the request.

It is considered that the request for information under both s. 36 and s. 37 are a form of questioning and should be undertaken during the interview at the police station. The request for such information prior to this would be an exception to the rule.

The interviewing officer is required to give the accused a 'special warning' for an inference to be drawn from a suspect's failure or refusal to answer a question about one of these matters or to answer it satisfactorily. This 'special warning' is provided by PACE Code C, para. 10.5B, which states that the interviewing officer must first tell the suspect *in ordinary language*:

- what offence is being investigated;
- what fact the suspect is being asked to account for;
- that the interviewing officer believes this fact may be due to the suspect's taking part in the commission of the offence in question;
- that a court may draw a proper inference if the suspect fails or refuses to account for the fact about which he/she is being questioned;
- that a record is being made of the interview and that it may be given in evidence at any subsequent trial.

As with the preceding two sections, in relation to s. 36 the accused cannot be convicted solely on an inference drawn from a failure or refusal (s. 38(3)) (see 4.12.9).

4.12.8 **Inferences from Silence: Failure to Account for Presence**

Section 37 of the Criminal Justice and Public Order Act 1994 provides that inferences can be drawn from an accused's failure to give evidence or refusal to answer any question about his/her presence at a place or time when the offence for which he/she was arrested was committed.

Section 37 states:

(1) Where—
  (a) a person arrested by a constable was found by him at a place at or about the time the offence for which he was arrested is alleged to have been committed; and
  (b) that or another constable investigating the offence reasonably believes that the presence of the person at that place and at that time may be attributable to his participation in the commission of the offence; and
  (c) the constable informs the person that he so believes, and requests him to account for that presence; and
  (d) the person fails or refuses to do so,
then if, in any proceedings against the person for the offence, evidence of those matters is given, subsection (2) below applies.

(2) Where this subsection applies—
  (a) a magistrates' court inquiring into the offence as examining justices;
  (b) a judge, in deciding whether to grant an application made by the accused under—
    (i) section 6 of the Criminal Justice Act 1987 (application for dismissal of charge of serious fraud in respect of which notice of transfer has been given under section 4 of that Act); or
    (ii) paragraph 5 of Schedule 6 to the Criminal Justice Act 1991 (application for dismissal of charge of violent or sexual offence involving child in respect of which notice of transfer has been given under section 53 of that Act);
  (c) the court, in determining whether there is a case to answer; and
  (d) the court or jury, in determining whether the accused is guilty of the offence charged, may draw such inferences from the failure or refusal as appear proper.

(3) Subsections (1) and (2) do not apply unless the accused was told in ordinary language by the constable when making the request mentioned in subsection (1)(c) above what the effect of this section would be if he failed or refused to comply with the request.

(4) This section applies in relation to officers of customs and excise as it applies in relation to constables.

(5) This section does not preclude the drawing of any inference from a failure or refusal of the accused to account for his presence at a place which could properly be drawn apart from this section.

(6) This section does not apply in relation to a failure or refusal which occurred before the commencement of this section.

KEYNOTE

Section 37 appears somewhat restrictive in that it is only concerned with the suspect's location at the time of arrest and applies only when he/she was found at the location of the crime at or about the relevant time.

PACE Code C, para. 10.5B also applies to s. 37 in relation to the 'special warning' required to be given by the interviewing officer.

Unlike s. 36, here the officer that sees the person at or near the scene of the alleged offence must be the arresting officer.

As with ss. 35 and 36, in relation to s. 37 the accused cannot be convicted solely on an inference drawn from a failure or refusal (s. 38(3)) (see 4.12.9).

4.12.9   **Inferences from Silence: No Conviction on Silence Alone**

Section 38 of the Criminal Justice and Public Order Act 1994 applies to all of the four provisions relating to inferences from silence (ss. 34, 35, 36 and 37) and provides that an inference cannot be the sole basis for a finding of a case to answer, issue or dismissal of a notice to transfer, or for a finding of guilt. Nothing in s. 38 prejudices the court's general powers to exclude evidence.

In *R* v *Gowland-Wynn* (2001) *The Times*, 7 December, the Court of Appeal held that in cases involving directions under s. 34, the burden of proof remained on the Crown despite the fact that a defendant chose to make no comment.

Appendix 1

PACE Code of Practice for the Exercise by Police Officers of Statutory Powers of Stop and Search (Code A)

Commencement—Transitional Arrangements

This code applies to any search by a police officer which commences after midnight on 31 March 2003.

General

This code of practice must be readily available at all police stations for consultation by police officers, detained persons and members of the public.

The notes for guidance included are not provisions of this code, but are guidance to police officers and others about its application and interpretation. Provisions in the annexes to the code are provisions of this code.

This code governs the exercise by police officers of statutory powers to search a person or a vehicle without first making an arrest. The main stop and search powers to which this code applies are set out in Annex A, but that list should not be regarded as definitive. [*See Note 1*]

This code does not apply to:

(a) the powers of stop and search under:
   (i) Aviation Security Act 1982, section 27(2);
   (ii) Police and Criminal Evidence Act 1984, section 6(1) (which relates specifically to powers of constables employed by statutory undertakers on the premises of the statutory undertakers);

(b) searches carried out for the purposes of examination under Schedule 7 to the Terrorism Act 2000 and to which the Code of Practice issued under paragraph 6 of Schedule 14 to the Terrorism Act 2000 applies.

1 Principles governing stop and search

1.1 Powers to stop and search must be used fairly, responsibly, with respect for people being searched and without unlawful discrimination. The Race Relations (Amendment) Act 2000 makes it unlawful for police officers to discriminate on the grounds of race, colour, ethnic origin, nationality or national origins when using their powers.

1.2 The intrusion on the liberty of the person stopped or searched must be brief and detention for the purposes of a search must take place at or near the location of the stop.

1.3 If these fundamental principles are not observed the use of powers to stop and search may be drawn into question. Failure to use the powers in the proper manner reduces their effectiveness. Stop and search can play an important role in the detection and prevention of crime, and using the powers fairly makes them more effective.

1.4 The primary purpose of stop and search powers is to enable officers to allay or confirm suspicions about individuals without exercising their power of arrest. Officers may be required to justify the use or authorisation of such powers, in relation both to individual searches and the overall pattern of their activity in this regard, to their supervisory officers or in court. Any misuse of the powers is likely to be harmful to policing and lead to mistrust of the police. Officers must also be able to explain their actions to the member of the public searched. The misuse of these powers can lead to disciplinary action.

1.5 An officer must not search a person, even with his or her consent, where no power to search is applicable. Even where a person is prepared to submit to a search voluntarily, the person must not be searched unless the necessary legal power exists, and the search must be in accordance with the relevant power and the provisions of this Code. The only exception, where an officer does not require a specific power, applies to searches of persons entering sports grounds or other premises carried out with their consent given as a condition of entry.

2 Explanation of powers to stop and search

2.1 This code applies to powers of stop and search as follows:

(a) powers which require reasonable grounds for suspicion, before they may be exercised; that articles unlawfully obtained or possessed are being carried, or under Section 43 of the Terrorism Act 2000 that a person is a terrorist;

(b) authorised under section 60 of the Criminal Justice and Public Order Act 1994, based upon a reasonable belief that incidents involving serious violence may take place or that people are carrying dangerous instruments or offensive weapons within any locality in the police area;

(c) authorised under section 44(1) and (2) of the Terrorism Act 2000 based upon a consideration that the exercise of one or both powers is expedient for the prevention of acts of terrorism;

(d) powers to search a person who has not been arrested in the exercise of a power to search premises (see Code B paragraph 2.3a).

Searches requiring reasonable grounds for suspicion

2.2 Reasonable grounds for suspicion depend on the circumstances in each case. There must be an objective basis for that suspicion based on facts, information, and/or intelligence which are relevant to the likelihood of finding an article of a certain kind or, in the case of searches under section 43 of the Terrorism Act 2000, to the likelihood that the person is a terrorist. Reasonable suspicion can never be supported on the basis of personal factors alone without reliable supporting intelligence or information or some specific behaviour by the person concerned. For example, a person's race, age, appearance, or the fact that the person is known to have a previous conviction, cannot be used alone or in combination with each other as the reason for searching that person. Reasonable suspicion cannot be based on generalisations or stereotypical images of certain groups or categories of people as more likely to be involved in criminal activity.

2.3 Reasonable suspicion can sometimes exist without specific information or intelligence and on the basis of some level of generalisation stemming from the behaviour of a person. For example, if an officer encounters someone on the street at night who is obviously trying to hide something, the officer may (depending on the other surrounding circumstances) base such suspicion on the fact that this kind of behaviour is often linked to stolen or prohibited articles being carried. Similarly, for the purposes of section 43 of the Terrorism Act 2000, suspicion that a person is a terrorist may arise from the person's behaviour at or near a location which has been identified as a potential target for terrorists.

2.4 However, reasonable suspicion should normally be linked to accurate and current intelligence or information, such as information describing an article being carried, a suspected offender, or a person who has been seen carrying a type of article known to have been stolen recently from premises in the area. Searches based on accurate and current intelligence or information are more likely to be effective. Targeting searches in a particular area at specified crime problems increases their effectiveness and minimises inconvenience to law-abiding members of the public. It also helps in justifying the use of searches both to those who are searched and to the general public. This does not however prevent stop and search powers being exercised in other locations where such powers may be exercised and reasonable suspicion exists.

2.5   Searches are more likely to be effective, legitimate, and secure public confidence when reasonable suspicion is based on a range of factors. The overall use of these powers is more likely to be effective when up to date and accurate intelligence or information is communicated to officers and they are well-informed about local crime patterns.

2.6   Where there is reliable information or intelligence that members of a group or gang habitually carry knives unlawfully or weapons or controlled drugs, and wear a distinctive item of clothing or other means of identification to indicate their membership of the group or gang, that distinctive item of clothing or other means of identification may provide reasonable grounds to stop and search a person. [*See Note 9*]

2.7   A police officer may have reasonable grounds to suspect that a person is in innocent possession of a stolen or prohibited article or other item for which he or she is empowered to search. In that case the officer may stop and search the person even though there would be no power of arrest.

2.8   Under section 43(1) of the Terrorism Act 2000 a constable may stop and search a person whom the officer reasonably suspects to be a terrorist to discover whether the person is in possession of anything which may constitute evidence that the person is a terrorist. These searches may only be carried out by an officer of the same sex as the person searched.

2.9   An officer who has reasonable grounds for suspicion may detain the person concerned in order to carry out a search. Before carrying out a search the officer may ask questions about the person's behaviour or presence in circumstances which gave rise to the suspicion. As a result of questioning the detained person, the reasonable grounds for suspicion necessary to detain that person may be confirmed or, because of a satisfactory explanation, be eliminated. [*See Notes 2 and 3*] Questioning may also reveal reasonable grounds to suspect the possession of a different kind of unlawful article from that originally suspected. Reasonable grounds for suspicion however cannot be provided retrospectively by such questioning during a person's detention or by refusal to answer any questions put.

2.10   If, as a result of questioning before a search, or other circumstances which come to the attention of the officer, there cease to be reasonable grounds for suspecting that an article is being carried of a kind for which there is a power to stop and search, no search may take place. [*See Note 3*] In the absence of any other lawful power to detain, the person is free to leave at will and must be so informed.

2.11   There is no power to stop or detain a person in order to find grounds for a search. Police officers have many encounters with members of the public which do not involve detaining people against their will. If reasonable grounds for suspicion emerge during such an encounter, the officer may search the person, even though no grounds existed when the encounter began. If an officer is detaining someone for the purpose of a search, he or she should inform the person as soon as detention begins.

Searches authorised under section 60 of the Criminal Justice and Public Order Act 1994

2.12   Authority for a constable in uniform to stop and search under section 60 of the Criminal Justice and Public Order Act 1994 may be given if the authorising officer reasonably believes:

(a) that incidents involving serious violence may take place in any locality in the officer's police area, and it is expedient to use these powers to prevent their occurrence, or

(b) that persons are carrying dangerous instruments or offensive weapons without good reason in any locality in the officer's police area.

2.13 An authorisation under section 60 may only be given by an officer of the rank of inspector or above, in writing, specifying the grounds on which it was given, the locality in which the powers may be exercised and the period of time for which they are in force. The period authorised shall be no longer than appears reasonably necessary to prevent, or seek to prevent incidents of serious violence, or to deal with the problem of carrying dangerous instruments or offensive weapons. It may not exceed 24 hours. [*See Notes 10–13*]

2.14 If an inspector gives an authorisation, he or she must, as soon as practicable, inform an officer of or above the rank of superintendent. This officer may direct that the authorisation shall be extended for a further 24 hours, if violence or the carrying of dangerous instruments or offensive weapons has occurred, or is suspected to have occurred, and the continued use of the powers is considered necessary to prevent or deal with further such activity. That direction must also be given in writing at the time or as soon as practicable afterwards. [*See Note 12*]

Powers to require removal of face coverings

2.15 Section 60AA of the Criminal Justice and Public Order Act 1994 also provides a power to demand the removal of disguises. The officer exercising the power must reasonably believe that someone is wearing an item wholly or mainly for the purpose of concealing identity. There is also a power to seize such items where the officer believes that a person intends to wear them for this purpose. There is no power to stop and search for disguises. An officer may seize any such item which is discovered when exercising a power of search for something else, or which is being carried, and which the officer reasonably believes is intended to be used for concealing anyone's identity. This power can only be used if an authorisation under section 60 or an authorisation under section 60AA is in force.

2.16 Authority for a constable in uniform to require the removal of disguises and to seize them under section 60AA may be given if the authorising officer reasonably believes that activities may take place in any locality in the officer's police area that are likely to involve the commission of offences and it is expedient to use these powers to prevent or control these activities.

2.17 An authorisation under section 60AA may only be given by an officer of the rank of inspector or above, in writing, specifying the grounds on which it was given, the locality in which the powers may be exercised and the period of time for which they are in force. The period authorised shall be no longer than appears reasonably necessary to prevent, or seek to prevent the commission of offences. It may not exceed 24 hours. [*See Notes 10–13*]

2.18 If an inspector gives an authorisation, he or she must, as soon as practicable, inform an officer of or above the rank of superintendent. This officer may direct that the authorisation shall be extended for a further 24 hours, if crimes have been committed, or are suspected to have been committed, and the continued use of the powers is considered necessary to prevent or deal with further such activity. This direction must also be given in writing at the time or as soon as practicable afterwards. [*See Note 12*]

Searches authorised under section 44 of the Terrorism Act 2000

2.19 An officer of the rank of assistant chief constable (or equivalent) or above, may give authority for the following powers of stop and search under section 44 of the Terrorism Act 2000 to be exercised in the whole or part of his or her police area if the officer considers it is expedient for the prevention of acts of terrorism:

(a) under section 44(1) of the Terrorism Act 2000, to give a constable in uniform power to stop and search any vehicle, its driver, any passenger in the vehicle and anything in or on the vehicle or carried by the driver or any passenger; and

(b) under section 44(2) of the Terrorism Act 2000, to give a constable in uniform power to stop and search any pedestrian and anything carried by the pedestrian.

An authorisation under section 44(1) may be combined with one under section 44(2)

2.20   If an authorisation is given orally at first, it must be confirmed in writing by the officer who gave it as soon as reasonably practicable.

2.21   When giving an authorisation, the officer must specify the geographical area in which the power may be used, and the time and date that the authorisation ends (up to a maximum of 28 days from the time the authorisation was given). [*See Notes 12 and 13*]

2.22   The officer giving an authorisation under section 44(1) or (2) must cause the Secretary of State to be informed, as soon as reasonably practicable, that such an authorisation has been given. An authorisation which is not confirmed by the Secretary of State within 48 hours of its having been given, shall have effect up until the end of that 48 hour period or the end of the period specified in the authorisation (whichever is the earlier). [*See Note 14*]

2.23   Following notification of the authorisation, the Secretary of State may:

(i)   cancel the authorisation with immediate effect or with effect from such other time as he or she may direct;

(ii)   confirm it but for a shorter period than that specified in the authorisation; or

(iii)   confirm the authorisation as given.

2.24   When an authorisation under section 44 is given, a constable in uniform may exercise the powers:

(a)   only for the purpose of searching for articles of a kind which could be used in connection with terrorism (see paragraph 2.25);

(b)   whether or not there are any grounds for suspecting the presence of such articles.

2.25   The selection of persons stopped under section 44 of the Terrorism Act 2000 should reflect an objective assessment of the threat posed by the various terrorist groups active in Great Britain. The powers must not be used to stop and search for reasons unconnected with terrorism. Officers must take particular care not to discriminate against members of minority ethnic groups in the exercise of these powers. There may be circumstances, however, where it is appropriate for officers to take account of a person's ethnic origin in selecting persons to be stopped in response to a specific terrorist threat (for example, some international terrorist groups are associated with particular ethnic identities). [*See Notes 12 and 13*]

2.26   The powers under sections 43 and 44 of the Terrorism Act 2000 allow a constable to search only for articles which could be used for terrorist purposes. However, this would not prevent a search being carried out under other powers if, in the course of exercising these powers, the officer formed reasonable grounds for suspicion.

Powers to search in the exercise of a power to search premises

2.27   The following powers to search premises also authorise the search of a person, not under arrest, who is found on the premises during the course of the search:

(a)   section 139B of the Criminal Justice Act 1988 under which a constable may enter school premises and search the premises and any person on those premises for any bladed or pointed article or offensive weapon; and

(b)   under a warrant issued under section s. 23(3) of the Misuse of Drugs Act 1971 to search premises for drugs or documents but only if the warrant specifically authorises the search of persons found on the premises.

2.28 Before the power under section 139B of the Criminal Justice Act 1988 may be exercised, the constable must have reasonable grounds to believe that an offence under section 139A of the Criminal Justice Act 1988 (having a bladed or pointed article or offensive weapon on school premises) has been or is being committed. A warrant to search premises and persons found therein may be issued under section s. 23(3) of the Misuse of Drugs Act 1971 if there are reasonable grounds to suspect that controlled drugs or certain documents are in the possession of a person on the premises.

2.29 The powers in paragraph 2.27(a) or (b) do not require prior specific grounds to suspect that the person to be searched is in possession of an item for which there is an existing power to search. However, it is still necessary to ensure that the selection and treatment of those searched under these powers is based upon objective factors connected with the search of the premises, and not upon personal prejudice.

3 Conduct of searches

3.1 All stops and searches must be carried out with courtesy, consideration and respect for the person concerned. This has a significant impact on public confidence in the police. Every reasonable effort must be made to minimise the embarrassment that a person being searched may experience. [*See Note 4*]

3.2 The co-operation of the person to be searched must be sought in every case, even if the person initially objects to the search. A forcible search may be made only if it has been established that the person is unwilling to co-operate or resists. Reasonable force may be used as a last resort if necessary to conduct a search or to detain a person or vehicle for the purposes of a search.

3.3 The length of time for which a person or vehicle may be detained must be reasonable and kept to a minimum. Where the exercise of the power requires reasonable suspicion, the thoroughness and extent of a search must depend on what is suspected of being carried, and by whom. If the suspicion relates to a particular article which is seen to be slipped into a person's pocket, then, in the absence of other grounds for suspicion or an opportunity for the article to be moved elsewhere, the search must be confined to that pocket. In the case of a small article which can readily be concealed, such as a drug, and which might be concealed anywhere on the person, a more extensive search may be necessary. In the case of searches mentioned in paragraph 2.1(b), (c), and (d), which do not require reasonable grounds for suspicion, officers may make any reasonable search to look for items for which they are empowered to search. [*See Note 5*]

3.4 The search must be carried out at or near the place where the person or vehicle was first detained. [*See Note 6*]

3.5 There is no power to require a person to remove any clothing in public other than an outer coat, jacket or gloves except under section 45(3) of the Terrorism Act 2000 (which empowers a constable conducting a search under section 44(1) or 44(2) of that Act to require a person to remove headgear and footwear in public) and under section 60AA of the Criminal Justice and Public Order Act 1994 (which empowers a constable to require a person to remove any item worn to conceal identity). [*See Notes 4 and 6*] A search in public of a person's clothing which has not been removed must be restricted to superficial examination of outer garments. This does not, however, prevent an officer from placing his or her hand inside the pockets of the outer clothing, or feeling round the inside of collars, socks and shoes if this is reasonably necessary in the circumstances to look for the object of the search or to remove and examine any item reasonably suspected to be the object of the search. For the same reasons, subject to the restrictions on the removal of headgear, a person's hair may also be searched in public (see paragraphs 3.1 and 3.3).

3.6 Where on reasonable grounds it is considered necessary to conduct a more thorough search (e.g. by requiring a person to take off a T-shirt), this must be done out of public view, for example, in a police van unless paragraph 3.7 applies, or police station if there is one nearby. [*See Note 6*] Any search involving the removal of more than an outer coat, jacket, gloves, headgear or footwear, or any other item concealing identity, may only be made by an officer of the same sex as the person searched and may not be made in the presence of anyone of the opposite sex unless the person being searched specifically requests it. [*See Notes 4, 7 and 8*]

3.7   Searches involving exposure of intimate parts of the body must not be conducted as a routine extension of a less thorough search, simply because nothing is found in the course of the initial search. Searches involving exposure of intimate parts of the body may be carried out only at a nearby police station or other nearby location which is out of public view (but not a police vehicle). These searches must be conducted in accordance with paragraph 11 of Annex A to Code C except that an intimate search mentioned in paragraph 11 (f) of Annex A to Code C may not be authorised or carried out under any stop and search powers. The other provisions of Code C do not apply to the conduct and recording of searches of persons detained at police stations in the exercise of stop and search powers. [*See Note 7*]

Steps to be taken prior to a search

3.8   Before any search of a detained person or attended vehicle takes place the officer must take reasonable steps to give the person to be searched or in charge of the vehicle the following information:

(a)   that they are being detained for the purposes of a search;

(b)   the officer's name (except in the case of enquiries linked to the investigation of terrorism, or otherwise where the officer reasonably believes that giving his or her name might put him or her in danger, in which case a warrant or other identification number shall be given) and the name of the police station to which the officer is attached;

(c)   the legal search power which is being exercised; and

(d)   a clear explanation of:
   (i)   the purpose of the search in terms of the article or articles for which there is a power to search; and
   (ii)   in the case of powers requiring reasonable suspicion (see paragraph 2.1(a)) the grounds for that suspicion; or
   (iii)   in the case of powers which do not require reasonable suspicion (see paragraph 2.1 (b), and (c)), the nature of the power and of any necessary authorisation and the fact that it has been given.

3.9   Officers not in uniform must show their warrant cards. Stops and searches under the powers mentioned in paragraphs 2.1 (b), and (c) may be undertaken only by a constable in uniform.

3.10   Before the search takes place the officer must inform the person (or the owner or person in charge of the vehicle that is to be searched) of his or her entitlement to a copy of the record of the search, including his entitlement to a record of the search if an application is made within 12 months, if it is wholly impracticable to make a record at the time. If a record is not made at the time the person should also be told how a copy can be obtained (see section 4). The person should also be given information about police powers to stop and search and the individual's rights in these circumstances.

3.11   If the person to be searched, or in charge of a vehicle to be searched, does not appear to understand what is being said, or there is any doubt about the person's ability to understand English, the officer must take reasonable steps to bring information regarding the person's rights and any relevant provisions of this Code to his or her attention. If the person is deaf or cannot understand English and is accompanied by someone, then the officer must try to establish whether that person can interpret or otherwise help the officer to give the required information.

4   **Recording requirements**

4.1   An officer who has carried out a search in the exercise of any power to which this Code applies, must make a record of it at the time, unless there are exceptional circumstances which would make this wholly impracticable (e.g. in situations involving public disorder or when the officer's presence is urgently required elsewhere). If a record is not made at the time, the officer must do so as soon as practicable afterwards. There may be situations in which it is not practicable to obtain the information necessary to complete a record, but the officer should make every reasonable effort to do so.

4.2 A copy of a record made at the time must be given immediately to the person who has been searched. The officer must ask for the name, address and date of birth of the person searched, but there is no obligation on a person to provide these details and no power of detention if the person is unwilling to do so.

4.3 The following information must always be included in the record of a search even if the person does not wish to provide any personal details:

(i)   the name of the person searched, or (if it is withheld) a description;

(ii)   a note of the person's self-defined ethnic background; [*See Note 18*]

(iii)   when a vehicle is searched, its registration number; [*See Note 17*]

(iv)   the date, time, and place that the person or vehicle was first detained;

(v)   the date, time and place the person or vehicle was searched (if different from (iv));

(vi)   the purpose of the search;

(vii)   the grounds for making it, or in the case of those searches mentioned in paragraph 2.1(b) and (c), the nature of the power and of any necessary authorisation and the fact that it has been given; [*See Note 17*]

(viii) its outcome (e.g. arrest or no further action);

(ix)   a note of any injury or damage to property resulting from it;

(x)   subject to paragraph 3.8(a), the identity of the officer making the search. [*See Note 15*]

4.4 Nothing in paragraph 4.3 (x) requires the names of police officers to be shown on the search record or any other record required to be made under this code in the case of enquiries linked to the investigation of terrorism or otherwise where an officer reasonably believes that recording names might endanger the officers. In such cases the record must show the officers' warrant or other identification number and duty station.

4.5 A record is required for each person and each vehicle searched. However, if a person is in a vehicle and both are searched, and the object and grounds of the search are the same, only one record need be completed. If more than one person in a vehicle is searched, separate records for each search of a person must be made. If only a vehicle is searched, the name of the driver and his or her self-defined ethnic background must be recorded, unless the vehicle is unattended.

4.6 The record of the grounds for making a search must, briefly but informatively, explain the reason for suspecting the person concerned, by reference to the person's behaviour and/or other circumstances.

4.7 Where officers detain an individual with a view to performing a search, but the search is not carried out due to the grounds for suspicion being eliminated as a result of questioning the person detained, a record must still be made in accordance with the procedure outlined above.

4.8 After searching an unattended vehicle, or anything in or on it, an officer must leave a notice in it (or on it, if things on it have been searched without opening it) recording the fact that it has been searched.

4.9 The notice must include the name of the police station to which the officer concerned is attached and state where a copy of the record of the search may be obtained and where any application for compensation should be directed.

4.10 The vehicle must if practicable be left secure.

5 Monitoring and supervising the use of stop and search powers

5.1 Supervising officers must monitor the use of stop and search powers and should consider in particular whether there is any evidence that they are being exercised on the basis of stereotyped images or inappropriate generalisations. Supervising officers should satisfy themselves that the practice of officers under their supervision in stopping, searching and recording is fully in accordance with this Code. Supervisors must also examine whether the records reveal any trends or patterns which give cause for concern, and if so take appropriate action to address this.

5.2 Senior officers with area or force-wide responsibilities must also monitor the broader use of stop and search powers and, where necessary, take action at the relevant level.

5.3 Supervision and monitoring must be supported by the compilation of comprehensive statistical records of stops and searches at force, area and local level. Any apparently disproportionate use of the powers by particular officers or groups of officers or in relation to specific sections of the community should be identified and investigated.

5.4 In order to promote public confidence in the use of the powers, forces in consultation with police authorities must make arrangements for the records to be scrutinised by representatives of the community, and to explain the use of the powers at a local level. [*See Note 19*]

Notes for guidance

Officers exercising stop and search powers

1   This code does not affect the ability of an officer to speak to or question a person in the ordinary course of the officer's duties without detaining the person or exercising any element of compulsion. It is not the purpose of the code to prohibit such encounters between the police and the community with the co-operation of the person concerned and neither does it affect the principle that all citizens have a duty to help police officers to prevent crime and discover offenders. This is a civic rather than a legal duty; but when a police officer is trying to discover whether, or by whom, an offence has been committed he or she may question any person from whom useful information might be obtained, subject to the restrictions imposed by Code C. A person's unwillingness to reply does not alter this entitlement, but in the absence of a power to arrest, or to detain in order to search, the person is free to leave at will and cannot be compelled to remain with the officer.

2   In some circumstances preparatory questioning may be unnecessary, but in general a brief conversation or exchange will be desirable not only as a means of avoiding unsuccessful searches, but to explain the grounds for the stop/search, to gain co-operation and reduce any tension there might be surrounding the stop/search.

3   Where a person is lawfully detained for the purpose of a search, but no search in the event takes place, the detention will not thereby have been rendered unlawful.

4   Many people customarily cover their heads or faces for religious reasons—for example, Muslim women, Sikh men, Sikh or Hindu women, or Rastafarian men or women. A police officer cannot order the removal of a head or face covering except where there is reason to believe that the item is being worn by the individual wholly or mainly for the purpose of disguising identity, not simply because it disguises identity. Where there may be religious sensitivities about ordering the removal of such an item, the officer should permit the item to be removed out of public view. Where practicable, the item should be removed in the presence of an officer of the same sex as the person and out of sight of anyone of the opposite sex.

5   A search of a person in public should be completed as soon as possible.

6   A person may be detained under a stop and search power at a place other than where the person was first detained, only if that place, be it a police station or elsewhere, is nearby. Such a place should be located within a reasonable travelling distance using whatever mode of travel (on foot or by car) is appropriate. This applies to all searches under stop and search powers, whether or not they involve the removal of clothing or exposure of intimate parts of the body (see paragraphs 3.6 and 3.7) or take place in or out of public view. It means, for example, that a search under the stop and search power in section 23 of the Misuse of Drugs Act 1971 which involves the compulsory removal of more than a person's outer coat, jacket or gloves cannot be carried out unless a place which is both nearby the place they were first detained and out of public view, is available. If a search involves exposure of intimate parts of the body and a police station is not nearby, particular care must be taken to ensure that the location is suitable in that it enables the search to be conducted in accordance with the requirements of paragraph 11 of Annex A to Code C.

7 A search in the street itself should be regarded as being in public for the purposes of paragraphs 3.6 and 3.7 above, even though it may be empty at the time a search begins. Although there is no power to require a person to do so, there is nothing to prevent an officer from asking a person voluntarily to remove more than an outer coat, jacket or gloves (and headgear or footwear under section 45(3) of the Terrorism Act 2000) in public.

8 Where there may be religious sensitivities about asking someone to remove headgear using a power under section 45(3) of the Terrorism Act 2000, the police officer should offer to carry out the search out of public view (for example, in a police van or police station if there is one nearby).

9 Other means of identification might include jewellery, insignias, tattoos or other features which are known to identify members of the particular gang or group.

Authorising officers

10 The powers under section 60 are separate from and additional to the normal stop and search powers which require reasonable grounds to suspect an individual of carrying an offensive weapon (or other article). Their overall purpose is to prevent serious violence and the widespread carrying of weapons which might lead to persons being seriously injured by disarming potential offenders in circumstances where other powers would not be sufficient. They should not therefore be used to replace or circumvent the normal powers for dealing with routine crime problems. The purpose of the powers under section 60AA is to prevent those involved in intimidatory or violent protests using face coverings to disguise identity.

11 Authorisations under section 60 require a reasonable belief on the part of the authorising officer. This must have an objective basis, for example: intelligence or relevant information such as a history of antagonism and violence between particular groups; previous incidents of violence at, or connected with, particular events or locations; a significant increase in knife-point robberies in a limited area; reports that individuals are regularly carrying weapons in a particular locality; or in the case of section 60AA previous incidents of crimes being committed while wearing face coverings to conceal identity.

12 It is for the authorising officer to determine the period of time during which the powers mentioned in paragraph 2.1 (b) and (c) may be exercised. The officer should set the minimum period he or she considers necessary to deal with the risk of violence, the carrying of knives or offensive weapons, or terrorism. A direction to extend the period authorised under the powers mentioned in paragraph 2.1 (b) may be given only once. Thereafter further use of the powers requires a new authorisation. There is no provision to extend an authorisation of the powers mentioned in paragraph 2.1(c); further use of the powers requires a new authorisation.

13 It is for the authorising officer to determine the geographical area in which the use of the powers is to be authorised. In doing so the officer may wish to take into account factors such as the nature and venue of the anticipated incident, the number of people who may be in the immediate area of any possible incident, their access to surrounding areas and the anticipated level of violence. The officer should not set a geographical area which is wider than that he or she believes necessary for the purpose of preventing anticipated violence, the carrying of knives or offensive weapons, acts of terrorism, or, in the case of section 60AA, the prevention of commission of offences. It is particularly important to ensure that constables exercising such powers are fully aware of where they may be used. If the area specified is smaller than the whole force area, the officer giving the authorisation should specify either the streets which form the boundary of the area or a divisional boundary within the force area. If the power is to be used in response to a threat or incident that straddles police force areas, an officer from each of the forces concerned will need to give an authorisation.

14 An officer who has authorised the use of powers under section 44 of the Terrorism Act 2000 must take immediate steps to send a copy of the authorisation to the National Joint Unit, Metropolitan Police Special Branch, who will forward it to the Secretary of State. The Secretary of State should be informed of the reasons for the authorisation. The National Joint Unit will inform the force concerned, within 48 hours of the authorisation being made, whether the Secretary of State has confirmed or cancelled or altered the authorisation.

Recording

15   Where a stop and search is conducted by more than one officer the identity of all the officers engaged in the search must be recorded on the record. Nothing prevents an officer who is present but not directly involved in searching from completing the record during the course of the encounter.

16   Where a vehicle has not been allocated a registration number (e.g. a rally car or a trials motorbike) that part of the requirement under 4.3(iii) does not apply.

17   It is important for monitoring purposes to specify whether the authority for exercising a stop and search power was given under section 60 of the Criminal Justice and Public Order Act 1994, or under section 44(1) or 44(2) of the Terrorism Act 2000.

18   Officers should record the self-defined ethnicity of every person stopped according to the categories used in the 2001 census question listed in Annex B. Respondents should be asked to select one of the five main categories representing broad ethnic groups and then a more specific cultural background from within this group. The ethnic classification should be coded for recording purposes using the coding system in Annex B. An additional 'Not stated' box is available but should not be offered to respondents explicitly. Officers should be aware and explain to members of the public, especially where concerns are raised, that this information is required to obtain a true picture of stop and search activity and to help improve ethnic monitoring, tackle discriminatory practice, and promote effective use of the powers. If the person gives what appears to the officer to be an 'incorrect' answer (e.g. a person who appears to be white states that they are black), the officer should record the response that has been given. Officers should also record their own perception of the ethnic background of every person stopped and this must be done by using the PNC/Phoenix classification system. If the 'Not stated' category is used the reason for this must be recorded on the form.

19   Arrangements for public scrutiny of records should take account of the right to confidentiality of those stopped and searched. Anonymised forms and/or statistics generated from records should be the focus of the examinations by members of the public.

ANNEX A   SUMMARY OF MAIN STOP AND SEARCH POWERS

Power	Object of Search	Extent of Search	Where Exercisable
Unlawful articles general			
1. Public Stores Act 1875, s. 6	HM Stores stolen or unlawfully obtained	Persons, vehicles and vessels	Anywhere where the constabulary powers are exercisable
2. Firearms Act 1968, s. 47	Firearms	Persons and vehicles	A public place, or anywhere in the case of reasonable suspicion of offences of carrying firearms with criminal intent or trespassing with firearms
3. Misuse of Drugs Act 1971, s. 23	Controlled drugs	Persons and vehicles	Anywhere
4. Customs and Excise Management Act 1979, s. 163	Goods: (a) on which duty has not been paid; (b) being unlawfully removed, imported or exported; (c) otherwise liable to forfeiture to HM Customs and Excise	Vehicles and vessels only	Anywhere
5. Aviation Security Act 1982, s. 27(1)	Stolen or unlawfully obtained goods	Airport employees and vehicles carrying airport employees or aircraft or any vehicle in a cargo area whether or not carrying an employee	Any designated airport

Annex A (Continued)

Power	Object of Search	Extent of Search	Where Exercisable
6. Police and Criminal Evidence Act 1984, s. 1	Stolen goods; articles for use in certain Theft Act offences; offensive weapons, including bladed or sharply-pointed articles (except folding pocket knives with a bladed cutting edge not exceeding 3 inches)	Persons and vehicles	Where there is public access
Police and Criminal Evidence Act 1984, s. 6(3) (by a constable of the United Kingdom Atomic Energy Authority Constabulary in respect of property owned or controlled by British Nuclear Fuels plc)	HM Stores (in the form of goods and chattels belonging to British Nuclear Fuels plc)	Persons, vehicles and vessels	Anywhere where the constabulary powers are exercisable
7. Sporting events (Control of Alcohol etc.) Act 1985, s. 7	Intoxicating liquor	Persons, coaches and trains	Designated sports grounds or coaches and trains travelling to or from a designated sporting event
8. Crossbows Act 1987, s. 4	Crossbows or parts of crossbows (except crossbows with a draw weight of less than 1.4 kilograms)	Persons and vehicles	Anywhere except dwellings
9. Criminal Justice Act 1988, s. 139B	Offensive weapons, bladed or sharply pointed article	Persons	School premises

Evidence of game and wildlife offences

Power	Object of Search	Extent of Search	Where Exercisable
10. Poaching Prevention Act 1862, s. 2	Game or poaching equipment	Persons and vehicles	A public place
11. Deer Act 1991, s. 12	Evidence of offences under the Act	Persons and vehicles	Anywhere except dwellings
12. Conservation of Seals Act 1970, s. 4	Seals or hunting equipment	Vehicles only	Anywhere
13. Protection of Badgers Act 1992, s. 11	Evidence of offences under the Act	Persons and vehicles	Anywhere
14. Wildlife and Countryside Act 1981, s. 19	Evidence of wildlife offences	Persons and vehicles	Anywhere except dwellings

Other

Power	Object of Search	Extent of Search	Where Exercisable
15. Terrorism Act 2000, s. 43	Evidence of liability to arrest under section 14 of the Act	Persons	Anywhere
16. Terrorism Act 2000, s. 44(1)	Articles which could be used for a purpose connected with the commission, preparation or instigation of acts of terrorism	Vehicles, driver and passengers	Anywhere within the area or locality authorised under subsection (1)
17. Terrorism Act 2000, s. 44(2)	Articles which could be used for a purpose connected with the commission, preparation or instigation of acts of terrorism	Pedestrians	Anywhere within the area of locality authorised

Annex A   (Continued)

Power	Object of Search	Extent of Search	Where Exercisable
18. Paragraphs 7 and 8 of Schedule 7 to the Terrorism Act 2000	Anything relevant to determining if a person being examined falls within paragraph 2(1)(a) to (c) of Schedule 5	Persons, vehicles, vessels etc.	Ports and airports
19. Section 60 Criminal Justice and Public Order Act 1994, as amended by s. 8 of the Knives Act 1997	Offensive weapons or dangerous instruments to prevent incidents of serious violence or to deal with the carrying of such items	Persons and vehicles	Anywhere within a locality authorised under subsection (1)

ANNEX B   SELF-DEFINED ETHNIC CLASSIFICATION CATEGORIES

White	*W*
A. White–British	W1
B. White–Irish	W2
C. Any other White background	W9

Mixed	*M*
D. White and Black Caribbean	M1
E. White and Black African	M2
F. White and Asian	M3
G. Any other Mixed Background	M9

Asian/Asian–British	*A*
H. Asian–Indian	A1
I. Asian–Pakistani	A2
J. Asian–Bangladeshi	A3
K. Any other Asian background	A9

Black/Black–British	*B*
L. Black–Caribbean	B1
M. Black African	B2
N. Any other Black background	B9

Other	*O*
O. Chinese	O1
P. Any other	O9
Not Stated	NS

Appendix 2

PACE Code of Practice for Searches of Premises by Police Officers and the Seizure of Property found by Police Officers on Persons or Premises (Code B)

Commencement—Transitional Arrangements

This Code applies to applications for warrants made after 31 March 2003 and to searches and seizures taking place after midnight on 31 March 2003.

1 Introduction

1.1   This Code of Practice deals with police powers to:

- search premises
- seize and retain property found on premises and persons

1.1A   These powers may be used to find:

- property and material relating to a crime
- wanted persons
- children who abscond from local authority accommodation where they have been remanded or committed by a court

1.2   A justice of the peace may issue a search warrant granting powers of entry, search and seizure, e.g. warrants to search for stolen property, drugs, firearms and evidence of serious offences. Police also have powers without a search warrant. The main ones provided by the Police and Criminal Evidence Act 1984 (PACE) include powers to search premises:

- to make an arrest
- after an arrest

1.3   The right to privacy and respect for personal property are key principles of the Human Rights Act 1998. Powers of entry, search and seizure should be fully and clearly justified before use because they may significantly interfere with the occupier's privacy. Officers should consider if the necessary objectives can be met by less intrusive means.

1.4   In all cases, police should:

- exercise their powers courteously and with respect for persons and property
- only use reasonable force when this is considered necessary and proportionate to the circumstances

1.5   If the provisions of PACE and this Code are not observed, evidence obtained from a search may be open to question.

2   General

2.1   This Code must be readily available at all police stations for consultation by:

- police officers
- detained persons
- members of the public

2.2   The *Notes for Guidance* included are not provisions of this Code.

2.3   This Code applies to searches of premises:

(a) by police for the purposes of an investigation into an alleged offence, with the occupier's consent, other than:
- routine scene of crime searches;
- calls to a fire or burglary made by or on behalf of an occupier or searches following the activation of fire or burglar alarms or discovery of insecure premises;
- searches when *paragraph 5.4* applies;
- bomb threat calls;

(b) under powers conferred on police officers by PACE, sections 17,18 and 32;

(c) undertaken in pursuance of search warrants issued to and executed by constables in accordance with PACE, sections 15 and 16. See *Note 2A*;

(d) subject to *paragraph 2.6*, under any other power given to police to enter premises with or without a search warrant for any purpose connected with the investigation into an alleged or suspected offence. See *Note 2B*.

For the purposes of this Code, 'premises' as defined in PACE, section 23, includes any place, vehicle, vessel, aircraft, hovercraft, tent or movable structure and any offshore installation as defined in the Mineral Workings (Offshore Installations) Act 1971, section 1. See *Note 2D*

2.4   A person who has not been arrested but is searched during a search of premises should be searched in accordance with Code A. See *Note 2C*

2.5   This Code does not apply to the exercise of a statutory power to enter premises or to inspect goods, equipment or procedures if the exercise of that power is not dependent on the existence of grounds for suspecting that an offence may have been committed and the person exercising the power has no reasonable grounds for such suspicion.

2.6   This Code does not affect any directions of a search warrant or order, lawfully executed in England or Wales that any item or evidence seized under that warrant or order be handed over to a police force, court, tribunal, or other authority outside England or Wales. For example, warrants and orders issued in Scotland or Northern Ireland, see *Note 2B(f)* and search warrants issued under the Criminal Justice (International Co-operation) Act 1990, section 7.

2.7   When this Code requires the prior authority or agreement of an officer of at least inspector or superintendent rank, that authority may be given by a sergeant or chief inspector authorised to perform the functions of the higher rank under PACE, section 107.

2.8   Written records required under this Code not made in the search record shall, unless otherwise specified, be made:

- in the recording officer's pocket book ('pocket book' includes any official report book issued to police officers) or
- on forms provided for the purpose

2.9 Nothing in this Code requires the identity of officers (or anyone accompanying them during a search of premises) to be recorded or disclosed:

(a) in the case of enquiries linked to the investigation of terrorism; or

(b) if officers reasonably believe recording or disclosing their names might put them in danger.

In these cases officers should use warrant or other identification numbers and the name of their police station. See *Note 2E*

2.10 The 'officer in charge of the search' means the officer assigned specific duties and responsibilities under this Code. Whenever there is a search of premises to which this Code applies one officer must act as the officer in charge of the search. See *Note 2F*

2.11 In this Code:

(a) 'designated person' means a person other than a police officer, designated under the Police Reform Act 2002, Part 4 who has specified powers and duties of police officers conferred or imposed on them;

(b) any reference to a police officer includes a designated person acting in the exercise or performance of the powers and duties conferred or imposed on them by their designation.

2.12 If a power conferred on a designated person:

(a) allows reasonable force to be used when exercised by a police officer, a designated person exercising that power has the same entitlement to use force;

(b) includes power to use force to enter any premises, that power is not exercisable by that designated person except:
(i) in the company and under the supervision of a police officer; or
(ii) for the purpose of:
– saving life or limb; or
– preventing serious damage to property.

2.13 Designated persons must have regard to any relevant provisions of the Codes of Practice.

Notes for guidance

2A PACE sections 15 and 16 apply to all search warrants issued to and executed by constables under any enactment, e.g. search warrants issued by a:

(a) justice of the peace under the:
– Theft Act 1968, section 26—stolen property;
– Misuse of Drugs Act 1971, section 23—controlled drugs;
– PACE, section 8—evidence of serious arrestable offence
– Terrorism Act 2000, Schedule 5, paragraph 1;

(b) circuit judge under the:
– PACE, Schedule 1;
– Terrorism Act 2000, Schedule 5, paragraph 11.

2B Examples of the other powers in paragraph 2.3(d) include:

(a) Road Traffic Act 1988 giving police power to enter premises:
(i) under section 4(7) to:
– arrest a person for driving or being in charge of a vehicle when unfit;
(ii) under section 6(6) to:
– require a person to provide a specimen of breath; or
– arrest a person following:
– a positive breath test;
– failure to provide a specimen of breath;

(b) *Transport and Works Act 1992, sections 30(3) and 30(4) giving police powers to enter premises mirroring the powers in (a) in relation to specified persons working on transport systems to which the Act applies;*

(c) *Criminal Justice Act 1988, section 139B giving police power to enter and search school premises for offensive weapons, bladed or pointed articles;*

(d) *Terrorism Act 2000, Schedule 5, paragraphs 3 and 15 empowering a superintendent in urgent cases to give written authority for police to enter and search premises for the purposes of a terrorist investigation;*

(e) *Explosives Act 1875, section 73(b) empowering a superintendent to give written authority for police to enter premises, examine and search them for explosives;*

(f) *search warrants and production orders or the equivalent issued in Scotland or Northern Ireland endorsed under the Summary Jurisdiction (Process) Act 1881 or the Petty Sessions (Ireland) Act 1851 respectively for execution in England and Wales.*

2C   The Criminal Justice Act 1988, section 139B provides that a constable who has reasonable grounds to believe an offence under the Criminal Justice Act 1988, section 139A has or is being committed may enter school premises and search the premises and any persons on the premises for any bladed or pointed article or offensive weapon. Persons may be searched under a warrant issued under the Misuse of Drugs Act 1971, section 23(3) to search premises for drugs or documents only if the warrant specifically authorises the search of persons on the premises.

2D   The Immigration Act 1971, Part III and Schedule 2 gives immigration officers powers to enter and search premises, seize and retain property, with and without a search warrant. These are similar to the powers available to police under search warrants issued by a justice of the peace and without a warrant under PACE, sections 17, 18, 19 and 32 except they only apply to specified offences under the Immigration Act 1971 and immigration control powers. For certain types of investigations and enquiries these powers avoid the need for the Immigration Service to rely on police officers becoming directly involved. When exercising these powers, immigration officers are required by the Immigration and Asylum Act 1999, section 145 to have regard to this Code's corresponding provisions. When immigration officers are dealing with persons or property at police stations, police officers should give appropriate assistance to help them discharge their specific duties and responsibilities.

2E   The purpose of paragraph 2.9(b) is to protect those involved in serious organised crime investigations or arrests of particularly violent suspects when there is reliable information that those arrested or their associates may threaten or cause harm to the officers. In cases of doubt, an officer of inspector rank or above should be consulted.

2F   For the purposes of paragraph 2.10, the officer in charge of the search should normally be the most senior officer present. Some exceptions are:

(a) *a supervising officer who attends or assists at the scene of a premises search may appoint an officer of lower rank as officer in charge of the search if that officer is:*
   – more conversant with the facts;
   – a more appropriate officer to be in charge of the search;

(b) *when all officers in a premises search are the same rank. The supervising officer if available must make sure one of them is appointed officer in charge of the search, otherwise the officers themselves must nominate one of their number as the officer in charge;*

(c) *a senior officer assisting in a specialist role. This officer need not be regarded as having a general supervisory role over the conduct of the search or be appointed or expected to act as the officer in charge of the search.*

Except in (c), nothing in this Note diminishes the role and responsibilities of a supervisory officer who is present at the search or knows of a search taking place.

3 Search warrants and production orders

(a) Before making an application

3.1 When information appears to justify an application, the officer must take reasonable steps to check the information is accurate, recent and not provided maliciously or irresponsibly. An application may not be made on the basis of information from an anonymous source if corroboration has not been sought. See *Note 3A*

3.2 The officer shall ascertain as specifically as possible the nature of the articles concerned and their location.

3.3 The officer shall make reasonable enquiries to:

(i) establish if:
  – anything is known about the likely occupier of the premises and the nature of the premises themselves;
  – the premises have been searched previously and how recently;

(ii) obtain any other relevant information.

3.4 An application:

(a) to a justice of the peace for a search warrant or to a circuit judge for a search warrant or production order under PACE, Schedule 1

must be supported by a signed written authority from an officer of inspector rank or above:

Note: If the case is an urgent application to a justice of the peace and an inspector or above is not readily available, the next most senior officer on duty can give the written authority.

(b) to a circuit judge under the Terrorism Act 2000, Schedule 5 for
  – a production order;
  – search warrant; or
  – an order requiring an explanation of material seized or produced under such a warrant or
  – production order
  must be supported by a signed written authority from an officer of superintendent rank or above.

3.5 Except in a case of urgency, if there is reason to believe a search might have an adverse effect on relations between the police and the community, the officer in charge shall consult the local police/community liaison officer:

– before the search; or

– in urgent cases, as soon as practicable after the search

(b) Making an application

3.6 A search warrant application must be supported in writing, specifying:

(a) the enactment under which the application is made, see *Note 2A*;

(b) the premises to be searched;

(c) the object of the search, see *Note 3B*;

(d) the grounds for the application, including, when the purpose of the proposed search is to find evidence of an alleged offence, an indication of how the evidence relates to the investigation;

(e) there are no reasonable grounds to believe the material to be sought, when making application to a:
  (i) justice of the peace or a circuit judge, consists of or includes items subject to legal privilege;
  (ii) justice of the peace, consists of or includes excluded material or special procedure material;

Note: this does not affect the additional powers of seizure in the Criminal Justice and Police Act 2001, Part 2 covered in *paragraph 7.7*, see *Note 3B*;

(f) if applicable, a request for the warrant to authorise a person or persons to accompany the officer who executes the warrant, see *Note 3C*.

3.7 A search warrant application under PACE, Schedule 1, *paragraph 12(a)*, shall if appropriate indicate why it is believed service of notice of an application for a production order may seriously prejudice the investigation. Applications for search warrants under the Terrorism Act 2000, Schedule 5, paragraph 11 must indicate why a production order would not be appropriate.

3.8 If a search warrant application is refused, a further application may not be made for those premises unless supported by additional grounds.

Notes for guidance

3A The identity of an informant need not be disclosed when making an application, but the officer should be prepared to answer any questions the magistrate or judge may have about:

- *the accuracy of previous information from that source*

- *any other related matters*

3B The information supporting a search warrant application should be as specific as possible, particularly in relation to the articles or persons being sought and where in the premises it is suspected they may be found. The meaning of 'items subject to legal privilege', 'special procedure material' and 'excluded material' are defined by PACE, sections 10, 11 and 14 respectively.

3C Under PACE, section 16(2), a search warrant may authorise persons other than police officers to accompany the constable who executes the warrant. This includes, e.g. any suitably qualified or skilled person or an expert in a particular field whose presence is needed to help accurately identify the material sought or to advise where certain evidence is most likely to be found and how it should be dealt with. It does not give them any right to force entry, to search for or seize property but it gives them the right to be on the premises during the search without the occupier's permission.

4 Entry without warrant—particular powers

(a) Making an arrest etc

4.1 The conditions under which an officer may enter and search premises without a warrant are set out in PACE, section 17. It should be noted that this section does not create or confer any powers of arrest. See other powers in *Note 2B(a)*.

(b) Search of premises where arrest takes place or the arrested person was immediately before arrest

4.2 The powers of an officer to search premises where that officer arrested a person or where the person was immediately before being arrested are set out in PACE, section 32.

(c) Search of premises occupied or controlled by the arrested person

4.3 The specific powers to search premises occupied or controlled by an arrested person are set out in PACE, section 18. They may not be exercised, except if section 18 (5) applies, unless an officer of inspector rank or above has given written authority. That authority should only be given when the authorising officer is satisfied the necessary grounds exist. If possible the authorising officer should record the authority on the Notice of Powers and Rights and, subject to *paragraph 2.9*, sign the Notice. The record of the grounds for the search and the nature of the evidence sought as required by section 18(7) of the Act should be made in:

- the custody record if there is one, otherwise
- the officer's pocket book, or
- the search record

5 Search with consent

5.1 Subject to *paragraph 5.4*, if it is proposed to search premises with the consent of a person entitled to grant entry the consent must, if practicable, be given in writing on the Notice of Powers and Rights before the search. The officer must make any necessary enquiries to be satisfied the person is in a position to give such consent. See *Notes 5A and 5B*

5.2 Before seeking consent the officer in charge of the search shall state the purpose of the proposed search and its extent. This information must be as specific as possible, particularly regarding the articles or persons being sought and the parts of the premises to be searched. The person concerned must be clearly informed they are not obliged to consent and anything seized may be produced in evidence. If at the time the person is not suspected of an offence, the officer shall say this when stating the purpose of the search.

5.3 An officer cannot enter and search or continue to search premises under *paragraph 5.1* if consent is given under duress or withdrawn before the search is completed.

5.4 It is unnecessary to seek consent under *paragraphs 5.1* and *5.2* if this would cause disproportionate inconvenience to the person concerned. See *Note 5C*

Notes for guidance

5A In a lodging house or similar accommodation, every reasonable effort should be made to obtain the consent of the tenant, lodger or occupier. A search should not be made solely on the basis of the landlord's consent unless the tenant, lodger or occupier is unavailable and the matter is urgent.

5B If the intention is to search premises under the authority of a warrant or a power of entry and search without warrant, and the occupier of the premises co-operates in accordance with paragraph 6.4, there is no need to obtain written consent.

5C Paragraph 5.4 is intended to apply when it is reasonable to assume innocent occupiers would agree to, and expect, police to take the proposed action, e.g. if:

- *a suspect has fled the scene of a crime or to evade arrest and it is necessary quickly to check surrounding gardens and readily accessible places to see if the suspect is hiding*
- *police have arrested someone in the night after a pursuit and it is necessary to make a brief check of gardens along the pursuit route to see if stolen or incriminating articles have been discarded*

6 Searching premises—general considerations

(a) Time of searches

6.1 Searches made under warrant must be made within one calendar month of the date of the warrant's issue.

6.2 Searches must be made at a reasonable hour unless this might frustrate the purpose of the search.

6.3 A warrant authorises an entry on one occasion only. When the extent or complexity of a search mean it is likely to take a long time, the officer in charge of the search may consider using the seize and sift powers referred to in section 7.

(b) Entry other than with consent

6.4 The officer in charge of the search shall first try to communicate with the occupier, or any other person entitled to grant access to the premises, explain the authority under which entry is sought and ask the occupier to allow entry, unless:

   (i)   the search premises are unoccupied;

   (ii) the occupier and any other person entitled to grant access are absent;

   (iii) there are reasonable grounds for believing that alerting the occupier or any other person entitled to grant access would frustrate the object of the search or endanger officers or other people.

6.5   Unless *sub-paragraph 6.4(iii)* applies, if the premises are occupied the officer, subject to *paragraph 2.9*, shall, before the search begins:

   (i)   identify him or herself, show their warrant card (if not in uniform) and state the purpose of and grounds for the search;

   (ii) identify and introduce any person accompanying the officer on the search (such persons should carry identification for production on request) and briefly describe that person's role in the process.

6.6   Reasonable and proportionate force may be used if necessary to enter premises if the officer in charge of the search is satisfied the premises are those specified in any warrant, or in exercise of the powers described in *paragraphs 4.1* to *4.3*, and if:

   (i)   the occupier or any other person entitled to grant access has refused entry;

   (ii) it is impossible to communicate with the occupier or any other person entitled to grant access; or

   (iii) any of the provisions of *paragraph 6.4* apply.

(c)   Notice of Powers and Rights

6.7   If an officer conducts a search to which this Code applies the officer shall, unless it is impracticable to do so, provide the occupier with a copy of a Notice in a standard format:

   (i)   specifying if the search is made under warrant, with consent, or in the exercise of the powers described in *paragraphs 4.1* to *4.3*. Note: the notice format shall provide for authority or consent to be indicated, see *paragraphs 4.3* and *5.1*;

   (ii) summarising the extent of the powers of search and seizure conferred by PACE;

   (iii) explaining the rights of the occupier, and the owner of the property seized;

   (iv) explaining compensation may be payable in appropriate cases for damages caused entering and searching premises, and giving the address to send a compensation application, see *Note 6A*;

   (v) stating this Code is available at any police station.

6.8   If the occupier is:

   –   present, copies of the Notice and warrant shall, if practicable, be given to them before the search begins, unless the officer in charge of the search reasonably believes this would frustrate the object of the search or endanger officers or other people

   –   not present, copies of the Notice and warrant shall be left in a prominent place on the premises or appropriate part of the premises and endorsed, subject to *paragraph 2.9* with the name of the officer in charge of the search, the date and time of the search

The warrant shall be endorsed to show this has been done.

(d)   Conduct of searches

6.9   Premises may be searched only to the extent necessary to achieve the object of the search, having regard to the size and nature of whatever is sought.

6.9A A search may not continue under:

   –   a warrant's authority once all the things specified in that warrant have been found

   –   any other power once the object of that search has been achieved

6.9B   No search may continue once the officer in charge of the search is satisfied whatever is being sought is not on the premises. See *Note 6B*. This does not prevent a further search of the same premises if additional grounds come to light supporting a further application for a search warrant or exercise or further exercise of another power. For example, when, as a result of new information, it is believed articles previously not found or additional articles are on the premises.

6.10   Searches must be conducted with due consideration for the property and privacy of the occupier and with no more disturbance than necessary. Reasonable force may be used only when necessary and proportionate because the co-operation of the occupier cannot be obtained or is insufficient for the purpose. See *Note 6C*

6.11   A friend, neighbour or other person must be allowed to witness the search if the occupier wishes unless the officer in charge of the search has reasonable grounds for believing the presence of the person asked for would seriously hinder the investigation or endanger officers or other people. A search need not be unreasonably delayed for this purpose. A record of the action taken should be made on the premises search record including the grounds for refusing the occupier's request.

6.12   A person is not required to be cautioned prior to being asked questions that are solely necessary for the purpose of furthering the proper and effective conduct of a search, see *Code C, paragraph 10.1(c)*. For example, questions to discover the occupier of specified premises, to find a key to open a locked drawer or cupboard or to otherwise seek co-operation during the search or to determine if a particular item is liable to be seized.

6.12A   If questioning goes beyond what is necessary for the purpose of the exemption in Code C, the exchange is likely to constitute an interview as defined by *Code C, paragraph 11.1A* and would require the associated safeguards included in *Code C, section 10*.

(e)   Leaving premises

6.13   If premises have been entered by force, before leaving the officer in charge of the search must make sure they are secure by:

- arranging for the occupier or their agent to be present
- any other appropriate means

(f)   Searches under PACE Schedule 1 or the Terrorism Act 2000, Schedule 5

6.14   An officer of inspector rank or above shall be the officer in charge of the search, see *paragraph 2.10*, in respect of any search made under a warrant issued under PACE Act 1984, Schedule 1 or the Terrorism Act 2000, Schedule 5. They are responsible for making sure the search is conducted with discretion and in a manner that causes the least possible disruption to any business or other activities carried out on the premises.

6.15   Once the officer in charge of the search is satisfied material may not be taken from the premises without their knowledge, they shall ask for the documents or other records concerned. The officer in charge of the search may also ask to see the index to files held on the premises, and the officers conducting the search may inspect any files which, according to the index, appear to contain the material sought. A more extensive search of the premises may be made only if:

- the person responsible for them refuses to:
  - produce the material sought, or
  - allow access to the index
- it appears the index is:
  - inaccurate, or
  - incomplete

for any other reason the officer in charge of the search has reasonable grounds for believing such a search is necessary in order to find the material sought

Notes for guidance

6A   Whether compensation is appropriate depends on the circumstances in each case. Compensation for damage caused when effecting entry is unlikely to be appropriate if the search was lawful, and the force used can be shown to be reasonable, proportionate and necessary to effect entry. If the wrong premises are searched by mistake everything possible should be done at the earliest opportunity to allay any sense of grievance and there should normally be a strong presumption in favour of paying compensation.

6B   It is important that, when possible, all those involved in a search are fully briefed about any powers to be exercised and the extent and limits within which it should be conducted.

6C   In all cases the number of officers and other persons involved in executing the warrant should be determined by what is reasonable and necessary according to the particular circumstances.

7   Seizure and retention of property

(a)   Seizure

7.1   Subject to *paragraph 7.2*, an officer who is searching any person or premises under any statutory power or with the consent of the occupier may seize anything:

(a)   covered by a warrant

(b)   the officer has reasonable grounds for believing is evidence of an offence or has been obtained in consequence of the commission of an offence but only if seizure is necessary to prevent the items being concealed, lost, disposed of, altered, damaged, destroyed or tampered with

(c)   covered by the powers in the Criminal Justice and Police Act 2001, Part 2 allowing an officer to seize property from persons or premises and retain it for sifting or examination elsewhere

See Note 7B

7.2   No item may be seized which an officer has reasonable grounds for believing to be subject to legal privilege, as defined in PACE, section 10, other than under the Criminal Justice and Police Act 2001, Part 2.

7.3   Officers must be aware of the provisions in the Criminal Justice and Police Act 2001, section 59, allowing for applications to a judicial authority for the return of property seized and the subsequent duty to secure in section 60, see *paragraph 7.12(iii)*.

7.4   An officer may decide it is not appropriate to seize property because of an explanation from the person holding it but may nevertheless have reasonable grounds for believing it was obtained in consequence of an offence by some person. In these circumstances, the officer should identify the property to the holder, inform the holder of their suspicions and explain the holder may be liable to civil or criminal proceedings if they dispose of, alter or destroy the property.

7.5   An officer may arrange to photograph, image or copy, any document or other article they have the power to seize in accordance with *paragraph 7.1*. This is subject to specific restrictions on the examination, imaging or copying of certain property seized under the Criminal Justice and Police Act 2001, Part 2. An officer must have regard to their statutory obligation to retain an original document or other article only when a photograph or copy is not sufficient.

7.6   If an officer considers information stored in any electronic form and accessible from the premises could be used in evidence, they may require the information to be produced in a form:

–   which can be taken away and in which it is visible and legible; or

–   from which it can readily be produced in a visible and legible form

(b)   Criminal Justice and Police Act 2001: Specific procedures for seize and sift powers

7.7   The Criminal Justice and Police Act 2001, Part 2 gives officers limited powers to seize property from premises or persons so they can sift or examine it elsewhere. Officers must be careful they only exercise these powers when it is essential and they do not remove any more material than necessary. The removal of large volumes of material, much of which may not ultimately be retainable, may have serious implications for the owners, particularly when they are involved in business or activities such as journalism or the provision of medical services. Officers must carefully consider if removing copies or images of relevant material or data would be a satisfactory alternative to removing originals. When originals are taken, officers must be prepared to facilitate the provision of copies or images for the owners when reasonably practicable. See *Note 7C*

7.8   Property seized under the Criminal Justice and Police Act 2001, sections 50 or 51 must be kept securely and separately from any material seized under other powers. An examination under section 53 to determine which elements may be retained must be carried out at the earliest practicable time, having due regard to the desirability of allowing the person from whom the property was seized, or a person with an interest in the property, an opportunity of being present or represented at the examination.

7.8A   All reasonable steps should be taken to accommodate an interested person's request to be present, provided the request is reasonable and subject to the need to prevent harm to, interference with, or unreasonable delay to the investigatory process. If an examination proceeds in the absence of an interested person who asked to attend or their representative, the officer who exercised the relevant seizure power must give that person a written notice of why the examination was carried out in those circumstances. If it is necessary for security reasons or to maintain confidentiality officers may exclude interested persons from decryption or other processes which facilitate the examination but do not form part of it. See *Note 7D*

7.9   It is the responsibility of the officer in charge of the investigation to make sure property is returned in accordance with sections 53 to 55. Material which there is no power to retain must be:

- separated from the rest of the seized property

- returned as soon as reasonably practicable after examination of all the seized property

7.9A   Delay is only warranted if very clear and compelling reasons exist, e.g. the:

- unavailability of the person to whom the material is to be returned

- need to agree a convenient time to return a large volume of material

7.9B   Legally privileged, excluded or special procedure material which cannot be retained must be returned:

- as soon as reasonably practicable

- without waiting for the whole examination

7.9C   As set out in section 58, material must be returned to the person from whom it was seized, except when it is clear some other person has a better right to it. See *Note 7E*

7.10   When an officer involved in the investigation has reasonable grounds to believe a person with a relevant interest in property seized under section 50 or 51 intends to make an application under section 59 for the return of any legally privileged, special procedure or excluded material, the officer in charge of the investigation should be informed as soon as practicable and the material seized should be kept secure in accordance with section 61. See *Note 7C*

7.11   The officer in charge of the investigation is responsible for making sure property is properly secured. Securing involves making sure the property is not examined, copied, imaged or put to any other use except at the request, or with the consent, of the applicant or in accordance with the directions of the appropriate judicial authority. Any request, consent or directions must be recorded in writing and signed by both the initiator and the officer in charge of the investigation. See *Notes 7F and 7G*

7.12   When an officer exercises a power of seizure conferred by sections 50 or 51 they shall provide the occupier of the premises or the person from whom the property is being seized with a written notice:

(i)   specifying what has been seized under the powers conferred by that section;

(ii)   specifying the grounds for those powers;

(iii) setting out the effect of sections 59 to 61 covering the grounds for a person with a relevant interest in seized property to apply to a judicial authority for its return and the duty of officers to secure property in certain circumstances when an application is made;

(iv) specifying the name and address of the person to whom:
  – notice of an application to the appropriate judicial authority in respect of any of the seized property must be given;
  – an application may be made to allow attendance at the initial examination of the property.

7.13   If the occupier is not present but there is someone in charge of the premises, the notice shall be given to them. If no suitable person is available, so the notice will easily be found it should either be:

–   left in a prominent place on the premises

–   attached to the exterior of the premises

(c)   Retention

7.14   Subject to *paragraph 7.15*, anything seized in accordance with the above provisions may be retained only for as long as is necessary. It may be retained, among other purposes:

(i)   for use as evidence at a trial for an offence;

(ii) to facilitate the use in any investigation or proceedings of anything to which it is inextricably linked, see *Note 7H*;

(iii) for forensic examination or other investigation in connection with an offence;

(iv) in order to establish its lawful owner when there are reasonable grounds for believing it has been stolen or obtained by the commission of an offence.

7.15   Property shall not be retained under *paragraph 7.14(i), (ii)* or *(iii)* if a copy or image would be sufficient.

(d)   Rights of owners etc

7.16   If property is retained, the person who had custody or control of it immediately before seizure must, on request, be provided with a list or description of the property within a reasonable time.

7.17   That person or their representative must be allowed supervised access to the property to examine it or have it photographed or copied, or must be provided with a photograph or copy, in either case within a reasonable time of any request and at their own expense, unless the officer in charge of an investigation has reasonable grounds for believing this would:

(i) prejudice the investigation of any offence or criminal proceedings; or

(ii) lead to the commission of an offence by providing access to unlawful material such as pornography.

A record of the grounds shall be made when access is denied.

Notes for guidance

7A   Any person claiming property seized by the police may apply to a magistrates' court under the Police (Property) Act 1897 for its possession and should, if appropriate, be advised of this procedure.

7B   The powers of seizure conferred by PACE, sections 18(2) and 19(3) extend to the seizure of the whole premises when it is physically possible to seize and retain the premises in their totality and practical considerations make seizure desirable. For example, police may remove premises such as tents, vehicles or caravans to a police station for the purpose of preserving evidence.

7C   Officers should consider reaching agreement with owners and/or other interested parties on the procedures for examining a specific set of property, rather than awaiting the judicial authority's determination. Agreement can sometimes give a quicker and more satisfactory route for all concerned and minimise costs and legal complexities.

7D   *What constitutes a relevant interest in specific material may depend on the nature of that material and the circumstances in which it is seized. Anyone with a reasonable claim to ownership of the material and anyone entrusted with its safe keeping by the owner should be considered.*

7E   *Requirements to secure and return property apply equally to all copies, images or other material created because of seizure of the original property.*

7F   *The mechanics of securing property vary according to the circumstances; 'bagging up', i.e. placing material in sealed bags or containers and strict subsequent control of access is the appropriate procedure in many cases.*

7G   *When material is seized under the powers of seizure conferred by PACE, the duty to retain it under the Code of Practice issued under the Criminal Procedure and Investigations Act 1996 is subject to the provisions on retention of seized material in PACE, section 22.*

7H *Paragraph 7.14 (ii) applies if inextricably linked material is seized under the Criminal Justice and Police Act 2001, sections 50 or 51. Inextricably linked material is material it is not reasonably practicable to separate from other linked material without prejudicing the use of that other material in any investigation or proceedings. For example, it may not be possible to separate items of data held on computer disk without damaging their evidential integrity. Inextricably linked material must not be examined, imaged, copied or used for any purpose other than for proving the source and/or integrity of the linked material.*

8   **Action after searches**

8.1   If premises are searched in circumstances where this Code applies, unless the exceptions in *paragraph 2.3(a)* apply, on arrival at a police station the officer in charge of the search shall make or have made a record of the search, to include:

- (i)   the address of the searched premises;
- (ii)   the date, time and duration of the search;
- (iii)   the authority used for the search:
  - – if the search was made in exercise of a statutory power to search premises without warrant, the power which was used for the search:
  - – if the search was made under a warrant or with written consent;
    - – a copy of the warrant and the written authority to apply for it, see *paragraph 3.4*; or
    - – the written consent;

  shall be appended to the record or the record shall show the location of the copy warrant or consent.
- (iv)   subject to *paragraph 2.9*, the names of:
  - – the officer(s) in charge of the search;
  - – all other officers who conducted the search;
- (v)   the names of any people on the premises if they are known;
- (vi)   any grounds for refusing the occupier's request to have someone present during the search, see *paragraph 6.11*;
- (vii)   a list of any articles seized or the location of a list and, if not covered by a warrant, the grounds for their seizure;
- (viii) whether force was used, and the reason;
- (ix)   details of any damage caused during the search, and the circumstances;
- (x)   if applicable, the reason it was not practicable;
  - (a) to give the occupier a copy of the Notice of Powers and Rights, see *paragraph 6.7*;
  - (b) before the search to give the occupier a copy of the Notice, see *paragraph 6.8*;
- (xi)   when the occupier was not present, the place where copies of the Notice of Powers and Rights and search warrant were left on the premises, see *paragraph 6.8*.

8.2 When premises are searched under warrant, the warrant shall be endorsed to show:

(i) if any articles specified in the warrant were found;

(ii) if any other articles were seized;

(iii) the date and time it was executed;

(iv) subject to *paragraph 2.9*, the names of the officers who executed it;

(v) if a copy, together with a copy of the Notice of Powers and Rights was:
  – handed to the occupier; or
  – endorsed as required by *paragraph 6.8*; and left on the premises and where.

8.3 Any warrant shall be returned within one calendar month of its issue, if it was issued by a:

– justice of the peace, to the clerk to the justices for the petty sessions area concerned

– judge, to the appropriate officer of the court concerned

9 Search registers

9.1 A search register will be maintained at each sub-divisional or equivalent police station. All search records required under *paragraph 8.1* shall be made, copied, or referred to in the register. See *Note 9A*

Note for guidance

9A Paragraph 9.1 also applies to search records made by immigration officers. In these cases, a search register must also be maintained at an immigration office. See also Note 2D

Appendix 3

PACE Code of Practice for the Detention, Treatment and Questioning of Persons by Police Officers (Code C)

This Code applies to people in police detention after midnight on 31st March 2003, notwithstanding that their period of detention may have commenced before that time.

1 General

1.1   All persons in custody must be dealt with expeditiously, and released as soon as the need for detention no longer applies.

1.1A   A custody officer must perform the functions in this Code as soon as practicable. A custody officer will not be in breach of this Code if delay is justifiable and reasonable steps are taken to prevent unnecessary delay. The custody record shall show when a delay has occurred and the reason. See *Note 1H.*

1.2   This Code of Practice must be readily available at all police stations for consultation by:

–   police officers

–   detained persons

–   members of the public.

1.3   The provisions of this Code:

–   include the *Annexes*

–   do not include the *Notes for Guidance.*

1.4   If an officer has any suspicion, or is told in good faith, that a person of any age may be mentally disordered or otherwise mentally vulnerable, in the absence of clear evidence to dispel that suspicion, the person shall be treated as such for the purposes of this Code. See *Note 1G*

1.5   If anyone appears to be under 17, they shall be treated as a juvenile for the purposes of this Code in the absence of clear evidence that they are older.

1.6   If a person appears to be blind, seriously visually impaired, deaf, unable to read or speak or has difficulty orally because of a speech impediment, they shall be treated as such for the purposes of this Code in the absence of clear evidence to the contrary.

1.7   'The appropriate adult' means, in the case of a:

(a) juvenile:
   (i)   the parent, guardian or, if the juvenile is in local authority or voluntary organisation care, or is otherwise being looked after under the Children Act 1989, a person representing that authority or organisation;
   (ii)   a social worker of a local authority social services department;
   (iii) failing these, some other responsible adult aged 18 or over who is not a police officer or employed by the police.

(b) person who is mentally disordered or mentally vulnerable: See *Note 1D*

    (i)   a relative, guardian or other person responsible for their care or custody;

    (ii) someone experienced in dealing with mentally disordered or mentally vulnerable people but who is not a police officer or employed by the police;

    (iii) failing these, some other responsible adult aged 18 or over who is not a police officer or employed by the police.

1.8   If this Code requires a person be given certain information, they do not have to be given it if at the time they are incapable of understanding what is said, are violent or may become violent or in urgent need of medical attention, but they must be given it as soon as practicable.

1.9   References to a custody officer include those performing the functions of a custody officer.

1.9A   When this Code requires the prior authority or agreement of an officer of at least inspector or superintendent rank, that authority may be given by a sergeant or chief inspector authorised to perform the functions of the higher rank under the Police and Criminal Evidence Act 1984 (PACE), section 107.

1.10   Subject to *paragraph 1.12*, this Code applies to people in custody at police stations in England and Wales, whether or not they have been arrested, and to those removed to a police station as a place of safety under the Mental Health Act 1983, sections 135 and 136. Section 15 applies solely to people in police detention, e.g. those brought to a police station under arrest or arrested at a police station for an offence after going there voluntarily.

1.11   People in police custody include anyone detained under the Terrorism Act 2000, Schedule 8 and section 41, having been taken to a police station after being arrested under the Terrorism Act 2000, section 41. In these cases, reference to an offence in this Code includes the commission, preparation and instigation of acts of terrorism.

1.12   This Code's provisions do not apply to people in custody:

    (i)   arrested on warrants issued in Scotland by officers under the Criminal Justice and Public Order Act 1994, section 136(2), or arrested or detained without warrant by officers from a police force in Scotland under section 137(2). In these cases, police powers and duties and the person's rights and entitlements whilst at a police station in England or Wales are the same as those in Scotland;

    (ii) arrested under the Immigration and Asylum Act 1999, section 142(3) in order to have their fingerprints taken;

    (iii) whose detention is authorised by an immigration officer under the Immigration Act 1971;

    (iv) who are convicted or remanded prisoners held in police cells on behalf of the Prison Service under the Imprisonment (Temporary Provisions) Act 1980;

    (v) detained for examination under the Terrorism Act 2000, Schedule 7 and to whom the Code of Practice issued under that Act, Schedule 14, paragraph 6 applies;

    (vi) detained for searches under stop and search powers except as required by Code A.

The provisions on conditions of detention and treatment in section 8 and 9 must be considered as the minimum standards of treatment for such detainees.

1.13   In this Code:

(a) 'designated person' means a person other than a police officer, designated under the Police Reform Act 2002, Part 4 who has specified powers and duties of police officers conferred or imposed on them;

(b) reference to a police officer includes a designated person acting in the exercise or performance of the powers and duties conferred or imposed on them by their designation.

1.14   If a power conferred on a designated person:

(a) allows reasonable force to be used when exercised by a police officer, a person exercising that power has the same entitlement to use force;

(b) includes power to use force to enter any premises, that power is not exercisable by that designated person except:

(i) in the company, and under the supervision, of a police officer;

(ii) for the purpose of:

– saving life or limb; or

– preventing serious damage to property.

1.15   Nothing in this Code prevents the custody officer, or other officer given custody of the detainee, from allowing civilian support staff who are not designated persons to carry out individual procedures or tasks at the police station if the law allows. However, the officer remains responsible for making sure the procedures and tasks are carried out correctly in accordance with the Codes of Practice. Any such civilian must be:

(a) a person employed by a police authority maintaining a police force and under the control and direction of the Chief Officer of that force;

(b) employed by a person with whom a police authority has a contract for the provision of services relating to persons arrested or otherwise in custody.

1.16   Designated persons and other civilian support staff must have regard to any relevant provisions of the Codes of Practice.

1.17   References to pocket books include any official report book issued to police officers or civilian support staff.

Notes for guidance

1A   Although certain sections of this Code apply specifically to people in custody at police stations, those there voluntarily to assist with an investigation should be treated with no less consideration, e.g. offered refreshments at appropriate times, and enjoy an absolute right to obtain legal advice or communicate with anyone outside the police station.

1B   A person, including a parent or guardian, should not be an appropriate adult if they:

–   are

–   suspected of involvement in the offence

–   the victim

–   a witness

–   involved in the investigation

–   received admissions prior to attending to act as the appropriate adult.

Note: If a juvenile's parent is estranged from the juvenile, they should not be asked to act as the appropriate adult if the juvenile expressly and specifically objects to their presence.

1C   If a juvenile admits an offence to, or in the presence of, a social worker or member of a youth offending team other than during the time that person is acting as the juvenile's appropriate adult, another appropriate adult should be appointed in the interest of fairness.

1D   In the case of people who are mentally disordered or otherwise mentally vulnerable, it may be more satisfactory if the appropriate adult is someone experienced or trained in their care rather than a relative lacking such qualifications. But if the detainee prefers a relative to a better qualified stranger or objects to a particular person their wishes should, if practicable, be respected.

1E   A detainee should always be given an opportunity, when an appropriate adult is called to the police station, to consult privately with a solicitor in the appropriate adult's absence if they want.

1F   A solicitor or independent custody visitor (formerly a lay visitor) present at the police station in that capacity may not be the appropriate adult.

1G   'Mentally vulnerable' applies to any detainee who, because of their mental state or capacity, may not understand the significance of what is said, of questions or of their replies. 'Mental disorder' is defined in the Mental Health Act 1983, section 1(2) as 'mental illness, arrested or incomplete development of mind, psychopathic disorder and any other disorder or disability of mind'. When the custody officer has any doubt about the mental state or capacity of a detainee, that detainee should be treated as mentally vulnerable and an appropriate adult called.

1H   Paragraph 1.1A is intended to cover delays which may occur in processing detainees e.g. if:

- *a large number of suspects are brought into the station simultaneously to be placed in custody;*
- *interview rooms are all being used;*
- *there are difficulties contacting an appropriate adult, solicitor or interpreter.*

1I   The custody officer must remind the appropriate adult and detainee about the right to legal advice and record any reasons for waiving it in accordance with section 6.

2   Custody records

2.1   A separate custody record must be opened as soon as practicable for each person brought to a police station under arrest or arrested at the station having gone there voluntarily. All information recorded under this Code must be recorded as soon as practicable in the custody record unless otherwise specified. Any audio or video recording made in the custody area is not part of the custody record.

2.2   If any action requires the authority of an officer of a specified rank, subject to *paragraph 2.6A*, their name and rank must be noted in the custody record.

2.3   The custody officer is responsible for the custody record's accuracy and completeness and for making sure the record or copy of the record accompanies a detainee if they are transferred to another police station. The record shall show the:

- time and reason for transfer;
- time a person is released from detention.

2.4   A solicitor or appropriate adult must be permitted to consult a detainee's custody record as soon as practicable after their arrival at the station and at any other time whilst the person is detained. Arrangements for this access must be agreed with the custody officer and may not unreasonably interfere with the custody officer's duties.

2.4A   When a detainee leaves police detention or is taken before a court they, their legal representative or appropriate adult shall be given, on request, a copy of the custody record as soon as practicable. This entitlement lasts for 12 months after release.

2.5   The detainee, appropriate adult or legal representative shall be permitted to inspect the original custody record after the detainee has left police detention provided they give reasonable notice of their request. Any such inspection shall be noted in the custody record.

2.6   Subject to *paragraph 2.6A*, all entries in custody records must be timed and signed by the maker. Records entered on computer shall be timed and contain the operator's identification.

2.6A   Nothing in this Code requires the identity of officers or civilian support staff to be recorded or disclosed:

- (a) in the case of enquiries linked to the investigation of terrorism; or
- (b) if the officer or civilian support staff reasonably believe recording or disclosing their name might put them in danger.

In these cases, they shall use their warrant or other identification numbers and the name of their police station. See *Note 2A*

2.7   The fact and time of any detainee's refusal to sign a custody record, when asked in accordance with this Code, must be recorded.

Note for guidance

2A   The purpose of paragraph 2.6A(b) is to protect those involved in serious organised crime investigations or arrests of particularly violent suspects when there is reliable information that those arrested or their associates may threaten or cause harm to those involved. In cases of doubt, an officer of inspector rank or above should be consulted.

(a) Detained persons—normal procedure

3.1   When a person is brought to a police station under arrest or arrested at the station having gone there voluntarily, the custody officer must make sure the person is told clearly about the following continuing rights which may be exercised at any stage during the period in custody:

(i)   the right to have someone informed of their arrest as in section 5;

(ii)   the right to consult privately with a solicitor and that free independent legal advice is available;

(iii)   the right to consult these Codes of Practice. See *Note 3D*

3.2   The detainee must also be given:

–   a written notice setting out:
  – the above three rights;
  – the arrangements for obtaining legal advice;
  – the right to a copy of the custody record as in *paragraph 2.4A*;
  – the caution in the terms prescribed in section 10.

–   an additional written notice briefly setting out their entitlements while in custody, see *Notes 3A and 3B*.

Note: The detainee shall be asked to sign the custody record to acknowledge receipt of these notices. Any refusal must be recorded on the custody record.

3.3   A citizen of an independent Commonwealth country or a national of a foreign country, including the Republic of Ireland, must be informed as soon as practicable about their rights of communication with their High Commission, Embassy or Consulate. See section 7

3.4   The custody officer shall:

–   note on the custody record any comment the detainee makes in relation to the arresting officer's account but shall not invite comment. If the custody officer authorises a person's detention the detainee must be informed of the grounds as soon as practicable and before they are questioned about any offence;

–   note any comment the detainee makes in respect of the decision to detain them but shall not invite comment;

–   not put specific questions to the detainee regarding their involvement in any offence, nor in respect of any comments they may make in response to the arresting officer's account or the decision to place them in detention. Such an exchange is likely to constitute an interview as in *paragraph 11.1A* and require the associated safeguards in section 11.

See *paragraph 11.13* in respect of unsolicited comments.

3.5   The custody officer shall:

(a) ask the detainee, whether at this time, they:
  (i) would like legal advice, see *paragraph 6.5*;
  (ii) want someone informed of their detention, see section 5;

(b) ask the detainee to sign the custody record to confirm their decisions in respect of (a);

(c) determine whether the detainee:
  (i) is, or might be, in need of medical treatment or attention, see section 9;
  (ii) requires:
    – an appropriate adult;
    – help to check documentation;
    – an interpreter;

(d) record the decision in respect of (c).

3.6   When determining these needs the custody officer is responsible for initiating an assessment to consider whether the detainee is likely to present specific risks to custody staff or themselves. Such assessments should always include a check on the Police National Computer, to be carried out as soon as practicable, to identify any risks highlighted in relation to the detainee. Although such assessments are primarily the custody officer's responsibility, it may be necessary for them to consult and involve others, e.g. the arresting officer or an appropriate health care professional, see *paragraph 9.13*. Reasons for delaying the initiation or completion of the assessment must be recorded.

3.7   Chief Officers should ensure that arrangements for proper and effective risk assessments required by *paragraph 3.6* are implemented in respect of all detainees at police stations in their area.

3.8   Risk assessments must follow a structured process which clearly defines the categories of risk to be considered and the results must be incorporated in the detainee's custody record. The custody officer is responsible for making sure those responsible for the detainee's custody are appropriately briefed about the risks. If no specific risks are identified by the assessment, that should be noted in the custody record. See *Note 3E* and *paragraph 9.14*.

3.9   The custody officer is responsible for implementing the response to any specific risk assessment, e.g.:

- – reducing opportunities for self harm;
- – calling a health care professional;
- – increasing levels of monitoring or observation.

3.10   Risk assessment is an ongoing process and assessments must always be subject to review if circumstances change.

3.11   If video cameras are installed in the custody area, notices shall be prominently displayed showing cameras are in use. Any request to have video cameras switched off shall be refused.

(b)   Detained persons—special groups

3.12   If the detainee appears deaf or there is doubt about their hearing or speaking ability or ability to understand English, and the custody officer cannot establish effective communication, the custody officer must, as soon as practicable, call an interpreter for assistance in the action under *paragraphs 3.1–3.5*. See section 13.

3.13   If the detainee is a juvenile, the custody officer must, if it is practicable, ascertain the identity of a person responsible for their welfare. That person:

- – may be:
  - – the parent or guardian;
  - – if the juvenile is in local authority or voluntary organisation care, or is otherwise being looked after under the Children Act 1989, a person appointed by that authority or organisation to have responsibility for the juvenile's welfare;
  - – any other person who has, for the time being, assumed responsibility for the juvenile's welfare.
- – must be informed as soon as practicable that the juvenile has been arrested, why they have been arrested and where they are detained. This right is in addition to the juvenile's right in section 5 not to be held incommunicado. See *Note 3C*

3.14   If a juvenile known to be subject to a court order under which a person or organisation is given any degree of statutory responsibility to supervise or otherwise monitor them, reasonable steps must also be taken to notify that person or organisation (the 'responsible officer'). The responsible officer will normally be a member of a Youth Offending Team, except for a curfew order which involves electronic monitoring when the contractor providing the monitoring will normally be the responsible officer.

3.15   If the detainee is a juvenile, mentally disordered or otherwise mentally vulnerable, the custody officer must, as soon as practicable:

- – inform the appropriate adult, who in the case of a juvenile may or may not be a person responsible for their welfare, as in *paragraph 3.13*, of:
  - – the grounds for their detention;
  - – their whereabouts.
- – ask the adult to come to the police station to see the detainee.

3.16   It is imperative a mentally disordered or otherwise mentally vulnerable person, detained under the Mental Health Act 1983, section 136, be assessed as soon as possible. If that assessment is to take place at the police station, an approved social worker and a registered medical practitioner shall be called to the station as soon as possible in order to interview and examine the detainee. Once the detainee has been interviewed, examined and suitable arrangements made for their treatment or care, they can no longer be detained under section 136. A detainee must be immediately discharged from detention under section 136 if a registered medical practitioner, having examined them, concludes they are not mentally disordered within the meaning of the Act.

3.17   If the appropriate adult is:

- already at the police station, the provisions of *paragraphs 3.1 to 3.5* must be complied with in the appropriate adult's presence;

- not at the station when these provisions are complied with, they must be complied with again in the presence of the appropriate adult when they arrive.

3.18   The detainee shall be advised that:

- the duties of the appropriate adult include giving advice and assistance;

- they can consult privately with the appropriate adult at any time.

3.19   If the detainee, or appropriate adult on the detainee's behalf, asks for a solicitor to be called to give legal advice, the provisions of section 6 apply.

3.20   If the detainee is blind, seriously visually impaired or unable to read, the custody officer shall make sure their solicitor, relative, appropriate adult or some other person likely to take an interest in them and not involved in the investigation is available to help check any documentation. When this Code requires written consent or signing the person assisting may be asked to sign instead, if the detainee prefers. This paragraph does not require an appropriate adult to be called solely to assist in checking and signing documentation for a person who is not a juvenile, or mentally disordered or otherwise mentally vulnerable (see *paragraph 3.15*).

(c)   Persons attending a police station voluntarily

3.21   Anybody attending a police station voluntarily to assist with an investigation may leave at will unless arrested. If it is decided they shall not be allowed to leave, they must be informed at once that they are under arrest and brought before the custody officer, who is responsible for making sure they are notified of their rights in the same way as other detainees. If they are not arrested but are cautioned as in section 10, the person who gives the caution must, at the same time, inform them they are not under arrest, they are not obliged to remain at the station but if they remain at the station they may obtain free and independent legal advice if they want. They shall be told the right to legal advice includes the right to speak with a solicitor on the telephone and be asked if they want to do so.

3.22   If a person attending the police station voluntarily asks about their entitlement to legal advice, they shall be given a copy of the notice explaining the arrangements for obtaining legal advice. See *paragraph 3.2*

(d)   Documentation

3.23   The grounds for a person's detention shall be recorded, in the person's presence if practicable.

3.24   Action taken under *paragraphs 3.12 to 3.20* shall be recorded.

Notes for guidance

3A   The notice of entitlements should:

- *list the entitlements in this Code, including:*
  - *visits and contact with outside parties, including special provisions for Commonwealth citizens and foreign nationals;*

- *reasonable standards of physical comfort;*
- *adequate food and drink;*
- *access to toilets and washing facilities, clothing, medical attention, and exercise when practicable.*
- *mention the:*
  - *provisions relating to the conduct of interviews;*
  - *circumstances in which an appropriate adult should be available to assist the detainee and their statutory rights to make representation whenever the period of their detention is reviewed.*

3B   In addition to notices in English, translations should be available in Welsh, the main minority ethnic languages and the principal European languages, whenever they are likely to be helpful.

3C   If the juvenile is in local authority or voluntary organisation care but living with their parents or other adults responsible for their welfare, although there is no legal obligation to inform them, they should normally be contacted, as well as the authority or organisation unless suspected of involvement in the offence concerned. Even if the juvenile is not living with their parents, consideration should be given to informing them.

3D   The right to consult the Codes of Practice does not entitle the person concerned to delay unreasonably any necessary investigative or administrative action whilst they do so. Examples of action which need not be delayed unreasonably include:

- *procedures requiring the provision of breath, blood or urine specimens under the Road Traffic Act 1988 or the Transport and Works Act 1992*
- *searching detainees at the police station*
- *taking fingerprints or non-intimate samples without consent for evidential purposes.*

3E   Home Office Circular 32/2000 provides more detailed guidance on risk assessments and identifies key risk areas which should always be considered.

4   Detainee's property

(a)   Action

4.1   The custody officer is responsible for:

(a) ascertaining what property a detainee:
  (i) has with them when they come to the police station, whether on:
    - arrest or re-detention on answering to bail;
    - commitment to prison custody on the order or sentence of a court;
    - lodgement at the police station with a view to their production in court from prison custody;
    - transfer from detention at another station or hospital;
    - detention under the Mental Health Act 1983, section 135 or 136;
  (ii) might have acquired for an unlawful or harmful purpose while in custody;

(b) the safekeeping of any property taken from a detainee which remains at the police station.

The custody officer may search the detainee or authorise their being searched to the extent they consider necessary, provided a search of intimate parts of the body or involving the removal of more than outer clothing is only made as in *Annex A*. A search may only be carried out by an officer of the same sex as the detainee. See *Note 4A*

4.2   Detainees may retain clothing and personal effects at their own risk unless the custody officer considers they may use them to cause harm to themselves or others, interfere with evidence, damage property, effect an escape or they are needed as evidence. In this event the custody officer may withhold such articles as they consider necessary and must tell the detainee why.

4.3   Personal effects are those items a detainee may lawfully need, use or refer to while in detention but do not include cash and other items of value.

(b) Documentation

4.4   The custody officer is responsible for recording all property brought to the police station which a detainee had with them, or had taken from them on arrest. The detainee shall be allowed to check and sign the record of property as correct. Any refusal to sign shall be recorded.

4.5   If a detainee is not allowed to keep any article of clothing or personal effects, the reason must be recorded.

Notes for guidance

4A   PACE, Section 54(1) and paragraph 4.1 require a detainee to be searched when it is clear the custody officer will have continuing duties in relation to that detainee or when that detainee's behaviour or offence makes an inventory appropriate. They do not require every detainee to be searched, e.g. if it is clear a person will only be detained for a short period and is not to be placed in a cell, the custody officer may decide not to search them. In such a case the custody record will be endorsed 'not searched', paragraph 4.4 will not apply, and the detainee will be invited to sign the entry. If the detainee refuses, the custody officer will be obliged to ascertain what property they have in accordance with paragraph 4.1.

4B   Paragraph 4.4 does not require the custody officer to record on the custody record property in the detainee's possession on arrest if, by virtue of its nature, quantity or size, it is not practicable to remove it to the police station.

4C   Paragraph 4.4 does not require items of clothing worn by the person be recorded unless withheld by the custody officer as in paragraph 4.2.

5   Right not to be held incommunicado

(a) Action

5.1   Any person arrested and held in custody at a police station or other premises may, on request, have one person known to them or likely to take an interest in their welfare informed at public expense of their whereabouts as soon as practicable. If the person cannot be contacted the detainee may choose up to two alternatives. If they cannot be contacted, the person in charge of detention or the investigation has discretion to allow further attempts until the information has been conveyed. See *Notes 5C and 5D*

5.2   The exercise of the above right in respect of each person nominated may be delayed only in accordance with *Annex B.*

5.3   The above right may be exercised each time a detainee is taken to another police station.

5.4   The detainee may receive visits at the custody officer's discretion. See *Note 5B*

5.5   If a friend, relative or person with an interest in the detainee's welfare enquires about their whereabouts, this information shall be given if the suspect agrees and *Annex B* does not apply. See *Note 5D*

5.6   The detainee shall be given writing materials, on request, and allowed to telephone one person for a reasonable time, see *Notes 5A and 5E.* Either or both these privileges may be denied or delayed if an officer of inspector rank or above considers sending a letter or making a telephone call may result in any of the consequences in:

   (a) *Annex B paragraphs 1 and 2* and the person is detained in connection with an arrestable or serious arrestable offence; or

   (b) *Annex B paragraphs 8 and 9* and the person is detained under the Terrorism Act 2000, Schedule 7 or section 41

For the purposes of this paragraph, any reference to a serious arrestable offence in *Annex B* includes an arrestable offence. However, nothing in this paragraph permits the restriction or denial of the rights in *paragraphs 5.1 and 6.1.*

5.7   Before any letter or message is sent, or telephone call made, the detainee shall be informed that what they say in any letter, call or message (other than in a communication to a solicitor) may be read or listened to and may be given in evidence. A telephone call may be terminated if it is being abused. The costs can be at public expense at the custody officer's discretion.

(b)   Documentation

5.8   A record must be kept of any:

(a) request made under this section and the action taken;

(b) letters, messages or telephone calls made or received or visit received;

(c) refusal by the detainee to have information about them given to an outside enquirer. The detainee must be asked to countersign the record accordingly and any refusal recorded.

Notes for guidance

5A   A person may request an interpreter to interpret a telephone call or translate a letter.

5B   At the custody officer's discretion, visits should be allowed when possible, subject to having sufficient personnel to supervise a visit and any possible hindrance to the investigation.

5C   If the detainee does not know anyone to contact for advice or support or cannot contact a friend or relative, the custody officer should bear in mind any local voluntary bodies or other organisations who might be able to help. *Paragraph 6.1* applies if legal advice is required.

5D   In some circumstances it may not be appropriate to use the telephone to disclose information under *paragraphs 5.1* and *5.5*.

5E   The telephone call at *paragraph 5.6* is in addition to any communication under *paragraphs 5.1 and 6.1*.

6   Right to legal advice

(a)   Action

6.1   Unless *Annex B* applies, all detainees must be informed that they may at any time consult and communicate privately with a solicitor, whether in person, in writing or by telephone, and that free independent legal advice is available from the duty solicitor. See *paragraph 3.1, Note 6B and Note 6J*

6.2   Not Used

6.3   A poster advertising the right to legal advice must be prominently displayed in the charging area of every police station. See *Note 6H*

6.4   No police officer should, at any time, do or say anything with the intention of dissuading a detainee from obtaining legal advice.

6.5   The exercise of the right of access to legal advice may be delayed only as in *Annex B*. Whenever legal advice is requested, and unless *Annex B* applies, the custody officer must act without delay to secure the provision of such advice. If, on being informed or reminded of this right, the detainee declines to speak to a solicitor in person, the officer should point out that the right includes the right to speak with a solicitor on the telephones. If the detainee continues to waive this right the officer should ask them why and any reasons should be recorded on the custody record or the interview record as appropriate. Reminders of the right to legal advice must be given as in *paragraphs 3.5, 11.2, 15.4, 16.4 and 16.5* and *Code D, paragraphs 3.17(ii) and 6.3*. Once it is clear a detainee does not want to speak to a solicitor in person or by telephone they should cease to be asked their reasons. See *Note 6K*

6.6   A detainee who wants legal advice may not be interviewed or continue to be interviewed until they have received such advice unless:

(a) *Annex B* applies, when the restriction on drawing adverse inferences from silence in *Annex C* will apply because the detainee is not allowed an opportunity to consult a solicitor; or

(b) an officer of superintendent rank or above has reasonable grounds for believing that:

    (i) the consequent delay might:

       – lead to interference with, or harm to, evidence connected with an offence;

       – lead to interference with, or physical harm to, other people;

       – lead to serious loss of, or damage to, property;

       – lead to alerting other people suspected of having committed an offence but not yet arrested for it;

       – hinder the recovery of property obtained in consequence of the commission of an offence.

    (ii) when a solicitor, including a duty solicitor, has been contacted and has agreed to attend, awaiting their arrival would cause unreasonable delay to the process of investigation.

Note: In these cases the restriction on drawing adverse inferences from silence in *Annex C* will apply because the detainee is not allowed an opportunity to consult a solicitor;

(c) the solicitor the detainee has nominated or selected from a list:

    (i)   cannot be contacted;

    (ii) has previously indicated they do not wish to be contacted; or

    (iii) having been contacted, has declined to attend; and

    the detainee has been advised of the Duty Solicitor Scheme but has declined to ask for the duty solicitor.

    In these circumstances the interview may be started or continued without further delay provided an officer of inspector rank or above has agreed to the interview proceeding.

Note: The restriction on drawing adverse inferences from silence in *Annex C* will not apply because the detainee is allowed an opportunity to consult the duty solicitor;

(d) the detainee changes their mind, about wanting legal advice.

In these circumstances the interview may be started or continued without delay provided that:

    (i) the detainee agrees to do so, in writing or on tape; and

    (ii) an officer of inspector rank or above has inquired about the detainee's reasons for their change of mind and gives authority for the interview to proceed.

Confirmation of the detainee's agreement, their change of mind, the reasons for it if given and, subject to *paragraph 2.6A*, the name of the authorising officer shall be recorded in the taped or written interview record. See *Note 6I*. Note: In these circumstances the restriction on drawing adverse inferences from silence in *Annex C* will not apply because the detainee is allowed an opportunity to consult a solicitor if they wish.

6.7   If *paragraph 6.6(b)(i)* applies, once sufficient information has been obtained to avert the risk, questioning must cease until the detainee has received legal advice unless *paragraph 6.6(a), (b)(ii), (c) or (d)* applies.

6.8   A detainee who has been permitted to consult a solicitor shall be entitled on request to have the solicitor present when they are interviewed unless one of the exceptions in *paragraph 6.6* applies.

6.9   The solicitor may only be required to leave the interview if their conduct is such that the interviewer is unable properly to put questions to the suspect. See *Notes 6D and 6E*

6.10   If the interviewer considers a solicitor is acting in such a way, they will stop the interview and consult an officer not below superintendent rank, if one is readily available, and otherwise an officer not below inspector rank not connected with the investigation. After speaking to the solicitor, the officer consulted will decide if the interview should continue in the presence of that solicitor. If they decide it should not, the suspect will be given the opportunity to consult another solicitor before the interview continues and that solicitor given an opportunity to be present at the interview. See *Note 6E*

6.11   The removal of a solicitor from an interview is a serious step and, if it occurs, the officer of superintendent rank or above who took the decision will consider if the incident should be reported to the Law Society. If the decision to remove the solicitor has been taken by an officer below superintendent rank, the facts must be reported to an officer of superintendent rank or above who will similarly consider whether a report to the Law Society would be appropriate. When the solicitor concerned is a duty solicitor, the report should be both to the Law Society and to the Legal Services Commission.

6.12   'Solicitor' in this Code means:

- a solicitor who holds a current practising certificate;
- a trainee solicitor;
- a duty solicitor representative;
- an accredited representative included on the register of representatives maintained by the Legal Services Commission.

6.12A   A non-accredited or probationary representative sent to provide advice by, and on behalf of, a solicitor shall be admitted to the police station for this purpose unless an officer of inspector rank or above considers such a visit will hinder the investigation and directs otherwise. Hindering the investigation does not include giving proper legal advice to a detainee as in *Note 6D*. Once admitted to the police station, *paragraphs 6.6 to 6.10* apply.

6.13   In exercising their discretion under *paragraph 6.12A*, the officer should take into account in particular:

- whether:
  - the identity and status of the non-accredited or probationary representative have been satisfactorily established;
  - they are of suitable character to provide legal advice, e.g. a person with a criminal record is unlikely to be suitable unless the conviction was for a minor offence and not recent.
- any other matters in any written letter of authorisation provided by the solicitor on whose behalf the person is attending the police station. See *Note 6F*

6.14   If the inspector refuses access to a non-accredited or probationary representative or a decision is taken that such a person should not be permitted to remain at an interview, the inspector must notify the solicitor on whose behalf the representative was acting and give them an opportunity to make alternative arrangements. The detainee must be informed and the custody record noted.

6.15   If a solicitor arrives at the station to see a particular person, that person must, unless *Annex B* applies, be so informed whether or not they are being interviewed and asked if they would like to see the solicitor. This applies even if the detainee has declined legal advice or, having requested it, subsequently agreed to be interviewed without receiving advice. The solicitor's attendance and the detainee's decision must be noted in the custody record.

(b)   **Documentation**

6.16   Any request for legal advice and the action taken shall be recorded.

6.17   A record shall be made in the interview record if a detainee asks for legal advice and an interview is begun either in the absence of a solicitor or their representative, or they have been required to leave an interview.

Notes for guidance

6A   In considering if paragraph 6.6(b) applies, the officer should, if practicable, ask the solicitor for an estimate of how long it will take to come to the station and relate this to the time detention is permitted, the time of day (i.e. whether the rest period under paragraph 12.2 is imminent) and the requirements of other investigations. If the solicitor is on their way or is to set off immediately, it will not normally be appropriate to begin an interview before they arrive. If it appears necessary to begin an interview before the solicitor's arrival, they should be given an indication of how long the police would be able to wait before 6.6(b) applies so there is an opportunity to make arrangements for someone else to provide legal advice.

6B   A detainee who asks for legal advice should be given an opportunity to consult a specific solicitor or another solicitor from that solicitor's firm or the duty solicitor. If advice is not available by these means, or they do not want to consult the duty solicitor, the detainee should be given an opportunity to choose a solicitor from a list of those willing to provide legal advice. If this solicitor is unavailable, they may choose up to two alternatives. If these attempts are unsuccessful, the custody officer has discretion to allow further attempts until a solicitor has been contacted and agrees to provide legal advice. Apart from carrying out these duties, an officer must not advise the suspect about any particular firm of solicitors.

6C   Not Used

6D   A detainee has a right to free legal advice and to be represented by a solicitor. The solicitor's only role in the police station is to protect and advance the legal rights of their client. On occasions this may require the solicitor to give advice which has the effect of the client avoiding giving evidence which strengthens a prosecution case. The solicitor may intervene in order to seek clarification, challenge an improper question to their client or the manner in which it is put, advise their client not to reply to particular questions, or if they wish to give their client further legal advice. Paragraph 6.9 only applies if the solicitor's approach or conduct prevents or unreasonably obstructs proper questions being put to the suspect or the suspect's response being recorded. Examples of unacceptable conduct include answering questions on a suspect's behalf or providing written replies for the suspect to quote.

6E   An officer who takes the decision to exclude a solicitor must be in a position to satisfy the court the decision was properly made. In order to do this they may need to witness what is happening.

6F   If an officer of at least inspector rank considers a particular solicitor or firm of solicitors is persistently sending non-accredited or probationary representatives who are unsuited to provide legal advice, they should inform an officer of at least superintendent rank, who may wish to take the matter up with the Law Society.

6G   Subject to the constraints of Annex B, a solicitor may advise more than one client in an investigation if they wish. Any question of a conflict of interest is for the solicitor under their professional code of conduct. If, however, waiting for a solicitor to give advice to one client may lead to unreasonable delay to the interview with another, the provisions of paragraph 6.6(b) may apply.

6H   In addition to a poster in English, a poster or posters containing translations into Welsh, the main minority ethnic languages and the principal European languages should be displayed wherever they are likely to be helpful and it is practicable to do so.

6I   Paragraph 6.6(d) requires the authorisation of an officer of inspector rank or above to the continuation of an interview when a detainee who wanted legal advice changes their mind. It is permissible for such authorisation to be given over the telephone, if the authorising officer is able to satisfy themselves about the reason for the detainee's change of mind and is satisfied it is proper to continue the interview in those circumstances.

6J   Whenever a detainee exercises their right to legal advice by consulting or communicating with a solicitor, they must be allowed to do so in private. This right to consult or communicate in private is fundamental. Except as allowed by the Terrorism Act 2000, Schedule 8, paragraph 9, if the requirement for privacy is compromised because what is said or written by the detainee or solicitor for the purpose of giving and receiving legal advice is overheard, listened to, or read by others without the informed consent of the detainee, the right will effectively have been denied. When a detainee chooses to speak to a solicitor on the telephone, they should be allowed to do so in private unless this is impractical because of the design and layout of the custody area or the location of telephones. However, the normal expectation should be that facilities will be available, unless they are being used, at all police stations to enable detainees to speak in private to a solicitor either face to face or over the telephone.

6K   A detainee is not obliged to give reasons for declining legal advice and should not be pressed to do so.

7 Citizens of independent Commonwealth countries or foreign nationals

(a) Action

7.1 Any citizen of an independent Commonwealth country or a national of a foreign country, including the Republic of Ireland, may communicate at any time with the appropriate High Commission, Embassy or Consulate. The detainee must be informed as soon as practicable of:

– this right;

– their right, upon request, to have their High Commission, Embassy or Consulate told of their whereabouts and the grounds for their detention. Such a request should be acted upon as soon as practicable.

7.2 If a detainee is a citizen of a country with which a bilateral consular convention or agreement is in force requiring notification of arrest, the appropriate High Commission, Embassy or Consulate shall be informed as soon as practicable, subject to *paragraph 7.4*. The countries to which this applies as at 1st April 2003 are listed in *Annex F*.

7.3 Consular officers may visit one of their nationals in police detention to talk to them and, if required, to arrange for legal advice. Such visits shall take place out of the hearing of a police officer.

7.4 Notwithstanding the provisions of consular conventions, if the detainee is a political refugee whether for reasons of race, nationality, political opinion or religion, or is seeking political asylum, consular officers shall not be informed of the arrest of one of their nationals or given access or information about them except at the detainee's express request.

(b) Documentation

7.5 A record shall be made when a detainee is informed of their rights under this section and of any communications with a High Commission, Embassy or Consulate.

Note for guidance

7A   The exercise of the rights in this section may not be interfered with even though Annex B applies.

8 Conditions of detention

(a) Action

8.1 So far as it is practicable, not more than one detainee should be detained in each cell.

8.2 Cells in use must be adequately heated, cleaned and ventilated. They must be adequately lit, subject to such dimming as is compatible with safety and security to allow people detained overnight to sleep. No additional restraints shall be used within a locked cell unless absolutely necessary and then only restraint equipment, approved for use in that force by the Chief Officer, which is reasonable and necessary in the circumstances having regard to the detainee's demeanour and with a view to ensuring their safety and the safety of others. If a detainee is deaf, mentally disordered or otherwise mentally vulnerable, particular care must be taken when deciding whether to use any form of approved restraints.

8.3 Blankets, mattresses, pillows and other bedding supplied shall be of a reasonable standard and in a clean and sanitary condition. See *Note 8A*

8.4 Access to toilet and washing facilities must be provided.

8.5 If it is necessary to remove a detainee's clothes for the purposes of investigation, for hygiene, health reasons or cleaning, replacement clothing of a reasonable standard of comfort and cleanliness shall be provided. A detainee may not be interviewed unless adequate clothing has been offered.

8.6 At least two light meals and one main meal should be offered in any 24 hour period. See *Note 8B*. Drinks should be provided at meal times and upon reasonable request between meals. Whenever necessary, advice shall be sought from the appropriate health care professional, see *Note 9A*, on medical and dietary matters. As far as practicable, meals provided shall offer a varied diet and meet any specific dietary needs or religious beliefs the detainee may have. The detainee may, at the custody officer's discretion, have meals supplied by their family or friends at their expense.

See *Note 8A*

8.7 Brief outdoor exercise shall be offered daily if practicable.

8.8 A juvenile shall not be placed in a police cell unless no other secure accommodation is available and the custody officer considers it is not practicable to supervise them if they are not placed in a cell or that a cell provides more comfortable accommodation than other secure accommodation in the station. A juvenile may not be placed in a cell with a detained adult.

(b) Documentation

8.9 A record must be kept of replacement clothing and meals offered.

8.10 If a juvenile is placed in a cell, the reason must be recorded.

8.11 The use of any restraints on a detainee whilst in a cell, the reasons for it and, if appropriate, the arrangements for enhanced supervision of the detainee whilst so restrained, shall be recorded.

See *paragraph 3.9*

Notes for guidance

8A The provisions in paragraph 8.3 and 8.6 respectively are of particular importance in the case of a person detained under the Terrorism Act 2000, immigration detainees and others likely to be detained for an extended period. In deciding whether to allow meals to be supplied by family or friends, the custody officer is entitled to take account of the risk of items being concealed in any food or package and the officer's duties and responsibilities under food handling legislation.

8B Meals should, so far as practicable, be offered at recognised meal times, or at other times that take account of when the detainee last had a meal.

9 Care and treatment of detained persons

(a) General

9.1 Nothing in this section prevents the police from calling the police surgeon or, if appropriate, some other health care professional, to examine a detainee for the purposes of obtaining evidence relating to any offence in which the detainee is suspected of being involved. See *Note 9A*

9.2 If a complaint is made by, or on behalf of, a detainee about their treatment since their arrest, or it comes to notice that a detainee may have been treated improperly, a report must be made as soon as practicable to an officer of inspector rank or above not connected with the investigation. If the matter concerns a possible assault or the possibility of the unnecessary or unreasonable use of force, an appropriate health care professional must also be called as soon as practicable.

9.3 Detainees should be visited at least every hour. If no reasonably foreseeable risk was identified in a risk assessment, see *paragraphs 3.6–3.10*, there is no need to wake a sleeping detainee. Those suspected of being intoxicated through drink or drugs or whose level of consciousness causes concern must, subject to any clinical directions given by the appropriate health care professional, see *paragraph 9.13*:

- be visited and roused at least every half hour

- have their condition assessed as in *Annex H*

- and clinical treatment arranged if appropriate

See *Notes 9B, 9C and 9H*

9.4 When arrangements are made to secure clinical attention for a detainee, the custody officer must make sure all relevant information which might assist in the treatment of the detainee's condition is made available to the responsible health care professional. This applies whether or not the health care professional asks for such information. Any officer or civilian support staff with relevant information must inform the custody officer as soon as practicable.

(b) Clinical treatment and attention

9.5   The custody officer must make sure a detainee receives appropriate clinical attention as soon as reasonably practicable if the person:

(a) appears to be suffering from physical illness; or

(b) is injured; or

(c) appears to be suffering from a mental disorder; or

(d) appears to need clinical attention.

This applies even if the detainee makes no request for clinical attention and whether or not they have already received clinical attention elsewhere. If the need for attention appears urgent, e.g. when indicated as in *Annex H*, the nearest available health care professional or an ambulance must be called immediately. See *Note 9C*

9.6   *Paragraph 9.5* is not meant to prevent or delay the transfer to a hospital if necessary of a person detained under the Mental Health Act 1983, section 136. See *Note 9D*. When an assessment under that Act takes place at a police station, see *paragraph 3.16*, the custody officer must consider whether an appropriate health care professional should be called to conduct an initial clinical check on the detainee. This applies particularly when there is likely to be any significant delay in the arrival of a suitably qualified medical practitioner.

9.7   If it appears to the custody officer, or they are told, that a person brought to a station under arrest may be suffering from an infectious disease or condition, the custody officer must take reasonable steps to safeguard the health of the detainee and others at the station. In deciding what action to take, advice must be sought from an appropriate health care professional. See *Note 9E*. The custody officer has discretion to isolate the person and their property until clinical directions have been obtained.

9.8   If a detainee requests a clinical examination, an appropriate health care professional must be called as soon as practicable to assess the detainee's clinical needs. If a safe and appropriate care plan cannot be provided, the police surgeon's advice must be sought. The detainee may also be examined by a medical practitioner of their choice at their expense.

9.9   If a detainee is required to take or apply any medication in compliance with clinical directions prescribed before their detention, the custody officer must consult the appropriate health care professional before the use of the medication. Subject to the restrictions in *paragraph 9.10*, the custody officer is responsible for the safekeeping of any medication and for making sure the detainee is given the opportunity to take or apply prescribed or approved medication. Any such consultation and its outcome shall be noted in the custody record.

9.10   No police officer may administer or supervise the self-administration of controlled drugs of the types and forms listed in the Misuse of Drugs Regulations 2001, Schedule 1, 2 or 3. A detainee may only self-administer such drugs under the personal supervision of the registered medical practitioner authorising their use. Drugs listed in Schedule 4 or 5 may be distributed by the custody officer for self-administration if they have consulted the registered medical practitioner authorising their use, this may be done by telephone, and both parties are satisfied self-administration will not expose the detainee, police officers or anyone else to the risk of harm or injury.

9.11   When appropriate health care professionals administer drugs or other medications, or supervise their self-administration, it must be within current medicines legislation and the scope of practice as determined by their relevant professional body.

9.12   If a detainee has in their possession, or claims to need, medication relating to a heart condition, diabetes, epilepsy or a condition of comparable potential seriousness then, even though *paragraph 9.5* may not apply, the advice of the appropriate health care professional must be obtained.

9.13   Whenever the appropriate health care professional is called in accordance with this section to examine or treat a detainee, the custody officer shall ask for their opinion about:

–   any risks or problems which police need to take into account when making decisions about the detainee's continued detention;

–   when to carry out an interview if applicable; and

–   the need for safeguards.

9.14   When clinical directions are given by the appropriate health care professional, whether orally or in writing, and the custody officer has any doubts or is in any way uncertain about any aspect of the directions, the custody officer shall ask for clarification. It is particularly important that directions concerning the frequency of visits are clear, precise and capable of being implemented. See *Note 9F.*

(c)   Documentation

9.15   A record must be made in the custody record of:

(a)   the arrangements made for an examination by an appropriate health care professional under *paragraph 9.2* and of any complaint reported under that paragraph together with any relevant remarks by the custody officer;

(b)   any arrangements made in accordance with *paragraph 9.5*;

(c)   any request for a clinical examination under *paragraph 9.8* and any arrangements made in response;

(d)   the injury, ailment, condition or other reason which made it necessary to make the arrangements in (a) to (c), see *Note 9G*;

(e)   any clinical directions and advice, including any further clarifications, given to police by a health care professional concerning the care and treatment of the detainee in connection with any of the arrangements made in (a) to (c), see *Note 9F*;

(f)   if applicable, the responses received when attempting to rouse a person using the procedure in *Annex H*, see *Note 9H*.

9.16   If a health care professional does not record their clinical findings in the custody record, the record must show where they are recorded. See *Note 9G*. However, information which is necessary to custody staff to ensure the effective ongoing care and well being of the detainee must be recorded openly in the custody record, see *paragraph 3.8* and *Annex G, paragraph 7*.

9.17   Subject to the requirements of Section 4, the custody record shall include:

–   a record of all medication a detainee has in their possession on arrival at the police station;

–   a note of any such medication they claim to need but do not have with them.

Notes for guidance

9A   A 'health care professional' means a clinically qualified person working within the scope of practice as determined by their relevant professional body. Whether a health care professional is 'appropriate' depends on the circumstances of the duties they carry out at the time.

9B   Whenever possible juveniles and mentally vulnerable detainees should be visited more frequently.

9C   A detainee who appears drunk or behaves abnormally may be suffering from illness, the effects of drugs or may have sustained injury, particularly a head injury which is not apparent. A detainee needing or dependent on certain drugs, including alcohol, may experience harmful effects within a short time of being deprived of their supply. In these circumstances, when there is any doubt, police should always act urgently to call an appropriate health care professional or an ambulance. Paragraph 9.5 does not apply to minor ailments or injuries which do not need attention. However, all such ailments or injuries must be recorded in the custody record and any doubt must be resolved in favour of calling the appropriate health care professional.

9D   Whenever practicable, arrangements should be made for persons detained for assessment under the Mental Health Act 1983, section 136 to be taken to a hospital. There is no power under that Act to transfer a person detained under section 136 from one place of safety to another place of safety for assessment.

9E   It is important to respect a person's right to privacy and information about their health must be kept confidential and only disclosed with their consent or in accordance with clinical advice when it is necessary to protect the detainee's health or that of others who come into contact with them.

9F   The custody officer should always seek to clarify directions that the detainee requires constant observation or supervision and should ask the appropriate health care professional to explain precisely what action needs to be taken to implement such directions.

9G   Paragraphs 9.15 and 9.16 do not require any information about the cause of any injury, ailment or condition to be recorded on the custody record if it appears capable of providing evidence of an offence.

9H   The purpose of recording a person's responses when attempting to rouse them using the procedure in Annex H is to enable any change in the individual's consciousness level to be noted and clinical treatment arranged if appropriate.

10   Cautions

(a)   When a caution must be given

10.1   A person whom there are grounds to suspect of an offence, see *Note 10A*, must be cautioned before any questions about an offence, or further questions if the answers provide the grounds for suspicion, are put to them if either the suspect's answers or silence, (i.e. failure or refusal to answer or answer satisfactorily) may be given in evidence to a court in a prosecution. A person need not be cautioned if questions are for other necessary purposes, e.g.:

(a)   solely to establish their identity or ownership of any vehicle;

(b)   to obtain information in accordance with any relevant statutory requirement, see *paragraph 10.9*;

(c)   in furtherance of the proper and effective conduct of a search, e.g. to determine the need to search in the exercise of powers of stop and search or to seek co-operation while carrying out a search;

(d)   to seek verification of a written record as in *paragraph 11.13*;

(e)   when examining a person in accordance with the Terrorism Act 2000, Schedule 7 and the Code of Practice for Examining Officers issued under that Act, Schedule 14, *paragraph 6*.

10.2   Whenever a person not under arrest is initially cautioned, or reminded they are under caution, that person must at the same time be told they are not under arrest and are free to leave if they want to. See *Note 10C*

10.3   A person who is arrested, or further arrested, must be informed at the time, or as soon as practicable thereafter, that they are under arrest and the grounds for their arrest, see *Note 10B*.

10.4   A person who is arrested, or further arrested, must also be cautioned unless:

(a)   it is impracticable to do so by reason of their condition or behaviour at time;

(b)   they have already been cautioned immediately prior to arrest as in *paragraph 10.1*.

(b)   Terms of the cautions

10.5   The caution which must be given on:

(a)   arrest;

(b)   all other occasions before a person is charged or informed they may be prosecuted, see section 16, should, unless the restriction on drawing adverse inferences from silence applies, see *Annex C*, be in the following terms:

> "You do not have to say anything. But it may harm your defence if you do not mention when questioned something which you later rely on in Court. Anything you do say may be given in evidence."

See *Note 10G*

10.6   *Annex C, paragraph 2* sets out the alternative terms of the caution to be used when the restriction on drawing adverse inferences from silence applies.

10.7   Minor deviations from the words of any caution given in accordance with this Code do not constitute a breach of this Code, provided the sense of the relevant caution is preserved. See *Note 10D*

10.8   After any break in questioning under caution, the person being questioned must be made aware they remain under caution. If there is any doubt the relevant caution should be given again in full when the interview resumes. See *Note 10E*

10.9   When, despite being cautioned, a person fails to co-operate or to answer particular questions which may affect their immediate treatment, the person should be informed of any relevant consequences and that those consequences are not affected by the caution. Examples are when a person's refusal to provide:

- their name and address when charged may make them liable to detention;

- particulars and information in accordance with a statutory requirement, e.g. under the Road Traffic Act 1988, may amount to an offence or may make the person liable to a further arrest.

(c)   Special warnings under the Criminal Justice and Public Order Act 1994, sections 36 and 37

10.10   When a suspect interviewed at a police station or authorised place of detention after arrest fails or refuses to answer certain questions, or to answer satisfactorily, after due warning, see *Note 10F*, a court or jury may draw such inferences as appear proper under the Criminal Justice and Public Order Act 1994, sections 36 and 37. Such inferences may only be drawn when:

(a)   the restriction on drawing adverse inferences from silence, see *Annex C*, does not apply; and

(b)   the suspect is arrested by a constable and fails or refuses to account for any objects, marks or substances, or marks on such objects found:
- on their person;
- in or on their clothing or footwear;
- otherwise in their possession; or
- in the place they were arrested;

(c)   the arrested suspect was found by a constable at a place at or about the time the offence for which that officer has arrested them is alleged to have been committed, and the suspect fails or refuses to account for their presence there.

When the restriction on drawing adverse inferences from silence applies, the suspect may still be asked to account for any of the matters in (b) or (c) but the special warning described in *paragraph 10.11* will not apply and must not be given.

10.11   For an inference to be drawn when a suspect fails or refuses to answer a question about one of these matters or to answer it satisfactorily, the suspect must first be told in ordinary language:

(a)   what offence is being investigated;

(b)   what fact they are being asked to account for;

(c)   this fact may be due to them taking part in the commission of the offence;

(d)   a court may draw a proper inference if they fail or refuse to account for this fact;

(e)   a record is being made of the interview and it may be given in evidence if they are brought to trial.

(d) Juveniles and persons who are mentally disordered or otherwise mentally vulnerable

10.12 If a juvenile or a person who is mentally disordered or otherwise mentally vulnerable is cautioned in the absence of the appropriate adult, the caution must be repeated in the adult's presence.

(e) Documentation

10.13 A record shall be made when a caution is given under this section, either in the interviewer's pocket book or in the interview record.

Notes for guidance

10A   There must be some reasonable, objective grounds for the suspicion, based on known facts or information which are relevant to the likelihood the offence has been committed and the person to be questioned committed it.

10B   An arrested person must be given sufficient information to enable them to understand they have been deprived of their liberty and the reason they have been arrested, e.g. when a person is arrested on suspicion of committing an offence they must be informed of the suspected offence's nature, when and where it was committed. If the arrest is made under the general arrest conditions in PACE, section 25, the grounds for arrest must include an explanation of the conditions which make the arrest necessary. Vague or technical language should be avoided.

10C   The restriction on drawing inferences from silence, see Annex C, paragraph 1, does not apply to a person who has not been detained and who therefore cannot be prevented from seeking legal advice if they want, see paragraph 3.21.

10D   If it appears a person does not understand the caution, the person giving it should explain it in their own words.

10E   It may be necessary to show to the court that nothing occurred during an interview break or between interviews which influenced the suspect's recorded evidence. After a break in an interview or at the beginning of a subsequent interview, the interviewing officer should summarise the reason for the break and confirm this with the suspect.

10F   The Criminal Justice and Public Order Act 1994, sections 36 and 37 apply only to suspects who have been arrested by a constable or Customs and Excise officer and are given the relevant warning by the police or customs officer who made the arrest or who is investigating the offence. They do not apply to any interviews with suspects who have not been arrested.

10G   Nothing in this Code requires a caution to be given or repeated when informing a person not under arrest they may be prosecuted for an offence. However, a court will not be able to draw any inferences under the Criminal Justice and Public Order Act 1994, section 34, if the person was not cautioned.

11   Interviews—general

(a) Action

11.1A   An interview is the questioning of a person regarding their involvement or suspected involvement in a criminal offence or offences which, under *paragraph 10.1*, must be carried out under caution. Whenever a person is interviewed they must be informed of the nature of the offence, or further offence. Procedures under the Road Traffic Act 1988, section 7 or the Transport and Works Act 1992, section 31 do not constitute interviewing for the purpose of this Code.

11.1   Following a decision to arrest a suspect, they must not be interviewed about the relevant offence except at a police station or other authorised place of detention, unless the consequent delay would be likely to:

   (a) lead to:
      – interference with, or harm to, evidence connected with an offence;
      – interference with, or physical harm to, other people; or

– serious loss of, or damage to, property;

(b) lead to alerting other people suspected of committing an offence but not yet arrested for it; or

(c) hinder the recovery of property obtained in consequence of the commission of an offence.

Interviewing in any of these circumstances shall cease once the relevant risk has been averted or the necessary questions have been put in order to attempt to avert that risk.

11.2   Immediately prior to the commencement or re-commencement of any interview at a police station or other authorised place of detention, the interviewer should remind the suspect of their entitlement to free legal advice and that the interview can be delayed for legal advice to be obtained, unless one of the exceptions in *paragraph 6.6* applies. It is the interviewer's responsibility to make sure all reminders are recorded in the interview record.

11.3   Not Used

11.4   At the beginning of an interview the interviewer, after cautioning the suspect, see section 10, shall put to them any significant statement or silence which occurred in the presence and hearing of a police officer or civilian interviewer before the start of the interview and which have not been put to the suspect in the course of a previous interview. See *Note 11A*. The interviewer shall ask the suspect whether they confirm or deny that earlier statement or silence and if they want to add anything.

11.4A   A significant statement is one which appears capable of being used in evidence against the suspect, in particular a direct admission of guilt. A significant silence is a failure or refusal to answer a question or answer satisfactorily when under caution, which might, allowing for the restriction on drawing adverse inferences from silence, see *Annex C*, give rise to an inference under the Criminal Justice and Public Order Act 1994, Part III.

11.5   No interviewer may try to obtain answers or elicit a statement by the use of oppression. Except as in *paragraph 10.9*, no interviewer shall indicate, except to answer a direct question, what action will be taken by the police if the person being questioned answers questions, makes a statement or refuses to do either. If the person asks directly what action will be taken if they answer questions, make a statement or refuse to do either, the interviewer may inform them what action the police propose to take provided that action is itself proper and warranted.

11.6   The interview or further interview of a person about an offence with which that person has not been charged or for which they have not been informed they may be prosecuted, must cease when the officer in charge of the investigation:

(a) is satisfied all the questions they consider relevant to obtaining accurate and reliable information about the offence have been put to the suspect, this includes allowing the suspect an opportunity to give an innocent explanation and asking questions to test if the explanation is accurate and reliable, e.g. to clear up ambiguities or clarify what the suspect said;

(b) has taken account of any other available evidence; and

(c) the officer in charge of the investigation, or in the case of a detained suspect, the custody officer, see *paragraph 16.1*, reasonably believes there is sufficient evidence to provide a realistic prospect of conviction for that offence if the person was prosecuted for it. See *Note 11B*

This paragraph does not prevent officers in revenue cases or acting under the confiscation provisions of the Criminal Justice Act 1988 or the Drug Trafficking Act 1994 from inviting suspects to complete a formal question and answer record after the interview is concluded.

(b)   Interview records

11.7 (a)   An accurate record must be made of each interview, whether or not the interview takes place at a police station

(b)   The record must state the place of interview, the time it begins and ends, any interview breaks and, subject to *paragraph 2.6A*, the names of all those present; and must be made on the forms provided for this purpose or in the interviewer's pocket book or in accordance with the Codes of Practice E or F;

(c)   Any written record must be made and completed during the interview, unless this would not be practicable or would interfere with the conduct of the interview, and must constitute either a verbatim record of what has been said or, failing this, an account of the interview which adequately and accurately summarises it.

11.8   If a written record is not made during the interview it must be made as soon as practicable after its completion.

11.9   Written interview records must be timed and signed by the maker.

11.10   If a written record is not completed during the interview the reason must be recorded in the interview record.

11.11   Unless it is impracticable, the person interviewed shall be given the opportunity to read the interview record and to sign it as correct or to indicate how they consider it inaccurate. If the person interviewed cannot read or refuses to read the record or sign it, the senior interviewer present shall read it to them and ask whether they would like to sign it as correct or make their mark or to indicate how they consider it inaccurate. The interviewer shall certify on the interview record itself what has occurred. See *Note 11E*

11.12   If the appropriate adult or the person's solicitor is present during the interview, they should also be given an opportunity to read and sign the interview record or any written statement taken down during the interview.

11.13   A written record shall be made of any comments made by a suspect, including unsolicited comments, which are outside the context of an interview but which might be relevant to the offence. Any such record must be timed and signed by the maker. When practicable the suspect shall be given the opportunity to read that record and to sign it as correct or to indicate how they consider it inaccurate. See *Note 11E*

11.14   Any refusal by a person to sign an interview record when asked in accordance with this Code must itself be recorded.

(c)   Juveniles and mentally disordered or otherwise mentally vulnerable people

11.15   A juvenile or person who is mentally disordered or otherwise mentally vulnerable must not be interviewed regarding their involvement or suspected involvement in a criminal offence or offences, or asked to provide or sign a written statement under caution or record of interview, in the absence of the appropriate adult unless *paragraphs 11.1, 11.18 to 11.20* apply. See *Note 11C*

11.16   Juveniles may only be interviewed at their place of education in exceptional circumstances and only when the principal or their nominee agrees. Every effort should be made to notify the parent(s) or other person responsible for the juvenile's welfare and the appropriate adult, if this is a different person, that the police want to interview the juvenile and reasonable time should be allowed to enable the appropriate adult to be present at the interview. If awaiting the appropriate adult would cause unreasonable delay, and unless the juvenile is suspected of an offence against the educational establishment, the principal or their nominee can act as the appropriate adult for the purposes of the interview.

11.17   If an appropriate adult is present at an interview, they shall be informed:

- they are not expected to act simply as an observer; and
- the purpose of their presence is to:
  - advise the person being interviewed;
  - observe whether the interview is being conducted properly and fairly;
  - facilitate communication with the person being interviewed.

(d)   Vulnerable suspects—urgent interviews at police stations

11.18   The following persons may not be interviewed unless an officer of superintendent rank or above considers delay will lead to the consequences in *paragraph 11.1(a) to (c)*, and is satisfied the interview would not significantly harm the person's physical or mental state (see *Annex G*):

(a)   a juvenile or person who is mentally disordered or otherwise mentally vulnerable if at the time of the interview the appropriate adult is not present;

   (b) anyone other than in (a) who at the time of the interview appears unable to:
- appreciate the significance of questions and their answers; or
- understand what is happening because of the effects of drink, drugs or any illness, ailment or condition;

   (c) a person who has difficulty understanding English or has a hearing disability, if at the time of the interview an interpreter is not present.

11.19   These interviews may not continue once sufficient information has been obtained to avert the consequences in *paragraph 11.1(a) to (c)*.

11.20   A record shall be made of the grounds for any decision to interview a person under *paragraph 11.18*.

Notes for guidance

11A   Paragraph 11.4 does not prevent the interviewer from putting significant statements and silences to a suspect again at a later stage or a further interview.

11B   The Criminal Procedure and Investigations Act 1996 Code of Practice, paragraph 3.4 states 'In conducting an investigation, the investigator should pursue all reasonable lines of enquiry, whether these point towards or away from the suspect. What is reasonable will depend on the particular circumstances.' Interviewers should keep this in mind when deciding what questions to ask in an interview.

11C   Although juveniles or people who are mentally disordered or otherwise mentally vulnerable are often capable of providing reliable evidence, they may, without knowing or wishing to do so, be particularly prone in certain circumstances to provide information that may be unreliable, misleading or self-incriminating. Special care should always be taken when questioning such a person, and the appropriate adult should be involved if there is any doubt about a person's age, mental state or capacity. Because of the risk of unreliable evidence it is also important to obtain corroboration of any facts admitted whenever possible.

11D   Juveniles should not be arrested at their place of education unless this is unavoidable. When a juvenile is arrested at their place of education, the principal or their nominee must be informed.

11E   Significant statements described in paragraph 11.4 will always be relevant to the offence and must be recorded. When a suspect agrees to read records of interviews and other comments and sign them as correct, they should be asked to endorse the record with, e.g. 'I agree that this is a correct record of what was said' and add their signature. If the suspect does not agree with the record, the interviewer should record the details of any disagreement and ask the suspect to read these details and sign them to the effect that they accurately reflect their disagreement. Any refusal to sign should be recorded.

12   Interviews in police stations

(a) Action

12.1   If a police officer wants to interview or conduct enquiries which require the presence of a detainee, the custody officer is responsible for deciding whether to deliver the detainee into the officer's custody.

12.2   Except as below, in any period of 24 hours a detainee must be allowed a continuous period of at least 8 hours for rest, free from questioning, travel or any interruption in connection with the investigation concerned. This period should normally be at night or other appropriate time which takes account of when the detainee last slept or rested. If a detainee is arrested at a police station after going there voluntarily, the period of 24 hours runs from the time of their arrest and not the time of arrival at the police station. The period may not be interrupted or delayed, except:

   (a) when there are reasonable grounds for believing not delaying or interrupting the period would:
- (i)   involve a risk of harm to people or serious loss of, or damage to, property;
- (ii)   delay unnecessarily the person's release from custody;
- (iii)   otherwise prejudice the outcome of the investigation;

   (b) at the request of the detainee, their appropriate adult or legal representative;

(c) when a delay or interruption is necessary in order to:
  (i) comply with the legal obligations and duties arising under section 15;
  (ii) to take action required under section 9 or in accordance with medical advice.

If the period is interrupted in accordance with (a), a fresh period must be allowed. Interruptions under (b) and (c), do not require a fresh period to be allowed.

12.3   Before a detainee is interviewed the custody officer, in consultation with the officer in charge of the investigation and appropriate health care professionals as necessary, shall assess whether the detainee is fit enough to be interviewed. This means determining and considering the risks to the detainee's physical and mental state if the interview took place and determining what safeguards are needed to allow the interview to take place. See *Annex G*. The custody officer shall not allow a detainee to be interviewed if the custody officer considers it would cause significant harm to the detainee's physical or mental state. Vulnerable suspects listed at *paragraph 11.18* shall be treated as always being at some risk during an interview and these persons may not be interviewed except in accordance with *paragraphs 11.18 to 11.20*.

12.4   As far as practicable interviews shall take place in interview rooms which are adequately heated, lit and ventilated.

12.5   A suspect whose detention without charge has been authorised under PACE, because the detention is necessary for an interview to obtain evidence of the offence for which they have been arrested, may choose not to answer questions but police do not require the suspect's consent or agreement to interview them for this purpose. If a suspect takes steps to prevent themselves being questioned or further questioned, e.g. by refusing to leave their cell to go to a suitable interview room or by trying to leave the interview room, they shall be advised their consent or agreement to interview is not required. The suspect shall be cautioned as in section 10, and informed if they fail or refuse to co-operate, the interview may take place in the cell and that their failure or refusal to co-operate may be given in evidence. The suspect shall then be invited to co-operate and go into the interview room.

12.6   People being questioned or making statements shall not be required to stand.

12.7   Before the interview commences each interviewer shall, subject to *paragraph 2.6A*, identify themselves and any other persons present to the interviewee.

12.8   Breaks from interviewing should be made at recognised meal times or at other times that take account of when an interviewee last had a meal. Short refreshment breaks shall be provided at approximately two hour intervals, subject to the interviewer's discretion to delay a break if there are reasonable grounds for believing it would:

  (i)   involve a:
    – risk of harm to people;
    – serious loss of, or damage to, property;

  (ii) unnecessarily delay the detainee's release;

  (iii) otherwise prejudice the outcome of the investigation.

See *Note 12B*

12.9   If during the interview a complaint is made by or on behalf of the interviewee concerning the provisions of this Code, the interviewer should:

  (i)   record it in the interview record;

  (ii) inform the custody officer, who is then responsible for dealing with it as in section 9.

(b) Documentation

12.10   A record must be made of the:

  –   time a detainee is not in the custody of the custody officer, and why

  –   reason for any refusal to deliver the detainee out of that custody

12.11   A record shall be made of:

(a) the reasons it was not practicable to use an interview room; and

(b) any action taken as in *paragraph 12.5*.

The record shall be made on the custody record or in the interview record for action taken whilst an interview record is being kept, with a brief reference to this effect in the custody record.

12.12   Any decision to delay a break in an interview must be recorded, with reasons, in the interview record.

12.13   All written statements made at police stations under caution shall be written on forms provided for the purpose.

12.14   All written statements made under caution shall be taken in accordance with *Annex D*. Before a person makes a written statement under caution at a police station they shall be reminded about the right to legal advice. See *Note 12A*

Notes for guidance

12A   It is not normally necessary to ask for a written statement if the interview was recorded or taped at the time and the record signed by the interviewee in accordance with paragraph 11.11. Statements under caution should normally be taken in these circumstances only at the person's express wish. A person may however be asked if they want to make such a statement.

12B   Meal breaks should normally last at least 45 minutes and shorter breaks after two hours should last at least 15 minutes. If the interviewer delays a break in accordance with paragraph 12.8 and prolongs the interview, a longer break should be provided. If there is a short interview, and another short interview is contemplated, the length of the break may be reduced if there are reasonable grounds to believe this is necessary to avoid any of the consequences in paragraph 12.8(i) to (iii).

13   **Interpreters**

(a)   **General**

13.1   Chief officers are responsible for making sure appropriate arrangements are in place for provision of suitably qualified interpreters for people who:

–   are deaf;

–   do not understand English.

(b)   **Foreign languages**

13.2   Unless *paragraphs 11.1, 11.18 to 11.20* apply, a person must not be interviewed in the absence of a person capable of interpreting if:

(a) they have difficulty understanding English;

(b) the interviewer cannot speak the person's own language;

(c) the person wants an interpreter present.

13.3   The interviewer shall make sure the interpreter makes a note of the interview at the time in the person's language for use in the event of the interpreter being called to give evidence, and certifies its accuracy. The interviewer should allow sufficient time for the interpreter to note each question and answer after each is put, given and interpreted. The person should be allowed to read the record or have it read to them and sign it as correct or indicate the respects in which they consider it inaccurate. If the interview is tape-recorded or visually recorded, the arrangements in Code E or F apply.

13.4   In the case of a person making a statement other than in English:

(a) the interpreter shall record the statement in the language it is made;

(b) the person shall be invited to sign it;

(c) an official English translation shall be made in due course.

(c)   Deaf people and people with speech difficulties

13.5   If a person appears to be deaf or there is doubt about their hearing or speaking ability, they must not be interviewed in the absence of an interpreter unless they agree in writing to being interviewed without one or *paragraphs 11.1, 11.18 to 11.20* apply.

13.6   An interpreter should also be called if a juvenile is interviewed and the parent or guardian present as the appropriate adult appears to be deaf or there is doubt about their hearing or speaking ability, unless they agree in writing to the interview proceeding without one or *paragraphs 11.1, 11.18 to 11.20* apply.

13.7   The interviewer shall make sure the interpreter is allowed to read the interview record and certify its accuracy in the event of the interpreter being called to give evidence. If the interview is tape-recorded or visually recorded, the arrangements in Code E or F apply.

(d)   Additional rules for detained persons

13.8   All reasonable attempts should be made to make the detainee understand that interpreters will be provided at public expense.

13.9   If *paragraph 6.1* applies and the detainee cannot communicate with the solicitor because of language, hearing or speech difficulties, an interpreter must be called. The interpreter may not be a police officer or civilian support staff when interpretation is needed for the purposes of obtaining legal advice. In all other cases a police officer or civilian support staff may only interpret if the detainee and the appropriate adult, if applicable, give their agreement in writing or if the interview is tape-recorded or visually recorded as in Code E or F.

13.10   When the custody officer cannot establish effective communication with a person charged with an offence who appears deaf or there is doubt about their ability to hear, speak or to understand English, arrangements must be made as soon as practicable for an interpreter to explain the offence and any other information given by the custody officer.

(e)   Documentation

13.11 Action taken to call an interpreter under this section and any agreement to be interviewed in the absence of an interpreter must be recorded.

14   Questioning – special restrictions

14.1   If a person is arrested by one police force on behalf of another and the lawful period of detention in respect of that offence has not yet commenced in accordance with PACE, section 41 no questions may be put to them about the offence while they are in transit between the forces except to clarify any voluntary statement they make.

14.2   If a person is in police detention at a hospital they may not be questioned without the agreement of a responsible doctor. See *Note 14A*

Note for guidance

14A   If questioning takes place at a hospital under paragraph 14.2, or on the way to or from a hospital, the period of questioning concerned counts towards the total period of detention permitted.

15   Reviews and extensions of detention

(a)   Persons detained under PACE

15.1   The review officer is responsible under PACE, section 40 for periodically determining if a person's detention, before or after charge, continues to be necessary. This requirement continues throughout the detention period and except as in *paragraph 15.10*, the review officer must be present at the police station holding the detainee. See *Notes 15A and 15B*

15.2   Under PACE, section 42, an officer of superintendent rank or above who is responsible for the station holding the detainee may give authority any time after the second review to extend the maximum period the person may be detained without charge by up to 12 hours. Further detention without charge may be authorised only by a magistrates' court in accordance with PACE, sections 43 and 44. See *Notes 15C, 15D and 15E*

15.3   Before deciding whether to authorise continued detention the officer responsible under *paragraphs 15.1 or 15.2* shall give an opportunity to make representations about the detention to:

(a) the detainee, unless in the case of a review as in *paragraph 15.1*, the detainee is asleep;

(b) the detainee's solicitor if available at the time; and

(c) the appropriate adult if available at the time.

15.3A   Other people having an interest in the detainee's welfare may also make representations at the authorising officer's discretion.

15.3B   Subject to *paragraph 15.10*, the representations may be made orally in person or by telephone or in writing. The authorising officer may, however, refuse to hear oral representations from the detainee if the officer considers them unfit to make representations because of their condition or behaviour. See *Note 15C*

15.4   Before conducting a review or determining whether to extend the maximum period of detention without charge, the officer responsible must make sure the detainee is reminded of their entitlement to free legal advice, see *paragraph 6.5*, unless in the case of a review the person is asleep.

15.5   If, after considering any representations, the officer decides to keep the detainee in detention or extend the maximum period they may be detained without charge, any comment made by the detainee shall be recorded. If applicable, the officer responsible under *paragraph 15.1 or 15.2* shall be informed of the comment as soon as practicable. See also *paragraphs 11.4 and 11.13*

15.6   No officer shall put specific questions to the detainee:

–   regarding their involvement in any offence; or

–   in respect of any comments they may make;
      – when given the opportunity to make representations; or
      – in response to a decision to keep them in detention or extend the maximum period of detention.

Such an exchange could constitute an interview as in *paragraph 11.1A* and would be subject to the associated safeguards in section 11 and, in respect of a person who has been charged, *paragraph 16.5*.

See also *paragraph 11.13*.

15.7   A detainee who is asleep at a review, see *paragraph 15.1*, and whose continued detention is authorised must be informed about the decision and reason as soon as practicable after waking.

(b)   Persons detained under the Terrorism Act 2000

15.8 In terrorism cases:

(a) the powers and duties of the review officer are in the Terrorism Act 2000, Schedule 8, Part II;

(b) a police officer of at least superintendent rank may apply to a judicial authority for a warrant of further detention under the Terrorism Act 2000, Schedule 8, Part III.

(c)   Telephone review of detention

15.9   PACE, section 40A provides that the officer responsible under section 40 for reviewing the detention of a person who has not been charged, need not attend the police station holding the detainee and may carry out the review by telephone if:

(a) it is not reasonably practicable for the officer to be present;

(b) PACE, section 45A, in respect of the use of video conferencing facilities, does not apply or it is not reasonably practicable to use such facilities.

See *Note 15F*

15.10   When a telephone review is carried out, an officer at the station holding the detainee shall be required by the review officer to fulfil that officer's obligations under PACE section 40 or this Code by:

(a) making any record connected with the review in the detainee's custody record;

(b) if applicable, making a record in (a) in the presence of the detainee; and

(c) giving the detainee information about the review.

15.11   When a telephone review is carried out, the requirement in *paragraph 15.3* will be satisfied:

(a) if facilities exist for the immediate transmission of written representations to the review officer, e.g. fax or email message, by giving the detainee an opportunity to make representations:
(i)   orally by telephone; or
(ii) in writing using those facilities; and

(b) in all other cases, by giving the detainee an opportunity to make their representations orally by telephone.

(d)   Documentation

15.12   It is the officer's responsibility to make sure all reminders given under *paragraph 15.4* are noted in the custody record.

15.13   The grounds for, and extent of, any delay in conducting a review shall be recorded.

15.14   When a telephone review is carried out, a record shall be made of:

(a) the reason the review officer did not attend the station holding the detainee;

(b) the place the review officer was;

(c) the method representations, oral or written, were made to the review officer, see *paragraph 15.11*.

15.15   Any written representations shall be retained.

15.16   A record shall be made as soon as practicable about the outcome of each review or determination whether to extend the maximum detention period without charge or an application for a warrant of further detention or its extension. If *paragraph 15.7* applies, a record shall also be made of when the person was informed and by whom. If an authorisation is given under PACE, section 42, the record shall state the number of hours and minutes by which the detention period is extended or further extended. If a warrant for further detention, or extension, is granted under section 43 or 44, the record shall state the detention period authorised by the warrant and the date and time it was granted.

Notes for guidance

15A   Review officer for the purposes of:

– *PACE, sections 40 and 40A means, in the case of a person arrested but not charged, an officer of at least inspector rank not directly involved in the investigation and, if a person has been arrested and charged, the custody officer;*

– *the Terrorism Act 2000, means an officer not directly involved in the investigation connected with the detention and of at least inspector rank, for reviews within 24 hours of the detainee's arrest or superintendent for all other reviews.*

15B   The detention of persons in police custody not subject to the statutory review requirement in paragraph 15.1 should still be reviewed periodically as a matter of good practice. The purpose of such reviews is to check the particular power under which a detainee is held continues to apply, any associated conditions are complied with and to make sure appropriate action is taken to deal with any changes. This includes the detainee's prompt release when the power no longer applies, or their transfer if the power requires the detainee be taken elsewhere as soon as the necessary arrangements are made. Examples include persons:

(a) *arrested on warrant because they failed to answer bail to appear at court;*

(b) *arrested under the Bail Act 1976, section 7(3) for breaching a condition of bail granted after charge;*

(c) *in police custody for specific purposes and periods under the Crime (Sentences) Act 1997, Schedule 1;*

(d) *convicted, or remand prisoners, held in police stations on behalf of the Prison Service under the Imprisonment (Temporary Provisions) Act 1980, section 6;*

(e) *being detained to prevent them causing a breach of the peace;*

(f) *detained at police stations on behalf of the Immigration Service.*

The detention of persons remanded into police detention by order of a court under the Magistrates' Courts Act 1980, section 128 is subject to a statutory requirement to review that detention. This is to make sure the detainee is taken back to court no later than the end of the period authorised by the court or when the need for their detention by police ceases, whichever is the sooner.

15C In the case of a review of detention, but not an extension, the detainee need not be woken for the review. However, if the detainee is likely to be asleep, e.g. during a period of rest allowed as in paragraph 12.2, at the latest time a review or authorisation to extend detention may take place, the officer should, if the legal obligations and time constraints permit, bring forward the procedure to allow the detainee to make representations. A detainee not asleep during the review must be present when the grounds for their continued detention are recorded and must at the same time be informed of those grounds unless the review officer considers the person is incapable of understanding what is said, violent or likely to become violent or in urgent need of medical attention.

15D An application to a Magistrates' Court under PACE, sections 43 or 44 for a warrant of further detention or its extension should be made between 10am and 9pm, and if possible during normal court hours. It will not usually be practicable to arrange for a court to sit specially outside the hours of 10am to 9pm. If it appears a special sitting may be needed outside normal court hours but between 10am and 9pm, the clerk to the justices should be given notice and informed of this possibility, while the court is sitting if possible.

15E In paragraph 15.2, the officer responsible for the station holding the detainee includes a superintendent or above who, in accordance with their force operational policy or police regulations, is given that responsibility on a temporary basis whilst the appointed long-term holder is off duty or otherwise unavailable.

15F The provisions of PACE, section 40A allowing telephone reviews do not apply to reviews of detention after charge by the custody officer or to reviews under the Terrorism Act 2000, Schedule 8, Part II in terrorism cases. When video conferencing is not required, they allow the use of a telephone to carry out a review of detention before charge if it is not reasonably practicable for the review officer to attend the station holding the detainee, e.g. when severe weather conditions or an unforeseen operational emergency prevent the review officer from attending. The procedure under PACE, section 42 must be done in person.

16 Charging detained persons

(a) Action

16.1 When the officer in charge of the investigation reasonably believes there is sufficient evidence to provide a realistic prospect of the detainee's conviction, see *paragraph 11.6*, they shall without delay, and subject to the following qualification, inform the custody officer who will be responsible for considering whether the detainee should be charged. See *Notes 11B and 16A*. When a person is detained in respect of more than one offence it is permissible to delay informing the custody officer until the above conditions are satisfied in respect of all the offences, but see *paragraph 11.6*. If the detainee is a juvenile, mentally disordered or otherwise mentally vulnerable, any resulting action shall be taken in the presence of the appropriate adult if they are present at the time. See *Note 16B and 16C*

16.2 When a detainee is charged with or informed they may be prosecuted for an offence, see *Note 16B*, they shall, unless the restriction on drawing adverse inferences from silence applies, see *Annex C*, be cautioned as follows:

'You do not have to say anything. But it may harm your defence if you do not mention now something which you later rely on in court. Anything you do say may be given in evidence.'

Annex C, paragraph 2 sets out the alternative terms of the caution to be used when the restriction on drawing adverse inferences from silence applies.

16.3   When a detainee is charged they shall be given a written notice showing particulars of the offence and, subject to *paragraph 2.6A*, the officer's name and the case reference number. As far as possible the particulars of the charge shall be stated in simple terms, but they shall also show the precise offence in law with which the detainee is charged. The notice shall begin:

'You are charged with the offence(s) shown below.' Followed by the caution.

If the detainee is a juvenile, mentally disordered or otherwise mentally vulnerable, the notice should be given to the appropriate adult.

16.4   If, after a detainee has been charged with or informed they may be prosecuted for an offence, an officer wants to tell them about any written statement or interview with another person relating to such an offence, the detainee shall either be handed a true copy of the written statement or the content of the interview record brought to their attention. Nothing shall be done to invite any reply or comment except to:

   (a)   caution the detainee, 'You do not have to say anything, but anything you do say may be given in evidence.'; and

   (b)   remind the detainee about their right to legal advice.

16.4A   If the detainee:

   –   cannot read, the document may be read to them

   –   is a juvenile, mentally disordered or otherwise mentally vulnerable, the appropriate adult shall also be given a copy, or the interview record shall be brought to their attention

16.5   A detainee may not be interviewed about an offence after they have been charged with, or informed they may be prosecuted for it, unless the interview is necessary:

   –   to prevent or minimise harm or loss to some other person, or the public

   –   to clear up an ambiguity in a previous answer or statement

   –   in the interests of justice for the detainee to have put to them, and have an opportunity to comment on, information concerning the offence which has come to light since they were charged or informed they might be prosecuted

Before any such interview, the interviewer shall:

   (a)   caution the detainee, 'You do not have to say anything, but anything you do say may be given in evidence.';

   (b)   remind the detainee about their right to legal advice.

See *Note 16B*

16.6   The provisions of *paragraphs 16.2 to 16.5* must be complied with in the appropriate adult's presence if they are already at the police station. If they are not at the police station then these provisions must be complied with again in their presence when they arrive unless the detainee has been released.

See *Note 16C*

16.7   When a juvenile is charged with an offence and the custody officer authorises their continued detention after charge, the custody officer must try to make arrangements for the juvenile to be taken into the care of a local authority to be detained pending appearance in court unless the custody officer certifies it is impracticable to do so or, in the case of a juvenile of at least 12 years old, no secure accommodation is available and there is a risk to the public of serious harm from that juvenile, in accordance with PACE, section 38(6). See *Note 16D*

(b) Documentation

16.8   A record shall be made of anything a detainee says when charged.

16.9   Any questions put in an interview after charge and answers given relating to the offence shall be recorded in full during the interview on forms for that purpose and the record signed by the detainee or, if they refuse, by the interviewer and any third parties present. If the questions are tape recorded or visually recorded the arrangements in Code E or F apply.

16.10   If it is not practicable to make arrangements for a juvenile's transfer into local authority care as in *paragraph 16.7*, the custody officer must record the reasons and complete a certificate to be produced before the court with the juvenile. See *Note 16D*

Notes for guidance

16A   The custody officer must take into account alternatives to prosecution under the Crime and Disorder Act 1998, reprimands and warning applicable to persons under 18, and in national guidance on the cautioning of offenders, for persons aged 18 and over.

16B   The giving of a warning or the service of the Notice of Intended Prosecution required by the Road Traffic Offenders Act 1988, section 1 does not amount to informing a detainee they may be prosecuted for an offence and so does not preclude further questioning in relation to that offence.

16C   There is no power under PACE to detain a person and delay action under paragraphs 16.2 to 16.5 solely to await the arrival of the appropriate adult. After charge, bail cannot be refused, or release on bail delayed, simply because an appropriate adult is not available, unless the absence of that adult provides the custody officer with the necessary grounds to authorise detention after charge under PACE, section 38.

16D   Except as in paragraph 16.7, neither a juvenile's behaviour nor the nature of the offence provides grounds for the custody officer to decide it is impracticable to arrange the juvenile's transfer to local authority care. Similarly, the lack of secure local authority accommodation does not make it impracticable to transfer the juvenile. The availability of secure accommodation is only a factor in relation to a juvenile aged 12 or over when the local authority accommodation would not be adequate to protect the public from serious harm from them. The obligation to transfer a juvenile to local authority accommodation applies as much to a juvenile charged during the daytime as to a juvenile to be held overnight, subject to a requirement to bring the juvenile before a court under PACE, section 46.

ANNEX A—INTIMATE AND STRIP SEARCHES

A   Intimate search

1.   An intimate search consists of the physical examination of a person's body orifices other than the mouth. The intrusive nature of such searches means the actual and potential risks associated with intimate searches must never be underestimated.

(a) Action

2.   Body orifices other than the mouth may be searched only if authorised by an officer of inspector rank or above who has reasonable grounds for believing that:

  (a) the person may have concealed on themselves
    (i) anything which they could and might use to cause physical injury to themself or others at the station; or
    (ii) a Class A drug which they intended to supply to another or to export; and

  (b) an intimate search is the only means of removing those items.

2A.   The reasons an intimate search is considered necessary shall be explained to the person before the search begins.

3.   An intimate search may only be carried out by a registered medical practitioner or registered nurse, unless an officer of at least inspector rank considers this is not practicable and the search is to take place under *paragraph 2(a)(i)*, in which case a police officer may carry out the search. See *Notes A1 to A5*

3A.   Any proposal for a search under *paragraph 2(a)(i)* to be carried out by someone other than a registered medical practitioner or registered nurse must only be considered as a last resort and when the authorising officer is satisfied the risks associated with allowing the item to remain with the detainee outweigh the risks associated with removing it. See *Notes A1 to A5*

4.   An intimate search under:

– *paragraph 2(a)(i)* may take place only at a hospital, surgery, other medical premises or police station

– *paragraph 2(a)(ii)* may take place only at a hospital, surgery or other medical premises and must be carried out by a registered medical practitioner or a registered nurse

5.   An intimate search at a police station of a juvenile or mentally disordered or otherwise mentally vulnerable person may take place only in the presence of an appropriate adult of the same sex, unless the detainee specifically requests a particular adult of the opposite sex who is readily available. In the case of a juvenile the search may take place in the absence of the appropriate adult only if the juvenile signifies in the presence of the appropriate adult they do not want the adult present during the search and the adult agrees. A record shall be made of the juvenile's decision and signed by the appropriate adult.

6.   When an intimate search under *paragraph 2(a)(i)* is carried out by a police officer, the officer must be of the same sex as the detainee. A minimum of two people, other than the detainee, must be present during the search. Subject to *paragraph 5*, no person of the opposite sex who is not a medical practitioner or nurse shall be present, nor shall anyone whose presence is unnecessary. The search shall be conducted with proper regard to the sensitivity and vulnerability of the detainee.

(b)   Documentation

7.   In the case of an intimate search the custody officer shall as soon as practicable, record:

– which parts of the detainee's body were searched

– who carried out the search

– who was present

– the reasons for the search including the reasons to believe the article could not otherwise be removed

– the result.

8.   If an intimate search is carried out by a police officer, the reason why it was impracticable for a registered medical practitioner or registered nurse to conduct it must be recorded.

B   Strip search

9.   A strip search is a search involving the removal of more than outer clothing. In this Code, outer clothing includes shoes and socks.

(a)   Action

10. A strip search may take place only if it is considered necessary to remove an article which a detainee would not be allowed to keep, and the officer reasonably considers the detainee might have concealed such an article. Strip searches shall not be routinely carried out if there is no reason to consider that articles are concealed.

The conduct of strip searches

11.   When strip searches are conducted:

(a)   a police officer carrying out a strip search must be the same sex as the detainee;

(b)   the search shall take place in an area where the detainee cannot be seen by anyone who does not need to be present, nor by a member of the opposite sex except an appropriate adult who has been specifically requested by the detainee;

(c)   except in cases of urgency, where there is risk of serious harm to the detainee or to others, whenever a strip search involves exposure of intimate body parts, there must be at least two people present other than the detainee, and if the search is of a juvenile or mentally disordered or otherwise mentally vulnerable person, one of the people must be the appropriate adult. Except in urgent cases as above, a search of a juvenile may take place in the absence of the appropriate adult only if the juvenile signifies in the presence of the appropriate adult that they do not want the adult to be present during the search and the adult agrees. A record shall be made of the juvenile's decision and signed by the appropriate adult. The presence of more than two people, other than an appropriate adult, shall be permitted only in the most exceptional circumstances;

(d)   the search shall be conducted with proper regard to the sensitivity and vulnerability of the detainee in these circumstances and every reasonable effort shall be made to secure the detainee's co-operation and minimise embarrassment. Detainees who are searched shall not normally be required to remove all their clothes at the same time, e.g. a person should be allowed to remove clothing above the waist and redress before removing further clothing;

(e)   if necessary to assist the search, the detainee may be required to hold their arms in the air or to stand with their legs apart and bend forward so a visual examination may be made of the genital and anal areas provided no physical contact is made with any body orifice;

(f)   if articles are found, the detainee shall be asked to hand them over. If articles are found within any body orifice other than the mouth, and the detainee refuses to hand them over, their removal would constitute an intimate search, which must be carried out as in Part A;

(g)   a strip search shall be conducted as quickly as possible, and the detainee allowed to dress as soon as the procedure is complete.

(b)   Documentation

12.   A record shall be made on the custody record of a strip search including the reason it was considered necessary, those present and any result.

Notes for guidance

A1   Before authorising any intimate search, the authorising officer must make every reasonable effort to persuade the detainee to hand the article over without a search. If the detainee agrees, a registered medical practitioner or registered nurse should whenever possible be asked to assess the risks involved and, if necessary, attend to assist the detainee.

A2   If the detainee does not agree to hand the article over without a search, the authorising officer must carefully review all the relevant factors before authorising an intimate search. In particular, the officer must consider whether the grounds for believing an article may be concealed are reasonable.

A3   If authority is given for a search under paragraph 2(a)(i), a registered medical practitioner or registered nurse shall be consulted whenever possible. The presumption should be that the search will be conducted by the registered medical practitioner or registered nurse and the authorising officer must make every reasonable effort to persuade the detainee to allow the medical practitioner or nurse to conduct the search.

A4   A constable should only be authorised to carry out a search as a last resort and when all other approaches have failed. In these circumstances, the authorising officer must be satisfied the detainee might use the article for one or more of the purposes in paragraph 2(a)(i) and the physical injury likely to be caused is sufficiently severe to justify authorising a constable to carry out the search.

A5   If an officer has any doubts whether to authorise an intimate search by a constable, the officer should seek advice from an officer of superintendent rank or above.

ANNEX B—DELAY IN NOTIFYING ARREST OR ALLOWING

Access to Legal Advice

A   Persons detained under PACE

1.   The exercise of the rights in Section 5 or Section 6, or both, may be delayed if the person is in police detention, as in PACE, section 118(2), in connection with a serious arrestable offence, has not yet been charged with an offence and an officer of superintendent rank or above, or inspector rank or above only for the rights in Section 5, has reasonable grounds for believing their exercise will:

   (i)   lead to:
      – interference with, or harm to, evidence connected with a serious arrestable offence; or
      – interference with, or physical harm to, other people; or

   (ii)   lead to alerting other people suspected of having committed a serious arrestable offence but not yet arrested for it; or

   (iii)   hinder the recovery of property obtained in consequence of the commission of such an offence.

2.   These rights may also be delayed if the serious arrestable offence is:

   (i)   a drug trafficking offence and the officer has reasonable grounds for believing the detainee has benefited from drug trafficking, and the recovery of the value of the detainee's proceeds from drug trafficking will be hindered by the exercise of either right;

   (ii)   an offence to which the Criminal Justice Act 1988, Part VI (confiscation orders) applies and the officer has reasonable grounds for believing the detainee has benefited from the offence, and the exercise of either right will hinder the recovery of the value of the:
      – property obtained by the detainee from or in connection with the offence
      – pecuniary advantage derived by the detainee from or in connection with it.

3.   Authority to delay a detainee's right to consult privately with a solicitor may be given only if the authorising officer has reasonable grounds to believe the solicitor the detainee wants to consult will, inadvertently or otherwise, pass on a message from the detainee or act in some other way which will have any of the consequences specified under *paragraphs 1 or 2*. In these circumstances the detainee must be allowed to choose another solicitor. See *Note B3*

4.   If the detainee wishes to see a solicitor, access to that solicitor may not be delayed on the grounds they might advise the detainee not to answer questions or the solicitor was initially asked to attend the police station by someone else. In the latter case the detainee must be told the solicitor has come to the police station at another person's request, and must be asked to sign the custody record to signify whether they want to see the solicitor.

5.   The fact the grounds for delaying notification of arrest may be satisfied does not automatically mean the grounds for delaying access to legal advice will also be satisfied.

6.   These rights may be delayed only for as long as grounds exist and in no case beyond 36 hours after the relevant time as in PACE, section 41. If the grounds cease to apply within this time, the detainee must, as soon as practicable, be asked if they want to exercise either right, the custody record must be noted accordingly, and action taken in accordance with the relevant section of the Code.

7. A detained person must be permitted to consult a solicitor for a reasonable time before any court hearing.

B Persons detained under the Terrorism Act 2000

8. The rights as in sections 5 or 6, may be delayed if the person is detained under the Terrorism Act 2000, section 41 or Schedule 7, has not yet been charged with an offence and an officer of superintendent rank or above has reasonable grounds for believing the exercise of either right will:

  (i)   lead to:
        – interference with, or harm to, evidence connected with a serious arrestable offence;
        – interference with, or physical harm to, other people; or

  (ii) lead to the alerting of other people suspected of having committed a serious arrestable offence but not yet arrested for it; or

  (iii) hinder the recovery of property:
        – obtained in consequence of the commission of such an offence; or
        – in respect of which a forfeiture order could be made under that Act, section 23;

  (iv) lead to interference with the gathering of information about the commission, preparation or instigation of acts of terrorism; or

  (v)   by alerting any person, make it more difficult to prevent an act of terrorism or secure the apprehension, prosecution or conviction of any person in connection with the commission, preparation or instigation of an act of terrorism.

9. These rights may also be delayed if the officer has reasonable grounds for believing:

  (a) the detainee:
      (i) has committed an offence to which the Criminal Justice Act 1988, Part VI (confiscation orders) applies;
      (ii) has benefited from the offence; and

  (b) the exercise of either right will hinder the recovery of the value of that benefit.

10. In these cases *paragraphs 3* (with regards to the consequences specified at *paragraphs 8 and 9*), *4 and 5* apply.

11. These rights may be delayed only for as long as is necessary but not beyond 48 hours from the time of arrest if arrested under section 41, or if detained under the Terrorism Act 2000, Schedule 7 when arrested under section 41, from the beginning of their examination. If the above grounds cease to apply within this time the detainee must as soon as practicable be asked if they wish to exercise either right, the custody record noted accordingly, and action taken in accordance with the relevant section of this Code.

12. In this case *paragraph 7* applies.

C Documentation

13. The grounds for action under this Annex shall be recorded and the detainee informed of them as soon as practicable.

14. Any reply given by a detainee under *paragraphs 6 or 11* must be recorded and the detainee asked to endorse the record in relation to whether they want to receive legal advice at this point.

D Cautions and special warnings

When a suspect detained at a police station is interviewed during any period for which access to legal advice has been delayed under this Annex, the court or jury may not draw adverse inferences from their silence.

Notes for guidance

B1 Even if Annex B applies in the case of a juvenile, or a person who is mentally disordered or otherwise mentally vulnerable, action to inform the appropriate adult and the person responsible for a juvenile's welfare if that is a different person, must nevertheless be taken as in paragraph 3.13 and 3.15.

B2 In the case of Commonwealth citizens and foreign nationals, see Note 7A.

B3 A decision to delay access to a specific solicitor is likely to be a rare occurrence and only when it can be shown the suspect is capable of misleading that particular solicitor and there is more than a substantial risk that the suspect will succeed in causing information to be conveyed which will lead to one or more of the specified consequences.

ANNEX C—RESTRICTION ON DRAWING ADVERSE INFERENCES FROM SILENCE AND TERMS OF THE CAUTION WHEN THE RESTRICTION APPLIES

(a) The restriction on drawing adverse inferences from silence

1. The Criminal Justice and Public Order Act 1994, sections 34, 36 and 37 as amended by the Youth Justice and Criminal Evidence Act 1999, section 58 describe the conditions under which adverse inferences may be drawn from a person's failure or refusal to say anything about their involvement in the offence when interviewed, after being charged or informed they may be prosecuted. These provisions are subject to an overriding restriction on the ability of a court or jury to draw adverse inferences from a person's silence. This restriction applies:

   (a) to any detainee at a police station, see *Note 10C* who, before being interviewed, see section 11 or being charged or informed they may be prosecuted, see section 16, has:
      (i) asked for legal advice, see section 6, *paragraph 6.1*;
      (ii) not been allowed an opportunity to consult a solicitor, including the duty solicitor, as in this Code; and
      (iii) not changed their mind about wanting legal advice, see section 6, *paragraph 6.6(d)*

      Note the condition in (ii) will

      – apply when a detainee who has asked for legal advice is interviewed before speaking to a solicitor as in section 6, *paragraph 6.6(a) or (b)*.
      – not apply if the detained person declines to ask for the duty solicitor, see section 6, *paragraphs 6.6(c) and (d)*;

   (b) to any person charged with, or informed they may be prosecuted for, an offence who:
      (i) has had brought to their notice a written statement made by another person or the content of an interview with another person which relates to that offence, see section 16, *paragraph 16.4*;
      (ii) is interviewed about that offence, see *section 16, paragraph 16.5*; or
      (iii) makes a written statement about that offence, see *Annex D paragraphs 4 and 9.*

(b) Terms of the caution when the restriction applies

2. When a requirement to caution arises at a time when the restriction on drawing adverse inferences from silence applies, the caution shall be:

   'You do not have to say anything, but anything you do say may be given in evidence.'

3. Whenever the restriction either begins to apply or ceases to apply after a caution has already been given, the person shall be re-cautioned in the appropriate terms. The changed position on drawing inferences and that the previous caution no longer applies shall also be explained to the detainee in ordinary language. See *Note C2*

Notes for guidance

C1   The restriction on drawing inferences from silence does not apply to a person who has not been detained and who therefore cannot be prevented from seeking legal advice if they want to, see paragraphs 10.2 and 3.15.

C2   The following is suggested as a framework to help explain changes in the position on drawing adverse inferences if the restriction on drawing adverse inferences from silence:

(a) *begins to apply:*

'The caution you were previously given no longer applies. This is because after that caution:
(i) *you asked to speak to a solicitor but have not yet been allowed an opportunity to speak to a solicitor.' See paragraph 1(a); or*
(ii) *you have been charged with/informed you may be prosecuted.' See paragraph 1(b).*

'This means that from now on, adverse inferences cannot be drawn at court and your defence will not be harmed just because you choose to say nothing. Please listen carefully to the caution I am about to give you because it will apply from now on. You will see that it does not say anything about your defence being harmed.'

(b) *ceases to apply before or at the time the person is charged or informed they may be prosecuted, see paragraph 1(a);*

'The caution you were previously given no longer applies. This is because after that caution you have been allowed an opportunity to speak to a solicitor. Please listen carefully to the caution I am about to give you because it will apply from now on. It explains how your defence at court may be affected if you choose to say nothing.'

ANNEX D—WRITTEN STATEMENTS UNDER CAUTION

(a) Written by a person under caution

1.   A person shall always be invited to write down what they want to say.

2.   A person who has not been charged with, or informed they may be prosecuted for, any offence to which the statement they want to write relates, shall:

(a) unless the statement is made at a time when the restriction on drawing adverse inferences from silence applies, see *Annex C*, be asked to write out and sign the following before writing what they want to say:

'I make this statement of my own free will. I understand that I do not have to say anything but that it may harm my defence if I do not mention when questioned something which I later rely on in court. This statement may be given in evidence.';

(b) if the statement is made at a time when the restriction on drawing adverse inferences from silence applies, be asked to write out and sign the following before writing what they want to say;

'I make this statement of my own free will. I understand that I do not have to say anything. This statement may be given in evidence.'

3.   When a person, on the occasion of being charged with or informed they may be prosecuted for any offence, asks to make a statement which relates to any such offence and wants to write it they shall:

(a) unless the restriction on drawing adverse inferences from silence, see *Annex C*, applied when they were so charged or informed they may be prosecuted, be asked to write out and sign the following before writing what they want to say:

'I make this statement of my own free will. I understand that I do not have to say anything but that it may harm my defence if I do not mention when questioned something which I later rely on in court. This statement may be given in evidence.';

(b) if the restriction on drawing adverse inferences from silence applied when they were so charged or informed they may be prosecuted, be asked to write out and sign the following before writing what they want to say:

'I make this statement of my own free will. I understand that I do not have to say anything. This statement may be given in evidence.'

4.   When a person, who has already been charged with or informed they may be prosecuted for any offence, asks to make a statement which relates to any such offence and wants to write it they shall be asked to write out and sign the following before writing what they want to say:

'I make this statement of my own free will. I understand that I do not have to say anything. This statement may be given in evidence.';

5.   Any person writing their own statement shall be allowed to do so without any prompting except a police officer or civilian interviewer may indicate to them which matters are material or question any ambiguity in the statement.

(b)   Written by a police officer or civilian interviewer

6.   If a person says they would like someone to write the statement for them, a police officer, or civilian interviewer shall write the statement.

7.   If the person has not been charged with, or informed they may be prosecuted for, any offence to which the statement they want to make relates they shall, before starting, be asked to sign, or make their mark, to the following:

(a) unless the statement is made at a time when the restriction on drawing adverse inferences from silence applies, see *Annex C*:

'I, _____ , wish to make a statement. I want someone to write down what I say. I understand that I do not have to say anything but that it may harm my defence if I do not mention when questioned something which I later rely on in court. This statement may be given in evidence.'

(b) if the statement is made at a time when the restriction on drawing adverse inferences from silence applies:

'I, _____ , wish to make a statement. I want someone to write down what I say. This statement may be given in evidence.'

8.   If, on the occasion of being charged with or informed they may be prosecuted for any offence, the person asks to make a statement which relates to any such offence they shall before starting be asked to sign, or make their mark to, the following:

(a) unless the restriction on drawing adverse inferences from silence applied, see *Annex C*, when they were so charged or informed they may be prosecuted:

'I, _____ , wish to make a statement. I want someone to write down what I say. I understand that I do not have to say anything but that it may harm my defence if I do not mention when questioned something which I later rely on in court. This statement may be given in evidence.';

(b) if the restriction on drawing adverse inferences from silence applied when they were so charged or informed they may be prosecuted:

'I, _____ , wish to make a statement. I want someone to write down what I say. This statement may be given in evidence.'

9. If, having already been charged with or informed they may be prosecuted for any offence, a person asks to make a statement which relates to any such offence they shall before starting, be asked to sign, or make their mark to:

'I, _____ , wish to make a statement. I want someone to write down what I say. This statement may be given in evidence.'

10. The person writing the statement must take down the exact words spoken by the person making it and must not edit or paraphrase it. Any questions that are necessary, e.g. to make it more intelligible, and the answers given must be recorded at the same time on the statement form.

11. When the writing of a statement is finished the person making it shall be asked to read it and to make any corrections, alterations or additions they want. When they have finished reading they shall be asked to write and sign or make their mark on the following certificate at the end of the statement:

'I have read the above statement, and I have been able to correct, alter or add anything I wish. This statement is true. I have made it of my own free will.'

12. If the person making the statement cannot read, or refuses to read it, or to write the above mentioned certificate at the end of it or to sign it, the person taking the statement shall read it to them and ask them if they would like to correct, alter or add anything and to put their signature or make their mark at the end. The person taking the statement shall certify on the statement itself what has occurred.

ANNEX E—SUMMARY OF PROVISIONS RELATING TO MENTALLY DISORDERED AND OTHERWISE MENTALLY VULNERABLE PEOPLE

1. If an officer has any suspicion, or is told in good faith, that a person of any age may be mentally disordered or otherwise mentally vulnerable, or mentally incapable of understanding the significance of questions or their replies that person shall be treated as mentally disordered or otherwise mentally vulnerable for the purposes of this Code. See *paragraph 1.4*

2. In the case of a person who is mentally disordered or otherwise mentally vulnerable, 'the appropriate adult' means:

(a) a relative, guardian or other person responsible for their care or custody;

(b) someone experienced in dealing with mentally disordered or mentally vulnerable people but who is not a police officer or employed by the police;

(c) failing these, some other responsible adult aged 18 or over who is not a police officer or employed by the police.

See *paragraph 1.7(b)* and *Note 1D*

3. If the custody officer authorises the detention of a person who is mentally vulnerable or appears to be suffering from a mental disorder, the custody officer must as soon as practicable inform the appropriate adult of the grounds for detention and the person's whereabouts, and ask the adult to come to the police station to see them. If the appropriate adult:

– is already at the station when information is given as in *paragraphs 3.1 to 3.5* the information

– must be given in their presence

– is not at the station when the provisions of *paragraph 3.1 to 3.5* are complied with these provisions must be complied with again in their presence once they arrive.

See *paragraphs 3.15 to 3.17*

4. If the appropriate adult, having been informed of the right to legal advice, considers legal advice should be taken, the provisions of section 6 apply as if the mentally disordered or otherwise mentally vulnerable person had requested access to legal advice. See *paragraph 3.19* and *Note E1*

5.   The custody officer must make sure a person receives appropriate clinical attention as soon as reasonably practicable if the person appears to be suffering from a mental disorder or in urgent cases immediately call the nearest health care professional or an ambulance. It is not intended these provisions delay the transfer of a detainee to a place of safety under the Mental Health Act 1983, section 136 if that is applicable. If an assessment under that Act is to take place at a police station, the custody officer must consider whether an appropriate health care professional should be called to conduct an initial clinical check on the detainee. See *paragraph 9.5 and 9.6*

6.   It is imperative a mentally disordered or otherwise mentally vulnerable person detained under the Mental Health Act 1983, section 136 be assessed as soon as possible. If that assessment is to take place at the police station, an approved social worker and registered medical practitioner shall be called to the station as soon as possible in order to interview and examine the detainee. Once the detainee has been interviewed, examined and suitable arrangements been made for their treatment or care, they can no longer be detained under section 136. A detainee should be immediately discharged from detention if a registered medical practitioner having examined them, concludes they are not mentally disordered within the meaning of the Act. See *paragraph 3.16*

7.   If a mentally disordered or otherwise mentally vulnerable person is cautioned in the absence of the appropriate adult, the caution must be repeated in the appropriate adult's presence. See *paragraph 10.12*

8.   A mentally disordered or otherwise mentally vulnerable person must not be interviewed or asked to provide or sign a written statement in the absence of the appropriate adult unless the provisions of *paragraphs 11.1 or 11.18 to 11.20* apply. Questioning in these circumstances may not continue in the absence of the appropriate adult once sufficient information to avert the risk has been obtained. A record shall be made of the grounds for any decision to begin an interview in these circumstances. See *paragraphs 11.1, 11.15 and 11.18 to 11.20*

9.   If the appropriate adult is present at an interview, they shall be informed they are not expected to act simply as an observer and the purposes of their presence are to:

– advise the interviewee

– observe whether or not the interview is being conducted properly and fairly

– facilitate communication with the interviewee

See *paragraph 11.17*

10.   If the detention of a mentally disordered or otherwise mentally vulnerable person is reviewed by a review officer or a superintendent, the appropriate adult must, if available at the time, be given an opportunity to make representations to the officer about the need for continuing detention.

See *paragraph 15.3*

11.   If the custody officer charges a mentally disordered or otherwise mentally vulnerable person with an offence or takes such other action as is appropriate when there is sufficient evidence for a prosecution this must be done in the presence of the appropriate adult. The written notice embodying any charge must be given to the appropriate adult. See *paragraphs 16.1 to 16.4A*

12.   An intimate or strip search of a mentally disordered or otherwise mentally vulnerable person may take place only in the presence of the appropriate adult of the same sex, unless the detainee specifically requests the presence of a particular adult of the opposite sex. A strip search may take place in the absence of an appropriate adult only in cases of urgency when there is a risk of serious harm to the detainee or others. See *Annex A, paragraphs 5 and 11(c)*

13.   Particular care must be taken when deciding whether to use any form of approved restraints on a mentally disordered or otherwise mentally vulnerable person in a locked cell. See *paragraph 8.2*

Notes for guidance

E1   The purpose of the provision at paragraph 3.19 is to protect the rights of a mentally disordered or otherwise mentally vulnerable detained person who does not understand the significance of what is said to them. If the detained person wants to exercise the right to legal advice, the appropriate action should be taken and not delayed until the appropriate adult arrives. A mentally disordered or otherwise mentally vulnerable detained person should always be given an opportunity, when an appropriate adult is called to the police station, to consult privately with a solicitor in the absence of the appropriate adult if they want.

E2   Although people who are mentally disordered or otherwise mentally vulnerable are often capable of providing reliable evidence, they may, without knowing or wanting to do so, be particularly prone in certain circumstances to provide information that may be unreliable, misleading or self-incriminating. Special care should always be taken when questioning such a person, and the appropriate adult should be involved if there is any doubt about a person's mental state or capacity. Because of the risk of unreliable evidence, it is important to obtain corroboration of any facts admitted whenever possible.

E3   Because of the risks referred to in Note E2, which the presence of the appropriate adult is intended to minimise, officers of superintendent rank or above should exercise their discretion to authorise the commencement of an interview in the appropriate adult's absence only in exceptional cases, if it is necessary to avert an immediate risk of serious harm. See paragraphs 11.1, 11.18 to 11.20

ANNEX F—COUNTRIES WITH WHICH BILATERAL CONSULAR CONVENTIONS OR AGREEMENTS REQUIRING NOTIFICATION OF THE ARREST AND DETENTION OF THEIR NATIONALS ARE IN FORCE AS AT 1 APRIL 2003

Armenia	Kazakhstan
Austria	Macedonia
Azerbaijan	Mexico
Belarus	Moldova
Belgium	Mongolia
Bosnia-Herzegovina	Norway
Bulgaria	Poland
China*	Romania
Croatia	Russia
Cuba	Slovak Republic
Czech Republic	Slovenia
Denmark	Spain
Egypt	Sweden
France	Tajikistan
Georgia	Turkmenistan
German Federal Republic	Ukraine
Greece	USA
Hungary	Uzbekistan
Italy	Yugoslavia
Japan	

* Police are required to inform Chinese officials of arrest/detention in the Manchester consular district only. This comprises Derbyshire, Durham, Greater Manchester, Lancashire, Merseyside, North South and West Yorkshire, and Tyne and Wear.

ANNEX G—FITNESS TO BE INTERVIEWED

1.   This Annex contains general guidance to help police officers and health care professionals assess whether a detainee might be at risk in an interview.

2. A detainee may be at risk in an interview if it is considered that:

(a) conducting the interview could significantly harm the detainee's physical or mental state;

(b) anything the detainee says in the interview about their involvement or suspected involvement in the offence about which they are being interviewed might be considered unreliable in subsequent court proceedings because of their physical or mental state.

3. In assessing whether the detainee should be interviewed, the following must be considered:

(a) how the detainee's physical or mental state might affect their ability to understand the nature and purpose of the interview, to comprehend what is being asked and to appreciate the significance of any answers given and make rational decisions about whether they want to say anything;

(b) the extent to which the detainee's replies may be affected by their physical or mental condition rather than representing a rational and accurate explanation of their involvement in the offence;

(c) how the nature of the interview, which could include particularly probing questions, might affect the detainee.

4. It is essential health care professionals who are consulted consider the functional ability of the detainee rather than simply relying on a medical diagnosis, e.g. it is possible for a person with severe mental illness to be fit for interview.

5. Health care professionals should advise on the need for an appropriate adult to be present, whether reassessment of the person's fitness for interview may be necessary if the interview lasts beyond a specified time, and whether a further specialist opinion may be required.

6. When health care professionals identify risks they should be asked to quantify the risks. They should inform the custody officer:

 – whether the person's condition:

 – is likely to improve

 – will require or be amenable to treatment; and

 – indicate how long it may take for such improvement to take effect

7. The role of the health care professional is to consider the risks and advise the custody officer of the outcome of that consideration. The health care professional's determination and any advice or recommendations should be made in writing and form part of the custody record.

8. Once the health care professional has provided that information, it is a matter for the custody officer to decide whether or not to allow the interview to go ahead and if the interview is to proceed, to determine what safeguards are needed. Nothing prevents safeguards being provided in addition to those required under the Code. An example might be to have an appropriate health care professional present during the interview, in addition to an appropriate adult, in order constantly to monitor the person's condition and how it is being affected by the interview.

Annex H—Detained Person: Observation List

1. If any detainee fails to meet any of the following criteria, an appropriate health care professional or an ambulance must be called.

2. When assessing the level of rousability, consider:

Rousability—can they be woken?

 – go into the cell

 – call their name

 – shake gently

Response to questions—can they give appropriate answers to questions such as:

- What's your name?
- Where do you live?
- Where do you think you are?

Response to commands—can they respond appropriately to commands such as:

- Open your eyes!
- Lift one arm, now the other arm!

3. Remember to take into account the possibility or presence of other illnesses, injury, or mental condition, a person who is drowsy and smells of alcohol may also have the following:

- Diabetes
- Epilepsy
- Head injury
- Drug intoxication or overdose
- Stroke

Appendix 4

PACE Code of Practice for the Identification of Persons by Police Officers (Code D)

This code has effect in relation to any identification procedure carried out after midnight on 31st March 2003.

1 Introduction

1.1   This Code of Practice concerns the principal methods used by police to identify people in connection with the investigation of offences and the keeping of accurate and reliable criminal records.

1.2   Identification by witnesses arises, e.g., if the offender is seen committing the crime and a witness is given an opportunity to identify the suspect in a video identification, identification parade or similar procedure. The procedures are designed to:

–   test the witness' ability to identify the person they saw on a previous occasion

–   provide safeguards against mistaken identification.

While this Code concentrates on visual identification procedures, it does not preclude the police making use of aural identification procedures such as a 'voice identification parade', where they judge that appropriate.

1.3   Identification by fingerprints applies when a person's fingerprints are taken to:

–   compare with fingerprints found at the scene of a crime

–   check and prove convictions

–   help to ascertain a person's identity.

1.4   Identification by body samples and impressions includes taking samples such as blood or hair to generate a DNA profile for comparison with material obtained from the scene of a crime, or a victim.

1.5   Taking photographs of arrested people applies to recording and checking identity and locating and tracing persons who:

–   are wanted for offences

–   fail to answer their bail.

1.6   Another method of identification involves searching and examining detained suspects to find, e.g., marks such as tattoos or scars which may help establish their identity or whether they have been involved in committing an offence.

1.7   The provisions of the Police and Criminal Evidence Act 1984 (PACE) and this Code are designed to make sure fingerprints, samples, impressions and photographs are taken, used and retained, and identification procedures carried out, only when justified and necessary for preventing, detecting or investigating crime. If these provisions are not observed, the application of the relevant procedures in particular cases may be open to question.

2 General

2.1   This Code must be readily available at all police stations for consultation by:

- police officers
- detained persons
- members of the public

2.2   The provisions of this Code:

- include the *Annexes*
- do not include the *Notes for guidance*.

2.3   *Code C, paragraph 1.4*, regarding a person who may be mentally disordered or otherwise mentally vulnerable and the *Notes for guidance* applicable to those provisions apply to this Code.

2.4   *Code C, paragraph 1.5*, regarding a person who appears to be under the age of 17 applies to this Code.

2.5   *Code C, paragraph 1.6*, regarding a person who appears blind, seriously visually impaired, deaf, unable to read or speak or has difficulty orally because of a speech impediment applies to this Code.

2.6   In this Code:

- 'appropriate adult' means the same as in *Code C, paragraph 1.7*,
- 'solicitor' means the same as in *Code C, paragraph 6.12*

and the *Notes for guidance* applicable to those provisions apply to this Code.

2.7   References to custody officers include those performing the functions of custody officer.

2.8   When a record of any action requiring the authority of an officer of a specified rank is made under this Code, subject to *paragraph 2.18*, the officer's name and rank must be recorded.

2.9   When this Code requires the prior authority or agreement of an officer of at least inspector or superintendent rank, that authority may be given by a sergeant or chief inspector who has been authorised to perform the functions of the higher rank under PACE, section 107.

2.10   Subject to *paragraph 2.18*, all records must be timed and signed by the maker.

2.11   Records must be made in the custody record, unless otherwise specified. References to 'pocket book' include any official report book issued to police officers or civilian support staff.

2.12   If any procedure in this Code requires a person's consent, the consent of a:

- mentally disordered or otherwise mentally vulnerable person is only valid if given in the presence of the appropriate adult
- juvenile, is only valid if their parent's or guardian's consent is also obtained unless the juvenile is under 14, when their parent's or guardian's consent is sufficient in its own right. If the only obstacle to an identification procedure in section 3 is that a juvenile's parent or guardian refuses consent or reasonable efforts to obtain it have failed, the identification officer may apply the provisions of *paragraph 3.21*. See *Note 2A*.

2.13   If a person is blind, seriously visually impaired or unable to read, the custody officer or identification officer shall make sure their solicitor, relative, appropriate adult or some other person likely to take an interest in them and not involved in the investigation is available to help check any documentation. When this Code requires written consent or signing, the person assisting may be asked to sign instead, if the detainee prefers. This paragraph does not require an appropriate adult to be called solely to assist in checking and signing documentation for a person who is not a juvenile, or mentally disordered or otherwise mentally vulnerable (see *Note 2B and Code C paragraph 3.15*).

2.14   If any procedure in this Code requires information to be given to or sought from a suspect, it must be given or sought in the appropriate adult's presence if the suspect is mentally disordered, otherwise mentally vulnerable or a juvenile. If the appropriate adult is not present when the information is first given or sought, the procedure must be repeated in the presence of the appropriate adult when they arrive. If the suspect appears deaf or there is doubt about their hearing or speaking ability or ability to understand English, and effective communication cannot be established, the information must be given or sought through an interpreter.

2.15   Any procedure in this Code involving the participation of a person (whether as a suspect or a witness) who is mentally disordered, otherwise mentally vulnerable or a juvenile, must take place in the presence of the appropriate adult. However, the adult must not be allowed to prompt any identification of a suspect by a witness.

2.16   References to:

–   'taking a photograph', include the use of any process to produce a single, still, visual image

–   'photographing a person', should be construed accordingly

–   'photographs', 'films', 'negatives' and 'copies' include relevant visual images recorded, stored, or reproduced through any medium

–   'destruction' includes the deletion of computer data relating to such images or making access to that data impossible.

2.17   Except as described, nothing in this Code affects the powers and procedures:

(i)   for requiring and taking samples of breath, blood and urine in relation to driving offences, etc, when under the influence of drink, drugs or excess alcohol under the:
  – Road Traffic Act 1988, sections 4 to 11
  – Road Traffic Offenders Act 1988, sections 15 and 16
  – Transport and Works Act 1992, sections 26 to 38;

(ii)   under the Immigration Act 1971, Schedule 2, paragraph 18, for taking photographs and fingerprints from persons detained under that Act, Schedule 2, paragraph 16 (Administrative Controls as to Control on Entry etc.); for taking fingerprints in accordance with the Immigration and Asylum Act 1999; sections 141 and 142(3), or other methods for collecting information about a person's external physical characteristics provided for by regulations made under that Act, section 144;

(iii)   under the Terrorism Act 2000, Schedule 8, for taking photographs, fingerprints, skin impressions, body samples or impressions from people:
  – arrested under that Act, section 41,
  – detained for the purposes of examination under that Act, Schedule 7, and to whom the Code of Practice issued under that Act, Schedule 14, paragraph 6, applies ('the terrorism provisions')

  See *Note 2C*

(iv)   for taking photographs, fingerprints, skin impressions, body samples or impressions from people who have been:
  – arrested on warrants issued in Scotland, by officers exercising powers under the Criminal Justice and Public Order Act 1994, section 136(2)
  – arrested or detained without warrant by officers from a police force in Scotland exercising their powers of arrest or detention under the Criminal Justice and Public Order Act 1994, section 137(2), (Cross Border powers of arrest etc.).

Note: In these cases, police powers and duties and the person's rights and entitlements whilst at a police station in England and Wales are the same as if the person had been arrested in Scotland by a Scottish police officer.

2.18   Nothing in this Code requires the identity of officers or civilian support staff to be recorded or disclosed:

(a)   in the case of enquiries linked to the investigation of terrorism;

(b)   if the officers or civilian support staff reasonably believe recording or disclosing their names might put them in danger.

In these cases, they shall use warrant or other identification numbers and the name of their police station. See *Note 2D*

2.19   In this Code:

(a) 'designated person' means a person other than a police officer, designated under the Police Reform Act 2002, Part 4, who has specified powers and duties of police officers conferred or imposed on them;

(b) any reference to a police officer includes a designated person acting in the exercise or performance of the powers and duties conferred or imposed on them by their designation.

2.20   If a power conferred on a designated person:

(a) allows reasonable force to be used when exercised by a police officer, a designated person exercising that power has the same entitlement to use force;

(b) includes power to use force to enter any premises, that power is not exercisable by that designated person except:
   (i) in the company, and under the supervision, of a police officer; or
   (ii) for the purpose of:
       – saving life or limb; or
       – preventing serious damage to property.

2.21   Nothing in this Code prevents the custody officer, or other officer given custody of the detainee, from allowing civilian support staff who are not designated persons to carry out individual procedures or tasks at the police station if the law allows. However, the officer remains responsible for making sure the procedures and tasks are carried out correctly in accordance with the Codes of Practice. Any such civilian must be:

(a) a person employed by a police authority maintaining a police force and under the control and direction of the Chief Officer of that force;

(b) employed by a person with whom a police authority has a contract for the provision of services relating to persons arrested or otherwise in custody.

2.22   Designated persons and other civilian support staff must have regard to any relevant provisions of the Codes of Practice.

Notes for guidance

2A   For the purposes of paragraph 2.12, the consent required from a parent or guardian may, for a juvenile in the care of a local authority or voluntary organisation, be given by that authority or organisation. In the case of a juvenile, nothing in paragraph 2.12 requires the parent, guardian or representative of a local authority or voluntary organisation to be present to give their consent, unless they are acting as the appropriate adult under paragraphs 2.14 or 2.15. However, it is important that a parent or guardian not present is fully informed before being asked to consent. They must be given the same information about the procedure and the juvenile's suspected involvement in the offence as the juvenile and appropriate adult. The parent or guardian must also be allowed to speak to the juvenile and the appropriate adult if they wish. Provided the consent is fully informed and is not withdrawn, it may be obtained at any time before the procedure takes place.

2B   People who are seriously visually impaired or unable to read may be unwilling to sign police documents. The alternative, i.e. their representative signing on their behalf, seeks to protect the interests of both police and suspects.

2C   Photographs, fingerprints, samples and impressions may be taken from a person detained under the terrorism provisions to help determine whether they are, or have been, involved in terrorism, as well as when there are reasonable grounds for suspecting their involvement in a particular offence.

2D   The purpose of paragraph 2.18(b) is to protect those involved in serious organised crime investigations or arrests of particularly violent suspects when there is reliable information that those arrested or their associates may threaten or cause harm to the officers. In cases of doubt, an officer of inspector rank or above should be consulted.

3   Identification by witnesses

3.1   A record shall be made of the suspect's description as first given by a potential witness. This record must:

(a)   be made and kept in a form which enables details of that description to be accurately produced from it, in a visible and legible form, which can be given to the suspect or the suspect's solicitor in accordance with this Code; and

(b)   unless otherwise specified, be made before the witness takes part in any identification procedures under *paragraphs 3.5 to 3.10, 3.21 or 3.23.*

A copy of the record shall where practicable, be given to the suspect or their solicitor before any procedures under *paragraphs 3.5 to 3.10, 3.21 or 3.23* are carried out. See *Note 3E*

(a)   Cases when the suspect's identity is not known

3.2   In cases when the suspect's identity is not known, a witness may be taken to a particular neighbourhood or place to see whether they can identify the person they saw. Although the number, age, sex, race, general description and style of clothing of other people present at the location and the way in which any identification is made cannot be controlled, the principles applicable to the formal procedures under *paragraphs 3.5 to 3.10* shall be followed as far as practicable. For example:

(a)   where it is practicable to do so, a record should be made of the witness' description of the suspect, as in *paragraph 3.1(a)*, before asking the witness to make an identification;

(b)   care must be taken not to direct the witness' attention to any individual unless, taking into account all the circumstances, this cannot be avoided. However, this does not prevent a witness being asked to look carefully at the people around at the time or to look towards a group or in a particular direction, if this appears necessary to make sure that the witness does not overlook a possible suspect simply because the witness is looking in the opposite direction and also to enable the witness to make comparisons between any suspect and others who are in the area; See *Note 3F*

(c)   where there is more than one witness, every effort should be made to keep them separate and witnesses should be taken to see whether they can identify a person independently;

(d)   once there is sufficient information to justify the arrest of a particular individual for suspected involvement in the offence, e.g., after a witness makes a positive identification, the provisions set out from *paragraph 3.4* onwards shall apply for any other witnesses in relation to that individual. Subject to *paragraphs 3.12 and 3.13*, it is not necessary for the witness who makes such a positive identification to take part in a further procedure;

(e)   the officer or civilian support staff accompanying the witness must record, in their pocket book, the action taken as soon as, and in as much detail, as possible. The record should include:
   – the date, time and place of the relevant occasion the witness claims to have previously seen the suspect; where any identification was made; how it was made and the conditions at the time (e.g., the distance the witness was from the suspect, the weather and light); if the witness's attention was drawn to the suspect; the reason for this; and anything said by the witness or the suspect about the identification or the conduct of the procedure.

3.3   A witness must not be shown photographs, computerised or artist's composite likenesses or similar likenesses or pictures (including 'E-fit' images) if the identity of the suspect is known to the police and the suspect is available to take part in a video identification, an identification parade or a group identification. If the suspect's identity is not known, the showing of such images to a witness to obtain identification evidence must be done in accordance with *Annex E.*

(b)   Cases when the suspect is known and available

3.4   If the suspect's identity is known to the police and they are available, the identification procedures set out in *paragraphs 3.5 to 3.10* may be used. References in this section to a suspect being 'known' mean there is sufficient information known to the police to justify the arrest of a particular person for suspected involvement in the offence. A suspect being 'available' means they are immediately available or will be within a reasonably short time and willing to take an effective part in at least one of the following which it is practicable to arrange;

- – video identification;
- – identification parade; or
- – group identification.

Video identification

3.5   A 'video identification' is when the witness is shown moving images of a known suspect, together with similar images of others who resemble the suspect. See *paragraph 3.21* for circumstances in which still images may be used.

3.6   Video identifications must be carried out in accordance with *Annex A*.

Identification parade

3.7   An 'identification parade' is when the witness sees the suspect in a line of others who resemble the suspect.

3.8   Identification parades must be carried out in accordance with *Annex B*.

Group identification

3.9   A 'group identification' is when the witness sees the suspect in an informal group of people.

3.10   Group identifications must be carried out in accordance with *Annex C*.

Arranging identification procedures

3.11   Except for the provisions in *paragraph 3.19*, the arrangements for, and conduct of, the identification procedures in *paragraphs 3.5 to 3.10* and circumstances in which an identification procedure must be held shall be the responsibility of an officer not below inspector rank who is not involved with the investigation, 'the identification officer'. Unless otherwise specified, the identification officer may allow another officer or civilian support staff, see *paragraph 2.21*, to make arrangements for, and conduct, any of these identification procedures. In delegating these procedures, the identification officer must be able to supervise effectively and either intervene or be contacted for advice. No officer or any other person involved with the investigation of the case against the suspect, beyond the extent required by these procedures, may take any part in these procedures or act as the identification officer. This does not prevent the identification officer from consulting the officer in charge of the investigation to determine which procedure to use. When an identification procedure is required, in the interest of fairness to suspects and witnesses, it must be held as soon as practicable.

Circumstances in which an identification procedure must be held

3.12   Whenever:

(i)   a witness has identified a suspect or purported to have identified them prior to any identification procedure set out in *paragraphs 3.5 to 3.10* having been held; or

(ii)   there is a witness available, who expresses an ability to identify the suspect, or where there is a reasonable chance of the witness being able to do so, and they have not been given an opportunity to identify the suspect in any of the procedures set out in *paragraphs 3.5 to 3.10*,

and the suspect disputes being the person the witness claims to have seen, an identification procedure shall be held unless it is not practicable or it would serve no useful purpose in proving or disproving whether the suspect was involved in committing the offence. For example, when it is not disputed that the suspect is already well known to the witness who claims to have seen them commit the crime.

3.13   Such a procedure may also be held if the officer in charge of the investigation considers it would be useful.

Selecting an identification procedure

3.14   If, because of *paragraph 3.12*, an identification procedure is to be held, the suspect shall initially be offered either a video identification or identification unless:

a)   a video identification is not practicable; or

b)   an identification parade is both practicable and more suitable than a video identification; or

c)   *paragraph 3.16* applies.

The identification officer and the officer in charge of the investigation shall consult each other to determine which option is to be offered. An identification parade may not be practicable because of factors relating to the witnesses, such as their number, state of health, availability and travelling requirements. A video identification would normally be more suitable if it could be arranged and completed sooner than an identification parade.

3.15   A suspect who refuses the identification procedure first offered shall be asked to state their reason for refusing and may get advice from their solicitor and/or if present, their appropriate adult. The suspect, solicitor and/or appropriate adult shall be allowed to make representations about why another procedure should be used. A record should be made of the reasons for refusal and any representations made. After considering any reasons given, and representations made, the identification officer shall, if appropriate, arrange for the suspect to be offered an alternative which the officer considers suitable and practicable. If the officer decides it is not suitable and practicable to offer an alternative identification procedure, the reasons for that decision shall be recorded.

3.16   A group identification may initially be offered if the officer in charge of the investigation considers it is more satisfactory than a video identification or an identification parade and the identification officer considers it practicable to arrange.

Notice to suspect

3.17   Unless *paragraph 3.20* applies, before a video identification, an identification parade or group identification is arranged, the following shall be explained to the suspect:

(i)   the purposes of the video identification, identification parade or group identification;

(ii)   their entitlement to free legal advice; see *Code C, paragraph 6.5*;

(iii)   the procedures for holding it, including their right to have a solicitor or friend present;

(iv)   that they do not have to consent to or co-operate in a video identification, identification parade or group identification;

(v)   that if they do not consent to, and co-operate in, a video identification, identification parade or group identification, their refusal may be given in evidence in any subsequent trial and police may proceed covertly without their consent or make other arrangements to test whether a witness can identify them, see *paragraph 3.21*

(vi)   whether, for the purposes of the video identification procedure, images of them have previously been obtained, see *paragraph 3.20*, and if so, that they may co-operate in providing further, suitable images to be used instead;

(vii)   if appropriate, the special arrangements for juveniles;

(viii)   if appropriate, the special arrangements for mentally disordered or otherwise mentally vulnerable people;

(ix)   that if they significantly alter their appearance between being offered an identification procedure and any attempt to hold an identification procedure, this may be given in evidence if the case comes to trial, and the identification officer may then consider other forms of identification, see *paragraph 3.21* and *Note 3C*;

(x)   that a moving image or photograph may be taken of them when they attend for any identification procedure;

(xi)   whether, before their identity became known, the witness was shown photographs, a computerised or artist's composite likeness or similar likeness or image by the police; see *Note 3B*

(xii) that if they change their appearance before an identification parade, it may not be practicable to arrange one on the day or subsequently and, because of the appearance change, the identification officer may consider alternative methods of identification; see *Note 3C*

(xiii) that they or their solicitor will be provided with details of the description of them as first given by any witnesses who are to attend the video identification, identification parade, group identification or confrontation, see *paragraph 3.1.*

3.18   This information must also be recorded in a written notice handed to the suspect. The suspect must be given a reasonable opportunity to read the notice, after which, they should be asked to sign a second copy to indicate if they are willing to co-operate with the making of a video or take part in the identification parade or group identification. The signed copy shall be retained by the identification officer.

3.19   The duties of the identification officer under *paragraphs 3.17 and 3.18* may be performed by the custody officer or other officer not involved in the investigation if:

(a) it is proposed to hold an identification procedure at a later date, e.g., if the suspect is to be bailed to attend an identification parade; and

(b) an inspector is not available to act as the identification officer, see *paragraph 3.11*, before the suspect leaves the station.

The officer concerned shall inform the identification officer of the action taken and give them the signed copy of the notice. See *Note 3C*

3.20   If the identification officer and officer in charge of the investigation suspect, on reasonable grounds that if the suspect was given the information and notice as in *paragraphs 3.17 and 3.18*, they would then take steps to avoid being seen by a witness in any identification procedure, the identification officer may arrange for images of the suspect suitable for use in a video identification procedure to be obtained before giving the information and notice. If suspect's images are obtained in these circumstances, the suspect may, for the purposes of a video identification procedure, co-operate in providing suitable new images to be used instead, see *paragraph 3.17(vi).*

(c)   Cases when the suspect is known but not available

3.21   When a known suspect is not available or has ceased to be available, see *paragraph 3.4*, the identification officer may make arrangements for a video identification (see *Annex A*). If necessary, the identification officer may follow the video identification procedures but using still images. Any suitable moving or still images may be used and these may be obtained covertly if necessary. Alternatively, the identification officer may make arrangements for a group identification. See *Note 3D*. These provisions may also be applied to juveniles where the consent of their parent or guardian is either refused or reasonable efforts to obtain that consent have failed (see *paragraph 2.12*).

3.22   Any covert activity should be strictly limited to that necessary to test the ability of the witness to identify the suspect.

3.23   The identification officer may arrange for the suspect to be confronted by the witness if none of the options referred to in *paragraphs 3.5 to 3.10 or 3.21* are practicable. A 'confrontation' is when the suspect is directly confronted by the witness. A confrontation does not require the suspect's consent. Confrontations must be carried out in accordance with *Annex D*.

3.24   Requirements for information to be given to, or sought from, a suspect or for the suspect to be given an opportunity to view images before they are shown to a witness, do not apply if the suspect's lack of co-operation prevents the necessary action.

(d)   Documentation

3.25   A record shall be made of the video identification, identification parade, group identification or confrontation on forms provided for the purpose.

3.26   If the identification officer considers it is not practicable to hold a video identification or identification parade requested by the suspect, the reasons shall be recorded and explained to the suspect.

3.27   A record shall be made of a person's failure or refusal to co-operate in a video identification, identification parade or group identification and, if applicable, of the grounds for obtaining images in accordance with *paragraph 3.20.*

(e)   Showing films and photographs of incidents and information released to the media

3.28   Nothing in this Code inhibits showing films or photographs to the public through the national or local media, or to police officers for the purposes of recognition and tracing suspects. However, when such material is shown to potential witnesses, including police officers, see *Note 3A*, to obtain identification evidence, it shall be shown on an individual basis to avoid any possibility of collusion, and, as far as possible, the showing shall follow the principles for video identification if the suspect is known, see *Annex A*, or identification by photographs if the suspect is not known, see *Annex E*.

3.29   When a broadcast or publication is made, see *paragraph 3.28*, a copy of the relevant material released to the media for the purposes of recognising or tracing the suspect, shall be kept. The suspect or their solicitor shall be allowed to view such material before any procedures under *paragraphs 3.5 to 3.10, 3.21 or 3.23* are carried out, provided it is practicable and would not unreasonably delay the investigation. Each witness involved in the procedure shall be asked, after they have taken part, whether they have seen any broadcast or published films or photographs relating to the offence or any description of the suspect and their replies shall be recorded. This paragraph does not affect any separate requirement under the Criminal Procedure and Investigations Act 1996 to retain material in connection with criminal investigations.

(f)   Destruction and retention of photographs and images taken or used in identification procedures

3.30   PACE, section 64A, provides powers to take photographs of suspects detained at police stations and allows these photographs to be used or disclosed only for purposes related to the prevention or detection of crime, the investigation of offences or the conduct of prosecutions by, or on behalf of, police or other law enforcement and prosecuting authorities inside and outside the United Kingdom. After being so used or disclosed, they may be retained but can only be used or disclosed for the same purposes.

3.31   Subject to *paragraph 3.33*, the photographs (and all negatives and copies), of suspects not detained and any moving images, (and copies), of suspects whether or not they have been detained which are taken for the purposes of, or in connection with, the identification procedures *in paragraphs 3.5 to 3.10, 3.21 or 3.23* must be destroyed unless the suspect:

(a) is charged with, or informed they may be prosecuted for, a recordable offence;

(b) is prosecuted for a recordable offence;

(c) is cautioned for a recordable offence or given a warning or reprimand in accordance with the Crime and Disorder Act 1998 for a recordable offence; or

(d) gives informed consent, in writing, for the photograph or images to be retained for purposes described in *paragraph 3.30.*

3.32   When *paragraph 3.31* requires the destruction of any photograph or images, the person must be given an opportunity to witness the destruction or to have a certificate confirming the destruction if they request one within five days of being informed that the destruction is required.

3.33   Nothing in *paragraph 3.31* affects any separate requirement under the Criminal Procedure and Investigations Act 1996 to retain material in connection with criminal investigations.

Notes for guidance

3A   Except for the provisions of Annex E, paragraph 1, a police officer who is a witness for the purposes of this part of the Code is subject to the same principles and procedures as a civilian witness.

3B   When a witness attending an identification procedure has previously been shown photographs, or been shown or provided with computerised or artist's composite likeness, or similar likenesses or pictures, it is the officer in charge of the investigation's responsibility to make the identification officer aware of this.

3C   The purpose of paragraph 3.19 is to avoid or reduce delay in arranging identification procedures by enabling the required information and warnings, see sub-paragraphs 3.17(ix) and 3.17(xii), to be given at the earliest opportunity.

3D   Paragraph 3.21 would apply when a known suspect deliberately makes themself 'unavailable' in order to delay or frustrate arrangements for obtaining identification evidence. It also applies when a suspect refuses or fails to take part in a video identification, an identification parade or a group identification, or refuses or fails to take part in the only practicable options from that list. It enables any suitable images of the suspect, moving or still, which are available or can be obtained, to be used in an identification procedure.

3E   When it is proposed to show photographs to a witness in accordance with Annex E, it is the responsibility of the officer in charge of the investigation to confirm to the officer responsible for supervising and directing the showing, that the first description of the suspect given by that witness has been recorded. If this description has not been recorded, the procedure under Annex E must be postponed. See Annex E paragraph 2.

3F   The admissibility and value of identification evidence obtained when carrying out the procedure under paragraph 3.2 may be compromised if:

(a) before a person is identified, the witness' attention is specifically drawn to that person; or

(b) the suspect's identity becomes known before the procedure.

4   Identification by fingerprints

(A)   Taking fingerprints in connection with a criminal investigation

(a)   General

4.1   References to 'fingerprints' means any record, produced by any method, of the skin pattern and other physical characteristics or features of a person's:

(i) fingers; or

(ii) palms.

(b)   Action

4.2   A person's fingerprints may be taken in connection with the investigation of an offence only with their consent or if *paragraph 4.3* applies. If the person is at a police station consent must be in writing.

4.3   PACE, section 61, provides powers to take fingerprints without consent from any person over the age of ten years:

(a) under section 61(3)(a), from a detainee at a police station if authorised by an officer of at least inspector rank who has reasonable grounds for suspecting that person is involved in a criminal offence and for believing their fingerprints will tend to confirm or disprove involvement, or assist in establishing their identity (including showing that they are not a particular person), or both. However, authority may not be given solely to establish the person's identity unless they have refused to identify themselves or the authorising officer has reasonable grounds to suspect the person is not who they claim to be.

(b) under section 61(3)(b), from a detainee at a police station who has been charged with a recordable offence, see *Note 4A*, or informed they will be reported for such an offence if, in the course of the investigation of that offence:

(i) they have not had their fingerprints taken; or

(ii) the fingerprints taken do not constitute a complete set of their fingerprints or some, or all, of the fingerprints are not of sufficient quality to allow satisfactory analysis, comparison or matching;

(c) under section 61(4A), from a person who has been bailed to appear at a court or police station if the person:

    (i) has answered to bail for a person whose fingerprints were taken previously and there are reasonable grounds for believing they are not the same person; or

    (ii) who has answered to bail claims to be a different person from a person whose fingerprints were previously taken;

and in either case, the court or an officer of inspector rank or above, authorises the fingerprints to be taken at the court or police station;

(d) under section 61(6), from a person who has been:

    (i) convicted of a recordable offence;

    (ii) given a caution in respect of a recordable offence which, at the time of the caution, the person admitted; or

    (iii) warned or reprimanded under the Crime and Disorder Act 1998, section 65, for a recordable offence.

4.4 PACE, section 27, provides power to:

(a) require the person as in *paragraph 4.3(d)* to attend a police station to have their fingerprints taken if the:

    (i) person has not been in police detention for the offence and has not had their fingerprints taken in the course of the investigation of that offence; or

    (ii) fingerprints that were taken from the person in the course of the investigation of that offence, do not constitute a complete set or some, or all, of the fingerprints are not of sufficient quality to allow satisfactory analysis, comparison or matching; and

(b) arrest, without warrant, a person who fails to comply with the requirement.

Note: The requirement must be made within one month of the date the person is convicted, cautioned, warned or reprimanded and the person must be given a period of at least 7 days within which to attend. This 7 day period need not fall during the month allowed for making the requirement.

4.5 A person's fingerprints may be taken, as above, electronically.

4.6 Reasonable force may be used, if necessary, to take a person's fingerprints without their consent under the powers as in *paragraphs 4.3 and 4.4*.

4.7 Before any fingerprints are taken with, or without, consent as above, the person must be informed:

(a) of the reason their fingerprints are to be taken;

(b) of the grounds on which the relevant authority has been given if the powers mentioned in *paragraph 4.3(a) or (c)* apply;

(c) that their fingerprints may be retained and may be subject of a speculative search against other fingerprints, see *Note 4B*, unless destruction of the fingerprints is required in accordance with *Annex F, Part (a)*; and

(d) that if their fingerprints are required to be destroyed, they may witness their destruction as provided for in *Annex F, Part (a)*.

(c) Documentation

4.8 A record must be made as soon as possible, of the reason for taking a person's fingerprints without consent. If force is used, a record shall be made of the circumstances and those present.

4.9 A record shall be made when a person has been informed under the terms of *paragraph 4.7(c)*, of the possibility that their fingerprints may be subject of a speculative search.

(B) Taking fingerprints in connection with immigration enquiries

Action

4.10 A person's fingerprints may be taken for the purposes of Immigration Service enquiries in accordance with powers and procedures other than under PACE and for which the Immigration

Service (not the police) are responsible, only with the person's consent in writing or if *paragraph 4.11* applies.

4.11   Powers to take fingerprints for these purposes without consent are given to police and immigration officers under the:

(a) Immigration Act 1971, Schedule 2, paragraph 18(2), when it is reasonably necessary for the purposes of identifying a person detained under the Immigration Act 1971, Schedule 2, paragraph 16 (Detention of person liable to examination or removal);

(b) Immigration and Asylum Act 1999, section 141(7)(a), from a person who fails to produce, on arrival, a valid passport with a photograph or some other document satisfactorily establishing their identity and nationality if an immigration officer does not consider the person has a reasonable excuse for the failure;

(c) Immigration and Asylum Act 1999, section 141(7)(b), from a person who has been refused entry to the UK but has been temporarily admitted if an immigration officer reasonably suspects the person might break a condition imposed on them relating to residence or reporting to a police or immigration officer, and their decision is confirmed by a chief immigration officer;

(d) Immigration and Asylum Act 1999, section 141(7)(c), when directions are given to remove a person:
   – as an illegal entrant,
   – liable to removal under the Immigration and Asylum Act 1999, section 10,
   – who is the subject of a deportation order from the UK;

(e) Immigration and Asylum Act 1999, section 141(7)(d), from a person arrested under UK immigration laws under the Immigration Act 1971, Schedule 2, paragraph 17;

(f) Immigration and Asylum Act 1999, section 141(7)(e), from a person who has made a claim:
   – for asylum
   – under Article 3 of the European Convention on Human Rights; or

(g) Immigration and Asylum Act 1999, section 141(7)(f), from a person who is a dependant of someone who falls into (b) to (f) above.

4.12   The Immigration and Asylum Act 1999, section 142(3), gives a police and immigration officer power to arrest, without warrant, a person who fails to comply with a requirement imposed by the Secretary of State to attend a specified place for fingerprinting.

4.13   Before any fingerprints are taken, with or without consent, the person must be informed:

(a) of the reason their fingerprints are to be taken;

(b) the fingerprints, and all copies of them, will be destroyed in accordance with *Annex F, Part B*.

4.14   Reasonable force may be used, if necessary, to take a person's fingerprints without their consent under powers as in *paragraph 4.11*.

4.15   *Paragraphs 4.1 and 4.8* apply.

Notes for guidance

4A   References to 'recordable offences' in this Code relate to those offences for which convictions, cautions, reprimands and warnings may be recorded in national police records. See PACE, section 27(4). The recordable offences current at the time when this Code was prepared, are any offences which carry a sentence of imprisonment on conviction (irrespective of the period, or the age of the offender or actual sentence passed) as well as the non-imprisonable offences under the Street Offences Act 1959, section 1 (loitering or soliciting for purposes of prostitution), the Telecommunications Act 1984, section 43 (improper use of public telecommunications systems), the Road Traffic Act 1988, section 25 (tampering with motor vehicles), the Malicious Communications Act 1988, section 1 (sending letters, etc. with intent to cause distress or anxiety) and others listed in the National Police Records (Recordable Offences) Regulations 2000.

4B   Fingerprints or a DNA sample (and the information derived from it) taken from a person arrested on suspicion of being involved in a recordable offence, or charged with such an offence, or informed they will be reported for such an offence, may be subject of a speculative search. This means the fingerprints or DNA sample may be checked against other fingerprints and DNA records held by, or on behalf of, the police and other law enforcement authorities in, or outside, the UK, or held in connection with, or as a result of, an investigation of an offence inside or outside the UK. Fingerprints and samples taken from a person suspected of committing a recordable offence but not arrested, charged or informed they will be reported for it, may be subject to a speculative search only if the person consents in writing. The following is an example of a basic form of words:

> *"I consent to my fingerprints and DNA sample and information derived from it being retained and used only for purposes related to the prevention and detection of a crime, the investigation of an offence or the conduct of a prosecution either nationally or internationally.*
>
> *I understand that my fingerprints or this sample may be checked against other fingerprint and DNA records held by or on behalf of relevant law enforcement authorities, either nationally or internationally.*
>
> *I understand that once I have given my consent for the sample to be retained and used I cannot withdraw this consent."*

See Annex F regarding the retention and use of fingerprints taken with consent for elimination purposes.

5   Examinations to establish identity and the taking of photographs

(A)   Detainees at police stations

(a)   Searching or examination of detainees at police stations

5.1   PACE, section 54A (1), allows a detainee at a police station to be searched or examined or both, to establish:

  (a)   whether they have any marks, features or injuries that would tend to identify them as a person involved in the commission of an offence and to photograph any identifying marks, see *paragraph 5.5*; or

  (b)   their identity, see *Note 5A*.

A person detained at a police station to be searched under a stop and search power, see *Code A*, is not a detainee for the purposes of these powers.

5.2   A search and/or examination to find marks under section 54A (1) (a) may be carried out without the detainee's consent, see *paragraph 2.12*, only if authorised by an officer of at least inspector rank when consent has been withheld or it is not practicable to obtain consent, see *Note 5D*.

5.3   A search or examination to establish a suspect's identity under section 54A (1) (b) may be carried out without the detainee's consent, see *paragraph 2.12*, only if authorised by an officer of at least inspector rank when the detainee has refused to identify themselves or the authorising officer has reasonable grounds for suspecting the person is not who they claim to be.

5.4   Any marks that assist in establishing the detainee's identity, or their identification as a person involved in the commission of an offence, are identifying marks. Such marks may be photographed with the detainee's consent, see *paragraph 2.12*; or without their consent if it is withheld or it is not practicable to obtain it, see *Note 5D*.

5.5   A detainee may only be searched, examined and photographed under section 54A, by a police officer of the same sex.

5.6   Any photographs of identifying marks, taken under section 54A, may be used or disclosed only for purposes related to the prevention or detection of crime, the investigation of offences or the conduct of prosecutions by, or on behalf of, police or other law enforcement and prosecuting authorities inside, and outside, the UK. After being so used or disclosed, the photograph may be retained but must not be used or disclosed except for these purposes, see *Note 5B*.

5.7   The powers, as in *paragraph 5.1*, do not affect any separate requirement under the Criminal Procedure and Investigations Act 1996 to retain material in connection with criminal investigations.

5.8   Authority for the search and/or examination for the purposes of *paragraphs 5.2 and 5.3* may be given orally or in writing. If given orally, the authorising officer must confirm it in writing as soon as practicable. A separate authority is required for each purpose which applies.

5.9   If it is established a person is unwilling to co-operate sufficiently to enable a search and/or examination to take place or a suitable photograph to be taken, an officer may use reasonable force to:

(a) search and/or examine a detainee without their consent; and

(b) photograph any identifying marks without their consent.

5.10   The thoroughness and extent of any search or examination carried out in accordance with the powers in section 54A must be no more than the officer considers necessary to achieve the required purpose. Any search or examination which involves the removal of more than the person's outer clothing shall be conducted in accordance with *Code C, Annex A, paragraph 11.*

5.11   An intimate search may not be carried out under the powers in section 54A.

(b)   Photographing detainees at police stations

5.12   Under PACE, section 64A, an officer may photograph a detainee at a police station:

(a) with their consent; or

(b) without their consent if it is:
   (i) withheld; or
   (ii) not practicable to obtain their consent.

See *Note 5E*

and *paragraph 5.6* applies to the retention and use of photographs taken under this section as it applies to the retention and use of photographs taken under section 54A, see *Note 5B*.

5.13   The officer proposing to take a detainee's photograph may, for this purpose, require the person to remove any item or substance worn on, or over, all, or any part of, their head or face. If they do not comply with such a requirement, the officer may remove the item or substance.

5.14   If it is established the detainee is unwilling to co-operate sufficiently to enable a suitable photograph to be taken and it is not reasonably practicable to take the photograph covertly, an officer may use reasonable force:

(a) to take their photograph without their consent; and

(b) for the purpose of taking the photograph, remove any item or substance worn on, or over, all, or any part of, the person's head or face which they have failed to remove when asked.

5.15   For the purposes of this Code, a photograph may be obtained without the person's consent by making a copy of an image of them taken at any time on a camera system installed anywhere in the police station.

(c)   Information to be given

5.16   When a person is searched, examined or photographed under the provisions as in *paragraph 5.1 and 5.12*, or their photograph obtained as in *paragraph 5.15*, they must be informed of the:

(a) purpose of the search, examination or photograph;

(b) grounds on which the relevant authority, if applicable, has been given; and

(c) purposes for which the photograph may be used, disclosed or retained.

This information must be given before the search or examination commences or the photograph is taken, except if the photograph is:

(i) to be taken covertly;

(ii) obtained as in *paragraph 5.15*, in which case the person must be informed as soon as practicable after the photograph is taken or obtained.

(d)   Documentation

5.17   A record must be made when a detainee is searched, examined, or a photograph of the person, or any identifying marks found on them, are taken. The record must include the:

(a) identity, subject to *paragraph 2.18*, of the officer carrying out the search, examination or taking the photograph;

(b) purpose of the search, examination or photograph and the outcome;

(c) detainee's consent to the search, examination or photograph, or the reason the person was searched, examined or photographed without consent;

(d) giving of any authority as in *paragraphs 5.2 and 5.3*, the grounds for giving it and the authorising officer.

5.18   If force is used when searching, examining or taking a photograph in accordance with this section, a record shall be made of the circumstances and those present.

(B)   Persons at police stations not detained

5.19   When there are reasonable grounds for suspecting the involvement of a person in a criminal offence, but that person is at a police station voluntarily and not detained, the provisions of *paragraphs 5.1 to 5.18* should apply, subject to the modifications in the following paragraphs.

5.20   References to the 'person being detained' and to the powers mentioned in *paragraph 5.1* which apply only to detainees at police stations shall be omitted.

5.21   Force may not be used to:

(a) search and/or examine the person to:
  (i) discover whether they have any marks that would tend to identify them as a person involved in the commission of an offence; or
  (ii) establish their identity, see *Note 5A*;

(b) take photographs of any identifying marks, see *paragraph 5.4*; or

(c) take a photograph of the person.

5.22   Subject to *paragraph 5.24*, the photographs or images, of persons not detained, or of their identifying marks, must be destroyed (together with any negatives and copies) unless the person:

(a) is charged with, or informed they may be prosecuted for, a recordable offence;

(b) is prosecuted for a recordable offence;

(c) is cautioned for a recordable offence or given a warning or reprimand in accordance with the Crime and Disorder Act 1998 for a recordable offence; or

(d) gives informed consent, in writing, for the photograph or image to be retained as in *paragraph 5.6*.

5.23   When *paragraph 5.22* requires the destruction of any photograph or image, the person must be given an opportunity to witness the destruction or to have a certificate confirming the destruction provided they so request the certificate within five days of being informed the destruction is required.

5.24   Nothing in *paragraph 5.22* affects any separate requirement under the Criminal Procedure and Investigations Act 1996 to retain material in connection with criminal investigations.

Notes for guidance

5A   The conditions under which fingerprints may be taken to assist in establishing a person's identity, are described in Section 4.

5B   Examples of purposes related to the prevention or detection of crime, the investigation of offences or the conduct of prosecutions include:

(a) checking the photograph against other photographs held in records or in connection with, or as a result of, an investigation of an offence to establish whether the person is liable to arrest for other offences;

(b) when the person is arrested at the same time as other people, or at a time when it is likely that other people will be arrested, using the photograph to help establish who was arrested, at what time and where;

(c) when the real identity of the person is not known and cannot be readily ascertained or there are reasonable grounds for doubting a name and other personal details given by the person, are their real name and personal details. In these circumstances, using or disclosing the photograph to help to establish or verify their real identity or determine whether they are liable to arrest for some other offence, e.g. by checking it against other photographs held in records or in connection with, or as a result of, an investigation of an offence;

(d) when it appears any identification procedure in section 3 may need to be arranged for which the person's photograph would assist;

(e) when the person's release without charge may be required, and if the release is:
   (i) on bail to appear at a police station, using the photograph to help verify the person's identity when they answer their bail and if the person does not answer their bail, to assist in arresting them; or
   (ii) without bail, using the photograph to help verify their identity or assist in locating them for the purposes of serving them with a summons to appear at court in criminal proceedings;

(f) when the person has answered to bail at a police station and there are reasonable grounds for doubting they are the person who was previously granted bail, using the photograph to help establish or verify their identity;

(g) when the person arrested on a warrant claims to be a different person from the person named on the warrant and a photograph would help to confirm or disprove their claim;

(h) when the person has been charged with, reported for, or convicted of, a recordable offence and their photograph is not already on record as a result of (a) to (f) or their photograph is on record but their appearance has changed since it was taken and the person has not yet been released or brought before a court.

5C   There is no power to arrest a person convicted of a recordable offence solely to take their photograph. The power to take photographs in this section applies only where the person is in custody as a result of the exercise of another power, e.g. arrest for fingerprinting under PACE, section 27.

5D   Examples of when it would not be practicable to obtain a detainee's consent, see paragraph 2.12, to a search, examination or the taking of a photograph of an identifying mark include:

(a) when the person is drunk or otherwise unfit to give consent;

(b) when there are reasonable grounds to suspect that if the person became aware a search or examination was to take place or an identifying mark was to be photographed, they would take steps to prevent this happening, e.g. by violently resisting, covering or concealing the mark etc and it would not otherwise be possible to carry out the search or examination or to photograph any identifying mark;

(c) in the case of a juvenile, if the parent or guardian cannot be contacted in sufficient time to allow the search or examination to be carried out or the photograph to be taken.

5E   Examples of when it would not be practicable to obtain the person's consent, see paragraph 2.12, to a photograph being taken include:

(a) when the person is drunk or otherwise unfit to give consent;

(b) when there are reasonable grounds to suspect that if the person became aware a photograph, suitable to be used or disclosed for the use and disclosure described in paragraph 5.6, was to be taken, they would take steps to prevent it being taken, e.g. by violently resisting, covering or distorting their face etc, and it would not otherwise be possible to take a suitable photograph;

(c) when, in order to obtain a suitable photograph, it is necessary to take it covertly; and

(d) in the case of a juvenile, if the parent or guardian cannot be contacted in sufficient time to allow the photograph to be taken.

6   **Identification by body samples and impressions**

(A)   **General**

6.1   References to:

(a) an 'intimate sample' mean a dental impression or sample of blood, semen or any other tissue fluid, urine, or pubic hair, or a swab taken from a person's body orifice other than the mouth;

(b) a 'non-intimate sample' means:
  (i)   a sample of hair, other than pubic hair, which includes hair plucked with the root, see *Note 6A*;
  (ii) a sample taken from a nail or from under a nail;
  (iii) a swab taken from any part of a person's body including the mouth but not any other body orifice;
  (iv) saliva;
  (v)   a skin impression which means any record, other than a fingerprint, which is a record, in any form and produced by any method, of the skin pattern and other physical characteristics or features of the whole, or any part of, a person's foot or of any other part of their body.

(B)   **Action**

(a)   **Intimate samples**

6.2   PACE, section 62, provides that intimate samples may be taken under:

(a) section 62(1), from a person in police detention only:
  (i)   if a police officer of inspector rank or above has reasonable grounds to believe such an impression or sample will tend to confirm or disprove the suspect's involvement in a recordable offence, see *Note 4A*, and gives authorisation for a sample to be taken; and
  (ii) with the suspect's written consent;

(b) section 62(1A), from a person not in police detention but from whom two or more non-intimate samples have been taken in the course of an investigation of an offence and the samples, though suitable, have proved insufficient if:
  (i)   a police officer of inspector rank or above authorises it to be taken; and
  (ii) the person concerned gives their written consent. See *Notes 6B and 6C*

6.3   Before a suspect is asked to provide an intimate sample, they must be warned that if they refuse without good cause, their refusal may harm their case if it comes to trial, see *Note 6D*. If the suspect is in police detention and not legally represented, they must also be reminded of their entitlement to have free legal advice, see *Code C, paragraph 6.5*, and the reminder noted in the custody record. If *paragraph 6.2(b)* applies and the person is attending a station voluntarily, their entitlement to free legal advice as in *Code C, paragraph 3.21* shall be explained to them.

6.4   Dental impressions may only be taken by a registered dentist. Other intimate samples, except for samples of urine, may only be taken by a registered medical practitioner or registered health care professional.

(b)   **Non-intimate samples**

6.5   A non-intimate sample may be taken from a detainee only with their written consent or if *paragraph 6.6* applies.

6.6   A non-intimate sample may be taken from a person without consent in accordance with PACE. The principal circumstances provided for are as follows:

(a) under section 63(3), from a person in police detention, or police custody on the authority of a court, if a police officer of inspector rank or above has reasonable grounds to believe the sample will tend to confirm or disprove the suspect's involvement in a recordable offence, see

Note 4A, and gives authorisation for a sample to be taken. However, the officer may not give authorisation to take a non-intimate sample consisting of a skin impression if a skin impression of the same part of the body has already been taken from that person in the course of the investigation of the offence and the impression previously taken is not one that has proved insufficient;

(b) under section 63(3A), from a person charged with a recordable offence or informed they will be reported for such an offence: and
  (i) that person has not had a non-intimate sample taken from them in the course of the investigation; or
  (ii) if they have had a sample taken, it proved unsuitable or insufficient for the same form of analysis, see *Note 6B*; or

(c) under section 63(3B), from a person convicted of a recordable offence after the date on which that provision came into effect. PACE, section 63A, describes the circumstances in which a police officer may require a person convicted of a recordable offence to attend a police station for a non-intimate sample to be taken.

6.7   Reasonable force may be used, if necessary, to take a non-intimate sample from a person without their consent under the powers mentioned in *paragraph 6.6*.

6.8   Before any intimate sample is taken with consent or non-intimate sample is taken with, or without, consent, the person must be informed:

(a) of the reason for taking the sample;

(b) of the grounds on which the relevant authority has been given, including, if appropriate, the nature of the suspected offence;

(c) that the sample or information derived from the sample may be retained and subject of a speculative search, see *Note 6E*, unless their destruction is required as in *Annex F, Part A*.

6.9   When clothing needs to be removed in circumstances likely to cause embarrassment to the person, no person of the opposite sex who is not a registered medical practitioner or registered health care professional shall be present, (unless in the case of a juvenile, mentally disordered or mentally vulnerable person, that person specifically requests the presence of an appropriate adult of the opposite sex who is readily available) nor shall anyone whose presence is unnecessary. However, in the case of a juvenile, this is subject to the overriding proviso that such a removal of clothing may take place in the absence of the appropriate adult only if the juvenile signifies, in their presence, that they prefer the adult's absence and they agree.

(c)   Documentation

6.10   A record of the reasons for taking a sample or impression and, if applicable, of its destruction must be made as soon as practicable. If force is used, a record shall be made of the circumstances and those present. If written consent is given to the taking of a sample or impression, the fact must be recorded in writing.

6.11   A record must be made of a warning given as required by *paragraph 6.3*.

6.12   A record shall be made of the fact that a person has been informed as in *paragraph 6.8(c)* that samples may be subject of a speculative search.

Notes for guidance

6A   When hair samples are taken for the purpose of DNA analysis (rather than for other purposes such as making a visual match), the suspect should be permitted a reasonable choice as to what part of the body the hairs are taken from. When hairs are plucked, they should be plucked individually, unless the suspect prefers otherwise and no more should be plucked than the person taking them reasonably considers necessary for a sufficient sample.

6B   (a) An insufficient sample is one which is not sufficient either in quantity or quality to provide information for a particular form of analysis, such as DNA analysis. A sample may also be insufficient if enough information cannot be obtained from it by analysis because of loss, destruction, damage or contamination of the sample or as a result of an earlier, unsuccessful attempt at analysis.

(b) An unsuitable sample is one which, by its nature, is not suitable for a particular form of analysis.

6C   Nothing in paragraph 6.2 prevents intimate samples being taken for elimination purposes with the consent of the person concerned but the provisions of paragraph 2.12 relating to the role of the appropriate adult, should be applied. Paragraph 6.2(b) does not, however, apply where the non-intimate samples were previously taken under the Terrorism Act 2000, Schedule 8, paragraph 10.

6D   In warning a person who is asked to provide an intimate sample as in paragraph 6.3, the following form of words may be used:

> *"You do not have to provide this sample/allow this swab or impression to be taken, but I must warn you that if you refuse without good cause, your refusal may harm your case if it comes to trial."*

6E   Fingerprints or a DNA sample and the information derived from it taken from a person arrested on suspicion of being involved in a recordable offence, or charged with such an offence, or informed they will be reported for such an offence, may be subject of a speculative search. This means they may be checked against other fingerprints and DNA records held by, or on behalf of, the police and other law enforcement authorities in or outside the UK or held in connection with, or as a result of, an investigation of an offence inside or outside the UK. Fingerprints and samples taken from any other person, e.g. a person suspected of committing a recordable offence but who has not been arrested, charged or informed they will be reported for it, may be subject to a speculative search only if the person consents in writing to their fingerprints being subject of such a search. The following is an example of a basic form of words:

> *"I consent to my fingerprints/DNA sample and information derived from it being retained and used only for purposes related to the prevention and detection of a crime, the investigation of an offence or the conduct of a prosecution either nationally or internationally.*
>
> *I understand that this sample may be checked against other fingerprint/DNA records held by or on behalf of relevant law enforcement authorities, either nationally or internationally.*
>
> *I understand that once I have given my consent for the sample to be retained and used I cannot withdraw this consent."*

See Annex F regarding the retention and use of fingerprints and samples taken with consent for elimination purposes.

ANNEX A—VIDEO IDENTIFICATION

(a)   General

1.   The arrangements for obtaining and ensuring the availability of a suitable set of images to be used in a video identification must be the responsibility of an identification officer, who has no direct involvement with the case.

2.   The set of images must include the suspect and at least eight other people who, so far as possible, resemble the suspect in age, height, general appearance and position in life. Only one suspect shall appear in any set unless there are two suspects of roughly similar appearance, in which case they may be shown together with at least twelve other people.

3.   The images used to conduct a video identification shall, as far as possible, show the suspect and other people in the same positions or carrying out the same sequence of movements. They shall also show the suspect and other people under identical conditions unless the identification officer reasonably believes:

   (a) because of the suspect's failure or refusal to co-operate or other reasons, it is not practicable for the conditions to be identical; and

   (b) any difference in the conditions would not direct a witness' attention to any individual image.

4. The reasons identical conditions are not practicable shall be recorded on forms provided for the purpose.

5. Provision must be made for each person shown to be identified by number.

6. If police officers are shown, any numerals or other identifying badges must be concealed. If a prison inmate is shown, either as a suspect or not, then either all, or none of, the people shown should be in prison clothing.

7. The suspect or their solicitor, friend, or appropriate adult must be given a reasonable opportunity to see the complete set of images before it is shown to any witness. If the suspect has a reasonable objection to the set of images or any of the participants, the suspect shall be asked to state the reasons for the objection. Steps shall, if practicable, be taken to remove the grounds for objection. If this is not practicable, the suspect and/or their representative shall be told why their objections cannot be met and the objection, the reason given for it and why it cannot be met shall be recorded on forms provided for the purpose.

8. Before the images are shown in accordance with *paragraph 7*, the suspect or their solicitor shall be provided with details of the first description of the suspect by any witnesses who are to attend the video identification. When a broadcast or publication is made, as in *paragraph 3.28*, the suspect or their solicitor must also be allowed to view any material released to the media by the police for the purpose of recognising or tracing the suspect, provided it is practicable and would not unreasonably delay the investigation.

9. The suspect's solicitor, if practicable, shall be given reasonable notification of the time and place the video identification is to be conducted so a representative may attend on behalf of the suspect. If a solicitor has not been instructed, this information shall be given to the suspect. The suspect may not be present when the images are shown to the witness(es). In the absence of the suspect's representative, the viewing itself shall be recorded on video. No unauthorised people may be present.

(b) Conducting the video identification

10. The identification officer is responsible for making the appropriate arrangements to make sure, before they see the set of images, witnesses are not able to communicate with each other about the case or overhear a witness who has already seen the material. There must be no discussion with the witness about the composition of the set of images and they must not be told whether a previous witness has made any identification.

11. Only one witness may see the set of images at a time. Immediately before the images are shown, the witness shall be told that the person they saw on a specified earlier occasion may, or may not, appear in the images they are shown and that if they cannot make a positive identification, they should say so. The witness shall be advised that at any point, they may ask to see a particular part of the set of images or to have a particular image frozen for them to study. Furthermore, it should be pointed out to the witness that there is no limit on how many times they can view the whole set of images or any part of them. However, they should be asked not to make any decision as to whether the person they saw is on the set of images until they have seen the whole set at least twice.

12. Once the witness has seen the whole set of images at least twice and has indicated that they do not want to view the images, or any part of them, again, the witness shall be asked to say whether the individual they saw in person on a specified earlier occasion has been shown and, if so, to identify them by number of the image. The witness will then be shown that image to confirm the identification, see *paragraph 17*.

13. Care must be taken not to direct the witness' attention to any one individual image or give any indication of the suspect's identity. Where a witness has previously made an identification by photographs, or a computerised or artist's composite or similar likeness, the witness must not be reminded of such a photograph or composite likeness once a suspect is available for identification by other means in accordance with this Code. Nor must the witness be reminded of any description of the suspect.

14.   After the procedure, each witness shall be asked whether they have seen any broadcast or published films or photographs, or any descriptions of suspects relating to the offence and their reply shall be recorded.

(c)   Image security and destruction

15.   Arrangements shall be made for all relevant material containing sets of images used for specific identification procedures to be kept securely and their movements accounted for. In particular, no-one involved in the investigation shall be permitted to view the material prior to it being shown to any witness.

16.   As appropriate, *paragraph 3.30 or 3.31* applies to the destruction or retention of relevant sets of images.

(d)   Documentation

17.   A record must be made of all those participating in, or seeing, the set of images whose names are known to the police.

18.   A record of the conduct of the video identification must be made on forms provided for the purpose. This shall include anything said by the witness about any identifications or the conduct of the procedure and any reasons it was not practicable to comply with any of the provisions of this Code governing the conduct of video identifications.

ANNEX B—IDENTIFICATION PARADES

(a)   General

1.   A suspect must be given a reasonable opportunity to have a solicitor or friend present, and the suspect shall be asked to indicate on a second copy of the notice whether or not they wish to do so.

2.   An identification parade may take place either in a normal room or one equipped with a screen permitting witnesses to see members of the identification parade without being seen. The procedures for the composition and conduct of the identification parade are the same in both cases, subject to *paragraph 8* (except that an identification parade involving a screen may take place only when the suspect's solicitor, friend or appropriate adult is present or the identification parade is recorded on video).

3.   Before the identification parade takes place, the suspect or their solicitor shall be provided with details of the first description of the suspect by any witnesses who are attending the identification parade. When a broadcast or publication is made as in *paragraph 3.28*, the suspect or their solicitor should also be allowed to view any material released to the media by the police for the purpose of recognising or tracing the suspect, provided it is practicable to do so and would not unreasonably delay the investigation.

(b)   Identification parades involving prison inmates

4.   If a prison inmate is required for identification, and there are no security problems about the person leaving the establishment, they may be asked to participate in an identification parade or video identification.

5.   An identification parade may be held in a Prison Department establishment but shall be conducted, as far as practicable under normal identification parade rules. Members of the public shall make up the identification parade unless there are serious security, or control, objections to their admission to the establishment. In such cases, or if a group or video identification is arranged within the establishment, other inmates may participate. If an inmate is the suspect, they are not required to wear prison clothing for the identification parade unless the other people taking part are other inmates in similar clothing, or are members of the public who are prepared to wear prison clothing for the occasion.

(c)   Conduct of the identification parade

6.   Immediately before the identification parade, the suspect must be reminded of the procedures governing its conduct and cautioned in the terms of *Code C, paragraphs 10.5 or 10.6*, as appropriate.

7.   All unauthorised people must be excluded from the place where the identification parade is held.

8.   Once the identification parade has been formed, everything afterwards, in respect of it, shall take place in the presence and hearing of the suspect and any interpreter, solicitor, friend or appropriate adult who is present (unless the identification parade involves a screen, in which case everything said to, or by, any witness at the place where the identification parade is held, must be said in the hearing and presence of the suspect's solicitor, friend or appropriate adult or be recorded on video).

9.   The identification parade shall consist of at least eight people (in addition to the suspect) who, so far as possible, resemble the suspect in age, height, general appearance and position in life. Only one suspect shall be included in an identification parade unless there are two suspects of roughly similar appearance, in which case they may be paraded together with at least twelve other people. In no circumstances shall more than two suspects be included in one identification parade and where there are separate identification parades, they shall be made up of different people.

10.   If the suspect has an unusual physical feature, e.g., a facial scar, tattoo or distinctive hairstyle or hair colour which cannot be replicated on other members of the identification parade, steps may be taken to conceal the location of that feature on the suspect and the other members of the identification parade if the suspect and their solicitor, or appropriate adult, agree. For example, by use of a plaster or a hat, so that all members of the identification parade resemble each other in general appearance.

11.   When all members of a similar group are possible suspects, separate identification parades shall be held for each unless there are two suspects of similar appearance when they may appear on the same identification parade with at least twelve other members of the group who are not suspects. When police officers in uniform form an identification parade any numerals or other identifying badges shall be concealed.

12.   When the suspect is brought to the place where the identification parade is to be held, they shall be asked if they have any objection to the arrangements for the identification parade or to any of the other participants in it and to state the reasons for the objection. The suspect may obtain advice from their solicitor or friend, if present, before the identification parade proceeds. If the suspect has a reasonable objection to the arrangements or any of the participants, steps shall, if practicable, be taken to remove the grounds for objection. When it is not practicable to do so, the suspect shall be told why their objections cannot be met and the objection, the reason given for it and why it cannot be met, shall be recorded on forms provided for the purpose.

13.   The suspect may select their own position in the line, but may not otherwise interfere with the order of the people forming the line. When there is more than one witness, the suspect must be told, after each witness has left the room, that they can, if they wish, change position in the line. Each position in the line must be clearly numbered, whether by means of a number laid on the floor in front of each identification parade member or by other means.

14.   Appropriate arrangements must be made to make sure, before witnesses attend the identification parade, they are not able to:

   (i)   communicate with each other about the case or overhear a witness who has already seen the identification parade;

   (ii)   see any member of the identification parade;

   (iii)   see, or be reminded of, any photograph or description of the suspect or be given any other indication as to the suspect's identity; or

   (iv)   see the suspect before or after the identification parade.

15.   The person conducting a witness to an identification parade must not discuss with them the composition of the identification parade and, in particular, must not disclose whether a previous witness has made any identification.

16.   Witnesses shall be brought in one at a time. Immediately before the witness inspects the identification parade, they shall be told the person they saw on a specified earlier occasion may, or may not, be present and if they cannot make a positive identification, they should say so. The witness must also be told they should not make any decision about whether the person they saw is on the identification parade until they have looked at each member at least twice.

17.   When the officer or civilian support staff (see *paragraph 3.11*) conducting the identification procedure is satisfied the witness has properly looked at each member of the identification parade, they shall ask the witness whether the person they saw on a specified earlier occasion is on the identification parade and, if so, to indicate the number of the person concerned, see *paragraph 28*.

18.   If the witness wishes to hear any identification parade member speak, adopt any specified posture or move, they shall first be asked whether they can identify any person(s) on the identification parade on the basis of appearance only. When the request is to hear members of the identification parade speak, the witness shall be reminded that the participants in the identification parade have been chosen on the basis of physical appearance only. Members of the identification parade may then be asked to comply with the witness' request to hear them speak, see them move or adopt any specified posture.

19.   If the witness requests that the person they have indicated remove anything used for the purposes of *paragraph 10* to conceal the location of an unusual physical feature, that person may be asked to remove it.

20.   If the witness makes an identification after the identification parade has ended, the suspect and, if present, their solicitor, interpreter or friend shall be informed. When this occurs, consideration should be given to allowing the witness a second opportunity to identify the suspect.

21.   After the procedure, each witness shall be asked whether they have seen any broadcast or published films or photographs or any descriptions of suspects relating to the offence and their reply shall be recorded.

22.   When the last witness has left, the suspect shall be asked whether they wish to make any comments on the conduct of the identification parade.

(d)   **Documentation**

23.   A video recording must normally be taken of the identification parade. If that is impracticable, a colour photograph must be taken. A copy of the video recording or photograph shall be supplied, on request, to the suspect or their solicitor within a reasonable time.

24.   As appropriate, *paragraph 3.30 or 3.31*, should apply to any photograph or video taken as in *paragraph 23*.

25.   If any person is asked to leave an identification parade because they are interfering with its conduct, the circumstances shall be recorded.

26.   A record must be made of all those present at an identification parade whose names are known to the police.

27.   If prison inmates make up an identification parade, the circumstances must be recorded.

28.   A record of the conduct of any identification parade must be made on forms provided for the purpose. This shall include anything said by the witness or the suspect about any identifications or the conduct of the procedure, and any reasons it was not practicable to comply with any of this Code's provisions.

ANNEX C—GROUP IDENTIFICATION

(a) General

1. The purpose of this Annex is to make sure, as far as possible, group identifications follow the principles and procedures for identification parades so the conditions are fair to the suspect in the way they test the witness' ability to make an identification.

2. Group identifications may take place either with the suspect's consent and co-operation or covertly without their consent.

3. The location of the group identification is a matter for the identification officer, although the officer may take into account any representations made by the suspect, appropriate adult, their solicitor or friend.

4. The place where the group identification is held should be one where other people are either passing by or waiting around informally, in groups such that the suspect is able to join them and be capable of being seen by the witness at the same time as others in the group. For example people leaving an escalator, pedestrians walking through a shopping centre, passengers on railway and bus stations, waiting in queues or groups or where people are standing or sitting in groups in other public places.

5. If the group identification is to be held covertly, the choice of locations will be limited by the places where the suspect can be found and the number of other people present at that time. In these cases, suitable locations might be along regular routes travelled by the suspect, including buses or trains or public places frequented by the suspect.

6. Although the number, age, sex, race and general description and style of clothing of other people present at the location cannot be controlled by the identification officer, in selecting the location the officer must consider the general appearance and numbers of people likely to be present. In particular, the officer must reasonably expect that over the period the witness observes the group, they will be able to see, from time to time, a number of others whose appearance is broadly similar to that of the suspect.

7. A group identification need not be held if the identification officer believes, because of the unusual appearance of the suspect, none of the locations it would be practicable to use satisfy the requirements of *paragraph 6* necessary to make the identification fair.

8. Immediately after a group identification procedure has taken place (with or without the suspect's consent), a colour photograph or video should be taken of the general scene, if practicable, to give a general impression of the scene and the number of people present. Alternatively, if it is practicable, the group identification may be video recorded.

9. If it is not practicable to take the photograph or video in accordance with *paragraph 8*, a photograph or film of the scene should be taken later at a time determined by the identification officer if the officer considers it practicable to do so.

10. An identification carried out in accordance with this Code remains a group identification even though, at the time of being seen by the witness, the suspect was on their own rather than in a group.

11. Before the group identification takes place, the suspect or their solicitor shall be provided with details of the first description of the suspect by any witnesses who are to attend the identification. When a broadcast or publication is made, as in *paragraph 3.28*, the suspect or their solicitor should also be allowed to view any material released by the police to the media for the purposes of recognising or tracing the suspect, provided that it is practicable and would not unreasonably delay the investigation.

12. After the procedure, each witness shall be asked whether they have seen any broadcast or published films or photographs or any descriptions of suspects relating to the offence and their reply recorded.

(b) Identification with the consent of the suspect

13. A suspect must be given a reasonable opportunity to have a solicitor or friend present. They shall be asked to indicate on a second copy of the notice whether or not they wish to do so.

14. The witness, the person carrying out the procedure and the suspect's solicitor, appropriate adult, friend or any interpreter for the witness, may be concealed from the sight of the individuals in the group they are observing, if the person carrying out the procedure considers this assists the conduct of the identification.

15. The person conducting a witness to a group identification must not discuss with them the forthcoming group identification and, in particular, must not disclose whether a previous witness has made any identification.

16. Anything said to, or by, the witness during the procedure about the identification should be said in the presence and hearing of those present at the procedure.

17. Appropriate arrangements must be made to make sure, before witnesses attend the group identification, they are not able to:

   (i) communicate with each other about the case or overhear a witness who has already been given an opportunity to see the suspect in the group;

   (ii) see the suspect; or

   (iii) see, or be reminded of, any photographs or description of the suspect or be given any other indication of the suspect's identity.

18. Witnesses shall be brought one at a time to the place where they are to observe the group. Immediately before the witness is asked to look at the group, the person conducting the procedure shall tell them that the person they saw may, or may not, be in the group and that if they cannot make a positive identification, they should say so. The witness shall be asked to observe the group in which the suspect is to appear. The way in which the witness should do this will depend on whether the group is moving or stationary.

Moving group

19. When the group in which the suspect is to appear is moving, e.g. leaving an escalator, the provisions of *paragraphs 20 to 24* should be followed.

20. If two or more suspects consent to a group identification, each should be the subject of separate identification procedures. These may be conducted consecutively on the same occasion.

21. The person conducting the procedure shall tell the witness to observe the group and ask them to point out any person they think they saw on the specified earlier occasion.

22. Once the witness has been informed as in *paragraph 21* the suspect should be allowed to take whatever position in the group they wish.

23. When the witness points out a person as in *paragraph 21* they shall, if practicable, be asked to take a closer look at the person to confirm the identification. If this is not practicable, or they cannot confirm the identification, they shall be asked how sure they are that the person they have indicated is the relevant person.

24. The witness should continue to observe the group for the period which the person conducting the procedure reasonably believes is necessary in the circumstances for them to be able to make comparisons between the suspect and other individuals of broadly similar appearance to the suspect as in *paragraph 6*.

Stationary groups

25. When the group in which the suspect is to appear is stationary, e.g. people waiting in a queue, the provisions of *paragraphs 26 to 29* should be followed.

26. If two or more suspects consent to a group identification, each should be subject to separate identification procedures unless they are of broadly similar appearance when they may appear in

the same group. When separate group identifications are held, the groups must be made up of different people.

27.   The suspect may take whatever position in the group they wish. If there is more than one witness, the suspect must be told, out of the sight and hearing of any witness, that they can, if they wish, change their position in the group.

28.   The witness shall be asked to pass along, or amongst, the group and to look at each person in the group at least twice, taking as much care and time as possible according to the circumstances, before making an identification. Once the witness has done this, they shall be asked whether the person they saw on the specified earlier occasion is in the group and to indicate any such person by whatever means the person conducting the procedure considers appropriate in the circumstances. If this is not practicable, the witness shall be asked to point out any person they think they saw on the earlier occasion.

29.   When the witness makes an indication as in *paragraph 28*, arrangements shall be made, if practicable, for the witness to take a closer look at the person to confirm the identification. If this is not practicable, or the witness is unable to confirm the identification, they shall be asked how sure they are that the person they have indicated is the relevant person.

All cases

30.   If the suspect unreasonably delays joining the group, or having joined the group, deliberately conceals themselves from the sight of the witness, this may be treated as a refusal to co-operate in a group identification.

31.   If the witness identifies a person other than the suspect, that person should be informed what has happened and asked if they are prepared to give their name and address. There is no obligation upon any member of the public to give these details. There shall be no duty to record any details of any other member of the public present in the group or at the place where the procedure is conducted.

32.   When the group identification has been completed, the suspect shall be asked whether they wish to make any comments on the conduct of the procedure.

33.   If the suspect has not been previously informed, they shall be told of any identifications made by the witnesses.

(c)   Identification without the suspect's consent

34.   Group identifications held covertly without the suspect's consent should, as far as practicable, follow the rules for conduct of group identification by consent.

35.   A suspect has no right to have a solicitor, appropriate adult or friend present as the identification will take place without the knowledge of the suspect.

36.   Any number of suspects may be identified at the same time.

(d)   Identifications in police stations

37.   Group identifications should take place in police stations only for reasons of safety, security or because it is not practicable to hold them elsewhere.

38.   The group identification may take place either in a room equipped with a screen permitting witnesses to see members of the group without being seen, or anywhere else in the police station that the identification officer considers appropriate.

39.   Any of the additional safeguards applicable to identification parades should be followed if the identification officer considers it is practicable to do so in the circumstances.

(e)   Identifications involving prison inmates

40.   A group identification involving a prison inmate may only be arranged in the prison or at a police station.

41.   When a group identification takes place involving a prison inmate, whether in a prison or in a police station, the arrangements should follow those in *paragraphs 37 to 39*. If a group identification takes place within a prison, other inmates may participate. If an inmate is the suspect, they do not have to wear prison clothing for the group identification unless the other participants are wearing the same clothing.

(f)   Documentation

42.   When a photograph or video is taken as in *paragraph 8 or 9*, a copy of the photograph or video shall be supplied on request to the suspect or their solicitor within a reasonable time.

43.   *Paragraph 3.30 or 3.31*, as appropriate, shall apply when the photograph or film taken in accordance with *paragraph 8 or 9* includes the suspect.

44.   A record of the conduct of any group identification must be made on forms provided for the purpose. This shall include anything said by the witness or suspect about any identifications or the conduct of the procedure and any reasons why it was not practicable to comply with any of the provisions of this Code governing the conduct of group identifications.

ANNEX D—CONFRONTATION BY A WITNESS

1.   Before the confrontation takes place, the witness must be told that the person they saw may, or may not, be the person they are to confront and that if they are not that person, then the witness should say so.

2.   Before the confrontation takes place the suspect or their solicitor shall be provided with details of the first description of the suspect given by any witness who is to attend. When a broadcast or publication is made, as in *paragraph 3.28*, the suspect or their solicitor should also be allowed to view any material released to the media for the purposes of recognising or tracing the suspect, provided it is practicable to do so and would not unreasonably delay the investigation.

3.   Force may not be used to make the suspect's face visible to the witness.

4.   Confrontation must take place in the presence of the suspect's solicitor, interpreter or friend unless this would cause unreasonable delay.

5.   The suspect shall be confronted independently by each witness, who shall be asked "Is this the person?". If the witness identifies the person but is unable to confirm the identification, they shall be asked how sure they are that the person is the one they saw on the earlier occasion.

6.   The confrontation should normally take place in the police station, either in a normal room or one equipped with a screen permitting a witness to see the suspect without being seen. In both cases, the procedures are the same except that a room equipped with a screen may be used only when the suspect's solicitor, friend or appropriate adult is present or the confrontation is recorded on video.

7.   After the procedure, each witness shall be asked whether they have seen any broadcast or published films or photographs or any descriptions of suspects relating to the offence and their reply shall be recorded.

ANNEX E—SHOWING PHOTOGRAPHS

(a)   Action

1.   An officer of sergeant rank or above shall be responsible for supervising and directing the showing of photographs. The actual showing may be done by another officer or civilian support staff, see *paragraph 3.11*.

2. The supervising officer must confirm the first description of the suspect given by the witness has been recorded before they are shown the photographs. If the supervising officer is unable to confirm the description has been recorded they shall postpone showing the photographs.

3. Only one witness shall be shown photographs at any one time. Each witness shall be given as much privacy as practicable and shall not be allowed to communicate with any other witness in the case.

4. The witness shall be shown not less than twelve photographs at a time, which shall, as far as possible, all be of a similar type.

5. When the witness is shown the photographs, they shall be told the photograph of the person they saw may, or may not, be amongst them and if they cannot make a positive identification, they should say so. The witness shall also be told they should not make a decision until they have viewed at least twelve photographs. The witness shall not be prompted or guided in any way but shall be left to make any selection without help.

6. If a witness makes a positive identification from photographs, unless the person identified is otherwise eliminated from enquiries or is not available, other witnesses shall not be shown photographs. But both they, and the witness who has made the identification, shall be asked to attend a video identification, an identification parade or group identification unless there is no dispute about the suspect's identification.

7. If the witness makes a selection but is unable to confirm the identification, the person showing the photographs shall ask them how sure they are that the photograph they have indicated is the person they saw on the specified earlier occasion.

8. When the use of a computerised or artist's composite or similar likeness has led to there being a known suspect who can be asked to participate in a video identification, appear on an identification parade or participate in a group identification, that likeness shall not be shown to other potential witnesses.

9. When a witness attending a video identification, an identification parade or group identification has previously been shown photographs or computerised or artist's composite or similar likeness (and it is the responsibility of the officer in charge of the investigation to make the identification officer aware that this is the case), the suspect and their solicitor must be informed of this fact before the identification procedure takes place.

10. None of the photographs shown shall be destroyed, whether or not an identification is made, since they may be required for production in court. The photographs shall be numbered and a separate photograph taken of the frame or part of the album from which the witness made an identification as an aid to reconstituting it.

(b) Documentation

11. Whether or not an identification is made, a record shall be kept of the showing of photographs on forms provided for the purpose. This shall include anything said by the witness about any identification or the conduct of the procedure, any reasons it was not practicable to comply with any of the provisions of this Code governing the showing of photographs and the name and rank of the supervising officer.

12. The supervising officer shall inspect and sign the record as soon as practicable.

ANNEX F—FINGERPRINTS AND SAMPLES—DESTRUCTION AND SPECULATIVE SEARCHES

(a) Fingerprints and samples taken in connection with a criminal investigation

1. When fingerprints or DNA samples are taken from a person in connection with an investigation and the person is not suspected of having committed the offence, see *Note F1*, they must be

destroyed as soon as they have fulfilled the purpose for which they were taken unless:

(a) they were taken for the purposes of an investigation of an offence for which a person has been convicted; and

(b) fingerprints or samples were also taken from the convicted person for the purposes of that investigation.

However, subject to *paragraph 2*, the fingerprints and samples, and the information derived from samples, may not be used in the investigation of any offence or in evidence against the person who is, or would be, entitled to the destruction of the fingerprints and samples, see *Note F2*.

2.   The requirement to destroy fingerprints and DNA samples, and information derived from samples, and restrictions on their retention and use in *paragraph 1* do not apply if the person gives their written consent for their fingerprints or sample to be retained and used after they have fulfilled the purpose for which they were taken, see *Note F1*.

3.   When a person's fingerprints or sample are to be destroyed:

(a) any copies of the fingerprints must also be destroyed;

(b) the person may witness the destruction of their fingerprints or copies if they ask to do so within five days of being informed destruction is required;

(c) access to relevant computer fingerprint data shall be made impossible as soon as it is practicable to do so and the person shall be given a certificate to this effect within three months of asking; and

(d) neither the fingerprints, the sample, or any information derived from the sample, may be used in the investigation of any offence or in evidence against the person who is, or would be, entitled to its destruction.

4.   Fingerprints or samples, and the information derived from samples, taken in connection with the investigation of an offence which are not required to be destroyed, may be retained after they have fulfilled the purposes for which they were taken but may be used only for purposes related to the prevention or detection of crime, the investigation of an offence or the conduct of a prosecution in, as well as outside, the UK and may also be subject to a speculative search. This includes checking them against other fingerprints and DNA records held by, or on behalf of, the police and other law enforcement authorities in, as well as outside, the UK.

(b)   Fingerprints taken in connection with Immigration Service enquiries

5.   Fingerprints taken for Immigration Service enquiries in accordance with powers and procedures other than under PACE and for which the Immigration Service, not the police, are responsible, must be destroyed as follows:

(a) fingerprints and all copies must be destroyed as soon as practicable if the person from whom they were taken proves they are a British or Commonwealth citizen who has the right of abode in the UK under the Immigration Act 1971, section 2(1)(b);

(b) fingerprints taken under the power as in *paragraph 4.11(g)* from a dependant of a person in *4.11(b) to (f)* must be destroyed when that person's fingerprints are to be destroyed;

(c) fingerprints taken from a person under any power as in *paragraph 4.11* or with the person's consent which have not already been destroyed as above, must be destroyed within ten years of being taken or within such period specified by the Secretary of State under the Immigration and Asylum Act 1999, section 143(5).

Notes for guidance

F1   Fingerprints and samples given voluntarily for the purposes of elimination play an important part in many police investigations. It is, therefore, important to make sure innocent volunteers are not deterred from participating and their consent to their fingerprints and DNA being used for the purposes of a specific investigation is fully informed and voluntary. If the police or volunteer seek to have the sample or fingerprints retained for use after the specific investigation ends, it is important the volunteer's consent to this is also fully informed and voluntary.

Examples of consent for:

- *DNA/fingerprints—to be used only for the purposes of a specific investigation;*
- *DNA/fingerprints—to be used in the specific investigation and retained by the police for future use.*

To minimise the risk of confusion, each consent should be physically separate and the volunteer should be asked to sign one or the other, not both.

    (a) DNA:

        (i) DNA sample taken for the purposes of elimination or as part of an intelligence-led screen and to be used only for the purposes of that investigation and destroyed afterwards:

        "I consent to my DNA/mouth swab being taken for forensic analysis. I understand that the sample will be destroyed at the end of the case and that my profile will only be compared to the crime stain profile from this enquiry. I have been advised that the person taking the sample may be required to give evidence and/or provide a written statement to the police in relation to the taking of it".

        (ii) DNA sample to be retained on the National DNA database and used in the future:

        "I consent to my DNA sample and information derived from it being retained and used only for purposes related to the prevention and detection of a crime, the investigation of an offence or the conduct of a prosecution either nationally or internationally."

        "I understand that this sample may be checked against other DNA records held by, or on behalf of, relevant law enforcement authorities, either nationally or internationally".

        "I understand that once I have given my consent for the sample to be retained and used I cannot withdraw this consent."

    (b) Fingerprints:

        (i) Fingerprints taken for the purposes of elimination or as part of an intelligence-led screen and to be used only for the purposes of that investigation and destroyed afterwards:

        "I consent to my fingerprints being taken for elimination purposes. I understand that the fingerprints will be destroyed at the end of the case and that my fingerprints will only be compared to the fingerprints from this enquiry. I have been advised that the person taking the fingerprints may be required to give evidence and/or provide a written statement to the police in relation to the taking of it."

        (ii) Fingerprints to be retained for future use:

        "I consent to my fingerprints being retained and used only for purposes related to the prevention and detection of a crime, the investigation of an offence or the conduct of a prosecution either nationally or internationally".

        "I understand that my fingerprints may be checked against other records held by, or on behalf of, relevant law enforcement authorities, either nationally or internationally."

        "I understand that once I have given my consent for my fingerprints to be retained and used I cannot withdraw this consent."

F2   The provisions for the retention of fingerprints and samples in paragraph 1 allow for all fingerprints and samples in a case to be available for any subsequent miscarriage of justice investigation.

Appendix 5

PACE Code of Practice on Tape Recording Interviews with Suspects (Code E)

This code applies to interviews carried out after midnight on 31st March 2003, notwithstanding that the interview may have commenced before that time.

1 General

1.1 This Code of Practice must be readily available for consultation by:

- police officers
- detained persons
- members of the public.

1.2 The *Notes for Guidance* included are not provisions of this Code.

1.3 Nothing in this Code shall detract from the requirements of Code C, the Code of Practice for the detention, treatment and questioning of persons by police officers.

1.4 This Code does not apply to those people listed in Code C, *paragraph 1.12*.

1.5 The term:

- 'appropriate adult' has the same meaning as in Code C, *paragraph 1.7*
- 'solicitor' has the same meaning as in Code C, *paragraph 6.12*.

1.6 In this Code:

(a) 'designated person' means a person other than a police officer, designated under the Police Reform Act 2002, Part 4 who has specified powers and duties of police officers conferred or imposed on them;

(b) any reference to a police officer includes a designated person acting in the exercise or performance of the powers and duties conferred or imposed on them by their designation.

1.7 If a power conferred on a designated person:

(a) allows reasonable force to be used when exercised by a police officer, a designated person exercising that power has the same entitlement to use force;

(b) includes power to use force to enter any premises, that power is not exercisable by that designated person except:
  (i) in the company, and under the supervision, of a police officer; or
  (ii) for the purpose of:
    - saving life or limb; or
    - preventing serious damage to property.

1.8 Nothing in this Code prevents the custody officer, or other officer given custody of the detainee, from allowing civilian support staff who are not designated persons to carry out individual procedures or tasks at the police station if the law allows. However, the officer remains responsible for making sure the procedures and tasks are carried out correctly in accordance with these Codes.

Any such civilian must be:

(a) a person employed by a police authority maintaining a police force and under the control and direction of the Chief Officer of that force; or

(b) employed by a person with whom a police authority has a contract for the provision of services relating to persons arrested or otherwise in custody.

1.9 Designated persons and other civilian support staff must have regard to any relevant provisions of the Codes of Practice.

1.10 References to pocket book include any official report book issued to police officers or civilian support staff.

1.11 References to a custody officer include those performing the functions of a custody officer.

2 Recording and sealing master tapes

2.1 Tape recording of interviews shall be carried out openly to instil confidence in its reliability as an impartial and accurate record of the interview.

2.2 One tape, the master tape, will be sealed in the suspect's presence. A second tape will be used as a working copy. The master tape is either of the two tapes used in a twin deck machine or the only tape in a single deck machine. The working copy is either the second/third tape used in a twin/triple deck machine or a copy of the master tape made by a single deck machine. See Notes 2A and 2B.

2.3 Nothing in this Code requires the identity of officers or civilian support staff conducting interviews to be recorded or disclosed:

(a) in the case of enquiries linked to the investigation of terrorism; or

(b) if the interviewer reasonably believes recording or disclosing their name might put them in danger.

In these cases interviewers should use warrant or other identification numbers and the name of their police station. *See Note 2C.*

Notes for guidance

2A The purpose of sealing the master tape in the suspect's presence is to show the tape's integrity is preserved. If a single deck machine is used the working copy of the master tape must be made in the suspect's presence and without the master tape leaving their sight. The working copy shall be used for making further copies if needed.

2B Reference to 'tapes' includes 'tape', if a single deck machine is used.

2C The purpose of paragraph 2.3(b) is to protect those involved in serious organised crime investigations or arrests of particularly violent suspects when there is reliable information that those arrested or their associates may threaten or cause harm to those involved. In cases of doubt, an officer of inspector rank or above should be consulted.

3 Interviews to be tape recorded

3.1 Subject to *paragraphs 3.3 and 3.4*, tape recording shall be used at police stations for any interview:

(a) with a person cautioned under Code C, *section 10* in respect of any indictable offence, including an offence triable either way; see Note 3A

(b) which takes place as a result of an interviewer exceptionally putting further questions to a suspect about an offence described in *paragraph 3.1(a)* after they have been charged with, or told they may be prosecuted for, that offence, see Code C, *paragraph 16.5*

(c) when an interviewer wants to tell a person, after they have been charged with, or informed they may be prosecuted for, an offence described in *paragraph 3.1(a)*, about any written statement or interview with another person, see Code C, *paragraph 16.4*.

3.2   The Terrorism Act 2000 makes separate provision for a Code of Practice for the tape recording of interviews of those arrested under Section 41 or detained under Schedule 7 of the Act. The provisions of this Code do not apply to such interviews.

3.3   The custody officer may authorise the interviewer not to tape record the interview when it is:

(a) not reasonably practicable because of equipment failure or the unavailability of a suitable interview room or recorder and the authorising officer considers, on reasonable grounds, that the interview should not be delayed; or

(b) clear from the outset there will not be a prosecution.

Note: In these cases the interview should be recorded in writing in accordance with Code C, *section 11*. In all cases the custody officer shall record the specific reasons for not tape recording. *See Note 3B.*

3.4   If a person refuses to go into or remain in a suitable interview room, see Code C *paragraph 12.5*, and the custody officer considers, on reasonable grounds, that the interview should not be delayed the interview may, at the custody officer's discretion, be conducted in a cell using portable recording equipment or, if none is available, recorded in writing as in Code C, *section 11*. The reasons for this shall be recorded.

3.5   The whole of each interview shall be tape recorded, including the taking and reading back of any statement.

Notes for guidance

3A   Nothing in the Code is intended to preclude tape recording at police discretion of interviews at police stations with people cautioned in respect of offences not covered by paragraph 3.1, or responses made by persons after they have been charged with, or told they may be prosecuted for, an offence, provided this Code is complied with.

3B   A decision not to tape record an interview for any reason may be the subject of comment in court. The authorising officer should be prepared to justify that decision.

4   The interview

(a)   General

4.1   The provisions of Code C:

– *sections 10 and 11*, and the applicable Notes for Guidance apply to the conduct of interviews to which this Code applies

– *paragraphs 11.7 to 11.14* apply only when a written record is needed.

4.2   Code C, *paragraphs 10.10, 10.11 and Annex C* describe the restriction on drawing adverse inferences from a suspect's failure or refusal to say anything about their involvement in the offence when interviewed or after being charged or informed they may be prosecuted, and how it affects the terms of the caution and determines if and by whom a special warning under sections 36 and 37 can be given.

(b)   Commencement of interviews

4.3   When the suspect is brought into the interview room the interviewer shall, without delay but in the suspect's sight, load the recorder with clean tapes and set it to record. The tapes must be unwrapped or opened in the suspect's presence.

4.4   The interviewer should tell the suspect about the tape recording. The interviewer shall:

(a) say the interview is being tape recorded

(b) subject to *paragraph 2.3*, give their name and rank and that of any other interviewer present

(c) ask the suspect and any other party present, e.g. a solicitor, to identify themselves

(d) state the date, time of commencement and place of the interview

(e) state the suspect will be given a notice about what will happen to the tapes.

See *Note 4A*

4.5   The interviewer shall:

–   caution the suspect, see Code C, *section 10*

–   remind the suspect of their entitlement to free legal advice, see Code C, *paragraph 11.2*.

4.6   The interviewer shall put to the suspect any significant statement or silence; see Code C, *paragraph 11.4*.

(c)   Interviews with deaf persons

4.7   If the suspect is deaf or is suspected of having impaired hearing, the interviewer shall make a written note of the interview in accordance with Code C, at the same time as tape recording it in accordance with this Code. See *Notes 4B and 4C*

(d)   Objections and complaints by the suspect

4.8   If the suspect objects to the interview being tape recorded at the outset, during the interview or during a break, the interviewer shall explain that the interview is being tape recorded and that this Code requires the suspect's objections be recorded on tape. When any objections have been tape recorded or the suspect has refused to have their objections recorded, the interviewer shall say they are turning off the recorder, give their reasons and turn it off. The interviewer shall then make a written record of the interview as in Code C, *section 11*. If, however, the interviewer reasonably considers they may proceed to question the suspect with the tape still on, the interviewer may do so. See *Note 4D*

4.9   If in the course of an interview a complaint is made by or on behalf on the person being questioned concerning the provisions of this Code or Code C, the interviewer shall act as in Code C, *paragraph 12.9*. See *Notes 4E and 4F*

4.10   If the suspect indicates they want to tell the interviewer about matters not directly connected with the offence and they are unwilling for these matters to be tape recorded, the suspect should be given the opportunity to tell the interviewer at the end of the formal interview.

(e)   Changing tapes

4.11   When the recorder shows the tapes have only a short time left, the interviewer shall tell the suspect the tapes are coming to an end and round off that part of the interview. If the interviewer leaves the room for a second set of tapes, the suspect shall not be left unattended. The interviewer will remove the tapes from the tape recorder and insert the new tapes which shall be unwrapped or opened in the suspect's presence. The tape recorder should be set to record on the new tapes. To avoid confusion between the tapes, the interviewer shall mark the tapes with an identification number immediately they are removed from the tape recorder.

(f)   Taking a break during interview

4.12   When a break is taken, the fact that a break is to be taken, the reason for it and the time shall be recorded on tape.

4.12A When the break is taken and the interview room vacated by the suspect, the tapes shall be removed from the tape recorder and the procedures for the conclusion of an interview followed; see *paragraph 4.18*.

4.13   When a break is a short one and both the suspect and an interviewer remain in the interview room, the tape recorder may be turned off. There is no need to remove the tapes and when the interview recommences the tape recording should continue on the same tapes. The time the interview recommences shall be recorded on tape.

4.14   After any break in the interview the interviewer must, before resuming the interview, remind the person being questioned that they remain under caution or, if there is any doubt, give the caution in full again. See *Note 4G*

(g)   Failure of recording equipment

4.15   If there is an equipment failure which can be rectified quickly, e.g. by inserting new tapes, the interviewer shall follow the appropriate procedures as in *paragraph 4.11*. When the recording is resumed the interviewer shall explain what happened and record the time the interview recommences. If, however, it will not be possible to continue recording on that tape recorder and no replacement recorder is readily available, the interview may continue without being tape recorded. If this happens, the interviewer shall seek the custody officer's authority as in *paragraph 3.3*. See *Note 4H*

(h)   Removing tapes from the recorder

4.16 When tapes are removed from the recorder during the interview, they shall be retained and the procedures in *paragraph 4.18* followed.

(i)   Conclusion of interview

4.17   At the conclusion of the interview, the suspect shall be offered the opportunity to clarify anything he or she has said and asked if there is anything they want to add.

4.18   At the conclusion of the interview, including the taking and reading back of any written statement, the time shall be recorded and the tape recorder switched off. The interviewer shall seal the master tape with a master tape label and treat it as an exhibit in accordance with force standing orders. The interviewer shall sign the label and ask the suspect and any third party present during the interview to sign it. If the suspect or third refuse to sign the label an officer of at least inspector rank, or if not available the custody officer, shall be called into the interview room and asked, subject to *paragraph 2.3*, to sign it.

4.19   The suspect shall be handed a notice which explains:

 –   how the tape recording will be used

 –   the arrangements for access to it

 –   that if the person is charged or informed they will be prosecuted, a copy of the tape will be

 –   supplied as soon as practicable or as otherwise agreed between the suspect and the police.

Notes for guidance

4A   For the purpose of voice identification the interviewer should ask the suspect and any other people present to identify themselves.

4B   This provision is to give a person who is deaf or has impaired hearing equivalent rights of access to the full interview record as far as this is possible using audio recording.

4C   The provisions of Code C, section 13 on interpreters for deaf persons or for interviews with suspects who have difficulty understanding English continue to apply. However, in a tape recorded interview the requirement on the interviewer to make sure the interpreter makes a separate note of the interview applies only to paragraph 4.7 (interviews with deaf persons).

4D   The interviewer should remember that a decision to continue recording against the wishes of the suspect may be the subject of comment in court.

4E   If the custody officer is called to deal with the complaint, the tape recorder should, if possible, be left on until the custody officer has entered the room and spoken to the person being interviewed. Continuation or

termination of the interview should be at the interviewer's discretion pending action by an inspector under Code C, paragraph 9.2.

4F If the complaint is about a matter not connected with this Code or Code C, the decision to continue is at the interviewer's discretion. When the interviewer decides to continue the interview, they shall tell the suspect the complaint will be brought to the custody officer's attention at the conclusion of the interview. When the interview is concluded the interviewer must, as soon as practicable, inform the custody officer about the existence and nature of the complaint made.

4G The interviewer should remember that it may be necessary to show to the court that nothing occurred during a break or between interviews which influenced the suspect's recorded evidence. After a break or at the beginning of a subsequent interview, the interviewer should consider summarising on tape the reason for the break and confirming this with the suspect.

4H If one of the tapes snaps during the interview it should be sealed as a master tape in the suspect's presence and the interview resumed where it left off. The unbroken tape should be copied and the original sealed as a master tape in the suspect's presence, if necessary after the interview. If equipment for copying the un-broken tape is not readily available, both tapes should be sealed in the suspect's presence and the interview begun again. If the tape breaks when a single deck machine is being used and the machine is one where a broken tape cannot be copied on available equipment, the tape should be sealed as a master tape in the suspect's presence and the interview begun again.

5 After the interview

5.1   The interviewer shall make a note in their pocket book that the interview has taken place, was tape recorded, its time, duration and date and the master tape's identification number.

5.2   If no proceedings follow in respect of the person whose interview was recorded, the tapes must be kept securely as in *paragraph 6.1* and *Note 6A*.

Note for guidance

5A Any written record of a tape recorded interview should be made in accordance with national guidelines approved by the Secretary of State.

6 Tape security

6.1   The officer in charge of each police station at which interviews with suspects are recorded shall make arrangements for master tapes to be kept securely and their movements accounted for on the same basis as material which may be used for evidential purposes, in accordance with force standing orders. See *Note 6A*

6.2   A police officer has no authority to break the seal on a master tape required for criminal trial or appeal proceedings. If it is necessary to gain access to the master tape, the police officer shall arrange for its seal to be broken in the presence of a representative of the Crown Prosecution Service. The defendant or their legal adviser should be informed and given a reasonable opportunity to be present. If the defendant or their legal representative is present they shall be invited to reseal and sign the master tape. If either refuses or neither is present this should be done by the representative of the Crown Prosecution Service. See *Notes 6B and 6C*

6.3   If no criminal proceedings result or the criminal trial and, if applicable, appeal proceedings to which the interview relates have been concluded, the chief officer of police is responsible for establishing arrangements for breaking the seal on the master tape, if necessary.

6.4   When the master tape seal is broken, a record must be made of the procedure followed, including the date, time, place and persons present.

Notes for guidance

6A   This section is concerned with the security of the master tape sealed at the conclusion of the interview. Care must be taken of working copies of tapes because their loss or destruction may lead to the need to access master tapes.

6B   If the tape has been delivered to the crown court for their keeping after committal for trial the crown prosecutor will apply to the chief clerk of the crown court centre for the release of the tape for unsealing by the crown prosecutor.

6C   Reference to the Crown Prosecution Service or to the crown prosecutor in this part of the Code should be taken to include any other body or person with a statutory responsibility for prosecution for whom the police conduct any tape recorded interviews.

Appendix 6

PACE Code of Practice on Visual Recordings with Sound of Interviews with Suspects (Code F)

1 General

1.1   This code of practice must be readily available for consultation by police officers, detained persons and members of the public.

1.2   The Notes for guidance included are not provisions of this code. They form guidance to police officers and others about its application and interpretation.

1.3   Nothing in this Code shall be taken as detracting in any way from the requirements of the Code of Practice for the Detention, Treatment and Questioning of Persons by Police Officers (Code C). [See *Note 1A*]

1.4   The interviews to which this Code applies are set out in paragraphs 3.1 to 3.3.

1.5   In this Code, the terms "appropriate adult", "solicitor" and "interview" have the same meaning as those set out in Code C. The corresponding provisions and notes for guidance in Code C applicable to those terms shall also apply where appropriate.

1.6   Any reference in this Code to visual recording shall be taken to mean visual recording with sound.

1.7   References to "pocket book" in this Code include any official report book issued to police officers.

Note for guidance

1A   As in Code C, references to custody officers include those carrying out the functions of a custody officer.

2 Recording and sealing of master tapes

2.1   The visual recording of interviews shall be carried out openly to instil confidence in its reliability as an impartial and accurate record of the interview. [See *Note 2A*]

2.2   The camera(s) shall be placed in the interview room so as to ensure coverage of as much of the room as is practicably possible whilst the interviews are taking place.

2.3   The certified recording medium will be of a high quality, new and previously unused. When the certified recording medium is placed in the recorder and switched on to record, the correct date and time, in hours, minutes and seconds, will be superimposed automatically, second by second, during the whole recording. [See *Note 2B*]

2.4   One copy of the certified recording medium, referred to in this Code as the master copy, will be sealed before it leaves the presence of the suspect. A second copy will be used as a working copy. [See *Notes 2C* and *2D*]

2.5   Nothing in this code requires the identity of an officer to be recorded or disclosed if:

(a) the interview or record relates to a person detained under the Terrorism Act 2000; or

(b) otherwise where the officer reasonably believes that recording or disclosing their name might put them in danger.

In these cases, the officer will have their back to the camera and shall use their warrant or other identification number and the name of the police station to which they are attached. Such instances and the reasons for them shall be recorded in the custody record. [See *Note 2E*]

Notes for guidance

2A   Interviewing officers will wish to arrange that, as far as possible, visual recording arrangements are unobtrusive. It must be clear to the suspect, however, that there is no opportunity to interfere with the recording equipment or the recording media.

2B   In this context, the certified recording media will be of either a VHS or digital CD format and should be capable of having an image of the date and time superimposed upon them as they record the interview.

2C   The purpose of sealing the master copy before it leaves the presence of the suspect is to establish their confidence that the integrity of the copy is preserved.

2D   The recording of the interview is not to be used for any identification purpose.

2E   The purpose of the paragraph 2.5 is to protect police officers and others involved in the investigation of serious organised crime or the arrest of particularly violent suspects when there is reliable information that those arrested or their associates may threaten or cause harm to the officers, their families or their personal property.

3   Interviews to be visually recorded

3.1   Subject to paragraph 3.2 below, visual recording shall be used for any interview:

(a) with a suspect in respect of an indictable offence (including an offence triable either way) [see Notes 3A and 3B];

(b) which takes place as a result of an interviewer exceptionally putting further questions to a suspect about an offence described in sub-paragraph (a) above after they have been charged with, or informed they may be prosecuted for, that offence [see Note 3C];

(c) in which an interviewer wishes to bring to the notice of a person, after that person has been charged with, or informed they may be prosecuted for an offence described in sub-paragraph (a) above, any written statement made by another person, or the content of an interview with another person [see Note 3D]

(d) with, or in the presence of, a deaf or deaf/blind or speech impaired person who uses sign language to communicate;

(e) with, or in the presence of anyone who requires an 'appropriate adult'; or

(f) in any case where the suspect or their representative requests that the interview be recorded visually.

3.2   The Terrorism Act 2000 makes separate provision for a code of practice for the video recording of interviews in a police station of those detained under Schedule 7 or section 41 of the Act. The provisions of this code do not therefore apply to such interviews [see Note 3E].

3.3   The custody officer may authorise the interviewing officer not to record the interview visually:

(a) where it is not reasonably practicable to do so because of failure of the equipment, or the non-availability of a suitable interview room, or recorder, and the authorising officer considers on reasonable grounds that the interview should not be delayed until the failure has been rectified or a suitable room or recorder becomes available. In such cases the custody officer may authorise the interviewing officer to audio record the interview in accordance with the guidance set out in Code E;

(b) where it is clear from the outset that no prosecution will ensue; or

(c) where it is not practicable to do so because at the time the person resists being taken to a - suitable interview room or other location which would enable the interview to be recorded, or otherwise fails or refuses to go into such a room or location, and the authorising officer considers on reasonable grounds that the interview should not be delayed until these conditions cease to apply.

In all cases the custody officer shall make a Note in the custody records of the reasons for not taking a visual record. [See *Note 3F*]

3.4   When a person who is voluntarily attending the police station is required to be cautioned in accordance with Code C prior to being interviewed, the subsequent interview shall be recorded, unless the custody officer gives authority in accordance with the provisions of paragraph 3.3 above for the interview not to be so recorded.

3.5   The whole of each interview shall be recorded visually, including the taking and reading back of any statement.

3.6   A visible illuminated sign or indicator will light and remain on at all times when the recording equipment is activated or capable of recording or transmitting any signal or information.

Notes for guidance

3A   Nothing in the Code is intended to preclude visual recording at police discretion of interviews at police stations with people cautioned in respect of offences not covered by paragraph 3.1, or responses made by interviewees after they have been charged with, or informed they may be prosecuted for, an offence, provided that this code is complied with.

3B   Attention is drawn to the provisions set out in Code C about the matters to be considered when deciding whether a detained person is fit to be interviewed.

3C   Code C sets out the circumstances in which a suspect may be questioned about an offence after being charged with it.

3D   Code C sets out the procedures to be followed when a person's attention is drawn after charge, to a statement made by another person. One method of bringing the content of an interview with another person to the notice of a suspect may be to play him a recording of that interview.

3E   When it only becomes clear during the course of an interview which is being visually recorded that the interviewee may have committed an offence to which paragraph 3.2 applies, the interviewing officer should turn off the recording equipment and the interview should continue in accordance with the provisions of the Terrorism Act 2000.

3F   A decision not to record an interview visually for any reason may be the subject of comment in court. The authorising officer should therefore be prepared to justify their decision in each case.

4   The Interview

(a)   General

4.1   The provisions of Code C in relation to cautions and interviews and the notes for guidance applicable to those provisions shall apply to the conduct of interviews to which this Code applies.

4.2   Particular attention is drawn to those parts of Code C that describe the restrictions on drawing adverse inferences from a suspect's failure or refusal to say anything about their involvement in the offence when interviewed, or after being charged or informed they may be prosecuted and how those restrictions affect the terms of the caution and determine whether a special warning under sections 36 and 37 of the Criminal Justice and Public Order Act 1994 can be given.

(b) Commencement of interviews

4.3   When the suspect is brought into the interview room the interviewer shall without delay, but in sight of the suspect, load the recording equipment and set it to record. The recording media must be unwrapped or otherwise opened in the presence of the suspect. [See Note 4A]

4.4   The interviewer shall then tell the suspect formally about the visual recording. The interviewer shall:

(a) explain the interview is being visually recorded;

(b) subject to paragraph 2.5, give his or her name and rank, and that of any other interviewer present;

(c) ask the suspect and any other party present (*e.g.* his solicitor) to identify themselves;

(d) state the date, time of commencement and place of the interview; and

(e) state that the suspect will be given a notice about what will happen to the recording.

4.5   The interviewer shall then caution the suspect, which should follow that set out in Code C, and remind the suspect of their entitlement to free and independent legal advice and that they can speak to a solicitor on the telephone.

4.6   The interviewer shall then put to the suspect any significant statement or silence (*i.e.* failure or refusal to answer a question or to answer it satisfactorily) which occurred before the start of the interview, and shall ask the suspect whether they wish to confirm or deny that earlier statement or silence or whether they wish to add anything. The definition of a "significant" statement or silence is the same as that set out in Code C.

(c) Interviews with the deaf

4.7   If the suspect is deaf or there is doubt about their hearing ability, the provisions of Code C on interpreters for the deaf or for interviews with suspects who have difficulty in understanding English continue to apply.

(d) Objections and complaints by the suspect

4.8   If the suspect raises objections to the interview being visually recorded either at the outset or during the interview or during a break in the interview, the interviewer shall explain the fact that the interview is being visually recorded and that the provisions of this Code require that the suspect's objections shall be recorded. The suspect's objections shall be noted.

4.9   If in the course of an interview a complaint is made by the person being questioned, or on their behalf, concerning the provisions of this Code or of Code C, then the interviewer shall act in accordance with Code C, record it in the interview record and inform the custody officer. [See Notes 4B and 4C]

4.10   If the suspect indicates that they wish to tell the interviewer about matters not directly connected with the offence of which they are suspected and that they are unwilling for these matters to be recorded, the suspect shall be given the opportunity to tell the interviewer about these matters after the conclusion of the formal interview.

(e) Changing the recording media

4.11   In instances where the recording medium is not of sufficient length to record all of the interview with the suspect, further certified recording media will be used. When the recording equipment indicates that the recording medium has only a short time left to run, the interviewer shall advise the suspect and round off that part of the interview. If the interviewer wishes to continue the interview but does not already have further certified recording media with him, they shall obtain a set. The suspect should not be left unattended in the interview room. The interviewer will remove the recording media from the recording equipment and insert the new ones which have been unwrapped or otherwise opened in the suspect's presence. The recording equipment shall then be set to record. Care must be taken, particularly when a number of sets of recording media have been used, to ensure that there is no confusion between them. This could be achieved by marking the sets of recording media with consecutive identification numbers.

(f) Taking a break during the interview

4.12   When a break is to be taken during the course of an interview and the interview room is to be vacated by the suspect, the fact that a break is to be taken, the reason for it and the time shall be recorded. The recording equipment must be turned off and the recording media removed. The procedures for the conclusion of an interview set out in paragraph 4.19, below, should be followed.

4.13   When a break is to be a short one, and both the suspect and a police officer are to remain in the interview room, the fact that a break is to be taken, the reasons for it and the time shall be recorded on the recording media. The recording equipment may be turned off, but there is no need to remove the recording media. When the interview is recommenced the recording shall continue on the same recording media and the time at which the interview recommences shall be recorded.

4.14   When there is a break in questioning under caution, the interviewing officer must ensure that the person being questioned is aware that they remain under caution. If there is any doubt, the caution must be given again in full when the interview resumes. [See *Notes 4D* and *4E*].

(g) Failure of recording equipment

4.15   If there is a failure of equipment which can be rectified quickly, the appropriate procedures set out in paragraph 4.12 shall be followed. When the recording is resumed the interviewer shall explain what has happened and record the time the interview recommences. If, however, it is not possible to continue recording on that particular recorder and no alternative equipment is readily available, the interview may continue without being recorded visually. In such circumstances, the procedures set out in paragraph 3.3 of this Code for seeking the authority of the custody officer will be followed. [See *Note 4F*]

(h) Removing used recording media from recording equipment

4.16   Where used recording media are removed from the recording equipment during the course of an interview, they shall be retained and the procedures set out in paragraph 4.18 below followed.

(i) Conclusion of interview

4.17   Before the conclusion of the interview, the suspect shall be offered the opportunity to clarify anything he or she has said and asked if there is anything that they wish to add.

4.18   At the conclusion of the interview, including the taking and reading back of any written statement, the time shall be recorded and the recording equipment switched off. The master tape or CD shall be removed from the recording equipment, sealed with a master copy label and treated as an exhibit in accordance with the force standing orders. The interviewer shall sign the label and also ask the suspect and any appropriate adults or other third party present during the interview to sign it. If the suspect or third party refuses to sign the label, an officer of at least the rank of inspector, or if one is not available, the custody officer, shall be called into the interview room and asked to sign it.

4.19   The suspect shall be handed a notice which explains the use which will be made of the recording and the arrangements for access to it. The notice will also advise the suspect that a copy of the tape *or CD* shall be supplied as soon as practicable if the person is charged or informed that he will be prosecuted.

Notes for guidance

4A   The interviewer should attempt to estimate the likely length of the interview and ensure that an appropriate quantity of certified recording media and labels with which to seal the master copies are available in the interview room.

4B   Where the custody officer is called immediately to deal with the complaint, wherever possible the recording equipment should be left to run until the custody officer has entered the interview room and spoken to the person being interviewed. Continuation or termination of the interview should be at the discretion of the interviewing officer pending action by an inspector as set out in Code C.

4C   Where the complaint is about a matter not connected with this Code of Practice or Code C, the decision to continue with the interview is at the discretion of the interviewing officer. Where the interviewing officer decides to continue with the interview, the person being interviewed shall be told that the complaint will be brought to the attention of the custody officer at the conclusion of the interview. When the interview is concluded, the interviewing officer must, as soon as practicable, inform the custody officer of the existence and nature of the complaint made.

4D   In considering whether to caution again after a break, the officer should bear in mind that he may have to satisfy a court that the person understood that he was still under caution when the interview resumed.

4E   The officer should bear in mind that it may be necessary to satisfy the court that nothing occurred during a break in an interview or between interviews which influenced the suspect's recorded evidence. On the recommencement of an interview, the officer should consider summarising on the tape or CD the reason for the break and confirming this with the suspect.

4F   If any part of the recording media breaks or is otherwise damaged during the interview, it should be sealed as a master copy in the presence of the suspect and the interview resumed where it left off. The undamaged part should be copied and the original sealed as a master copy in the suspect's presence, if necessary after the interview. If equipment for copying is not readily available, both parts should be sealed in the suspect's presence and the interview begun again.

5   After the Interview

5.1   The interviewer shall make a Note in his or her pocket book of the fact that the interview has taken place and has been recorded, its time, duration and date and the identification number of the master copy of the recording media.

5.2   Where no proceedings follow in respect of the person whose interview was recorded, the recording media must nevertheless be kept securely in accordance with paragraph 6.1 and Note 6A.

Note for guidance

5A   Any written record of a recorded interview shall be made in accordance with national guidelines approved by the Secretary of State, and with regard to the advice contained in the Manual of Guidance for the preparation, processing and submission of files.

6   Tape Security

(a)   General

6.1   The officer in charge of the police station at which interviews with suspects are recorded shall make arrangements for the master copies to be kept securely and their movements accounted for on the same basis as other material which may be used for evidential purposes, in accordance with force standing orders [See *Note 6A*]

(b)   Breaking master copy seal for criminal proceedings

6.2   A police officer has no authority to break the seal on a master copy which is required for criminal trial or appeal proceedings. If it is necessary to gain access to the master copy, the police officer shall arrange for its seal to be broken in the presence of a representative of the Crown Prosecution Service. The defendant or their legal adviser shall be informed and given a reasonable opportunity to be present. If the defendant or their legal representative is present they shall be invited to reseal and sign the master copy. If either refuses or neither is present, this shall be done by the representative of the Crown Prosecution Service. [See *Notes 6B* and *6C*]

(c) Breaking master copy seal: other cases

6.3 The chief officer of police is responsible for establishing arrangements for breaking the seal of the master copy where no criminal proceedings result, or the criminal proceedings, to which the interview relates, have been concluded and it becomes necessary to break the seal. These arrangements should be those which the chief officer considers are reasonably necessary to demonstrate to the person interviewed and any other party who may wish to use or refer to the interview record that the master copy has not been tampered with and that the interview record remains accurate. [See *Note 6D*]

6.4 Subject to paragraph 6.6, a representative of each party must be given a reasonable opportunity to be present when the seal is broken, the master copy copied and re-sealed.

6.5 If one or more of the parties is not present when the master copy seal is broken because they cannot be contacted or refuse to attend or paragraph 6.6 applies, arrangements should be made for an independent person such as a custody visitor to be present. Alternatively, or as an additional safeguard, arrangement should be made for a film or photographs to be taken of the procedure.

6.6 Paragraph 6.5 does not require a person to be given an opportunity to be present when:

(a) it is necessary to break the master copy seal for the proper and effective further investigation of the original offence or the investigation of some other offence; and

(b) the officer in charge of the investigation has reasonable grounds to suspect that allowing an opportunity might prejudice any such an investigation or criminal proceedings which may be brought as a result or endanger any person. [See *Note 6E*]

(e) Documentation

6.7 When the master copy seal is broken, copied and re-sealed, a record must be made of the procedure followed, including the date, time and place and persons present.

Notes for guidance

6A This section is concerned with the security of the master copy which will have been sealed at the conclusion of the interview. Care should, however, be taken of working copies since their loss or destruction may lead unnecessarily to the need to have access to master copies.

6B If the master copy has been delivered to the crown court for their keeping after committal for trial the crown prosecutor will apply to the chief clerk of the crown court centre for its release for unsealing by the crown prosecutor.

6C Reference to the Crown Prosecution Service or to the crown prosecutor in this part of the Code shall be taken to include any other body or person with a statutory responsibility for prosecution for whom the police conduct any recorded interviews.

6D The most common reasons for needing access to master copies that are not required for criminal proceedings arise from civil actions and complaints against police and civil actions between individuals arising out of allegations of crime investigated by police.

6E Paragraph 6.6 could apply, for example, when one or more of the outcomes or likely outcomes of the investigation might be: (i) the prosecution of one or more of the original suspects; (ii) the prosecution of someone previously not suspected, including someone who was originally a witness; and (iii) any original suspect being treated as a prosecution witness and when premature disclosure of any police action, particularly through contact with any parties involved, could lead to a real risk of compromising the investigation and endangering witnesses.

Appendix 7

Criminal Procedure and Investigations Act 1996: Code of Practice Under Part II

Introduction

1.1   This code of practice is issued under part II of the Criminal Procedure and Investigations Act 1996 ('the Act'). It applies in respect of criminal investigations conducted by police officers which begin on or after the day on which this code comes into effect. Persons other than police officers who are charged with the duty of conducting an investigation as defined in the Act are to have regard to the relevant provisions of the code, and should take these into account in applying their own operating procedures.

1.2   This code does not apply to persons who are not charged with the duty of conducting an investigation as defined in the Act.

1.3   Nothing in this code applies to material intercepted in obedience to a warrant issued under section 2 of the Interception of Communications Act 1985, or to any copy of that material as defined in section 10 of that Act.

1.4   This code extends only to England and Wales.

Definitions

2.1   In this code:

–   a *criminal investigation* is an investigation conducted by police officers with a view to it being ascertained whether a person should be charged with an offence, or whether a person charged with an offence is guilty of it. This will include
  – investigations into crimes that have been committed;
  – investigations whose purpose is to ascertain whether a crime has been committed, with a view to the possible institution of criminal proceedings; and
  – investigations which begin in the belief that a crime may be committed, for example when the police keep premises or individuals under observation for a period of time, with a view to the possible institution of criminal proceedings;

–   charging a person with an offence includes prosecution by way of summons;

–   an i*nvestigator* is any police officer involved in the conduct of a criminal investigation. All investigators have a responsibility for carrying out the duties imposed on them under this code, including in particular recording information, and retaining records of information and other material;

–   the *officer in charge of an investigation* is the police officer responsible for directing a criminal investigation. He is also responsible for ensuring that proper procedures are in place for recording information, and retaining records of information and other material, in the investigation;

- the *disclosure officer* is the person responsible for examining material retained by the police during the investigation; revealing material to the prosecutor during the investigation and any criminal proceedings resulting from it, and certifying that he has done this; and disclosing material to the accused at the request of the prosecutor;

- the *prosecutor* is the authority responsible for the conduct of criminal proceedings on behalf of the Crown. Particular duties may in practice fall to individuals acting on behalf of the prosecuting authority;

- *material* is material of any kind, including information and objects, which is obtained in the course of a criminal investigation and which may be relevant to the investigation;

- material may be *relevant to an investigation* if it appears to an investigator, or to the officer in charge of an investigation, or to the disclosure officer, that it has some bearing on any offence under investigation or any person being investigated, or on the surrounding circumstances of the case, unless it is incapable of having any impact on the case;

- *sensitive material* is material which the disclosure officer believes, after consulting the officer in charge of the investigation, it is not in the public interest to disclose;

- references to *primary prosecution disclosure* are to the duty of the prosecutor under section 3 of the Act to disclose material which is in his possession or which he has inspected in pursuance of this code, and which in his opinion might undermine the case against the accused;

- references to *secondary prosecution disclosure* are to the duty of the prosecutor under section 7 of the Act to disclose material which is in his possession or which he has inspected in pursuance of this code, and which might reasonably be expected to assist the defence disclosed by the accused in a defence statement given under the Act;

- references to the disclosure of material to a person accused of an offence include references to the disclosure of material to his legal representative;

- references to police officers and to the chief officer of police include those employed in a police force as defined in section 3(3) of the Prosecution of Offences Act 1985.

General responsibilities

3.1   The functions of the investigator, the officer in charge of an investigation and the disclosure officer are separate. Whether they are undertaken by one, two or more persons will depend on the complexity of the case and the administrative arrangements within each police force. Where they are undertaken by more than one person, close consultation between them is essential to the effective performance of the duties imposed by this code.

3.2   The chief officer of police for each police force is responsible for putting in place arrangements to ensure that in every investigation the identity of the officer in charge of an investigation and the disclosure officer is recorded.

3.3   The officer in charge of an investigation may delegate tasks to another investigator or to civilians employed by the police force, but he remains responsible for ensuring that these have been carried out and for accounting for any general policies followed in the investigation. In particular, it is an essential part of his duties to ensure that all material which may be relevant to an investigation is retained, and either made available to the disclosure officer or (in exceptional circumstances) revealed directly to the prosecutor.

3.4   In conducting an investigation, the investigator should pursue all reasonable lines of inquiry, whether these point towards or away from the suspect. What is reasonable in each case will depend on the particular circumstances.

3.5   If the officer in charge of an investigation believes that other persons may be in possession of material that may be relevant to the investigation, and if this has not been obtained under paragraph 3.4 above, he should ask the disclosure officer to inform them of the existence of the investigation and to invite them to retain the material in case they receive a request for its disclosure. The disclosure officer should inform the prosecutor that they may have such material. However, the officer in charge of an investigation is not required to make speculative enquiries of other persons: there must be some reason to believe that they may have relevant material. That reason may come from information provided to the police by the accused or from other inquiries made or from some other source.

3.6   If, during a criminal investigation, the officer in charge of an investigation or disclosure officer for any reason no longer has responsibility for the functions falling to him, either his supervisor or the police officer in charge of criminal investigations for the police force concerned must assign someone else to assume that responsibility. That person's identity must be recorded, as with those initially responsible for these functions in each investigation.

Recording of information

4.1   If material which may be relevant to the investigation consists of information which is not recorded in any form, the officer in charge of an investigation must ensure that it is recorded in a durable or retrievable form (whether in writing, on video or audio tape, or on computer disk).

4.2   Where it is not practicable to retain the initial record of information because it forms part of a larger record which is to be destroyed, its contents should be transferred as a true record to a durable and more easily-stored form before that happens.

4.3   Negative information is often relevant to an investigation. If it may be relevant it must be recorded. An example might be a number of people present in a particular place at a particular time who state that they saw nothing unusual.

4.4   Where information which may be relevant is obtained, it must be recorded at the time it is obtained or as soon as practicable after that time. This includes, for example, information obtained in house-to-house enquiries, although the requirement to record information promptly does not require an investigator to take a statement from a potential witness where it would not otherwise be taken.

Retention of material

(a)   Duty to retain material

5.1   The investigator must retain material obtained in a criminal investigation which may be relevant to the investigation. This includes not only material coming into the possession of the investigator (such as documents seized in the course of searching premises) but also material generated by him (such as interview records). Material may be photographed, or retained in the form of a copy rather than the original, if the original is perishable, or was supplied to the investigator rather than generated by him and is to be returned to its owner.

5.2   Where material has been seized in the exercise of the powers of seizure conferred by the Police and Criminal Evidence Act 1984, the duty to retain it under this code is subject to the provisions on the retention of seized material in section 22 of that Act.

5.3   If the officer in charge of an investigation becomes aware as a result of developments in the case that material previously examined but not retained (because it was not thought to be relevant) may now be relevant to the investigation, he should, wherever practicable, take steps to obtain it or ensure that it is retained for further inspection or for production in court if required.

5.4   The duty to retain material includes in particular the duty to retain material falling into the following categories, where it may be relevant to the investigation:

- crime reports (including crime report forms, relevant parts of incident report books or police officers' notebooks);
- custody records;

- records which are derived from tapes of telephone messages (for example, 999 calls) containing descriptions of an alleged offence or offender;

- final versions of witness statements (and draft versions where their content differs from the final version), including any exhibits mentioned (unless these have been returned to their owner on the understanding that they will be produced in court if required);

- interview records (written records, or audio or video tapes, of interviews with actual or potential witnesses or suspects);

- communications between the police and experts such as forensic scientists, reports of work carried out by experts, and schedules of scientific material prepared by the expert for the investigator, for the purposes of criminal proceedings;

- any material casting doubt on the reliability of a confession;

- any material casting doubt on the reliability of a witness;

- any other material which may fall within the test for primary prosecution disclosure in the Act.

5.5   The duty to retain material falling into these categories does not extend to items which are purely ancillary to such material and possess no independent significance (for example, duplicate copies of records or reports).

(b)   Length of time for which material is to be retained

5.6   All material which may be relevant to the investigation must be retained until a decision is taken whether to institute proceedings against a person for an offence.

5.7   If a criminal investigation results in proceedings being instituted, all material which may be relevant must be retained at least until the accused is acquitted or convicted or the prosecutor decides not to proceed with the case.

5.8   Where the accused is convicted, all material which may be relevant must be retained at least until:

- the convicted person is released from custody, or discharged from hospital, in cases where the court imposes a custodial sentence or a hospital order;

- six months from the date of conviction, in all other cases.

If the court imposes a custodial sentence or hospital order and the convicted person is released from custody or is discharged from hospital earlier than six months from the date of conviction, all material which may be relevant must be retained at least until six months from the date of conviction.

5.9   If an appeal against conviction is in progress when the release or discharge occurs, or at the end of the period of six months specified in paragraph 5.8, all material which may be relevant must be retained until the appeal is determined. Similarly, if the Criminal Cases Review Commission is considering an application at that point in time, all material which may be relevant must be retained at least until the Commission decides not to refer the case to the Court of Appeal, or until the Court determines the appeal resulting from the reference by the Commission.

5.10   Material need not be retained by the police as required in paragraph 5.8 if it was seized and is to be returned to its owner.

Preparation of material for prosecutor

(a)   Introduction

6.1   The officer in charge of the investigation, the disclosure officer or an investigator may seek advice from the prosecutor about whether any particular item of material may be relevant to the investigation.

6.2   Material which may be relevant to an investigation, which has been retained in accordance with this code, and which the disclosure officer believes will not form part of the prosecution case, must be listed on a schedule.

6.3   Material which the disclosure officer does not believe is sensitive must be listed on a schedule of non-sensitive material. The schedule must include a statement that the disclosure officer does not believe the material is sensitive.

6.4   Any material which is believed to be sensitive must be either listed on a schedule of sensitive material or, in exceptional circumstances, revealed to the prosecutor separately.

6.5   Paragraphs 6.6 to 6.11 below apply to both sensitive and non-sensitive material. Paragraphs 6.12 to 6.14 apply to sensitive material only.

(b)   Circumstances in which a schedule is to be prepared

6.6   The disclosure officer must ensure that a schedule is prepared in the following circumstances:

- the accused is charged with an offence which is triable only on indictment;
- the accused is charged with an offence which is triable either way, and it is considered either that the case is likely to be tried on indictment or that the accused is likely to plead not guilty at a summary trial;
- the accused is charged with a summary offence, and it is considered that he is likely to plead not guilty.

6.7   In respect of either way and summary offences, a schedule may not be needed if a person has admitted the offence, or if a police officer witnessed the offence and that person has not denied it.

6.8   If it is believed that the accused is likely to plead guilty at a summary trial, it is not necessary to prepare a schedule in advance. If, contrary to this belief, the accused pleads not guilty at a summary trial, or the offence is to be tried on indictment, the disclosure officer must ensure that a schedule is prepared as soon as is reasonably practicable after that happens.

(c)   Way in which material is to be listed on schedule

6.9   The disclosure officer should ensure that each item of material is listed separately on the schedule, and is numbered consecutively. The description of each item should make clear the nature of the item and should contain sufficient detail to enable the prosecutor to decide whether he needs to inspect the material before deciding whether or not it should be disclosed.

6.10   In some enquiries it may not be practicable to list each item of material separately. For example, there may be many items of a similar or repetitive nature. These may be listed in a block and described by quantity and generic title.

6.11   Even if some material is listed in a block, the disclosure officer must ensure that any items among that material which might meet the test for primary prosecution disclosure are listed and described individually.

(d)   Treatment of sensitive material

6.12   Subject to paragraph 6.13 below, the disclosure officer must list on a sensitive schedule any material which he believes it is not in the public interest to disclose, and the reason for that belief. The schedule must include a statement that the disclosure officer believes the material is sensitive. Depending on the circumstances, examples of such material may include the following among others:

- material relating to national security;
- material received from the intelligence and security agencies;
- material relating to intelligence from foreign sources which reveals sensitive intelligence gathering methods;
- material given in confidence;
- material which relates to the use of a telephone system and which is supplied to an investigator for intelligence purposes only;

- material relating to the identity or activities of informants, or under-cover police officers, or other persons supplying information to the police who may be in danger if their identities are revealed;

- material revealing the location of any premises or other place used for police surveillance, or the identity of any person allowing a police officer to use them for surveillance;

- material revealing, either directly or indirectly, techniques and methods relied upon by a police officer in the course of a criminal investigation, for example covert surveillance techniques, or other methods of detecting crime;

- material whose disclosure might facilitate the commission of other offences or hinder the prevention and detection of crime;

- internal police communications such as management minutes;

- material upon the strength of which search warrants were obtained;

- material containing details of persons taking part in identification parades;

- material supplied to an investigator during a criminal investigation which has been generated by an official of a body concerned with the regulation or supervision of bodies corporate or of persons engaged in financial activities, or which has been generated by a person retained by such a body;

- material supplied to an investigator during a criminal investigation which relates to a child or young person and which has been generated by a local authority social services department, an Area Child Protection Committee or other party contacted by an investigator during the investigation.

6.13   In exceptional circumstances, where an investigator considers that material is so sensitive that its revelation to the prosecutor by means of an entry on the sensitive schedule is inappropriate, the existence of the material must be revealed to the prosecutor separately. This will apply where compromising the material would be likely to lead directly to the loss of life, or directly threaten national security.

6.14   In such circumstances, the responsibility for informing the prosecutor lies with the investigator who knows the detail of the sensitive material. The investigator should act as soon as is reasonably practicable after the file containing the prosecution case is sent to the prosecutor. The investigator must also ensure that the prosecutor is able to inspect the material so that he can assess whether it needs to be brought before a court for a ruling on disclosure.

Revelation of material to prosecutor

7.1   The disclosure officer must give the schedules to the prosecutor. Wherever practicable this should be at the same time as he gives him the file containing the material for the prosecution case (or as soon as is reasonably practicable after the decision on mode of trial or the plea, in cases to which paragraph 6.8 applies).

7.2   The disclosure officer should draw the attention of the prosecutor to any material an investigator has retained (whether or not listed on a schedule) which may fall within the test for primary prosecution disclosure in the Act, and should explain why he has come to that view.

7.3   At the same time as complying with the duties in paragraphs 7.1 and 7.2, the disclosure officer must give the prosecutor a copy of any material which falls into the following categories (unless such material has already been given to the prosecutor as part of the file containing the material for the prosecution case):

- records of the first description of a suspect given to the police by a potential witness, whether or not the description differs from that of the alleged offender;

- information provided by an accused person which indicates an explanation for the offence with which he has been charged;

- any material casting doubt on the reliability of a confession;

- any material casting doubt on the reliability of a witness;

   – any other material which the investigator believes may fall within the test for primary prosecution disclosure in the Act.

7.4   If the prosecutor asks to inspect material which has not already been copied to him, the disclosure officer must allow him to inspect it. If the prosecutor asks for a copy of material which has not already been copied to him, the disclosure officer must give him a copy. However, this does not apply where the disclosure officer believes, having consulted the officer in charge of the investigation, that the material is too sensitive to be copied and can only be inspected.

7.5   If material consists of information which is recorded other than in writing, whether it should be given to the prosecutor in its original form as a whole, or by way of relevant extracts recorded in the same form, or in the form of a transcript, is a matter for agreement between the disclosure officer and the prosecutor.

Subsequent action by disclosure officer

8.1   At the time a schedule of non-sensitive material is prepared, the disclosure officer may not know exactly what material will form the case against the accused, and the prosecutor may not have given advice about the likely relevance of particular items of material. Once these matters have been determined, the disclosure officer must give the prosecutor, where necessary, an amended schedule listing any additional material:

   – which may be relevant to the investigation,

   – which does not form part of the case against the accused,

   – which is not already listed on the schedule, and

   – which he believes is not sensitive,

unless he is informed in writing by the prosecutor that the prosecutor intends to disclose the material to the defence.

8.2   After a defence statement has been given, the disclosure officer must look again at the material which has been retained and must draw the attention of the prosecutor to any material which might reasonably be expected to assist the defence disclosed by the accused; and he must reveal it to him in accordance with paragraphs 7.4 and 7.5 above.

8.3   Section 9 of the Act imposes a continuing duty on the prosecutor, for the duration of criminal proceedings against the accused, to disclose material which meets the tests for disclosure (subject to public interest considerations). To enable him to do this, any new material coming to light should be treated in the same way as the earlier material.

Certification by disclosure officer

9.1   The disclosure officer must certify to the prosecutor that, to the best of his knowledge and belief, all material which has been retained and made available to him has been revealed to the prosecutor in accordance with this code. He must sign and date the certificate. It will be necessary to certify not only at the time when the schedule and accompanying material is submitted to the prosecutor, but also when material which has been retained is reconsidered after the accused has given a defence statement.

Disclosure of material to accused

10.1   If material has not already been copied to the prosecutor, and he requests its disclosure to the accused on the ground that:

   – it falls within the test for primary or secondary prosecution disclosure, or

   – the court has ordered its disclosure after considering an application from the accused,

the disclosure officer must disclose it to the accused.

10.2   If material has been copied to the prosecutor, and it is to be disclosed, whether it is disclosed by the prosecutor or the disclosure officer is a matter for agreement between the two of them.

10.3   The disclosure officer must disclose material to the accused either by giving him a copy or by allowing him to inspect it. If the accused person asks for a copy of any material which he has been allowed to inspect, the disclosure officer must give it to him, unless in the opinion of the disclosure officer that is either not practicable (for example because the material consists of an object which cannot be copied, or because the volume of material is so great), or not desirable (for example because the material is a statement by a child witness in relation to a sexual offence).

10.4   If material which the accused has been allowed to inspect consists of information which is recorded other than in writing, whether it should be given to the accused in its original form or in the form of a transcript is a matter for the discretion of the disclosure officer. If the material is transcribed, the disclosure officer must ensure that the transcript is certified to the accused as a true record of the material which has been transcribed.

10.5   If a court concludes that it is in the public interest that an item of sensitive material must be disclosed to the accused, it will be necessary to disclose the material if the case is to proceed. This does not mean that sensitive documents must always be disclosed in their original form: for example, the court may agree that sensitive details still requiring protection should be blocked out, or that documents may be summarised, or that the prosecutor may make an admission about the substance of the material under section 10 of the Criminal Justice Act 1967.

ATTORNEY-GENERAL'S GUIDELINES: DISCLOSURE OF INFORMATION IN CRIMINAL PROCEEDINGS

Introduction

1.   Every accused person has a right to a fair trial, a right long embodied in our law and guaranteed under Article 6 of the European Convention on Human Rights. A fair trial is the proper object and expectation of all participants in the trial process. Fair disclosure to an accused is an inseparable part of a fair trial.

2.   The scheme set out in the Criminal Procedure and Investigations Act 1996 (the Act) is designed to ensure that there is fair disclosure of material which may be relevant to an investigation and which does not form part of the prosecution case. Disclosure under the Act should assist the accused in the timely preparation and presentation of their case and assist the court to focus on all the relevant issues in the trial. Disclosure which does not meet these objectives risks preventing a fair trial taking place.

3.   Fairness does, however, recognise that there are other interests that need to be protected, including those of victims and witnesses who might otherwise be exposed to harm. The scheme of the Act protects those interests. It should also ensure that material is not disclosed which overburdens the participants in the trial process, diverts attention from the relevant issues, leads to unjustifiable delay, and is wasteful of resources.

4.   These guidelines build upon the existing law to help to ensure that the legislation is operated more effectively. In some areas guidance is given which goes beyond the requirements of the legislation, where experience has suggested that such guidance is desirable.

General principles

Investigators and disclosure officers

5.   Investigators and disclosure officers must be fair and objective and must work together with prosecutors to ensure that disclosure obligations are met. A failure to take action leading to proper disclosure may result in a wrongful conviction. It may alternatively lead to a successful abuse of process argument or an acquittal against the weight of the evidence.

6.   In discharging their obligations under the statute, code, common law and any operational instructions, investigators should always err on the side of recording and retaining material where they have any doubt as to whether it may be relevant.

7.   An individual must not be appointed as disclosure officer, or continue in that role, if that is likely to result in a conflict of interest, for instance, if the disclosure officer is the victim of the alleged crime which is the subject of criminal proceedings. The advice of a more senior officer must always be sought if there is doubt as to whether a conflict of interest precludes an individual acting as the disclosure officer. If thereafter the doubt remains, the advice of a prosecutor should be sought.

8.   Disclosure officers, or their deputies, must inspect, view or listen to all material that has been retained by the investigator, and the disclosure officer must provide a personal declaration to the effect that this task has been done. The obligation does not apply, however, in the circumstances set out in paragraph 9 below.

9.   In some cases, out of an abundance of caution, investigators seize large volumes of material which may not, because of its source, general nature or other reasons, seem likely ever to be relevant. In such circumstances, the investigator may consider that it is not an appropriate use of resources to examine such large volumes of material seized on a precautionary basis. If such material is not examined by the investigator or disclosure officer, and it is not intended to examine it, but the material is nevertheless retained, its existence should be made known to the accused in general terms at the primary stage and permission granted for its inspection by him or his legal advisers. A section 9 statement will be completed by the investigating officer or disclosure officer describing the material by general category and justifying it not having been examined. This statement will itself be listed as unused material and automatically disclosed to the defence.

10.   In meeting the obligations in paragraph 6.9 and 8.1 of the Code, it is crucial that descriptions by disclosure officers in non-sensitive schedules are detailed, clear and accurate. The descriptions may require a summary of the contents of the retained material to assist the prosecutor to make an informed decision on disclosure. The same applies to sensitive schedules, to the extent possible without compromising the confidentiality of the information.

11.   Disclosure officers must specifically draw material to the attention of the prosecutor for consideration where they have any doubt as to whether it might undermine the prosecution case or might reasonably be expected to assist the defence disclosed by the accused.

12.   Disclosure officers must seek the advice and assistance of prosecutors when in doubt as to their responsibility, and must deal expeditiously with requests by the prosecutor for further information on material which may lead to disclosure.

Prosecutors generally

13.   Prosecutors must do all that they can to facilitate proper disclosure, as part of their general and personal professional responsibility to act fairly and impartially, in the interests of justice. Prosecutors must also be alert to the need to provide advice to disclosure officers on disclosure issues and to advise on disclosure procedure generally.

14.   Prosecutors must review schedules prepared by disclosure officers thoroughly and must be alert to the possibility that material may exist which has not been revealed to them. If no schedules have been provided, or there are apparent omissions from the schedules, or documents or other items are insufficiently described or are unclear, the prosecutor must at once take action to obtain properly completed schedules. If, following this, prosecutors remain dissatisfied with the quality or content of the schedules they must raise the matter with a senior officer, and if necessary, persist, with a view to resolving the matter satisfactorily.

15.   Where prosecutors have reason to believe that the disclosure officer has not discharged the obligation in paragraph 8 to inspect, view or listen to material, they must at once raise the matter with the disclosure officer and, if it is believed that the officer has not inspected, viewed or listened to the material, request that it be done.

16. When the prosecutor or disclosure officer believes that material might undermine the prosecution case or assist the defence case, for instance in the case of records of previous statements by witnesses, prosecutors must always inspect, view or listen to the material and satisfy themselves that the prosecution can properly be continued. Their judgment as to what other material to inspect, view or listen to will depend on the circumstances of each case.

17. Prosecutors should inform the investigator if, in their view, reasonable and relevant lines of further inquiry exist.

18. Prosecutors should not adduce evidence of the contents of a defence statement other than in the circumstances envisaged by section 11 of the Act or to rebut alibi evidence. Where evidence may be adduced in these circumstances, this can be done through cross-examination as well as through the introduction of evidence. There may be occasions when a defence statement points the prosecution to other lines of inquiry. Further investigation in these circumstances is possible and evidence obtained as a result of inquiring into a defence statement may be used as part of the prosecution case or to rebut the defence.

19. Prosecutors must ensure that they record in writing all actions and decisions they make in discharging their disclosure responsibilities, and this information is to be made available to the prosecution advocate if requested or if relevant to an issue.

20. In deciding what material should be disclosed (at any stage of the proceedings) prosecutors should resolve any doubt they may have in favour of disclosure, unless the material is on the sensitive schedule and will be placed before the court for the issue of disclosure to be determined.

21. If prosecutors are satisfied that a fair trial cannot take place because of a failure to disclose which cannot or will not be remedied, they must not continue with the case.

Prosecution advocates

22. Prosecution advocates should use their best endeavours to ensure that all material that ought properly to be made available is either presented by the prosecution or disclosed to the defence. However, the prosecution cannot be expected to disclose material if they are not aware of its existence. As far as is possible, prosecution advocates must place themselves in a fully informed position to enable them to make decisions on disclosure.

23. Upon receipt of instructions, prosecution advocates should consider as a priority all the information provided regarding disclosure of material. Prosecution advocates should consider, in every case, whether they can be satisfied that they are in possession of all relevant documentation and that they have been instructed fully regarding disclosure matters. Decisions already made regarding disclosure should be reviewed. If as a result the advocate considers that further information or action is required, written advice should be promptly provided setting out the aspects that need clarification or action. If necessary and where appropriate a conference should be held to determine what is required.

24. The prosecution advocate must continue to keep under review until the conclusion of the trial decisions regarding disclosure. The prosecution advocate must in every case specifically consider whether he or she can satisfactorily discharge the duty of continuing review on the basis of the material supplied already, or whether it is necessary to inspect further material or to reconsider material already inspected.

25. Prior to the commencement of a trial, the prosecuting advocate should always make decisions on disclosure in consultation with those instructing him and it is desirable that the disclosure officer should also be consulted. After a trial has started, it is recognised that in practice consultation on disclosure issues may not be practicable; it continues to be desirable, however, whenever this can be achieved without affecting unduly the conduct of the trial.

26. The practice of 'counsel to counsel' disclosure should cease: it is inconsistent with the requirement of transparency in the prosecution process.

Defence practitioners

27.   A defence statement should set out the nature of the defence, the matters on which issue is taken and the reasons for taking issue. A comprehensive defence statement assists the participants in the trial to ensure that it is fair. It provides information that the prosecutor needs to identify any remaining material that falls to be disclosed at the secondary stage. The more detail a defence statement contains the more likely it is that the prosecutor will make a properly informed decision about whether any remaining material might assist the defence case, or whether to advise the investigator to undertake further inquiries. It also helps in the management of the trial by narrowing down and focusing the issues in dispute. It may result in the prosecution discontinuing the case. Defence practitioners should be aware of these considerations in advising their clients.

28.   Defence solicitors should ensure that statements are agreed by the accused before being served. Wherever possible, the accused should sign the defence statement to evidence his or her agreement.

Involvement of other agencies

(a)   Material held by Government departments or other Crown bodies

29.   Where it appears to an investigator, disclosure officer or prosecutor that a Government department or other Crown body has material that may be relevant to an issue in the case, reasonable steps should be taken to identify and consider such material. Although what is reasonable will vary from case to case, prosecutors should inform the department or other body of the nature of its case and of relevant issues in the case in respect of which the department or body might possess material, and ask whether it has any such material. Departments in England and Wales have established Enquiry Points to deal with issues concerning the disclosure of information in criminal proceedings. Further guidance for prosecutors and investigators seeking information (including documents) from Government departments or other Crown bodies may be found in the pamphlet 'Giving Evidence or Information about suspected crimes: Guidance for Departments and Investigators' (March, 1997, Cabinet Office).

(b)   Material held by other agencies

30.   There may be cases where the investigator, disclosure officer or prosecutor suspects that a non-government agency or other third party (for example, a local authority, a social services department, a hospital, a doctor, a school, providers of forensic services) has material or information which might be disclosable if it were in the possession of the prosecution. In such cases consideration should be given as to whether it is appropriate to seek access to the material or information and if so, steps should be taken by the prosecution to obtain such material or information. It will be important to do so if the material or information is likely to undermine the prosecution case, or assist a known defence.

31.   If the investigator, disclosure officer or prosecutor seeks access to the material or information but the third party declines or refuses to allow access to it, the matter should not be left. If despite any reasons offered by the third party it is still believed that it is reasonable to seek production of the material or information, and the requirements of section 2 of the Criminal Procedure (Attendance of Witnesses) Act 1965 or as appropriate section 97 of the Magistrates Courts Act 1980 are satisfied, then the prosecutor or investigator should apply for a witness summons causing a representative of the third party to produce the material to the Court.

32.   Information which might be disclosable if it were in the possession of the prosecution which comes to the knowledge of investigators or prosecutors as a result of liaison with third parties should be recorded by the investigator or prosecutor in a durable or retrievable form (for example potentially relevant information revealed in discussions at a child protection conference attended by police officers).

33.   Where information comes into the possession of the prosecution in the circumstances set out in paragraphs 30–32 above, consultation with the other agency should take place before disclosure

is made: there may be public interest reasons which justify withholding disclosure and which would require the issue of disclosure of the information to be placed before the court.

Disclosure prior to primary disclosure under the CPIA 1996

34.   Prosecutors must always be alive to the need, in the interests of justice and fairness in the particular circumstances of any case, to make disclosure of material after the commencement of proceedings but before the prosecutor's duty arises under the Act. For instance, disclosure ought to be made of significant information that might affect a bail decision or that might enable the defence to contest the committal proceedings.

35.   Where the need for such disclosure is not apparent to the prosecutor, any disclosure will depend on what the defendant chooses to reveal about the defence. Clearly, such disclosure will not normally exceed that which is obtainable after the duties under the 'Act' arise.

Primary disclosure

36.   Generally, material can be considered to potentially undermine the prosecution case if it has an adverse effect on the strength of the prosecution case. This will include anything that tends to show a fact inconsistent with the elements of the case that must be proved by the prosecution. Material can have an adverse effect on the strength of the prosecution case:

   (a) by the use made of it in cross-examination; and
   (b) by its capacity to suggest any potential submissions that could lead to:
      (i)   the exclusion of evidence;
      (ii) a stay of proceedings;
      (iii) a court or tribunal finding that any public authority had acted incompatibly with the defendant's rights under the ECHR.

37.   In deciding what material might undermine the prosecution case, the prosecution should pay particular attention to material that has potential to weaken the prosecution case or is inconsistent with it. Examples are:

   i.   Any material casting doubt upon the accuracy of any prosecution evidence.
   ii. Any material which may point to another person, whether charged or not (including a co-accused) having involvement in the commission of the offence.
   iii. Any material which may cast doubt upon the reliability of a confession.
   iv. Any material that might go to the credibility of a prosecution witness.
   v.   Any material that might support a defence that is either raised by the defence or apparent from the prosecution papers. If the material might undermine the prosecution case it should be disclosed at this stage even though it suggests a defence inconsistent with or alternative to one already advanced by the accused or his solicitor.
   vi. Any material which may have a bearing on the admissibility of any prosecution evidence.

It should also be borne in mind that while items of material viewed in isolation may not be considered to potentially undermine the prosecution case, several items together can have that effect.

38.   Experience suggests that any item which relates to the defendant's mental or physical health, his intellectual capacity, or to any ill-treatment which the defendant may have suffered when in the investigator's custody is likely to have the potential for casting doubt on the reliability of an accused's purported confession, and prosecutors should pay particular attention to any such item in the possession of the prosecution.

Secondary disclosure

39.   Prosecutors should be open, alert and promptly responsive to requests for disclosure of material supported by the comprehensive defence statement. Conversely, if no defence statement has been served or if the prosecutor considers that the defence statement is lacking specific and/or clarity, a letter should be sent to the defence indicating that secondary disclosure will not take place or will be limited (as appropriate), and inviting the defence to specify and/or clarify the accused's case. The prosecutor should consider raising the issue at a preliminary hearing if the position is not resolved satisfactorily to enable the court to give directions.

40.   Experience suggests that material of the description set out below might reasonably be expected to be disclosed to the defence where it relates to the defence being put forward. Accordingly, following the delivery of a defence statement and on receipt of a request specifically linking the material sought with the defence being put forward, such linked material should be disclosed unless there is good reason not to do so. However, if defences put forward in a defence statement are inconsistent within the meaning of section 11 of the Act, then the preceding guidance set out in this paragraph will not apply. Conversely, if material of the description set out below might undermine the prosecution case, and does not justify an application to the court to withhold disclosure, prosecutors must disclose it at the primary stage. The material is:

   i.   Those recorded scientific or scenes of crime findings retained by the investigator which:
        relate to the defendant; and
        are linked to the point at issue; and
        have not previously been disclosed.

   ii. where identification is or may be in issue, all previous descriptions of suspects, however recorded, together with all records of identification procedures in respect of the offence(s) and photographs of the accused taken by the investigator around the time of his arrest;

   iii. information that any prosecution witness has received, has been promised or has requested any payment or reward in connection with the case;

   iv. plans of crime scenes or video recordings made by investigators of crime scenes;

   v.   names, within the knowledge of investigators, of individuals who may have relevant information and whom investigators do not intend to interview;

   vi. records which the investigator has made of information which may be relevant, provided by any individual (such information would include, but not be limited to, records of conversation and interviews with any such person).

Disclosure of video recordings or scientific findings by means of supplying copies may well involve delay or otherwise not be practicable or desirable, in which case the investigator should make reasonable arrangements for the video, recordings or scientific findings to be viewed by the defence.

Applications for non-disclosure in the public interest

41.   Before making an application to the court to withhold material which would otherwise fall to be disclosed, on the basis that to disclose would not be in the public interest, a prosecutor should aim to disclose as much of the material as he properly can (by giving the defence redacted or edited copies of summaries).

42.   Prior to or at the hearing, the court must be provided with full and accurate information. The prosecution advocate must examine all material which is the subject matter of the application and make any necessary enquiries of the prosecutor and/or investigator. The prosecutor (or representative) and/or investigator should attend such applications.

Summary trial

43.   The prosecutor should, in addition to complying with the obligations under the CPIA, provide to the defence all evidence upon which the Crown proposes to rely in a summary trial. Such provision should allow the accused or their legal advisers sufficient time properly to consider the evidence before it is called. Exceptionally, statements may be withheld for the protection of witnesses or to avoid interference with the course of justice.

Material relevant to sentence

44.   In all cases the prosecutor must consider disclosing in the interests of justice any material which is relevant to sentence (e.g. information which might mitigate the seriousness of the offence or assist the accused to lay blame in whole or in part upon a co-accused or another person).

Applicability of these guidelines

45.   These guidelines should be adopted with immediate effect in relation to all cases submitted in future to the prosecuting authorities in receipt of these guidelines. They should also be adopted as regards cases already submitted to which the Act applies, so far as they relate to stages in the proceedings that have not yet been reached.

Appendix 8

Joint CPS/Police Disclosure Project JOPI Guidelines (2003)

The following sections are set out below

SECTION TWO   POLICE ACTIONS
ANNEX J   THIRD PARTY PROCEDURE

SECTION TWO: POLICE ACTIONS

Introduction

2.1   This section contains instructions and guidance explaining how police officers should meet the requirements of the Act and the Code. The Code provides the framework for the roles of police officers in the disclosure process, and it forms the basis of this guidance. These instructions should also be read in conjunction with the Manual of Guidance for the Preparation, Processing and Submission of Files and other agreements on operational issues reached between ACPO and the CPS.

Roles and responsibilities

2.2   The **chief officer of police** for each police force is responsible for putting in place arrangements to ensure that in every investigation the identity of the officer in charge of an investigation and that of the disclosure officer is recorded.

2.3   An investigator, a disclosure officer, and an officer in charge of an investigation perform different functions. The three roles may be performed by different people or by one person. The person who is performing the role of disclosure officer and officer in charge of the investigation must be identifiable.

2.4   Where the three roles are undertaken by more than one person, close consultation between them will be essential to ensure compliance with the statutory duties imposed by the Act and the Code.

2.5   The **officer in charge of the investigation** is responsible for directing an investigation. This officer's responsibilities under the Act and the Code are to:

–   account for any general policies followed in the investigation

–   ensure that all reasonable steps are taken for the purposes of the investigation and, in particular, that all reasonable lines of enquiries are pursued

–   ensure that proper procedures are in place for recording and retention of material obtained in the course of the investigation

–   appoint the disclosure officer

–   ensure that tasks delegated to civilians employed by the police force have been carried out in accordance with the requirements of the Code

–   ensure that material which is relevant to an investigation is retained and recorded in a durable and retrievable form

- ensure that all retained material is either made available to the disclosure officer, or in exceptional circumstances revealed directly to the prosecutor
- ensure that all practicable steps are taken to recover any material that was inspected and not retained, if as a result of developments in the case it later becomes relevant.

2.6   An **investigator** is any police officer or civilian employee involved in a criminal investigation. All officers, including those who may not view themselves as investigators, have a responsibility for carrying out the duties imposed under the Code. All officers, in particular must retain material obtained in a criminal investigation which is either created or discovered during the investigation, and which may be relevant to the investigation.

2.7   The investigator must notify the disclosure officer of the existence and whereabouts of material that has been retained.

2.8   The **disclosure officer** (or **officers**, see paragraphs 2.164–66 below) has a statutory duty to discharge disclosure responsibilities throughout a criminal investigation. The officer(s) must:

- examine, inspect, view or listen to all material that has been retained by the investigator and that does not form part of the prosecution case unless the material comes within paragraph 9 of the Attorney General's Guidelines 2000 (see paragraph 2.145 below)
- create schedules that fully describe the material
- identify to the prosecutor all material which might undermine the prosecution case
- pass the schedules to the prosecutor
- at the same time, supply to the prosecutor a copy of material falling into any of the categories described in paragraph 7.3 of the Code and copies of the documents described in 2.120 below, if the prosecutor does not have them already
- consult with and allow the prosecutor to inspect the retained material
- review the schedules and the retained material after the defence statement has been received, identify to the prosecutor material that might reasonably be expected to assist the accused's defence, and supply a copy of any such material not already provided
- certify that all retained material has been revealed to the prosecutor in accordance with the Code at both the primary and secondary stages of prosecution disclosure
- schedule and reveal to the prosecutor any relevant additional unused material pursuant to the continuing duty of disclosure
- where the prosecutor requests disclosure of any material to the accused, give the accused a copy of the material or allow the accused to inspect it.

2.9   The disclosure officer may be a police officer or a civilian. In order to perform the duties under the Code properly, the disclosure officer will need to become fully familiar with the facts and background to the case. The investigator(s) and the officer in charge of the investigation (where these roles are performed by a different individual to the disclosure officer) must provide assistance to the disclosure officer in performing this function.

2.10   In some cases it will be desirable to appoint a disclosure officer at the outset of the investigation. In making this decision, the officer in charge of the investigation should have regard to the nature and seriousness of the case, the volume of material which may be obtained or created, and the likelihood of a committal or a not guilty plea. If not appointed at the start of an investigation, a disclosure officer must be appointed in sufficient time to be able to prepare the unused material schedules for inclusion in the full file submitted to CPS.

2.11   An individual must not be appointed as disclosure officer, or continue in that role, if that is likely to result in a conflict of interest, for instance, if the disclosure officer is the victim of the alleged crime which is the subject of criminal proceedings. The advice of a more senior officer must always be sought if there is doubt as to whether a conflict of interest precludes an individual acting as the disclosure officer. If thereafter the doubt remains, the advice of the prosecutor should be sought.

2.12   The officer in charge of an investigation may delegate certain tasks to civilians employed by the police such as SOCO and fingerprint officers. The officer in charge of an investigation must ensure that those tasks have been carried out in accordance with the Code.

Retention

2.13   The Code requires that material of any kind, including information and objects, which **is obtained in the course of a criminal investigation and which may be relevant to the investigation** must be retained.

2.14   If material with an evidential value has been destroyed, there is a danger that a court may stop the prosecution for abuse of process. Thus while it is not necessary to retain every item obtained or generated during the course of an investigation, any doubt should be resolved in favour of retention.

2.15   Material includes information given orally. Where relevant material is not recorded in any way, it will need to be reduced into a suitable form (see paragraphs 2.28 onwards below).

2.16   Material which may be **relevant to the investigation** is defined in the Code as anything that: **has some bearing on any offence under investigation or any person being investigated, or to the surrounding circumstances of the case, unless it is incapable of having any impact on the case.**

2.17   Care is needed when exercising judgement and discretion to decide what should be retained. Material or information which may not appear to have any significance at the outset of an investigation may have a bearing at a later stage.

2.18   The issue of relevance is especially important where an investigator is considering whether to throw something away, or to return an item to the owner, or not to record information; or where not keeping material or recording information would result in the permanent loss or alteration of the material (as with control room tapes, shop videos etc).

2.19   In discharging their obligations under the Act, Code, Attorney General's Guidelines, the common law and these operational instructions, investigators should always err on the side of recording and retaining material where they have any doubt as to whether it may be relevant.

2.20   Factors that may influence the decision to record information or retain material may be the size of the enquiry, the number of potential suspects, and the stage that the enquiry has reached. Early in an enquiry it may not be possible to make a considered decision on the relevance of an item until later in the case when the facts are clearer. However, considerations that the investigator should bear in mind will include:

- whether the information adds to the total knowledge of how the offence was committed, who may have committed it, and why
- whether the information could support an alternative explanation, given the current understanding of events surrounding the offence
- what the potential consequences will be if the material is not preserved.

2.21   If there is any question whatsoever that the material or information might have an impact on the case, either now or at some time in the future, the investigator should exercise his judgement in favour of recording and retaining the material.

2.22   Negative results can sometimes be as significant to an investigation as positive ones. It is impossible to define precisely when a negative result may be significant, as every case is different. However it will include the result of any enquiry that differs from what might be expected, given the prevailing circumstances. An example is given in paragraph 4.3 of the Code. Not only must material or information which points towards a fact or an individual be retained, but also that which casts doubt on the suspect's guilt, or implicates another person. Examples of negative information include:

- a CCTV camera that did not function, had no videotape loaded or did not record the crime/ location/suspect. This comprises three separate and distinct scenarios for potential negative information, but it is only the last of these that may usually be considered relevant
- where a number of people present at a particular location at the particular time that an offence is alleged to have taken place state they saw nothing unusual
- where a finger-mark from a crime scene cannot be identified as belonging to a known suspect, or is of insufficient value to determine identity
- any other failure to match a crime scene sample with one taken from a known suspect.

2.23   Material may come into an investigator's possession during an investigation, or be generated during the course of the investigation: for example an interview record. Whatever the source, if it is relevant, it must be retained. If it is not possible or practicable to retain an item, a copy or a photograph may be taken. In indictable cases, and those other cases where a not guilty plea is likely, investigators should seek the advice of the officer in charge of the investigation, and if necessary, the prosecutor, particularly when the investigator is minded to return any material to its owner or otherwise dispose of it.

2.24   A **criminal investigation** is defined in the Code as an investigation conducted by a police officer with a view to it being ascertained whether a person should be charged with an offence, or whether a person charged with an offence is guilty of it.

2.25   This includes investigations which are begun in the belief that a crime is about to be committed. For example, a surveillance operation is part of an investigation even if it is directed to a target without there being a specific offence in mind.

2.26   This means that information and material arising out of operations conducted purely for intelligence purposes **might become disclosable** (subject to Public Interest Immunity (PII) considerations). Officers involved in intelligence operations should regularly and actively consider whether the information that they have impacts upon any live investigations or prosecutions, and if so, act quickly to ensure it is brought to the attention of the disclosure officer and prosecutor.

2.27   Particular categories of material that **must** be retained are listed in paragraph 5.4 of the Code. The list is not exhaustive, and there may be other material which requires retaining because it may be relevant. Examples of specific items which fall into these categories are listed in Annex D and the disclosure wall chart.

Recording of information

2.28   It is important to record promptly any information from any source, which might later become relevant to the investigation. A record should be made at the time the information is obtained, or as soon as practicable after that time.

2.29   It is the responsibility of the officer in charge of the investigation to ensure that the material is recorded in a durable or retrievable form, for instance, in writing, on video or audio tape, or computer disk.

2.30   Sometimes it is not practicable to retain the initial record because it forms part of a larger record which is to be destroyed, for example, control room audio tapes, custody suite video tapes, traffic car videos of speeding offences, or other similar recordings. Where this is the situation, the officer in charge of the investigation should identify information that should be retained, and ensure that it is transferred accurately to a durable and more easily stored form before the tapes are destroyed.

2.31   Investigators should be alert to the potential relevance and evidential value of information contained in messages that might not normally be retained; for example, running commentaries and details of pursuit. Investigators should also consider making a record of conversations with experts and other investigators, where the information discussed is likely to be relevant to the case.

2.32   Whether in original or copy form, details of preserved messages should be listed on the schedule(s) in the normal way.

Information recorded on computer

2.33   It is difficult to give clear-cut guidance on the approach to be adopted when dealing with information recorded on computer, owing to the wide range of investigative computer systems employed throughout the Police Service. But many computer systems (for example, HOLMES) generate material in the form of hard copy. This should be treated in the same way as relevant material from any other source.

2.34   The prosecutor will need to be informed of the use of such systems, and any hard copies produced listed on the schedules by the disclosure officer. Local arrangements may need to be agreed as to the means by which the prosecutor can inspect material held on computer systems. Where material is to be disclosed to the defence under the Act, supervised access to a terminal screen may be appropriate. Material may be supplied on a disk where this is acceptable to the accused and the disclosure officer.

2.35   Information contained in emails may amount to relevant unused material, particularly if the information is not recorded elsewhere. It should be recorded, retained and scheduled in the same way as other relevant material. (Where however, emails are intercepted under section 17 of the Regulation of Investigatory Powers Act 2000, disclosure is specifically prohibited.)

2.36   On a major crime enquiry, investigators may find it helpful to identify potentially sensitive material at the input stage. The final decision as to sensitivity at this stage will be the responsibility of the officer in charge of the investigation.

Recovering material not retained

2.37   Material may be examined during the course of an investigation, but not retained because it does not appear to be relevant at that stage. This will include material that has been returned to its owner without a copy being taken.

2.38   If during the lifetime of a case, the officer in charge of an investigation becomes aware that such material may become relevant as a result of new developments, paragraph 5.3 of the Code will apply. That officer should take steps to recover the material wherever practicable, or ensure that it is preserved by the person in possession of it.

Material in the possession of third parties

2.39   The Act only imposes duties of disclosure upon the investigator and the prosecutor. The term 'third party' applies to any person or agency who does not have a duty under the Act.

2.40   A third party has no obligation under the Act to reveal material to the investigator or to the prosecutor, nor is there any duty on the third party to retain material which may be relevant to the investigation. In some circumstances, the third party may not be aware of the investigation or prosecution.

2.41   However, there is a duty under the Code for an investigator to pursue all reasonable lines of enquiry, whether these point towards or away from a suspect. What is reasonable will depend upon the particular case, but it may include enquiries as to the existence of material relevant to the investigation in the possession of a third party. It is not necessary to make speculative enquiries, but frequently the existence of the material will be known or can be deduced from the circumstances. For example, where a child witness is in the care of the local authority, the social services may have relevant material relating to the allegation under investigation.

2.42   If the officer in charge of the investigation, the investigator or the disclosure officer suspects that a third party holds material that may be relevant to the investigation, that person or body should be told of the investigation. They should be alerted to the need to preserve relevant material. Consideration should be given as to whether it is appropriate to seek access to the material, and if so, steps should be taken to obtain such material. It will be important to do so if the material or information is likely to undermine the prosecution case, or to assist a known defence. A letter should be sent to the third party together with the explanatory leaflet, specimens of which are at Annex J.

2.43   The disclosure officer should inform the prosecutor of the identity of the third party and the nature of the material the third party is believed to possess by way of the MG6. In some circumstances it may be appropriate for the disclosure officer and the investigator to consider with the prosecutor whether the third party should be approached and further material sought or inspected.

2.44   If material relevant to the investigation comes to the knowledge of the investigator or is inspected or obtained from a third party, it will become unused material or information within the terms of the Code. This applies particularly to relevant information conveyed verbally by the third party. This should be recorded in a durable or retrievable form (for example potentially relevant information revealed in discussions at a child protection conference attended by police officers). It will have to be recorded on the appropriate schedule and revealed to the prosecutor in the usual way.

2.45   Where access to the material is declined or refused by the third party and the investigator believes that it is reasonable to seek production of the material before a suspect is charged because he or she believes it is likely to be relevant evidence and of substantial value, the investigator should consider making an application under Schedule 1 of the Police and Criminal Evidence Act (PACE) 1984, (Special Procedure Material). The investigator may seek advice of the prosecutor before such an application is made.

2.46   Where there are proceedings before a court and the requirements of section 2 of the Criminal Procedure (Attendance of Witnesses) Act 1965 or section 97 of the Magistrates' Court Act 1980 as appropriate are satisfied, then the investigator or the prosecutor should apply for a witness summons causing a representative of the third party to produce the material to the court.

2.47   The statutory requirements in 2.46 above are more stringent than those for the primary and secondary disclosure tests. Items sought under the summons procedure must be 'likely to be material evidence,' (which the House of Lords in *R* v *Derby Magistrates' Court ex parte B* [1995] 4 All ER 526 has construed to mean 'immediately admissible per se.') Accordingly, there should be consultation between the investigator and the prosecutor before any application to the court is made to assess whether it can properly proceed. (The transcript of *R* v *Brushett* (2001) Crim LR 471, illustrates an approach, commended by the Court of Appeal, where a pragmatic and co-operative stance was taken by social services and material revealed to the prosecution.)

2.48   Any reports prepared by a third party at the request of the investigator and supplied to the investigator will also be subject to the requirements of the Act relating to disclosure.

2.49   Where material is obtained from third parties, the investigator should discuss with them whether any sensitivities attach to the material that might influence whether it is used as evidence, or otherwise disclosed to the defence, or whether there may be public interest reasons that justify withholding disclosure. The third party's view must be passed to the prosecutor using the MG6.

2.50   Where material is held by a Government department or other Crown body that may be relevant to an issue in the case, reasonable steps should be taken to identify and consider such material. Investigators and disclosure officers should refer to paragraph 3.145 below for the procedure to follow.

Retention periods

2.51   Paragraphs 5.6 to 5.10 of the Code provide for the period of retention. This is the minimum period of retention and individual force policy may provide for a longer period.

2.52   Material seized under the provisions of PACE will be subject to the retention provisions of section 22 PACE.

Preparation of schedules

2.53   The disclosure officer is responsible for preparing the schedules and submitting them to the prosecutor. The schedules, dated by the disclosure officer, should be submitted to the prosecutor with a full file.

2.54   It is not necessary to maintain schedule(s) of unused material from the start of all investigations. During the course of the investigation it may not be possible to decide whether particular material will eventually form part of the prosecution case, or will remain unused. In some cases there may be advantages in starting the schedule(s) at an early stage. The officer in charge of the investigation will need to consider at what stage the schedules should be prepared, and when to appoint a disclosure officer.

2.55   Where working schedules or draft lists have been created as the enquiry progressed, the disclosure officer must check the contents and consolidate the items into two schedules for the prosecutor listing:

- – any non-sensitive unused material (MG6C)
- – any sensitive unused material (MG6D).

2.56   Draft schedules or lists used to prepare the final schedule need not be retained or listed on the MG6C.

2.57   Any comments, observations or explanations about the contents of the schedules should be made on the MG6, which should accompany the submission of the MG6C and MG6D. The disclosure officer must also indicate on the MG6E whether the investigation started before 1 April 1997. This will be of relevance to the prosecutor in deciding how to go about disclosing material to the accused, see **Pre-CPIA investigations** at paragraphs 1.48–49 above.

2.58   **All** items of material relevant to the investigation must be listed on one of the above schedules for the prosecutor, unless the material is so sensitive that it cannot even be listed on a schedule. This is dealt with at paragraph 2.86 below.

2.59   The table at Annex D provides some help as to whether the material should be listed as sensitive or otherwise. If in doubt, consult the prosecutor.

2.60   Correspondence or advice between the CPS and the police should not ordinarily be listed on either schedule, see paragraph 2.85 below.

2.61   As a general rule, pure opinion or speculation, for example police officers' theories about who committed the crime, is not unused material. However, if the opinion or speculation is based on some other information or fact, not otherwise apparent to the prosecutor, that information or fact might well be relevant to the investigation and should be notified to the prosecutor in accordance with these instructions.

2.62   Where the disclosure officer is unsure whether an item is relevant to the investigation and thus requires listing on a schedule, the prosecutor should be consulted as soon as practicable.

The non-sensitive material schedule

2.63   Non-sensitive unused material should be listed on the MG6C. **This form will be disclosed to the defence**.

2.64   In the description column of every schedule, each item should be individually listed and consecutively numbered throughout all schedules. Thus, where continuation sheets are used or additional schedules sent in later submissions, item numbering must be consecutive to all items on earlier schedules.

2.65   The descriptions in non-sensitive schedules should be detailed, clear and accurate. **They should include a summary of the contents of the retained material to allow the prosecutor to make an informed decision on disclosure**. The same applies to sensitive schedules to the extent possible without compromising the confidentiality of the information. It is not sufficient merely to refer to a document by way of a form number which may be meaningless outside the Police Service. Example schedules are given on the disclosure wall chart.

2.66   In cases where there are many items of a similar or repetitive nature (messages for example) it is permissible to describe them by quantity and generic title. However, inappropriate use of generic listing (such as 'correspondence 1.4.02 to 10.12.02') is likely to lead to requests from the prosecutor and the defence to see the items. This may result in wasted resources and unnecessary delay. The preparation of properly detailed schedules at this stage will save time and resources throughout the disclosure process, and will promote confidence in its integrity.

2.67   When items are described by generic titles or quantities, the disclosure officer must ensure that items which might meet the test for disclosure are listed individually.

2.68   The disclosure officer should keep a copy of the schedules that are sent to the prosecutor, in case there are any queries that need to be resolved. A copy will also assist the disclosure officer to keep track of the items listed, should the schedules need to be updated.

Phoenix input documents

2.69   Frequently, Phoenix input documents and fingerprint forms contain information that replicates exactly that which appears in other documents which have been used as evidence or are unused material. Not all information recorded on Phoenix forms will be material relevant to the investigation within the meaning of the Code: for example, information recorded for intelligence purposes only.

2.70   However, there will be circumstances where relevant information on these documents does not appear elsewhere, or is inconsistent with other material. Where this occurs, the disclosure officer should seek advice from the prosecutor as to whether the material may be relevant before listing the item on a schedule. A copy of the document should be sent to the prosecutor. The disclosure officer should explain why the information is thought to be relevant in the particular case.

2.71   It will not normally be necessary to list these documents on a schedule unless the prosecutor considers that they may be relevant. The prosecutor will decide whether the material is relevant, and whether it requires disclosure to the accused under the Act. If the item is relevant, but does not require disclosure to the accused, the prosecutor will request that it be added to the appropriate schedule.

2.72   If the document contains relevant information that must be disclosed to the accused because it undermines the prosecution case, or assists the defence at secondary stage, the prosecutor and the disclosure officer may need to consider whether the document should be edited if it contains sensitive material.

Offences taken into consideration (TICs)

2.73   Offences not charged but prepared as matters to be taken into consideration by the court on sentence will be treated in accordance with the Manual of Guidance. Normally, material relating to TICs need not be scheduled as individual items. However, if the investigating officer or the disclosure officer forms the view that a confession is unreliable, and this undermines the prosecution case, the CPS must be informed using the MG6. In this event the material relating to proposed TICs should be listed in the same way as all other unused material.

The sensitive material schedule

2.74   This schedule should be used to reveal to the prosecutor the existence of unused material which the disclosure officer, after consulting with the officer in charge of the investigation, believes should be withheld from the defence because it is not in the public interest to disclose it. Such material must none the less be revealed to the prosecutor.

2.75   The disclosure officer must list such material on the MG6D, and indicate on the form why the item(s) should not be disclosed. **This form will not be disclosed to the defence.**

2.76   In those cases where there is no sensitive unused material, the disclosure officer should endorse and sign an MG6D to this effect and should submit this with the MG6C and MG6E.

2.77   It is not possible to provide an exhaustive list of items which may be withheld. The proper test to apply is whether disclosure of the item would cause **real harm to the public interest**. Some examples are given at paragraph 6.12 of the Code.

2.78   Some items by their very nature will reveal why disclosure should be withheld, for example, information concerning intelligence sources. Others require more explanation. Careful attention to this element of the schedule will avoid further enquiries and consequent delay. Both the 'Description of item' and the 'Reasons for sensitivity' sections must contain sufficient information to enable the prosecutor to make an informed decision as to whether or not the material itself should be viewed. Schedules containing insufficient information will be returned by the prosecutor. If there is any doubt about the sensitivity of the material, the prosecutor should be consulted.

2.79   The police and CPS will always take care to protect intelligence information and information given to the police in confidence. That will be so whether or not it is thought likely that the court will order its disclosure. If the investigator is unsure whether information was given in confidence, the position should be clarified with the person who provided the information.

2.80   When the schedule and any material is sent to the prosecutor, a protective marking should be applied to it consistent with the level of sensitivity of its contents. This will determine the manner in which the material is conveyed to, and stored by the CPS. Reference should be had to the police policy guidance issued in October 2001 as to the detailed categorisation of different types of sensitive material as **Restricted, Confidential, Secret** or **Top Secret**. Guidance is given in Annex K below.

2.81   In deciding sensitivity it is important to bear in mind that the sensitivity of the schedule and the sensitivity of the information may differ. It may be possible to describe a highly sensitive piece of material adequately on the schedule without disclosing the information (for example, a name), which makes the material sensitive. The security marking will depend on what is being submitted to the prosecutor; if the material itself is to accompany the schedule the material will determine the marking. If the schedule alone is submitted the content of the schedule will determine its security marking.

2.82   Sensitive unused material and schedules relating to informants, observation posts or undercover operations will normally be treated as **Confidential**. They should be sent to the prosecutor in a sealed envelope marked 'Sensitive unused material—**Confidential** and bearing the name and URN of the defendant(s). Any other material which the police consider to meet the requirements of a **Confidential** marking should be submitted in the same way.

2.83   If a third party gives material to investigators, or allows material to be inspected, but indicates that material is sensitive in any way, the material must be listed on the MG6D. The third party's view must be passed on to the prosecutor via the MG6.

2.84   In order to make a proper assessment of the material which is said to be sensitive, the prosecutor will need either to see the material or part of it, or to be fully informed of its contents. In many cases it will be possible to attach a copy of the material (or part of it) to the schedule. But there will be occasions when this will not be feasible, either because the bulk of the material makes it impractical, or because the material is too sensitive to be copied and transmitted. In this event it will be for the disclosure officer to make arrangements with the prosecutor to view the material with an appropriate level of physical and personal security.

2.85   There is no need to list reports, advice or other communications between the CPS and police. Most in themselves will have no bearing on the case and thus will not be relevant. Those that are relevant will usually be protected by PII. When in doubt, guidance should be sought from the prosecutor.

Handling highly sensitive material

2.86   All relevant sensitive unused material should be included on the MG6D unless the exceptional circumstances identified in paragraph 6.13 of the Code exist. Paragraph 6.13 recognises that there may be material of such sensitivity that it would be inappropriate even to list it on the

MG6D. Examples of such highly sensitive material would include information that, should it be compromised, would:

- lead directly to the loss of life
- directly threaten national security.

The small number of such cases where this situation may arise are likely to involve investigations into organised crime or into terrorist offences. This material is likely to be in the **Secret** or **Top Secret** categories.

2.87   Where there is unused material that is so sensitive that it cannot be itemised on the MG6D but the disclosure officer is aware of it, the disclosure officer should refer to the existence of such material on the MG6D without identifying it. The disclosure officer should notify the prosecutor of the existence of such material as soon as possible after a full file has been submitted to the prosecutor and should identify the person holding the material to enable the prosecutor to contact that person to discuss the nature of the material and to arrange to inspect it. Inspection should be at an appropriate location having regard to the sensitivity of the material.

2.88   Where the material in question is considered by police to be too sensitive even for a reference to its existence to be included on the MG6D, or it is considered too sensitive to reveal to the disclosure officer, the person holding the material should make contact with the prosecutor to discuss the material which **must** be viewed by the prosecutor.

2.89   It is likely that there will need to be an early consultation to discuss whether sensitive material may require disclosure and to decide whether the direction of the court should be sought. Where the police contend that material comes within paragraph 2.86 above, initial contact with the CPS to discuss the material should be with the appropriate Unit Head or Special Casework Lawyer.

Applications to the court: sensitive material

2.90   The prosecutor has a duty under the Act to consider whether sensitive material might undermine the prosecution case or assist the defence. Where the prosecutor decides that the sensitive material requires disclosure to the accused because it falls within the tests set out in the Act, and the prosecutor in consultation with the police considers that disclosure should be withheld on public interest grounds, the direction of the court must be sought.

2.91   Before an application is made to the court, the prosecutor will need to consult the police. This should take place at a senior level, and a senior officer (who may be independent of the investigation) should be involved (see paragraphs 3.120 and 3.123 for levels of authority). Others may also be consulted, including the officer in charge of the investigation, and in Crown court cases, the prosecution advocate.

2.92   Consultation will include a careful examination of the circumstances of the case and the nature of the sensitive material. In particular, the prosecutor will require information dealing with the following issues:

- **the reasons why the material is said to be sensitive**
- **the degree of sensitivity said to attach to the material, in other words, why it is considered that real harm would be caused to the public interest by disclosure**
- **the consequences of revealing to the defence**
  (i)   the material itself
  (ii)   the category of the material
  (iii) the fact that an application is being made
- **the significance of the material to the issues in the trial**
- **the involvement of any third parties in bringing the material to the attention of the police**
- **where the material is likely to be the subject of an order for disclosure, what the police view is regarding continuance of the prosecution.**

2.93   For consultation to be effective, the officer in charge of the investigation should ensure that the prosecutor is provided with the information necessary to make a proper decision on how the application is to be made. This should be in documentary form, unless the information is so sensitive that it would be inappropriate to put it into writing.

2.94   On the basis of the information provided at the consultation, the prosecutor will decide whether an application should be made, and the form of application required. The editing of a document, or other methods of disclosing the relevant information without compromising the sensitive material may be considered appropriate.

2.95   Following consultation, the prosecutor will set out in writing the submission to be made to the court (see paragraph 3.124 below). The submission will be signed by the prosecutor (at Unit Head or Special Casework Lawyer level), and by a Detective Chief Inspector, unless a Detective Inspector has specific delegated authority to do so. The officer will state that to the best of his or her knowledge and belief the assertions of fact on which the submission is based are correct. The officer may be required to attend court to give evidence in support of the application.

Editing

2.96   Some documents may contain a mixture of sensitive and non-sensitive material. For example, a witness address or personal telephone number may appear on a document that otherwise is entirely non-sensitive.

2.97   In these cases there may be no objection to the sensitive part being blocked out, using a dark marker pen (not correcting fluid), on the copy document which is to be sent to the prosecutor. The original should not be marked in any way. A description of the document should be listed on the MG6C. (The unedited version should **not** be listed on the MG6D, but made available to the prosecutor for inspection if required). The prosecutor should be informed of the nature of the edited material, if not obvious, on the MG6.

2.98   Decisions about editing documents should only be made after consultation between the disclosure officer and the prosecutor, other than for the simple deletion of the personal addresses or telephone numbers of witnesses.

Amending the schedules

2.99   On occasions it may be necessary to amend the schedules. When the schedules are first submitted with a full file, the disclosure officer may not know exactly what material the prosecutor intends to use as part of the prosecution case. The prosecutor may create unused material by extracting statements or documents from the evidence bundle, in which case the prosecutor may disclose material directly to the defence without waiting for the disclosure officer to amend the schedule, but should advise the officer accordingly. Police officers should ensure that obviously non-evidential material is not included in the evidence bundle.

2.100   The prosecutor is required to advise the disclosure officer of: items listed on the MG6C that should properly be on the MG6D; any apparent omissions or amendments required; where there are insufficient or unclear descriptions; or where there has been a failure to provide schedules at all. The disclosure officer must then take all necessary remedial action and provide properly completed schedules to the prosecutor. Failure to do so may result in the matter being raised with a senior officer.

2.101   The Code places the responsibility for creating the schedules and keeping them accurate and up to date on the disclosure officer. Consequently, the prosecutor will not amend them. In these circumstances the prosecutor will inform the disclosure officer of the changes required, and will return the schedules for amendment where appropriate.

2.102   The disclosure officer should effect the amendments promptly and return the amended or fresh schedules to the prosecutor as soon as possible with an MG6E as appropriate.

Continuing duties

2.103   The duties of revelation to the prosecutor and disclosure to the accused are continuing obligations. Any new material coming to light after primary or secondary disclosure has been completed should be treated in the same way as earlier material. The new material should be listed on a further MG6C, MG6D or a continuation sheet. To avoid confusion, numbering of items submitted at a later stage must be consecutive to those on the previously submitted schedules.

2.104   A further MG6E should also be submitted irrespective of whether or not any of the new material is considered by the disclosure officer to come within the appropriate primary or secondary disclosure test.

Revelation of the material to the prosecutor: common law

2.105   Investigators and disclosure officers must be mindful of the prosecutor's duty, in the interests of justice and fairness in the particular circumstances of any case, to make disclosure of material after the commencement of proceedings but **before** the duty arises under the Act. For instance, the investigator or disclosure officer must inform the prosecutor of significant information, such as a victim's previous convictions, that might affect a bail decision or that might enable the defence to contest committal proceedings.

2.106   Similarly, the investigator or disclosure officer must reveal to the prosecutor any material that is relevant to sentence (for example, information which might mitigate the seriousness of the offence or assist the defendant in laying blame in whole or in part upon a co-defendant or another).

Revelation of the material to the prosecutor: primary stage

2.107   Revealing material to the prosecutor does not mean automatic disclosure to the defence. The prosecutor will only disclose material to the defence if it falls within the tests for disclosure set out in the Act. If the material is sensitive, and must otherwise be disclosed under the Act, the prosecutor will either apply to the court for a ruling as to whether the public interest requires disclosure or disclose the material after consultation with police or withdraw the prosecution.

2.108   The MG6C will be disclosed to the defence at primary stage.

2.109   Revelation to the prosecutor involves:

–   promptly sending the completed schedules

–   pointing out any material which might undermine the prosecution case and therefore fall within the test for primary disclosure

–   copying certain material to the prosecutor (see paragraphs 2.119–2.125 below)

–   allowing the prosecutor to inspect material.

2.110   Disclosure at the primary stage requires the disclosure of material which **in the prosecutor's opinion might undermine the case for the prosecution**. The disclosure officer will need to carefully check the material listed on **both** schedules and assist the prosecutor to identify anything which **potentially** might need disclosing to the defence. The case against each accused must be considered separately.

2.111   In large or complicated cases or in any case where particular difficulties are anticipated, an early discussion between the disclosure officer or the officer in charge of the investigation, the prosecutor and prosecution advocate, if instructed, may be extremely beneficial. For example, they may agree to look at the material together before the schedules are prepared. In such circumstance, the disclosure officer or the officer in charge of the investigation, should not hesitate to contact the prosecutor for advice.

2.112   The disclosure officer should bring to the prosecutor's attention any material which might have the potential to undermine the prosecution case. Examples will include:

-   records of previous convictions and cautions for prosecution witnesses (see Annex A and Annex B)

-   any other information which casts doubt on the reliability of a witness or on the accuracy of

-   any prosecution evidence

-   any motives for the making false of allegations by a prosecution witness

-   any material which may have a bearing on the admissibility of any prosecution evidence

-   the fact that a witness has sought, been offered or received a reward

-   any material that might go to the credibility of a prosecution witness

-   any information which may cast doubt on the reliability of a confession. Any item which relates to the defendant's mental or physical health, his intellectual capacity, or to any ill-treatment which the defendant may have suffered when in the investigators custody is likely to have the potential for casting doubt on the reliability of a purported confession

-   information that a person other than the defendant was or might have been responsible or which points to another person whether charged or not (including a co-defendant) having involvement in the commission of the offence.

2.113   Any material that has an adverse effect on the strength of the prosecution case should be pointed out by the disclosure officer. This will include anything that may weaken an essential part of the prosecution case. Any material that supports or is consistent with a defence put forward in interview or before charge or which is apparent from the prosecution papers should be provided to the prosecutor at this stage. It also includes anything that points away from the defendant, such as information about a possible alibi. If the material might undermine the prosecution case it should be brought to the prosecutor's attention at this stage even though it suggests a defence inconsistent with or alternative to the one already advanced by the defendant or solicitor. Items of material viewed in isolation may not be considered to have potential to undermine the prosecution case, however several items together can have that effect.

2.114   Such material must be brought to the prosecutor's attention regardless of any views about the accuracy or truth of the information, although where appropriate the disclosure officer may express an opinion on what weight should be given to it.

2.115   A wide interpretation should be given when identifying material that might fall within the test. A thorough and careful check at primary stage may save time later on. The disclosure officer should consult with the prosecutor where necessary to help identify material that may require disclosure at this stage, and must specifically draw material to the attention of the prosecutor where the disclosure officer has any doubt as to whether it might have potential to undermine the prosecution case.

2.116   Disclosure officers must deal expeditiously with requests by the prosecutor for further information on material which may lead to disclosure.

2.117   The MG6E should be used to draw the attention of the prosecutor to material that might undermine the prosecution case. The disclosure officer should also explain on form MG6E (by referring to the relevant item's number on the schedule) why he or she has come to that view. The MG6C itself should not be marked or highlighted in any way, as it will be provided to the defence.

2.118   Where it is the case that the disclosure officer believes there is no material that might have the potential to undermine the prosecution case, the officer should endorse the MG6E in the following terms: '**I have reviewed all the material which has been retained and made available to me and there is nothing to the best of my knowledge and belief that might undermine the prosecution case.**'

2.119   As well as describing the material on the schedule(s), there is a duty to copy certain material to the prosecutor. The types of material that should **always** be sent are described in paragraph 7.3 of the Code.

2.120   In addition to this, and as an aid to prosecutors in their case review function, copies of the crime report and the log of messages should also be routinely copied to the prosecutor in every case in which a full file is provided. (These documents are known in different police forces by different names, for example OIS or CAD for the log of messages.)

2.121   The documents should be fully described in accordance with 2.65 above to enable a properly informed decision by the prosecutor as to disclosure.

2.122   If the disclosure officer believes that these documents might have the potential to undermine the prosecution case, they should be listed on the MG6E in the usual way. However, copies should be provided to the prosecutor irrespective of whether they are considered to be potentially disclosable to the defence.

2.123   The copy of the crime report and log of messages should be edited by the police in accordance with paragraphs 2.96 and 2.97 above, before they are sent to the prosecutor. If it is impossible to edit any sensitive parts of the material, then it should be listed on the MG6D and be sent to the prosecutor with that schedule.

2.124   **Revealing this material to the prosecutor does not mean it will be automatically disclosed to the defence**. The prosecutor will only disclose unused material if it falls within the test for disclosure set out in the Act, and will advise the police of any such decision by endorsing the MG6C with reasons as to why the material meets the disclosure test.

2.125   This requirement to routinely reveal the crime report and the log of messages does not prejudice any other locally agreed arrangements between the police and the CPS that allow for the similar treatment of other additional categories or types of document.

2.126   The task of indicating material that might undermine the prosecution case, and the submission of copies of that material, involves a proper consideration of all the retained material. That obligation cannot be discharged by simply sending to the prosecutor material which has not been so considered.

2.127   Considering the unused material against the primary disclosure test does not mean that material not thought to be capable of undermining the prosecution case can be omitted from the schedule(s). **All retained unused material or information must be scheduled**, save in those rare cases where paragraphs 2.86–2.89 apply.

2.128   A prosecutor may ask to inspect material, or request a copy of material where one has not been sent. The disclosure officer is responsible for arranging this. Material should be copied to the prosecutor on request unless it is too sensitive or too bulky, or can only be inspected. This applies to both stages of disclosure.

2.129   After the prosecutor has considered each schedule, it will be endorsed with the decisions as to whether each listed item will be disclosed to the defence. A copy of the endorsed schedule will be sent to the disclosure officer.

Revelation of material to the prosecutor: secondary stage

2.130   The prosecutor will give the disclosure officer a copy of any defence statement received as soon as possible following its receipt.

2.131   The defence statement should set out the nature of the defence in general terms, indicate the matters on which the defendant takes issue with the prosecution and the reasons why he takes issue. There may be a note from the prosecutor, providing guidance on what material might have to be disclosed at the secondary stage, advice on whether any further lines of enquiry need to be followed (for example, where an alibi has been given) or suggestions for when the officer reconsiders the unused material. These may arise where the prosecutor (unlike the disclosure officer) is aware of issues raised by the defence during the progress of the case, for example at bail hearings or during committal proceedings.

2.132   At the secondary stage, the prosecutor must serve upon the defence material which might be reasonably expected to assist the accused's defence as disclosed by the defence statement. This must be done as soon as reasonably practicable after receipt of the defence statement.

2.133   The disclosure officer should promptly look again at the retained material and must draw the attention of the prosecutor to any material which **might reasonably be expected to assist the accused's defence as disclosed by the defence statement**. Both sensitive and non-sensitive material must be considered.

2.134   Material that might assist the defence may already have been identified at primary stage. It will include anything that might help the defence in preparing or presenting their case, as outlined in the defence statement. The disclosure officer should consult with the prosecutor where necessary to help identify any material which may require disclosure at this stage, as for primary disclosure.

2.135   The disclosure officer's observations should be submitted to the prosecutor on a fresh MG6E. If there is no material that the disclosure officer believes will assist the defence, the disclosure officer should endorse the second MG6E in the following terms: '**I have reviewed all the retained material made available to me and there is nothing to the best of my knowledge and belief to assist the defence in the light of the defence statement.**'

2.136   Any items that might assist should be referred to by quoting the item number from the schedule(s). If material identified has not previously been supplied to the prosecutor, a copy should be forwarded by the disclosure officer, except where the material is considered to be too sensitive to copy and arrangements are to be made for the prosecutor to inspect the material.

2.137   The disclosure officer should ensure that it is clear that the MG6E has been completed in response to a defence statement (secondary disclosure). The disclosure officer should explain why the material might reasonably be expected to assist the defence. The disclosure officer must sign and date the MG6E to comply with paragraph 9.1 of the Code.

2.138   The defence statement may on occasion point the prosecution to other lines of inquiry, for example, the investigation of an alibi, or where forensic expert evidence is involved. The disclosure officer should inform the officer in charge of the investigation and copy the defence statement to him or her, together with any advice provided by the prosecutor, if appropriate. Further investigation in these circumstances is possible and evidence obtained as a result of inquiring into a defence statement may be used as part of the prosecution case or to rebut the defence. However, an investigator should not show a defence statement to a witness. The extent to which the detail of a defence case statement is made known to a witness will depend upon the extent to which it is necessary to clarify the issues disputed by the defence, assist the prosecutor to identify any further disclosable material and/or to identify any further reasonable lines of inquiry. The officer should seek guidance from the prosecutor if there is any doubt as to permissible usage of the defence statement in conducting further inquiries.

2.139   If enquiries are carried out in response to the defence statement, the disclosure officer in consultation with the officer in charge of the investigation should notify the prosecutor of the results of those enquiries. This should be done on an MG20, and given to the prosecutor together with any additional schedules and a further MG6E as appropriate. If no enquiries were made, particularly when the defence statement has given details of an alibi, the disclosure officer should explain why.

2.140   Once the prosecutor has decided whether there is material that should be disclosed at secondary stage, a letter will be sent to the defence. The disclosure officer will be sent a copy of the letter, which will contain details of any items that require disclosure.

Large or complex cases

2.141   Some investigations may involve a large quantity of material, both used and unused. Examples of cases where this may occur include the following:

– substantial frauds

– large scale conspiracies

–   drug related offences involving manufacture, importation or supply

–   homicide or other major enquiries.

2.142   Such cases will inevitably need close and early liaison between the disclosure officer and the prosecutor. Where appropriate, they may agree to look at the material together before the schedules are prepared. Alternatively, they may need to work closely to identify material listed on the schedules that may require disclosure under the Act, and to agree arrangements for its disclosure to the accused. Such early discussion between the Police and the prosecutor may be extremely beneficial to effective case preparation.

2.143   In any cases where there is a large amount of unused material, it may not be possible or desirable to copy all necessary material to the prosecutor. The disclosure officer should inform the prosecutor that a large quantity of material exists, and should make any necessary arrangements to facilitate inspection of the items by the prosecutor.

2.144   The disclosure officer and the prosecutor must consider the unused material, and decide what items require disclosure to the accused. Once a decision has been reached on what should be disclosed, the disclosure officer and the prosecutor may agree that it would be more practicable to allow the defence to inspect all or part of the material that should be disclosed. This is more likely to occur at secondary stage in cases where there is potentially a lot of material that may assist the defence put forward, but it may occur at primary stage.

2.145   In some cases, investigators may seize large volumes of material that may not, for whatever reason, seem likely ever to be relevant. In such circumstances, the investigator may consider that it is not an appropriate use of resources to examine such large volumes of material seized on a precautionary basis. If such material is not examined by the investigator or disclosure officer, and it is not intended to examine it, but the material is nevertheless retained, its existence should be made known to the accused in general terms at the primary stage and permission granted for its inspection by him or his legal advisers. A section 9 statement will be completed by the investigator or the disclosure officer describing the material by general category and justifying it not having been examined. This statement will itself be listed as unused material and automatically disclosed to the defence.

2.146   The prosecutor should be informed of any arrangements made with the defence and should also be informed of defence requests for copies of items. The disclosure officer must comply with defence requests for copies unless it is neither practicable nor desirable. Examples of such circumstances are given in paragraph 10.3 of the Code.

Certification by disclosure officer

2.147   The disclosure officer is required to certify to the prosecutor that: **To the best of my knowledge and belief, all material which has been retained and made available to me has been inspected, viewed or listened to (other than unexamined irrelevant material) and revealed to the prosecutor in accordance with the Criminal Procedure and Investigations Act 1996, Code of Practice and the Attorney General's Guidelines 2000.** The purpose of certification is to provide an assurance to the prosecutor on behalf of the police investigating team that all relevant material has been identified, considered and revealed to the prosecutor.

2.148   The officer in charge of the investigation must ensure that all relevant material that has been retained is either made available to the disclosure officer, or in exceptional circumstances revealed directly to the prosecutor. The disclosure officer must be able to perform the duties of scheduling the material and revealing it to the prosecutor accurately and efficiently.

2.149   The disclosure officer must make certification when the schedules are submitted at primary stage, and again at secondary stage when a defence statement has been supplied and the retained material is reviewed again. The signed and dated MG6E should be used to provide certification to the prosecutor at both stages.

2.150   If the disclosure officer is uncertain as to whether all the retained material has been made available, enquiries should be made of the officer in charge of the investigation to resolve the matter.

Disclosure to the accused

2.151   Disclosure of material that falls within the tests for disclosure to the accused can be achieved either by copying the item, or by allowing the accused to inspect it. Where the item to be disclosed is a document, and has been copied to the CPS, the prosecutor will usually copy it to the defence.

2.152   There will be situations where this is not possible or appropriate, for example where the quality of the copy supplied is inadequate, or where the item is in a form requiring specialist copying equipment (such as audio or video tapes), or where the prosecutor considers that the material is not suitable for copying for other reasons (such as the sexual content). Sometimes it will not be possible to copy the item at all, for example where the item is a physical object.

2.153   In these circumstances the prosecutor may decide that the item should be inspected, or that the disclosure officer should arrange for a copy to be given to the defence. Where the item is a video or an audio tape, the police will be responsible for providing copies.

2.154   The prosecutor will indicate on the MG6C whether the item is to be disclosed by way of inspection, and should discuss with the disclosure officer the appropriate method of disclosure before that decision is taken. Where the prosecutor requests that the item to be disclosed should be made available for the accused (or his legal representative) to inspect, the disclosure officer is responsible for arranging this.

2.155   If the accused asks for a copy of any material which he has been allowed to inspect, the disclosure officer must give it to him, unless in the opinion of the disclosure officer it is either not practicable or desirable. Examples of these circumstances are given in paragraph 10.3 of the Code.

2.156   Where a copy of any disclosable item is given to the accused, the disclosure officer should inform the prosecutor, and supply a copy to the prosecutor, if one has not already been provided. It is important that a careful record is kept by the disclosure officer of what items are inspected by or copied to the accused or his legal representatives.

2.157   For information that is not recorded in writing, the disclosure officer may decide in what form the material should be disclosed. If a transcript is provided, the disclosure officer must ensure that the transcript is certified as a true record, for example by way of a short statement by the transcriber. It is not necessary for the disclosure officer to personally certify the accuracy of the transcript.

Summary trials

2.158   In summary trials, the time available for the investigator and the prosecutor to carry out their respective functions under the Act will be limited, particularly where the accused is in custody.

2.159   To make best use of available time, it is therefore essential that:

–   potential not guilty pleas are identified so that the preparation of full files can start as soon as possible

–   file upgrades are commenced as soon as possible

–   full files should be submitted on time, complete with the schedules and copies of any items that must be supplied to the prosecutor.

2.160   In summary trials, the defence need not provide a defence statement. This means that there may not be a secondary stage to prosecution disclosure, and no opportunity to provide assisting material. In the interests of justice, the identification of material which might undermine the prosecution case should be interpreted as widely as possible.

2.161   In summary only matters, there is no requirement to provide schedules unless and until a formal not guilty plea is entered by the accused. However, as soon as the police receive notification of a not guilty plea in such cases, all appropriate disclosure schedules should be prepared and submitted to the prosecutor. This also applies to minor traffic offences.

Special problems with disclosure

2.162   There are a number of difficult areas that require specific and detailed guidance in relation to the handling of material for disclosure purposes. These are dealt with in the following annexes:

- previous convictions and disciplinary findings against police officers: Annex A
- previous convictions and cautions against other prosecution witnesses: Annex B
- debriefing sessions: Annex E
- pre-trial meetings with witnesses: Annex F
- financial investigation material: Annex G
- scientific support disclosure: Annexes H and I
- third party material procedures: Annex J
- the security of sensitive material schedules and unused material: Annex K (**Restricted**).

2.163   Investigators and disclosure officers should refer to the appropriate annex when dealing with these issues.

2.164   There will occasionally be cases where the unused material is revealed to the prosecutor by someone other than the disclosure officer. In some cases, for example, where the police investigation has been intelligence led, there may be an additional disclosure officer appointed just to deal with intelligence material which, by its very nature, is likely to be sensitive.

2.165   Where more than one disclosure officer has been appointed to deal with different aspects of the case, a principal disclosure officer should be identified as the single point of contact for the prosecutor. Where an officer other than the principal disclosure officer submits a disclosure schedule to the prosecutor, that officer should inform the principal disclosure officer.

2.166   Where the prosecutor consults with the principal disclosure officer, for example, when he provides a copy of the defence statement, the principal disclosure officer should inform any other officer who has provided unused material schedules to the prosecutor.

ANNEX J THIRD PARTY PROCEDURES

Explanatory leaflet on the principles and procedures relating to third parties under the Criminal Procedures and Investigation Act 1996 and the disclosure of material in their possession.

Letter from the Police Disclosure Officer to Local Authority Legal Department.

AN EXPLANATORY LEAFLET ON THE PRINCIPLES AND PROCEDURES RELATING TO THIRD PARTIES UNDER THE CRIMINAL PROCEDURE AND INVESTIGATIONS ACT 1996 AND THE DISCLOSURE OF MATERIAL IN THEIR POSSESSION

Introduction

1.   This document explains the procedures to be followed by the prosecution in seeking to obtain relevant material held by individuals and organisations that are regarded as third parties in criminal proceedings.

2.   The law governing material held by third parties is contained in the Criminal Procedure and Investigations Act 1996 (CPIA) and the Attorney General's Guidelines published in November 2000.

Who are third parties?

3.   In the course of an investigation to determine whether an offence has been committed, the police may become aware of relevant material in the possession of persons or organisations which may have a bearing on the investigation. It is only the investigator and the prosecutor who have statutory duties of revelation and disclosure under the CPIA. All other categories of persons are third parties so far as the conduct of the case is concerned.

The Legal Requirements of the Prosecution

4.   Every accused person has a right to a fair trial, a right enshrined in our law and guaranteed under the European Convention on Human Rights. This right to a fair trial is fundamental and the accused's right to fair disclosure is an inseparable part of it.

5.   The scheme set out in the CPIA is designed to ensure that there is fair disclosure of material to the accused which may be relevant to an investigation and which does not form part of the prosecution case. This is known as 'unused material'. Fairness does, however, recognise that there are other interests that need to be protected, including those of the victims and witnesses who might otherwise be exposed to harm. The CPIA protects those interests.

6.   Investigators are under a duty to pursue all reasonable lines of enquiry, whether these point towards or away from the accused. What is reasonable in each case will depend on the particular circumstances. Investigators and prosecutors must do all they can to facilitate proper disclosure, as part of their general and professional responsibility to act fairly and impartially, in the interests of justice.

7.   Where you possess material, which has not been obtained by the police, they are under a duty to inform you of the existence of the investigation and to invite you to retain the material in case they receive a request for its disclosure. Where the police inspect material with your agreement and do not retain it, they are under a duty to record details of that material and to reveal it to the prosecutor.

8.   Where you do not allow the prosecution access to the material, the prosecution may apply to the court for a witness summons, and if granted would require you to attend court to produce the material to the court. Application for a witness summons will only be made where the prosecution considers that the material sought is likely to be material to the proceedings. You do have the right to make representations to the court against the issue of a witness summons.

9.   Where the relevant material held by you or owned by you but in the possession of the prosecution is sensitive, in that it is not in the public interest to disclose, then the prosecution will treat that material in confidence. Where that material might undermine the prosecution case or might reasonably assist the defence case, a public interest immunity application must be made to prevent disclosure to the defence. Where you have an interest in that material, the prosecution is under a duty to notify you in writing of the time and place of any public interest immunity application. You have a right to make representations to the court.

10.   Failure by the prosecution to take action leading to the disclosure of relevant material may result in a wrongful conviction or dismissal of the proceedings.

The Prosecution Procedures in dealing with Third Parties

11.   In the course of an investigation, the investigator will write to you setting out the circumstances of the case and specifying the relevant material that he believes is in your possession.

12.   Where you acknowledge that you hold relevant material which may have some bearing on the issues in the case, the investigator will request a copy from you or request to inspect the material.

13.   Where you provide the material to the police in the course of the investigation, the police will discuss with you whether any sensitivity attaches to the material. Your view will be passed on to the Crown Prosecution Service.

14.   Where the material is sensitive, and a public interest immunity application is made to withhold the material from the defence, you have a right to make representations to the court on issues of the sensitivity of the material. The Crown Prosecution Service will notify you of the time and place of the application.

15.   Where you refuse to provide all or part of the material, or refuse to allow the police to inspect it, the police will request you to retain the material in case they receive a request for its disclosure or the court later requires the material to be disclosed.

16.   Where an accused has been charged with an offence and you have refused to reveal the material to the police, or failed to respond to the request for the material, the Crown Prosecution Service may consider applying to the court for a witness summons. The procedure relating to witness summonses is set out below.

Rules relating to witness summonses in the Crown Court (Criminal Procedure (Attendance of Witnesses) Act 1965)

17.   An application for a summons for a person to produce a document or thing to the court must be made in writing, where the trial has not commenced, to the appropriate officer of the Crown Court. The application should contain:

- A brief description of the required document or thing;
- Reasons why the person will not voluntarily produce it;
- Reasons why the document or thing is likely to be material evidence;
- A supporting affidavit setting out the charge and specifying: the evidence which will enable the person to identify it; the grounds for believing that the person is likely to be able to produce the document or thing; and the grounds for believing that it will be material evidence.

18.   A copy of the application and the supporting affidavit will be served on the person by the Crown Prosecution Service/Police. It will inform the person of their right to make representations in writing and at the hearing, and that they have 7 days to inform the court if they wish to make representations.

19.   If the person does not request a hearing, the appropriate officer of the Crown Court will refer the papers to the judge. The judge will decide whether or not to issue a witness summons in the light of the information before him.

20.   If the person requests a hearing, the court will set a time, place and date and will notify both the person and the Crown Prosecution Service. The hearing shall be in private unless the judge directs otherwise.

21.   Where the person produces the document or thing prior to the hearing of the summons, the Crown Prosecution Service will notify the court that the requirements imposed by the summons are no longer needed.

22.   A person may make an application to the Crown Court to make a summons which has been issued ineffective on the grounds that he had not received a notice of application to issue the summons and that he had not been present or represented at any hearing of the application and would not be able to produce any document or thing likely to be material evidence.

Rules Relating to Witness Summonses in the Magistrates' Court

23.   If the proceedings are before the Magistrates' Court, an application can be made for a witness summons for a person to produce a document or thing under section 97 or 97A (committal proceedings) of the Magistrates' Court Act 1980.

24.   Where an indictable only offence has been sent to the Crown Court and before service of the prosecution case, an application can be made to the Magistrates' Court for a person to produce a document or other exhibit, Schedule 3, paragraph 4 of the Crime and Disorder Act 1998.

DRAFT LETTER TO THIRD PARTIES

Dear Sir/Madam

REQUEST FOR DISCLOSURE OF MATERIAL HELD BY …

( ) Police are conducting a criminal investigation into allegations made against (*name and address, if appropriate, of the alleged offender*).

The allegations being investigated are, in general terms, that (*set out the nature of the allegations and the issues in the case*).

I believe that you hold material which may be relevant to the investigation, namely (*set out what material it is believed the third party holds*).

The reasons why I am seeking access to this material is because I believe that (*list the reasons which may include; material which might affect the credibility and reliability of a witness; material which might undermine the prosecution case; and material which might reasonably assist the defence case*).

I would be grateful if you would confirm whether or not you hold any such material and if so, whether you are prepared to disclose it for the purposes of the investigation. I would also be grateful if you could let me know whether you consider the material to be sensitive and the reasons for any sensitivity.

If you object to disclosing the material, I would be grateful if you could specify your reasons.

I request that you retain the material in case the court requires you to disclose some or all of the material.

I enclose for your assistance, an explanatory leaflet that sets out the role of the prosecution in dealing with material in the possession of third parties. It explains what will happen with the material if you disclose it. Further, it explains what may happen if you refuse to disclose it.

It would be of great assistance if you could reply by (*insert date*).

If you wish to discuss this request, or any further information, please do not hesitate to contact me on (*insert contact number*).

Thank you in advance for your assistance.

Yours faithfully,

(Officer in charge of the investigation/investigator/disclosure officer).

Index